# New Perspectives on Witchcraft, Magic and Demonology

## Volume 3
### Witchcraft in the British Isles and New England

# Series Content

# New Perspectives on Witchcraft, Magic and Demonology

## Volume 3
### Witchcraft in the British Isles and New England

Edited with introductions by

Brian P. Levack
*University of Texas*

ROUTLEDGE
*New York/London*

Published in 2001 by

Routledge
270 Madison Avenue
New York, NY 10016

Published in Great Britain by
Routledge
2 Park Square
Milton Park, Abingdon
Oxon OX14 4RN

Routledge is an Imprint of Taylor & Francis Books, Inc.

10 9 8 7 6 5 4 3 2 1

Library of Congress Cataloging-in-Publication Data

New perspectives on witchcraft / edited with introductions by Brian P. Levack.
   p. cm.
   Contents: v. 1. Demonology, religion, and witchcraft -- v. 2. Witchcraft in continental
Europe -- v. 3. Witchcraft in the British Isles and New England -- v. 4. Gender and
witchcraft -- v. 5. Witchcraft, disease, and popular healing -- v. 6. Witchcraft in the
modern world, 1750-2000.
   ISBN 0-8153-3668-3 (set)
   1. Witchcraft--History. I. Levack, Brian P.

BF1566 .N48 2002
133.4--dc21
ISBN 978-0-4158-8503-4 (POD set)          2001048489

ISBN 978-0-8153-3668-6 (set)
ISBN 978-0-8153-3669-3 (v.1)
ISBN 978-0-8153-3671-6 (v.2)
ISBN 978-0-8153-3672-3 (v.3)
ISBN 978-0-8153-3673-0 (v.4)
ISBN 978-0-8153-3674-7 (v.5)
ISBN 978-0-8153-3670-9 (v.6)

# Contents

# Introduction

This volume brings together a selection of recent articles on accusations of witchcraft and on and prosecutions in the British Isles (England, Scotland, Wales, and Ireland) and colonial New England. The main reason for grouping these geographical areas together, aside from their isolation from the European continent, is that after 1603, when James VI of Scotland became James I of England, all of them owed allegiance to the same king. This dynastic unity did not give these countries a single government, but it did make them part of a loosely structured "empire" that possessed common religious, social, and cultural bonds. These countries were not exclusively English-speaking, but political elites in all of them, including English and Scottish settlers in Ireland, spoke English.

As an area of study in the history of witchcraft, the British Isles and New England possess only a fragile unity. There were considerable variations in the intensity of witchcraft prosecutions from one country to another. Scotland, a country with only one-quarter of the population of England, probably executed three times as many witches. The Scottish pattern of prosecutions had more similarities with some continental European countries, especially the German lands, than with England. Prosecutions were also more intense in New England than in England, especially in Massachusetts, but that intensity owes much of its strength to the large-scale witch-hunt that took place at Salem, Massachusetts, in 1692. There were relatively few prosecutions and even fewer executions in Wales and in Ireland.

Despite this broad variation in the number and the intensity of prosecutions, witchcraft trials in all these countries shared some similarities. The most significant was the absence of a fully developed image of the witch's sabbath--the alleged nocturnal gathering of witches--in the trial records. In England there was little mention of the pact with the Devil and no mention of the sabbath until 1612, and it was only during the witch trials instigated by the professional witch-finders Matthew Hopkins and John Stearne in the 1640s that such references appeared more than occasionally. Even then, the sabbaths described in these confessions were relatively tame affairs. In Scotland confessions to witches' gatherings occur as early as the 1590s, but the reported meetings did not include promiscuous sexual activity, the sacrifice of children, or the cannibalistic eating of dismembered children's bodies. Nor did witches allegedly fly to these assemblies. In New England a few references to the sabbath occurred in the trials, especially in 1692, but the details did not conform to the continental European stereotype.

The absence of graphic depictions of the sabbath in the British Isles and New England can be explained in part by the distinctive features of the criminal procedures used in their courts. Most continental European countries followed inquisitorial procedure under which professional judges controlled the entire judicial process and determined guilt or innocence by weighing pieces of evidence to determine if they satisfied prescribed standards of judicial proof. In England, Scotland, and Ireland, however, lay juries played an important role in determining guilt or innocence, and the entire system of criminal justice in these areas was characterized by an adversarial encounter between the defendant and his or her accusers. This system resulted in a number of acquittals, especially in England. Even more important, in none of these countries was torture a regular instrument of judicial interrogation. In England and Scotland torture could be used only if authorized by a special warrant from the Privy Council, as it was in the Scottish witch trials of 1591. In Scotland, however, it was used in an informal, illegal way at the time of the witches arrest, very often in connection with the pricking of the witches skin by long pins in order to discover the Devil's mark. This mark was a spot on the witch's body, allegedly given at the time of the negotiation of the demonic pact, that demonologists claimed was insensitive to pain and did not bleed. Torture administered in this way resulted in the production of a number of confessions that would not otherwise have been forthcoming. The use of this type of legal coercion provides the best explanation not only for the higher number of convictions in Scotland but for the admission by Scottish witches that they had attended the sabbath.

The history of witchcraft prosecutions in England continues to be the subject of new scholarship. Three of the articles in this collection deal with different aspects of the legal process. C. R. Unsworth provides a comprehensive study of English criminal procedure in the trial of witches, which he views as possessing some of the features of inquisitorial justice. Brian Levack studies the role played by the Court of Star Chamber in prosecuting people who falsely accused others of witchcraft. He sees the prosecution of Brian and Anne Gunter for accusing three women of causing the possession of Anne as the turning point in the history of English witch-hunting. Jim Sharpe's article on women and witchcraft focuses on the role played by women in the legal process, mainly in searching for the Devil's mark and as witnesses in the trials.

Another group of articles, all based on materials in local archives, deals in different ways with the social and economic foundations of accusations of witchcraft, which came from women as well as men. J. T. Swain studies the economic foundations of the famous Lancashire witch-hunts of 1612 and 1634. Anabel Gregory explores the way in which conflict between two political factions in the town of Rye in Sussex led to charges of witchcraft at a time when a slump in trade during the 1590s had caused a change in the relative fortunes of the two factions. The witches were believed to have challenged prevailing standards of good neighborliness. Anne Reiber de Windt explores the competing visions of community that found expression in the famous witchcraft case at Warboys, Huntingtonshire, in 1593. Malcolm Gaskill provides a thorough study of the social characteristics of witches brought to trial in the county of Kent, and J. A. Sharpe studies the depositions taken against witches in the county of Yorkshire in the seventeenth century. These articles also address the question of gender, which is the subject of Volume 4 in this series.

Another group of articles deals in one way or another with witch-beliefs, reflected not so much in the demonological literature written by clerics but in witchcraft accusations and confessions. Some of these articles also contribute to a scholarly discourse on the role of gender and sexuality in the prosecutions. Deborah Willis's article on Shakespeare and the English witch-hunts uses material from Shakespeare's plays to advance her argument that many English witches were mothers or caretakers of small children. Gillian Bennett also draws on the literature of the period to show that beliefs in ghosts and witches were so closely linked that they formed intrinsic parts of the same belief system. Diane Purkiss focuses on fantasies regarding witches and witchcraft during the English Civil War of 1642-1646. She interprets these fantasies as reflections of anxieties among soldiers and noncombatants regarding their masculinity. Much of her material comes from the witchcraft narratives of Matthew Hopkins, who conducted a major witch-hunt in southeastern England in 1645 and 1646. Malcolm Gaskill writes about the charges against one woman, Margaret Moore, who was tried as a witch during this hunt. James Sharpe also contributes a revisionist interpretation article on Hopkins's hunt, which among other things explores the sexual content of the accusations. The article by Ian Bostridge on the repeal of witchcraft laws also deals with witchcraft beliefs, especially those that prevailed in Scotland in 1736, when the British parliament repealed the English witchcraft statute of 1604 and the Scottish statute of 1563.

Bostridge's article is one of three in this volume that deals with witchcraft in Scotland. P. G. Maxwell-Stuart contributes a piece on the famous witchcraft trials of 1590-1591 in which King James VI was the intended victim. Maxwell-Stuart emphasizes the king's fear of an alliance between the witches of East Lothian and the earl of Bothwell, who was rebelling against the king at that time. S. W. Macdonald, A. Thom, and A. Thom offer a psychiatric reassessment of a Scottish witch-hunt involving demonic possession that took place more than 100 years after the East Lothian trials. The case, which involved the demonic possession of Christian Shaw, attributes her violent seizures to a dissociative disorder. The article by Elwyn Lapoint addresses the question why so few witchcraft prosecutions took place in Ireland.

The final set of essays all deal with witchcraft in New England and focus on the large-scale hunt that took place at Salem in 1692. Michael Clark uses the writings of Cotton Mather to explore the interaction of the natural and the supernatural realms that underlies all manifestations of witchcraft. Bernard Rosenthal's article on Tituba, the Indian slave whose confession played a crucial role in the Salem witch-hunt, questions many of the myths that have arisen surrounding this woman, including her identification as a black from Barbados. Wendel D. Craker minimizes the importance of spectral evidence in the Salem trials, showing that no one was convicted on the basis of spectral evidence alone. Philip Gould's article on the politics of reason in the early American republic explores the early nineteenth-century characterization of Puritan witch-hunting as delusional, zealous, and irrational and the result of unbridled human passions. The article by Louis Kern deals with the important demonological question of the sexual relationship between demons and human beings, especially women. He places the sexual elements of witchcraft in England and New England within a broader Europeans framework.

## Chapter 5

## Witchcraft Beliefs and Criminal Procedure in Early Modern England

### C R Unsworth

The relationship between the witch-hunt which took place in Europe in the early modern period and the machinery, procedure and conceptual apparatus of the law was especially intimate. The following analysis explores the contribution of legal culture and institutions to England's distinctive experience of the witch-hunt, focusing in particular upon the various respects in which trial and pre-trial procedures were adapted to take account of the exceptional nature of the crime of witchcraft, which was perceived as posing special problems of evidence and proof.

### 1. Law and Witchcraft: The General Relationship

The role of law in the witch-hunt has three main aspects, which will be considered in turn. Firstly, witchcraft beliefs did not simply form the basis of prosecutions as a pre-existing component of the mental fabric of early modern European society. Rather they were themselves in an important sense legally constructed. Pollock and Maitland conclude their survey of the legal history of the subject with the paradox that 'Sorcery is a crime created by the measures taken for its suppression'.[1] This proposition anticipates the work of the sociological school of labelling theory in the 1950s and 1960s in according priority to the role of the agencies of social control in producing, shaping and ironically amplifying the deviance they purport to eradicate, a perspective applied to witchcraft by, amongst others, Thomas Szasz[2] and Thomas Scheff.[3] It was, however, an insight shared by contemporary sceptics. In 1610, the Spanish Inquisitor, Antonio de Salazar, observed that 'there were neither witches nor bewitched until they were talked and written about',[4] – and a crucial site for this talking and writing was the courtroom. Confession evidence

---

[1] Sir F. Pollock and F.W. Maitland, *The History of English Law*, 2nd edn. (Cambridge, 1968), p.556.

[2] T.S. Szasz, *The Manufacture of Madness* (London, 1970).

[3] T. Scheff, *Being Mentally Ill* (Chicago, 1966).

[4] B. Levack, *The Witch-Hunt in Early Modern Europe* (London, 1987), p.150.

extracted by torture, or in England by less formalized means of judicial coercion, was the primary form in which suggestion, delusion, fantasy and fabrication (in addition to an unquantifiable proportion of naturalistic evidence relating to the actualities of occult activity) acquired the status of legally validated official knowledge. Trial and pre-trial proceedings generated and disseminated knowledge of the nature and extent of witchcraft practices, systematically exposing the workings of this subterranean threat to social order. Contemporaries employed the term 'discovery' of witches to describe the object of legal proceedings, as in Matthew Hopkins's *The Discovery of Witches* and Reginald Scot's *The Discoverie of Witchcraft*.[5] By virtue of the trials, the reality of witchcraft was constantly reaffirmed, and religious dogma and peasant belief vindicated. Legal proceedings provided a fertile source of the witchcraft lore which became incorporated in formal knowledge as a department of law, divinity and physic, for legal, clerical and medical treatise writers relied significantly upon experience and accounts of the trials. It was, however, a corollary of the interconnection of witchcraft belief and legal process that the growth of scepticism within the legal culture was a cardinal factor in the decline of the witch-hunt. An example is Mr. Justice Powell's reported remark at the trial at Hertford in 1712 of Jane Wenham – the last convicted witch in England[6] – that there was no law against flying.[7]

The substantiation and elaboration of witchcraft beliefs within the criminal process lends itself to analysis as a case of the interdependence of power and knowledge as conceived in the later work of Michael Foucault. For Foucault, instances of power entail knowledge, which itself reinforces power in a circular process.[8] He traces the origins of the human sciences in the practice of techniques of discipline, examination and observation upon captive populations in proliferating institutional settings such as prisons, schools, hospitals and asylums mainly from the late eighteenth century onwards. So, for example, when public asylums for the insane were established under medical control in early and mid-nineteenth century England, sometimes on the basis of Jeremy Bentham's model prison, the Panopticon, they functioned as medical observatories of insanity, fostering the development of a body of knowledge which laid the foundations for a formal science of medical psychology. The possession of

---

[5] Matthew Hopkins, self-styled 'witch-finder general' was in the forefront of England's most highly developed and large-scale witch-hunting campaign, in the south eastern counties of England in 1645-7. *The Discovery of Witches* was an account and defence of his activities published in 1647, the year of his death. Reginald Scot, on the other hand, was an early sceptic. His *Discoverie of Witchcraft*, which appeared in 1584, was much despised by James VI of Scotland, who, it seems, ordered its burning when he became king of England.

[6] She was, however, reprieved and saved from execution.

[7] K. Thomas, *Religion and the Decine of Magic* (London, 1971), p.547.

[8] M. Foucault, *Discipline and Punish* (London, 1977), p.224.

this block of positive knowledge in turn legitimated doctors' claims to exclusive authority in the treatment of the insane.[9] Adapting this analysis to a different type of power-knowledge relationship at an earlier historical juncture, witchcraft trials, especially in those jurisdictions where inquisitorial methods and torture were deployed, effectively involved courts in functioning as workshops for the production of witchcraft knowledge. The resultant revelations reinforced public fear and so further legitimated the enterprise of the witch-hunters, creating a circle which it was difficult, but not impossible, to break. Foucault himself considers the contribution of the inquisitorial investigative process to the formation of knowledge, identifying in it the model for the deployment of the empirical natural sciences. As the inquisitorial technique, derived from tax collection and administration, came to dominate European judicial process in harness with the rise of church and state power, he describes it as providing the 'juridico-political matrix' of the natural sciences.[10] In the context of witchcraft trials inquisitorial technique may be credited with having played an immediate and direct role in the constitution of a corpus of knowledge which was concerned partly with man, partly with the natural world, and partly with the spiritual world: the investigation of the witch was directed to the exposure of her capacity to work magic for malign purposes as a result of having entered into a league with Satan.

Secondly, it was through the invocation of the powers of the law that the social denunciation of witches was given effect in the imposition of legitimately sanctioned penalties, primarily physical extermination, which, so it was believed, destroyed the witch's power enabling victims to recover, while those accused of witchcraft were able to retaliate by taking legal countermeasures in the form of actions for defamation, assault and false imprisonment. As Levack has recently stated, 'the great European witch-hunt was essentially a judicial operation'.[11] As a means of combating bewitchment, law represented one of a range of options available to a victim or potential victim. One other possibility was private vengeance. When an incredulous parliament adopted the Witchcraft Act in 1736 (against the eighteenth century's trend of increasing the number of capital offences) witchcraft ceased to be a crime of occult power and was brought down to earth as a mere crime of deceit. The result was that from then on local communities within which witchcraft belief persisted were forced back into private vengeance. A notorious incident of this took place in 1751. Thomas Colley, a chimney sweep, conducted a witch-swimming in which a woman was drowned and as a result of which her husband later

[9] See H. Dreyfus and P. Rabinow, *Michel Foucault: Beyond Structuralism and Hermeneutics* (Brighton, 1982); P.Q. Hirst, 'Constructed Space and the Subject', in R. Fardon (ed.), *Power and Knowledge: Anthropological and Sociological Approaches* (Edinburgh, 1985), p.171.

[10] Foucault, p.225.

[11] Levack, p.63.

died. Tried at Hertford Assizes and convicted, he was returned to the scene of the crime under an escort of 108 men, 7 officers and 2 trumpeters, and hanged, his body swinging there in chains for many years.[12]

Another option was countermagic. This could take many forms, including the wearing of amulets or charms, the assistance of white witches or wizards, and direct action against the witch of types that were believed to cancel her magic, such as scratching her, or burning some of her hair or thatch from her roof. In line with a current theory that both ecclesiastical and secular judges were protected from her powers once the witch was apprehended and the subject of legal process,[13] James I in his *Daemonologie* depicted law itself as possessing magical properties, divine disarming demonic intervention:

> If they be apprehended and deteined by anie private person, upon other private respects, their power no doubt either in escaping, or in doing hurte, is no lesse nor ever it was before. But if on the other parte, their apprehending and detention be by the lawfull Magistrate, upon the just respectes of their guiltinesse in that craft, their power is then no greater then before that ever they medled with their master. For where God beginnes justlie to strike by his lawful Lieutennents, it is not in the Devilles power to defraude or bereave him of his office, or effect of his powerfull and revenging Scepter.[14]

A further resource was religion, in the form of religious magic (exorcism), or, in the Reformed Church, prayer and faith, the supplication of the deity. The co-involvement of religious powers makes the point that legal authorities took part in the processing of witchcraft accusations as one sector of the elite. This is strikingly evident in the famous Warboys case in Huntingdonshire in 1592-3, where the victims themselves were of somewhat elevated social status. The case concluded with the execution of an old woman, her husband and her daughter. It arose from the insistence of a sick child, one of the daughters of Sir Robert Throckmorton, a prominent Huntingdonshire landowner, that a humble neighbour, Alice Samuel, looked just like a witch. Here, medical authority was the initial basis for granting credence to the claim, as Dr. Barrow, a Cambridge physician who was consulted regarding the child's illness, gave it as his opinion that she was bewitched, witchcraft providing a convenient explanation when a malaise did not fall within available diagnostic categories. Lady Cromwell (step-grandmother of Oliver Cromwell), coming to visit the children, took up the accusation and cut off a lock of Alice Samuel's hair to burn it as a countermeasure. Afterwards she became afflicted with a strange illness, languished and died. Throckmorton's other four daughters and seven maidservants resident at

---

[12] See J.H. Langbein, *Torture and the Law of Proof* (Chicago, 1977), p.210, n.49; C. Hole, *Witchcraft in Britain* (London, 1980), pp.169-71.

[13] E. Peters, *The Magician, the Witch and the Law* (Philadelphia, 1978), p.153.

[14] James VI, *Daemonologie* (Edinburgh, 1597), pp.50-1

the house also suffered otherwise inexplicable fits. The Cambridge scholars, colleagues of Henry Pickering, a relat sought, and confessions were eventually forthcoming before, fir clergyman and then the bishop of Lincoln. In the formal proceedings which followed the bishop joined two justices, _.ancıs Cromwell and Richard Tryce, in the examination, an instance of the auxiliary role played by ecclesiastical figures in secular tribunals charged with judging witchcraft. Three different clerics gave evidence. The issue therefore involved medical, academic, social and ecclesiastical as well as, and in conjunction with, legal authority.[15]

Before witchcraft became a statutory crime in 1542,[16] it had been treated as essentially a matter for the ecclesiastical courts, where usually minor witchcraft offences fell for decision and sanctions had been lenient and directed more to penance and atonement than punishment. These courts retained a substantial role in the determination of witchcraft accusations until the beginning of the seventeenth century.[17] However, although clerical authorities participated in the resolution of witchcraft cases, in the early modern period it was secular law that dominated, punitive displacing reformative justice. The decline of ecclesiastical jurisdiction in this area has indeed been identified as one of the preconditions of the witch-hunt.[18] We can say that in the medieval period witchcraft was treated primarily as a pastoral matter, in the early modern period predominantly as a legal matter, and in the modern period as a myth, or, to the extent that confessions have been explained as the product of derangement, senility or drug-induced fantasy, as a medico-scientific matter.[19] Effectively, after the early modern period, witchcraft was

---

[15] *The most strange and admirable discoverie of the three witches of Warboys . . .* (London, 1593), reprinted in R. Boulton, *A Compleat History of Magick* (1715), vol.i, 49-152; C.L. Ewen, *Witchcraft and Demonianism* (London, 1933), pp. 169-73; W. Notestein, *A History of Witchcraft in England from 1558-1718* (Washington, 1911), p.47 *et seq.*

[16] 32 Henry VIII, c.8.

[17] A. Macfarlane, *Witchcraft in Tudor and Stuart England* (London, 1970), p.68.

[18] Levack, pp.77-84. Three other statutes of the second half of Henry VIII's reign imposed secular penalties for moral or ecclesiastically related offences:
(1) 23 Henry VIII, c.11: 'an acte for breking of prison by Clerks convicte:
(2) 25 Henry VIII, c.6: this classified buggery 'with mankind or beast' as a felony, there being as yet no 'condigne' punishment.
(3) 31 Henry VIII, c.14: a statute for 'abolishing diversity in Opynions'.

[19] Although the so-called Zilboorg thesis (G. Zilboorg, *The Medical Man and the Witch during the Renaissance* (Baltimore, 1935), which asserts that witchcraft was the misrecognition of mental illness in a less rational age, should be rejected, as should the thesis of Thomas Szasz which stands this on its head by portraying modern psychiatry as a social functional substitute for persecutory witch-hunting, a position which, despite the fact that it highlights some arresting parallels, denies the irreducible historical specificity of witchcraft as concept and practice. See P.Q. Hirst and P. Woolley, *Social Relations and Human Attributes* (London, 1982), pp.219-23, 236, 240; G.R. Quaife, *Godly Zeal and Furious Rage* (London, 1987), pp.204-6, 209, n.8.

blotted from social reality by a revised conception of the possible.

In terms of the role of law in the witch-hunt in Continental Europe the most important features were the adoption of inquisitorial procedure and the use of torture. Both of these were generally formally absent in English secular courts.[20] One characteristic of witch trials which was common to England was the phenomenon Hirst and Woolley term 'disorderly legality':

> Witchcraft trials are a part of conditions of *disorderly legality*. They are desperate measures and by their very form they undermine the possibility of creating a stable, useful and pacified population. Although conducted by authority, and serving as a means to enforce religious conformity, they threaten both political order and religious conformity. For if the courts of authority provide the theatre, popular accusations and the confessions of the accused determine the cast, and those accusations are not limited by considerations of social standing or outward belief. Beggar women can denounce merchants and councillors . . . Witch trials, like the disorder of festivals and organized licenced begging, threaten to give rise to an institutionalized anarchy in which popular forces rather than state agencies set the norms of conduct.[21]

The most intense moments and phases of the witch-hunt tended to take place where and when local courts were least subject to corrective central control and able to improvise in ways prejudicial to suspected witches, spawning a legality that was unstable, elastic and volatile. The point was made early in the modern historiography of witchcraft by Wallace Notestein, an American historian in the liberal humanist tradition, that a significant proportion of English witch trials took place in towns possessing separate rights of jurisdiction, citing Yarmouth, King's Lynn, Newcastle-upon-Tyne, Berwick and Canterbury.[22] The virulence of England's most notorious witch-hunting episode, promoted by Matthew Hopkins, assisted by John Stearne, in the south eastern counties in 1645-7, may be attributed in part to the interruption of normal government and legality by the conditions of the Civil War. This campaign, which yielded a total of about 200 executions, entailed something of a continentalization of the legal process, with oppressive procedure and *de facto* torture being brought to bear upon the accused. The trial of Essex witches at

[20] Exceptions are dealt with below in the body of the article.

[21] Hirst and Woolley, p.254; hence the link between the rise of absolutism and the decline of witch-hunting as inimical to strong central control. On the subject of the lowly directing accusations at the mighty, this could rapidly induce an attack of scepticism in the elite, as in the case of the accusation of Lady Phips, wife of the governor of the Bay Colony and Samuel Willard, president of Harvard College and pastor of the First Church of Boston in the Salem trials in New England in 1692: J. Bednarski, 'The Salem Witch-Scene Viewed Sociologically', in M. Marwick (ed.), *Witchcraft and Sorcery*, 2nd edn. (Harmondsworth, 1982), pp.193-4.

[22] Notestein, p.201.

Chelmsford in late July 1645 was conducted, not by judges of assize, but before the J.P.s presided over by Robert Rich, earl of Warwick, who had no clear judicial status.

That the political centre did from time to time intervene correctively is illustrated by the fact that Parliament constituted a special commission of oyer and terminer to try witches imprisoned at Bury gaol in August 1645 because of suspicion of Hopkins' and his confederates' methods. As a result the swimming of witches was abandoned and a new evidential emphasis upon genuinely voluntary confession and clear proof introduced.[23] Another example of central intervention to restrain a witch-hunt in danger of spiralling out of control took place in Lancashire in 1634. A boy of ten, Edmund Robinson, was set up by his father as a witch-finder and made a series of remarkable allegations. After the assizes, where twenty were found guilty, execution was stayed and proceedings reported to the king in council. The bishop of Chester was ordered to examine seven of the convicted. Four witches were later ordered to be brought to London for examination by physicians and midwives under the direction of Dr. William Harvey, and nothing incriminating was found. The boy witch-finder was also ordered by Sir Francis Windebank, Secretary of State, to be examined by George Long, J.P. for Middlesex, and admitted his allegations were fabricated.[24]

The third aspect of the relationship between law and the witch-hunt to be considered is the notion of the demonic pact. This concept was a core element in the continental European elite's composite picture of witchcraft and exerted influence in English trials from the early seventeenth century. The Jacobean statute against witchcraft of 1604[25] imposed the death penalty for anyone who 'shall consult *covenant with* entertaine employ feede or rewarde any evill and wicked Spirit to or for any intent or purpose'.[26] Parliamentary recognition was thereby given to the Continental concept of witchcraft as arising from an heretical bargain between the witch and the devil, the demonic pact. This pact was contractually conceived and discussed in legalistic terms.

In the medieval notion of the pact between sorcerer and the devil, the sorcerer obtained mastery over demons and emerged with reward from the bargain. In the early modern era the witch was portrayed as cheated by the devil, the victim of a trick. Matthew Hopkins in his *The Discovery of Witches* provides an account of witchcraft in which *maleficium* (the harm done by witches) is itself treated as an illusion, the product of 'the great deceiver's' own sleight of hand. Hopkins' explanation runs as follows. The

---

[23] C.L. Ewen, *Witchcraft and Demonianism*, p.260.

[24] *Ibid.*, pp.244-51. There are European examples of the centre promoting a witch hunt in the face of local inaction. See Quaife, p.118.

[25] 1 Jas. I, c.12.

[26] Author's italics.

devil knows X is fatally diseased. He tells the witches that X is conspiring against them. They call upon him to dispose of X. X dies a natural death but the witches believe the Devil has granted their request and so are further wedded to him.[27] For Hopkins the illusory quality of *maleficium* was not a problem: the pact with Satan was the essence of the crime. This pact could be merely oral, or take written form, being signed and sealed in blood. The witch might commit herself for life, or for a fixed term of years. The relationship thus initiated has been characterized as a replica of that between feudal lord and vassal.[28]

An interesting quasi-legal discussion of the demonic pact is to be found in William Perkins' *A Discourse of the Dammed Art of Witchcraft* (1608) and repays quotation at length. Perkins is concerned to refute three arguments advanced by 'the patrons of witches':

I.     In every league and contract the parties must be mutually bound each to the other: now betweene man and woman, and the devill, there can be no bond made, and though there could, yet man is bound in conscience to God, to renounce the bond of obedience to Satan, and to break the covenant. *Ans.* There be two sorts of Leagues; lawfull, and unlawfull: in all lawfull leagues it is true, that there must be a mutuall bond of both parties, each to other, which may not be dissolved; but in unlawfull compacts it is otherwise. And no man can say that this league between a Witch and the Devill is lawfull, but wicked, and damnable, yet being once made, howsoever unlawfully, it is a league and compact. This therefore prooveth not, that there can be no covenant at all, but that there can be no lawfull covenant betwixt them, which no man will denie.

II.    Satan and the Witch are of divers natures: he is spirituall, they are corporall substances: therefore there can be no league made betweene them. *Ans.* The reason is not good. For even God himselfe, who is of nature most simple and spirituall made a covenant with Adam, renued the same unto Abraham, Isaac and Jacob: and continueth it with his Church on earth from age to age. Hence it appeareth, that diversitie of nature in the parties, can not hinder the making of a covenant. And therefore if man may make covenant with God himselfe, who is most spirituall; then may he likewise come in league with the devill, whose substance is not so pure and spirituall. Againe, we must remember, that in making of a covenant, it is sufficient, that the parties consent and agree in will and understanding, though other circumstances and rites, which are but signes of confirmation be wanting. Be it then, that Satan hath not a bodily substance, as man hath, yet considering that man is indued with understanding to conceive of things as the devill doth, and hath also will to yield consent, and approbation thereunto, though in a corrupt and wicked manner, there may passe a confederacie, and a covenant may be made, and stand in force betweene them.

[27] Hopkins, p.10.
[28] Quaife, p.55.

III. Whatsoever the devil doth in this compact, he doth it in fraud and deceit, never meaning in his promises, as man doth, and when both parties mean not one and the same thing, how can they grow to agreement in any kind? *Ans.* Suppose this be true, yet it only prooveth, that the covenant made between them, was deceitful and unlawfull. But what of that? Still it remaineth a bargain howsoever: for it faileth only in the circumstance, the substance, which is the consent of the parties was not wanting.[29]

In this extract, Perkins, a Puritan divine, addresses a series of issues of an essentially legal nature relating to the validity of contracts, as they apply to the demonic pact: the possibility of illegal contracts, the capacity of the parties to contract, the sufficiency of consensus between the parties to found a contract in the absence of formalities, and the effect of deceit upon the contractual relationship. These issues are rationally resolved on the basis of the combination of a Biblically sanctioned conception of cosmic order and a theory of contract.

## 2. The Modesty of England's Witch-Hunt

Having examined these general features of the relationship between law and witchcraft with principal reference to English experience, the rest of the discussion will be concerned with the impact of witchcraft beliefs upon English criminal law and procedure. Before the last years of Henry VIII the position regarding the legal basis of witch prosecutions appears confused. It seems that witchcraft could be dealt with in the secular courts where fraud, treason, murder or injury were involved,[30] and following *De Haeretico Comburendo* (1401), witches could be handed over by the ecclesiastical courts to be executed. In 1542 the first of a series of statutes was enacted, remaining in force only until 1547 when it fell as part of a general repeal. It became a capital offence to conjure spirits or practise witchcraft, enchantment or sorcery in order to find lost treasure, waste or destroy a person's body, members or goods, provoke to unlawful love, or for any other unlawful intent or purpose. Benefit of clergy and sanctuary were lost, and land and goods forfeit. A second statute,[31] enacted in 1563, imposed the death penalty for 'any Invocacons or Conjuracons of evill and wicked Spirites, to or for *any* Intent or Purpose',[32] but where the victim of witchcraft, enchantment, charming or sorcery merely suffered injury rather than death; where there was only an attempted murder or injury; where animals or goods were damaged or the purpose was to find lost

---

[29] London, 1610 edn. pp.188-90.
[30] Thomas, pp.557-8.
[31] 5 Eliz., c.16.
[32] Author's italics.

treasure or provoke to unlawful love, the penalty was reduced to one year's imprisonment with quarterly appearances in the pillory and confession of error. In the case of a second offence in these categories, however, actual injury to person or property attracted the death penalty, while the other crimes were punishable by life imprisonment. This statute also protected wives and successors against forfeiture, but loss of goods was introduced as a sanction in certain of the lesser categories of offence. The third statute, enacted in 1604, imposed more severe penalties. Injury to the person by witchcraft, enchantment, charm or sorcery became a capital crime, as did a repeated transgression in the other lesser categories. Further, the employment of a corpse 'or the skin bone or any other parte' thereof in witchcraft or allied practices became a capital offence. All three Acts encompassed not only the direct practitioners of witchcraft but also their 'counsellors, abettors and procurers'.[33] The Jacobean statute was repealed in 1736 when the Witchcraft Act abolished witchcraft as a crime consisting in the exercise of occult powers for personal ends and introduced instead a penalty of one year's imprisonment for pretending to exercise such powers.[34]

Compared with some other areas of Europe, notably France, Switzerland, parts of Germany, and Poland, England underwent a modest and only semi-developed witch-hunt. The witch-hunt in England remained preoccupied with *maleficium*, the infliction of harm by occult power, rather than with heresy and the demonic pact, even after the raising of evil spirits per se had been criminalized by statute. The demand for prosecutions arose substantially from the populace of local communities rather than being stoked by the elite. It therefore rested upon the traditional peasant stereotype of the witch as an ill-disposed, indigent and aged woman, rather than upon the learned concept of a diabolical compact rooted in demonological theory, although the latter did exert significant influence. Witch-hunts based upon the demonological conception were more liable, because of the collective nature of witchcraft as a criminal activity celebrated at the sabbath, and particularly when fuelled by torture, to snowball out of control and so engulf men, children and other members of the elite, whereas in England the proportion of women amongst accused witches was exceptionally

---

[33] An Act of 1582 (23 Eliz., c.2) is also relevant. The casting of horoscopes to predict the length of the Queen's reign and who should succeed her was made punishable by death.

[34] This statute remained in force for more than two centuries, and its use was revived as late as 1944 in the prosecution of a spiritualist medium, Helen Duncan. After a campaign by the Spiritualist National Union, the act was repealed and replaced by the Fraudulent Mediums Act 1951, which made it clear that merely purporting to contact the spirit world was not an offence: there must be an intent to deceive and it must be done for reward..

high, Macfarlane recording a figure of 92% for the cou·
Another index of moderation is that the character of the ʻ
supporting evidence was less florid than in the Continentaⁱ
the witch-hunt, where elements such as the sabbath, nocturⁿ.
sexual relations with demons, cannibalism and infanticide were ·
entrenched. Taking the example of flight, which was central to the
continental concept, as it accounted for rapid journeying over long
distances to the sabbath, mention in the learned literature or the trials in
England was very rare. One reference is made by William West in a legal
treatise, *Symbolaeographie* (1594), listing the practices of a witch to include
being

> conveyed of her familiar which hath taken upon him the deceitful shape of a
> goate, swine or calfe etc. into some mountaine farre distant, in a wonderfull
> short space of time. And sometimes to flie upon a staffe or forke, or some other
> instrument.[36]

Mention of a broom-stick occurs only once in an account of an English
trial. This was in the case of Julian Cox, a woman of about 70, who was
indicted for bewitching a servant maid. The defendant confessed that
'there came riding towards her three persons upon three broomstaves
borne up about a yard and a half from the ground'. The third person, in
the shape of a black man, tempted her to sign a compact with her own
blood, agreeing to give him her soul in return for help in 'carrying out
revenge', but she had refused. Having prejudiced herself by error in
reciting the Lord's Prayer, she was found guilty and executed.[37]

Another sign of restraint was that the witch-hunt in England began
later than in most of the European countries affected, but ended earlier.[38]

---

[35] *Witchcraft in Tudor and Stuart England*, p.160. In qualification of this picture, it should
be noted that Christina Larner found that when Scottish witch-hunts escalated, the
proportion of women witches rose. She gives the explanation that male witches needed
more time to build up a reputation, so in times of panic, accusers, and convicted witches
pressed to incriminate accomplices, felt more secure in denouncing women: *Enemies of God:
The Witch-Hunt in Scotland* (London, 1981), p.92; see also Quaife, p.81; Levack, p.24; and A.
Anderson and R. Gordon, 'Witchcraft and the Status of Women – the Case of England',
*British Journal of Sociology*, 29 (1978), p.171. In a neat demonstration of sex discrimination,
Larner points out in relation to a ratio of 80 women to 20 men amongst Scottish witch
suspects that men enjoyed a similar preponderance over women amongst thirteenth and
fourteenth century saints: *Enemies of God*, p.94.

[36] C.L. Ewen, *Witch-Hunting and Witch Trials* (London, 1919), p.22.

[37] C.L. Ewen, *Witchcraft and Demonianism*, p.337. The judge allowed the test, whilst
cautioning against its being taken into account.

[38] Witch prosecutions in England accelerated from the mid-sixteenth century as
opposed to the mid-fifteenth century (although there was a period of dormancy in Europe
in the first half of the sixteenth century). The last official execution in England was that of
Alice Mulholland at Exeter in 1685, the last conviction in 1712 and the last trial in 1717.
The last execution in Scotland was in 1722 and in some areas of Europe executions
continued well into the eighteenth century, the last taking place, possibly illegally, in
Poland in 1793.

Further, there were proportionately fewer trials and executions. England probably provided less than 1,000 of upwards of 60,000 executions in Europe as a whole.[39] There were other interesting differences. In England the death penalty for witchcraft took the form of hanging rather than burning, which is perhaps reflective of the lesser link with heresy, although there was an exception in cases of petty treason (including *inter alia* murder of husband by wife, parent by child and master or mistress by servant), where men were to be drawn and hanged, but women burned alive.[40] Thus Mother Lakeland was burned at Ipswich in September 1645 for bewitching to death her husband. The concept of the witch's animal familiar was uniquely prominent in England, a divergence from European practice as remarkable as the virtual absence of the animal trials which were such an exotic aspect of continental juridical reason.[41] Finally, in contrast to European experience, there is scant evidence in England of witch-finding being taken up as a species of entrepreneurial profit-seeking.[42]

This profile of restraint can partly be explained by the legal situation in England, notably the persistence of accusatorial as opposed to inquisitorial criminal procedure, and the normal exclusion of judicial torture. The categorization of witchcraft as an exceptional crime creating special evidential problems was used to justify adaptations and innovations in both European and English systems.[43] The exceptionality of the crime of witchcraft flowed from its occult, that is its secret and supernatural, quality. The witch need not be present at the time of injury or death, so it was unlikely that there would be witnesses to the offence, conceived as *maleficium*. This lack of direct witness applied even more strongly when the crime was defined to consist of a pact with the Devil. However, there was a prosecutorial advantage here in that an alibi for the time of death or injury was of no value. These evidential characteristics were shared by the crime of poisoning, with which witchcraft possessed close affinities. Both involved the artful concoction and application of noxious substances. While poisoning depended upon natural processes, witchcraft depended upon supernatural effects. The line between the two could be difficult to draw.[44] Significantly, the Latin term *veneficium* was

---

[39] This estimate is given by Levack, at p.21. Geoffrey Scarre in *Witchcraft and Magic in Sixteenth and Seventeenth-Century Europe* (London, 1987), estimates 100,000 while Quaife sets the figure at about 200,000.

[40] M. Dalton, *The countrey justice, conteyning the practice of the justices of the peace out of their sessions* (London, 1618), pp.204-6.

[41] See K. Thomas, *Man and the Natural World*, p.97; E.P. Evans, *The Criminal Prosecution and Capital Punishment of Animals* (London, 1987) (originally published 1906).

[42] An English example is Samuel Cocwra in Salop, Worcester and Montgomery: see C.L. Ewen, *Witch-Hunting and Witch Trials*, pp.69-70.

[43] See C. Larner, 'Crimen Exceptum', in *Witchcraft and Religion* (Oxford, 1984).

[44] See R. Kieckhefer, *European Witch Trials* (London, 1976), p.34.

used for both.[45]

If witchcraft was evidentially problematic because it was secret, the answer was to rely upon indirect evidence; and if it was problematic because it was supernatural, the answer was to admit evidence of a supernatural or quasi-miraculous character. English judicial practice responded as follows. Firstly, an important part was played by circumstantial evidence. The suspect's association with an animal or insect could be interpreted as the entertaining of a familiar spirit. Witnesses willing to testify to this were a convenient substitute for witnesses to the demonic pact itself when the legal emphasis shifted from *maleficium* to heresy in the early seventeenth century.[46] If some contact with the suspected witch, together with a history of bad relations, were to be followed by mishap, a causal connection could be imputed. Thus Richard Bernard in his *A Guide to Grand Jury Men* (1627) took the view that if a woman gave a child an apple and the recipient quickly fell ill after eating it, then given a background of ill will, there was a sufficient basis for the accused to be condemned and executed.[47] Secondly, various categories of physical evidence were accepted. There might be residual physical evidence of witchcraft practices, such as a waxen image of the victim found in the accused's possession after a misfortune had been suffered. This type of evidence would of course be convincing in a modern sceptical culture as a demonstration that witchcraft had been practised against the victim, with the difference that in the absence of some belief supportive of the efficacy of image-magic, such as, in the early modern period, Renaissance Neoplatonism, it would not be acceptable as evidence that the victim had thereby been harmed. In a more radical departure, however, physical evidence was admitted which involved attributing various supernatural properties to the witch's body. If there was one source of evidence which was at the disposal of the court it was the witch's body, and investigation of its physical qualities would provide a means of judging the witch's spiritual status. This entailed the legal recognition and incorporation in the judicial process of traditional peasant witch beliefs and a primitively magical brand of Christianity which drew censorship from learned commentators.[48] The manifestation

---

[45] Again, poisoning was conceived as characteristically a female crime as its commission did not require physical strength. Terminologically there is an analogy with the use of the term 'buggery' to refer both to heresy and sodomy: see T. Szasz, *Manufacture of Madness*, p.38.

[46] This was the central evidential concern of commentaries on the law in the first half of the seventeenth century, following upon the 1604 statute's specification of the covenant. Bernard, for example, states 'to convict anyone of witchcraft, is to prove a league made with the devil . . . Now, they that make this league, have a familiar spirit. For this is true, as soone as the league is made . . .': *A Guide to Grand Jury Men*, pp.216-17.

[47] Macfarlane, p.18.

[48] See e.g. discussion below of Dr. John Cotta's opinions on the use of the water ordeal.

of certain of the supernatural bodily properties which provided a judicial litmus test required the witch's active participation. Thus if the accused's alleged crime was to have committed murder by witchcraft and the corpse bled at her touch, this was evidence of guilt. Similarly a witch was deemed incapable of standing up in court and giving voice to a particular religious form of words – reciting the Lord's Prayer, the creed, or some other scriptural passage – without faltering or failing. In other cases, the witch was the passive object of an experimental test. The medieval water ordeal was resuscitated as a mode of proof in cases of witchcraft. As the symbol of purity and instrument of baptism, water would reject the witch, and therefore if the accused floated it was evidence of guilt. Another more obscure oracular practice was to weigh the witch in a pair of scales against the weight of a Bible and if she was outweighed it was a sign of guilt.[49] If a victim scratched the witch responsible drawing blood, and the harm ceased forthwith, this also connoted guilt. Then there was physical evidence which involved the observation of the witch's body rather than the revelation of its properties by some proceeding. Thus witches were thought incapable of shedding tears, when so accused, and were searched for the witch's mark, conceived according to the demonic model as bestowed by Satan as a sign of his dominion over the witch, or more traditionally as providing a place at which her familiars would suck blood to gain sustenance, and sometimes consisting of an insensible spot of flesh detectable by pricking with needles. Thirdly, on occasion spectral evidence, testimony relating to demonic apparitions, was treated as admissible.[50]

Most highly valued, though, was the extraction of a confession, and pressure was also sometimes exerted upon those who confessed guilt to implicate other witches. So there was an impetus to judicial coercion, inquisitorial investigative techniques and strategies, and, in Continental Europe, legalized torture. Procedures tended to presuppose guilt: they were designed to unmask or 'discover' witches.[51] It must be appreciated

---

[49] See R.D. Hunt (ed.), 'Henry Townshend's "Notes of the Office of a Justice of the Peace" 1661-3' in Worcestershire Historical Society, *Miscellany II* (1967), p.118.

[50] As in the case of that given by Matthew Hopkins regarding the appearance of imps at the trial of Elizabeth Clarke of Manningtree in 1645.

[51] This is one of many parallels with the modern treatment of psychiatric illness. The 1959 Mental Health Act (now replaced by the more liberal Mental Health Act 1983) introduced a system of Mental Health Review Tribunals to consider the discharge of long-term detained patients in part substitution for the safeguard of reference to a magistrate before commitment, which was being abolished. Although these were the only tribunals in the English legal system to be vested with the power to determine issues of individual liberty, they were designed to proceed with the minimum of formality. The assumption was that a more formal procedure would be disturbing for the mentally disordered. Mental Health Review Tribunals were devised to operate as an outlet for the frustrations of 'paranoid' patients and to provide a therapeutic second opinion rather than to function in

that, despite the influence of the comforting notions that bringing her within the control of legal authorities disarmed the witch and that the Devil himself malignantly betrayed witches into the hands of temporal justice, witch trials, compared with trials of other types of offence, were perceived to be peculiarly vulnerable. Earthly courts, as they took on board the demonic conception of witchcraft, saw themselves as confronted by malign spiritual powers, creating an atmosphere of tension and apprehension of spectacular supernatural interference, especially during episodes of panic when multiple trials were in progress. With supernatural assistance a witch could carry a hot iron several paces further than was necessary to prove her innocence,[52] make her Devil's mark disappear to frustrate the searchers,[53] torture her child accusers with violent fits in the courtroom itself[54] and even break the leg of a justice as he sat in judgement on the bench.[55] The witch trial became a contest beween the forces of light and those of darkness, which sixteenth-century Christianity portrayed as unprecedently powerful, sinister and socially pervasive. What was being dispensed was very much an emergency justice and procedures were tailored accordingly.

In assessing the legal contribution to the witch-hunt of the sixteenth and seventeenth centuries, we may consider two contrasting theses, those of Keith Thomas in *Religion and the Decline of Magic* (1971) and Norman Cohn in *Europe's Inner Demons* (1976). Thomas asks why, if English popular witch beliefs were much the same as they had been in the Middle Ages, it was only in this epoch that legal action against witchcraft really took off. There are two explanations on offer. One is that the demand for witchcraft prosecutions suddenly grew, the second that the legal situation itself changed in such a way as to encourage an upsurge in prosecutions. The latter explanation is smartly dismissed because it would seem that 'a woman who killed a man by sorcery was in medieval law as liable to prosecution as if she had used a hatchet!'[56] The former proposition – that it was demand for legal redress that increased – is preferred, the growth in demand being related to the decline of magic within the church as a result of the Reformation, depriving the populace of a major source of magical

---

the manner of a court of law. Therefore tribunal procedure presupposed the character of the standard applicant, and so denied him or her the benefits of earlier more 'legalistic' machinery for the protection of individual liberty.

[52] See R. Bartlett, *Trial by Fire and Water* (Oxford, 1986), pp.145-6, in reference to a case in the Black Forest in 1485 which is treated in the *Malleus Maleficarum*.

[53] J.W. Willis Bund (ed.), *The Diary of Henry Townshend of Elmley Lovett 1640-1663*, Worcestershire Historical Society (1915), p.40.

[54] This was a common feature of the Warboys trial in 1593 and the Salem trials in 1692.

[55] Reginald Scot recorded this claim made by an Essex Justice: see A. Macfarlane, *Witchcraft in Tudor and Stuart England*, p.88.

[56] K. Thomas, *Religion and the Decline of Magic*, p.548.

protection and pointing it in the alternative direction of the law.[57] Norman Cohn, on the other hand, emphasises that the legal situation itself *had* changed. From the early thirteenth century, in its drive to combat heresy, the church, its example quick to be followed by secular powers, had replaced an accusatorial tradition of judicial procedure favourable to the accused with an inquisitorial procedure facilitative of successful prosecution, and judicial torture had replaced trial by ordeal. The installation of the inquisition and torture constituted the legal preconditions of the Great Witch-Hunt.[58] Cohn treats this proposition as diminishing the cogency of Thomas's argument, but however compelling the Cohn thesis may be as a contributory explanation of the European witch-hunt, English circumstances were of course here as in so many other regards culturally discrepant. A basically accusatorial model of criminal justice was preserved and torture only selectively authorized under the royal prerogative. Nevertheless once the crime of witchcraft was taken seriously in a legal context and dealt with punitively there were inherent pressures towards the assumption, even within an accusatorial system, of inquisitorial features. This facilitated the witch-hunt and propelled English experience towards the continental model. The Hopkins campaign was the most advanced episode of the English witch-hunt in this respect. It is therefore legitimate to classify English witch trials as to a greater or a lesser extent, depending upon their circumstances, 'sub-inquisitorial' in character, and to arrive at a conclusion in relation to the situation in England which represents a compromise between the positions of Thomas and Cohn, that is that the decline of ecclesiastical magic stimulated an upsurge in popular demand for witch prosecutions, while the criminal process underwent inquisitorial modifications which eased the legal accommodation of that demand.

The possible methods of proceeding against a witch can be arranged in a spectrum running from informal, which might variously be termed immediate popular justice, remedial crime, private vengeance or lynching, to highly formal and structured, with built-in procedural protections for the accused. Commencing with the informal proceeding, this might take on features borrowed from or also integral to the formal criminal process. For example, a lynch mob might submit a suspected witch to the swimming test or oppressive interrogation to name other witches. Such an overlap was possible because the witch trial furnished a setting for the expression of popular hostility. It was the climax of a cumulative process of community denunciation, whereby social

---

[57] *Ibid.*, p.594: 'What the religious changes in the mid sixteenth century did was to eliminate protective ecclesiastical magic which had kept the threat of sorcery under control . . . Ecclesiastical magic crumbled, and society was forced to take legal action against a peril which for the first time threatened to get seriously out of hand.'

[58] N. Cohn, *Europe's Inner Demons* (London, 1976), pp.160-3.

ostracization could be translated into judicially mediated physical extermination.[59] Witch trials were organic to the local community, a dark manifestation of popular democracy. Thus there was no sharp disjunction between formal and informal proceedings: each influenced the other. Formal proceedings reflected popular belief in admitting types of evidence and modes of proof regarded as vulgar and superstitious by sections of the elite, while the elite's conception of witchcraft as heresy filtered downwards partly as a result of the involvement of learned lawyers, doctors and divines in the trials, an exchange now widely recognized as lying at the heart of the Great Witch-Hunt.[60] Meanwhile acts of private vengeance mirrored official conceptions of appropriate methods for the identification and disposal of witches.

If informal, non-judicial methods of proceeding against witches are ranked as most prejudicial to, and placing greatest pressure on, the accused, then, of the formal methods available, the inquisitorial mode must be ranked next.[61] Michel Foucault describes it as 'an authoritarian search for truth observed or attested'.[62] The object of the proceedings is to extract the truth of the issue. To this end, the judge occupies an unfettered position and pursues an investigative and directive course. As Max Weber characterizes it, 'the trial is dominated by the presiding judge whose position it is to ascertain what has happened and who is, therefore, alone or primarily entitled to call and examine the witnesses and to require such

---

[59] George Gifford's *A Discourse of the Subtill Practices by Devilles by Witches and Sorcerers* (1587) is quoted to this effect by Alan Macfarlane in 'Witchcraft in Tudor and Stuart Essex' in J.S. Cockburn (ed.), *Crime in England 1550-1800* (London, 1977), at pp.83-4:
'Some woman doth fall out bitterly with her neighbour; there followeth some great hurt, either that God hath permitted the devil to vex him, or otherwise. There is a suspicion conceived. Within a few years after she is in some jar with another. He is also plagued. This is noted of all. Great fame is spread of the matter. Mother W is a witch. She hath bewitched goodman B. Two hogs which died strangely; or else he is taken lame. Well, mother W doth begin to be very odious and terrible unto many. Her neighbours dare say nothing but yet in their hearts they wish she were hanged. Shortly after another falleth sick and doth pine; he can have no stomach unto his meat; now he can not sleep. The neighbours come to visit him. "Well neighbour", sayth one, "do ye not suspect some naughty dealing; did ye never anger mother W?" "Truly neighbour" (sayth he) "I have not liked the woman a long time. I can not tell how I should displease her, unless it were this other day, my wife prayed her, and so did I, that she would keep her hens out of my garden. We spake her as fair as we could for our lives. I think verily she hath bewitched me." Everybody sayth now that mother W is a witch indeed, and hath bewitched the good man E. He cannot eat his meat. It is out of all doubt: for there were (those) who saw a weasel run from her house-ward into his yard even a little before he fell sick. The sick man dieth, and taketh it upon his death that he is bewitched. Then is mother W apprehended, and sent to prison.'
[60] See Cohn, p.xiii; Kieckhefer, p.ix.
[61] See A. Esmein, *A History of Continental Criminal Procedure with Special Reference to France*, trans. J. Simpson (London, 1914).
[62] *Discipline and Punish*, p.225.

proof as he thinks necessary'.[63] Apart from judicial activism, the hallmarks of inquisitorial process are that accusations emanate from public officials rather than private citizens and that the accused is subject to extensive judicial interrogation beyond the public gaze. The truth is established by judicial agents on the basis of a rational assessment of the assembled evidence rather than by submission of the issue to a panel of unaccountable lay jurors. Historically the quest for truth in inquisitorial systems has been lubricated by the systematic and regulated administration of torture. As the adoption of inquisitorial procedure was pioneered by the church to hound down heresy, it was peculiarly fitting for the trial of witchcraft as a species, indeed the ultimate embodiment, of heresy, representing as it did a parodic total inversion of Christianity.[64] The most significant feature of early modern inquisitorial practice in the present context was that on the continent of Europe, where this procedure was the norm, in the case of witchcraft exceptional measures were held to be justified and what can be termed a 'super-inquisitorial' procedure prevailed weighing even more heavily upon the accused than standard inquisitorial trial. Thus rules regarding the qualification of witnesses were relaxed, torture could be applied without first establishing that a crime had been committed, and repetition of torture, normally forbidden, was permitted.[65] Super-inquisitorial procedure accordingly ranks between non-judicial and inquisitorial modes of proceeding.

The accusatorial form of criminal process should be ranked as least directed to imposing pressure to reveal the truth upon the accused. It rests upon the accusation of a private citizen, the trial taking the form of a contest between two formally equal adversaries who choose their own witnesses, the judge acting as umpire. There is an emphasis upon public, oral testimony. Whereas the inquisitorial mode aspires to establish the absolute truth of the matter, the accusatorial system is formalistic. It makes a fetish of the rules of the game, and arrives at a relative, synthetic truth sufficient for practical legal purposes. Where the inquisition ranges state, church or some other concentration of power against the individual, the accusatorial mode entails the formal equality of the parties, a feature underscored in the medieval period by the *lex talionis*, which threatened accusers that if they failed to prove their case they faced a similar penalty to that the accused escaped. This concept of balance preempts the use of torture to assist in proof of the case of one side, and this form of procedure has evolved historically in association with the common law institution of jury trial, celebrated in liberal democratic political cultures as an

---

[63] M. Rheinstein, *Max Weber on Law in Economy and Society*, (Cambridge, Mass., 1954), p.46, n.12.

[64] J. Gaule, *Select Cases of Conscience Touching Witches and Witchcrafts* (London, 1646), p.57 *et seq.*, p.68.

[65] Levack, pp.73-5.

important safeguard for the accused.

In characterizing these two systems, the one influential in Roman law-based continental legal orders, and the other in common law jurisdictions, it is desirable to avoid any simplistic ideological representation of the latter as inherently more 'fair'. The criminal process in any given historically developing legal system consists of a complex and shifting ensemble of arrangements. The foregoing characterizations are typological, and operational legal systems combine elements of both. Thus police interrogation of suspects is an inquisitorial component of the English 'accusatorial' system of criminal justice – and one which many civil libertarians might well prefer to see made subject to magisterial supervision on the continental model. It is by no means the case that inquisitorially inclined systems inevitably leave the accused bereft of procedural guarantees. The Italian Code of Criminal Procedure, for example, secures that failure to observe any provision relating to the defence of the accused leads to the absolute nullity of the proceedings.[66] When comparing the English and continental European criminal justice systems historically, it must be appreciated that before the eighteenth century, an 'age of legalism' when a rational, formal justice was emergent,[67] the accused's position in an English trial for felony was anyway precarious, and only slowly improved thereafter. The lack of a developed law of evidence meant that hearsay was frequently allowed; the testimony of one eye witness was sufficient for conviction of felony compared with the two required by the romano-canonical law of proof; the right of the accused to call witnesses was subject to limitations that did not apply to the prosecution; and counsel for the defence was not allowed unless a point of law arose on indictment.[68] The self-satisfaction of the English with their common law liberties and disdain for the barbarism of continental juridical and penal practices, a style of cultural nationalism evident as early as the fourteenth and fifteenth centuries, could be countered with the charge that evidence which on the mainland of Europe might bring defendants to the threshold of torture frequently in England led straight to the scaffold. This was a point made by Dr. Samuel Johnson in debate with a Dutchman at Colchester in 1763:

> The Dutchman . . . thinking to recommend himself to us by expatiating on the superiority of the criminal jurisprudence of this country over that of Holland . . . inveighed against the barbarity of putting an accused person to the torture, in order to force a confession. But Johnson (responded) 'Why, Sir, you do not, I find, understand the law of your own country. The torture in Holland is

[66] Article 185(1) n.3; see G. Certoma, *The Italian Legal System* (London, 1985).

[67] See D. Hay 'Property, Authority and the Criminal Law' in D. Hay *et al.*, *Albion's Fatal Tree* (London, 1975).

[68] The latter two disabilities were removed by the Criminal Law Amendment Act 1867, section 3 and the Trials for Felony Act 1836 (6 and 7 Will. IV, c.114) respectively.

considered as a favour to an accused person; for no man is put to the torture there, unless there is as much evidence against him as would amount to conviction in England. An accused person among you, therefore, has one chance more to escape punishment, than those who are tried among us.[69]

It has been seen that in witchcraft trials continental inquisitorial practice and the application of techniques of torture were procedurally unshackled so that they might stand a better chance of success in the prosecution of occult crime. While English practice remained distinctly more moderate, the theoretical insulation of the defendant from concentrated pressure by the accusatorial tradition could be significantly eroded in proceedings against witches. We shall now turn to examine the respects in which English criminal proceedings developed tendencies which led them to resemble an inquisitorial process, sometimes intensified by de facto torture.

### 3. Sub-Inquisitorial Trial

Inquisitorial procedure was officially installed in certain corners of England's complex tapestry of courts. This was true of secular courts: the Star Chamber, which tried a number of witchcraft cases, but did not have a substantial role in the witch-hunt,[70] the Chancery, the court of Requests and coroners' courts, and, most relevantly, justices of the peace conducting preliminary examinations, as well as ecclesiastical courts. In the latter, judges themselves acted as accusers on the basis of common fame or personal knowledge, or proceeded upon accusations by promoters, or denunciation.[71] The potential of these inquisitorial forms to colour the evidence extracted was offset by four factors: the lack of gravity of many of the complaints, the use of purgation, the absence of torture and the purpose of the proceedings, which remained one of reclamation rather than punishment. In the event of a conclusion unfavourable to the accused witch, common practice was that she be ordered to attend the parish church on the Lord's day wearing a white sheet and carrying a white wand, and confess, committing herself to lead a reformed life.[72] The great majority of trials in the secular courts were conducted at the assize courts. Quarter sessions did not try capital felonies, but certified examinations of suspected witches to the justices of Gaol Delivery.[73] The usual procedure was for a complainant to lay an information before a justice in which personal misfortunes were recited and responsibility

[69] J. Boswell, *The Life of Samuel Johnson* (Harmondsworth, 1979), p.119.
[70] C.L. Ewen, *Witchcraft in the Star Chamber* (1938).
[71] W. Holdsworth, *A History of English Law*, 7th edn. (London, 1956), 1, 619-20.
[72] A. Macfarlane, *Witchcraft in Tudor and Stuart England*, p.69.
[73] *Ibid.*, p.23.

attributed to the accused witch. The suspect would be brought under examination and witnesses might be called. If the matter came to trial, the resultant written depositions would be read out in court, forming a major part of the evidence. Pending the next assizes, the accused witch might be committed to gaol. At the assizes, the complainant preferred a bill of indictment. Evidence was presented to the grand jury to determine whether the issue should go to trial. If a majority consisting of twelve, jurors found a true bill, the accused was then indicted. The prisoner being arraigned before the court and the indictment read, she was called upon to enter a plea. Where the charge was witchcraft this was normally a plea of not guilty. Suspected felons who refused to plead were subject to a judicial torture, *peine forte et dure*, involving pressing with heavy weights until the victim either relented or died, thought to have been last applied in 1741, and finally abolished in 1772.[74] This allowed those who saw conviction as practically inevitable to die without conviction and so protect their families against forfeiture of property,[75] thus opting for a form of judicial suicide, a rationale which did not however pertain to witchcraft after 1563 as wives and successors were already so protected by statute. Once a plea of not guilty was entered, the petty jury or 'jury of life or death' was empanelled, evidence taken, a verdict reached and sentence passed.

One inquisitorial element demonstrable in English witch trials and affecting the quality of the evidence and the chance of conviction was judicial activism. Several judges acted oppressively towards accused witches in order to secure a confession or otherwise managed the trials in such a way as strongly to promote conviction, in particular Brian D'Arcy at St. Osyth in Essex in 1582; Edward Fenner at the Warboys trial in 1593; Sir Edmund Anderson, C.J. of the Common Pleas at the trial of Elizabeth Jackson in 1602 and in several other cases in the 1590s and early 1600s; Sir Edmund Bromley in the trial of the Pendle witches in 1612; and Humphrey Winch and Sargeant Ranulph Crewe at Leicester in 1616.[76] In contrast George Gifford, a perceptive critic of witch-hunting, prefaced his *Dialogue concerning Witches* (1593) with a dedication to Robert Clarke, Baron of the Exchequer, praising him for his discrimination in the conduct of witchcraft trials.[77] Keith Thomas emphasizes that 'the judges as a class do not seem to have been any more vindictive towards witches than their contemporaries'.[78] Although they may not have been entrepreneurs of witch-hunting in the manner of their continental

[74] 12 Geo. III, c.20.

[75] J.W. Baker, *An Introduction to English Legal History*, 2nd edn. (London, 1979), p.415. Giles Cory, a witch suspect in the Salem episode, stood mute at his trial and was crushed to death under a pile of stones.

[76] K. Thomas, p.546; C.L. Ewen, *Witchcraft and Demonianism*, pp.126-8.

[77] Although Ewen points out that he was responsible for a proportion of witches convicted or hanged which was quite up to the average.

[78] Thomas, p.546.

counterparts, the signal importance of the fact that they shared the hostility of their contemporaries is thrown into relief by the central contribution of the reversal in judicial opinion to the decline of the witch-hunt in the latter half of the seventeenth and early eighteenth centuries; entrepreneurial activity by sceptical judges then barred off legal avenues of redress for the victims of witchcraft.

Zealous judges were not the only inquisitors. Bernard recommended as follows:

> Now while these sorts (witches) are in examining, it were very good, in the meanspace, to have a godly and learned Divine, and somewhat well read in the discourses of Witchcraft and impieties thereof, to be instructing the suspected, of the points of salvation, of the damnable cursednesse of witchcraft, and his or her fearfull state of death eternall, if guilty and not repentent: That thus . . . the suspected may be haply prepared to confession before Authority, when he or shee is examined.[79]

This recommendation lent further support to a practice which intensified the pressure upon the accused, Ewen describing the victims as being 'harassed almost to dementia by the divines'.[80] It is another respect in which religious authority combined with legal authority in the determination of witchcraft allegations, participating in the transformation of the judicial instance from a supposedly neutral arbiter into an engine for discovering the truth of witchcraft.

Another group awarded privileged access to the prisoners were the panels of women searchers whose function it was to investigate the bodies of accused female witches for the witch's or Devil's mark, and who make their first recorded appearance at the court leet of Southampton in 1579. These parels, frequently appointed by the court or as part of a preliminary or post-trial inquiry, and sometimes remunerated, were recruited from the ranks of 'honest matrons', 'women of credit' or midwives, and were akin to the panels appointed to warrant pregnancy when raised as a ground for the stay of execution.[81] Clearly women of maturity and experience, at least in 1645 they were in the nature of professional witnesses, experts in the location and recognition of the mark, the Manningtree witch Elizabeth Clarke being 'searched by women who had for many yeares known the Devill's marks'.[82] For it was not every uncommon bodily marking that necessarily sufficed as evidence, at least in theory.[83] As the anthropological literature systematically demonstrates

---

[79] Bernard, pp.237-8.

[80] C.L. Ewen, *Witchcraft and Demonianism*, p.126.

[81] Alice Samuel of Warboys pleaded pregnancy and was examined by a 'jury of matrons', although eighty years of age.

[82] Notestein, p.167.

[83] J. Stearne, *A Confirmation and Discovery of Witchcraft* (1648), pp.46-7; M. Hopkins, *The Discovery of Witches*, p.4.

for developing societies, witchcraft beliefs possess a sophisticated internal rationality. Thus Evans-Pritchard provides us with an exposition of the logic whereby the Azande differentiate misfortune attributable to witchcraft powers from that to be assigned to natural causes.[84] So in Stuart England, various brands of expertise were acknowledged as relevant in the forensic detection of witchcraft, including medical knowledge to demarcate sickness attributable to occult intervention from other sickness, and special knowledge in the identification of the Devil's mark to distinguish it from other bodily excrescences. The search itself may be classified as an inquisitorial process, comprising not this time an inquisition of the individual as legal personality, but an inquisition of the body, an experienced reading of the body for signs of Satanic dominion. It was also characteristically inquisitorial in the sense that it was, inevitably, an examination in private, ancillary to the court-bound proceedings determinant of guilt. In the Hopkins campaign, a domestic crusade against witches which Macfarlane has linked to the millenarian currents[85] at their strongest during this phase of the English Revolution,[86] Goodwife Mary Phillips, one of his disciples, performed the role of an itinerant searcher, organizing local assistants as the bandwagon rolled from place to place.[87]

As in continental Europe, rules relating to the giving of evidence were modified for the exceptional crime of witchcraft. Bernard thought that the testimony of 'fearfull, superstitious, or children, or old silly persons' should be admissible though it should be 'not easily credited',[88] while in his three-tiered scheme of evidence, accusation by another witch counted as conclusive proof, being placed alongside the Devil's mark, two witnesses of the pact or entertaining familiars, the discovery of images of the victim in the witch's house, bleeding of the corpse, and confession, in the third and highest category.[89] In practice, children below the normal age of competence for witnesses, fourteen, frequently gave evidence in witchcraft trials, including against their own parents, as in the cases of the Essex witch Ellen Smythe's thirteen-year-old son in 1579, and Elizabeth Device's nine-year-old daughter Jennet at Lancaster assizes in 1612. Wives also gave evidence against their husbands contrary to the usual rule. This deregulation of the capacity to give evidence further weighted judicial proceedings against the accused, conspiring with established

---

[84] E.E. Evans-Pritchard, *Witchcraft, Oracles and Magic among the Azande* (Oxford, 1937), abridged with an introduction by E. Gillies (Oxford, 1976), pp.25-30.

[85] A. Macfarlane, *Witchcraft in Tudor and Stuart England*, p.141.

[86] C. Hill, *The World Turned Upside Down: Radical Ideas During The English Revolution* (Harmondsworth, 1975), p.96.

[87] John Stearne was the leading searcher in the case of male suspects.

[88] Bernard, p.230.

[89] *Ibid.*, pp.226-7.

structural features such as denial of legal counsel, and the social circumstances of the trials, which were sometimes marked by such popular clamour that the suspected witch could not follow the proceedings.

Roles in the judicial process could become blurred. Magistrates anxious for conviction, in presenting evidence from the initial inquiry to the trial court, were in a strategic position to prejudice the later proceedings. A major trial at Chelmsford in 1566 was conducted by the Reverend Thomas Cole, a local rector, Sir John Fortescue, keeper of the Queen's wardrobe, John Southcote, justice of the King's Bench, with Sir Gilbert Gerard, the Queen's Attorney. It was unclear whether the last of these eminent figures was in charge of the prosecution or sitting in judgement, some of the evidence suggesting the latter.[90] On occasion it seems that testimony was taken from the bench. In the trials at Chelmsford promoted by Matthew Hopkins and John Stearne in 1645, one of the justices, Sir Thomas Bowes, testified that a glover, 'a very reliable man', had witnessed three or four imps emerging by moonlight from the house of one of the suspects, Anne West, an 'old Beldam'. At St. Osyth in 1582 one of those appointed to search for the Devil's mark had given evidence for the prosecution,[91] and the searches which took place under the auspices of Hopkins in 1645 were clearly an integral part of a promotional campaign.

The inquisitorial reorientation of legality could be reinforced by torture of the accused. Torture was a part of English criminal justice, but more marginal than on the continent. Although not recognized by the common law, it could lawfully be authorized under the prerogative. This was done where sorcery or magic were practised against the person of the monarch, and under Mary I and in the late Tudor and Stuart periods also in cases of non-treasonable witchcraft.[92] Kingly and queenly fear of treason by witchcraft was a factor in the accumulation of concern over the power of witches.[93] In 1620, Peacock, a schoolmaster, was committed to the Tower and subjected to torture for practising sorcery against James I.[94] But it was *de facto* rather than *de jure* torture which influenced the course of the English witch-hunt. Suspected witches, regarded with great hostility by the community, were often brutally served and physical hardship no doubt helped to bring them to confess. Matthew Hopkins and his associate raised maltreatment to a new level, forcing suspects to endure solitary confinement, constant intense observation, extended deprivation

---

[90] Notestein, pp.34-5.

[91] *Ibid.*, p.45.

[92] J.G. Bellamy, *The Tudor Law of Treason* (London, 1979), pp.111, 120; D. Veall, *The Popular Movement for Law Reform* (Oxford, 1970), p.26.

[93] See n.34, and C. Larner, 'James VI and I and Witchcraft' in *Witchcraft and Religion*, which deals with the trials for treason by sorcery in Scotland in 1590-1.

[94] C.L. Ewen, *Witch-Hunting and Witch Trials*, p.65.

of sleep, and starvation. John Gaule, a powerful critic of Hopkins' campaign, who declared that the office of witch-finder ought not to be assumed by a private person in a Christian church or state,[95] and who opposed the excesses of populism with the proposal that the petty jury of laymen of modest status be replaced by a tribunal of 'Eminent Physicians, Lawyers and Divines',[96] provides us with the following account of these practices:

> Having taken the suspected witch, she is placed in the middle of the room upon a stool or table, crosslegged, or in some other uneasy posture, to which if she submits not, she is then bound with cords; there is she watched and kept without meat or sleep for the space of twenty four hours for within that time they shall see her impe come and suck. A little hole is likewise made at the door for the imp to come in at; and lest it might come in some discernible shape, they that watch are taught to be ever and anon sweeping the room, and if they see any spiders or flies, to kill them. And if they cannot kill them, then they may be sure they are her imps.[97]

The function of observation generated circles of professional watchers who gave evidence of the materialization of familiars and other unnatural happenings in the course of their vigil.[98] This parallels the way in which the function of detecting the Devil's mark generated clusters of professional searchers, and was again a procedure closed off from public scrutiny. Witchcraft beliefs thus proliferated the categories of personnel engaged in the judicial process.

John Lowes, vicar of Brandeston in East Suffolk, was a particular victim of these methods. Lowes, possibly nearly eighty years of age at the time of his ordeal, was an obstreperous, turbulent and uncomfortable character, who had a long history of conflict with sections of his parishioners, on a number of occasions reaching the courts.[99] His case illustrates the utility of witchcraft accusations, or the fear of provoking them, as a means of imposing accountability upon or else disposing of unpopular or divisive figures in authority within the local community. A milder example is the treatment of Richard Alchurch, a controversial headmaster of King Edward VI Grammar School, Stourbridge in Worcestershire, who was dismissed at the end of the sixteenth century *inter alia* upon charges of occult activity.[100] Lowes was searched for marks,

---

[95] Gaule, p.88 *et seq.*

[96] *Ibid.*, p.195.

[97] *Ibid.*, p.78.

[98] C.L. Ewen, *Witchcraft and Demonianism*, p.275.

[99] C.L. Ewen, *The Trials of John Lowes, Clerk*, 1937.

[100] See R.L. Chambers, *The Headmasters of King Edward's School, Stourbridge from 1552 to 1691* (1960), pp.17-22, 25-9. Vulgar distrust of learned engagement with the occult was violently manifested when John Dee, Elizabeth I's astrologer, sometimes consulted in connection with witch trials, suffered the sacking of his house at Mortlake at the hands of a mob in 1583. On Dee, see F. Yates, *The Occult Philosophy of the Elizabethan Age* (London, 1979), Chapter 8.

25

forced to undergo the swimming test, and kept awake for several nights in succession by being constantly walked up and down. Eventually he admitted to having covenanted with the Devil and having bade a yellow imp sink 'a new vessel sailing in the middle of a large fleet', killing fourteen, near Harwich,[101] and so paved the way for his execution.

· Although enforced sleeplessness was a recognized mode of torture on the continent,[102] its English perpetrators compiled an apologetic justifying it in terms of the logic of witchcraft belief. John Stearne maintained that 'the watching is not to use violence or extremity to force them to confess, but only the keeping awake is first to see whether any of their spirits or familiars come to or neere them'. Solitary confinement was similarly defended on the basis that it was 'also to the end that Godly Divines might discourse with them . . . For if any of their society come to them to discourse with them, they will never confess'.[103] The pricking or prodding of witches' skin with needles to locate the Devil's mark, much used in Scotland, and occasionally in England,[104] was also a form of de facto torture motivated and legitimated by a specific witchcraft belief. So we may contrast a continental practice of torture limited by legalism (albeit significantly attenuated in witchcraft cases) with an English torture limited by belief, mitigated only by the self-restraint, if any, of its technicians.

A final element of interest in the early modern trial of witchcraft is the revival of trial by ordeal as a contributory mode of proof. In later medieval times the hot iron had been the usual form of ordeal for suspected witches, but it was the water ordeal which found favour as the vehicle for this anomalous and anachronistic re-enchantment of the trial.[105] The swimming of witches in connection with criminal proceedings against them was in recorded use in England from 1590, its incidence increasing in the seventeenth century, especially during the Hopkins episode. When trial by ordeal was abandoned with the withdrawal of clerical support in 1215, it was succeeded by divergent strategies probative: on the continent by the inquisition and torture; in England by jury trial, jurors initially presenting from their own knowledge and later coming to be seen as qualified triers of fact precisely by virtue of their lack of personal knowledge. Max Weber saw the English solution to the problem of proof as expressive of the persistent archaism of the common law tradition, classifying the jury as itself an oracular method of judicial resolution, a reincarnation of the ordeal, the jurors being unconfined by any

---

[101] C.L. Ewen, *The Trials of John Lowes, Clerk*, pp.6-7.

[102] Levack, p.75.

[103] Notestein, pp.189-90; Stearne, pp.13-14.

[104] Ewen cites a case at Newcastle-upon-Tyne in 1649.

[105] Bartlett, p.146. The water ordeal was also employed in the trial of witches during the medieval period: see G. Kittredge, *Witchcraft in Old and New England* (Cambridge, Mass., 1929), p.233.

requirement to indicate reasons for their decision,[106] (and therefore positioned to return 'perverse' verdicts and refract or defeat the formal law). From this perspective, English legal culture could be seen as providing a uniquely favourable environment for the recrudescence of the ordeal, especially in witchcraft cases, where proof on the basis of witness was problematic and the operation of supernatural powers was anyway at issue. Trial by ordeal was particularly indicated in intractable cases.[107] However, the swimming test was also in vogue on the continent where it appeared as early as the 1560s, and its propriety was vigorously contested in England as in Roman-based jurisdictions.

Stripped of the clerical superintendence and sacramental trappings of its medieval precursor, the procedure was carried out in a perfunctory fashion. Bernard provides us with a description of the ritual as performed upon Mary Sutton, who was executed with her mother at Bedford in 1612: 'She was . . . cast into a Mill-damme very deep, then bound; her right thumbe to her left toe, and her left thumbe to her right toe, who sat upon the water, and turned round like a wheele, as in a whirlepoole, yet they had her tyed in a rope, lest she should have sunke'.[108] The practice was commended by James I in his *Daemonologie*: '. . . so it appears that God hath appoynted (for a super-natural signe of the monstrous impietie of the Witches) that the water shal refuse to receive them in her bosom, that have shaken off them the sacred Water of Baptism and wilfullie refused the benefite thereof'.[109] But it was vilified by semi-sceptical treatise writers of the first half of the seventeenth century, who represented a transitional stage towards scepticism; recognizing that many convictions were unsafe by dint of the procedures adopted whilst maintaining a firm belief in the evil reality of witchcraft. Their arguments echo those advanced by critics of the ordeal in the middle ages.[110] Bernard himself did so in endorsing condemnation of the test for tempting God: 'There needs no miraculous meanes more to detect witches, then other secret practises, as it is an adulterous, and unbelieving generation to look for a signe: and what is this but a presumptuous expectation of an extraordinary revelation from God without warrant'.[111]

Dr. John Cotta, entering a plea for rationalism, deduced the correct mode of proceeding to proof at law from man's position in the cosmic order. Man's imperfection was to be contrasted with God's perfection. Man was confined to the use of natural means to discover witchcraft, even though it partook of a supernatural character. Reason was 'the sole eye

---

[106] M. Rheinstein, pp.79-80, 229; A. Hunt, *The Sociological Movement in Law* (London, 1978), pp.122-7.

[108] Bartlett, p.144.

[108] Bernard, p.214.

[109] James VI, *Daemonologie*, p.81.

[110] For these arguments, see Bartlett, pp.70-90.

[111] Bernard, p.215.

and light of natural understanding which God hath given to reasonable man'. Accordingly, trial must proceed on the basis of an evaluation of testimony in the light of a system of presumptions and proofs, and the water ordeal be excluded.[112] These texts depended very much upon the authority of the Bible, but scripture could be turned to liberal ends – there was no Biblical warrant for the water ordeal – and in time the authoritative mode of argument itself was to give way to analytical and experimental methods of reasoning.[113]

The swimming test did not always have to be imposed, for it attracted volunteers.[114] No doubt an important motivation to undergo the test was to restore a reputation damaged by local rumour. Once in the clutches of the law, the ordeal could provide a possible life-line for those protesting their innocence. Jane Wenham offered to be searched or cast into the water in order to establish her freedom of guilt. Trial could be precipitated by the victims of witchcraft accusations as a positive aid to rehabilitation, and superstitious modes of proof appeared to avail an opportunity for vindication, especially where the defendant's faith led her to believe that the divinity would intervene to save her. On the other hand such tests did not necessarily yield determinate results, and provided a persuasive source of evidence rather than a legal decision of guilt or innocence. In concert with the inquisitorial elements of the witch trial, they increased the physical and psychological pressure upon the accused.

### 4. Conclusion

The witch trial may be envisioned as a multi-layered site of interaction or exchange: between class cultures, affording a forum in which authority could speak and an outlet for popular expression in a pre-democratic political order; between the mundane and spiritual dimensions; between distinct but overlapping orders of discourse: scripture and demonology, natural philosophy, medicine and the law itself; between different terrains of political struggle, reflecting social, economic, religious, sexual, professional and community division; and ultimately, in the period of its decline, as judicial scepticism deepened, between competing magical and mechanistic world-views. It thus helped to effect a transition from one hegemonic conception of natural order to another. The formal and abstract qualities of the legal process enabled it to accommodate and negotiate these diversities, whilst its ritual and dramaturgical qualities equipped it to celebrate and sanctify a quasi-military victory over witchcraft in spectacular, public, physical modes of punishment calculated to repair the fabric of society and the authority of princes.

[112] J. Cotta, *The Triall of Witchcraft, shewing the True and Right Methode of the Discovery: with a Confutation of Erroneous Waves* (London, 1616), p.19.

[113] S. Anglo, 'The Desiderata of Belief' in S. Anglo (ed.) *The Damned Art: Essays in the Literature of Witchcraft* (London, 1977), pp.246-7.

[114] A. Macfarlane, *Witchcraft in Tudor and Stuart England*, p.141.

# Possession, Witchcraft, and the La..
# Jacobean England

Brian P. Levack[*]

In 1606, three years after the accession of King James I, the English government prosecuted a Berkshire gentleman, Brian Gunter, and his teen-aged daughter, Anne, for conspiracy to indict two women for the crime of witchcraft. Sir Edward Coke, the greatest jurist of the seventeenth century, initiated the case in the Court of Star Chamber, and many of the witnesses were members of the country's academic elite. This fascinating trial, which lasted more than eighteen months, involved demonic possession as well as witchcraft, and it had a lasting effect upon the prosecution of the crime of witchcraft in England for the remainder of the seventeenth century.[1]

In the mental world of the early seventeenth century, witchcraft and demonic possession were considered to be distinct but related phenomena. Witchcraft was, in its most basic form, harmful or black magic: the alleged infliction of physical harm or misfortune by one person on another through some kind of preternatural, supernatural, or mysterious means. It often took the form of a spell or a curse, and it was referred to in Latin as *maleficium*. The witch's maleficent power was believed, at least by educated Europeans during the early modern period, to have been acquired by a pact with the Devil. This meant that the witch was not only a felon who murdered her enemies, inflicted illness on children, killed cattle, started fires, and caused

---

* John E. Green Regents Professor of History, University of Texas at Austin; Scholar-in-Residence, Frances Lewis Law Center, Washington and Lee University School of Law, Fall 1994.

1. The interrogatories and depositions of the case are preserved in the Public Record Office, London, STAC 8/4/10, a volume consisting of 230 folios. The information was exhibited on January 20, 1606, and the last deposition was taken on April 25, 1607. Further interrogatories and depositions, taken on July 29, 1607, are preserved in the Ellesmere manuscripts at the Huntington Library in San Marino, California, EL MS. 5955/1-2. There is no record of a decree or sentence because the order and decree books have been lost. For a brief summary of the case, see C. L'ESTRANGE EWEN, WITCHCRAFT IN THE STAR CHAMBER 28-36 (1938).

sexual impotence in bridegrooms but also a heretic and apostate, one who had sold her soul to the Devil and who, according to widespread learned belief, worshiped her master with other witches at nocturnal orgies known as sabbaths. In some countries, although not in England, these same Devil-worshiping magicians were believed to have flown to these sabbaths, transported not so much by their brooms with which witches are still depicted today but by the power of the Devil with whom they were allied.[2]   Both ecclesiastical and secular authorities declared witchcraft to be a crime, and somewhere between 100,000 and 200,000 persons, the great majority of them women, were tried for this offense between 1450 and 1750. More than half of those tried were executed, usually by burning at the stake.[3]

The second phenomenon, demonic possession, is the process whereby, according to Christian belief, a demonic spirit invades the body of a human being, assumes control of its physical movements, and alters its personality. This assault upon the possessed person resulted in bodily contortions and convulsions, the performance of great feats of strength, clairvoyance, the vomiting of foreign objects, insensitivity to pain, the knowledge of previously unknown foreign languages, and speaking in strange voices. Those individuals who were possessed, whom we refer to as demoniacs, also exhibited a horror and revulsion of sacred things or the words of Scripture, and they frequently uttered obscenities and blasphemies.

Demonologists of the sixteenth century usually made a sharp distinction between demoniacs and witches on the grounds that possession, unlike witchcraft, was an involuntary condition and was not considered sinful or criminal.[4]   Demoniacs, unlike witches, were not held legally or morally

---

2.  Accusations or confessions that witches flew to the sabbath are rare in England. C. L'ESTRANGE EWEN, WITCHCRAFT AND DEMONIANISM 84 (1933). Flight was implied in some of the testimony against the Lancashire witches in 1612 and against Anne Baites in 1661. *See* THE TRIAL OF THE LANCASTER WITCHES, 1612, at 61-62 (G. B. Harrison ed., 1929); DEPOSITIONS FROM THE CASTLE OF YORK 191 (J. Raine ed., London, Surtees Society 1861). The belief in flight was in large part dependent upon a belief that witches gathered in large numbers and at great distances from their homes to worship the Devil, and such beliefs were uncommon in English witch-trials. The English prohibition of judicial torture, which on the Continent was instrumental in securing confessions to both Devil-worship and flight, explains the paucity of such references in English witch-trials.

3.  For different estimates of the total number of prosecutions and executions throughout Europe, see BRIAN P. LEVACK, THE WITCH-HUNT IN EARLY MODERN EUROPE 19-22 (1987), and ANNE L. BARSTOW, WITCHCRAZE: A NEW HISTORY OF THE EUROPEAN WITCH-HUNTS 20-23, 179-81 (1994).

4.  Despite the distinction, possessed persons did occasionally incur the suspicion of witchcraft, while some women accused of witchcraft actually manifested signs of possession after they had been accused. *See* CAROL KARLSEN, THE DEVIL IN THE SHAPE OF A WOMAN

responsible for their actions. They could, therefore, violate cultural norms with impunity. They could shout and scream, disobey their superiors, and exhibit sexually immodest behavior, claiming in effect that the Devil, rather than they themselves, was responsible for their actions. This fact helps to explain why possession tended to occur among subordinate groups in society, especially young women who would not otherwise engage in unconventional or rebellious behavior.[5] Possession allowed these women to acknowledge illicit impulses in themselves without according those impulses any legitimate status.[6]

Yet however distinct witchcraft and possession may have been, there was a close connection between the two phenomena because witches were often accused of causing the possession of another person. Traditional demonological theory acknowledged two methods of possession: A demon could enter a person's body either directly, with God's permission but without any human agency, or as the result of a witch's command. In the latter case, demonic possession became just one of many maleficent deeds that a witch might be accused of.[7] The afflictions that the demoniac suffered were thus classified as acts of harmful magic. The classic illustration of the connection between the two phenomena occurred at Salem, Massachusetts, in 1692, when a group of girls, manifesting various signs of demonic affliction, accused scores of women and men of harming them by means of witchcraft and ultimately sent nineteen of those accused witches to their deaths.[8]

---

243-44 (1987); H.C. Erik Midelfort, *The Devil and the German People: Reflections on the Popularity of Demon Possession in Sixteenth Century*, 11 RELIGION & CULTURE IN THE RENAISSANCE & REFORMATION, SIXTEENTH CENTURY ESSAYS & STUDIES 116-17 (1989). The girls in a home founded by Antoinette Bourignon in the early seventeenth century experienced hallucinations and underwent exorcism, but they also declared that they could practice witchcraft and worship the Devil. *See* 3 HENRY C. LEA, MATERIALS TOWARD A HISTORY OF WITCHCRAFT 1044 (1957).

5. On the gender and social status of demoniacs, see KARLSEN, *supra* note 4, at 231-36, and Midelfort, *supra* note 4, at 109-12.

6. KARLSEN, *supra* note 4, at 249-51. *See generally* Michael MacDonald, *Introduction* to WITCHCRAFT AND HYSTERIA IN ELIZABETHAN LONDON (Michael MacDonald ed., 1990).

7. On the connection between possession and witchcraft, see KEITH THOMAS, RELIGION AND THE DECLINE OF MAGIC 478 (1971). Occasionally contemporaries challenged the belief that a man could send a Devil into another person's body. For the opinion of a skeptical Jesuit in 1555, see 3 LEA, *supra* note 4, at 1051.

8. A total of 78 possessed persons, all but twelve of whom were women, were responsible for only a small percentage of the witchcraft accusations at Salem, but they made the initial accusations and played a decisive role in the progress of the hunt by directing accusations at more than one suspect. KARLSEN, *supra* note 4, at 223-25. The possessed girls,

At the beginning of the seventeenth century, the time of the trial with which we are concerned, both witchcraft and possession appeared to be on the rise. The number of reported cases of possession had risen significantly during the late sixteenth century, and now, as a result of the demonization of European culture that accompanied the Protestant and Catholic Reformations, Europe was about to enter what has been referred to as the "golden age of the demoniac," a period when literally thousands of instances of possession would be observed.[9] During the same period of time the number of witchcraft trials had also been steadily increasing and would soon reach an all-time high.[10] Many of the witchcraft trials of the seventeenth century, such as that of Urbain Grandier at Loudun in France in 1634, originated in charges brought by demoniacs, in that case a convent of possessed Ursuline nuns.[11]

England conformed fairly closely to this general European pattern. Although the prosecution of witches never became as intense in England as it did in Germany, Switzerland, Poland, or Scotland, there had been a large increase in the number of trials during the 1570s and 1580s.[12] The number of trials dropped in the 1590s and in the first years of the seventeenth century, but the percentage of trials resulting in executions rose precipitously after 1597.[13] In 1602, a record number of executions occurred in the county of Essex, and there were signs that the trend would continue.[14] The accession of James I in 1603 certainly pointed in this direction because James, as king of Scotland, had published a treatise on witchcraft, entitled *Daemon-*

---

together with the confessing witches, were exclusively responsible for making accusations regarding the worship of the Devil; all the other witnesses accused witches simply of *maleficium*. RICHARD GODBEER, THE DEVIL'S DOMINION: MAGIC AND RELIGION IN EARLY NEW ENGLAND 205 (1992).

9. E. WILLIAM MONTER, WITCHCRAFT IN FRANCE AND SWITZERLAND 60 (1977). In Geneva, possessed women became a problem at the beginning of the seventeenth century. For a listing of some of the most prominent cases, see TRAUGOTT K. OESTERREICH, POSSESSION, DEMONIACAL AND OTHER, AMONG PRIMITIVE RACES IN ANTIQUITY, THE MIDDLE AGES, AND MODERN TIMES 188-89 (D. Ibberson trans., 1966).

10. Witchcraft prosecutions peaked at different times in different countries and regions, but the height of the entire European phenomenon was the period from 1580 to 1650. *See* LEVACK, *supra* note 3, at 170-75.

11. *See generally* ALDOUS HUXLEY, THE DEVILS OF LOUDUN (1952).

12. *See* C. L'ESTRANGE EWEN, WITCH HUNTING AND WITCH TRIALS 101 (1929) (charting numbers of prosecutions for home circuit during entire period of witch-hunting).

13. *Id.* at 100.

14. ALAN MACFARLANE, WITCHCRAFT IN TUDOR AND STUART ENGLAND 58 (1970). The annual number of accusations and indictments had been significantly higher in a number of years during the 1580s and 1590s. *Id.* at 26-27.

*ologie*, which refuted the views of skeptics such as Reginald Scot and encouraged the vigorous prosecution of the crime.[15] During the first year of James's reign in England, moreover, Parliament had passed a new witchcraft statute, which extended the scope of the crime specifically to include commerce with demons as well as maleficent magic and established stricter penalties for those convicted.[16] Witchcraft and possession were also becoming more closely associated. During the reign of Elizabeth, a number of witchcraft prosecutions, including the widely publicized trial of Elizabeth Jackson in 1602, had originated in accusations made by demoniacs.[17]

With a demonologist like James on the throne and with a new statute at the disposal of the justices of the peace, we would expect that a person tried for witchcraft in 1604 or shortly thereafter would incur the full wrath of state power. Everything would suggest that we would find the government using the system to root out witches and prosecute them to the full extent of the law. Much has been made of the connection between the rise of witch-hunting on the one hand and the development of state power on the other. Some have argued that witchcraft was one of the means by which the early modern state disciplined and Christianized the masses, suppressed rebellion, and contributed to the advance of that Leviathan, the secular, absolutist state.[18] Because James, like the French political theorist Jean Bodin, had written in support of royal absolutism as well as witch-hunting, the vigorous prosecution of witchcraft seemed all the more likely.[19] But as events

---

15. *See generally* JAMES VI, DAEMONOLOGIE (G. B. Harrison ed., 1924) (Edinburgh 1597).

16. 1 Jam., ch. 12 (1604) (Eng.). This act was more severe than the Elizabethan statute, 5 Eliz., ch. 16 (1563) (Eng.), which it replaced in four respects: 1) It declared it to be a felony if the victim of witchcraft was merely injured rather than killed; 2) it replaced life imprisonment with death for the second offense in cases involving the use of magic to locate lost treasure or an unsuccessful attempt to kill someone by magical means; 3) it made it felonious to use a dead body for magical purposes; and 4) it made it a felony to "consult, covenant with, entertain, employ, feed, or reward an evil and wicked spirit." *Id.* The act is summarized in MATTHEW HALE, PLEAS OF THE CROWN: A METHODICAL SUMMARY 1678, at 6-8 (1972). For a comparison of the penalties enumerated in the statutes of 1563 and 1604, see MACFARLANE, *supra* note 14, at 14-15.

17. On the sixteenth-century English cases of possession, see D. P. WALKER, UNCLEAN SPIRITS: POSSESSION AND EXORCISM IN FRANCE AND ENGLAND IN THE LATE SIXTEENTH AND EARLY SEVENTEENTH CENTURIES 42-73 (1981). For the Mary Glover Case of 1602, which resulted in the trial of Elizabeth Jackson, see generally MacDonald, *supra* note 6.

18. For a discussion and critique of these theories, see Brian P. Levack, *State-Building and Witch Hunting in Early Modern Europe*, in WITCHCRAFT IN EARLY MODERN EUROPE: STUDIES IN CULTURE AND BELIEF 96-115 (J. Barry et al. eds., 1996).

19. *See generally* JEAN BODIN, DE LA DÉMONOMANIE DES SORCIERS (Paris 1580).

unfolded in England between 1604 and 1606, the government of James I surprisingly used its secular judicial power for very different purposes.

### The Possession of Anne Gunter

The case began in 1604 with an instance of demonic possession. Anne Gunter, the fourteen-year-old daughter of Brian Gunter, a gentleman from North Moreton, Berkshire, displayed many of the symptoms that had become common in both English and Continental cases of possession. She experienced convulsive fits in which her body writhed, quivered, and shook; she acquired temporary deafness and blindness; her body became extraordinarily stiff; she sneezed up, voided, and vomited pins — sometimes numbering in the hundreds — while still more pins exuded from her breasts and fingers; she foamed at the mouth; her pulse was temporarily interrupted; and she went as many as twelve days without eating. She physically assaulted those around her, throwing her sisters against the walls of their house. Her shoes, stockings, petticoats, and garters all displayed the remarkable ability to untie themselves, come out from under her clothes of their own power, crawl around the ground, and return to her body, tying themselves neatly in place. She also told people who were brought before her how much money they had in their purses.[20]

Like so many alleged demoniacs, Anne also claimed that witches were responsible for her afflictions. In fact, she named three women: Elizabeth Gregory, Mary Pepwell, and Agnes Pepwell. Anne further claimed that she had had visions of these women's familiar spirits. Familiar spirits or imps were common features of English witchcraft. Appearing in the form of domestic animals who often possessed unusual features, they were believed to be the demonic source of the witch's power. They were also believed to have received nourishment from the witch, usually by sucking an extra nipple on the witch's body, a nipple that when examined could be shown to be insensitive to pain. Location of this extra teat had become a main concern of those who were responsible for arresting and interrogating suspected witches, and the identification of such a nipple, known as the witch's mark, could provide grounds for the indictment and sometimes even the conviction of the accused.[21] In the case of the North Moreton witches, Anne Gunter

---

20. STAC 8/4/10, fol. 201 & *passim*. The fits began shortly after mid-summer 1604.

21. On familiars and the witch's mark, see EWEN, *supra* note 2, at 70-76. William Perkins claimed that the mark constituted sufficient presumptive evidence for examining a witch, a claim that Sir Robert Filmer later challenged. *See* [Sir Robert Filmer], AN ADVERTISEMENT TO THE JURY MEN OF ENGLAND TOUCHING WITCHES 9-10 (London 1653).

identified the three familiars as a white mouse with a man's face, a black rat with a swine's face, and a white toad (presumably with a toad's face).[22] Because Anne made this identification in a vision, her evidence was considered to be spectral, the same type of evidence that was to become so controversial in the Salem witchcraft trials and ultimately rejected as unreliable, it being possibly the product of demonic illusion. At this time, however, such evidence was admissible, and it remained so in English witchcraft cases well into the 1660s.[23]

It is not entirely clear why the Gunters preferred charges of witchcraft against these three women. We do know, however, that witchcraft accusations served the function not only of explaining misfortune but also of eliminating socially undesirable people or one's personal rivals. Evidence from later depositions in Star Chamber suggests that the Gunter family had long been at odds with the three accused women and their families. Testimony from various sources revealed that Gunter had been involved in a fight with members of Elizabeth Gregory's family at a football match and that his neighbors held him to be responsible for the death of her two brothers-in-law.[24] Indeed, Elizabeth Gregory, upon coming to the Gunter residence, accused Brian of being a "murdering bloodsucker" and demanded revenge.[25]

---

RICHARD BERNARD, A GUIDE TO GRAND JURY MEN 214-15 (London 1627), considered discovery of the witch's mark one of seven proofs sufficient to convict a person of witchcraft, since it established "a league made with the Devil." On the use of language borrowed from Continental law regarding presumptive and convictive evidence in witchcraft cases, see BARBARA J. SHAPIRO, BEYOND REASONABLE DOUBT AND PROBABLE CAUSE: HISTORICAL PERSPECTIVES ON THE ANGLO-AMERICAN LAW OF EVIDENCE 51-54, 164-68 (1991).

22. STAC 8/4/10, fols. 101, 144v, 210.

23. Sir Matthew Hale allowed the use of spectral evidence in the trial of Amy Duny and Rose Collender in 1662. *See generally* A TRYAL OF WITCHES AT THE ASSIZES HELD AT BURY ST. EDMONDS FOR THE COUNTY OF SUFFOLK (London 1682) [hereinafter A TRYAL OF WITCHES]. On spectral evidence at the Salem witchcraft trials in 1692, see generally Daniel G. Payne, *Defending Against the Indefensible: Spectral Evidence at the Salem Witchcraft Trials*, 129 ESSEX INST. HIST. COLLECTIONS 62 (1993). For a list of English cases in which spectral evidence was admitted, either in examination or actual trial, see GEORGE L. KITTREDGE, WITCHCRAFT IN OLD AND NEW ENGLAND 363-64 (1929). The most important question was not whether such evidence would be admitted but whether it should pass for proof.

24. STAC 8/4/10, fols. 2b, 167v, 178. The parish register of North Moreton confirms that in May 1598 John and Richard Gregory were killed by "old Gunter and his sons" at a football match. Gunter "drew his dagger and broke both their heads." Berkshire Record Office, D/P 86/1/1. Gunter's three sons are identified as Brian, Harvey, and William. STAC 8/4/10, fol. 11.

25. STAC 8/4/10, fol. 178; *see also id.* fol. 168 (recording deposition of William Sawyer).

Further tension might have arisen from the fact that the three women, being from the lower classes of society, threatened to drain the resources of the more well-to-do members of society, such as the Gunters, or simply that they, being aggressive and contentious women, did not conform to the ideal of feminine conduct that was being proclaimed at the time. Agnes Pepwell had in fact been suspected of witchcraft for many years, while Elizabeth Gregory, whose mother-in-law, Katherine Gregory, was reputed to be a witch, was a "notorious scold."[26] When Brian Gunter had himself been gravely ill in the summer of 1604, he had suspected Elizabeth Gregory as the cause of his misfortune, and indeed, after scratching her head, he had quickly recovered, thereby confirming his suspicion.[27]

In the course of her afflictions, Anne also accused a godly minister, Reverend Thomas Bird from the neighboring parish of Brightwell, of coming to her parish to preach and "choke me with his pins."[28] This charge suggests a possible source of Anne's possession. Ministers, especially those of the godly or Puritan persuasion, could be particularly effective in making the members of their congregations aware of their moral shortcomings and of creating moral anxiety regarding salvation. We know that many demoniacs came from environments in which strict moral standards were enforced. In Europe, hundreds of demoniacs were nuns from cloistered convents, while in England and America a consistent pattern of possession occurred within families known for their piety.[29] The Gunter family probably conforms to this pattern, as does that of the Throckmorton girls, who were dispossessed by the charismatic Puritan minister and healer John Darrel in 1593. In these situations, the demands created moral pressures that the children or nuns could not bear, resulting in a hysterical reaction. The fact that Anne railed against Bird and other godly ministers who came to observe her fits would be consistent with this analysis.[30]

---

26. *Id.* fols. 160, 196, 226.

27. *Id.* fols. 88, 106.

28. *Id.* fol. 209 (recording deposition of Thomas Bird).

29. On the possession of nuns in European convents, see the incidents reported in JOHANN WEYER, WITCHES, DEVILS, AND DOCTORS IN THE RENAISSANCE 304-12 (George Mora & Benjamin Kohl eds. & John Shea trans., Medieval & Renaissance Text & Studies 1991) (1583), and generally in HUXLEY, *supra* note 11. In England and America, possession often occurred in the households of Puritans. THOMAS, *supra* note 7, at 481. One commentator argues that possession occurred among women who experienced crises regarding conversion. GODBEER, *supra* note 8, at 114-15

30. There is no direct evidence of the piety practiced in the Gunter household, although during her fits at Oxford Anne did ask to receive the sacrament. She also requested that her brother-in-law, Thomas Holland, the regius professor of divinity, first give a sermon, noting

The possibility that Anne was responding, either consciously or subconsciously, to the pressures of her moral training raises the more general question of whether she was suffering from some sort of psychiatric disorder. Scholars who do not believe that demons can actually possess the bodies of human beings have traditionally advanced two explanations of the symptoms that demoniacs manifested. The first is that they were engaged in deliberate deception, faking their symptoms in order that they could either behave in an unconventional manner or retaliate against their rivals. The second is that they were experiencing some sort of natural illness, whether it be physical or psychological in origin. Epilepsy, St. Vitus Dance, Tourette's Syndrome, ergot poisoning, and hysteria have all been advanced as the "real" cause of the afflictions suffered by demoniacs. These two explanations are not mutually exclusive. Even if Anne were feigning some of her symptoms, which she later admitted to having done, that does not exclude the possibility that other symptoms, particularly her convulsive fits, were genuine. Anne herself ultimately adopted this position, admitting to deception while insisting that she had not faked her convulsions.[31]

The problem of distinguishing between fakery and natural illness in these circumstances is compounded by the fact that in both cases cultural traditions and expectations shape the demoniac's behavior. Anne and the other members of her family clearly were fully familiar with the behavior of other demoniacs, and this knowledge allowed her to feign certain activities, such as reacting violently to the reading of the Lord's Prayer. But that same body of knowledge also explains why her "natural" convulsive fits took the form that they did. Demoniacs in all societies act the way their religious culture tells them they should act. Either consciously or unconsciously, they *learn* how to act like possessed persons. This is not as surprising as it may seem. Anthropologists and many psychiatrists would argue that psychiatric illness tends to manifest itself in forms that reflect the cultural expectations of the society in which it occurs.[32] What we are probably witnessing in 1604 are the symptoms of a psychiatric disorder that was taking its most common cultural form in seventeenth-century Europe.

---

that while the Devil could deny food to her body, he could not do likewise to her soul. STAC 4/8/10, fol. 207v (recording deposition of Susanna Holland).

31. *Id.* fols. 112-129v (recording deposition of Anne Gunter).

32. MacDonald, *supra* note 6, at xxxiv-xxxv & n.65. The possibility that individuals can learn to be possessed or hysterical explains why many instances of demonic possession in the early modern period spread from one person to another, often afflicting large groups. For examples of such contagious and collective possessions, besides the well-known ones at Loudun and Salem, see 3 LEA, *supra* note 4, at 1045-46.

When Anne began to exhibit the symptoms of possession, her father arranged for a number of doctors from nearby Oxford and Newbury to examine her. Their inability to find any natural cause of her ailment strengthened the suspicion that witchcraft had been responsible.[33] Not everyone, however, was convinced that Anne was the victim of a supernatural illness. As in many cases of possession, the suspicion of deception naturally arose. The strength of that suspicion became apparent after Anne was moved first to Staunton, Oxfordshire, where she spent some time at the house of her brother Harvey, and then to the University of Oxford, where she stayed with Dr. Thomas Holland, the regius professor of divinity and the rector of Exeter College. The reason for the selection of Holland's residence is that Holland's wife, Susan, was Anne's sister.[34] Anne apparently already knew many of the members of the college, some of whom later accompanied her to Abington.[35]

While staying at Holland's residence, Anne continued to exhibit her symptoms of possession, and it is quite possible that they became more pronounced as she became the main theatrical attraction in Oxford, sometimes commanding an audience of forty people at one time. The similarities between possession and theater have been noted before: Both possession and attempts to end it by means of exorcism involved the recitation of a script and the staging of an action.[36] The main question was whether God or the human actors wrote the script. This is the question that the large number of

---

33. STAC 8/4/10, fols. 95v, 96, 105, 140v, 156.

34. Holland had married Susan Gunter in North Moreton on July 22, 1593. Berkshire Record Office, D/P 86/1/1. DIARY OF WALTER YONGE, ESQ. 12 (George Roberts ed., London, J.B. Nichols & Son 1848) refers to Anne as "a near kinswoman" to Holland's wife. John Harding, D.D., in his deposition before Star Chamber, specifically identified Anne as Mistress Holland's sister. STAC 8/4/10, fol. 6. In a Star Chamber case in 1621, Brian Gunter was accused together with William Holland, gent., who was identified as his grandchild, and with one Susan Holland, widow, and her spinster daughter Susan, in a dispute over tithes due to Gilbert Bradshawe. STAC 8/80/6. The younger Susan was baptized as "Susanna, daughter of Mr. Thomas Holland, Doctor in Divinity," at North Moreton on December 3, 1601. Berkshire Record Office, D/P 86/1/1.

35. STAC 8/4/10, fol. 18, refers to her "being supported on either side and behind her with some of her friends and scholars of Oxford." John Hall, MA, held one of Anne's hands during her fits at Exeter College. *See* STAC 8/4/10, fol. 207 (recording deposition of Susanna Holland). A number of the fellows of Exeter later gave testimony in Star Chamber *ex parte* Brian Gunter.

36. KARLSEN, *supra* note 4, at 231, discusses possession as "cultural performance" in which shared meanings were communicated by the demoniacs, the ministers, and the audience. For a discussion of exorcism as theater, see STEPHEN GREENBLATT, SHAKESPEAREAN NEGOTIATIONS 96-114 (1988).

fellows, students, and dons who visited Holland's home to view Anne's behavior were asking. Many of these visitors noted inconsistencies in the demoniac's actions or discovered that she could not pass various tests they devised to prove the authenticity of her fits. Dr. John Harding, the Hebrew reader for the University and the president of Magdalen College, observed that, while claiming to be able to read while blind, she could not continue her reading once the lights went out.[37] A student at the college, the second son of the Scottish earl of Murray, discovered the different means she used to untie her shoes and garters and move them along the floor.[38] As we shall see, the list of skeptics grew steadily during the next year and eventually included the king himself.

### The Abington Witchcraft Trial

Although suspicion of Anne was growing, Brian Gunter proceeded to have the women whom his daughter had named as the cause of her afflictions charged with witchcraft. The trial of Elizabeth Gregory and Agnes Pepwell (Mary Pepwell had fled) took place at the Lent assizes held at Abington on March 1, 1605.[39] The trial was by all standards unusual, not the least because of its length. At a time when trials were often handled with great haste and juries decided many cases at one sitting, this one trial lasted at least eight hours, with the jury not withdrawing to "confer of the issue and the proofs thereof made by the evidence" until after 10 p.m. Although Gunter marshaled some fifteen witnesses, and the presentation of the evidence involved some "very long discourses," the jury decided on a verdict of not guilty.

Two developments during the trial appear to have been decisive in producing this verdict. The first was the determination of Thomas Hinton of Chilton Park, a cousin of one of the judges, to expose Anne's fits as counterfeit. Not only did he succeed in making a declaration of his incredulity before the court, but he also spoke with others who attended the proceedings, including Sir Francis Knowles and Alexander Chokke, a justice of the peace.[40] The second development was the selection of Chokke and

---

37. STAC 8/4/10, fol. 21 (recording deposition of John Harding). Harding and Holland were both members of the commission that prepared the King James version of the Bible.

38. Examination of Murray by Lord Ellesmere, July 29, 1607, Huntington Library, EL MS. 5955/2.

39. The depositions of Thomas Hinton and Alexander Chokke in the later trial of Anne and Brian in Star Chamber, STAC 8/4/10, fols. 9-18, remain the only source for the proceedings of this trial. The assize records for the Oxfordshire circuit are no longer extant.

40. STAC 8/4/10, fol. 18v (recording examination of Alexander Chokke).

two other justices of the peace as members of the jury. Chokke, who was appointed foreman of the jury, became increasingly skeptical regarding the authenticity of Anne's fits when he observed Anne's behavior during the trial. The same was true of the other two justices of the peace, who interviewed Anne just before the trial began.

As unusual as the conduct of this trial may have been, its outcome was by no means exceptional, at least not in England. An accused witch had a better chance of securing an acquittal in England than in any other country in western Europe, with the possible exception of the Netherlands and Finland. In the early seventeenth century, more than fifty percent of all English witchcraft trials ended in acquittals.[41] The absence of inquisitorial procedure and the prohibition of torture in English common-law courts had a great deal to do with this high acquittal rate. In criminal trials at the common law, the officers of the court could not force defendants to confess to deeds they had not in fact performed. The method of proof that the common-law courts did use, trial by jury, by no means guaranteed acquittal, especially when a witch's neighbors believed that she possessed malevolent powers. But in this particular trial, as in many others in which the jury became skeptical, the system worked to the defendant's advantage.

Perhaps the main reason for the relatively low conviction rate in England was the supervision of local justice by judges from the central courts. Throughout Europe a fairly close correlation existed between the exercise of central control over witchcraft trials and the maintenance of a fairly low percentage of convictions and executions.[42] In England most trials took place in the local assizes, but the circuit judges who heard these cases were the judges of the central common-law courts at Westminster. Regarding themselves as the conservators of the law, these men were in large part responsible for preventing some of the procedural abuses that reportedly took place in many German and Scottish regions

---

41. MACFARLANE, *supra* note 14, at 57. This figure is based on an analysis of the Essex assizes and includes those whose bill of presentment was dismissed. In Österbotten, Finland, at least 57% of those tried for witchcraft between 1666 and 1685 were acquitted. *See* Antero Heikkinen & Timo Kervinen, *Finland: The Male Domination, in* EARLY MODERN EUROPEAN WITCHCRAFT 319, 335 (Bengt Ankarloo & Gustav Henningsen eds., 1990). On acquittals in Holland, see generally Hans de Waardt, *Prosecution or Defense: Procedural Possibilities Following a Witchcraft Accusation in the Province of Holland Before 1800, in* WITCHCRAFT IN THE NETHERLANDS: FROM THE FOURTEENTH TO THE TWENTIETH CENTURY 79 (Marijke Gijswijt-Hofstra & Willem Frijhoff eds. & Rachel van der Wilden-Fall trans., 1991).

42. *See* LEVACK, *supra* note 3, at 85-90 (comparing central courts' leniency towards witchcraft prosecutions with local courts' harsher approach).

when local officials — often without legal training — conducted witchcraft trials.

A few English assize judges, to be sure, did use their power and
influence to secure the conviction and execution of witches.  At the trial of
Elizabeth Jackson held in London in 1602, for example, the judge, Edmund
Anderson, in summing up the evidence, assured the jury that "the land was
full of witches" and claimed that he had hanged more than twenty of them.[43]
But it was far more common for English judges to exercise caution and
restraint in witchcraft cases.  In the trial of Gregory and Pepwell, David
Williams, a justice from the Court of King's Bench, served as one of the
assize judges, and his actions during the trial certainly contributed to the
acquittal of the two women.[44]  Williams allowed Thomas Hinton to declare
his skepticism before the court; he appointed three skeptical justices of the
peace to the jury; and when Brian Gunter entreated him to have the court
hear Elizabeth Gregory pronounce the spell that allegedly would relieve
Anne of her fits, the judge deliberately substituted a different spell from the
one Gunter had given him.[45]

### The Investigation of Anne Gunter

The acquittal of Gregory and Pepwell by no means settled the issue.  In
the following months Anne Gunter came under the care or observation of
many different persons, all of whom became more skeptical of the authenticity of her alleged demonic affliction.  The first were the members of the
Royal College of Physicians.  Just before the trial, the newly appointed
bishop of London, Richard Vaughan, asked the fellows of the College to
examine the young demoniac.  Three of the fellows visited Anne and concluded on March 4 that she was feigning possession.[46]  A few weeks later,

---

43.  Regarding Anderson's conduct in 1602, see Clive Holmes, *Popular Culture?
Witches, Magistrates and Divines in Early Modern England*, in UNDERSTANDING POPULAR
CULTURE 86, 91 (Steven L. Kaplan ed., 1984).

44.  The other assize judge was Sir Christopher Yelverton, also a justice on King's
Bench.  It is apparent from the testimony of Alexander Chokke that both judges presided at
the trial.  STAC 8/4/10, fol. 18.  More commonly, one of the assize judges adjudicated civil
cases while the other heard criminal trials.

45.  *Id.* fol. 9v.  Williams at first denied Gunter's request, leading Gunter to complain
that his daughter "could not have that justice which Mr. Throckmorton's children had," a
reference to the conviction of three witches from Warboys, Huntingdonshire, for causing the
Throckmorton girls' possession in 1593.

46.  1 GEORGE CLARK, A HISTORY OF THE ROYAL COLLEGE OF PHYSICIANS OF LONDON
198 (1964).  William Harvey, then a candidate of the College and a friend of one of Anne's
examiners, later used this case in his Anatomical Lectures of 1616 to illustrate how a person

Dr. Richard Haddock, a physician in Salisbury, reached a similar conclusion regarding the authenticity of Anne's malady. Acting at the request of Henry Cotton, the bishop of the diocese, Haddock examined Anne and concluded that the pins she vomited up were the same ones that he had secretly marked beforehand.[47]

Anne's fits continued through the summer of 1605, and at the end of August they attracted the attention of King James himself when he visited Oxford.[48] It is not surprising that the king, having already written a treatise on demonology while king of Scotland, would express interest in a case of this sort. James had been highly credulous of witchcraft in that book, an understandable position because he himself had been the alleged victim of a conspiracy of witches from North Berwick who were in league with the treasonous earl of Bothwell. Those witches had purportedly thrown some hexed cats into the North Sea, thereby causing a storm that had delayed the arrival of the king's new bride, Princess Anne of Denmark, in 1590. They also were accused of plotting to kill the king. The king's personal interest in that case had led to one of the most severe witch-hunts in Scottish history.[49] Since that time, however, especially since his arrival in England in 1603, James had become more skeptical regarding witchcraft, and he had already begun to take delight in exposing hoaxes.[50] The Gunter case, therefore, offered him an opportunity to explore one of his long-standing interests as well as to play the role of enlightened monarch.

---

could make herself insensitive to pain. THE ANATOMICAL LECTURES OF WILLIAM HARVEY 46-47 (Gweneth Whitteridge ed. & trans., 1964). In Richard A. Hunter & Ida MacAlpine, *A Note on William Harvey's "Nan Gunter" (1616)*, 12 J. OF THE HIST. OF MED. 512 (1957), the authors suggest that Anne may have first drawn Harvey's attention to patients who showed disturbances of sensation accompanying mental illness. Harvey did not, however, claim that Anne was mentally ill. He simply claimed that she made herself insensitive to pain.

47. STAC 8/4/10, fols. 3v, 20v, 23, 100. This Richard Haddock is the same Haddock or Haydock, M.D., of New College, Oxford, who attracted considerable attention in 1605 by allegedly preaching in his sleep. Ironically he, like Anne Gunter, was exposed as a fraud. DIARY OF WALTER YONGE, ESQ., *supra* note 34, at 12; 9 DICTIONARY OF NATIONAL BIOGRAPHY 281 (Leslie Stephen & Sidney Lee eds., 1921-22). On the swallowing of indigestible objects by demoniacs see 3 LEA, *supra* note 4, at 1046-47.

48. STAC 8/4/10, fols. 151v, 163. Brian Gunter brought his daughter to Oxford again at this time with the specific purpose of securing James's interest in the case.

49. Christina Larner, *James VI and Witchcraft, in* THE REIGN OF JAMES VI AND I, at 74, 78-80 (Alan G. R. Smith ed., 1973).

50. *See* KITTREDGE, *supra* note 23, at 276-328; HENRY N. PAUL, THE ROYAL PLAY OF MACBETH 90-130 (1950). On James's caution in such matters before he left Scotland, see Stuart Clark, *King James VI's DAEMONOLOGIE, in* THE DAMNED ART: ESSAYS IN THE LITERATURE OF WITCHCRAFT 156, 162-64 (Sydney Anglo ed., 1977).

The king interviewed Anne Gunter on at least four separate occasions between August and October 1605 — at Oxford in August, twice at Windsor in October, and one more time at Whitehall.[51] At some point between the first and second interviews the king referred the case to Richard Bancroft, the archbishop of Canterbury. Bancroft in turn placed Anne in the custody of his chaplain and main assistant, Samuel Harsnett. Harsnett, like Bancroft, had a special interest in cases of possession. During the previous ten years Harsnett had spearheaded a clerical campaign to discredit a rash of exorcisms that were being performed both by Jesuit seminary priests like William Weston and by Puritan ministers like John Darrell. The purpose of the Roman Catholic exorcisms was to prove to a heretical English nation that the Catholic Church was the one true church, one of the marks of which was the power to perform miracles. The greatest of these so-called miracles was the casting out of Devils. The Puritans, on the other hand, using only the scripturally warranted methods of prayer and fasting, were conducting their exorcisms to counter the claims of the Papists. The motive of the Anglican clerical establishment was to discredit both groups of exorcists by revealing the fraudulence of their efforts.[52]

The position that Harsnett took in his treatise on the subject, *A Declaration of Egregious Popish Impostures* (London 1603), was that the power of the Devil is greatly limited in this world and that he generally works through natural causes. Appealing in good Protestant fashion to the sovereignty of God, Harsnett asserted that the age of miracles is past. He claimed that Christ and the apostles had performed exorcisms, but there was no longer any need for such signs of divine power.[53] This position could easily lead

---

51. The first interview was at Oxford on August 27, while two more took place at Finchingbrooke, near Windsor, on October 9 and 10. The date of the meeting at Whitehall is uncertain. *See* PAUL, *supra* note 50, at 121 (claiming Whitehall meeting occurred in September, at which time the king referred the girl to Edward Jorden); *see also* Thomas Guidott, *Preface to the Third Edition* of EDWARD JORDEN, DISCOURSE OF NATURAL BATHS (London 1669) (reporting meeting without date). Edward Jorden later testified that Anne "came from Court" within a month after being committed to Harsnett's custody, thus suggesting some time in September as the date of the meeting at Whitehall. Anne refers to all these interviews, but without dates, in STAC 8/4/10, fol. 128v. James requested yet another meeting at Ware on October 30, but Dr. Richard Neile claimed that Anne could not be delivered to him at that time. Letter from Richard Neile to the earl of Salisbury (Oct. 30, 1605), *in* 17 CALENDAR OF THE MANUSCRIPTS OF THE MOST HONOURABLE THE MARQUESS OF SALISBURY PRESERVED AT HATFIELD HOUSE 471, 471-72 (M.S. Giuseppi ed., 1938).

52. On this campaign, see MacDonald, *supra* note 6, at xix-xxvi.

53. *See* SAMUEL HARSNETT, A DECLARATION OF EGREGIOUS POPISH IMPOSTURES (London 1603), *reprinted in* F. W. BROWNLOW, SHAKESPEARE, HARSNETT, AND THE DEVILS OF DENHAM 191 (Associated Univ. Presses 1993).

to a denial of the reality of both possession and witchcraft.[54]   Indeed, Harsnett was so skeptical on these points that his critics associated him with Reginald Scot, who in 1584 had written an uncompromising criticism of witch-hunting which came close to denying the reality of demonic power.[55] Both Harsnett and Scot were in fact accused of atheism, a common charge against critics of witch-hunting throughout the seventeenth century.[56]

With Anne committed directly to his charge at Lambeth Palace, Harsnett was eventually able to extract from her an admission to the fraud she and her father had perpetrated.  She admitted that her father had made her fake many of her alleged symptoms and accuse Gregory and the Pepwells of witchcraft.  It has been suggested that Harsnett may have coerced her into making this confession.[57]  That is unlikely, however, since Anne made confessions on numerous occasions, not only at Lambeth Palace but also before the king at Finchingbrooke and later in the Court of Star Chamber.  At the end of October, Harsnett reported to James that the girl had confessed on oath to what she had already admitted voluntarily.[58]  Anne had also admitted her trickery to one Asheley, a servant of the archbishop, with whom she had fallen in love while in detention at Lambeth Palace. Harsnett had apparently encouraged this romance in order to obtain Anne's unsuspecting admission to her deceptive behavior.[59]

---

54. Harsnett referred to those persons who have "their fancies distempered with the imaginations and apprehensions of witches, conjurers, and fairies, and all that lymphatical chimera," and he cited Chaucer's opinion that "all these brainless imaginations of witchings, possessings, house-haunting, and the rest, were the forgeries, cosenages, impostures, and legerdemain of crafty priests and lecherous friars." *Id.* at 309. KITTREDGE, *supra* note 23, at 299, is in error when he claims that Harsnett, Deacon, and Walker "did not attack the witchcraft dogma." Harsnett did not unequivocally deny the possibility of witchcraft, but he ridiculed those who believed in it and challenged its existence in numerable instances. WALKER, *supra* note 17, at 71, argues that Harsnett very strongly implied the denial of witchcraft. *See also* PAUL, *supra* note 50, at 124.

55. *See generally* REGINALD SCOT, THE DISCOVERIE OF WITCHCRAFT (Dover Publications 1972) (1930). Scot also discussed the cessation of miracles. *Id.* at 89-90. For Harsnett's reliance on Scot, see PAUL H. KOCHER, SCIENCE AND RELIGION IN ELIZABETHAN ENGLAND 132 (1953), and PAUL, *supra* note 50, at 100.

56. Darrell, among others, made the charge. *See* WALKER, *supra* note 17, at 72.

57. EWEN, *supra* note 1, at 36.

58. Letter from Richard Neile to the earl of Salisbury (Oct. 30, 1605), *in* 17 CALENDAR OF THE MANUSCRIPTS OF THE MOST HONOURABLE THE MARQUESS OF SALISBURY PRESERVED AT HATFIELD HOUSE 471, 471-72 (M.S. Giuseppi ed., 1938).

59. Robert Johnston, in his HISTORIA RERUM BRITANNICARUM (n.p. 1655), claimed that Harsnett deliberately sued Asheley "to entice the girl into love" and that Anne, "inclined to lust," revealed all of her tricks to him. PAUL, *supra* note 50, at 125-26.

At some point during Anne's stay at Lambeth Place, Harsnett called in a London physician, Dr. Edward Jorden, to examine her.[60] Jorden had also had previous experience with demoniacs, having only three years before testified in court that the fits of another possessed girl, Mary Glover, were the result of hysteria — or what was then referred to as the suffocation of the mother. In that same year Jorden had published a treatise on the subject.[61] Somewhat surprisingly, he did not reach the same conclusion regarding Anne's affliction, possibly because the girl had ceased having fits when he examined her so that he lacked direct evidence of her malady. All Jorden possessed was the information that pins and pieces of glass had been discovered in Anne's stools, leading him to conclude that she had swallowed the objects, perhaps in her fits. There was clearly nothing supernatural about her behavior, but the evidence seemed to point more to fraud than to disease as the cause of Anne's affliction. Indeed, in his testimony Jorden referred to Anne's "sundry feigned fits" while in the custody of Harsnett.[62]

Having interviewed Anne directly and having received reports from Harsnett and others, the king concluded in a letter to the earl of Salisbury on October 10 that the star demoniac of Oxford and Berkshire was "never possessed with any devil, nor bewitched." He based his diagnosis on the fact that she appeared to have been cured by a nonmedicinal potion given her by a physician, either Haddock or Jorden, together with a tablet to be hung around her neck.[63] He also claimed that her vomiting of pins was the result of various pinpranks and that the swelling of her belly was attributable to the disease called suffocation of the mother.[64] Finally, he reported that Anne,

---

60. PAUL, *supra* note 50, at 120-21, claims that the king referred the girl directly to Jorden in September. Jorden's deposition in Star Chamber, however, refers to examination one month after the girl was committed to Harsnett's custody, and that commitment probably did not take place until early September. STAC 8/4/10, fol. 57.

61. EDWARD JORDEN, A BRIEFE DISCOURSE OF A DISEASE CALLED SUFFOCATION OF THE MOTHER (London 1603). The treatise is photographically reproduced in WITCHCRAFT AND HYSTERIA IN ELIZABETHAN LONDON (Michael MacDonald ed., 1990).

62. STAC 8/4/10, fol. 57 (recording deposition of Edward Jorden). Jorden's testimony was given *ex parte* Gunter. Jorden reported that the last of Anne's fits took place about two weeks before Michaelmas day 1605, placing it about September 15.

63. Most authors, following Thomas Guidott, assume that Jorden was the physician mentioned in this letter. There is nothing in Jorden's deposition in Star Chamber, however, that would indicate that he gave the girl a potion, much less tied a tablet around her neck. *Id.*

64. Letter from James I to the earl of Salisbury (Oct. 10, 1605), *in* RICHARD HUNTER & IDA MACALPINE, THREE HUNDRED YEARS OF PSYCHIATRY, 1535-1860, at 76, 76-77 (1963). The authors suggest that this may be the only psychiatric report by a king of England. *Id.* at 76.

who had sought Asheley's "love most importunately and immodestly," was now asking permission to marry him. James's report, therefore, while admitting the possibility of illness, emphasized the girl's deceit. It is even possible that Anne was the "little counterfeit wench" whom James later referred to in an undated letter to his son.[65]

When the king wrote this letter to Salisbury, he already suspected that Anne's counterfeit possession was part of a plot "against one Gregory for some former hatred . . . borne unto her." In a draft of his letter to the earl of Salisbury, he indicated that he was planning to have Agnes Pepwell examined by the archbishop of Canterbury and by certain legal officials in order to press her to confess the truth, claiming that she had previously lied when she had been given the benefit of royal protection. In particular, the king wanted to know what had been admitted to her in a conversation with William Gunter, Anne's brother.[66] The king also had in his possession an incriminating letter from Anne Gunter to her father.[67] As early as October 1605, therefore, the government was contemplating legal action against the Gunters.

### Prosecution in Star Chamber

This prosecution of the Gunters finally commenced in February 1606, when Sir Edward Coke exhibited an information against Brian and Anne Gunter in the Court of Star Chamber. The charge was that the two had conspired "by false and wicked devices to bring [Gregory and the two Pepwells] into infamy and cause them to be reputed and taken for witches and thereupon also to cause them to be indicted and arraigned for witchcraft."[68] It was claimed that Master Gunter, who by now was imprisoned in Lambeth Palace, had put his daughter's head in the smoke of burning brimstone, administered intoxicating drinks to her, forced her to swallow salad oil to

---

65. Walker, *supra* note 17, at 80-81.

66. Deleted portion of a draft of James's letter to the earl of Salisbury, October 10, 1605, in the hand of Sir Julius Caesar. British Library, Additional MS. 12,497, fols. 197-197v. Pepwell is referred to as "the old Pepwell" in this letter, the name by which she was known in North Moreton. *See* Berkshire Record Office, D/P 86/1/1, burial of Old Agnes Pepwell, August 2, 1610. Despite their acquittal in March, both Agnes Pepwell and Elizabeth Gregory remained in custody during the entire episode. The reason for their continued custody was apparently the sentence, given at the same time as their trial, for another offense. *See* STAC 8/4/10, fol. 18 (examination of Alexander Chokke). Anne was eventually brought to London and committed to the custody of William Gwyllyam. *Id.* fol. 203.

67. British Library, Additional MS. 12,497, fol. 197v.

68. STAC 8/4/10, fol. 75.

make her vomit, beat her, thrust pins into her while she was asleep, and then, as in modern cases of child abuse, sworn her to secrecy.[69]

The choice of Star Chamber as the court in which to bring this action made sense from the government's point of view. Star Chamber derived its authority from that of the Privy Council; it was in effect the Council acting in a judicial capacity, meeting in a chamber of the Palace of Westminster whose ceiling was decorated with gold stars. The court acquired a distinct institutional identity in the early sixteenth century, when the judicial and administrative functions of the council were separated.[70] Intended originally to proceed expeditiously against those who violated the king's peace, it developed a jurisdiction over crimes not easily prosecuted in the common-law courts, especially sedition, riot, unlawful assembly, perjury, fraud, libel, and conspiracy. Star Chamber also served to prosecute those who corrupted the legal process, as in this case, in which the charge was conspiracy to indict a person of felony.[71]

This particular set of charges took the form of a written information preferred by Coke, who was then attorney general, the chief law officer of the Crown. Star Chamber was the only secular court in the realm in which prosecution of a serious crime could commence by mere information, without an indictment from a grand jury.[72] An indictment at common law would be necessary if the defendant were to be tried for a felony and thereby risk life or limb, but all crimes triable in Star Chamber were technically misdemeanors, even if they were referred to as "gross misdemeanors" or "high crimes," and the most severe punishments were cutting off the guilty party's ears or slitting his nose.[73] Procedure by information possessed obvious

---

69. *Id.* fols. 97, 103. For the swearing her to secrecy, see *id.* fols. 104, 124, 128.

70. On the origins and development of the court, see J. A. GUY, THE COURT OF STAR CHAMBER AND ITS RECORDS TO THE REIGN OF ELIZABETH I, at 1-17 (1985).

71. For a full list of the offenses prosecuted in Star Chamber, see 1 LIST AND INDEX TO THE PROCEEDINGS IN STAR CHAMBER FOR THE REIGN OF JAMES I (1603-1625) IN THE PUBLIC RECORD OFFICE, LONDON, CLASS STAC8, at 34-36 (Thomas G. Barnes et al. eds., 1975).

72. In the Middle Ages, informations could originate only in the Court of King's Bench and were used when a person committed "a gross misdemeanor, either personally against the king or his government, or against the public peace and good order." In those cases the form of trial was by jury. In the sixteenth century, however, jurisdiction in such cases and the authority to initiate them by information passed from King's Bench to Star Chamber. 4 WILLIAM BLACKSTONE, COMMENTARIES *305-06.

73. Other more common punishments were fines or imprisonment. *See* GUY, *supra* note 70, at 46-47. Occasionally the court tried felonies as misdemeanors and inflicted punishments appropriate to misdemeanors. *See* Thomas G. Barnes, *Star Chamber Mythology*, 5

attractions to a government when, as in this case, it wished to ensure that a prosecution would take place. The other advantage of trying the case in Star Chamber, at least from the government's point of view, is that it would be decided by the judges of the court, who were members of the Privy Council or justices of the central common-law courts, without having to submit the facts to a trial jury.

It might strike one as odd that Coke, the great defender of common-law procedure, especially trial by jury, would participate in the operation of a court that followed this type of inquisitorial procedure and that was associated with arbitrary government. Within forty years of the Gunter case, the Court of Star Chamber would be abolished by statute, mainly because of its enforcement of Charles I's unpopular and allegedly tyrannical religious and financial policies.[74] At the beginning of the seventeenth century, however, few complained about the court's procedure — not even the common lawyers, who were engaged in jurisdictional rivalries with other prerogative or conciliar courts. Private parties initiated most of the litigation in Star Chamber, and the procedure in those suits was similar to that followed in the Court of Chancery and the other courts of equity, with a suit commencing upon an individual's complaint, known as an English bill. Most of the suits heard before the court were in fact civil cases, even if they were technically classified as criminal proceedings.[75] Coke himself had a fairly brisk business representing clients in such suits.[76] The government would initiate genuine criminal prosecutions by information only in special circumstances like this, and Coke does not seem to have been bothered by the occasional operation of such an inquisitorial policy.[77] Indeed, as attorney general it was his responsibility to lay such informations before the court.

In any event, Coke was not the person responsible for the decision to charge the Gunters. Good reason exists to believe that Archbishop Bancroft, who as a member of the Privy Council could serve as a judge in the court,

---

AM. J. LEG. HIST. 4 (1961).

74. 16 Car., ch. 10 (1640) (Eng.). The statute referred to the proceedings of the court as "the means to introduce an arbitrary power and government." *Id.*

75. During the reign of James I, about 80% of all cases heard in Star Chamber involved real or personal property, even though the civil jurisdiction of the court had been eliminated by 1600. *See* GUY, *supra* note 70, at 47.

76. Barnes, *supra* note 73, at 5.

77. Of 8,228 actions brought in Star Chamber during the reign of James I, only 52 were informations brought on behalf of the king; the attorney general brought some 600 informations, but most of those were not *pro rege* and were indistinguishable from private party bills. Thomas G. Barnes, *Star Chamber Litigants and their Counsel, 1596-1641, in* LEGAL RECORDS AND THE HISTORIAN 7, 9 (J. H. Baker ed., 1978).

took the initiative in this regard and may have even secured the support of the king himself.[78] Nor was Coke the man responsible for directing the prosecution.[79] That duty fell to Bancroft's subordinates, Harsnett and Richard Neile, the dean of Westminster. The role these two men played in the trial became clear when Harsnett, who had been chosen vice-chancellor of the University of Cambridge, was asked to travel to the university to be admitted. Neile protested this absence on the grounds that it would "greatly hinder the prosecution of Anne Gunter's business." The problem was that neither his Majesty's counsel nor the clerks of the Star Chamber could "do anything longer than myself or Mr. Harsnett do ourselves attend them."[80]

No small irony appears in the use of inquisitorial procedure in this case. Inquisitorial procedure, as employed on the European continent, greatly facilitated the prosecution of witches, whereas English criminal procedure at the common law, which prohibited the government from initiating cases by itself and which required conviction by a petty jury, helps to explain the relatively low conviction rates in English witchcraft trials.[81] Now, however, the government was using inquisitorial procedure not to prosecute witches but to prosecute those who had accused them.

Whatever the drawbacks of inquisitorial procedure, it did provide certain protections to the accused that were unavailable at the common law. The defendants could, for example, have counsel, and they could call witnesses on their behalf. Moreover, those witnesses were sworn. Their testimony, therefore, carried more weight than in the common-law courts, in which only crown witnesses were sworn. During the two years this case consumed, more than fifty witnesses were deposed, and their testimony filled more than 450 manuscript pages. This group of witnesses included not only many of the residents of North Moreton and the surrounding area but also a large number of Oxford men, many of whom had come to see Anne when she was staying at Exeter College. Among them were six members of

---

78. On Bancroft's involvement in this case, see EWEN, *supra* note 1, at 33. On Bancroft's influence on the king's attitudes toward possession and witchcraft after his arrival in England, see MacDonald, *supra* note 6, at xlviii-l. Bancroft had probably commissioned Jorden's pamphlet on Hysteria. *Id.* at xxiii.

79. Coke left his position as attorney general during the period when depositions were being taken. He was appointed chief justice of the Court of Common Pleas on June 30, 1606.

80. Letter from Richard Neile to the earl of Salisbury (1606), *in* 18 CALENDAR OF THE MANUSCRIPTS OF THE MOST HONOURABLE THE MARQUESS OF SALISBURY PRESERVED AT HATFIELD HOUSE 422, 422-23 (M.S. Giuseppi ed., 1940). On March 1, 1606, Neile received £300 from the Exchequer to distribute to various persons who were involved in the case against the Gunters. EWEN, *supra* note 1, at 14.

81. LEVACK, *supra* note 3, at 64-70, 184.

Exeter college (two of them fellows), the regius professor of physic, and the Hebrew reader for the University. The group also included Dr. Jorden and his wife, the parson of St. Tolles in Oxford, and the chancellor of the diocese of Salisbury. Jorden, it should be mentioned, had been asked to testify in the Elizabeth Jackson case two years before, and he had published his treatise on hysteria at the prompting of Bancroft.

What is interesting about this testimony is that a great majority of it was given *ex parte* Gunter. Admittedly, many of these witnesses, in responding to interrogatories drafted by the prosecution, gave evidence that supported the prosecution's case. Nonetheless, the depositions produced a surprising amount of support for the Gunters. The vicar of North Moreton and many other witnesses claimed that they had seen Anne's clothes perform as described without human aid.[82] Curiously enough, Reverend Bird, despite being the object of one of Anne's charges, declared to the court that he thought her fits were genuine.[83] Apparently, Bird's belief in the reality of possession was more important to him than the prospect of retaliating against Anne by his testimony.

Even more surprising was the testimony of William Gwillyam and his wife, Anne, that Agnes Pepwell, who had been placed in their custody at Westminster toward the end of 1605, had confessed to them that she had in fact been a witch for fourteen years and possessed a black cat as her familiar spirit. According to the Gwillyams, Agnes had admitted that she and Elizabeth Gregory had bewitched Anne by having her spirit blow upon her "to make her sick and to swell"; that she would have also bewitched Brian Gunter but could not, having no power over him; and that Anne had not feigned her torments and pains. Agnes had also expressed sorrow for having bewitched Anne but explained that she could not undo the harm inflicted. She wished that Elizabeth Gregory would also repent yet knew that she could not because "her heart is so hardened."[84]

This remarkable testimony regarding Agnes Pepwell's alleged confession in the presence of the Gwillyams was itself suspect on the same grounds as Anne Gunter's confession to Harsnett: It may have been coerced. Pepwell had, after all, been in Gwillyam's custody when she made her alleged admission of guilt. Moreover, she herself did not testify in the case, raising the further possibility that the Gwillyams might have misrepresented

---

82. STAC 8/4/10, fols. 192, 208v.

83. *Id.* fol. 208v.

84. *Id.* fols. 203-06. An uncoerced admission of witchcraft was not unprecedented, especially when the accused party experienced guilt for hostility to a neighbor or for other sins.

what she had told them. In any event, Pepwell's reported confession was unlikely to serve as a counterweight to Anne's, which she had made before the court in answer to the information against her on February 23 and in her deposition of February 24.[85]

Conspicuous in his absence from this list of witnesses was Anne's brother-in-law, Thomas Holland. Although his wife testified on behalf of her sister, Holland did not. The reason for this is apparently Holland's own skepticism regarding possession. Known for his hostility to Catholicism,[86] he had on at least one occasion preached against the practice of exorcism, castigating those who "go about to show the truth of religion by casting out devils."[87] These actions would seem to identify him with the position of Bancroft and the ecclesiastical establishment regarding the phenomenon of possession.

Unfortunately, we do not have a formal record of the court's decision because most decrees of the court have been lost.[88] It is likely, however, that Brian Gunter was convicted and fined (although not mutilated), while Anne, having confessed to the king and the court, apparently received a royal pardon and a dowry.[89] Much more important than any sentence, however, was the discrediting of a counterfeit possession and the demonstrable proof, so often lacking even in mere acquittals for witchcraft, that an alleged practice of witchcraft had never taken place. The trial of the Gunters in Star Chamber did much more to support the arguments of the witchcraft skeptics such as Reginald Scot than had the acquittal of Elizabeth Gregory and Agnes Pepwell at the Berkshire assizes. It also strengthened the emerging skepticism of the new king of England. Once the scourge of Scottish witches, he took particular delight during the rest of his reign in England in exposing culprits who brought fraudulent charges against witches.[90]

---

85. *Id.* fols. 73, 122-29. Anne threw herself on the mercy of the court, appealing to the "weakness of her sex and of her young years." *Id.* fol. 73.

86. *See* RICHARD KILBIE, A SERMON PREACHED IN SAINT MARIES CHURCH IN OXFORD, MARCH 26, 1612, AT THE FUNERALL OF THOMAS HOLLAND (Oxford 1613). On Holland's hostility to Arminianism as a manifestation of popery, see NICHOLAS TYACKE, ANTI-CALVIN-ISTS 72 (1987).

87. THE DIARY OF JOHN MANNINGHAM OF THE MIDDLE TEMPLE 1602-1603, at 198 (Robert P. Sorlien ed., 1976).

88. GUY, *supra* note 70, at 19.

89. The king allegedly gave Anne a marriage portion after she confessed to him on October 10, 1605. Guidott, *supra* note 51.

90. PAUL, *supra* note 50, argues that James's skepticism began earlier.

## The Significance of the Trial

The Gunter trial was the first attempt by an English government, using the one central criminal court in which it could initiate criminal prosecutions, to bring the *accusers* of witches to trial.[91] Previously, the only way such persons could be prosecuted was by a charge of slander, brought by the wronged party, in either an ecclesiastical or a secular court.[92] Now the government itself, represented by members of the Privy Council, was undertaking this task and was using one of the most powerful courts in the realm to achieve its objectives. Ultimately all central governments would take such action, but not until they had first repealed the legislation that had originally facilitated the prosecution of the crime. What is striking about this case is that the process of counteraction began only two years after the passage of a new, more severe witchcraft statute and at a time when that statute was still being enforced.

The Gunter case did not bring an end to witchcraft prosecutions in England. Trials continued to be held for a full century after the Gunters were exposed. The Gunter trial did, however, mark a turning point in the history of English witch-hunting: After 1607 the number of witchcraft executions in England began to decline.[93] Part of the reason for this development was the growing skepticism of those who effectively controlled the judicial process:

---

91. In February 1603, Star Chamber had sentenced John Darling, the fourteen-year-old boy whom John Darrell had dispossessed, to be whipped and to lose his ears for libeling the vice-chancellor of the University of Oxford, not for falsely accusing individuals of witchcraft. 1 THE LETTERS OF JOHN CHAMBERLAIN 186-87 (Norman E. McClure ed., 1939).

92. On slander charges in the ecclesiastical courts, see generally J. A. Sharpe, *Defamation and Sexual Slander in Early Modern England: The Church Courts at York*, 58 BORTHWICK PAPERS 1 (1980). Slander for calling a person a witch could be actionable in the common-law courts, where the claim that a person had committed a felony was one of the few circumstances in which an action on the case for words was allowed. Occasionally such cases came before quarter sessions. For example, see 4 QUARTER SESSIONS RECORDS 182 (J. C. Atkinson ed., 1886). The common-law courts, however, usually interpreted such defamatory comments strictly, leaving them to be heard before the ecclesiastical courts. For example, see Markham v. Adamson, 82 Eng. Rep. 883 (K.B. 1681), in which the defendant accused the plaintiff of being a witch. The verdict was for the plaintiff, but judgment was given against him on the grounds that the slanderous words "did not import an accusation of any offence within the statute." *Id.* at 883. In the common-law courts a slandered party could collect damages, but in the ecclesiastical courts the only punishment could be public penance. *See* J. H. BAKER, AN INTRODUCTION TO ENGLISH LEGAL HISTORY 495-508 (3d ed. 1990).

93. Alfred Soman, *Decriminalizing Witchcraft: Does the French Experience Furnish a European Model?*, 10 CRIM. JUST. HIST. 1, 1-22 (1989); EWEN, *supra* note 12, at 100. The number rose again only for a brief period of time during the 1640s.

the king, the judges, and the clergy. During the 1630s, when men like Chief Justice John Finch dominated the bench, executions for witchcraft became more infrequent than at any time since the accession of Queen Elizabeth. Finch, the judge responsible for cropping William Prynne's ears in Star Chamber as a punishment for libel, was much more sympathetic to those accused of witchcraft. While riding the western circuit in 1630, he assigned four eminent barristers to counsel a poor woman accused of witchcraft on points of law.[94] During the same period of time, when William Laud was archbishop of Canterbury and Harsnett and Neile served on the episcopal bench, the clergy exhibited a comparable skepticism. In 1633, the efforts of John Bridgeman, the bishop of Chester, exposed one of the greatest cases of witchcraft fraud, the Pendle Swindle. Two of the suspects in that case were sent to London, where King Charles I and his physician, William Harvey, who had demonstrated skepticism in 1605 regarding Anne Gunter's calluses, searched in vain for the witches' marks on the suspects' bodies.[95]

The only serious witch-hunting to take place after this time occurred during the English Civil War, when the self-styled witch-hunters Matthew Hopkins and John Stearne conducted a major witch-hunt, resulting in the conviction and execution of more than 100 persons in the southeastern counties of the country. This hunt, the most intense in English history, would not have taken place if central justice had not broken down. Owing to the disruptions of the Civil War, the judges from the central common-law courts were unable to preside at the assizes in 1645, and as a result Hopkins and Stearne, acting with the permission of municipal authorities, were able to use methods of judicial coercion that had been strictly forbidden in previous English witchcraft trials.[96] For example, they subjected witches to the torture of forced sleeplessness — the dreaded *tormentum insomniae* — that had been used to great effect on the Continent to secure confessions that could not otherwise have been elicited.[97] One might also speculate that the

---

94. *See* J. S. COCKBURN, A HISTORY OF ENGLISH ASSIZES 1558-1714, at 121 (1972).

95. On this episode, see WALLACE NOTESTEIN, A HISTORY OF WITCHCRAFT IN ENGLAND FROM 1558 TO 1718, at 146-57 (1911).

96. THOMAS, *supra* note 7, at 458. For a full discussion of this witch-hunt, see generally RICHARD DEACON, MATTHEW HOPKINS: WITCH FINDER GENERAL (1976).

97. MATTHEW HOPKINS, THE DISCOVERY OF WITCHES (1647), *reprinted in* THE DISCOVERY OF WITCHES: A STUDY OF MASTER MATTHEW HOPKINS COMMONLY CALLED WITCH FINDER GENERAL 49, 54-55 (Montague Summers ed., Cayme Press 1928). Hopkins justified this procedure on the grounds that it was designed to encourage the witches' familiars to appear, since if the witches were awake, they "would be more the active to call their imps in open view the sooner to their help." *Id.* at 54. Hopkins denied that a confession adduced under torture had any validity and that if a witch confessed after being kept awake,

abolition of Star Chamber in 1641 and the elimination of episcopal judicial and political authority at the time of the Civil War removed further impediments to the type of intense witch-hunting that occurred in 1645.

After the Restoration, the number of witchcraft prosecutions and executions continued the downward trend that had developed in the first part of the century. The last execution took place in 1685, while the last conviction, that of Jane Wenham in 1712, was effectively reversed when the skeptical assize judge, Sir John Powell, granted a reprieve. An act of the British Parliament in 1736 finally repealed the witchcraft statute of 1604, together with the Scottish statute of 1563.[98]

Overall,. however, the decriminalization of witchcraft in England was a long and complex process. Ironically, it took longer to realize in England than in other European countries, especially those where inquisitorial procedure was employed. In those countries judges exercised tighter control of the judicial process than did their English counterparts, and they also acquired appellate authority in all witchcraft sentences. By exercising those powers they were thereby able to discourage prosecutions unilaterally.[99] In England, on the other hand, juries continued to establish the facts of the case and to make determinations of judicial proof, and there was no system of regular appeals. Judges might try to influence the jury by refusing to admit certain witnesses and by summing up the evidence, but with the law of evidence still in its infancy and with judges still respecting traditions of jury independence, occasional convictions and even executions occurred long after they had been abandoned in other parts of Europe.[100] The conviction and execution of Amy Duny and Rose Cullender at Bury St. Edmunds in 1662 and that of Temperance Lloyd, Susanna Edwards, and Mary Trembles at Exeter in 1682 can be attributed to the determination of juries to convict

---

the magistrate would examine them after sleep. *Id.* at 57-58.

98. 9 Geo. 2, ch. 5, §§ 1-2 (1736) (Eng.). The law made it an offense to "pretend to exercise or use any kind of witchcraft, sorcery, enchantment or conjuration, or undertake to tell fortunes" on the pain of imprisonment for one year. *Id.* § 4.

99. For example, see generally Soman, *supra* note 93.

100. *Id.* The last execution for witchcraft in England, the hanging of Alice Molland, occurred at Exeter in 1685, while the last conviction, in which Justice Powell reprieved the defendant, Jane Wenham, took place at Hertford in 1712. *See* THOMAS, *supra* note 7, at 452. By contrast the Netherlands had its last executions during the first decade of the seventeenth century. Marijke Gijswijt-Hofstra, *Six Centuries of Witchcraft in the Netherlands: Themes, Outlines, and Interpretations, in* WITCHCRAFT IN THE NETHERLANDS: FROM THE FOURTEENTH TO THE TWENTIETH CENTURY 1, 27 (Marijke Gijswijt-Hofstra & Willem Frijhoff eds. & Rachel van der Wilden-Fall trans., 1991).

and the reluctance of the judiciary to use their influence to persuade them otherwise.[101]

Although the English government did not succeed in preventing all witchcraft executions after 1604, it did take steps throughout the seventeenth century to discourage certain prosecutions. The tactic used in the Gunter case, of prosecuting those who brought false charges against innocent persons, was only one of the weapons at its disposal, but it was a particularly effective one. It was in fact the tactic employed by the government in one of the last witchcraft cases of the period, that of Richard Hathaway in 1702.

Hathaway, a laborer, had accused one Sarah Morduck, of Southwark, of bewitching him, preventing him from eating, and inflicting on him a number of diseases. As a means of curing himself he scratched Morduck to obtain blood, an action by which he claimed to be cured. In the ensuing trial Morduck was acquitted, and Hathaway was exposed as an impostor and a cheat. Nevertheless, Hathaway continued to claim that he was bewitched, and under his prodding, Morduck continued to be "abused by the rabble."[102] It was claimed that Hathaway had the support of a Surrey magistrate, as well as that of neighbors who took up collections for him. In order to put an end to the harassment of Morduck, the attorney general, Edward Northey, exhibited an information in King's Bench against Hathaway, claiming that he was an imposter and that he had maliciously intended "to bring [her] into the danger of losing her life."[103] Hathaway was convicted at the Surrey assizes. He was also tried and convicted, together with three other accomplices, of assaulting, beating, scratching, and wounding Sarah Morduck.[104]

There are of course numerous similarities between the Gunter and Hathaway trials. In both cases the attorney general filed an information against the defendant for falsely accusing individuals of witchcraft. In both cases the accused were charged with conspiracy to indict as well as with

---

101. For the trials at Bury St. Edmunds and the role played by Sir Matthew Hale, see generally A TRYAL OF WITCHES, *supra* note 23, and especially *id.* at 55-56. On the prosecutions at Exeter and the failure of Sir Thomas Raymond to instruct the jury regarding the use of confessions as evidence, see ROGER NORTH, THE LIVES OF THE RT. HON. FRANCIS NORTH; THE HON. SIR DUDLEY NORTH; AND THE HON. AND REV. DR. JOHN NORTH 9, 167-68 (London 1890), and see generally A TRUE AND IMPARTIAL RELATION OF THE INFORMATIONS AGAINST THREE WITCHES (London, F. Collins 1682), *reprinted in* 8 A COMPLETE COLLECTION OF STATE TRIALS AND PROCEEDINGS FOR HIGH TREASON AND OTHER CRIMES AND MISDEMEANORS FROM THE EARLIEST PERIOD TO THE YEAR 1783, at 1017 (T.B. Howell ed., London, T.C. Hansard 1816) [hereinafter A COMPLETE COLLECTION].

102.   14 A COMPLETE COLLECTION, *supra* note 101, at 644.

103.   *Id.* at 640. Hathaway was imprisoned and fined.

104.   *Id.* at 689-96.

imposture. The only difference is that the Gunters were tried in Star Chamber, whereas Hathaway and his associates were tried by a jury at the assizes after the information had been exhibited in the Court of King's Bench. The change can be accounted for by the destruction of the Star Chamber in 1641 and the transfer of its jurisdiction to the common-law courts, mainly to King's Bench, where all informations were to originate.[105]

The decline of witch-hunting after 1660, and its virtual termination by the Hathaway prosecution of 1702, can easily lead to the conclusion that the common-law courts, which triumphed over the prerogative courts at the time of the English Revolution, were primarily responsible for the decline and end of witch-hunting. Unquestionably, the Hathaway case, taken together with the refusal of skeptical judges like Sir Thomas Holt and Sir John Powell to countenance prosecutions for witchcraft brought into their courts, contributed significantly to that process.[106] But in discussing the end of witch-hunting in England, we must recognize that the first step in this process, the prosecution of the Gunters in 1606, occurred not in a common-law tribunal but in a prerogative court — a court that followed inquisitorial procedure and that was, for a short period of time, associated with "arbitrary power and government." ·

---

105. *See* 4 WILLIAM BLACKSTONE, COMMENTARIES *306-16. The statute abolishing Star Chamber, 16 Car., ch. 10 (1640) (Eng.), actually provided for the disablement of an officer convicted three times "by indictment, information or any other lawful means" for violating the act itself. *Id.* § 4.

106. For the negative effect of Holt on prosecutions for witchcraft, see NOTESTEIN, *supra* note 95, at 320-21.

*Chapter Five*

# Women, witchcraft and the legal process

## Jim Sharpe

The problem of gender is one that has only recently begun to attract the attention of historians of crime, of the law, and of the operation of legal systems. There have, of course, been a number of works that have demonstrated the potential fruitfulness of various lines of approach: the different participation rates of the two sexes in various types of offence; male and female involvement in litigation, perhaps most notably in church court slander cases; and on such gender related (or indeed gender specific) matters as infanticide and scolding.[1] Yet it remains clear that considerable work needs to be done both in charting the statistical contours of such matters as prosecutions brought against men and women, and the punishments inflicted upon them, as well as in using court records to help to understand gender as a social construct, as a bundle of assumptions or attitudes about how men and women should behave.[2] The difficulties in following such a course are, unfortunately, more severe when women are under consideration. The English legal system was run by men, the statutes it enforced were drawn up and promulgated by men, and the English common law seemed designed to constrain the rights of women as much as possible.[3] At first sight then, it would seem that historians studying the relationship between women and the legal process in the past have had their task restricted to doing little more than cataloguing the ways in which women were disadvantaged.

Nowhere would this premise, again at first sight, seem more conspicuously true than when considering the prosecution of witchcraft in Tudor and Stuart courts. As is well known, around 90 per cent of persons indicted for witchcraft at the Home Circuit assizes between the passing of the Elizabethan statute in 1563 and the abolition of laws against witchcraft in 1736 were women.[4] Work on comparable sources suggests that this rate was fairly usual for the indictment of malefic witchcraft in England.[5] Yet even the first step that might be taken beyond this simple counting exercise exposes complications. Reworking the figures for Essex, we discover that the 236 presentments for witchcraft or related matters made before the Archdeacons of Essex and Colchester between the 1560s and the 1630s reveal a male participation rate of 29 per cent.[6] Further complications arise when we examine cunning men and women, those "good" witches who attracted so much hostility from the writers of English demonological tracts, but whose services were so eagerly sought by the population at large. Whereas over 90 per cent of those accused at the Essex assizes for witchcraft were female, two-thirds of the cunning folk whom Macfarlane was able to identify in his Essex study were men.[7] These figures suggest that we will have to refine our standard notions of the connection between women and witchcraft at some future point. For the present, however, it seems safe to take as our starting point that the overwhelming majority of persons accused of malefic witchcraft were women, and that a study of witchcraft cases could offer a potentially fruitful approach to the study of women's involvement in the legal process in early modern England.

We must, however, pause to consider what we mean by the term "legal process". To understand the operation of the law in its full context, it is necessary to go beyond the courtroom and the strict rules of legal procedure, and even to speculate about what was going on outside areas covered by the legal record. The English criminal legal system was an accusatory one, and, in large measure, the prosecution of witches, along with other felons, was dependent on the initiative of the person offended against – the victim. As I have argued elsewhere, on the strength of Northern Circuit assize depositions, women showed no reluctance in accusing other women of being witches, or of giving evidence against alleged witches.[8] Indeed, in both these areas female participation in the legal system seemed to be at least equal to that of men. In this chapter I should like to take things further, and seek other points at which we can delineate a distinctive female contribution to the prosecution of witches: the rôle of women in searching for the witch's mark; wider evidence about female involvement as witnesses in witchcraft cases; the behaviour of both witches and their accusers in court; and the subsequent behaviour of condemned witches on the gallows. A consideration of these topics, based as it must be on imperfect and at times contradictory materials, can only lead to very tentative conclusions. What it does demonstrate is that witchcraft prosecutions cannot be interpreted purely as the oppression of women by a male dominated legal system.

★ ★ ★

One area where women were of unique importance in the judicial trial of witchcraft was in their being used to search for the witch's mark. The mark was seen as a method of establishing guilt in some fifteenth-century Continental trials, although the then current custom of shaving body hair from suspects to facilitate the search does not seem to have been followed in England.[9] The first pamphlet account of a witchcraft trial in England, published in 1566, stressed the importance of the mark as a means of establishing proof,[10] and as English trials progressed its importance remained central. It also seems that it gradually became accepted that the mark, with women, most commonly took the form of a teat-like growth in the pudenda, from which it was thought that the witch's familiar sucked blood. Contemporary usage dictated that if the discovery of such a mark was thought vital for proving witchcraft, the search for it should be made by women. The earliest known reference to appointing women for this task comes, perhaps a little unexpectedly, from the court leet of Southampton in 1579. The wording of the relevant order suggests that the practice was already a familiar one. The leet jury directed that half a dozen honest matrons should be appointed to strip widow Walker and to determine if she had "eny bludie marke on hir bodie which is a comon token to know all witches by".[11] That the practice was widely known at this time is confirmed by a tract describing the prosecution of several women in Essex in 1582. This incident involved the searching of a number of suspected witches by local women, including the alleged victims of witchcraft, one such group of searchers being described as "women of credite".[12]

The actual mechanics by which women were appointed to search witches varied enormously. Edward Fairfax, a Yorkshire gentleman who thought two of his daughters were being bewitched, recorded how in 1621 the suspected women were "by appointment, at the house of widow Pullens, at Fuystone, searched for marks upon their bodies", which suggests a degree of official sanctioning of the process. Some years later, in another Yorkshire case, Dorothy Rodes, another parent who thought her child to be bewitched, noted how the suspected witch, Mary Sikes, was "searched by weomen appointed by a justice of peace". A male witness recorded how he went with one of Rodes' sons to Henry Tempest, a West Riding justice who seems to have been much involved in witchcraft cases, "to procure a warrant for searching the said Mary Sikes and Susan Beaumont". Six women, three married and three widows, were appointed. Another Yorkshire witness, Alice Purston, told in 1655 how she and other women were appointed to search Katherine Earle on the direction of the constable of their township who was himself acting under direction from a justice. Four years earlier, in another Yorkshire case, the direction seems to have come simply from the local constable.[13] The decision to search seems, therefore, to have involved an interplay between official attitudes and the demands of the local community, whose members were aware of the need to search for the mark. This suggests that the legitimation for searching operated at both an official and a popular level.

Perhaps the most remarkable evidence we have of the dynamics of the search for the mark comes from the case of Elizabeth Sawyer, executed after trial at the Middlesex Sessions in 1621. Sawyer's trial was rather hanging fire, with neither the judge nor the jury apparently having much idea of what to make of the evidence before them. At that point a Justice who had taken considerable interest in the case, Arthur Robinson, intervened. He told the court that "information was given unto him by some of her neighbours, that this Elizabeth Sawyer had a private and strange marke on her body, by which suspition was confirmed against her". "The Bench", we are told, "commanded officers appointed for those purposes, to fetch in three women to search the body of Elizabeth Sawyer". One of these was Margaret Weaver, "that keepes the Session House for the City of London, a widdow of honest reputation". She was joined by "two grave matrons, brought in by the officer out of the streete, passing there by chance". Sawyer resisted the searchers, behaving "most sluttish and loathsomely towards them, intending thereby to prevent their search of her", but the women continued in their efforts, each of them deposing separately to court about the results of the exercise. They found a teat "the bignesse of the little finger, and the length of halfe a finger", which looked as though it had recently been sucked. This evidence proved decisive, and swung the jury against Sawyer.[14]

As this case suggests, the credentials needed by women searchers were those resulting from good character rather than technical expertise. Some other cases, however, suggested that women with some type of knowledge might be favoured. Midwives were, of course, uniquely qualified to comment on irregularities in the female genitals. The exceptionally rich documentation provided by the Matthew Hopkins trials of 1645–7 shows a number of them in action. A midwife named Bridget Reynolds searched one of the Essex witches, Elizabeth Harvey. Five women gave evidence against Joan Salter, one of those accused on the Isle of Ely, and deposed how they found three teats in her privy parts "which the midwife and the rest of these informants have not seen the like on the body of any other woman".[15] Later in the century, again in Essex, we find a midwife being appointed to search the body of a suspected witch "in the presence of some sober women". This she did, and informed the author of the narration of the case

> that she never saw the like in her life: that her fundament was open like a mouse hole, and that in it were two long biggs, out of which being pressed issued blood: that they were neither piles nor emrods (for she knew both) but excrescences like to biggs with nipples which seemed as if they had been frequently sucked.[16]

Some midwives clearly felt themselves able to give expert evidence in witchcraft cases.[17]

Others might claim a more general expertise. Hence, again during the Hopkins trials, Anne the wife of Thomas Savory of Upwell in Norfolk was examined by "some that were there who p[re]tended to have skill in the discovery of witches" who "sayd that some of the divles impes had sucked her".[18] The Hopkins episode also saw the emergence of a woman who clearly attained a regional reputation as a searcher for the witch's mark, Mary Philips. Philips was involved as a witness in some of the early Essex trials in the spring of 1645 and, for reasons which remain elusive, seems to have acquired a wider repute as a finder of the witch's mark. Certainly, she was brought in by the authorities of Aldeburgh in Suffolk to supervise other women searching suspected witches there, and was paid for such duties and also received expenses.[19]

Not all of the women searched, as the case of Elizabeth Sawyer suggests, submitted willingly, while several of them offered those searching them explanations for those physical peculiarities which risked being identified as the witch's mark. Joan Salter explained to an investigating justice that "the markes that she hath about her are not the markes of a witch but caused as it pleaseth God she beleaveth by child bearing". Mary Armitage, a Yorkshire witch, was searched by four women in 1658, and a suspicious hole a quarter of an inch deep was found on her right shoulder. The suspected witch attributed this to an injury sustained while carrying a bundle of thorns, one of which penetrated her shoulder. She explained that the thorn "continewed there about a yeare before itt could be gott out &

caused a great swelling & since that tyme there hath beene a little hole upon her shoulder". Something of the experience of the search for the witch's mark is conveyed in the examination of another Yorkshire witch, Katherine Earle. Earle, asked

> why she did not tell the woemen that searched . . . of a marke betweene here thighs as well as that of behind her eare she at first answered that she did not know of it, whereat the women laughing she p[re]sently after said it came by a burne and she had it 36 yeares.[20]

The frequency of references in surviving depositions to women searching for the mark suggests that the practice, existing as it did on the peripheries of the legal process, was widespread and culturally familiar. This point is reinforced by a remarkable case from Oxfordshire in 1687. Joan Walker of Bicester, the widow of a gentleman, petitioned the bench in that year, to the effect that despite her good reputation and good conduct,

> severall wicked & mallicious persons enveing the good name, fame, credit & reputacon of your peti[tioner] have uniustly & without any ground or collo[u]r of reason given out in speeches that your peti[tioner] is a witch which odious name yo[u]r peti[tioner] utterly abhors & detests & all the works of the devill.

To clear herself, widow Walker requested that the bench should order that she "may be searched by foure & twenty honest sober iudicious matrons & make report of their opinions at next sessions", and that the persons abusing her should be bound over to appear there. By this time, and at this social level, the attention of the jury of women searchers was clearly recognized, while Walker's suggestion that she should be searched by "foure & twenty" women is instructive. A criminal accusation at the sessions or assizes typically would be screened by a grand jury of twelve or so men, and then tried by a trial jury of another twelve. Walker obviously desired that the search that was intended to clear her name should mirror proper legal process as far as possible.[21]

This last case reminds us that the female searchers officially sanctioned to search women were but one of a number of types of juries, or near juries, of female experts who were called in to adjudicate in a number of legal matters, both criminal and civil. The English medieval ecclesiastical courts had sought female assistance in cases of annulment of marriage on the grounds of the husband's impotence, when the accuracy of the plea was tested by "honest women" who, by baring their breasts and kissing or fon-dling the man, attempted to arouse him sexually.[22] This practice seems to have been discontinued by the sixteenth century, but the operation of the church courts still made occasional use of women as experts in sexual cases. Thus when, in 1595, a man from Barking in Essex was presented for incest with his daughter, it was reported that the suspicion was not founded merely on "common report", but also "upon the assertion of honest women, who have had the examincion of the young wench".[23] Although the point needs further investigation, it seems certain that similar searches, sometimes with official sanction, would be made by women in infanticide and rape cases. Most familiar, perhaps, was the use made by female juries in examining women who claimed to be pregnant after conviction for felony, and who hence hoped to delay or evade being executed.[24] Together, this use of female juries or less formal groups of female investigators constitutes a part of the legal process that must modify the general assertion that women were excluded from official participation in it. They did not serve as magistrates or jurors but the authority derived from the crucial evidence of their "special knowledge" was a dramatic reversal of their generally powerless rôles as petitioners, witnesses or parties to litigation.

Women were also frequently involved as witnesses against witches. The Home Circuit assize records reveal that there were 1207 calls for witnesses at witch trials between 1600 and 1702. Of these, 631 (or 52 per cent) involved men and 576 (or 48 per cent) women, a nearly even split. In iso-lated cases, there might be a heavy preponderance of women witnesses: 14 women to 3 men in Kent in 1657, 10 women to 5 men in Surrey in 1664, 8 women alone in Essex in 1650. Such cases would seem to support the conclusion advanced elsewhere, on the strength of Northern Circuit assize depositions, that women felt no qualms about giving evidence against fe-male witches.[25] The Home Circuit records also suggest that the proportion of women witnesses increased over the seventeenth century, from 46 women to 80 men in 1600–1609, to a preponderance of women witnesses in the 1660s and 1670s. The importance of these figures is emphasized when we compare them to the gender ratio of all witnesses called to give evidence in felony cases in Hertfordshire between 1610 and 1619. In that decade 572 men and 36 women were called to give evidence in felony cases at the Hertfordshire assizes, a ratio of over twelve male witnesses to each female.[26] In the same decade, taking the Home Circuit as a whole, there 92 men and 82 women were called to give evidence in witchcraft cases. On these figures, women were over 11 times more likely to act as witnesses in witchcraft trials at the assizes than they were in all felony cases. We return to the notion that the connection between women and witchcraft lay not only in the gender of the accused, but also in a much wider, much more complex, and as yet barely investigated web of assumptions about gender, female power, and female interaction in early modern England.

★ ★ ★

It is possible to push beyond statistics occasionally, and to reconstruct something of the experience of women in the courtroom. Such instances throw light on what is still one of the problem areas of English legal history: the very basic issue of how trials were actually conducted, of what happened in the push and shove of a court in session. The official documentation engendered by an English criminal trial in this period rarely sheds much light on these matters. The indictment is a notoriously arid document, while depositions, although invaluable for illustrating other matters, were essentially pre-trial documents that by their very nature usually tell us nothing of what happened in court. Other sources can be more revealing and, as we shall see, something can be constructed from pamphlet accounts of trials, and from isolated references in letters, diaries, memoirs, and such like. The general point to be made is that court proceedings were more disorderly, more ramshackle, and less seemly than those obtaining in a modern court of law. Some notion of typical conditions can be gained from the case of Mary Spencer who, at her trial for witchcraft, complained that "the wind was so loud, and the throng so great, that she could not hear the evidence against her".[27] John Aubrey noted that at the trial of a witch in 1653 "the spectators made such a noise that the judge could not hear the prisoner nor the prisoner the judge, but the words were handed from one to the other by Mr R. Chandler, and sometimes not truly reported".[28] Sometimes the throng in the court during a witchcraft trial might be so oppressive, and demonstrate its hostility to the accused so forcefully, that, as Roger North recorded of one post-Restoration case in the south-west, the judge might be pressured into convicting against his inclinations.[29]

All this was bad enough for the accused, but even giving evidence could be a stressful experience. The century which witnessed the judicial style of Judge Jeffreys in 1685 was not one in which witnesses might usually expect indulgent attitudes from judges, and witnesses, male and female alike, were often browbeaten or ridiculed by the judiciary. In 1712 there occurred the last known assize trial for witchcraft in England, the accused being a Hertfordshire woman named Jane Wenham. One of those giving evidence against her was Elizabeth Field. She told how Wenham had bewitched a child of hers about nine years previously. The judge asked why she had not prosecuted Wenham immediately after this incident, to which she answered "she was a poor women, and the child had no friends able to bear the charges of such a prosecution". The judge, who was sceptical, and who was subsequently to reprieve Wenham after conviction, asked sarcastically if Field had now grown rich.[30] Conversely, there were signs of women witnesses being treated with politeness. In 1702 Richard Hathaway was tried as a cheat for accusing Sarah Morduck of witchcraft. Elizabeth Willoughby was one of those giving evidence on Hathaway's behalf before the sceptical Chief Justice Holt. Holt asked her what skill she had in matters of witchcraft, and she replied that she had been bewitched as a child, and that this experience had given her insight into such matters. An obviously unconvinced Judge Holt was very restrained in his subsequent questioning about this claim.[31]

If the treatment of women witnesses varied, so did that of the women accused of witchcraft. Low conviction rates at the assizes suggest that throughout the period of the operation of the English witch statutes, judges were, broadly speaking, sceptical about, if not the abstract possibility of witchcraft, at least of the guilt of the individual old women brought before them.[32] By the later seventeenth century, when convictions were very rare, judges must have played a major part in helping accused witches evade execution. Yet in other instances women accused of witchcraft in the confusing and hostile environment of the court might find themselves under heavy pressure. In many cases the accused were elderly women who had been cowed by the experiences of community hostility, examination by justices and mob pressure on the way to the place of trial. Such women were unlikely to mount much by way of a coherent defence against the charges levelled against them. Nevertheless, scattered evidence suggests that a few women were able to defend themselves in court. Thus in 1586 Joan Cason, a widow of Faversham in Kent, was tried at the borough sessions for invoking evil spirits and bewitching a child to death. Seven women and one man, poor people but her near neighbours, gave evidence against her. Cason, while admitting contact with what may have been familiars, denied bewitching the child to death, claiming that her adversaries were maliciously accusing her and that there were existing differences between them in which her accusers had already done her wrong. Her arguing convinced the Recorder of Faversham of her innocence, although a bungle over legal technicalities led to her execution.[33]

Other cases of what amounted almost to defiance were recorded. Anna Trapnel, the Interregnum religious visionary, recorded how during her travels in Cornwall she was investigated as a witch, and that a clergymen helped to frame an indictment against her, "but though he and the witch-trying woman looked steadfastly in my face, it did no way dismay me".[34] Margaret Landish, one of the Essex witches accused in 1645, alleged malice and an old grudge against her at her trial, and at one point made "a strange howling in the court to the great disturbance of the whole bench".[35] Temperance Lloyd, one of three witches executed at Exeter in 1682, although confessing her witchcraft at her trial, was "perfectly resolute, not minding what should become of her immortal soul, but rather impudently at, as well as after her tryal, so audacious".[36] Another distraction to the court was offered by Anne Ashby, tried at Maidstone in 1652. Ashby confessed to copulation with the devil, and in open court "fell into an extasie before the bench, and swelled into a monstrous and vast bigness, schreeching and crying out very dolefully", and on her recovery claimed that her familiar had entered her body.[37]

More commonly, the progress of witch trials was disturbed by sufferings of this last type on the part of the alleged victims of witchcraft. One of the recurring themes of English witchcraft was the possession of young people by spirits sent by a witch, or by curious diseases inflicted on them by witchcraft. The accounts of the sufferings of such possessed persons, frequently involving fits and convulsions, are some times very long and very harrowing. What is striking, however, is the number of occasions when such behaviour occurred in the courtroom, sometimes being regarded (at least by the accusers) as evidence of bewitchment. Although people of either sex might be possessed, it seems that most of the cases of fits and convulsions occurring in court of which details have come down to us involved young women. Frequently these took the form of dramatic interventions on the part of the alleged sufferer when the supposed witch entered the court or was first noticed by the supposedly possessed girl.

Thus in one well documented case we find Mary Glover, daughter of a London shopkeeper, who was thought to be bewitched in 1602, falling into a fit when she was called to give evidence in court. The three strong men who carried the girl out of court declared that they had "never carried a heavier burden". The Recorder of London and other officials tested the genuineness of her fit by burning her hand until it blistered: the girl remained insensible.[38] In another case, tried at the Berkshire assizes at almost the same time, Anne Gunter, a gentleman's daughter, similarly went into fits at the trial of two of the women who had allegedly bewitched her, one witness referring to the "gogling of hir heade & eyes, the turning of her armes and hands, the dubling & swelling of hir body" in court.[39] Two decades later two other daughters of the gentry, Helen and Elizabeth Fairfax, likewise "fell into a trance before the judge, and were carried out". Justices present followed the girls out, and "made experiments to prove if they counterfeited or not". The girls' father noted that "report said that it was not so civil as I expected from such men, yet their curiosity found nothing but sincerity in my children".[40]

The theme of the possession of adolescents is a major one in the history of English witchcraft in this period, and is too complex to go into here. What is obvious is that being possessed, whether in the courtroom or not, gave adolescents a unique opportunity to cast off their characteristically submissive and repressed rôle, and indulge in bad behaviour that was not only licensed, but also made them the centre of attention.[41] Given the probability that girls were more likely than boys to be deeply socialized into submissiveness, their behaviour when possessed attracted considerable comment from contemporary observers, and indeed may have been regarded as a deeper affront to social norms than that of young males. Something of the divergence in the normal expectations of a young woman's behaviour and that of the possessed adolescent girl in the presence of a judge can be glimpsed in the account of the sufferings of yet another daughter of the gentry, Margaret Muschamp. The girl and her mother were attempting to persuade a sceptical judge to prosecute the persons suspected of witchcraft, and the girl fell into fits before the judge, at one stage, as was typical in such cases, vomiting foreign bodies. But when she came out of her fits, she "did not know what was past, as all the beholders did see onely an innocent, bashfull girle, without any confidence at all when she was out of her fits".[42] When examining gender as an aspect of witchcraft, it is clear that being possessed and launching a witchcraft accusation gave many an "innocent, bashfull girle" the chance to become the centre of attention and to exercise power over adults.

After trial and condemnation the witch, like any other felon, would be prepared for death. Appropriately enough, this process would be entrusted to a clergyman. Hence Henry Goodcole worked on (to use the contemporary phrase) Elizabeth Sawyer in 1621 to accept her sinfulness and the death by hanging that it had drawn upon her, and to make a full confession. It was desirable that the condemned witch, like other convicted felons, should "make a good end", and die penitently and with dignity. In Sawyer's case, Goodcole officiated at the execution, and at the gallows read to her the confession that she had made earlier, which she declared to be true "in the hearing of many hundreds".[43] Sometimes this sort of clerical pressure could be excessive. Joan Peterson, executed at Tyburn in 1652, was, at the place of execution, exhorted nine or more times to confess by the Ordinary of Newgate. At this point the executioner commented that "the Ordinary might be ashamed to trouble a dying woman so much", to which the clergyman responded that "he was commanded to do so, and durst do no otherwise". This story does at least demonstrate that convicted witches could be obdurate at the gallows.[44] Ideally, however, as with Elizabeth Sawyer, an execution would involve the convicted witch making a "good end" and behaving in an appropriately edifying fashion. Thus when Joan Cason died at Faversham in 1586 she made a gallows speech accepting that her fate was the result of divine justice, and made so godly an end that many who had previously been her enemies lamented her death.[45]

But not all died so edifyingly. Ann Bodenham, executed at Salisbury, was worked on by a minister named Foster, "who comforted her to bear death Christianly, boldly, and chearfully". He managed to bring her "to that pitch as to promise him she would goe a true penitent to her place of execution, and to die as a lamb". She refused, however, to confess the matters for which she had been convicted, adding "that she wrongfully suffered death, and did lament extremely, and desired to die quietly". Her execution was, in fact, less than edifying. According to the pamphlet account, she was "very desirous for drink, and had not Mr Undersheriff's prudence been such as to restrain her from it she would have died drunk". As she walked to the gallows, "by every house she went by, she went with a small piece of silver in her hand, calling for beer, and was very passionate when denyed", while she was also, for unclear reasons, very annoyed when the sheriff told her she could not be buried at the gallows. In fact, at the gallows she refused to confess, and

> being asked whether she desired the prayers of any of the people; she answered, she had as many prayers already as she intended, and desired to have, but cursed those that detained her from her death, and was importunate to goe up the ladder.

She then tried to turn herself off on the gallows, but was restrained by the executioner, who asked her forgiveness, as was the custom. "She replyed forgive thee? A pox on thee, turn me off, which were the last words she spoke". "Thus", concluded the account of her trial, "you have her wicked life, her wofull death. Those that forsake God in their lives, shall be forsaken of him in their deaths". Those who have argued that witchcraft accusations were a means of controlling women can at least take consolation in Bodenham's case as one of hegemony's failures.[46]

* * *

This chapter has concentrated on witchcraft and the secular criminal law courts. But before moving to any conclusions on the evidence presented by this connection, we should remind ourselves that there were other tribunals involved with witchcraft cases, notably the ecclesiastical courts. Less serious forms of witchcraft, sorcery and charming might be presented before these courts, while, more importantly for our immediate purposes, defamation suits involving allegations of witchcraft might be pursued there. Ecclesiastical law gave women greater opportunities for litigating than did the common law, and some of the better documented cases reveal clearly how witchcraft accusations might form part of a wider body of tensions and conflicts between women.

One such case was tried before the Chester Consistory Court in 1662. It arose from problems between Mary Briscoe and Ann Wright. Wright's daughter, aged about twelve, had fallen ill, and "was very sadly afflicted and in a strange manner by fitts", during which time "she would many times say that Mary Briscoe pricked her to the heart with pins and would have her heart and the like, and she did swell much in the body and soe dyed". In consequence, as a witness named Cicely Winne deposed, "the said Mary Briscoe was suspected by many neighbours to be the cause both of her afflictinge and likewise of a brother of hers who was sadly afflicted before that & dyed in a strange manner".

Thus we have a case which resembles so many others: the strange death of a child, the allegation of witchcraft, the neighbourly evaluation, the focusing of suspicion, the defamation suit in defence of good name. Unusually, however, the surviving documentation allows us to piece together something of the background. Neither woman had an unblemished reputation. Briscoe was described as a "very troublesome and wrangling woman among her neighbours", or as a "very wilfull high spirited woman amongst her neighbours". Indeed, her husband, worried about the suspicion of witchcraft against his wife, had discussed the problem with Cicely Winne, and told her "he was much troubled at it but he could not rule her, and he was very much afraid that she would come to the same end as her moth[er] did". But Wright herself had given birth to an illegitimate child just after the Restoration, had refused to identify its father to the midwife and had refused to do penance for it. One witness, interestingly, deposed that Wright claimed Briscoe had bewitched her at the time of the child's conception. She also complained at about the same time of being compelled "to be a witness against her husband for speaking treason against the king". Another women, Margery Whishall, claimed that Wright had slandered her for adultery. With Wright and Briscoe we obviously have two rather contentious women, who had, in fact, already been locked into a dispute over a house in which Wright had dwelt, "which the said Mary had a great mind of". This dispute had already provoked a suit which had been arbitrated by a justice of the peace. This case, which ended in Wright performing public penance in her parish church, demonstrates how the ecclesiastical law helped women to become agents in legal matters. Wright and Briscoe were clearly not victims of a patriarchal legal system, but rather two women who were willing to use the law to pursue their own ends.[47]

This assertion reminds us of the problems of determining a specifically female experience before the courts and legal process. We are examining witchcraft, a crime which, correctly, has been regarded as having a peculiar connection with women. But much of what seems to have happened to women involved in witchcraft cases, whether as accused, accusers or witnesses, seems very similar to what happened to their male counterparts: men accused of felony, and male witnesses giving evidence in court, might be hectored or pressured by aggressive judges, and men convicted of felony, like women convicted of witchcraft, were "worked on" by clergymen before their execution in hopes that they might produce a model speech from the gallows. However, we must keep our minds open to the possibility that although women might have shared with men the experience of going through various stages of the judicial process, the quality of that experience and the reactions and emotions it might provoke could have been very different for them.

There were, however, aspects of the prosecution of felony which were either specific to or more marked in trials of witchcraft. The most obvious of these, as I have stressed, was the use of groups of women to search suspected witches for the mark. Another recurring theme in accounts of witchcraft cases was the frequent occurrence of something amounting to mob action, or at least popular pressure. Of course, the phenomenon of crowd action or popular attitudes towards criminals or at executions was not limited to witchcraft cases; but the frequency of references to hostile mobs is striking, especially since they were on the fringes of the legal process. Suspected witches might be subjected to swimming, scratching or other forms of popularly licensed violence. Further research into this issue might lead to some useful insights into attitudes to gender, given that most of the people towards whom such violence was directed were women.

The willingness of other women to act against alleged witches is also a constant theme. As I have suggested elsewhere, materials from Yorkshire demonstrate that witchcraft accusations were not simply foisted onto women by men, but rather were frequently generated from tensions between women, often arising from such traditional female concerns as childrearing, and were often formulated and refined in the world of female sociability, gossip among women, and female concern over reputation.[48] This creates problems for those investigating constraints on female behaviour in early modern England. Many witchcraft accusations, I would argue, reveal a social arena where channels of female force, female power, and female action could run. The high level of participation of women witnesses in witchcraft cases, and the ready participation of women in searching for the witch's mark, were areas in which women could enter the male dominated milieu of legal process, and in which women, perhaps within parameters dictated and maintained by men, could carve out some rôle for themselves in the public sphere. This would seem to be a line of investigation well worth pursuing.

This leads us to a final point. It is a commonplace that early modern England was a patriarchal society in which issues of gender, like everything else, were viewed in hierarchical terms, and in which women, not least in their status before the common law, were disadvantaged. This is especially relevant when we consider witchcraft, an offence which, even if we eschew some of the women's movement writings on the subject from the 1970s, is somehow connected with the male domination of women. Yet in the preceding pages we have seen women acting strongly: defying judges and executioners; accusing other women as witches; giving evidence against suspected women witches; and suing each other for defamation arising from allegations of witchcraft. Even though contemporary attitudes to gender probably made those experiences different for the women involved, they nonetheless establish women as active participants in the legal system. Like all of us, these women found themselves in a real world that imposed constraints upon them. Yet within those constraints and limitations, in the legal process and before the courts as elsewhere, they were historical actors.

# Notes

1. For participation rates, see C. Z. Weiner, Sex roles and crime in late Elizabethan Hertfordshire, *Journal of Social History*, **8**, 1975, pp. 18–37, and J. M. Beattie, The criminality of women in eighteenth-century England, *ibid.*, pp. 80–116; for defamation litigation, J. A. Sharpe, *Defamation and sexual slander in early modern England: the church courts at York*, Borthwick Papers, 58 (York, 1980); for infanticide, P. C. Hoffer & N. E. Hull, *Murdering mothers: infanticide in England and New England 1558–1803* (New York, 1981); for scolding, D. E. Underdown, The taming of the scold, in *Order and disorder in early modern England*, eds A. Fletcher & J. Stevenson (Cambridge, 1985), pp. 116–36.

2. Gender as a social construct has so far received little attention from historians of early modern England. For an important preliminary discussion, see S. Amussen, Gender, family and the social order, 1560–1725, in Fletcher & Stevenson (1985) pp. 196–218. The themes raised here are discussed further in Amussen's, *An ordered society: gender and class in early modern England* (Oxford, 1988). I am grateful to K. Cowman for discussing modern gender theory with me.

3. For a contemporary introduction to women and the common law, see *The lawes resolution of womens rights: or, the lawes provision for women. A methodicall collection of such statutes and customes, with the cases, opinions and points of learning in the law, as doe properly concern women* (London, 1652).

4. For a list of these indictments see C. L'Estrange Ewen, *Witch hunting and witch trials: the indictments for witchcraft from the records of 1373 assizes held for the Home Circuit AD 1559–1736* (London, 1929), pp. 117–265.

5. Cf. materials for the Western Circuit printed in C. L'Estrange Ewen, *Witchcraft and demonianism: a concise account derived from sworn depositions and confessions obtained in the courts of England and Wales* (London, 1933), appendix L, pp. 439–46.

6. A. Macfarlane, *Witchcraft in Tudor and Stuart England: a regional and comparative study* (London, 1970), pp. 278–93.

7. *Ibid.*, pp. 117–18.

8. J. A. Sharpe, Witchcraft and women in seventeenth-century England: some northern evidence, *Continuity and Change*, **6**, 1991, pp. 179–99. For a somewhat different perspective on these issues, see C. Holmes, Women: witnesses and witches, *Past & Present*, **140**, 1993, pp. 45–78. Unfortunately Dr Holmes' article appeared too late to have its findings addressed in this essay.

9. Ewen, *Witchcraft and demonianism*, p. 63.

10. *The examination and confession of certain wytches at Chensford in the countie of Essex before the queens maiesties judges, the xxvi day of July anno 1566* (London, 1566).

11. *Court leet records, vol. 1, part 2, AD 1578–1602*, eds F. J. C. Hearnshaw & D. M. Hearnshaw, Southampton Record Society, I (Southampton, 1906), p. 187.

12. *A true and just recorde of the information, examination and confession of all the witches*

taken at S. Oses in the countie of Essex, whereof some were executed and others treated according to the determination of the law (London, 1582), sig D4.

13. W. Grange (ed.), Daemonologia: a discourse on witchcraft, as it was acted in the family of Mr Edward Fairfax, of Fuyston, in the county of York, in the year 1621: along with the only two eclogues of the same author known to be in existence, (Harrogate, 1882), p. 78; PRO, Northern Circuit Depositions, ASSI 45/3/2/129; ASSI 45/5/2/30; ASSI 45/4/1/131.

14. H. Goodcole, The wonderfull discoverie of Elizabeth Sawyer a witch, late of Edmonton, her conviction and condemnation and death (London, 1621), Sig B2v.–B3v.

15. A true and exact relation of the severall informations, examinations and confessions of the late witches arraigned and executed in the county of Essex (London, 1645), p. 26; Camb UL, Ely Assize Depositions Michaelmas 1647, EDR 12/20.

16. J. Boys, The case of witchcraft at Coggeshall, Essex, in the year 1699 (London, 1909), pp. 21–2.

17. This is contrary to the opinion, which probably rests on an uncritical reading of the Malleus Maleficarum and other continental witchcraft treatises, that midwives were a group of women very much at risk to being accused of witchcraft: for a discussion of this point see D. Harley, Historians as demonologists: the myth of the midwife-witch, Journal of the Society for the Social History of Medicine, 3, 1990, pp. 1–26.

18. Camb UL, EDR 12/3.

19. Suffolk RO, Aldeburgh Borough Records, Chamberlain's Account Books, EE1/12/2, ff. 248, 249v.

20. PRO, ASSI 45/5/5/1; 45/5/2/30.

21. Oxon RO, Quarter Sessions Records, Q3/1687 Mi/14.

22. For a case of this type see R. H. Helmholz, Marriage litigation in medieval England (Cambridge, 1974), p. 89. Yorkshire medieval cases are discussed and a number of references to relevant secondary materials made in F. Pedersen, Marriage litigation and the ecclesiastical courts in York in the fourteenth century, PhD thesis, University of Toronto, 1991, pp. 133–41. I am grateful to Dr Pedersen for providing me with information on this subject.

23. P. Hair, Before the bawdy court: selections from the church court and other records relating to the correction of moral offences in England, Scotland and New England, 1300–1800 (London, 1972), p. 189.

24. This practice is discussed in A calendar of assize records: introduction, ed. J. S. Cockburn (London, 1985), pp. 121–3. See also J. C. Oldham, On pleading the belly: a history of the jury of matrons, Criminal Justice History, 6, 1985, pp. 1–64.

25. These figures are based on an analysis of abstracts of assize cases given in Ewen, Witch hunting and witch trials, pp. 187–264. For analysis of the Northern Circuit Depositions, see Sharpe, Witchcraft and women.

26. These figures are derived from abstracts of indictments given in A calendar of assize records: Hertfordshire indictments James I, ed. J. S. Cockburn (London,

1975), pp. 70–223.

27. *Calendar of State Papers, Domestic, 1634–5*, p. 79.

28. Ewen, *Witchcraft and demonianism*, p. 125.

29. R. North, *The lives of the right hon Francis North, Baron Guildford; the hon Sir Dudley North; and the hon and rev Dr John North*, 3 vols (London, 1890), III, pp. 130–31 describes this case, where the judge was "a mild, passive man, who had neither dexterity nor spirit to oppose a popular rage".

30. *A full and impartial account of the discovery of sorcery and witchcraft practis'd by Jane Wenham of Walkerne in Hertfordshire, upon the bodies of Anne Thorne, Anne Street, &c* (London, 1712), p. 28.

31. *The tryal of Richard Hathaway upon an information for being a cheat and imposter for endeavouring to take away the life of Sarah Morduck for being a witch* (London, 1702), p. 20.

32. Ewen, *Witch hunting and witch trials*, p. 99, shows that of 513 persons accused of witchcraft at the Home Circuit assizes, 112 (or 22 per cent) were executed. Many others, of course, suffered lesser penalties.

33. The contemporary account of this case is printed in B. Rosen, *Witchcraft* (London, 1969), pp. 163–7.

34. A. Trapnel, *Anna Trapnel's report and plea or a narrative of her journey from London to Cornwal, the occasion of it, the Lord's encouragements to it, and sign of presence with her in it* (London, 1654), p. 24.

35. Ewen, *Witchcraft and demonianism*, p. 256. Landish was sentenced to death, PRO, Home Circuit Assizes Files, ASSI 35/86/1/84.

36. *The tryal, condemnation and execution of three witches, viz Temperance Floyd, Mary Floyd and Susanna Edwards, who were arraigned at Exeter on the 18th of August 1682* (London, 1682), p. 4.

37. *A prodigious and tragicall history of the tryall, confession and condemnation of six witches at Maidstone, in Kent, att the assizes held there in July, Fryday 30, this present year 1652* (London, 1652), p. 4.

38. Ewen, *Witchcraft and demonianism*, p. 197. Materials relating to this case are brought together in M. MacDonald, *Witchcraft and hysteria in Elizabethan London: Edward Jordan and the Mary Glover case* (London, 1990).

39. PRO, Star Chamber Records, STAC 8 4/10, f. 9.

40. Fairfax, *Daemonologia*, pp. 123–4.

41. This phenomenon is perhaps most familiar in the context of the trials at Salem, Massachusetts, in 1692. For a work which, although now somewhat dated, does focus on this issue, see M. L. Starkey, *The devil in Massachusetts: a modern enquiry into the Salem witch trials* (New York, 1950).

42. M. Moore, *Wonderfull news from the North: or, a true relation of the sad and grievous torments, inflicted upon the bodies of three children of Mr George Muschamp, late of the county of Northumberland* (London, 1650), pp. 15–6.

43. Goodcole, *Wonderfull discoverie of Elizabeth Sawyer*, sig D2v.

44. Ewen, *Witch hunting and witch trials*, p. 276.

# THE LANCASHIRE WITCH TRIALS OF 1612 AND 1634 AND THE ECONOMICS OF WITCHCRAFT*

J. T. Swain

AN IMPORTANT THEORY was put forward by Alan Macfarlane and Keith Thomas to help explain the incidence of witchcraft accusations at a local level in early modern England.[1] They noted the fact that the witches were often poor old women who were usually accused by more prosperous younger neighbours, following a refusal of charity. Thomas and Macfarlane saw the economic changes of the sixteenth century, with rapid population growth putting pressure on limited resources and with enclosure increasing the number of the landless poor, as factors which accelerated the trend towards a cash economy. The medieval idea of voluntary charity towards the poor as a necessary Christian obligation was rendered obsolete by the advent of the Elizabethan Poor Law which discouraged begging. Thus the move away from a neighbourly, communal ethic to one based more on private property and commercial values led to increasing social tension, as the poor felt the full force of unfavourable market forces and the sanctions of the state. A rejected beggar would often curse his uncharitable neighbour, and, should something then go wrong, the neighbour might attribute his misfortune to witchcraft. Also present is the notion that the victim, aware that he had failed in his social obligations, sought to exonerate himself by transferring the guilt he felt to the beggar.

Macfarlane admitted that there were problems with this model, and later repudiated his original ideas, claiming instead that the individualistic characteristics of the English were present in medieval times and did not arise specifically in the sixteenth century along with witchcraft accusations.[2] Nevertheless, Macfarlane's original ideas, together with those of Thomas, remain very influential, whilst his later ideas have not

* An earlier version of this paper was read in October 1991 to a day school on 'Witchcraft in Seventeenth Century England' at Lancaster University. I am grateful to Angus Winchester for organizing the programme, and to all those who made helpful comments there, particularly Michael Mullett and Stephen Pumfrey. I am also very grateful for the comments of Paul Gladwish and John Hatcher. Final responsibility for any shortcomings and errors rests with the author.

[1] A. D. J. Macfarlane, *Witchcraft in Tudor and Stuart England. A Regional and Comparative Study* (1970), chs 10–16 and K. Thomas, *Religion and the Decline of Magic* (1971; Harmondsworth, 1973), pp. 638–77.

[2] A. D. J. Macfarlane, *The Origins of English Individualism. The Family, Property and Social Transition* (Oxford, 1978), pp. 1–2.

been as widely accepted. The purpose of this investigation is to assess the extent to which economic factors played a part in what are, arguably, the most famous witch trials in English history — those of the Lancashire witches.

I

The Lancashire or Pendle witches are justifiably famous. Two historical novels based on the events of the 1612 trial have contributed most to the legend: Harrison Ainsworth's *The Lancashire Witches* (1849) and Robert Neill's *Mist over Pendle* (1951). Neill's book has the merit of being based more heavily on the chief historical source, *The wonderful discovery of witches in the county of Lancaster*, published in 1613 by Thomas Potts, the judges' clerk at the fateful Assizes of August 1612 where the chief witches were condemned to death.[3]

During the early seventeenth century, however, it seems that it was the second trial of 1634 which attracted the most attention. In May 1634 Sir William Pelham wrote to Edward, Viscount Conway, saying that:

The greatest news from the country is of a huge pack of witches which are lately discovered in Lancashire, whereof it is said 19 are condemned, and that there are at least 60 already discovered, and yet daily there are more revealed; there are divers of them of good ability and they have done much harm. It is suspected that they had a hand in raising the great storm wherein his Majesty was in so great danger at sea in Scotland.[4]

Charles I's sister, Elizabeth, 'The Winter Queen' of Bohemia, had also heard about the witches by June 1634, despite being in exile at The Hague in Holland.[5] By October, a comedy entitled *The Late Lancashire Witches* by Thomas Heywood and Richard Broome was being enacted at the Globe Theatre in London.[6]

The immediate events which led to the first trial began on 18 March 1612 when Alizon Device met a Halifax pedlar called John Law near Colne. She wanted some pins, but he refused to sell or give her any. He

[3] W. H. Ainsworth, *The Lancashire Witches* (1849); R. Neill, *Mist over Pendle* (1951). T. Potts, *The wonderful discovery of witches in the county of Lancaster* (1613) (republished by the Chetham Society, old series, vi (1845), ed. J. Crossley). This more than compensates for the regrettable loss of the Assize records (those for 1634 have also been lost).

[4] C(alendar of) S(tate) P(apers) D(omestic), 1634–35, p. 26.

[5] Sir W. Brereton, *Travels in Holland, the United Provinces England, Scotland and Ireland, 1634–1635*, ed. E. Hawkins, Chetham Society, o.s., i (1844), 33–34.

[6] M. Tonge, 'The Lancashire Witches: 1612 and 1634', *Transactions of the Historic Society of Lancashire and Cheshire [THSLC]*, LXXXIII (1931), 171; E. Peel and P. Southern, *The Trials of the Lancashire Witches*, 3rd edn (Nelson, 1985), p. 99.

then suffered a stroke, and accused Alizon of bewitching him. Apparently, she later confessed to the crime of witchcraft both to Law and to his son, Abraham, a Halifax cloth dyer. On 30 March, a local J.P., Roger Nowell, Esq. of Read, questioned her together with her brother James and her mother Elizabeth Device. Nowell interrogated others and mutual recriminations followed; finally, on Saturday 4 April, he sent for trial at the next Lancaster Assizes, Alizon, her eighty-year-old grandmother Elizabeth Southerns alias Old Demdike, and two women from another family thought to be notorious witches, Anne Whittle alias Old Chattox (also aged about eighty) and her married daughter Anne Redfern. Old Demdike had confessed to Nowell that she had given her soul to the Devil twenty years before and let her familiar, called Tibb, suck her blood. Alizon also admitted to a demonic pact sealed two years previously, apparently at her grandmother's instigation. Anne Whittle similarly confessed to making a pact fourteen or fifteen years before with a devil called Fancy.[7]

The following Friday, Good Friday 10 April, relatives and friends met in Pendle Forest at Old Demdike's house called the Malkin Tower. No doubt they were alarmed and confused about the arrests and naturally wondered what to do next. Nowell got to hear of the meeting, assumed because of the day chosen that it was a witches' sabbat (despite the fact that no evidence of the Devil's presence was discovered) and, after further examinations, sent several more prisoners to join the other four in Lancaster Castle. There, they were interrogated again, and details of an incredible plot emerged, notably that they had intended to rescue the four prisoners, kill the Lancaster gaoler and blow up the castle.[8]

This was only seven years after the Gunpowder Plot, and so perhaps naturally the authorities took the case seriously, particularly since accusations of witchcraft were involved. On the other hand, to what extent did the authorities pressurize those who were accused? In theory, torture was not allowed in English trials that did not involve treason, but some of the confessions seem too incredible and far-fetched to be the result of anything other than the product of unscrupulous tactics by the prosecution, whether by the use of force, methods such as prolonged periods of sleep deprivation, threats, suggestions that others had already confessed or promises of leniency if the accused admitted to what the authorities wished to hear. Whatever did happen inside the dungeons at Lancaster, it was too much for Old Demdike, who died before the trial. At his trial in

---

[7] Potts, *Wonderful Discovery*, B–B3, C, D3, R3–4, S–S2 and passim.
[8] Ibid., C4, F2–F4, G2–G4, H3, I2–I3 and passim.

August, the labourer James Device 'was so insensible, weak and unable in all things as he could neither speak, hear or stand, but was holden up'.[9]

The star witness at the trials which followed in August was nine-year-old Jennet Device, the sister of Alizon and James. She provided evidence about those who had attended the Malkin Tower gathering, including information against her own mother, Elizabeth Device, and her elder brother and sister! The shock of this was too much for Elizabeth, who had refused to make any confession, but finally broke down in court when Jennet, backed up by James and Alizon, accused her of witchcraft. Not all the prisoners pleaded guilty, and one who refused to confess was Alice Nutter of Roughlee, whom Potts describes as standing out because, unlike the others, she was a rich woman. Not only was she charged with attending the Malkin Tower meeting, but, incredibly, she was also accused of consorting with Old Demdike and Elizabeth Device to kill Henry Mitton of Roughlee because Demdike, when on a begging expedition, had been refused a penny by Mitton! This is not the only piece of implausible evidence accepted by the court and Potts. Some were acquitted, including a further group of alleged witches from Samlesbury. Nine, however, were condemned to death and, together with a woman from Windle near St Helens, were taken out and hanged the following day. Another woman who had apparently attended the ill-fated Malkin Tower meeting, Jennet Preston of Gisburn in Craven, had been previously tried at the York Assizes in July and had been executed too.[10]

The second witch trial in 1634 is similar to the first in one important respect, namely that the chief witness was a child. His name was Edmund Robinson junior of Newchurch in Pendle, aged ten or eleven.[11] In February 1634 he made a statement to two J.P.s, Richard Shuttleworth and John Starkey Esqs, that the previous November, on All Saints' Day, he had seen two greyhounds change into human form, that of a woman and a boy. He claimed that the woman had then transformed the boy into a horse and had then taken Edmund on it to a house called Hoarstones in Wheatley Lane in Pendle. There, a large number of men and women were feasting and three women were to be seen with clay models full of thorns. Edmund escaped and told his father Edmund, a poor waller or

[9] Ibid., C4, H2.
[10] Ibid., F2–F3, O3–O4 and passim.
[11] *CSPD*, 1634–35, p. 141 gives Edmund's age in July 1634 as 'ten years or thereabouts', whereas a copy of the boy's examination taken the previous February states that he was eleven (J. Webster, *The Displaying of Supposed Witchcraft* (1677), p. 347).

mason, of his experience.[12] His father apparently took three months before going to the authorities — a peculiar and suspicious delay. Many individuals were rounded up, tried at the Lancaster Assizes and twenty-two were found guilty.[13]

Charles I and the Privy Council then intervened and instructed Henry Bridgeman, Bishop of Chester, to examine the prisoners.[14] One woman, Margaret Johnson of Marsden, a widow of sixty, admitted her guilt as a witch, saying that she had given her soul to a devil called Mamilion six years previously and had allowed it to suck her blood and commit 'wicked uncleanness'.[15] As with the earlier trial, the methods used by the authorities to extract confessions must be viewed with suspicion. They certainly suffered the indignity of being strip-searched for evidence of a witch's mark, where the witch's familiar or devil was supposed to suck her blood and which was supposed to be insensitive to pain. Most of the accused were found to have marks and nearly all of these were discovered in the genital areas.[16]

Margaret Johnson and three other women were summoned to London to be examined by the leading royal and London physicians and mid-wives, and later by Charles I and the Privy Council. Whilst the women were held in the Fleet Prison, they were put on show for public viewing, and apparently a large amount of money was raised in the process.[17] Unnatural marks were not found this time, yet, despite this, many of the witches were still in gaol in Lancaster in August 1636, and their ultimate fate is unknown.[18] This seems particularly unjust because the Robinsons had been examined separately in London. The boy eventually confessed that he made up the whole story to avoid a beating, since he had been

[12] Ibid., pp. 347–49; B(ritish) L(ibrary), Harleian MSS, 6854, fols 22–26 and Additional MSS, 36674, fol. 193 all give slightly different versions of Edmund's statement. For further details of these and other copies of Edmund's statement, see Tonge, *THSLC*, LXXXIII, 157.
[13] BL, Add. MSS, 36674, fol. 199.
[14] *CSPD*, 1634–35, pp. 77–79.
[15] BL, Add. MSS, 36674, fol. 196. As with Edmund Robinson's statement, there are several other copies with slight variations (e.g. BL, Harl. MSS, 6854, fols 27–29). For further details, see Tonge, *THSLC*, LXXXIII, 159.
[16] BL, Add. MSS, 36674, fol. 199. Other historians have noted similar findings with regard to witches' marks, e.g. Thomas, *Religion*, pp. 530, 657, 687; G. R. Quaife, *Godly Zeal and Furious Rage. The Witch in Early Modern Europe* (1987), pp. 55, 105, 142–43; J. Klaits, *Servants of Satan. The Age of Witch Hunts* (Bloomington, Indiana, 1985), pp. 56–57.
[17] *CSPD*, 1634–35, pp. 98, 129–30; Webster, *Displaying of Supposed Witchcraft*, pp. 277–78, 346; Peel and Southern, *Trials*, p. 97; Tonge, *THSLC*, LXXXIII, 168–69.
[18] *The Farington Papers*, ed. S. M. Farington, Chetham Society, o.s., XXXIX (1856), 27; Tonge, *THSLC*, LXXXIII, 174; C. Holmes, 'Women: Witnesses and Witches', *Past & Present*, 140 (Aug. 1993), 66.

playing with other children when he should have been bringing home the family's cows.[19] In 1677 John Webster published an account of the whole affair, including details of how the pair had attempted to discover witches amongst his congregation at Kildwick in Craven. Apparently, the pair had capitalized on their celebrity status and even travelled from parish to parish as expert witch-finders. Webster was sceptical of the Robinsons from the first, and claimed that when he grew up, Edmund junior acknowledged that he had been put up to making the accusations by his father and others.[20]

## II

What was the economic background to the Pendle witch trials? The term 'Forest of Pendle' is somewhat misleading because the area was not a forest at all in the modern sense of the word. Originally, the area was a forest or chase in the legal sense and was therefore reserved for hunting deer, but, in the later Middle Ages substantial vaccaries (cattle farms) were established. During the fourteenth century the area was leased, and farmers had the opportunity to develop the resources of the forest on their own account. Pendle Forest, as part of the Duchy of Lancaster's Honour of Clitheroe, became part of the Crown lands when Henry IV usurped the throne in 1399. Leasing continued throughout the fifteenth century until in 1507 the forests of the Honour of Clitheroe were granted to tenants by copy of court roll, according to the custom of the adjacent manors such as Colne and Ightenhill.

This was a decision which benefited the Crown in the short term — rents rose by 39 per cent in Pendle — but in the longer term prospects were more to the advantage of the tenants since they gained security of tenure with copies of their tenancy agreements which could be demonstrated if necessary in court. In addition, the forest copyholders were permitted to inherit their holdings automatically, provided that they paid an entry fine of just one year's rent. The rents themselves were fixed, so, in real terms, the copyholders became increasingly better off during the sixteenth century as prices rose. By contrast, many tenants in other areas faced great hardship, often being evicted if the landlord wished to enclose his lands, or at the very least were subjected to rapidly rising entry fines and rents.[21]

[19] *CSPD*, 1634–35, pp. 141, 152–53.
[20] Webster, *Displaying of Supposed Witchcraft*, pp. 276–78.
[21] J. T. Swain, *Industry Before the Industrial Revolution. North-East Lancashire c. 1500–1640*, Chetham Soicety, 3rd ser. xxxii (1986), 8–9, 56–57.

Not surprisingly, the opening up of these forest areas — in Pendle's case 7,289 acres — on such advantageous terms led to rapid population growth. There had been just twenty-four tenants in Pendle Forest in 1443 but the number had grown to exactly 100 by 1527. In response, a new corn mill was built at New Carr in 1542[22] and Newchurch itself was officially consecrated in 1544 and separated from St Michael's Clitheroe.[23] Other areas of Pendle Forest were contained in three adjacent chapelries: Barrowford in the north-east was in Colne chapelry; to the south-east, Burnley chapelry contained Reedley Hallows, Filly Close and New Laund; to the south-west, Higham, West Close and Heyhouses were part of Padiham chapelry. All formed part of the huge parish of Whalley.[24]

Exact population figures are impossible to obtain, but a total of 100 tenants in 1527 suggests a population of at least 400–500, and this must be regarded as an absolute minimum since it takes no account of families existing as subtenants or those officially landless but illegally squatting. Moreover, the population seems to have continued to grow. In Newchurch chapelry there were sixty-four households according to the communicants' returns of 1563, and 150 in 1650.[25] Making allowances for the sections of Pendle Forest in the other three chapelries gives an estimate of 145 households in the whole of Pendle Forest in 1563 and 340 in 1650. This suggests a total population of 580–725 in 1563, and of about 1,620 people living in Pendle Forest in 1650.[26] The communicants' returns may be somewhat unreliable, but the non-communicating and largely Catholic population was not very numerous in this area.[27] It seems reasonably safe to conclude that the population had more than doubled between 1563 and 1650.

The harshness of the climate and the unproductiveness of the land for arable crops meant that the predominant form of agriculture was

[22] Ibid., pp. 58, 71.
[23] *Victoria County History of Lancashire*, ed. W. Farrer and J. Brownhill, 8 vols (1906–14, reprinted 1966), vi, 517–18.
[24] Swain, *Industry*, pp. 3–4.
[25] Ibid., p. 17.
[26] For a very rough estimate the Protestation Oath of 1642 has been used, where Newchurch in Pendle constituted 44.1 per cent of the whole of Pendle Forest. L(ancashire) R(ecord) O(ffice), MF 25 (the original is in the House of Lords Record Office). The figures for 1563 show the possible range if average household size was between four and five; for 1650, average household size in Padiham chapelry was 4.767 and this figure has been used for the whole of Pendle Forest (*Lancashire and Cheshire Church Surveys, 1649–1655*, ed. H. Fishwick, Record Society of Lancashire and Cheshire, i (1878), 164).
[27] See below, section iv.

pastoral, taking the form largely of stock-raising with some dairying.[28] In 1608, four years before the first witch trial, the forest tenants of the Honour of Clitheroe pointed out that there were 'great and mountainous commons extremely barren and unprofitable' and since the disafforestation of 1507, the copyholders' had been put to considerable expense:

not only in the enclosure of the same copyholds and the continual manuring and tilling thereof, being before that time in respect both of the nature of the country and the soil thereabouts extremely barren and unprofitable and as yet capable of no other corn but oats and that but only in dry years and not without the continual charge of every third year's new manuring, but also in the building of their houses and habitations thereon having no timber there nor within many miles thereof, and having from time to time ever since enjoyed the same and therefore paid a rent and fine at the first as much or more and now very near the value thereof, have nearly disposed, employed and placed all the fruit and increase of their ancestors and their own labours and industries and the estates and maintenance of themselves, their families and posterities upon the same copyholds . . .[29]

The copyholders, needless to say, were exaggerating, for the petition was designed to persuade the Duchy that they were too poor to be able to pay a large sum of money for the confirmation of their copyholds. The picture was certainly not as bleak as they painted it; for example, probate inventories record crops other than oats growing in the Pendle area, such as barley and wheat.[30]

In the early years after the disafforestation of 1507, when land was plentiful, some copyholders chose to treat their sons equally and practise partible inheritance.[31] In 1532 the Duchy noted with alarm the subdivision of holdings, fearful that the small farms created would be incapable of supporting a tenantry sufficiently prosperous to pay their rents. A decree was therefore issued that no tenant in Pendle, Trawden or Rossendale forest was to sell, lease or surrender part of their lands unless the new tenant's lands were worth £1 6s. 8d. above all charges, on penalty of seizure of the holding by the steward.[32] No examples of seizure have been found and, since there were some extremely small holdings, perhaps the decree was ignored. It may have influenced the copyholders' to move away from partible inheritance, for the wills available for the late sixteenth and early seventeenth centuries reveal the universal practice of primogeniture, whereby the eldest son acquired the holding and the land

---

[28] Swain, *Industry*, ch. 3.
[29] P(ublic) R(ecord) O(ffice), DL 5/19 fol. 395; LRO, DDTa 216 fol. 3.
[30] Swain, *Industry*, pp. 37–38.
[31] Ibid., pp. 73, 77.
[32] PRO, DL 1/8/R7.

was only split if there were daughters but no sons. This was quite logical in an area where land was not particularly productive and where pressure on resources was becoming apparent. Moreover, the heir did not get everything his own way, for if his mother were still alive he was obliged by custom (and it was often stated in the father's will) that she should have a quarter of the holding as her dower; sometimes even more than this was left to the widow. She was also entitled to a third of the personal estate or moveable goods. If the heir had younger brothers and sisters too, he was often obliged to provide them with cash portions when they came of age.[33] All of these burdens might force an heir to sell or mortgage part of the holding, and so the years immediately following his father's death could be extremely difficult for the eldest son.

It is therefore not surprising that all types of household chose to try to earn a living by means other than simply agriculture in order to make ends meet. The inventories reveal a wide range of other activities, including coal-mining, quarrying of slate and limestone, tanning and brewing.[34] It is clothmaking, however, that was particularly widespread, notably production of a coarse woollen cloth called kersey. Some 70 per cent of 'supra' inventories (i.e., where the personal estate was valued at £40 or more) listed clothmaking tools. Over half of these Pendle households possessed cards or combs (52 per cent) and spinning wheels (56 per cent), and nearly two-fifths (38 per cent) owned looms.[35]

These inventories reflect the middling wealth levels of society; the very poor did not make wills and hence left no inventory, and few 'infra' inventories (less than £40 and proved locally) have survived, but those that are extant reveal a similar picture.[36] We know from the witchcraft evidence that the very poorest and youngest in society might be involved in textile production. For example, Anne Whittle alias Old Chattox was hired by the wife of James Robinson to card wool about six years before the trial of 1612, despite being in her seventies, almost blind and apparently a witch of eight years experience! She carded on a Friday, Saturday and the following Monday, but then apparently soured the ale after drinking from it — what did she do with it/in it?[37] Another example comes from the 1634 evidence. The star witness, Edmund Robinson

[33] Swain, *Industry*, pp. 73–78.

[34] Ibid., chs 7–8.

[35] LRO, WCW Supra, passim. The sample includes 101 inventories of Pendle Forest testators, 1559–1640.

[36] Of seven Infra inventories, two listed cards or combs, three noted spinning wheels and two recorded looms; LRO, WCW Infra, passim.

[37] Potts, *Wonderful Discovery*, E–E2.

junior, aged ten or eleven, said that his mother had brought him up to spin wool and fetch home the cattle.[38]

There are, however, no local examples of putting out, the system of production whereby a cloth merchant or capitalist clothier gave out the wool to be made up into cloth in the workers' own homes, paid piece rates and then sold the cloth and took the profit for himself. On the contrary, inventories and lawsuits reveal a picture of independent, small-scale producers, often buying their wool from merchants (or 'broggers' as they were called) and selling the finished material themselves.[39]

## III

Is it possible to tie in particular economic crises with the two Pendle witch trials of 1612 and 1634? Problems were certainly developing in the local cloth industry for two reasons. Firstly, the Cockayne Project of 1614–1617 banned the export of undyed cloth in an attempt to stimulate cloth finishing in England, but this had damaging consequences for the northern kersey industry which exported the bulk of its kerseys in an undyed state. Secondly, the Thirty Years' War seriously disturbed overseas markets, including those in the Baltic to which northern kerseys had traditionally been sent. Export data confirm the severity of the depression in the cloth trade in the sixteen-twenties and thirties.[40] Additional evidence is provided by a report to the Privy Council from the Bishop of Chester and Lancashire J.P.s who found in 1622 that the local cloth trade was in 'great decay . . . and the poor brought into great extremity for want of work therein'.[41] Whilst this no doubt exacerbated the crisis mortality of 1623,[42] the witch trial of 1612 preceded the first troubles induced by the Cockayne Project by two years, and difficulties had been experienced for twenty years before the second major trial — rather a long-delayed reaction! It does not seem therefore that problems in the cloth industry led directly to increased social tension and accusations of witchcraft.

Another source of crisis was the Duchy's decision to call into question the security of the copyholders' estates. Duchy lawyers found loopholes in the original grants of 1507 and in 1607 started proceedings against the tenants of the Blackburnshire forests for allegedly unlawful entry. This legal chicanery was really designed to produce a large cash sum from the

---

[38] *CSPD*, 1634–35, p. 141.
[39] Swain, *Industry*, pp. 113–17.
[40] Ibid., pp. 136–38, 142–44.
[41] PRO, SP 14/129, fol. 132.
[42] This seems to have been largely famine-induced (Swain, *Industry*, pp. 22–25).

tenants in return for confirmation of their titles. James I, always short of money, was exploiting every expedient he could. A settlement was reached whereby the tenants agreed to pay twelve years' rent in three instalments in 1609.[43] The total amount paid by the Pendle tenants was £1438 2s. 6d., and, large as this payment was, it should be noted that subtenants were often paying far larger sums to the copyholders.[44] Thus the Duchy's demand for twelve years' rent in a single year may not have caused a severe problem and certainly seems to have led to few copyholders being forced to sell or mortgage part of their holding.[45] Nevertheless, the Pendle composition, paid by the end of 1609, may well have contributed somewhat to the social tension which produced the accusations of witchcraft in March 1612. Some of those brought to trial, such as Old Demdike and her grand-daughter Alizon Device, seemed to have lived partly by begging and the accusation of acts of witchcraft sometimes centred on a curse following refusal of charity by a wealthier neighbour, who presumably had less to spare after the composition payment.[46]

The witchcraft accusations in 1612 and 1634 do not tie in neatly with other economic indicators such as periods of crisis mortality, high bread prices or data for sales and mortgages of land. The years 1612 and 1633–34 were not years of crisis mortality in this area. The worst year for this during the period 1600–1640 was 1623, which seems to have been largely famine-induced, and yet witches do not appear to have been blamed for this natural disaster.[47] Crop prices were certainly far higher than usual in 1612–13, but were not out of the ordinary in 1633–34, so the pattern here is inconsistent.[48] Transfers of land for money payment in Pendle Forest are more difficult to correlate since it was not necessary to register a land transaction which had been made out of court until up to the third halmote (manorial court) following, which might be eighteen

---

[43] Ibid., pp. 60–61, 64–65.

[44] In the period 1601–1620 the average payment from subtenants was twenty-five times the rent paid by the copyholders to the Duchy (LRO, DDHCl 3/82–103).

[45] There are few tranfers of Pendle land for cash in the years 1609, 1610, 1611 and 1612 — just 1, 3, 2 and 0 respectively (LRO, DDHCl 3/91–94).

[46] Swain, *Industry*, pp. 64, 82.

[47] Ibid., pp. 21, 23.

[48] For 'national' crop prices, see P. Bowden, 'Statistical Appendix', pp. 820–21, in *The Agrarian History of England and Wales, Vol. IV. 1500–1640*, ed. J. Thirsk (Cambridge, 1967), 814–70. Local wheat prices from the accounts of the Walmsleys of Dunkenhalgh, available only from 1612, are: 1612– 8s. 6d. per mett (a local measurement, equivalent to two pecks); 1613– 6s. 0¼d.; 1614– 7s. 3d. For the second trial: 1633– 9s. 1d. per mett; 1634– 8s. 6d.; 1635– 9s. 3d. (LRO, DDPt 1, passim). These data relate to harvest years, dated from the opening Michaelmas.

months away. Certainly there were more transactions in 1612–14 (nineteen) than in the period 1609–11 (six), but the three-year period 1615–17 produced still more transactions (twenty) rather than a return to 'normal'. Turning to 1634, the period 1633–35 produced forty-six transactions compared with thirty-two for 1630–32 and thirty-seven for 1636–38, so in this case the central period of the witchcraft accusations coincided with a peak in land sales and mortgages. Interpretation of this coincidence, however, is rather more problematic since sales and mortgages need not be due to economic difficulties, and so we should not necessarily regard peaks in these figures as simply indicative of economic crisis or social tension.[49]

Clearly, as the population grew, land increasingly became in short supply and therefore more valuable. The rental of 1650, which lists subtenants, records a total of 155 Duchy copyholders and 33 tenants who held land only from copyholders (18 per cent of the total).[50] This is far from a total record of all the subtenants in the Pendle area since only subtenancies for longer than a year and a day had to be registered before the halmote, at which an entry fine was also payable to the Duchy; leases for shorter periods might be agreed without surrender and fine at the halmote.[51] It is undoubtedly true that some of the prominent witches lived as subtenants. For example, Anne Redfern, Old Chattox's daughter, was a tenant of the Nutters of Greenhead in New Laund; one day, about eighteen or nineteen years before the trial of 1612, Robert Nutter junior made unwelcome advances towards her, and, on being rejected, rode off in a rage, saying, 'if ever the ground came to him, she should never dwell upon his land'. In revenge, Old Chattox allegedly procured Robert's death a few months later with the help of her spirit, rather ironically called Fancy.[52]

There was a sub-society of the landless or virtually landless that had to rely on charity, and many of the leading witches seem to have fallen into this category. An Act of 1589 prohibited the use of a cottage for habitation if it had fewer than four acres attached to it, or taking in more

[49] LRO, DDHCl 3/91–100, 112–21.
[50] PRO, E 317 Lancs. 8, m. 61–66.
[51] Swain, *Industry*, p. 84. Leasing land for longer than a year and a day was becoming increasingly common in Pendle Forest; there was a total of 38 such leases 1561–1580, which rose to 82, 1581–1600, and then to 114, 1601–1620, and finally to 123, 1621–1640 (*The Court Rolls of the Honor of Clitheroe in the County of Lancaster*, ed. W. Farrer, II (Edinburgh, 1912), 304–68; LRO, DDHCl 3/50–123, passim).
[52] Potts, *Wonderful Discovery*, D3.

than one family in a cottage as inmates.[53] Landlords could command huge rents for these tiny holdings and were consequently prepared to ignore the Act. Fines were commonly brought by the halmote juries in the fifteen-nineties and sixteen-twenties.[54] In October 1621, for example, thirty-one were presented for this offence; in addition, four were accused of receiving strangers or vagrants, and one of taking a pregnant woman into his house.[55]

Subtenants seem to have been finding it increasingly difficult to pay their rents, particularly in the period 1622–24. From the mid-1610s, the juries began to present individuals for 'detinue' of buildings and land; prior to 1615 this was extremely rare, though private suits for detinue were a common feature of court business. Usually, these fines were presented at the Easter rather than the Michaelmas halmote; 78 per cent of the eighty-eight Pendle cases occurred at the Easter court. Rents were usually paid twice a year at Michaelmas and Easter, and subtenants would have found it harder to pay their Easter dues when prices were generally higher and wage labour less available than in the period during and immediately following the harvest.[56] In this connexion, it is perhaps significant that both major Pendle witch outbreaks occurred in the spring, in March 1612 and February 1634, well after the harvest and when people had more time on their hands to allow petty arguments, resentment and jealousies to get out of hand. Perhaps the Devil does find work for idle hands! Macfarlane found from Essex assize records that the greatest number of bewitchings took place from February to June, and the least from August to October, but he noted that the differences were not significant and thus it was not simply a question of hunger which led to witchcraft accusations.[57]

## IV

It would be wrong to concentrate exclusively on economic factors in seeking to explain the incidence of witchcraft accusations. Clearly, the social and religious attitudes, both of the political and ecclesiastical leaders in the locality, as well as the beliefs of the mass of the population, must be explored. Roger Nowell was the J.P. whose thorough investigation in 1612 led to the trials at the Lancaster Assizes. He was described by

[53] 31 Eliz. c. 7.
[54] Swain, *Industry*, p. 89.
[55] LRO, DDHCl 3/104 (Higham, 25 Oct. 1621).
[56] Swain, *Industry*, p. 90.
[57] Macfarlane, *Witchcraft*, p. 152.

Potts as 'a very religious honest Gentleman'[58] and he came from a notable Protestant family — his great-uncles Alexander and Lawrence had been Marian exiles, and later became Dean of St Paul's and Dean of Lichfield respectively.[59] Willingness by the local political élite to take the witchcraft accusations seriously was obviously important. In the second trial of 1634 one of two J.P.s involved, John Starkie, may have been particularly receptive to witchcraft allegations because in 1597 he had been one of seven children allegedly possessed by demons.[60] It is clear, however, that the initiative for prosecution came not from the J.P.s but from ordinary people, the Laws in 1612 and the Robinsons in 1634.

What were the views of the local clergy? Some historians have stressed the huge size both of the diocese of Chester (R. C. Richardson described it as 'monstrously large'), and of the parish of Whalley, covering 180 square miles with the consequent difficulties of ecclesiastical administration and supervision.[61] This view ignores the existence of the chapelries into which Whalley parish was subdivided, each of which had its own curate. Nevertheless, the upland nature of the area, and the fact that the chapelries were still fairly large, must have caused considerable problems.

Rather more difficulties, however, were caused by the inadequacy of the curate's stipend. In September 1610, several witnesses in a lawsuit said that the minister of Colne was paid just £4 per annum and that this amount was totally inadequate.[62] Thus it is not surprising that the quality and commitment of some of the local incumbents was less than the church hierarchy would have liked. In 1640, for example, a number of charges were brought against the Newchurch curate, John Horrocks, including that he had:

---

[58] Potts, *Wonderful Discovery*, B2.
[59] *VCH Lancs*, vi, 504.
[60] Potts, *Wonderful Discovery*, introduction by J. Crossley, lx.
[61] R. C. Richardson, *Puritanism in North-West England. A Regional Study of the Diocese of Chester to 1642* (Manchester, 1972), pp. 1, 15; P. Collinson, *The Religion of Protestants, The Church in England Society 1559–1625* (Oxford, 1982), p. 231; C. Haigh, 'Puritan Evangelism in the Reign of Elizabeth I', *English Historical Review*, xcii (1977), 39; K. Wrightson, *English Society, 1580–1680* (1982), p. 208.
[62] PRO, DL 4/56/15. To put this in context, slaters were paid 4d. a day at this time, so their annual income, assuming regular work was available six days a week, forty-eight weeks a year was £4 16s. 0d., and, in addition, they were usually supplied with some food and drink (*The House and Farm Accounts of the Shuttleworths of Gawthorpe Hall in the County of Lancaster at Smithils and Gawthorpe, from September 1582 to October 1621*, ed. J. Harland, i, Chetham Society, o.s., xxxv (1856), 190).

been much given to excessive drinking of ale, wine and strong beer . . . and have lived and lodged and dieted in an alehouse of one Elizabeth Hargreaves of Fence Yate in Pendle and have made several affrays with several men and have oftentimes . . . beaten the said Elizabeth and one Henry Robinson son of John Robinson churchwarden of Newchurch aforesaid because he would not pay a drinking shot in the said alehouse.

That was not all, for Horrocks was also accused of slander, conducting a marriage in a private house, taking bribes for baptizing illegitimate children without inquiring into the father's identity or punishing the parents, and having sexual relations with Elizabeth Hargreaves.[63]

It would be wrong to paint a picture of totally dissolute or inefficient curates. In a survey of Lancashire clergy in 1604, Christopher Nutter or Nuttall was described as being in charge of the well-affected parochial chapelry of Pendle, and Richard Brierley, the minister of Colne chapelry, was also found to be 'well affected'.[64] Nevertheless, the same Christopher Nuttall was presented at the visitation of 1592 for marrying a couple without licence, and again in 1611 for marrying a couple in an alehouse when the woman was contracted to marry another man.[65] Clearly, if the minister was not beyond reproach himself, his flock had less reason to be.

There are many examples in the records of the ecclesiastical courts of irreligious behaviour. The problem is to assess how typical these cases were. Nicholas Hargreaves of Newchurch was presented in 1596 for 'playing upon organs in the house and drawing people from evening prayer upon the sabbath'.[66] In 1605 eight Colne men were accused of 'excessive ringing of the bells at burials and disturbing divine service'. In 1611 eight men from Colne chapelry, including one of the previous eight, James Ellingtrop, were presented for being in alehouses and elsewhere at service time. At the visitation of 1622 even the constable of Colne was presented for wandering in the streets at the time of divine service, and refusing to go to church, 'saying he was about greater business'. Newchurch in Pendle presentments were remarkably few before the first witch trial of 1612, for in October 1608, the only matter brought before the visitation was that a widow called Jane Whalley was a non-communicant,

---

[63] C(heshire) R(ecord) O(ffice), EDC 5 (1639), 127.

[64] *Historical Manuscripts Commission, Fourteenth Report, Appendix Part IV — Kenyon MSS* (1894), p. 10. In many documents, the Pendle minister's surname is given as 'Nuttall' (e.g. PRO DL 4/51/47, m. 3, where Christopher Nuttall, curate of Newchurch in Pendle, aged fifty-six, was a witness in a lawsuit in Sept. 1606).

[65] CRO, EDV 1/10, fol. 149; EDV 1/17, fol. 125.

[66] Haigh, *EHR*, xcii, 53.

and in October 1611 that Henry Standen kept two obstinate recusants in his house (and the previously mentioned case of the curate marrying a couple in an alehouse). On the other hand, some Pendle people were capable of expressing extremely unchristian ideas, such as Richard Moore, charged at the visitation of 1626 for 'saying that God where he did one good turn did two bad and that if God were there he would cut off his head'.[67]

Ronald Marchant has suggested that there was an irreligious subsociety, with perhaps as many as 15 per cent of the population of the diocese of Chester in 1633 in the excommunicate classes, and so he claimed that there was 'a seam of irreligious people lying below the greater mass of nominal Christians'.[68] This does not do justice to the various reasons why people may have been excommunicated, for no doubt some were Catholics. Whilst, however, there were a number of prominent Catholic families amongst the local gentry, notably the Towneleys of Towneley and Barnside, and the Bannisters of Parkhill, and naturally some of their servants and tenants followed their masters' lead, Catholicism does not seem to have been very prominent amongst the mass of the population. In October 1611, apart from the Newchurch case of Henry Standen keeping two recusants in his house, the chapelries of Burnley, Colne and Padiham only produced another five people presented for being recusants or non-communicants.[69] In the diocese of Chester as a whole in 1603 just over 1 per cent were found to be recusants, and it does not seem that the Catholic population locally would have been substantially greater.[70]

The halmote records provide further evidence of behaviour which the authorities found undesirable and wished to control. Bowling seems to have been a popular Sunday activity, for in November 1601, sixteen men, including four from Pendle, were fined at the Colne halmote for playing bowls on the Sabbath.[71] Bowling had been banned by a statute of

---

[67] CRO, EDV 1/14, fol. 159; 1/17, fol. 124; 1/24, fol. 175ᵛ; 1/15, fol. 152ᵛ; 1/17, fol. 125; 1/22 fol. 207ᵛ.

[68] R. A. Marchant, *The Church under the Law. Justice, Administration and Discipline in the Diocese of York 1560–1640* (Cambridge, 1969), p. 227.

[69] CRO, EDV 1/17, fols 121–25. At the visitations of December 1604, October 1605 and October 1608, Newchurch presentments as recusants or non-communicants were 0, 2 and 1 respectively, though the numbers were certainly greater in Colne and Burnley, amounting to twenty-six in Burnley and thirty-four in Colne in December 1604, for example (CRO, EDV 1/13, fols 168–72, 174ᵛ; 1/14 fols 156, 158–60; 1/15 fols 149–53).

[70] BL, Harl. MSS, 280, fol. 171ᵛ reported that there were 2,442 recusants and 178,190 communicants.

[71] LRO, DDHCl 3/84 (Colne, 18 Nov. 1601).

Henry VIII, since it was feared that it distracted men from archery practice.[72] Again, it is difficult to assess how typical these cases were — are they the tip of the iceberg or were the juries efficient at detecting and fining offenders? There is certainly nothing unusual in the Pendle halmote records which might tie in with the 1612 or 1634 trials.[73]

V

Just because several people preferred to play bowls on a Sunday or stay away from church does not mean that it is any more likely that a local witches' coven existed. What is undoubtedly true is that local people believed strongly in the existence of witches in the Pendle area and in their power to do evil. Although he finally admitted to fabricating the details of the witchcraft accusations in 1634, Edmund Robinson junior did say that he made up the stories against those accused 'because he heard the neighbours repute them for witches'.[74] As a further example, the son-in-law of Old Demdike, John Device, was so afraid of the spells of the other leading witch, Old Chattox, that he agreed to pay her a measure of meal each year in return for an undertaking that she would not harm him or his goods. It seems that he had insufficient confidence in the magical powers of his mother-in-law to protect him! On his death-bed, he attributed his condition to the non-payment of the meal.[75] There was bad blood between the two families which seems to have originated about eleven years before the trial when the Device house was burgled and goods worth £1 stolen, a crime which they attributed to Old Chattox's family.[76] The rivalry between these two families was important; Potts described Old Chattox as 'always opposite to Old Demdike, for whom the one favoured, the other hated deadly, and how they envy and accuse one another in their examinations may appear'. Conflict was only natural since the two families were in a very real sense competing for a limited market, as healers, beggars, and probably also as witches, and hence reputation was everything.

[72] J. Tait, 'The Declaration of Sports for Lancashire (1617)', *EHR*, xxxii (1917), 564.

[73] LRO, DDHCl 3/94 (Higham, 6 Dec. 1611; 25 July 1612); DDHCl 3/116 (Higham, 24 Oct. 1633, 22 Apr. 1634).

[74] *CSPD*, 1634–35, p. 152.

[75] Potts, *Wonderful Discovery*, E4. There were several other examples of men, on their death-bed, blaming witches for their condition (ibid., F, O).

[76] Ibid., E4. Old Chattox blamed Old Demdike for her decision about fourteen years previously to become a witch, so presumably the two had then been friends (ibid., B4). Similarly, according to James Device, the two women apparently shared eight teeth taken by Old Chattox from graves at Newchurch twelve years previously (ibid., E3).

There is strong evidence that some of those accused of witchcraft were thought to have the ability to heal the sick. Alizon Device said that although she did not have the power to cure the pedlar John Law, her grandmother, Old Demdike, could have done so if she had lived. Some of the local inhabitants seem to have been prepared to enlist the services of the witches to cure their sick animals: John Nutter of the Bull Hole apparently asked Old Demdike to cure a sick cow, but it died.[77] Some of those who were indicted may have been practitioners of herbal or folk remedies for curing human and animal ills; inevitably sometimes things went wrong, and they got the blame.

It seems likely that some of those accused of witchcraft actively fostered their reputations as witches since it enabled them to make a living by begging and extortion. They exploited and preyed on popular fears of witches and on the omnipresence of sudden and inexplicable illnesses and deaths of both man and beast. No doubt many people, such as John Device with his annual tribute of meal to Old Chattox, paid up a nominal amount rather than risk offending Old Demdike, Old Chattox or their broods. As Potts put it in his description of Old Demdike: 'no man escaped her, or her Furies, that ever gave them any occasion of offence, or denied them anything they stood in need of'.[78] Nature had not been kind to many of those who were accused — some were old, virtually blind widows such as Old Demdike and Old Chattox, whilst others such as Old Demdike's daughter Elizabeth Device suffered from physical deformity. As Potts says: 'This odious witch was branded with a preposterous mark in nature, even from her birth, which was her left eye standing lower than the other, the one looking down, the other looking up.'[79] Such people must have felt social outcasts. What better way to achieve social standing, or at least make themselves feared if not respected, and also repay folk

---

[77] Ibid., D2; S; C.

[78] Ibid., B2. Thomas cites several examples from other parts of the country in *Religion*, pp. 674–75, including the comment by the sceptic Reginald Scot that witches were 'so odious unto all their neighbours and so feared, as few dare offend them, or deny them anything they ask'. See also C. Holmes, 'Popular Culture? Witches, Magistrates and Divines in Early Modern England', in *Understanding Popular Culture. Europe from the Middle Ages to the Nineteenth Century*, ed. S. L. Kaplan (New York, 1984), pp. 96–97.

[79] Ibid., G. The pamphleteer, Thomas Potts, also commented on the prevailing attitude towards old age and physical deformity: 'For the wrinkles of an old wife's face is good evidence to the jury against a witch. And how often will the common people say " Her eyes are sunk in her head; God bless us from her". But Old Chattox had Fancy [her familiar], besides her withered face, to accuse her.' (ibid., M2).

for unkindness, than to cultivate a reputation for witchcraft?[80] They exploited popular fears and superstitions about witchcraft and perhaps used, or appeared to use, the paraphernalia of witchcraft, including clay or wax models. They may even have convinced themselves and each other of their supernatural powers.

The trial of 1634 provides clear evidence that accusations of witchcraft might also spring from financial motives. The Bishop of Chester had been told that Edmund Robinson senior had demanded £2 from Frances and John Dicconson in return for dropping the accusations against Frances, but she had advised her husband against paying anything. Edmund Robinson senior later denied that this had happened when questioned in London.[81] As John Webster wrote in 1677, however, Robinson had other charges to face:

the boy, his father and some others did make a practice to go from church to church that the boy might reveal and discover witches, pretending that there was a great number at the pretended meeting whose faces he could know, and by that means they got a good living, that in a short space the father bought a cow or two, when he had none before.[82]

And what of the Thomas/Macfarlane model, which focuses on the problems created by refusal of charity? Many allegations of injury or death were made in 1612, but in twelve cases the actual cause of the dispute is clearly stated. Only three originated from problems relating to refusal of charity. It seems that the initial incident which triggered off the whole chain of witchcraft accusations in 1612 may be attributed to a refused request for charity, i.e. the pedlar John Law's apparent unwillingness to hand over some pins to Alizon Device when her offer to pay for them was probably not genuine.[83] Secondly, the case of Henry Mitton (previously cited) fits into this pattern, since he was allegedly bewitched to death by an unholy alliance of Old Demdike, Elizabeth Device and Alice Nutter, for refusing to give Old Demdike a penny. Thirdly, James Device confessed to getting his spirit, Dandy, to kill John Duckworth of

---

[80] G. Scarre, *Witchcraft and Magic in 16th and 17th Century Europe* (1987), pp. 52–53; Thomas, *Religion*, pp. 674–75.

[81] *CSPD*, 1634–35, pp. 77–79. Frances Dicconson claimed that the enmity between the Robinsons and her family had arisen over the purchase of a cow.

[82] Webster, *Displaying of Supposed Witchcraft*, p. 277.

[83] Potts, *Wonderful Discovery*, R3–S. Alizon claimed that she wanted to *buy* some pins from John Law who refused to undo his pack; John Law said that Alizon 'was very earnest with him for pins, but he would give her none'; Abraham Law, John's son, said that Alizon had offered to buy some pins but had no money, but, despite this, John gave her some.

the Laund because Duckworth had promised him a shirt but subsequently refused to hand it over.

The other nine cases cover a wide range of allegations, none of which apparently concerns refusal of charity. Three spring from Old Chattox's confessions. The death of Robert Nutter at Old Chattox's hands for making unwanted advances to her daughter, Anne Redfern, and for threatening them with eviction, has already been quoted. Secondly, Old Chattox also claimed to have made her spirit, Fancy, kill a cow belonging to Anthony Nutter because he favoured Old Demdike rather than her. Thirdly, she maintained that she had killed a cow belonging to John Moore, a gentleman of Higham, because Moore's wife had nagged her, even after she had cured his bewitched drink.

Alizon Device referred to four other cases in her confessions. The death-bed claim by her father, John Device, that he was dying because of the non-payment of the meal to Old Chattox has already been quoted. In addition Old Chattox had apparently bewitched to death Anne Nutter for laughing at her, and Hugh Moore for accusing her of bewitching his cattle. Lastly, Alizon Device claimed that Old Chattox had bewitched to death a cow belonging to John Nutter because John's son disliked what she was doing with a can of milk which had been begged from his family.[84]

The two remaining cases refer to confessions made by Alizon's mother Elizabeth and by her brother James. Elizabeth Device claimed that her spirit, Ball, had made her make a clay model of John Robinson alias Swyer of Barley and kill him by drying it so that it crumbled away, all because he had insulted her by saying that she had a bastard child. Her son James confessed that Mistress Anne Towneley of Carr Hall, had been killed by the same method because she had accused James and his mother of stealing her turves and because she had hit James.[85]

Many other witch trials from this period do not provide significant evidence of problems arising because of refusal of charity. Several motives were alleged for witchcraft at Royston (1606), Milton (Bedfordshire, 1612), Northamptonshire (1612) and Belvoir (1619), amongst them being revenge for verbal insults suffered, injuries incurred and unfair dismissal from employment. Failure to provide appropriate charity was mentioned only once out of nine occasions when a motive was clearly

---

[84] Ibid., F4, G2, O4; H3–4; F; D3; E2–3; E4–F. In this last case, charity had not been refused, and the dispute centred around the use to which the can of milk was subsequently being put.

[85] Ibid., F4, H3.

stated.[86] J. A. Sharpe's work on seventeenth-century witchcraft in York-shire confirms the view that problems relating to refusal of charity did not play a central role in prompting allegations of witchcraft.[87] It therefore does not seem justified, at least for the early seventeenth century, for Thomas to assert that

the overwhelming majority of fully documented witch cases fall into this simple pattern. The witch is sent away empty-handed, perhaps mumbling a malediction; and in due course something goes wrong with the household, for which she is immediately held responsible.[88]

## VI

In conclusion, it appears that the early seventeenth century was a period of considerable economic difficulties for many who lived in the Pendle area, particularly, of course, the poor. There may have been increasing tension between rich and poor, and it is possibly true that the old medieval communal ethic of neighbourliness and charity was breaking down before the forces of capitalism and the agencies of the state, especially the apparatus set up under the Poor Law.[89] It is certainly the case that the Lancashire witch trials do not tie in very closely with periods of obvious economic distress.[90] Strong support for the Thomas/ Macfarlane model is difficult to sustain because refusal of charity did not play a part in three-quarters of the detailed allegations of witchcraft in 1612, nor in the main events of the 1634 trial, nor in most of the motives

---

[86] *Witchcraft*, ed. B. Rosen (1969), pp. 323–56, 369–84. The only problem relating to charity which is apparent from these four trials was when Anne Baker of Bottesford confessed that she had bewitched a woman to death for giving her 'alms of her second bread' (i.e. stale bread) when she felt that she deserved better because she was always going on errands for the woman. In this particular case, therefore, charity was not actually refused, but was felt to be insufficiently generous (ibid., p. 375).

[87] J. A. Sharpe, 'Witchcraft and Women in Seventeenth-Century England: some Northern evidence', *Continuity and Change*, VI (1991), 186–87; *Witchcraft in Seventeenth-Century Yorkshire: Accusations and Counter Measures* (Borthwick Paper 81. York, 1992), p. 8.

[88] Thomas, *Religion*, p. 661.

[89] The regrettable loss of the accounts of the local overseers of the poor for this period makes a detailed investigation of this matter impossible.

[90] The point that specific economic or demographic crises do not really tie in with outbreaks of witch persecutions has been made by several historians, including Klaits, *Servants of Satan*, pp. 89, 91–94; Macfarlane, *Witchcraft*, ch. 10; Scarre, *Witchcraft and Magic*, pp. 38–39; Thomas, *Religion*, p. 697.

alleged for acts of witchcraft in other contemporary trials.[91] The world of those who were accused of witchcraft seems to have revolved largely around the difficulties of making ends meet. Some seem to have tried to resolve their financial problems by cultivating a reputation for witchcraft, which enabled them to make a living by acting as healers, or by extorting money, food and drink or goods from their neighbours. In these circumstances no one had good reason to feel guilty about refusing charity, only fear at what might befall him at the witch's hands. Many of the Lancashire witches were no doubt completely innocent of the charges brought against them, but to some, witchcraft was a business, a livelihood with enormous risks, for failure meant not bankruptcy, nor the debtors' prison, but the gallows.

*Nottingham*

---

[91] For other criticism of the Thomas/Macfarlane model, see Klaits, *Servants of Satan*, pp. 89–94; C. Larner, *Witchcraft and Religion. The Politics of Popular Belief* (Oxford, 1984), pp. 50–53; Quaife, *Godly Zeal*, pp. 181, 189–90; Scarre, *Witchcraft and Magic*, pp. 40–43.

# WITCHCRAFT, POLITICS AND "GOOD NEIGHBOURHOOD" IN EARLY SEVENTEENTH-CENTURY RYE[*]

## I

### INTRODUCTION

> The European witch, unlike her African or American-Indian counterpart, was a transfigured creature who began her career in the farmyard as an enemy of her neighbour, and ended it in the courts as a public person, an enemy of God and of the godly society.[1]

In this passage Christina Larner expressed with characteristic lucidity an argument which has been gaining currency among historians. According to this approach, responsibility for the dramatic rise and decline in witchcraft prosecutions in early modern Europe lay primarily with the élites who controlled the courts rather than with the accusers, who were usually of lower status. Judges not only allowed cases to be prosecuted in their courts, but on occasion promoted witch-hunts, and it has been argued that they were motivated by a commitment to reform unchristian beliefs and disorderly behaviour, both aspects of "popular culture". Ideological zeal, whether Protestant or Catholic, provided a means of imposing order and legitimizing new regimes in an era of increasing political centralization. This approach (which I shall call the "social-control model") therefore has the great merit of relating this extraordinary European-wide phenomenon to major processes of historical change, although historians vary in the aspects which they emphasize.[2]

* I am very grateful to David Anderson, Miranda Chaytor, Anne DeWindt, Cynthia Herrup, Jos Hincks, Michael Hunter, Alex King, Lyndal Roper and George Yerby for many helpful comments on earlier versions of this article, as well as to participants at History Workshop 22 and the London Anthropology Society. I am also grateful to the British Academy for funding some of the research on which this article is based; a partial discussion of the case is included in Annabel Gregory, "Slander Accusations and Social Control in Late Sixteenth and Early Seventeenth Century England, with Particular Reference to Rye (Sussex), 1590-1615" (Univ. of Sussex D.Phil. thesis, 1985).

[1] C. Larner, *Enemies of God: The Witch-Hunt in Scotland* (Oxford, 1983), p. 5.

[2] Two of the three recent surveys of European witchcraft endorse this approach: J. Klaits, *Servants of Satan: The Age of the Witch-Hunts* (Bloomington, Ind., 1985); G. R. Quaife, *Godly Zeal and Furious Rage: The Witch in Early Modern Europe*

(cont. on p. 32)

These theories are rather more complex than those put forward twenty years ago by Keith Thomas and Alan Macfarlane in their pioneering works on English witchcraft.[3] Thomas and Macfarlane focused on the relationship between accuser and accused, and since their studies were only concerned with English cases, which were relatively uncomplicated, they were not prompted to consider in much detail such factors as legal changes and interaction between accusers and judges. Yet to one basic question they both suggested an answer which has not been improved upon by the newer theories. Why did people accuse others of causing harm by supernatural means (*maleficium*)? This question concerns popular attitudes more than those of the "judicial élites", since, as several studies have shown, it was the accusers who were primarily concerned about *maleficia*, while diabolism was of greater interest to magistrates. Thomas and Macfarlane's argument focused in particular on conflicts over traditional obligations of neighbourliness between those who benefited from economic changes and those who were impoverished by them. A modified version of this thesis is generally accepted, but the issue is regarded as having little significance for theories of social change, since the evidence for a shift in popular attitudes in this period is so limited.[4]

I would suggest that this exclusion of popular attitudes has been too extreme. Recent studies have shown that causing harm by supernatural means was an issue in witchcraft cases in all countries studied between Russia and white America, whereas diabolism was only of concern in some areas, and at some periods.[5]

*(n. 2 cont.)*
(London, 1987). B. P. Levack, *The Witch-Hunt in Early Modern Europe* (London, 1987), pp. 117-19, 147-8, also emphasizes the role of ideology among ruling élites. G. Scarre, whose term "social-control model" has been used in this article, provides a summary of different approaches in G. Scarre, *Witchcraft and Magic in Sixteenth and Seventeenth Century Europe* (Basingstoke, 1987).

[3] K. V. Thomas, *Religion and the Decline of Magic: Studies in Popular Beliefs in Sixteenth and Seventeenth Century England* (London, 1971), chs. 14-18; A. Macfarlane, *Witchcraft in Tudor and Stuart England: A Regional and Comparative Study* (London, 1970).

[4] Larner, *Enemies of God*, pp. 20-4, 60, 137-8; Levack, *Witch-Hunt in Early Modern Europe*, pp. 9, 118-19, 214-15, 226; Klaits, *Servants of Satan*, pp. 3-4, 161, 174, ch. 4; Quaife, *Godly Zeal*, pp. 4, 127, 206-7, chs. 11, 12. For the Middle Ages, see R. Kieckhefer, *European Witch Trials: Their Foundations in Popular and Learned Culture, 1300-1500* (London, 1976). Larner attributes the increasing popular concern with diabolism in seventeenth-century Scotland at least in part to the influence of the judiciary: Larner, *Enemies of God*, pp. 144-51.

[5] Levack, *Witch-Hunt in Early Modern Europe*, pp. 170-211.

Explanations for changing prosecution rates should therefore give some weight to concern about *maleficia* as well as to the issue of heresy, even though the worst witch-hunts involved diabolism. There is also a danger of overstating the contrast between "élite" and "popular" attitudes and producing stereotypes, so that the populace seem no more than passive receptacles of inherited beliefs, while the élite appear cynical manipulators of an acquired ideology.

The relation between the two theories therefore requires fuller examination, and as a contribution to this I will explore some relevant issues raised by an extended case-study from the town of Rye in Sussex. This example is particularly suited to the examination of accusers' motivations because not only is it unusually well documented — over twenty thousand words of evidence — but also there is excellent material which can be used to reconstruct the socio-economic context. The Thomas-Macfarlane thesis is not obviously relevant to the case because the underlying conflicts appear to be political rather than economic: the case was one episode in a series of conflicts between the two factions in the town. The social-control model looks more promising, because some of the accusers were local magistrates (not unknown elsewhere).[6] In addition the case had a rather un-English flavour because of a jurisdictional peculiarity in this corner of England. Most English witchcraft cases were tried in the centralized assize courts, but Rye was one of the Cinque Ports where the assizes had no jurisdiction, and the magistrates therefore had an unusual degree of authority. This situation is comparable to that in some German towns where jurisdictional issues exacerbated the witch-hunts.[7]

In several respects, however, the social-control model does not suit the Rye case. Members of the "judicial élite" themselves

[6] For example, R. Scot, *The Discoverie of Witchcraft* (Wakefield, 1973; repr. of 1886 edn.; first pubd. London, 1584), pp. 209-10; *A Rehearsall both Straung and True, of Hainous and Horrible Actes Committed by . . . Fower Notorious Witches, Apprehended at Winsore* (London, 1579); quoted in *Witchcraft*, ed. B. Rosen (London, 1969), p. 86; *The Examination of . . . Joan Williford . . . at Faversham in Kent* (London, 1645).

[7] Macfarlane, *Witchcraft in Tudor and Stuart England*, pp. 24-5; W. Holloway, *The History and Antiquities of the Ancient Town and Port of Rye in the County of Sussex* (London, 1847), pp. 52-6, 74-7, 83-5, 118-19; K. M. E. Murray, *The Constitutional History of the Cinque Ports* (Manchester, 1935), pp. 69-71; Levack, *Witch-Hunt in Early Modern Europe*, pp. 177-9; Quaife, *Godly Zeal*, pp. 115-20; H. C. E. Midelfort, *Witch-Hunting in South-Western Germany, 1562-1684: The Social and Intellectual Foundations* (Stanford, 1972), chs. 5-6.

made accusations of *maleficia,* they were not simply pressurizing others to make accusations; nor was diabolism an issue in the case. Instead of a clear distinction between "élite" and "popular" culture, there was a more complex use of different cultural idioms.

The explanatory framework which is finally adopted in this paper has, in fact, more in common with the Thomas-Macfarlane thesis than with the social-control model. It is founded on the "anthropological truism that witch-beliefs represent a direct inversion of the values of the society in which they are held".[8] Like Thomas and Macfarlane, I consider that neighbourliness was the principal value at issue, but suggest that the concept had a rather wider significance than they propose. They looked mostly at relations of mutual help between individuals, whereas I will be focusing more on communal and political issues. These include, first, the maintenance of solidarity in dealing with those outside the community; and, secondly, the reduction of dissension within it, in order to establish a social environment conducive to mutual help and solidarity. It will be argued that failure to maintain an adequate level of neighbourliness, or disagreements about what that level should be, could have exacerbated major factional divisions within the community as a whole. Accusations of witchcraft were one means of expressing and acting upon such conflicts.

Before turning to the case itself, it is necessary to note one obvious consequence of the peculiar legal context in Rye, which is that the accusations were taken to court much earlier than in most cases. Pamphlet accounts of English witchcraft cases often indicate that there had been a history of suspicions that a particular woman was a witch for years before an indictment was preferred against her, whereas in this case there are no references to suspicions before the year in which the indictment was preferred (1607). This suggests that the magistrates either suffered a minor witch panic, or else cynically calculated that they could get rid of the accused woman without having to collect all the evidence which would have been required by assize judges, who were not on the whole easily convinced.[9] The depositions do not, con-

---

[8] Larner, *Enemies of God,* p. 134. Macfarlane has since rejected his and Thomas's thesis, but his argument involved issues which, according to his account, were peculiar to English history. It is therefore less relevant now that the early modern witch-hunt is viewed from a European perspective: A. Macfarlane, *The Origins of English Individualism: The Family, Property and Social Transition* (Oxford, 1978), pp. 1-2.

[9] Macfarlane, *Witchcraft in Tudor and Stuart England,* ch. 7; Quaife, *Godly Zeal,* pp. 175, 191; Thomas, *Religion and the Decline of Magic,* pp. 544-8.

sequently, present a clear story, but rather an apparently aimless collection of anecdotes about fairies, buried treasure, unneighbourly opinions and, eventually, explicit accusations of black witchcraft — of harming and killing people in the town by the utterance of angry words or some other unspecified supernatural method. Only when I linked them with conflicts reconstructed from other local records did a story begin to emerge. The case illustrates how witchcraft accusations were articulated — starting with no clear distinction between good and evil, black and white witchcraft, suspicions gradually crystallized into a story depicting particular people as evil.

## II

### THE STORY IN BRIEF

Rye lies on the border of Sussex and Kent, and in the sixteenth century an estuary connected it with the sea. For a short period in the middle of the century it was in fact one of the main ports on the south coast, having not only a harbour of refuge, but also a good road to London, along which pack-loads of fish were carried daily to provision the London fishmarkets and the royal household. About half the population were fishermen, and the rest were craftsmen, victuallers and merchants. Graham Mayhew has disentangled the complicated series of factors which contributed to the dramatic decline of the port, one of which was the changing shape of the coastline and the consequent silting up of the harbour. At the end of the sixteenth century Rye was still, however, one of the four most populous towns in East Sussex, with a population of about two thousand.[10]

The two main focuses for business in the town were the fishmarket on the Strand and the butchery, where the town hall was located and the market for produce other than fish was held. It was here, in about 1604, that a poor sawyer and his wife, Roger and Susan Swapper, rented part of a house from old Anne Bennett, widow of a rich butcher. The widow lived next door with her daughter Anne, who had recently married a minor Kent gentle-

[10] G. Mayhew, *Tudor Rye* (Falmer, 1987), ch. 7, pp. 19, 22-3, 145-8; see also S. A. Hipkin, "The Economy and Social Stucture of Rye, 1600-60" (Univ. of Oxford D.Phil. thesis, 1986), chs. 1, 3; A. Fletcher, *A County Community in Peace and War: Sussex, 1600-60* (London, 1975), pp. 8-9; East Sussex Record Office, Lewes (hereafter E.S.R.O.), Rye Corporation MSS. (hereafter RYE), 47/54; C. E. Brent, "Urban Employment and Population in Sussex between 1550 and 1660", *Sussex Archaeol. Colls.*, cxiii (1975), pp. 35-50.

man named George Taylor. Both Anne and her mother were well
known in the town as healers, or "cunning folk", and it must
therefore have been a relief to the Swappers to have Anne Taylor
to attend on them when they both fell ill during Lent in 1607.[11]

Anne's expertise included the treatment of spiritual afflictions
as well as physical ones, and Susan sought her advice on how to
deal with four spirits who appeared to her when she was lying in
bed. The spirits consisted of two men and two women, dressed
in contemporary clothes and in the fairy colours of green and
white, which she described in detail for the benefit of the mayor
and jurats (aldermen) of Rye when they examined her the following September. The spirits were both alarming — threatening to
carry her away — and helpful, because she was told to go to
Anne Taylor (whom they always referred to as "young Anne
Bennett") and "Call her and goe into her garden with her and
digge and set sage and then you should be well".[12]

The following day, according to Susan, the two women dug in
a haunted place near the summer-house in Anne's garden, but
they were apparently looking for fairy treasure rather than "setting sage". Like a previous tenant in her house, one of Susan's
symptoms was being "troubled with treasure", but in spite of
the fact that they did not find any, her symptoms went away that
night. Both Susan and another witness said that Anne was also
very interested in the treasure, and Susan said that Anne believed
that she was "heir to it".

The following Whitsun Susan tried again, prompted by the
spirits, this time in a field belonging to a farm at Weeks Green,
just outside Rye, which had formerly belonged to Anne and her
mother. One of the spirits said that a pot of gold was buried
there, but Susan failed to find it. She did, however, meet the
queen of the fairies, and was told that if she knelt to her the
queen would give her a living. Susan refused to do so, and
returned to Rye very sick and frightened.[13]

This is a very typical account of confrontations with fairies, to

[11] Mayhew, *Tudor Rye*, pp. 40-1; E.S.R.O., RYE, 13/1, 11, 18-20; E.S.R.O.,
W/A10, fo. 31, Will of R. Bennett; W. Berry, *County Genealogies: Pedigrees of the
Families in the County of Kent* (London, 1830), pp. 162-3. Demographic and occupa-
tional data have been taken from transcripts of the Rye parish registers, E.S.R.O.,
PAR, 467/1/1-2, and many other sources listed in Gregory, "Slander Accusations and
Social Control", p. 106 table 5.2.
[12] E.S.R.O., RYE, 13/1.
[13] E.S.R.O., RYE, 13/1, 4, 15; W/A10, fo. 31, Will of R. Bennett.

judge from Thomas's survey of fairy beliefs in this period.[14] The revelations, however, caused alarm among some of the town's inhabitants, and several pages of evidence concerning Susan and Anne's dealings with spirits were collected by the mayor and jurats during the autumn of 1607. At the December sessions of the peace, two indictments were preferred against the women by unknown parties. Susan was accused of counselling with and feeding wicked spirits in order to obtain treasure, and Anne of aiding and abetting her. The indictments were based on the recent witchcraft statute of 1604, which made it a felony to "consult covenant with . . . feede or rewarde any evill and wicked Spirit to or for any intent or purpose". Susan was found guilty and sentenced to be hanged, which was unusual in a case which did not involve any damage to persons or goods. Anne had meanwhile escaped to her husband's relations in Kent, and her trial was therefore deferred until the next sessions, which in Rye were held biannually.[15]

At this point outside influence was brought to bear on the mayor and jurats to abandon the case, through the intervention of Henry Howard, earl of Northampton. As lord warden of the Cinque Ports, he had the duty of investigating any corrupt practices, and in this case complained that the mayor and jurats were personally involved in the accusations against Anne Taylor — Susan was not mentioned. He went further than this, however, and in what was clearly a move to further the interests of the government at the expense of the ancient privileges of the Cinque Ports, attempted to prevent them from trying the case at all. He claimed that the magistrates, whose authority rested on a town charter, did not have the full powers of those county magistrates named in a commission of the peace.

The right of the Rye magistrates to try the case was nevertheless upheld by the King's justices, and the trial was eventually held, after the collection of yet more evidence, in the summer of 1609. Anne Taylor was acquitted by a local jury on the original indictment, and also on another preferred by Martha Higgons, widow of two ex-mayors, who accused her of bewitching to death her first husband, Thomas Hamon. Susan Swapper, who was still in

---

[14] Thomas, *Religion and the Decline of Magic*, pp. 724-34.

[15] E.S.R.O., RYE, 13/1-10; 1/8, fos. 73-4; 47/75; Historical Manuscripts Commission (hereafter H.M.C.), *Thirteenth Report: Appendix*, iv (London, 1892), p. 140; the statute 1 Jac. I, c. 12; Thomas, *Religion and the Decline of Magic*, pp. 531-2.

prison at this time, was eventually released under a general pardon in 1611.[16]

## THE ACCUSERS AND THEIR MOTIVATIONS

It will be evident from the above summary that this case is unusually informative on beliefs about fairies. To a modern reader, however, the fairies seem innocuous, and it is not obvious from the depositions what motivated the accusers. The motives become more intelligible if occasional clues in the depositions are linked with disputes between the protagonists which have been reconstructed from other records. In this section I will look at these clues, and also show that these disputes were only the latest in a history of factional conflict which can be traced back at least a couple of generations.

One point which is evident both from Susan's accounts and from the interrogatories drawn up by the magistrates is that the accusers were mainly interested in accusing Anne. Susan appears to have been acceding to her interrogators' wishes when she made references at every opportunity to Anne's interest in, and knowledge about, the spirits. She did not accuse Anne of wickedness in her early evidence, however, and George Taylor said that she only did so after she had been imprisoned.[17] Her accusations just before the trial in 1607 consisted of anecdotes such as the following:

> Mres Tayler did then tell her [Susan] that she the said Mres Tayler heard that Mr Maior was taken sick and that he should dye of the said sickness for she knewe it well, and that she did knowe and could tell all what was done in Mr Maior's howse and in every howse in Rye yf that she the said Mres Tayler would troble herself aboute it. And she further said to this examinate that every body should see that after Mr Maior was dead, what an ugley corpse he should be to looke on . . . And after Mr Maiors death, the said Mres Tayler did further say to this examinate that it were no matter yf the dyvell did fetch away his body for, or to be, an example for others, for she doubted that the diveil had his soule alreddy, for that he was an evil Lyver.[18]

The mayor referred to in this passage was Thomas Hamon, who had died a few months earlier. Anne was later to be accused of

[16] E.S.R.O., RYE, 47/66, 71, 74-6 (also H.M.C., *Thirteenth Report: Appendix*, iv, pp. 139-40); E.S.R.O., RYE, 1/8, fos. 156-7ᵛ, 255ᵛ.
[17] E.S.R.O., RYE, 13/1, 2, 6-8.
[18] E.S.R.O., RYE, 13/8.

bewitching him to death, in the indictment preferred in 1609 by his widow Martha.

Why were the accusers so keen to convict Anne? We cannot get much idea of her attitude from the legal evidence, because she was unwilling to answer the interrogators' questions, unlike the voluble Susan. There is one clue to her interests in the evidence, however, relating to the farm at Weeks Green which had belonged to her father and grandfather, both butchers named Robert Bennett. According to Susan, Anne was hoping to repurchase it — if the fairies would only provide the necessary £100.

Anne and her mother had been forced to sell the farm to a rich tanner to whom her father had been indebted when he died of plague in the epidemic of 1596. The story has more than individual interest, however, since it can be seen as symptomatic of the political decline of the butchers and their allies, several of whom had been jurats in the middle years of the century when the town was prosperous, including Robert Bennett senior.[19] By the end of the century the town's butchers were all too poor to have been likely candidates for the magistracy (none were taxed on more than £50 in 1598, while eleven of the thirteen magistrates were taxed on £100 or more). It seems probable that this was a result of a loss of custom associated with the gradual deterioration of the harbour. Anne's father had been taxed on £120 in 1596, although the assessors must have been out of touch with his real circumstances, since his probate inventory totalled only £43 a year later.

The political and economic decline of the butchers was more than matched by the increasing dominance of the brewers, as indicated by the occupations of mayors in the later sixteenth century. (See Table 1.) The early 1580s constitute a dividing-line because this was the period when the balance of power in the town shifted from a faction led by the butcher John Fagge to the other faction, which was led first by the feeter (fish wholesaler) Henry Gaymer, and later by the brewers Robert Carpenter and Thomas Hamon. The membership of the two factions at this period is evident from a major clash at the mayoral election of 1579 (which was one among several conflicts), when some of the magistrates refused to be sworn into office in protest at the

[19] E.S.R.O., RYE, 13/1, 5, 12; 33/17, fos. 210-11; 58/11; W/A10, fo. 31, Will of R. Bennett; Public Record Office, London (hereafter P.R.O.), Prerogative Court of Canterbury, Wills (hereafter P.C.C.W.), 14 Stonarde.

## TABLE 1

### OCCUPATIONS OF MAYORS OF RYE IN THE LATER SIXTEENTH CENTURY*

|                          | 1563-82 | 1583-1608 |
|--------------------------|---------|-----------|
| Merchant                 | 6       | 4         |
| Brewer                   | 2       | 12        |
| Vintner                  | 0       | 4         |
| Butcher                  | 4       | 0         |
| Feeter (fish wholesaler) | 2       | 4         |
| Fisherman                | 3       | 1         |
| Unknown                  | 3       | 1         |
| Total                    | 20      | 26        |

*Notes and sources: East Sussex Record Office, Lewes (hereafter E.S.R.O.), Rye Corporation MSS. (hereafter RYE), 1/3-8; occupations taken from many different sources. The figures refer to mayoral years in which the mayors were drawn from each occupational group rather than to the number of individuals of each occupation who held office: note that the brewer Thomas Hamon held the office six times.

election of John Fagge as mayor for a third consecutive term. No mayor had held office for more than two terms in succession since the fifteenth century, and the protesters claimed that it was contrary to the customs of the town. It appears from a petition to the privy council by members of the Fagge faction that the protesters wanted Robert Carpenter to be mayor. Fagge nevertheless remained in office, and the mayor came from this faction in six of the ten years between 1573 and 1582. In two of the remaining four years, the mayor came from the other faction (in the ten years before 1573, the divisions were either less clear-cut, or less apparent from the records). From 1583 until 1608, however, the Gaymer/Carpenter/Hamon faction dominated — in at least nineteen of these twenty-six years, the mayor came from this faction.[20]

The last quarter of the sixteenth century, therefore, saw the emergence of one faction as politically dominant in the town, after a decade or two when the two factions had been fairly evenly

[20] E.S.R.O., RYE, 1/4, fo. 307; 47/25/22; L. A. Vidler, *A New History of Rye* (Hove, 1934), p. 159. For the factional conflicts in the 1570s and 1580s, see Mayhew, *Tudor Rye*, pp. 127-37. It will be apparent from what follows that Thomas Hamon was no longer a member of the Fagge faction by 1600. References for the local tax assessments of 1596, 1598 and 1610 are: E.S.R.O., RYE, 1/6, fos. 30ᵛ-43; 77/6; 1/6, fo. 209ᵛ; 77/7; 1/8, fos. 232ᵛ-233. Since the frequent tax assessments must have been impressionistic, they have been grouped according to the assessors' implicit categories, as indicated by the tax intervals used in 1598: "rich" = £100 and over (in intervals of £50 or £100); "middling" = £20-80 (in intervals of £10); "lower" = £1-12 (in intervals of £1-3).

matched. Did this development reflect economic changes? Such a connection is not obvious, since it is difficult to establish factional allegiance even among the magistracy at this period, and there was no division between a "richer" and "poorer" group among the magistrates. Brewers certainly monopolized the mayoral office and led the dominant faction, but it is not evident who if anybody was the leader of the other faction after John Fagge died. It may be suggested, however, that those trades which required some capital, either for equipment (brewers and tanners) or for merchandise (vintners, goldsmiths, mercers and drapers), would have been able to survive the declining prosperity of the port more easily than the butchers because they could exclude poorer competitors. If the character of factional conflict is determined as much by the followers as by the leaders, and if the brewers were acting as leaders of the majority of the capitalist tradesmen and merchants, then the richer butchers were likely to have taken on the leadership of those who were not included in this category — the ordinary artisans. The butchers had not needed to try and exclude their poorer competitors when the town had been prosperous, and later they had not the means to do so, because their trade did not require expensive tools or merchandise. The Bennetts were in fact closely related to artisans — Robert junior's wife was the daughter and sister of shoemakers (both named Thomas Radford, and of only lower or middling wealth). The political decline of this faction may therefore have been partly a consequence of the leaders' failure to prosper as much as the leaders of the other faction, and partly a result of a decline in wealth and solidarity among their supporters. In what follows, the two factions will be distinguished as the "brewers'" and "butchers'" factions for ease of reference. This is not to suggest, however, that these two trades predominated in the respective factions.

Before leaving the question of possible economic differences between the factions, I would like to emphasize that some of the richer inhabitants appear to have been not only surviving better than the others, but even prospering in the early 1590s, suggesting that the inflation of food prices which was widening the gap between rich and poor elsewhere in the country was having a similar effect even in declining Rye. This may seem surprising if we consider the extent of Rye's decline in the late sixteenth century, so graphically described by Mayhew, and I shall there-

## TABLE 2

### COMPARISON BETWEEN LOCAL TAX ASSESSMENTS FOR 1576, 1596 AND 1610 AND PROBATE INVENTORY TOTALS*

| | Tax rate | | | | |
|---|---|---|---|---|---|
| | £1-2 | £2.5-9 | £10-19 | £20 + | Overall |
| **1576** | | | | | |
| Median | 4 | 3 | 5 | 3 | |
| Mean | 5.6 | 6.6 | 4.8 | 4.3 | 5.9 |
| No. observations | 14 | 29 | 7 | 5 | 55 |
| **1596** | | | | | |
| Median | 4.0 | 3.0 | 2.1 | 1.2 | |
| Mean | 4.0 | 4.3 | 2.3 | 1.2[a] | 2.1 |
| No. observations | 2 | 7 | 6 | 22 | 37 |
| **1610** | | | | | |
| Median | 6.5 | 2.9 | 2.1 | 1.4 | |
| Mean | 6.5 | 5.1 | 3.4 | 1.5[a] | 3.5 |
| No. observations | 2 | 12 | 8 | 12 | 34 |
| **Total no. taxed** | | | | | |
| 1576 | 135 | 177 | 67 | 41 | 420 |
| 1596 | 165 | 91 | 38 | 122 | 416 |
| 1610 | 97[b] | 113 | 50 | 94 | 354 |

*Notes and sources: The format of the Table and the figures for 1576 are from G. Mayhew, *Tudor Rye* (Falmer, 1987), p. 142; other figures from E.S.R.O., RYE, 1/6, fos. 30ᵛ-43, 77/6-7; E.S.R.O., W/B2-4. The figures relate to inhabitants who died within seven years of one of the three tax assessments; each person's tax assessment has been divided by their probate inventory total. About half of those in the 1596 list died of plague in the same year as the tax. Probate inventories were of course not limited to goods in Rye, unlike the tax assessments, and those proved at the prerogative court of Canterbury have not survived.

[a] For the people taxed on £50 or over, these figures were 1.5 and 1.2 for the 1596 and 1610 groups respectively (no. of observations 11 and 6).

[b] £2 rather than £1 was the lower limit at this date.

fore present some figures to support this contention. Evidence from the 1596 tax list can be compared with that for 1576 (a time when the port was still prospering), which Mayhew has analysed. The assessments appear to have been more generous in the 1570s than in the 1590s, as Mayhew points out, and it is therefore necessary to repeat his comparison between tax assessments and probate inventory totals.[21] (See Table 2.) The figures indicate that the 1596 tax assessments for those taxed on £20 or more appear to have been closer to actual wealth by a factor of about four than the figures for 1576. An assessment of £50 in 1576 would therefore have been comparable to one of £200 in 1596. In 1576 eight (2 per cent) of the taxed population were assessed on £50 or over,

[21] C. G. A. Clay, *Economic Expansion and Social Change: England, 1500-1700*, 2 vols. (Cambridge, 1984), i, pp. 214-22; Mayhew, *Tudor Rye*, ch. 7, pp. 14-27, 139-42.

and in 1596 sixteen (4 per cent) on £200 or over, indicating that the richest group had not become less wealthy even though the prosperity of the town as a whole had been declining for over two decades. The assessments for 1610 show a relation to actual wealth similar to that for 1596.[22]

The increasing dominance of one faction may, therefore, have partly reflected a widening economic split between the richer inhabitants and others in the town. Let us now return to the witchcraft case, and the involvement in it of the two factions. The principal victim was the brewer Thomas Hamon, then the most senior jurat and probably the richest man in the town. The daughter and daughter-in-law of the former leader of the brewers' faction, Robert Carpenter (brewer), gave evidence after his death against Anne Taylor. Hamon's widow Martha was the daughter of the jurat William Tharpe (draper), and her second husband Thomas Higgons (merchant) succeeded Hamon as mayor. When he died shortly afterwards in 1608, his successor was a rich brewer (Richard Portriffe) who was probably also from this faction, since his policy over the witchcraft case appears to have been no different from his predecessor's, in spite of his being the client of the earl of Northampton.

This material suggests some motive for antagonism, but why should Anne Taylor have been singled out, and why did the accusation take the form of witchcraft? An examination of the religious differences which polarized the factions suggests a connection between Anne's claims to godliness and her expertise in dealing with spirits. It also shows how these claims could pose a threat to the other faction. Mayhew has described in detail the conflicts at the time of the Reformation, when Robert Bennett senior had been a member of the Protestant faction which had tried to get the traditionalist vicar removed.[23] He was one inhabitant who, in a rare personal touch to the preamble of a will, gave voice to godly sentiments: "I commend my soul into thandes of god the father, trusting assuredly to be saved by the merits of christ's passion, and to be raised upp agayne at the daye of Judgment with the righteous people: and this I protest before all

[22] The 1610 figures are referred to below, pp. 47–8.

[23] Thomas Hamon and John Fowtrell were taxed higher than any other inhabitants, at £400, in 1598; E.S.R.O., RYE, 13/18, 24; H.M.C., *Thirteenth Report: Appendix*, iv, p. 132; G. Mayhew, "Religion, Faction and Politics in Reformation Rye: 1530-59", *Sussex Archaeol. Colls.*, cxx (1982), pp. 139-60.

the whole world, to be my faithe".[24] By the time Bennett wrote his will in 1564 the commonalty of Rye appear to have become uniformly godly. It is noteworthy that although the arrival of large numbers of Huguenots fleeing from religious persecution in France caused occasional economic conflicts, these did not reveal any evidence of religious controversy.[25]

Anne's father also appears to have had godly pretensions, although this is only evident from the record of a confrontation between him and the magistrates in 1575, when he refused to swear on the holy evangelist. They were trying to question him about some "illrule" the previous Monday night, when, among other acts of destruction, the lattice had been pulled from a window belonging to a prominent member of the brewers' faction. He and his brother John had both been involved. Before being examined, he "swore, Layinge his hande upon his brest, by the Lyvinge god, that he wold saie the truth, as well as though they shuld swere him uppon a booke".[26] Robert and John Bennett were frequent troublemakers.[27]

From the 1570s the brewers' faction appear to have become less godly, while the godliness of the butchers' faction increased. This development is illustrated by the changing attitude of the leader of the brewers' faction, Robert Carpenter. In 1580 he was asked by a pious Huguenot glazier to act as one of the two executors of his will, but it was during Carpenter's mayoralty in 1590 that the magistrates wrote to the lord admiral complaining that "a small secte of purytanes, more holy in shew then in dede, is sprong up among us". They said that the "Puritans" were trying to get the preacher, who was one of the lord admiral's chaplains, removed. Those interrogated were mostly artisans, except for the servant of a rich man, Robert Wood, who may have expressed the views of his master. since Wood's claims to godliness are indicated by the names he gave two of his children: "Convert" and "Renewed". Wood was later made a jurat. These godly names were not at all common in Rye, and it is therefore

[24] P.R.O., P.C.C.W., 14 Stonarde.

[25] Mayhew, *Tudor Rye*, pp. 77-9, 84-5; P. Collinson, "Cranbrook and the Fletchers: Popular and Unpopular Religion in the Kentish Weald", in P. N. Brooks (ed.), *Reformation Principle and Practice: Essays in Honour of A. G. Dickens* (London, 1980), p. 194.

[26] E.S.R.O., RYE, 1/4/218.

[27] E.S.R.O., RYE, 1/4, fos. 183v, 214v-215v, 217v-218, 223-4v; see also Collinson, "Cranbrook and the Fletchers", p. 195.

significant that one of the accused "Puritans", a French surgeon, had similar names for some of his children — "Hopewell" and "Repente".[28]

Some evidence for the religious orientation of the brewers' faction comes from the witchcraft case. Anne is alleged to have said of Thomas Hamon that "he never did any man good but such as was of his Religion", a remark which suggests a real difference in values between them, even if it was quoted (by Susan) as evidence of Anne's derisiveness.[29]

The attitude of Anne herself can be ascertained from an account which she gave of two angels which had been seen by Susan Swapper:

> And she further said unto this examinate that those two Angells had each of them A prophett. And that those Angells would reveale unto the two prophets, to no other persons, the cause of their comeing, and that there coming was to cutt of the wicked from the yearth. And that this examinate and her husband should see the Angells hereafter.[30]

This was almost the only piece of information which she offered which was not elicited by the interrogators. George Taylor related another of Susan's sayings in a letter which he wrote to the mayor and jurats: "at Eleven months Ende I [Taylor] should have that Reveled unto mee that never Abraham nor Salloman hade nor any man Lyvinge uppon the Earthe. And that at Eleven munthes Ende ther should no mane Lyvinge be left to Trede uppon this Earthe".[31]

This was a more radical form of millenarianism than that current in most published works of the period, which placed the Day of Judgement at least several decades into the future. George was already related to a former member of the butchers' faction before he married Anne. The Taylors' account of the spirits differs markedly from Susan's own, who never referred in her evidence to angels, prophets, predestination or the coming millennium.

---

[28] The accused "Puritans" were George Martin, William Gyll (surgeon), John Baylye (shoemaker), Francis Godfrey (carpenter) and Richard Tate (servant of Robert Wood, merchant): E.S.R.O., W/A7, fo. 194, Will of A. Harry; H.M.C., *Thirteenth Report: Appendix*, iv, pp. 98-100; E.S.R.O., RYE, 1/5, fos. 216-17ᵛ; P.R.O., P.C.C.W., 74 Hayes, 33 Capell (and parish registers). See Gregory, "Slander Accusations and Social Control", appendix 1a, for a list of the godly and biblical names given to children in Rye in this period (first instance per family).

[29] Susan had been referring to the devil (see above, p. 38); E.S.R.O., RYE, 13/8.

[30] E.S.R.O., RYE, 13/5.

[31] E.S.R.O., RYE, 13/6.

None of the inhabitants, including the Taylors, claimed to have seen Susan's spirits, but the Taylors do appear to have placed particular importance on some "apparitions" which they saw in the glass windows of the house opposite theirs, and which they thought might be connected with Susan's spirits. As George described it in his letter (and also in some evidence recorded by the town clerk), these apparitions were a kind of tableau, which showed a man sitting "in majesterial sort", with other people ranged around him. The implication seems to have been that the man was Thomas Hamon, and that this was a forewarning of his death.[32]

The Taylors were so interested in these apparitions that they invited their neighbours in to see them, but according to the town clerk's wife, Margery Convers, no one else could see anything. In some evidence recorded by her husband two years later, Margery gave a detailed account of a conversation which she had had with Anne on this occasion. After commiserating with her on the recent sickness of her husband, Margery went on:

> "I see no cause, but by the grace of God, Mr. Taylor and you may lyve many faire yeares togethers." Then said Mres. Taylor to her againe:
> That Swapper was with her for the Lengthe of her husband in a Sheete, were it never so old. Then this deponent said unto her againe:
> "I hope you did not geve her the length of him in a sheete." "Why", said Mres. Taylor againe, "she asked of me for the length of myself in a hairlace!" Then said this deponent:
> "Trewly, Mres. Taylor, yf you will be ruled by me, you shall geve her nothinge." Then saide Mres. Taylor againe:
> "She hath come to me for Beefe out of my pott, and diverse other thinges, and she came the other day for Apples for one of them [spirits] that was with childe." And I asked her whether she gave her any, and she said:
> "I'faith, that I did, and a peece of suger too." And then this deponent asked Mres. Taylor what they were that shee sent the apples to, and she said she knewe not what they were. Then this deponent asked Mres. Taylor whether they could speake, and she said that Susan Swapper saieth that they can speake, and that they cry "yangh yanghe".[33]

This deposition would give the impression of being a simple account of a neighbourly conversation, were it not for the fact that it was recorded in the same month as the final trial of Anne Taylor, and the conversation had occurred two years previously.

[32] P. Christianson, *Reformers and Babylon: English Apocalyptic Visions from the Reformation to the Eve of the Civil War* (Toronto, 1978), ch. 3. George Taylor was the step-grandson of Richard Rucke: Berry, *County Genealogies*, pp. 162-3; Mayhew, *Tudor Rye*, p. 70; E.S.R.O., RYE, 13/5-6.

[33] E.S.R.O., RYE, 13/25.

The significance of this point is emphasized by an account at the end of the deposition of a quarrel between Anne and the Convers's maidservant, which concludes with Margery's opinion that Anne had bewitched the girl to death. This suggests that Margery had been making some point in the quoted passage which helped support this conclusion, but she did not spell out what that point was. One implication of her evidence, however, is that she was playing down the importance of the spirits, and suggesting that Susan was simply using them as a means of manipulating Anne. There may indeed have been some truth in this observation, since other evidence suggests that the pregnant woman who wanted apples was a sailor's wife, and not a spirit at all.

If Margery felt it necessary to belittle the spirits, this suggests that they held some threat. One might also expect that the threat was associated with godliness, since the Taylors were so interested in the spirits. Yet some descriptions of the spirits were notably ungodly. They were described as playing puckish practical jokes on inhabitants, such as bouncing a couple up and down in bed. When in the guise of fairies, these spirits seem in fact more suited to a remote, unreformed village than to godly Rye.[34]

The witnesses thus all provided different accounts of the spirits, perhaps articulating opinions through them which they would not have dared express in their own words. What could the magistrates do against such ephemeral beings, other than label them as devils — which they do not appear to have had the conviction to do — or dismiss them as of minor importance, as Margery Convers tried to do?

The richer inhabitants were perhaps particularly susceptible to this spiritual threat to their dominance because of a trade slump which had hit them a few years earlier. Mayhew has demonstrated that the dramatic decline in the town's trade in the 1590s was less a direct result of the silting up of the harbour than the shifting arena of war on the continent, and the consequent transfer of trade to other parts of the country seems to have affected the richer merchants more than other inhabitants.[35]

These changes were reflected in the local tax assessments, since the assessments for those individuals in the "rich" category declined much more between 1598 and 1610 than those in the "middling" category. (See Table 3.) People in the middling group

[34] E.S.R.O., RYE, 13/1, 6, 11, 13, 19.
[35] Mayhew, *Tudor Rye*, pp. 244-69.

TABLE 3

DECLINE IN WEALTH 1598-1610 OF RYE INHABITANTS ASSESSED ON
£20 OR MORE IN 1598*

|  | "Rich" (£100 + ) | "Middling" (£20-80) |
|---|---|---|
| Mean assessment in 1598 | £150 | £35 |
| Mean decline | £70 | £7 |
| Standard deviation | 45 | 21 |
| Decline as percentage of mean assessment | 47 | 20 |
| No. observations | 10 | 22 |

*Notes and source: E.S.R.O., RYE, 77/6-7. Mean decline = mean decline in assessed
wealth of individuals, 1598-1610.

were of course more likely to disappear into the realms of the
untaxed than those in the rich group, but on the other hand the
percentage decline in the middling group would be only 13 per
cent if one person were excluded who had been much richer (at
£68) in 1598 than the rest of this group.

At a more individual level, Robert Carpenter, the leader of the
brewers' faction, went bankrupt in 1601 and retired from the
bench; in the same year as he died, in 1606, another of the jurats
from the brewers' faction, Thomas Fisher, retired from the bench
when his son was accused of being a papist by some of the godly.
The earl of Northampton investigated the case, and Thomas
Fisher junior ended his life in Rye prison.[36]

Thomas Hamon's death in 1607 at the age of 58 may, therefore,
have seemed to members of the brewers' faction as the decisive
blow after a series of afflictions. The brass of Hamon placed in
Rye church by his widow is the only example from this period,
perhaps signifying that his death marked the final end to the
town's brief period of importance. If this calamity was the result
of malevolence, then who was a more likely suspect than a censori-
ous cunning woman from the rival butchers' faction, who was
claiming privileged access to the spirit world, as well as having
contrived an advantageous marriage which strengthened this
faction?

By 1609, however, the brewers' faction must have realized that
resistance to the butchers' faction was unprofitable, if only because their conflicts encouraged interference from outsiders such
as the earl of Northampton. The two factions now closed ranks —

[36] E.S.R.O., RYE, 1/7, fo. 357ᵛ; 47/70; 1/9, fos. 475ᵛ-476. "Some of the godly"
included Anne Taylor's cousin Noah Radford (shoemaker); a "Mr. Taylor", probably

(cont. on p. 49)

George Taylor was made a freeman and was employed with the vicar as a representative of the town in some negotiations with the government, and a member of the butchers' faction was chosen to be mayor.[37] The magistrates had to suppress some attempts to undermine this alliance, such as that by the butcher and innkeeper Francis Daniel, who told some visiting musicians "that wee have a Puritayne to or Maior, and therefore you may play as longe as you will at his doore, but he will geve you nothinge".[38] A rich freeman was disenfranchised for calling the magistrates "fools and sottes", and for saying such divisive things as "Mr. Convers and Mr. Mayor were never frendes till nowe".[39]

This truce was not long-lived, and there were violent clashes between the factions later in the century. As for the individuals, George Taylor soon withdrew from active involvement in Rye politics, for reasons which are unclear, and died in Rye in 1628. Anne left a will in 1644, in which she named a local butcher as the executor. The only subsequent reference to the Swappers in the corporation records is in connection with the theft of a sack of woad, for which they and a local fisherman and his wife were examined in 1613.[40]

Let us conclude this section by drawing out the themes which were important in the witchcraft case, before proceeding to analyse them. Political competition provided at least part of the motivation for the accusers. The prominent role given to George Taylor after the acquittal suggests that a major reason for the accusation against his wife was to discredit him, thus undermining the position of probably the richest and most influential member of the butchers' faction. Anne's position was particularly important for him because, like the many other outsiders who had married the daughters or widows of freemen, any claim on his part to political office (and hence also to a dominant role in the

(n. 36 cont.)
George, was present at one of the incidents. The initial accusations were made by two Cranbrook clothiers.

[37] E.S.R.O., RYE, 1/9, fos. 338ᵛ, 351-2, 355-6, 380, 382, 473. The new mayor, Richard Cockram, had been asked by the godly jurat Robert Wood (see above, p. 44) to be an overseer of his will: RYE, 1/8, fo. 181; P.R.O., P.C.C.W., 74 Hayes.

[38] H.M.C., *Thirteenth Report: Appendix*, iv, p. 144, or E.S.R.O., RYE, 47/77/2; 1/8, fo. 210ᵛ.

[39] E.S.R.O., RYE, 47/78; 1/8, fo. 181.

[40] Fletcher, *County Community*, pp. 116-20, 238-9; M. Hunter and A. Gregory, *An Astrological Diary of the Seventeenth Century: Samuel Jeake of Rye, 1652-99* (Oxford, 1988), pp. 28-34. E.S.R.O., W/U1; RYE, 47/84.

butchers' faction) would have been substantiated by the marriage.[41]

These political factors were, however, conditioned by economic factors. The political strength of the brewers' faction in the last quarter of the sixteenth century appears to have been based at least in part on the economic pre-eminence of the capitalist tradesmen, who could survive better than the other inhabitants, or even benefit from, the combined effects of the late sixteenth-century inflation and the decline of Rye harbour. This economic division may have been reflected in the increasing ideological divergence between the two factions.

The specific trigger for the witchcraft accusation, however, was the trade slump of the 1590s, which mainly affected the richer inhabitants and upset the position of the brewers' faction in town politics relative to the butchers' faction.

## IV

### CYNICISM AND POLITICAL STRATEGY

This reconstruction of the background to the witchcraft case has shown that it was only one episode in a series of factional conflicts in Rye. Demonstrating that it had political significance does not, however, take us very far in understanding the accusers' motivations. Why should an accusation of witchcraft have seemed an appropriate political strategy at this period for some of the richer inhabitants of a town in close contact with London, when it was unlikely to have done so a century later? To answer this question, we must consider what the strategy meant to the accusers. In the second half of this paper I will discuss what meanings could have been relevant in the cultural context of the period. One possibility might be that the accusers used the prosecution as an instrument of "moral discipline", along the lines of the social-control model. It will be argued, however, that such an explanation would be inadequate not only for this case, but for any case which involved factional conflicts. We therefore have to cast our net wider in a search for contemporary cultural concepts which might have legitimized such a strategy.

---

[41] For some other examples of accusations of witchcraft made against the wives of influential men, in towns in Norway and Germany, see Levack, *Witch-Hunt in Early Modern Europe*, p. 189; Quaife, *Godly Zeal*, p. 151. The "other outsiders" included Robert Convers, the town clerk, and Thomas Higgons, who succeeded Thomas Hamon as mayor.

Before beginning this discussion, however, a complicating factor must be considered which could make it redundant. The magistrates' main interest in the case after the first few months could have been deflected from prosecuting Anne Taylor to defending their privileges. Had the earl of Northampton's intervention after the trial of 1607, challenging the magistrates' right to try the case, changed their perspective?

If the magistrates and some, at least, of the deponents had been primarily concerned in 1608 and 1609 to defend the privileges of the town, they would probably have focused on substantiating the accusation against Anne Taylor of "aiding and abetting" Susan. Since this had not been a felony under witchcraft statues passed before 1604, they might also have been concerned to demonstrate that there was evidence of worse deeds of witchcraft perpetrated by Anne than were encompassed in this rather weak charge. It is this second objective which is most evident from depositions collected later than the 1607 trial, since they include accusations of black witchcraft against Anne, which had not been made before this date. We therefore need to consider whether the charge against her of killing Thomas Hamon by witchcraft could have been entirely cynical, in the sense of having no basis in common fame.

This seems unlikely, because all the evidence for Anne Taylor's antagonism towards Hamon, apart from his widow's, was collected (from Susan) *before* the trial in 1607, even though it had no relevance to the indictments preferred at this date. Accusations made by deponents after this date were, moreover, consistent with those made before it, since everyone agreed that it was only Susan who saw the spirits, and that Anne acted as her mentor. Accusations of black witchcraft were not made indiscriminately — only Anne was thus accused, even though Susan and Widow Bennett were more like the stereotype of the witch. Susan was poor, while Widow Bennett was old (age 59), both the daughter and sister of shoemakers, and her expertise in healing, astrology and dealing with spirits was referred to by her interrogators. If the accusers had been mainly concerned to make a charge of witchcraft against Anne seem feasible to sceptics — whether other inhabitants, or outsiders such as Northampton — they would have been better advised to prefer an indictment against her for a less major offence than causing death, such as dealing directly with spirits (on the same basis as Susan), or causing minor harm by witchcraft. Since they (or to be more exact, Hamon's widow) acted on suspicions which had been articulated before the trial of 1607, this suggests that suspicions among at least some inhabitants may have hardened by this time.[42] We may conclude that although the magistrates had the additional issue of defence of their privileges to consider after the trial of 1607, the evidence does not suggest that this caused them to fabricate new charges against Anne Taylor.

Let us now return to the question why a witchcraft accusation was considered an appropriate weapon to use against the opposite faction. This again raises an issue about cynicism and belief. Was the accusation made because the accusers "believed" it, or were they "unscrupulously using 'the system' to eliminate rivals"?[43] This question needs to be modified, since it is unlikely that the accusers' motives can be categorized in terms of a simple dichotomy. A political strategy is only effective if it attracts allies, and this will only be achieved if potential allies accept the principle underlying the strategy. What we need to ask, therefore, is what the accusers might have thought the accusation "meant" to others in the town. Whether, or to what extent, it meant the same to the accusers themselves can then be left open. At a broader level, the underlying principle was unlikely to have been peculiar to Rye, since it must have been drawn from a pool of shared cultural meanings for it to have been effective as propaganda.

It might be thought that one aspect of the propaganda in this case would have been the legitimization of those in authority, since the accusers were linked with the dominant brewers' faction. This is the central issue in the social-control model, and we therefore need to consider if it is applicable to Rye.[44] According to this model, witchcraft cases initiated by members of the populace were encouraged by judicial elites in order to help legitimize their politico-religious ideology and authority during the conflicts

---

[42] E.S.R.O., RYE, 13/6-8, 10, 20, 24-5. Anne was neither old (30 years) nor poor, but Sabean notes that in some German communities women were only accused of witchcraft when their influence in the community was on the wane. This suggests that if this case had not reached the courts under unusual circumstances, the accusers might have waited some years before preferring an indictment: D. W. Sabean, *Power in the Blood: Popular Culture and Village Discourse in Early Modern Germany* (Cambridge, 1984), pp. 108-9.

[43] Quaife, *Godly Zeal*, p. 151.

[44] Larner refers to this issue in a context relevant to this case, the competition for power between alternative ruling groups: Larner, *Enemies of God*, p. 196.

of the Reformation and Counter-Reformation. As G. R. Quaife puts it:

> This ideology, Protestant and Catholic, imposed an austere code of behaviour which was both a test of political loyalty and a rejection of traditional popular culture. Popular culture was undermined by these authorities through redefining as diabolic its key elements: peasant magic, public festivals such as May Day, and types of sexual behaviour.[45]

This approach might seem appropriate because the role played by fairies in the Rye case suggests a strong association with "popular culture", even though there was no explicit reference to diabolism in the evidence. Rye had been characterized as a godly town for the previous half-century, and popular festivities such as mumming, the "May game" and the Rye play had all been abolished by the 1560s. Even the annual parish festival, occasion for merriment in more remote areas, was now to be celebrated with gravity.[46]

A closer look at the case indicates, however, that the issues were more complex than this. The character of the spirits varied with the attitudes of different inhabitants — to some, they were traditional fairies; to others, they were the godly prophets of the coming millennium. They were not therefore simply identifiable with "popular culture". More importantly the cultural distinctions between different social groups in the town did not follow the lines of the social-control model. The judicial élite had certainly made determined efforts to impose moral discipline in the 1570s, but at this period it had been the godly butchers' faction who were in power. When the other faction began to consolidate their dominance in the 1580s, this policy of moral discipline was not continued, and a more positive attitude to popular festivities is suggested by an increase in the number of players invited to the town, although the numbers dropped sharply thereafter. An accusation of witchcraft directed against a member of the godly butchers' faction was not, therefore, likely to have been an attempt to suppress "popular culture". Anne Taylor would also have been an inappropriate choice of representative for the unreformed populace because she could at least sign her name, and

---

[45] Quaife, *Godly Zeal*, p. 207.
[46] Mayhew, *Tudor Rye*, ch. 2; E.S.R.O., RYE, 1/4, fo. 188ᵛ.

her mother wrote a sentence before signing the bottom of her
examination.[47]

It might be objected that special circumstances made the imposition of "moral discipline" an unimportant issue in this case,
since some of the accusers had close links with the magistracy.
There was therefore no distinction between the culture of the
"judicial élite" and that of the people who made accusations of
witchcraft. This consideration would apply, however, not only to
the Rye case, but also to *all* cases which involved factional conflicts, because it is improbable that one would find a cultural
dichotomy between the "judicial élite" and opponents who had
some political influence in the community.

Thus, in the hope that it would be effective as a political
strategy, some ethical principles other than "moral discipline"
were being invoked by the accusers through this witchcraft accusation; and this would probably also have been the case in other
communities in which witchcraft and factionalism were associated. In the next section I will therefore consider whether or not
this association was unusual, and, in the context of factionalism,
what type of issues were likely to have been considered important.

V

FACTIONALISM AND THE CONTROL OF CONFLICT

Was factionalism commonly associated with witchcraft accusations? This link has occasionally been mentioned in the literature
on witchcraft, but has been little discussed. Studies of witchcraft
in New England are an exception, since Paul Boyer and Stephen
Nissenbaum identify factionalism as a central issue in the Salem
witch-hunt, and John Demos has found that witchcraft accusations often followed a period of open factional conflicts (as well
as having direct links with them) in the early history of some
New England communities. Factionalism was also sometimes involved in the witch-hunts in south-west Germany.[48]

---

[47] Mayhew's figures show that the numbers of visits of players to the town decreased
steadily from sixty-three in the decade beginning in 1525, to nine in the decade
beginning in 1575; in the following decade this increased to twenty-four before
declining to four in the decade beginning in 1595: *Tudor Rye*, pp. 132, 59. For the
signatures, see E.S.R.O., RYE, 13/21.

[48] P. Boyer and S. Nissenbaum, *Salem Possessed: The Social Origins of Witchcraft*
(Cambridge, Mass., 1974), esp. pp. 92-109; J. P. Demos, *Entertaining Satan: Witchcraft and the Culture of Early New England* (Oxford, 1982), pp. 315-86, esp.
pp. 369-71; Midelfort, *Witch-Hunting in South-Western Germany*, chs. 5-6; Quaife,

(cont. on p. 55)

Thomas and Macfarlane did not include political factors in their explanations for the rise and decline in witchcraft accusations in England in the late sixteenth and early seventeenth centuries, but detailed analyses of political conflicts would have been difficult in their large-scale studies. Their conclusions do not preclude the possibility that factional conflicts might have been revealed in some cases, if sources other than those relating to the witchcraft cases had been used (assuming suitable records were available). The purpose of the witchcraft depositions was to give evidence that harm had been inflicted, not to recount the history of conflict between the parties, and it would not have been in the accusers' interests to air such conflicts in public. There are nevertheless clues that some of the conflicts may have involved groups and not just tensions between individuals. Macfarlane observes that pamphlet accounts of witchcraft cases (based on depositions) usually mention several accusers. He argues that accusations "were not merely the result of tension between two individuals, but rather between a group of villagers and an individual suspect". Pamphlet accounts do not indicate whether or not the suspect had supporters, since depositions in the secular courts were usually only taken from prosecution witnesses.[49]

A link between factionalism and witchcraft was therefore not unknown in early modern Europe and white America, and may have been more common than is at present recognized. What ethical principle is likely to have been involved in these cases? Witches were characterized as people with evil tongues who stirred up trouble among their neighbours, and I will argue that in the context of factionalism this implied not just a few bad words between individuals from the "poorer sort", but conflicts involving the whole community.[50] A witchcraft accusation denounced the evils of dissension, and could therefore be used as a means of suppressing opposition to a regime. This argument may seem functionalist, but it is being presented as only one aspect of early modern witchcraft, which will be discussed in a broader

*(n. 48 cont.)*
*Godly Zeal*, pp. 149-50. Political witchcraft among the nobility will not be discussed here.

[49] Macfarlane, *Witchcraft in Tudor and Stuart England*, pp. 86, 206; J. S. Cockburn, *Calendar of Assize Records: Home Circuit Indictments, Elizabeth I and James I: Introduction* (London, 1985), pp. 11, 96-7. Pamphlet accounts have to be used because most depositions were destroyed.

[50] See, for example, Larner, *Enemies of God*, pp. 97-8; Levack, *Witch-Hunt in Early Modern Europe*, pp. 136-9; Quaife, *Godly Zeal*, pp. 172-9.

context below. It should also be noted that the outcome of such a strategy could have been the opposite of what was intended. An accusation of witchcraft made in an unstable political situation could destabilize relations still further, rather than inducing people to sink their differences.

This argument rests not on objective standards of "peacefulness" or "conflict", but on contemporaries' perceptions of these states, and on the reasons why they perceived them in the way they did. We are therefore concerned with cultural concepts, and the English had a term which expressed the virtues of peacefulness — "good neighbourhood". Contemporary commentators emphasized both political and economic aspects of this term — the avoidance of strife and encouragement of amity on the one hand, and charity and hospitality on the other — but it is the political with which we are concerned here. As John Bossy has argued with respect to medieval England, "good neighbourhood" was not a description of social reality, but rather a desired state which by implication contrasted with reality, and with what contemporaries perceived as unacceptable levels of conflict.[51]

It may be argued that these values would have been of much greater importance in pre-Reformation communities, or those in remote areas, than in godly Rye. Similar values were, however, expressed in a decree by Rye corporation in the 1570s, which is particularly evocative because factional conflicts had at this time degenerated into rioting. It was a period when the silting up of the harbour had been greatly exacerbated by storms, and the decree indicates that this was thought to be God's punishment for quarrelsomeness (as well as other sins) in the town:

> it is agred, orderd and appointed by the worshipful Mr maior and the jurats his bretherne, that in consideration of this unseasonable wether, token of god's great displeasure, threatening no small miseries and Calamities to fall uppon us; and that for our Losse Liff and neglecting to do our duties as we ought to serve god, On Mondays next and so forth every Monday till it pleise god to staie this unseasonable wether, The people

[51] J. Bossy, "Blood and Baptism: Kinship, Community and Christianity in Western Europe from the Fourteenth to the Seventeenth Centuries", in D. Baker (ed.), *Sanctity and Secularity: The Church and the World* (Studies in Church History, x, Oxford, 1973), pp. 142-3; D. Underdown, *Revel, Riot and Rebellion: Popular Politics and Culture in England, 1603-60* (Oxford, 1985), ch. 3; W. Hunt, *The Puritan Moment: The Coming of Revolution in an English County* (Cambridge, Mass., 1983), pp. 130-5; C. Hill, *Society and Puritanism in Pre-Revolutionary England* (London, 1969), pp. 141-211; W. Vaughan, *The Spirit of Detraction* (London, 1611), p. 81, preface; H. Roberts, *An Earnest Complaint* (London, 1572); C. Fetherston, *A Dialogue against Light, Lewde and Lascivious Dauncing* (London, 1582).

and inhabitants of this town of all ages and sortes dilligently repair unto the church, both to call uppon god by praier, and also for the hering of his worde . . .

Item it is also agred and in godes feare consentid that uppon the next Saboth daie their be a general communion of all the honest inhabitants of the towne and their wyves and suche of their householde as they shall thinke most mete, therby to declare, to all the worlde, a generall reconsiliation of all offences whatsoever passed betwene eny of the inhabitants of this towne, As also to protest a godly christian and stedfast Love and unitie between the Inhabitantes. And farther by suche brotherly and Christian communicating togethers, to manifest their faith and godly agrement in the religion of Jesus Christ.[52]

This decree from the 1570s suggests that at this time the values of "good neighbourhood" were still alive in Rye, and not just among the "poorer sort". The connection between quarrelling and misfortune was a community issue, involving the control of factionalism, although in this instance the sin was attributed to everyone equally, rather than to a sharp-tongued butcher's daughter.

The decree demonstrates, however, a more specific continuity with past values than a general concern with reducing conflict. Links between the Eucharist and "good neighbourhood" in fifteenth- and early sixteenth-century thought have been demonstrated by several historians. Bossy has emphasized the social significance of taking communion, and the associated *pax* ceremony, as a statement of the abandonment of quarrels between neighbours. Similarly the use of the consecrated host in Corpus Christi celebrations to express the unity of the community, and in informal contexts to break up fights, has been described by Mervyn James.[53] The values connecting the Eucharist with the abandonment of quarrels are found in Rye as well as in these pre-Reformation communities, although in the Rye case they were actualized in a thoroughly godly manner, without popular rituals, and accompanied by fasting and prayers. This emphasis on continuity in values may seem incongruous, but it should be borne in mind that the main sources for the conceptualization of "good neighbourhood" (as opposed to behavioural evidence) are Puritan

[52] E.S.R.O., RYE, 1/4, fos. 121-2; the rioting is described in Mayhew, *Tudor Rye*, pp. 127-32.

[53] Bossy, "Blood and Baptism", pp. 140-2; M. James, "Ritual, Drama and Social Body in the Late Medieval English Town", in M. James, *Society, Politics and Culture: Studies in Early Modern England* (Cambridge, 1986), pp. 18-27, 23 n. 21. See also K. Wrightson, *English Society, 1580-1680* (London, 1982), p. 54; C. Haigh, *Reformation and Resistance in Tudor Lancashire* (Cambridge, 1975), p. 63; Sabean, *Power in the Blood*, pp. 45-8.

diatribes against popular festivities and rituals. It would not be surprising if the authors of these works, in trying to convince their readers of the evils of certain types of activity and behaviour, minimized the effectiveness of these activities.

The problem of quarrelsomeness in Rye was not simply internal, but involved external politics — on several occasions such conflicts had given outsiders the opportunity to intervene (usually at the invitation of one party) and challenge the autonomy of the town.[54] Linking quarrelling with misfortune was likely to be particularly effective as propaganda in communities where the maintenance of autonomy was a dominant issue, and this issue is very frequently raised in the literature on European and North American witchcraft — for example in relation to Salem, territories in the south-west of Germany, and regions on the borders of France.[55]

VI

### THE ABANDONMENT OF POPULAR FESTIVITIES IN CROSS-CULTURAL PERSPECTIVE

We have seen that an accusation of witchcraft was an appropriate tactic for suppressing political opposition in Rye because there was a continuing belief among at least some of the inhabitants that misfortune could result from excessive quarrelsomeness. The importance of this issue has been emphasized in the consideration of the rituals and festivities in pre-Reformation communities whose purpose was in part to reduce dissension. This leaves us, however, with a problem of chronology — why should the most flamboyant of these activities have been abandoned in Rye half a century earlier, if some of the associated beliefs and values had not greatly changed? In this final section I shall argue that we can gain a better understanding of this question if we consider in more general terms why good neighbourhood had been important in its heyday. I would suggest that studies of similar institutions in modern developing countries can offer different perspectives on this issue, and that they also provide examples of an association

---

[54] E.S.R.O., RYE, 1/4, fo. 321v; W. J. Jones, "Chancery and the Cinque Ports in the Reign of Elizabeth I", *Archaeol. Cantiana*, lxxvi (1961), pp. 143-51; H.M.C., *Thirteenth Report: Appendix*, iv, pp. 73-4.
[55] Quaile, *Godly Zeal*, pp. 115-22; Levack, *Witch-Hunt in Early Modern Europe*, pp. 176-82.

between fears about witchcraft and concern that these institutions were not being effective or adequately maintained.

The reasons for the abandonment of the annual cycle of festivities in many communities during the sixteenth and seventeenth centuries are of course a perennial source of debate. Discussion often focuses on the late sixteenth century, when the widening split between rich and poor in England, occasioned by rising prices and a series of bad harvests, is thought to have been associated with conflicts over popular festivities. It has been argued that the main instigators of these conflicts were a godly élite desirous of imposing moral discipline on their inferiors. Historians do not, however, usually apply this argument to the period before the social consequences of inflation had been manifested, and it is therefore not applicable to Rye.[56] As has already been argued, there is no evidence of substantial opposition to godliness in the town in the 1560s, and by the end of the century the leaders of the dominant brewers' faction appear to have become less rather than more godly.

A very different argument for the abandonment of popular festivities in towns, put forward by Charles Phythian-Adams, relates it to economic decline. He has provided striking evidence of the expense of these festivities, and concludes that the frequent complaints by office-holders about expense in the early sixteenth century are evidence of declining wealth on the part of these complainants and the towns in which they held office. Rye is a particularly notable example of the vulnerability of sixteenth-century English towns to sudden changes in economic fortune, but in the 1550s and 1560s the port was at its peak of prosperity, and the festivities were therefore likely to have been less of a financial burden than they would have been a couple of decades earlier.[57]

The issue of expense raised by Phythian-Adams can, however, point to a different type of explanation if it is considered in cross-

---

[56] See, for example, Wrightson, *English Society*, esp. pp. 206-28; Hunt, *Puritan Moment*, esp. pp. 130-55; Underdown, *Revel, Riot and Rebellion*, esp. pp. 20-63; P. Clark, *English Provincial Society from the Reformation to the Revolution: Religion, Politics and Society in Kent, 1500-1640* (Hassocks, 1977), esp. pp. 155-7, 176.

[57] C. Phythian-Adams, "Urban Decay in Late Medieval England", in P. Abrams and E. A. Wrigley (eds.), *Towns in Societies: Essays in Economic History and Historical Sociology* (Cambridge, 1978), pp. 174-8; C. Phythian-Adams, *Desolation of a City: Coventry and the Urban Crisis of the Late Middle Ages* (Cambridge, 1979), pp. 110, 112, 141.

cultural perspective. I will argue that the purpose which festivities served in the late fifteenth century may have been considered less important by the inhabitants in the early sixteenth century, and that the incentive to dispense with the cost of the festivities was a function of this. Such investment of material resources in social relations, not only through festivities, but also through gifts, loans and hospitality, is considered by anthropologists to be a strategy for exercising control over an unpredictable political and economic environment. The purpose is to establish a basis of goodwill so that when assistance (whether economic or political) is required in the future, allies will feel morally obliged not to betray trust at the crucial moment of need. Pierre Bourdieu therefore calls this the "good faith" economy, in which people have to constantly reaffirm and renegotiate these personal ties during the interactions of everyday life (with gifts, hospitality and so on) as well as on occasions of special ritual significance. Various methods of institutionalizing these ties, including neighbourliness, patronage, age-grading and kinship, have been developed in societies which differ widely in complexity. In general, however, it can be said that such investment in social relations is dominant in societies where the influence of the state is limited or non-existent, and where a market economy is imperfect or absent.[58]

A decision to abandon festivities would, therefore, depend not so much on levels of current wealth or power in a community, as on expectations of economic and political stability in the future. This is something which is not, unfortunately, easily ascertainable from urban records. Political centralization was, however, a dominant theme of the period, and internal markets in England were sufficiently integrated by the end of seventeenth century to prevent the occurrence of subsistence crises.[59]

The investment of material resources in social relations has

[58] P. Bourdieu, *Outline of a Theory of Practice*, trans. R. Nice (Cambridge, 1977), pp. 171-97. See also S. N. Eisenstadt and L. Roniger, *Patrons, Clients and Friends: Interpersonal Relations and the Structure of Trust in Society* (Cambridge, 1984), ch. 3; M. Sahlins, *Stone Age Economics* (London, 1974), ch. 5 (the subject of the book is much broader than the title suggests). For a general overview, see D. Pocock, *Understanding Social Anthropology* (London, 1975), ch. 4.

[59] Clay, *Economic Expansion and Social Change*, i, pp. 103-4. See Clark, *Provincial Society*, pp. 3-33, on the decline of disorder in Kent in the first thirty years of the sixteenth century — including references to the decline in magnate feuding, increasing economic expansion in the formerly backward areas of west Kent and the Weald, and expanding internal trade. His remarks on urban decline in Kent would not be applicable to Rye.

thus far been considered only from a behavioural angle, but it may be suggested that this also encouraged a certain psychological orientation, and that this psychology was likely to include a belief in witchcraft. I am here focusing on that aspect of witchcraft which can be usefully compared cross-culturally, that is to say the infliction of harm by supernatural means. It may be suggested that an emphasis on the destructive power of evil will through witchcraft is the obverse of the belief that the goodwill of others is essential for the achievement of survival or success. If someone feels that they need to make a considerable investment in personal ties in order to protect their commercial interests, this may predispose them to see commercial failure as in some circumstances due to the ill will of others. If such a suspicion gets articulated as an accusation of witchcraft, it can then be seen as some kind of negative statement about traditional obligations — that they are being abandoned, abused or imposed too strongly.

If we turn to early modern Europe, some associations between "good neighbourhood" and witchcraft can be discerned. Stuart Clark has described the similarities between one type of popular festivity, rituals of inversion, and contemporaries' accounts of the activities of witches. In Scotland witches were thought to take part in the kind of revelry which typified popular festivities, and, as Larner pointed out, the representation of the Demonic Pact in Scottish beliefs was in the form of a feudal relationship. Ties of "good lordship", like those of "good neighbourhood", were cemented by gifts, hospitality and festivities.[60]

The idea that there was a link between witchcraft and conflicts over neighbourliness originated with Thomas and Macfarlane in their very perceptive studies of English witchcraft. They emphasized that one aspect of neighbourliness — charity to the poor — was particularly likely to be a source of conflict at this period. Their argument was based on pamphlet accounts of witchcraft cases, in which those accused of witchcraft were often presented as old women who had asked for gifts, loans or hospitality, and

[60] S. Clark, "Inversion, Misrule and the Meaning of Witchcraft", *Past and Present*, no. 87 (May 1980), pp. 98-127; Larner, *Enemies of God*, pp. 148, 152-5. Underdown, *Revel, Riot and Rebellion*, pp. 63-8, suggests that clientage ties were linked with neighbourliness. On the use of gifts, hospitality and festivities to maintain ties of "good lordship", see, for example, the foreword by H. Trevor-Roper to *The Lisle Letters*, ed. M. St. Clare Byrne (Harmondsworth, 1985), pp. 13-16; L. Stone, *The Family, Sex and Marriage in England, 1500-1800* (London, 1977), pp. 124-5; S. R. Westfall, *Patrons and Performance: Early Tudor Household Revels* (Oxford, 1990).

had been refused. In the Rye case, also, there were many references to the giving of gifts, both to the spirits and between human
beings. The first reference to black witchcraft was in fact associated with a loan, but it should be noted that none of this gift-
giving involved charity to the poor — it expressed the quality of
relationship between neighbours of similar status rather than
conflicts associated with poverty.[61]

Similar points are made in discussions of witchcraft cases in
the assize and quarter sessions courts of East Sussex and Kent by
Cynthia Herrup and Adrian Pollock. Herrup suggests that the
East Sussex cases may have been rather unusual (there were only
ten in all) because accuser and accused were of similar status, and
"the charges seem to express ongoing competition rather than
guilt or anger born of spurned hospitality". Pollock observes that
begging was not often referred to in Kent cases (the examples
are mostly from quarter sessions depositions).[62]

Witches were often thought to be extreme examples of unneighbourly people, and some of the deponents in the Rye case
presented Anne Taylor in this way. Let us review some of the
points made about her. It has already been suggested that she
was accused of being unneighbourly not only because of her sharp
tongue, but also because she encouraged opposition to Thomas
Hamon, thereby threatening to revive the factional conflicts which
had paralysed Rye politics in the 1570s and early 1580s. In the
references to her activities as a healer, there are implications that
she used her powers to inflict harm rather than to cure.[63] There
are also intimations that she was unnaturally uncaring in the
following excerpt from Margery Convers's evidence, which relates to the occasion when a group of neighbours came to see the
apparitions in the windows opposite the Taylors' house. When
they were about to leave:

> Mres. Taylor requested this deponent to stay with her a little while, the
> which this deponent consented unto.
> Wheruppon Mres. Taylor desired her to sett downe by her, and then

[61] Thomas, *Religion and the Decline of Magic*, pp. 600-79; Macfarlane, *Witchcraft in Tudor and Stuart England*, pp. 170-6, 205-6; see also A. Macfarlane, "Witchcraft in Tudor and Stuart Essex", in M. Douglas (ed.), *Witchcraft Confessions and Accusations* (London, 1970), pp. 92-5; E.S.R.O., RYE, 13/1, 4-5, 7, 8, 10-11, 25.
[62] C. B. Herrup, *The Common Peace: Participation and the Criminal Law in Seven-teenth Century England* (Cambridge, 1987), pp. 27, 33; A. Pollock, "Regions of Evil: A Geography of Witchcraft and Social Change in Early Modern England" (Univ. of Michigan Ph.D. thesis, 1977), p. 164; see also Quaife, *Godly Zeal*, p. 190.
[63] E.S.R.O., RYE, 13/25.

entringe into communication aswell of the death of her children as of the later sicknes of her husband, this deponent said unto her that she was sorry for the death of her children and Leikwise for the sickness of her husband. And she [Anne Taylor] said [that] she was no whit sorry for the same, for as freel[y] [god] gave them [her as soon she] gave them to god againe. Then this deponent said unto [Mres.] Taylor:

"It is well that you can take it so lightly, for I assure you that I buryed a mayde of myne which was buryed that day that your sonne was buryed, which greeveth mee very much, and I thinke in regarde of her great paines and panges in her sickness, and the manner of her sickness, will be A cause that I shall never forgett her whilest I lyve." Then said she:

"Your maide was with mee for A medizen for her throte, and I was as Angry with her as Ever I was with maide in my Lyfe." Then this deponent asked her the cause, and Mres. Taylor Answered her:

"Why, woman, she tooke the upper hand of my childe!"[64]

Margery went on to recount Anne's complaints about possible financial problems if her husband died. To "take the upper hand" meant to claim superior status, as in seating arrangements, and from other evidence it appears that the maidservant said, or implied, that Anne's child was of lower status than herself.

Margery appears to be presenting herself as the one who cares, even for maidservants, while Anne does not even care about her husband and child. The implication seems to be that Anne's deference to the will of God is hypocritical, perhaps on the lines of the saying "a puritane is such a one as loves God with all his soule, but hates his neighbour with all his heart". Anne's main interest is presented as the acquisition of wealth and status. This was the occasion when the maidservant, according to Margery, was bewitched to death by Anne.[65]

If belief in witchcraft is often associated with a belief that investment in social relations is essential for survival or success (whether economic or political), what happens when such investment is withdrawn? Third World studies suggest that if there is general agreement that this investment is no longer necessary, witchcraft is unlikely to be a cause for concern. Problems arise, however, if there are different opinions on this question, and such disagreements often occur when the introduction of new resources — whether technological or commercial — exacerbates existing inequalities or creates new ones. Those who benefit from the changes usually have different attitudes to traditional obligations from those who suffer from them, and these conflicts and uncer-

[64] Ibid.
[65] See, for example, The Diary of John Manningham of the Middle Temple, 1602-03, ed. R. P. Sorlien (Hanover, N.H., 1976), pp. 164, 219. See above, pp. 46-7.

tainties are sometimes expressed in terms of fears or accusations of witchcraft. Accusations do not follow a uniform pattern, however: the relative social status and gender of accusers and accused vary in different societies.[66]

Before leaving Third World issues, I will describe one example, partly because it illustrates some of the themes discussed above, and partly because it demonstrates that even in tribal societies, witch-beliefs are not a static, unchanging part of oral tradition, but vary with social context. During the second half of the nineteenth century the Bakweri of Cameroon benefited from the introduction of a new food crop, the cocoyam, which both improved food supply and enabled them to take part in coastal trade. Details of witch-beliefs are limited for this period, but following the settlement of plantations on Bakweri lands by the Germans in the 1890s (later to be taken over by the British), the most horrific fantasies about witchcraft and zombies developed which appear to have had little basis in the traditional belief system (although similar ideas were found elsewhere in Africa). The minority who made profits from work connected with the plantations were thought to have achieved it with the labour of their apparently dead relatives, who, it was thought, had in fact been turned into zombies. The fears about zombies were, however, banished in the 1950s, at a time when co-operative banana farming was found to be profitable and reliable enough to benefit everyone. A slight resurgence of fears occurred in the 1960s when there was a slump in the banana market.[67]

These references to the Third World are intended to generate ideas, and do not assume that societies follow identical lines of

[66] See, for example, D. Parkin, "The Rhetoric of Responsibility: Bureaucratic Communications in a Kenya Farming Area", in M. Bloch (ed.), *Political Language and Oratory in Traditional Society* (London, 1975), pp. 120-1, 132-7; S. Epstein, "A Sociological Analysis of Witch-Beliefs in a Mysore Village", in J. Middleton (ed.), *Magic, Witchcraft and Curing* (New York, 1967), pp. 135-54; M. Rowlands and J.-P. Warnier, "Sorcery, Power and the Modern State in Cameroon", *Man*, xxiii (1988), pp. 130-1; M. G. Marwick, *Sorcery in its Social Setting: A Study of the Northern Rhodesian Cewa* (Manchester, 1965), pp. 248-54; J. Beattie, "Sorcery in Bunyoro", in J. Middleton and E. H. Winter (eds.), *Witchcraft and Sorcery in East Africa* (London, 1963), pp. 53-5; B. T. Van Velzen, "Bush Negro Regional Cults: A Materialist Explanation", in R. P. Werbner (ed.), *Regional Cults* (London, 1977), pp. 93-118. My observation that the gender of people most commonly accused of witchcraft varies in different societies is not intended to imply that gender is not a very important issue, nor that useful cross-cultural comparisons cannot be made.

[67] E. Ardener, "Witchcraft, Economics, and the Continuity of Belief", in Douglas (ed.), *Witchcraft Confessions and Accusations*, pp. 141-60.

"development". Changes in the Third World are often short term, piecemeal and introduced from outside. In addition, anthropological studies of witchcraft which are concerned with social change more commonly focus on economic rather than political aspects. We should therefore, as Natalie Zemon Davis argues, "consult anthropological writings not for prescriptions, but for suggestions". In the concluding paragraphs, I will consider how these ideas could help set a historical context for the Rye case.[68]

It has been shown that the most flamboyant institutions of "good neighbourhood", the annual cycle of festivities, were abandoned when Rye was prospering, in the 1550s and 1560s. Evidence of economic decline is present in the 1570s, when storms exacerbated the silting up of the harbour, and these occasioned the decree linking quarrelling with misfortune.[69] This suggests that although behavioural changes had occurred, the associated psychological attitudes had not been as easily banished. When misfortune struck, the old internalized values and fears reasserted themselves with renewed vigour, even if the suggested remedy was entirely spiritual, with no element of ritual. Where these values had previously been acted out and controlled through communal rituals, they were now under the control of the individual conscience, with much greater demands on self-discipline.

There is no evidence of scapegoating in the 1570s, perhaps in part because the storms affected all inhabitants. Later in the century, however, the economic changes (both local and national) affected different groups in different ways, and attitudes to "good neighbourhood" were therefore likely to have varied. It may be argued that those who suffered were more likely at this period than earlier to lay the blame on others, whose failure to uphold community values, as they saw it, threatened the prosperity of their neighbours.

The search for a scapegoat undertaken by members of the dominant brewers' faction could be seen as a gut reaction to economic and political catastrophe, but we need to consider not only their suspicions, but why they acted on them. Political strategy has to be taken into consideration as well as belief, and I will therefore leave it an open question as to whether the

[68] N. Z. Davis, "Anthropology and History in the 1980s", in T. K. Rabb and R. I. Rotberg (eds.), *The New History: The 1980s and Beyond: Studies in Interdisciplinary History* (Princeton, 1982), p. 273.
[69] See above, pp. 56–7.

accusers in the Rye case were primarily prompted by their own fears, or were more concerned to capitalize on the values and fears of others — perhaps of those commoners who had been most impoverished by the inflation and declining state of Rye harbour — in order to strengthen opposition to the godly butchers' faction.

This chronology of changing attitudes to "good neighbourhood" seems complex when viewed in a local context, and I will therefore conclude by looking at the issues in a broader perspective. I have argued that popular festivities were abandoned more because they were considered redundant than as part of a wholesale rejection of the values enacted in them. I do not mean to imply, however, that there was no change in values: people may have been prepared to pay lip-service to them, but not to invest much time, effort or money in maintaining them. Nor is an absence of change implicit in my argument that there could be a resurgence of old fears and values in periods of misfortune, sometimes manifested in witchcraft accusations. This was more likely to have been a confused response to changing economic and political circumstances, reflecting uncertainties, rather than any real desire for a return to old ways. The paper has emphasized continuity rather more than change because it has been focusing on communal issues, but from the point of view of some individuals, an increase in factionalism may have been an acceptable price to pay for less interference in their commercial activities.

*Birkbeck College, London*                    *Annabel Gregory*

# Witchcraft and Conflicting Visions of the Ideal Village Community

*Anne Reiber DeWindt*

In the fallen world, communities (patterns of interaction) are endlessly dying and being born. The historian's job is to specify what, at a given moment, is changing into or being annihilated by what.[1]

In the fall of 1589, ten-year-old Jane Throckmorton pointed to the old woman who had settled into a seat in her family's cavernous stone hearth and cried out, "Looke where the old witch sitteth . . . did you ever see . . . one more like a witch then she is?" With those words the child set in motion a four-year-long drama that culminated in the hanging of three of her neighbors from their fenland village of Warboys in north Huntingdonshire. Within weeks after the executions, Jane's father and uncle, with the help of a trial judge and the local parson, published their version of this tragic story in a pamphlet that now resides in the British Library.[2]

After Jane Throckmorton and her sisters had shared symptoms

ANNE REIBER DEWINDT teaches history at Wayne County Community College, Detroit. The author wishes to thank the following colleagues for comments and criticisms offered on the material in this article: Annabel Gregory, Donald Logan, Sarah Gravelle, Jutta Goheen, Edwin DeWindt, Hugh Culik, George Pickering, Kathleen Biddick, and Cynthia Herrup.

[1] William Hunt, *The Puritan Moment: The Coming of Revolution in an English County* (Cambridge, Mass., 1983), p. 131.

[2] "The Most Strange and admirable discoverie of the three Witches of Warboys, arraigned, convicted, and executed at the last Assises at Huntington, for the bewitching of the five daughters of Robert Throckmorton Esquire, and divers other persons with sundrie Divellish and grievous torments: And also for the bewitching to death of the Lady Crumwell, the like hath not been heard of in this age" (London: Printed by the Widdowe Orwin, for Thomas Man and John Winnington, 1593) (hereafter cited as "Witches of Warboys"). Copies survive in the British Library, the Bodleian Library, and the Norris Museum Library in St. Ives, Hunts. Page references in this study are from the British Library copy.

*Journal of British Studies* 34 (October 1995): 427–463
©1995 by The North American Conference on British Studies.
All rights reserved. 0021-9371/95/3404-0001$01.00

such as violent sneezing and grotesque seizures for several weeks, and
two medical doctors at Cambridge had suggested the possibility of
witchcraft, Gilbert Pickering—a relative from Northamptonshire—
arrived at the Warboys manor house to conduct numerous experiments
with Jane and her neighbor, Alice Samuel. His intention was to demonstrate that the old woman was the cause of the girl's symptoms. In
February 1590 one of the sisters was taken to the Pickering home
in Northamptonshire where the results of further experiments were
recorded for eventual inclusion in the pamphlet.

Soon after that child left Warboys, the wife of the lord of Warboys
arrived at the Throckmorton house to confront Mother Samuel. The
encounter between Alice Samuel and Lady Cromwell was tense and
highly charged, and words were exchanged whose horrible significance
became clearer as time passed.[3] In fact, Lady Cromwell herself became ill after this meeting and died about a year later.[4]

Robert Throckmorton dispersed his children to the households of
friends or relatives, and little information is provided about their activities during 1591 and early 1592. Tensions mounted again in September
of 1592 when one of the children's aunts gave birth at Warboys, and
Mother Samuel arrived with other neighbors to look in on the new
mother and her baby. Young Jane Throckmorton experienced a dramatic change in her own condition upon encountering the old woman,
and for the next several weeks one of the older sisters described a
series of encounters with spirits that were sent and controlled by
Mother Samuel. When those spirits, speaking through the girls, began
to accuse Mother Samuel, the girls' father brought the old woman into
their household, where she slept in the same room with her host and
hostess. While in such close quarters with the victims and their parents, Mother Samuel weakened to the point of confessing some form
of responsibility for the children's illnesses, and on Christmas Eve of
1592, she appeared in the Warboys parish church as a penitent sinner.

However, when she returned to her own home that night, her
husband and daughter vehemently reproached her weakness and gave
her the courage to recant on the following day, Christmas morning.
Robert Throckmorton then managed to arrange another confession and

---

[3] The speech by Mother Samuel: "Madame why doe you use me thus? I never did
you any harme as yet." The pamphlet authors then add, "These words were afterwards
remembred, and were not at that present time taken hold of by any"; "Witches of
Warboys," sig. D4r.

[4] The relevant entry in the Ramsey Parish registers located at the Huntingdon Record Office is difficult to decipher but refers to "My Ladye Susan[?] Cromwells funerall"
in an entry from July 12, 159?. If the pamphlet is accurate, then this date must be 1591.

turned her and her daughter Agnes over to the constable who took them to the Justices of the Peace. After the Huntingdon assizes in April 1593, all three members of the Samuel family were found guilty of bewitching Lady Cromwell to death, and they were all hanged.[5]

The plight of the Throckmorton and Samuel families has excited the attention of students of the witchcraft phenomenon since the time the pamphlet was first published in 1593.[6] Modern historians of the witchcraft persecutions have been struck by the relatively high status of the victims' family as well as of the witches themselves, by the pamphlet authors' meticulous descriptions of the symptoms of spirit possession, and, above all, by evidence for the mingling of popular and elite beliefs about witches, fueled as they were in this case by the medical establishment at Cambridge.[7] Furthermore, the active roles taken by the sick girls in this case and the suggestions of rivalries between two elderly female neighbors invite investigations into the role of gendered social networks in fueling this conflict.[8]

But the Warboys story is not just a witch story. In this essay no attempt will be made to suggest or describe the multiple and complex causes behind the accusations of witchcraft against the Samuels.[9] Instead I propose here that the evidence associated with the Warboys case makes an important contribution to historians' discussions of the evolving nature of community. Both medievalists and early modernists have participated in the task of describing "community" and tracing the various manifestations of its presumed existence over varying time spans. Important studies of individual villages and towns, on one hand,

[5] The 1563 statute establishing the death penalty is cited by Alan Macfarlane, *Witchcraft in Tudor and Stuart England* (London, 1970), p. 14.

[6] See Samuel Harsnet, *A Discovery of the Fraudulent Practices of John Darrel* (London, 1599), pp. 93, 97; John Cotta, *The Infallible True and Assured Witch* (London, 1625), p. 99; Thomas Heywood, *The Hierarchie of the Blessed Angels* (London, 1635), p. 598; Richard Boulton, *A Compleat History of Magick, Sorcery, and Witchcraft* (London, 1715), 1:49–152.

[7] See Clive Holmes, "Popular Culture? Witches, Magistrates, and Divines in Early Modern England," in *Understanding Popular Culture: Europe from the Middle Ages to the Nineteenth Century*, ed. Stephen L. Kaplan (Berlin, 1984), pp. 85–112; Leland L. Estes, "The Medical Origins of the European Witch Craze: A Hypothesis," *Journal of Social History* 17 (Winter 1983): 271–84.

[8] See J. A. Sharpe, "Witchcraft and Women in Seventeenth-Century England: Some Northern Evidence," *Continuity and Change* 6, no. 2 (1991): 179–99; Clive Holmes, "Women: Witnesses and Witches," *Past and Present*, no. 140 (August 1993), pp. 45–78. Also Lyndal Roper, "Witchcraft and Fantasy in Early Modern Germany," *History Workshop*, no. 32 (Autumn 1991), pp. 19–43; Peter Rushton, "Property Power and Family Networks: The Problem of Disputed Marriage in Early Modern England," *Journal of Family History* 11, no. 3 (1986): 205–19.

[9] The present writer plans a more complete study of this witchcraft case.

and county-wide networks of gentry families and their patronage and
tenant networks, on the other hand, have been offered to this end by
historians of the thirteenth through the seventeenth centuries. As a
result, the term "community" appears in the title of books and articles
with a wide variety of sociological concerns and historical themes. Put
most simply, a dichotomy has developed along spatial, or geographical, lines. For some historians, the English county provides the focus,
whereas for others, the community is confined to the boundaries of
the parish or village.[10] In each case, issues of definition and attempts
to analyze the characteristics of "community" are sometimes ignored
as the meaning of the term is taken for granted and is simply used to
refer to the geographical territory within parish or county boundaries.
In other studies, more attention is given to theoretical discussions
which draw upon sociological and anthropological analyses.[11]

Regardless of the geographical scope of the territory under study,
several themes have emerged from the scholarly debates. One of these
concerns the nature of the relationship between local (village or
county-wide) power elites and national legal and administrative institutions channeling power from Westminster to the "periphery." For
example, how did villagers become drawn into a genuinely national
framework of legal and administrative responsibility, and to what degree is there significant change over time in the intensity and nature
of that involvement?[12] Did the county gentry owe primary allegiance

[10] For example, David Gary Shaw, *The Creation of a Community: The City of
Wells in the Middle Ages* (Oxford, 1993); Marjorie Keniston McIntosh, *Autonomy and
Community: The Royal Manor of Havering, 1200–1500* (Cambridge, 1986); Margaret
Bonney, *Lordship and the Urban Community: Durham and Its Overlords, 1250–1540*
(Cambridge, 1990); David G. Hey, *An English Rural Community: Myddle under the
Tudors and Stuarts* (Leicester, 1974); Margaret Spufford, *Contrasting Communities:
English Villagers in the Sixteenth and Seventeenth Centuries* (Cambridge, 1974); An-
thony Fletcher, *A County Community in Peace and War: Sussex, 1600–1660* (London,
1975); Peter Clark, *English Provincial Society from the Reformation to the Revolution:
Religion, Politics and Society in Kent, 1500–1640* (Sussex: Harvester, 1977); Clive
Holmes, *Seventeenth-Century Lincolnshire* (Lincoln, 1980); Alan Everitt, *Change in the
Provinces: The Seventeenth Century* (Leicester, 1969); Ann Hughes, "Local History
and the Origins of the Civil War," in *Conflict in Early Stuart England: Studies in
Religion and Politics, 1603–1642,* ed. Richard Cust and Ann Hughes (London, 1989),
pp. 224–53.
[11] Anthony Fletcher, "National and Local Awareness in the County Communities,"
in *Before the English Civil War,* ed. Howard Tomlinson (London, 1983), p. 152; Shaw,
pp. 2–8; Susan Reynolds, *Kingdoms and Communities in Western Europe, 900–1300*
(Oxford, 1984), pp. 2–4; C. J. Calhoun, "Community: Toward a Variable Conceptualization for Comparative Research," *Social History* 5, no. 1 (1980): 105–29.
[12] See Richard M. Smith, "'Modernization' and the Corporate Medieval Village
Community in England: Some Sceptical Reflections," in *Explorations in Historical Geography,* ed. Alan R. H. Baker and Derek Gregory (Cambridge, 1984), pp. 140–79.

to their region rather than to their nation or monarch, and if so, what factors encouraged those attitudes to change over time?[13]

Other scholars are more interested in the changes taking place within parish and/or village boundaries and attempt to trace transformations in the institutions of local village and town government. They have noticed that access to the village court jury or to the status of town burgess became more restricted over time.[14] Associated with that development were dramatic economic and social changes that resulted in heightened tensions among the villagers themselves. Keith Wrightson and Martin Ingram, among others, have noted that the late sixteenth-century English countryside experienced a dramatic polarization between the wealthy and the poor. As the population increased, the ranks of the laboring poor doubled in size.[15] Both historians expected such social polarization to result in growing disagreements about the types of behavior required of successful community life.[16] In Terling, conflict developed between innovating yeomen and the families of laboring poor "whose behavior they regarded as morally and socially reprehensible." Puritan sentiment among those yeomen families exacerbated this sense of social alienation between the two groups.[17]

Related to that concern are the debates over the relationship in rural village life between the tendency to group action in pursuit of corporate or "communal" interests and the centrifugal forces of "individualism."[18] Alan Mcfariane and Keith Thomas suggested that con-

---

[13] For summaries of this discussion, see Fletcher, "National and Local Awareness in the County Communities," pp. 151–54; and Hughes.

[14] A. R. DeWindt, "Local Government in a Small Town: A Medieval Leet Jury and Its Constituents," *Albion* 23, no. 4 (1991): 627–54; Marjorie McIntosh, *A Community Transformed: The Manor and Liberty of Havering, 1500–1620* (Cambridge, 1991), p. 326.

[15] Keith Wrightson and David Levine, *Poverty and Piety in an English Village: Terling, 1525–1700* (New York, 1979), p. 175; Martin Ingram, *Church Courts, Sex and Marriage in England, 1570–1640* (Cambridge, 1987), pp. 32–33. Also, Barry Coward cites E. Kerridge's study of Wiltshire in *Social Change and Continuity in Early Modern England: 1550–1750* (London, 1988), p. 52. Also see Derek Hirst, *Authority and Conflict: England, 1603–1658* (London, 1986), pp. 14 ff. Victor Skipp's study *Crisis and Development: An Ecological Case Study of the Forest of Arden, 1570–1674* (Cambridge, 1978) points out that polarization could be caused by immigration as well as engrossment.

[16] See Wrightson and Levine, p. 176; and Ingram, pp. 32–33.

[17] Wrightson and Levine, pp. 175, 177. David Underdown also notes that "parish notables" had a sense of being a beleaguered minority "beset by chaos and disorder"; see *Revel, Riot, and Rebellion: Popular Politics and Culture in England, 1603–1660* (Oxford, 1985), p. 33.

[18] Along these lines, see Clive Holmes's discussion of "the closed corporate peasant community" as a concept discordant with his Lincolnshire evidence, *Seventeenth-Century Lincolnshire* (Lincoln, 1980), pp. 9 ff. Calhoun suggests that we be wary of

flicting ideals of community life inspired many of the Essex witchcraft prosecutions, as villagers clung to traditional communal values of mutual assistance while craving the economic opportunities promised by greater individual freedom—a freedom that required release from restrictive obligations to one's less fortunate neighbors.[19] Medievalists have noted similar tensions as far back as the fourteenth century.[20]

For some early modernists, changing religious beliefs are credited with important changes in ritual community identity and, in some cases, with the disintegration of older communal ideals. Many Puritans disapproved of traditional village rites and ceremonies such as church ales, or May revels. As William Hunt argues, "The Preachers proposed to substitute for the culture of neighborhood and good fellowship a new culture of discipline."[21] Spufford pointed out that in some Cambridge parishes Dissenters, as a small minority of the population, were forced to abandon their local parish churches and recreate religious communities of their own that transcended their traditional neighborhoods. But she also points out the dangers of assuming that issues of social control were new to the sixteenth century.[22]

The Warboys witchcraft case can contribute to several of these ongoing conversations. On the one hand, its drama arose from a highly localized dispute between neighbors within the boundaries of a single parish, but it also fed upon the Puritan zeal of gentry kin from another county and eventually attracted the full weight of royal justice. Boundaries were fluid, and communities of varying scope merged with one another and periodically reconstituted themselves as they became relevant.[23] Neighbors drew upon parish-wide witnesses in support of their cause. Kin from another county assisted in drawing the witches to the attention of a local Huntingdonshire J.P. who in turn prepared the case to be heard before assize judges sent from Westminster. Other kinds

---

efforts to set up a dichotomy between "individual" and "community," as "it suggests, misleadingly, the possibility of an asocial individual"; see Calhoun, p. 109.

[19] Macfarlane (n. 5 above).

[20] J. A. Raftis, *Warboys: Two Hundred Years in the Life of an English Mediaeval Village* (Toronto, 1974), chap. 7; E. B. DeWindt, *Land and People in Holywell-Cum-Needingworth* (Toronto, 1972), chap. 4; Edward Britton, *The Community of the Vill: A Study in the History of the Family and Village Life in Fourteenth-Century England* (Toronto, 1977), pp. 108–9.

[21] Hunt (n. 1 above), p. 140.

[22] Spufford, *Contrasting Communities* (n. 10 above), pp. 344–50, and also "Puritanism and Social Control?" in *Order and Disorder in Early Modern England*, ed. Anthony Fletcher and John Stevenson (Cambridge, 1985), pp. 41–57.

[23] Describing a parallel situation, Gervase Rosser found in Westminster that cooperation among individuals was periodic and arose in response to particular, and often temporary, needs; see *Medieval Westminster, 1200–1540* (Oxford, 1989), p. 327.

of boundaries were violated with tragic consequences. Witches violated the sanctuary of home and hearth, and strangers from outside the parish and county pressed felony charges that ultimately violated a yeoman family's fundamental right to survival.

Most important was the arrival of a gentry family into a village unaccustomed to making space for such a neighbor; this was the violation that preceded all the others. The Throckmortons were not simply the self-proclaimed victims of witchcraft—they were intruders. Mother Samuel's threatening penetration into the manor house hearthside on that fall day in 1589 was inadequate retribution for that even more disruptive invasion of a small rural village by a gentry family bearing a name with the faded hints of national fame and courtly connections.[24]

The Warboys witch case thus invites particular investigation into the relationships between fellow villagers. There is usually a moral dimension to discussions of community life, in the sense that individuals commonly assume that there are benefits to be achieved from participation in successful communities, but that the success of those communities depends upon the appropriate behavior and/or sentiment on the part of its constituents.[25] The Warboys "community" invoked in this discussion relates not so much to a sociological reality as to the "something imagined" that Gillian Rose recently described in her reference to historians' stubborn insistence on interpreting the term "community," "to be not a social structure but a structure of meaning." The focus of this essay on Warboys is "with community as a contested idea, as something imagined."[26] If modern nationalists have been ready to die for their "imagined communities," it is clear that Robert Throckmorton was certainly ready to kill for his.[27]

---

[24] For a similar situation in an eighteenth-century village, see David Rollison, "Property, Ideology and Popular Culture," *Past and Present,* no. 93 (1981), pp. 70–97.

[25] Notice Calhoun (n. 11 above), pp. 107 ff.

[26] Gillian Rose, "Imagining Poplar in the 1920s: Contested Concepts of Community," *Journal of Historical Geography* 16, no. 4 (1990): 425–37. Quotations above are from pp. 425 and 426. I owe this reference to Bruce Campbell, Queens University, Belfast.

[27] Recent research has demonstrated the usefulness of recognizing a broad variety of causal factors, from economic stress to class or gender conflicts to psychological trauma. For a few examples, see John Demos, *Entertaining Satan: Witchcraft and the Culture of Early New England* (Oxford, 1983); Carol Karlsen, *The Devil in the Shape of a Woman: Witchcraft in Colonial New England* (New York, 1987); Michael MacDonald, *Witchcraft and Hysteria in Elizabethan London: Edward Jorden and the Mary Glover Case* (London, 1991); Lyndal Roper, *Oedipus and the Devil: Witchcraft, Sexuality and Religion in Early Modern Europe* (London, 1994). For a study of witchcraft accusations with a background of disputes between neighbors and town factions, see Annabel Gregory, "Witchcraft, Politics and 'Good Neighbourhood' in Early Seventeenth-Century

The village of Warboys, Huntingdonshire, offers an opportunity to examine sixteenth-century concepts of the ideal community based on pamphlet evidence as well as on the traditional manorial sources associated with medieval and early modern village studies. The Warboys witchcraft narrative provides insights into the authors' ideas about the behavior required of village neighbors, but it also reveals clues to the attitudes that underlay the behavior of the authors' antagonists who were hanged.[28]

The Warboys evidence demonstrates that disagreements among villagers about the characteristics of a good neighbor took place at the upper end of the social scale, and furthermore, the pamphlet provides an opportunity to examine more specifically the nature of those disagreements. Although yeomen may have gravitated into the same camp with the gentry because "they were . . . less likely to share the interests and concerns of the numerous poor,"[29] in the Warboys case, the yeoman Samuels family, instead of allying itself with the Throckmortons, stood its ground in opposition to them.

The late sixteenth-century sources from Warboys offer two important advantages. First, my own research has revealed that thirty of the thirty-two personal names mentioned in the pamphlet text can be identified from a variety of contemporary fiscal and judicial documents, placing the main characters of this drama into a more precise social context than is usually possible with English witchcraft cases. Second, the pamphlet text itself is a rich narrative source, complete with carefully observed details surrounding those events deemed particularly significant by the authors and including extended passages of dialogue between the Samuels and their accusers from which the "witches' " voices can be excavated, buried as they are in the rhetoric

---

Rye," *Past and Present*, no. 133 (1991), pp. 31–66. J. A. Sharpe summarized the standard approach to English witchcraft by citing "the fundamental importance of stresses in interpersonal relations between villagers in generating witchcraft accusations": *Witchcraft in Seventeenth-Century Yorkshire: Accusations and Counter Measures*, Borthwick Paper no. 81 (York: University of York, 1992), p. 1.

[28] The Warboys case will also, of course, continue to provide contributions to those discussions and controversies about the witchcraft phenomenon. Indeed, this one case does suggest causal factors not yet fully explored. For summaries of current theories, see Geoffrey Scarre, *Witchcraft and Magic in Sixteenth- and Seventeenth-Century Europe* (Atlantic Highlands, N.Y., 1987); and Brian P. Levack, *The Witch-Hunt in Early Modern Europe* (London, 1987); Joseph Klaits, *Servants of Satan: The Age of the Witch Hunts* (Bloomington, Ind., 1985). Notice also Sharpe's appreciation of single cases which can provide qualitative evidence on witchcraft questions. See his *Witchcraft in Seventeenth-Century Yorkshire: Accusations and Counter Measures*, p. 23.

[29] Hirst (n. 15 above), p. 15.

of the staunchly unsympathetic authors. The Warboys pamphlet thus offers a rare opportunity to examine two points of view: those of the accusers as well as those of the witches themselves.

The purpose of the essay is to tease these opposing viewpoints out of the contemporary sources and to suggest that, in this case at least, a witchcraft accusation was nurtured within an environment in which neighbors held incompatible expectations about how best to share their community. This incompatibility was certainly not the sole reason for the witchcraft accusations, but it does represent another ingredient in the complex array of factors contributing to the Warboys tragedy.

This conflict between the Samuels and the Throckmorton party took place during a time when hundreds of English villages were experiencing the arrival of new residents claiming superior social status and taking great pains to demonstrate and validate their claims to deference through such means as the instruments of heraldry.[30] Control of vast amounts of crown and former monastic properties shifted into the hands of the gentry. In the early fifteenth century, approximately 25 percent of landed property in England was in the hands of gentry families. By the late seventeenth century this proportion had grown dramatically to between 45 and 50 percent.[31] And, perhaps more important, it has been estimated that fewer than half of all English villages had resident gentry at the beginning of the sixteenth century, and by the later seventeenth century this percentage had risen to three-quarters.[32]

Such an important change in the sociological map of local settlements must certainly have had profound effects on villagers. Warboys offers an opportunity to study individual personalities with direct experience of one such invasion. Robert Throckmorton, his wife, and their seven children made a tragically unsuccessful attempt to "fit" into the social landscape of their fenland village. Their struggle was certainly shared by hundreds of other purchasers of crown properties after the dissolution of the monasteries.[33] In the county of Huntingdonshire as

---

[30] John Bedells, "The Gentry of Huntingdonshire," *Local Population Studies* 44 (1990): 30–40.

[31] G. E. Mingay, *The Gentry: The Rise and Fall of a Ruling Class* (London, 1976), pp. 58–59.

[32] Underdown (n. 17 above), p. 21.

[33] For a summary of the work done on the fate of crown lands during the sixteenth century, see W. G. Hoskins, *The Age of Plunder, King Henry's England, 1500–47* (London, 1976), pp. 121–38.

a whole, for example, the number of resident gentry rose from nine in 1539 to sixty-one in 1613.[34]

My argument will begin with a look at the contemporary legal and fiscal sources in order to establish the identities and social strata of the main characters—their external personae. Next, the pamphlet language will be analyzed in order to unearth the Throckmorton and Samuel points of view—their internal, mental, personae.

The physical setting that provided home and inspiration for these conflicting views was a fenland village formerly belonging to Ramsey Abbey, "Ramsey the Rich." In 1540, Robert Throckmorton's father Gabriel had acquired the lease of the Warboys manor site from Richard Cromwell, who had purchased the Huntingdonshire estates of Ramsey Abbey.[35] Prior to the Throckmorton purchase of the Warboys manor site, that property had been leased by the abbot of Ramsey to a husbandman, John Mayhue, for a rent of £8 per year, the same rent paid by Throckmorton.[36] Gabriel died thirteen years after acquiring this property, leaving his widow and infant son residing in Warboys by the early 1550s.[37]

Robert was therefore raised in a village unaccustomed to rendering special place to a resident of his social class. Richard Cromwell himself had never resided in Warboys, and Gabriel probably resided in Warboys only thirteen years. The pamphlet insists that the adult Robert Throckmorton, "esquire,"[38] was a newcomer to Warboys in the fall of 1589, probably in order to eliminate the reader's possible suspicion that some long-standing feud between neighbors would explain Mother Samuel's hostility to the head of the Throckmorton family.[39] In fact, there is evidence that son Robert may have lived elsewhere when he was a very young man. Gabriel had purchased the manor of Ellington shortly before his death, and Robert was his only male heir. Wardship for Robert went to the crown and was accounted

---

[34] Bedells, table 1, p. 39. Huntingdonshire had a particularly large number of monastic estates.

[35] William Page, Granville Proby, and S. Inskip Ladds, eds., *The Victoria History of the County of Huntingdon* (London, 1932), 2:243.

[36] A 1540 Indenture, British Library Additional (Brit. Lib. Add.) MS 34397.

[37] The Inquest Post Mortem indicates that Gabriel was dead by January 6, 1553, Public Record Office (PRO) C142/98/27.

[38] "Witches of Warboys," sig. A3r.

[39] Ibid., sig. A4r. "This thing did something move the Parents, and strike into their minds a suspicion of witchcraft, yet devising with themselves for what cause it should be wrought upon them or their children, they could not imagine, for they were but newly come to the towne to inhabite, which was but at Michaelmas before, neither had they given any occasion (to their knowledge) either to her or any other, to practise any such malice against them."

for by Gabriel's brother, Simon Throckmorton of Brampton.[40] The young Robert Throckmorton thus probably spent much of his childhood in Ellington and Brampton and may have resided in Ellington when he first married, although his children were baptized in Titchmarsh and Warboys.[41] The reasons for Robert's presumed move back to Warboys in the fall of 1589 into the household of his widowed mother are not provided by the pamphlet authors. In any case, by the time Throckmorton's children were baptized at Warboys in the 1570s and 1580s, it had been about thirty years since an adult male representative of the Throckmorton family had resided in that village.

Prior to the arrival of Gabriel Throckmorton, and the eventual presence of his adult son, Warboys tenants had exercised considerable control over local affairs. Through their village leet court, presided over by the abbot's steward, but run by panels of jurors chosen from among Warboys tenants, villagers had regulated the plowing and harvesting of their fields, settled disputes over rights to common marsh and pasture, and had registered licenses for the selling of ale, land transfers, and debt obligations. In many ways, Warboys had been a self-governing community. There is no doubt but that the larger landholders in a village such as Warboys held sway over their poorer neighbors, and certainly over the landless laborers and servants, but these more substantial tenants did so through the institutions of the village court. It is unclear how a man such as Master Throckmorton could have found his place among those long-established power relationships.

Neither Robert Throckmorton, nor his father Gabriel, as far as can be known, ever served on the Warboys village jury. Taking a leadership role within the context of long-established village courts might have been unsuitable for a man who was not out in the fields plowing side by side with his neighbors. However, the jurors of the neighboring village of Upwood served side by side with a member of the gentry. He was sworn with eleven of his "fellow" villagers and listed at the head of the 1568 court roll as William Taylard "generosus." Whether Taylard's service was inspired by a sense of duty, or by some astute political calculation that this would be of personal benefit to him, there is no evidence that Robert Throckmorton was of like mind.[42] Perhaps the Throckmortons' illustrious family history of

---

[40] PRO Ward 8/8 fols. 359v.–360r.

[41] Parish registers of Titchmarsh, Northants., and Warboys, Hunts.: Titchmarsh: 1573. Warboys: 1574, 1575, 1577, 1579, 1583.

[42] Brit. Lib. Add. roll 34842. Marjorie McIntosh noted the presence of members of the gentry on Havering juries by the 1560s and 1570s; McIntosh (n. 14 above), p. 323.

connections at Court prevented the possibility of their sitting side by side with customary tenants in so lowly a forum as village politics.[43]

Warboys was a fairly small parish, and the Throckmortons were the wealthiest family among only about seventy resident families.[44] Even if the Throckmortons had wanted to retire into some sheltered and isolated obscurity, such a tactic could never have worked.

And so Robert Throckmorton was left to his own devices, with little guiding precedent, in the daunting task of finding his "place" in Warboys. Indeed, once his children were placed in danger from witchcraft, and direct action against the Samuels was required, he seemed determined to play a leadership role in a community with which he closely identified. The witchcraft accusations would have been inconceivable unless Robert and his family felt intimately tied to the Warboys villagers' reality in some way or other. Only as part of that community could they feel genuinely threatened by the web of psychic stresses within it.[45] One hundred years later, by the eighteenth century, resident gentry were further removed from the social and cultural life of their tenants, and the psychological proximity necessary for witchcraft accusations would be a thing of the past.[46]

Christina Larner suggested that witch hunts were "the pursuit of ideological crime in the process of legitimizing new regimes."[47] These new regimes are usually associated with national monarchies. However, the Warboys evidence demonstrates that a similar process had local significance much further down the social ladder. Many English villages through their leet and frankpledge courts had, in a practical sense, run most of their local affairs without the interfering presence of resident landlords, or from any member of the gentry, for that matter.[48] Gabriel Throckmorton and, soon thereafter, his son Robert had stepped into a

[43] Robert was the grandson of Richard Throckmorton, steward of the duke of Lancaster and great-grandson of Sir Robert Throckmorton, J.P., descended from the Throckmortons of Coughton, Warwickshire; see Henry Ellis, ed., *The Visitation of the County of Huntingdon*, Camden Society (London, 1849), pp. 123–24; also A. L. Rowse, *Ralegh and the Throckmortons* (London, 1962).

[44] Brit. Lib. Harl. MS 618 temp. Elizabeth.

[45] Mary Douglas, *Witchcraft Confessions and Accusations* (London, 1970), p. xxx; Demos (n. 27 above), pp. 275, 311–12.

[46] Lawrence Stone and Jeanne C. Fawtier Stone, *An Open Elite? England, 1540–1880* (Oxford, 1984), p. 329.

[47] Christina Larner discusses the phenomenon here in a European context, *Witchcraft and Religion: The Politics of Popular Belief* (Oxford: Blackwell, 1985), p. 139.

[48] For local studies within Huntingdonshire itself, see, e.g., E. DeWindt (n. 20 above), esp. discussions of the village court on pp. 206–11; Raftis (n. 20 above); and Britton (n. 20 above). For other regions, see, e.g., McIntosh (n. 10 above); and Spufford (n. 10 above).

village with years of experience in self-government. As cousins of royal courtiers, there is little wonder that the Throckmortons brought ideas and behavior patterns into a settlement of fenland villagers that were seen by at least some of the locals as alien and unwelcome.

Closely associated with the Throckmortons throughout the pamphlet, and a close ally in their efforts to bring the Warboys witch drama to a successful conclusion, was the Pickering family of Titchmarsh, Northamptonshire. Gilbert Pickering is described in the pamphlet as the afflicted girls' uncle, and the Northamptonshire visitation of 1618 testifies that Gilbert was the brother of Elizabeth Pickering, wife of Robert Throckmorton.[49] The "rise of the Pickerings" has been celebrated by one historian who cites their successful climb in social status, from husbandman to knight of the shire by 1625, as characteristic of the age.[50]

Because historians have noticed that Puritan affiliations could sometimes alienate families from traditional community ties, it is important to notice the evidence of Puritan leanings among members of the Pickering family.[51] As early as 1576 there is evidence that the Pickering family identified themselves unequivocally with the Puritan cause, and Shiels suggests that Gilbert I married Dorothy Brown, a member of the separatist family.[52] Pickering's home manor of Titchmarsh, Northamptonshire, was in a region profoundly influenced by Puritan sentiments by the end of the sixteenth century.[53] The grandmother of the sick girls, Emma Throckmorton, left a will whose preamble reflects her Puritan sympathies.[54] Perhaps she arranged her son Robert's marriage to the Titchmarsh Pickering family because of this shared religious commitment.

---

[49] Walter C. Metcalfe, ed., *The Visitations of Northamptonshire made in 1564 and 1618-19* (London, 1887), p. 126.

[50] W. J. Sheils, *The Puritans in the Diocese of Peterborough, 1558-1610* (Northampton, 1979), p. 12. See also Helen Belgion, *Titchmarsh Past and Present* (Northants.: Privately published by the author, 1979), pp. 38, 46.

[51] Hunt (n. 1 above), p. 140. See also Wrightson and Levine (n. 15 above), p. 175; Christopher Haigh, "The Church of England, the Catholics and the People," in *The Reign of Elizabeth I*, ed. C. Haigh (London, 1984), pp. 195-219.

[52] Sheils, p. 40.

[53] "From 1583 Titchmarsh remained a puritan centre" (ibid., p. 40).

[54] The will, dated 1600, requested that Bartholomew Chamberlain preach at her burial. "I committ my sowle into the handes of the almightie and most mercifull father my creator and to Jhesus Christe his onlie sonne my redemer and saviour. And to God the holie Ghost my comforter and of all the elect of God" (PRO B. 11/97 30 Woodhall). For a discussion of the use of will preambles as indicators of religious preference, along with a useful bibliography on the subject, see Patrick Collinson, *The Religion of Protestants: The Church in English Society, 1559-1625* (Oxford, 1982), p. 197, and notes on pp. 196-97; also Sheils.

The Throckmortons' antagonists in this witch drama, and near neighbors to the north of the manor house, were John, Alice, and Agnes Samuel. Unlike the Throckmortons, John and Alice had deep roots in the Huntingdonshire village milieu. There were Ramsey Abbey tenants bearing the Samuel name in nearby Bury as early as 1493, and several men and women of that name appear in Upwood court rolls and parish registers between 1560 and 1599. John Samuel married Alicia Ybbot in Upwood in 1561, when Alice would have been about forty-six years old.[55]

Mother Samuel may well have been a widow when she married John Samuel. In any case the surname Ybbot appears regularly in the Upwood manorial court rolls and parish registers between the 1520s and 1580s. Both they and the Samuels were probably fairly substantial tenants because their names appear now and then on the lists of village jurors. Furthermore, John Samuel was among the seven names listed in the Upwood lay subsidy of 1568, identifying him with the more substantial villagers.[56]

The key figures in the Warboys witch drama therefore represented social groups a little higher on the social scale than is often found in English witchcraft cases.[57] The trial of Mother Samuel before the Huntingdon assizes of 1593 pitted a local yeoman family with deep roots in the villages of northern Huntingdonshire against branches of two renowned gentle families with a history of court connections, the Throckmortons and Cromwells, and against a third Northamptonshire gentry family newly "risen" from the ranks of local husbandmen and exhibiting strong Puritan connections—the Pickerings.

We turn now to the Warboys pamphlet in an attempt to explore the inner lives and motives of these major actors in the witch drama. That pamphlet was written within a contentious social framework, fraught with ambiguities. The authors of the pamphlet describe in remarkable detail the Samuels' trial and the four years culminating in their convictions. Edward Fenner, the judge who sentenced the three accused witches, is cited by the authors as their patron, but the authors themselves are not named. Several clues within the text itself indicate

[55] "Witches of Warboys," sig. O2v. Upwood court rolls between 1560 and 1599: Brit. Lib. Add. Rolls 34841–34850, 34924–34928.

[56] PRO E179/122/161; seven were taxed out of a community of forty-seven households (Brit. Lib. Harl. Ms. 618).

[57] Macfarlane (n. 5 above). For another case involving daughters of a gentry family from Fewstone, West Riding, Yorkshire, in the year 1621, see R. M. Milnes, ed., *A Discourse of Witchcraft*, Miscellanies of the Philobiblon Soc., vol. 5 (London, 1858–59). Also see Sharpe (n. 27 above).

that Gilbert Pickering, Throckmorton's brother-in-law, was most likely one of the authors and that more than one person contributed to the narrative. Robert Throckmorton himself, the father of the bewitched girls, was probably a coauthor, with contributions from the parson of Warboys and Judge Fenner himself.[58]

The self-justifying tone of the pamphlet, designed to demonstrate the guilt of the Samuels and to dispel doubts about the justice of the court verdict, further indicates that the family of the young girls was responsible for the publication of this narrative.[59] Evidence of the Throckmorton/Pickering attitudes toward community life therefore will be more clearly and unambiguously reflected in the pamphlet language itself than will the attitudes of the accused witches, who did not have an opportunity to publish their own version of events. The Pickering/Throckmorton version of events and the resulting text which gives us access to their point of view will be explored first. The particular difficulties of unearthing the Samuel point of view from a text they did not create themselves will be discussed later on.

The pamphlet narrative unmasks Robert Throckmorton most powerfully and effectively by reproducing a speech he delivered to Alice Samuel at the climax of their deadly struggle. Poignantly self-revelatory, this speech confirms the power of those personal and psychological links that locked Robert into an increasingly unbearable relationship with the tormentors of his "innocent" daughters and the Warboys neighbors they all shared. Just when a Throckmorton victory by way of confession and reconciliation had seemed finally to be won, Alice rescinded her first confession of guilt. It was after that loss of a highly valued victory that Robert Throckmorton forced another encounter with Alice in order to say to her, "I will not let passe this matter thus, for seeing it is published, either you or I will beare the shame of it in the end."[60]

---

[58] See "Witches of Warboys," sig. F2v, for reference to the pamphlet's patron. There are several references in the text to plural authors: sigs. B4r, H2v, H3r, C2v. The pronouns "I" and "we" are both used on sig. A2r and A2v. Barbara Rosen, who has published a modernized and condensed version of the British Museum edition of the pamphlet, points out that the pamphlet must have been produced by several authors, *Witchcraft in England, 1558–1618* (Amherst, Mass., 1991), p. 240, n. 2.

[59] Notice the defensive tone established in this passage from "Witches of Warboys," sig. H1r: "These circumstances about her [Alice Samuel's] confession are therefore the more expresly set downe although they be not so pertinent to the matter, neither indeed should have bin declared at all, had it not bin reported by some in the countrey, and those that thought themselves wise, that this mother Samuel now in question, was an olde simple woman, and that one might make her by fayre words confesse what they would."

[60] Ibid., sig. G4r.

In that important speech Robert identifies himself with Mother
Samuel and the group of neighbors that they both share. To share
susceptibility to shame is to share an intimate sociological context.
Only individuals closely connected with one another can suffer shame
because of the behavior of that "other." The intimacy of this connection is revealed in some of the most important episodes of the pamphlet—those describing the intensely emotional moments of confession and temporary reconciliation, whereby the Throckmorton view
of reality had been, at least temporarily, imposed upon, and accepted
by, the "witch."

The old woman had been pressured into confessing her guilt after
a prolonged stay at the manor house with the Throckmorton family
when she was exposed regularly to the children's fits and was able to
see for herself that her own presence in the house had a direct effect
on their behavior. Mother Samuel made her original confession in a
very emotional scene in which she was presumably reconciled with
her accusers and received their forgiveness.

> O sir said she, I have been the cause of all this trouble to your
> children. Have you mother Samuel said he? and why so? what cause did
> I ever give you thus to use me and my children? None at all said she.
> Then said master Throckmorton, you have done mee the more wrong.
> Good master, said she, forgive me. God forgive you said he, and I doe.
> But tell me, how came you to be such a kinde of woman? Master, saide
> shee, I have forsaken my maker, and given my soule to the divell (these
> were her very wordes.) And olde mistresse Throcmorton their grand-
> mother, and mistresse Throcmorton their mother, being now in the hall
> (for this was done in the parlour), hearing them very loud (not understand-
> ing the matter perfectly) came into the parlour, of whom, (when mother
> Samuel saw her) shee asked likewise forgivenesse. Mistresse Throcmor-
> ton their mother, presently without any questions forgave her with all
> her heart, yet she could not well tell what the matter was. Mother Samuel
> asked those three children that were there forgivenes and afterwards the
> rest, kissing al of them: the children easily forgave her, for they knew
> not that shee had offended any of them, in their own persons: (except
> what they sawe in their sisters, when they themselves were out of their
> fits.) Master Throckmorton and his wife, perceiving the old woman thus
> penitent, and so greatly cast downe: for she did nothing but weep and
> lament al this time, comforted her by al the good meanes they could, and
> said that they would freely forgive her from their harts, so be it their
> children might never be more troubled.[61]

---

[61] Ibid., sig. G3r.

On the next day, Sunday, December 24, 1592, the parson delivered a sermon in church on the theme of the "penitent hart."[62] According to the pamphlet, Mother Samuel "answered before them all that it [her confession] came of her selfe, and desired all her neihbours to pray to God for her, and to forgive her."[63]

Shortly thereafter, on Christmas day, Alice Samuel "revolted." The pamphlet authors blame her husband and her daughter for talking her into denying her original confession. Her daughter Agnes was reported to have said to her mother, "Beleeve them not beleave them not, for all their faire speeches."[64] Throckmorton and the Warboys parson, Francis Dorrington, therefore felt compelled to press on with their formal prosecution of Mother Samuel in spite of the earlier reconciliation.

Alice Samuel's denial of her earlier confession elicited an immediate response from Robert. He understood her rejection of her confession and the resulting challenge to his own explanation for his family's suffering as a serious danger. Robert behaved as a man under attack. He went that very evening, along with the Warboys pastor, "to her house to know the truth." She answered that she would deny that she was a witch or any cause of the troubling of his children.

"Why, sayd he, did not you confess so much unto me? I sayd so (saith she), indeede, but it is nothing so. Why then, sayd he, I must not shew you that favour which I promised: I will surely have you before the Justices: but sayd he, why did you confesse it to be so to me, if it be not so?"[65]

The historian's task here is to identify the motives for those forceful words—"I will surely have you before the Justices."

Robert's concerns by that point transcended even the matter of his children's health. That issue had, at least for the moment, faded into relative insignificance, because the girls' fits had abated after the initial confession and reconciliation. Indeed, when Alice Samuel referred to "your children so presently well," Robert brushed aside that point—one that might appear critically important to a twentieth-century observer—by saying "I pray God so continue them, notwithstanding howsoever it bee, I will not let passe this matter thus, for

---

[62] On that occasion, Alice may have donned a white sheet and carried a wand as she made her public confession before her neighbors in the Warboys church. See Kathleen Major, "The Lincoln Diocesan Records," *Transactions of the Royal Historical Society*, 4th ser., 22 (1940): 63.

[63] "Witches of Warboys," sig. G3v.

[64] Ibid., sig. G3v–G4r.

[65] Ibid., sig. G4r.

seeing it is published, either you or I will beare the shame of it in the end."[66] If the children were at that point cured, why was the matter not dropped? Answering this question requires an understanding of Robert's use of the word "shame."

Robert seemed to believe that the two of them, he and Alice, had reached the most critical test for them both so far in their shared adventure. The decision he made at this point would determine who would bear the burden of some future shame. Either Alice would be shamed, or he would. Robert was not speaking here as a helpless observer. He was not throwing his hands up in the air and making the simple prediction—"One of us is guilty. When the truly guilty one is properly identified as such—that one will be assigned the inevitable shame (public censure) that is companion to all such guilt." Robert was not passive. He was as forceful and as active an agent as he ever was or ever would be again in the entire course of the pamphlet narrative. Robert felt that he had clearly been backed up against a wall at this point and must take action.

The clue to Robert's behavior lies in identifying properly the source of shame. Contrary to what a modern reader might assume, it never occurs to Robert that he could be guilty either of his children's suffering or of Mother Samuel's plight as accused witch. The pamphlet tells us that Robert went to Pastor Dorrington's house the day after his conversation with Mother Samuel about her recantation and repeated his assertion that "he would not suffer this matter thus to die in his hand, least the worser sorte of the people should imagine that this was but some devisse of theirs, to bring the olde woman into further danger."[67]

Suffering this matter to die in Throckmorton's hand must entail allowing Alice's rejection of her confession to remain unchallenged, with the result being that no prosecution is pursued. The danger referred to in the above quotation therefore could not be any danger to Alice resulting from her prosecution before the assize judges. In a reflection of Throckmorton's sensitivity to public opinion, he expresses the fear that the "worser sorte of the people" must be suspecting him and the parson of plotting some other "danger" for Mother Samuel rather than the dangers of a trial.

At first a modern reader might think that Robert meant that he could not bear the shame of being seen by others as a persecutor of innocent old women, and thus his own avoidance of shame required

[66] Ibid.
[67] Ibid.

him to prove once and for all that Alice was, indeed, guilty as a witch. But that is not what the pamphlet authors mean to say about Robert here. Robert knew Alice was guilty. He was not in danger of suffering any shame resulting from the persecution or prosecution of an innocent old woman for one very important reason—Alice simply was not innocent in his eyes. The pamphlet did not suggest that the worser sort might accuse him of persecuting an innocent woman. Throckmorton imagined that "the worser sorte" had some other danger in mind for Mother Samuel other than the hangman.

It might be helpful to look at the quotation again, in its complete form: "Then said Master Throckmorton unto her, . . . I will not let passe this matter thus, for seeing it is published, either you or I will beare the shame of it in the end; and so they departed for that night. The next morning betimes, master Throckmorton went to master Doctor Doringtons house, and tolde him, that he would not suffer this matter thus to die in his hand, least the worser sorte of the people should imagine that this was but some devisse of theirs, to bring the olde woman into further danger."

Robert's shame would lie in *failure* to prosecute. It would be failure to prosecute rather than the prosecution itself which would "bring the olde woman into further danger." The real "further" danger to Alice lay in her refusal to confess, not in any legal action Robert could bring down on her head. When the pamphlet says that people might imagine that "this" was but some device to bring the old woman into further danger, it is not referring to any plans to prosecute, but to the possibility that this matter should "thus to die in his hand." He says that letting the matter die would encourage some people to think that "this" was some device to endanger her. Prosecution is not the device in question, because "letting the matter die" involves just the opposite—letting the matter die means refusal to prosecute.

In other words, Alice Samuel's denial of her confession left the matter in Robert's hands. He could either acquiesce and accept her denial, thereby giving the false impression he had changed his mind and no longer believed her to be a witch, or he could challenge her again and stand by his original contention that she was, indeed, a witch. As Robert saw things, Alice (and probably all of Warboys as well) could only be brought to further danger if he, Robert, failed to challenge her denial. "So they agreed to approve [charge] her once agayne in this matter."[68] Throckmorton's self-respect, and therefore

[68] ibid.

his vulnerability to shame, rested on the fulfillment of his patriarchal responsibilities to Alice Samuel and to their shared community.

The key lies in recognizing that shame is an emotion that grows out of the realization that other people see us and judge us. Throckmorton's concern is with shame rather than with guilt and is therefore related to public esteem rather than private self-assessment. Shame is a public emotion that comes to life in response to public opinion (real or imagined). One is watched by others who judge. Unlike guilt, shame requires an audience in a world where the public and the private realm are hardly distinguished. Robert was not acting as a lone individual pursuing a vendetta against a private enemy. In his mind, the entire village, and even the entire county, was involved in his drama. He drew upon this perception of social interdependence to make sense of the drama and to pursue a strategy that would bring it to a satisfactory conclusion. The men and women of Warboys are assumed by Robert Throckmorton to value a standard of behavior by which they measure his actions. He suffers shame when he sees himself through their eyes. To lose the esteem of the members of one's "public" is to lose honor. For Throckmorton, the inhabitants of Warboys made up an important part of his honor group.[69]

Stepping into the paternalistic role assumed by his class, Throckmorton was forging an identity for himself within the context of Warboys sociology, and in that process, he was introducing a new niche into the social hierarchy of Warboys inhabitants. He was very sensitive to the necessity of living up to the expectations he assumed villagers would have for a member of his class.

The fact that Robert Throckmorton was vulnerable to shame underscores his dependence on the men and women of Warboys. As their social superior, he took upon himself the responsibility of living up to their presumed expectations. Indeed, paternalism, when successful, produces a system of interdependence that binds both the master and his social inferiors into a single honor group.[70]

Demonstrating his awareness of the powerful role played by the honor group that both he and Mother Samuel shared, Robert staged

---

[69] For a helpful discussion of the significance of the emotions of shame and guilt, see Gabriele Taylor, *Emotions of Self Assessment* (Oxford, 1985), esp. pp. 56–82. I owe this reference to Beatrice Beech. For references to studies of honor and shame in the Renaissance context, see J. A. Sharpe, *Defamation and Sexual Slander in Early Modern England: The Church Courts at York*, Borthwick Papers, no. 58 (York: University of York, 1980).

[70] Eugene D. Genovese, *Roll Jordan Roll: The World the Slaves Made* (New York, 1964).

Mother Samuel's second confession very carefully. After arranging to have the old woman confess to Pastor Dorrington in the front parlor of the manor house where Dorrington was to write down her words, Throckmorton walked through the neighboring churchyard and into the parish church where services were then being held. He led a number of worshipers outside and gathered them underneath the parlor window of his manor house to listen in secret to the proceedings within. He did this, not only because he wanted them all to be convinced of Alice's guilt, but so that they as a group could make it more difficult for her to deny that confession, once it was made. Indeed, the pamphlet reports that after her neighbors heard the confession, they said to her, "Nay, . . . it is too late to denie any thing now, for we heard all this with our eares."[71]

Robert recognized the power and importance of his neighbors in two ways. First, he used their presence to pressure Alice into sticking by her confession and owning up to her guilt. At some level, even though Robert was personally convinced of Alice's guilt, he still needed to know that his fellow villagers agreed with him. He may, in fact, have been vulnerable to the shame that would fall upon him if he failed to convince his neighbors that she was truly guilty of witchcraft. The efficacy of his leadership was at stake, but his vulnerability to shame operated on more than one level. The power of his community of neighbors was still operative in helping him create his own understanding of reality. The pamphlet authors reflect a sensitivity to the threatening presence of dissent in the following passage: "These circumstances about her confession are therefore the more expresly set downe although they be not so pertinent to the matter, neither indeed should have bin declared at all, had it not bin reported by some in the countrey, and those that thought themselves wise, that this mother Samuel now in question, was an olde simple woman, and that one might make her by fayre words confesse what they would."[72]

Robert Throckmorton thus took upon himself the responsibility for Alice Samuel's confession. His original intention had been to reconcile her with his own family and through them to bring about reconciliation with her family and the community as a whole. It was for this reason he had asked her, after her first confession, "before his neighbours, whether that confession which she over night had made

---

[71] Whether or not this is an accurate reporting of the villagers' comments, the speech is useful as a reflection of Throckmorton's motives for arranging a public confession: "Witches of Warboys," sig. G4v.

[72] Ibid., sig. H1r.

to him and master Doctor was wrested and wroong out of her, or whether it proceeded frankly and freely of and from her selfe. She answered before them all that it came of her selfe, and desired all her neighbours to pray to God for her, and to forgive her." Pastor Dorrington then offered to help reconcile her with her husband.[73]

Throckmorton's vision of community was based on his own paternalistic assumption of responsibility for the souls of his social inferiors and on his religious preoccupations with the necessity of purging sin from that community by means of public confession. Throckmorton appears to have desired a transformation of Warboys into a true community of believers, free of sin.

Throckmorton's ideal village would therefore be both hierarchical and communal. He saw his ideal community as a single entity expressing in a single voice, as would a tightly knit family, the need to acknowledge, and thus purge, sin so that a healed body politic could grow strong in virtue. This vision may well have come to Robert Throckmorton in part through the influence of his mother, because it seems to be a vision of godly community shared by many Puritans.[74]

Robert Throckmorton's vision, however, was flawed. He could not impose it successfully onto the reality of Warboys, and it was not only Alice who thwarted him. He was trying to impose his own idealistic vision of village unity and patriarchal deference onto a village far from unanimous in its acceptance of his personal leadership. He received only partial cooperation. The constable appeared to be a relatively passive tool of Throckmorton and dutifully hauled Alice and her daughter off to the bishop after her second confession, but individual villagers did voice sympathy for Alice, even in a narrative authored by her enemies. After Alice Samuel's second confession, when a group of villagers was brought to the Throckmorton parlor window to listen in secret to Alice's words, Alice collapsed in a "counterfeit swoune" upon the arrival of her husband on the scene. Another villager stepped forward at that point and offered assistance. "One of her neighbours standing by, peradventure better acquainted with her fashions then the rest, sayd, if they would let her alone, he would be their warrant, that she would doe well enough: so presently after, she came to her self again, and all was well."[75]

Finally, because Alice had refused to stick by her first confession, she had proven herself unreliable. This meant that reconciliation was impossible and Throckmorton's original agenda was irrevocably destroyed. Authorities outside the village were called in only because

[73] Ibid., sig. G3v.

[74] Hunt (n. 1 above), p. 91.

[75] "Witches of Warboys," sig. H1r.

Mother Samuel could not be trusted to take the burden of guilt and shame onto herself. From Throckmorton's point of view, he then had no choice but to transcend local village imperatives and turn to the bishop and justices of the peace as last resort.[76]

Indeed, Throckmorton turned to the justices of the peace only after a four-year-long effort to resolve the matter locally. But his own sphere of operations obviously transcended the parish of Warboys and demonstrates the "overlapping loyalties" a sixteenth-century English gentleman might experience as resident of a parish and participant in a county community as well.[77]

It will now be argued that the Throckmorton vision of community and how best it should be ordered was quite different from the understanding held by the Samuels and, probably, by many of their fellow villagers.[78]

At this point, the interpretation of the sources becomes more difficult. The detailed pamphlet narrative, complete with dialogue, was authored by men who were responsible for the prosecution of the Samuel family and does not allow us direct access to the Samuels' version of events, nor, therefore, to their prescriptions for harmonious community life. Speeches and motives attributed to the Samuels could well be dismissed by the historian as mere projections onto ultimately unknowable figures by self-serving authors. Historians are faced here with the challenge similar to that facing students of medieval heresy. How does one reconstruct the Cathar or Albigensian worldview when only their persecutors' voices can now be heard? In that sense, the Warboys pamphlet poses challenges similar to those of the inquisitorial evidence explored by Carlo Ginzburg.[79]

Indeed, at first glance, the pamphlet's portraits of Alice and her hus-

---

[76] Ibid. It looks as if the bishop of Lincoln was serving as Justice of the Peace in this context, rather than as an ecclesiastical official. In 1591, 1592, and 1600, the bishop sat with committees of justices, varying in size from five to seven at courts of Quarter Sessions (Brit. Lib. Add. rolls 39449, fol. 16; 39446, fols. 5, 10).

[77] See Fletcher, "National and Local Awareness in the County Communities" (n. 11 above), p. 152; also Hughes (n. 10 above).

[78] However, the question of whether the Samuels' views were representative of those of their Warboys neighbors is a complex one that cannot be pursued here. It is not possible to decide how much sympathy the Samuels received from their other neighbors. The trial was held in Huntingdon, not in Warboys, and the trial witnesses, aside from members of the Throckmorton family and their in-laws, were from outside the village ("Witches of Warboys," sigs. N4v–O1r).

[79] Carlo Ginzburg, *Night Battles: Witchcraft and Agrarian Cults in the Sixteenth and Seventeenth Centuries*, trans. John Tedeschi and Anne Tedeschi (New York, 1985), and *Clues, Myths, and the Historical Method*, trans. John Tedeschi and Anne Tedeschi (Baltimore, 1989).

band, John, appear to be blatant projections of harsh stereotypically
witch-like characteristics onto the Throckmorton neighbors. Alice's
husband John is portrayed as stubborn, abusive, and aggressively antisocial. The authors report that he beat his wife, and whenever he appears
on stage he is angry and uncooperative with his social superiors.

However, there are strong arguments in favor of reading the pamphlet narrative for signs of the survival, embedded in the Throckmor-
ton/Pickering text, of the Samuels' points of view. First of all, corroborating documentation demonstrates that all but two of the thirty-two
characters mentioned in the narrative were historical figures and definitely not figments of the Throckmorton/Pickering imagination. In
spite of the fact that the trial documents do not survive, it is clear that
the pamphlet narrative was based on events leading to an actual trial
and execution.[80] Furthermore, the pamphlet was written within weeks
of the April trial, and within four years of the earliest events included
in the narrative, so that memories of the most recent events (sometimes aided by notes) and of the testimony offered at the trial would
have been very fresh in the minds of the authors.

Second, analysis of the nature of the pamphlet text itself reveals
two types of descriptive passages. The first type was based on notes
that had been collected regularly and meticulously over a long period
of time in the course of direct observations made by either Throckmorton, Pastor Dorrington, or Gilbert Pickering. Those passages take on
the character of "clinical observation" and bring to the reader an
immediacy of experience in the present. Because so much of the force
of their case against the Samuels rested on careful descriptions of the
behavior of the afflicted girls, these accounts focus particularly on the
bizarre behavior of the children. But they do so with the clinical detail
of a natural philosopher, making every effort to avoid the impression
that their stories are fantastic inventions. In these passages especially,
the pamphlet authors made a concerted effort to convince their readers
that they were recording actual events and real conversations.[81] The
following sample quotations from the pamphlet illustrate this effort at
careful, firsthand observation, calling to mind entries from a diary.

> So mistresse Joane repeated the same words after the spirite which
> were then set downe in writing.[82]

---

[80] The earliest Huntingdonshire indictments in the PRO are from March 1694. See
also C. L'Estrange Ewen, *Witchcraft in the Norfolk Circuit* (Paignton: Printed for the
author, 1939). No evidence for the Norfolk circuit survives prior to 1690. Alan Macfarlane has commented on the accuracy of the Essex witch pamphlet narratives; Macfarlane (n. 5 above), chap. 5, esp. p. 85.
[81] "Witches of Warboys," sigs. J4v, B4v, C1r, D1r.
[82] Ibid., sig. J4v.

The observations of certaine daies follow, from the sixteenth of February to the 26. of the moneth, she was taken most commonly 5. or 6. times a day.[83]

On the 26. of February she read and sung Psalmes, . . . The 27. of Februarie, she was partly well.[84]

Now the 29. of July 1590. She had a fit from noone until night.[85]

It was hereupon therefore thought good by divers to make some trials and experiments (as they had oftentimes done before in such like cases).[86]

A second category of text within the pamphlet narrative is quite different. These passages consist of news that is filtered through the afflicted children in the form of prophecies, during the course of their "sermons," or during conversations with their spirits. This information takes on the import of that category of truth that is elevated by presumption to a level of validity that does not rely on individual experience. These descriptions match up most effectively with the stereotype of the witch. Alice was accused of failure to attend church services regularly, and in one scene with two young Cambridge theologians who traveled to Warboys to interrogate her, she is reported to have shown them the disdain and insubordination one might expect the authors to project onto a woman they have decided was a witch.[87] "Her answere to him was this, (for they were then in the streete hard by a pond) I had rather (said she) see you dowsed over head and eares in this pond, and so they parted."[88] That entire episode was revealed to one of the girls by their spirits. The girl was not present during the scholars' encounter with Mother Samuel, and the truth of her account had to be confirmed by interviewing the young scholars after the event.[89] The child demonstrates her prophetic powers, resulting from her contact with Mother Samuel's demons, by describing this scene for her audience while still in the manor house, and before news of it could presumably have reached her in any normal way. The purpose of this scene for the narrative is, therefore, primarily to demonstrate the effect of Mother Samuel's demons on the children.

In another example of this category of indirect testimony, one passage recreates the children's sermons which were delivered to Alice

---

[83] Ibid., sig. B4v.

[84] Ibid., sigs. B4v–C1r.

[85] Ibid., sig. C2v.

[86] Ibid., sig. D1r.

[87] Christina Larner, *Enemies of God: The Witch-Hunt in Scotland* (London, 1983), p. 97. Underdown (n. 17 above), p. 40; G. R. Quaife, *Godly Zeal and Furious Rage: The Witch in Early Modern Europe* (London, 1987), pp. 171–74.

[88] "Witches of Warboys," sigs. D4v.–E1r.

[89] Ibid., sig. E1v.

in a last ditch attempt to encourage her confession. Alice is condemned by the sermonizing girls for her "naughty manner of living, her usuall cursing and banning of all that displeased her, . . . her negligent comming to Church, and slacknesse in Gods service." The girls reprimand Alice for "her lewde bringing up of her Daughter, in suffering her to be her dame, both in controuling of her, and beating of her, which before had been proved to her face, and she herself had also confessed."[90]

There is a tension between these two types of pamphlet texts, and this tension is an important clue to the validity of the first category, the "clinical observations," as historical evidence.[91] This tension between those two genres, the "clinical observations" on one hand and the "prophecy-sermon" material on the other, produces a fault line through which an alternative version/vision of the "witches" appears—a version notably different from the one the pamphlet authors are attempting to create as their end product.[92] As a result, the historian is encouraged to accept and exploit these "clinical observations" as a valuable pathway to the Samuels' personalities and points of view.

Furthermore, these "clinical observations" succeed in painting portraits of three quite distinct personalities in the characters of Alice, daughter Agnes, and John Samuel. This achievement can more plausibly be attributed to the fact that something of those characters' personalities actually survives the decidedly biased perspective of the pamphlet authors than to the authors' sophisticated literary imaginations.

Because the discrepancy between the prophecy material and the clinical observations is strongest in the cases of the female witches, they will be discussed first. To begin with the older woman, Alice, several passages from the "prophecy-sermon" material in the pamphlet paint a portrait of this witch that conforms closely with the stereotypes of an angry, antisocial, quarrelsome, and disruptive personality. This sixteenth- and seventeenth-century stereotype has been noted and analyzed by modern scholars such as G. R. Quaife and Christina Larner. Alice's defiance during her interview with the two young Cambridge scholars was cited above, as was the "sermon" material in which she was harangued by the sick girls.

In contrast to this material, the "clinical observations" which take the form of direct reporting, based on the authors' own experiences,

---

[90] Ibid., sig. F4r.

[91] I owe this observation to Dr. Jutta Goheen from Carlton University, Ottawa.

[92] Calling to mind the "Bakhtinian sense of an unresolved clash of conflicting voices" cited by Ginzburg, *Clues, Myths, and the Historical Method* (n. 79 above), p. 164.

rather than on observations made by the witches' victims, present an Alice oddly out of tune with these stereotypes. For example, in one passage, Alice complains to Master Throckmorton and his wife that she suffers pains in her belly, giving her a chance to offer her own explanation for the troubles that have been afflicting the inhabitants of the manor house, and placing herself, alongside the girls, in the role of victim. The following exchange is reported between Robert Throckmorton and Alice:

> And one night amongst all the rest, she cryed out very pitifully of her belly, insomuch, that she disturbed and awakened both Master Throckmorton and his wife, that lay by her: saith Master Throckmorton, In Gods name Mother Samuel, what ayleth you, and why doe you grone so? Said shee, I have a marvellous great paine in my belly on the suddaine, and I know not how it should be caused. . . . But whosoever it was, she cried out to master Throckmorton of her belly, and said she was full of paine: and further shee said, that shee had often tolde him, that she thought there was some evill spirites haunted his house, which did thus torment his children, which thing he told her that he did easily beleeve was true: and now saith she, I verely beleeve, that one of them is gotten into my belly. Master Throcmorton said, that all this might very well bee true. So she said, that it was an evill house, and haunted with spirits, and wished that shee had never come into it: hee told her that if there were any evill spirits haunted the house, they were of her sending, and so he would grant all that she said.[93]

In tune with this more sympathetic caricature, prior to her sojourn in the Throckmorton house, the pamphlet authors had suggested that Alice conducted herself in a manner similar to that of most of those unremarkable neighbors who periodically stopped by to visit the Throckmorton family. Alice walked into the manor house parlor in the fall of 1589 in order to demonstrate concern for a sick child:

> [Jane] continuing in this case two or three daies, amongst other neighbours in the towne there came into the house of Master Throckmorton, the foresayd Alice Samuel to visite this sicke child, who dwelled in the next house on the Northside of the sayd Master Throckmorton.[94]

On another similar occasion, Alice, along with others, was ushered upstairs into one of the bedchambers in the Throckmorton manor

---

[93] "Witches of Warboys," sig. G1v.
[94] Ibid., sig. A3r.

house where Elizabeth Pickering lay after giving birth.[95] Alice was demonstrating, again, her neighborly interest in the new baby and its mother, and her presumption of a right, and/or duty, to be present in that house. On the surface, her behavior seems to have been similar to that of numerous other visitors whose actions failed to excite the fear and loathing that hers did. Her hosts were willing to allow her into their home initially but eventually came to see those visits as intrusions by malignant, contaminating forces that had to be rejected.[96]

Here we see Alice participating in a social world of women in which ease of movement from house to house was taken for granted by her, particularly in that sphere involving the care of children. As J. A. Sharpe has recently demonstrated, witchcraft accusations often arose from this female context of child care obligations and anxieties.[97] Unlike her husband John, who maintained a determined distance between himself and the Throckmorton household, Alice apparently had had regular contact with the Throckmorton girls and therefore with their mother and grandmother as well. Whether or not Alice was considered a local healer or cunning woman, and the pamphlet offers no evidence, or even hint, that this was so, it is clear that she expected to be received into the Throckmorton parlor at a comfortable seat by the fire when calling on the family to express interest in a sick daughter. It is also clear that even after that same child had expressed fears that Alice was a witch, the old woman was received into the bedchamber where a Pickering relative had recently given birth.

Alice's involvement in this female network of village social relations provided her with personal motives that were inverted by the pamphlet authors. She expected to continue her former role as neighbor, companion, adviser, helper to the women of her parish, including the women of the Throckmorton household. But accusations of witchcraft violated her own self-image and eventually threatened her confidence in her own interpretations of the events around her. Repeated experiments demonstrated, even to her, that her presence in the Throckmorton home had a direct affect on the young girls' health.

[95] The Warboys parish registers reveal that a Mr. John Pickering married Elizabeth Cervington on November 15, 1591. In September 1592, Gilbert, son of John Pickering, was baptized in Warboys.

[96] Interest in babies and children was feared as well as expected. The darker side of a neighbor's friendly concern was envy and jealous spite—dangerous emotions. See Roper (n. 8 above) for an important discussion of witchcraft accusations growing out of the psychic dramas of childbed. See Mary Douglas, *Purity and Danger* (New York, 1966), for analysis of the concept of pollution as it relates to witchcraft beliefs; notice particularly pp. 94–113.

[97] Sharpe, "Witchcraft and Women in Seventeenth-Century England: Some Northern Evidence" (n. 8 above).

For example, just prior to Mother Samuel's first confession, Robert Throckmorton commanded her to issue an order to the spirit controlling his children:

> Saith master Throckmorton, it is wel, thanks be to God, charge the spirit againe in the name of God, and speake from your heart, and be not afraid, that he depart from them all now at this present, and that he never returne to them againe, which words she uttered very lowde, and very boldly. So soone as she had ended, then those three children that were then in their fits, and had so continued for the space of three weekes, wiped their eyes, and at that instant thrust backe the stooles whereon they sat, and stood upon their legges, being as well as ever they were in their lives.[98]

Alice Samuel would have required remarkable strength to withstand the impact of such forceful evidence. Instead, she succumbed. Indeed, one of Alice's last speeches before the assize judges was that of a woman resigned at last to an absurd existence, devoid of the structure of meaning that had supported her in the past. She had tried to define herself as victim of the same evil forces attacking the Throckmorton children, but, after experiencing the effects her presence had on those children, little remained of her sense of self but absurd contradictions. She was somehow both victim and victimizer. In one last mad gesture, she, at the age of seventy, claimed to be pregnant. After the trial, just as she was about to climb the scaffold, the judge asked her if there were any reasons to stay the execution. At that point Alice said:

> Whereat shee aunswered, that shee was with childe: which set all the company on a great laughing, and shee her selfe more than any other, because as she thought, there should (for that cause) no iudgement have beene given. Her age was neere fourescore, . . . A jury of women were empaneled.[99]

The old woman's daughter Agnes also appears in two very different guises in the two types of pamphlet texts. In the prophecy-sermon texts, the girls accuse her of beating her mother, and the spirits describe her as violent and dangerous.[100]

In the girls' sermons directed at Alice, the children condemn Al-

---

[98] "Witches of Warboys," sig. G2v.
[99] Ibid., sig. O2v.
[100] Ibid., sig. H3v.

ice's "lewde bringing up of her Daughter, in suffering her to be her dame, both in controuling of her, and beating of her."[101]

In contrast to these texts, the authors' own direct experiences of Agnes are of a rather compliant woman who meekly submits to violent scratchings[102] and stumbles over her prayers. She is portrayed as backward in her religious training and slow to learn.[103]

However, this seemingly submissive and "backward" woman held fast to her sense of self, defending her personal integrity despite being abandoned by her village community. The pamphlet reports the following exchange between the judge and young Agnes just before the hangings:

> After all this, the Judge asked Agnes Samuel the daughter, what she had to say, why judgement of Death should not be given her. At which time there was one (being a prisoner) standing by her, that willed her to say that she was also with child. Nay, sayd she, that will I not do: it shall never be sayd, that I was both a Witch and a whore.[104]

Agnes shared Robert Throckmorton's determination to avoid shame, and she was strong enough at the end to be able to define herself in spite of the labels imposed upon her by her accusers. It may have been said that she was a witch, but her honor group would not be allowed to make her out to be a whore as well. Like her father, Agnes remained secure enough in her own vision of reality to be defiant in the face of death.

In contrast with his wife and daughter, John Samuel's death scene remains well in keeping with his earlier portraits in the pamphlet text—that of a cantankerous, obstreperous, disrespectful old man. For example, notice the attitude he displayed toward his wife even at the moment of their final defeat:

> And to draw to some ende, the Jury of life and death, in the afternoone, found all the Inditements Billa vera, which when old father Samuel heard, he said to his wife in the hearing of many: A plague of God light

---

[101] Ibid., sig. F4r.

[102] Ibid., sig. K2r-v.

[103] Just prior to her execution Agnes was unable to say the Lord's Prayer and the Creed, and earlier in the narrative, Master Throckmorton unsuccessfully tried to teach Agnes a grace (ibid., sigs. O3v, K2r). Perhaps the pamphlet authors mean to imply that Agnes is exercising willful ignorance here or that the devil has imposed hindrances to her ability to learn. I owe this suggestion to Annabel Gregory.

[104] Ibid., sig. O3r.

upon thee, for thou art she that hath brought us all to this, and wee may thanke thee for it.[105]

In fact, the discordance between the "prophecy-sermon" texts and the direct observations that was obvious in the cases of Alice and Agnes is much weaker in the case of the old man. For example, when the girls berate Mr. Samuel in one of their sermons, their description of him and the pamphlet author's account of his reactions to that sermon are quite compatible. The point seems to be that the girls do not feel the intimate psychological dependency on this old man as they had with Alice Samuel and her daughter. They fear him and are intimidated by him as the stranger that he was. Their relationship with him was quite different from the more intensely intimate and physical relationships they had with Alice and Agnes. The children's references to the old man are thus less pointed and quite generalized, and they shrink from any inclinations to scratch him, as they did the two women.[106]

John responded to the girls' accusations as follows:

> The man was so rude in his behaviour, and so lowde in his speeches, that the child could not be heard for him: His answers to the childe were, that she lyed, and so did all the companie, in saying hee was a Witch, and he sayd that she had been taught her lessons well enough, and that she was above seven yeares olde, (though indeed she was not twice seven) with many such like speeches, and would not bee silent, nor suffer the childe to speake for any thing untill he was almost forced unto it by the childes father.[107]

John Samuel is cited in the local Warboys village court rolls, and that record can be used to test the plausibility of the pamphlet account. The pamphlet portrait of an abusive, cantankerous old man may certainly be exaggerated to serve the propaganda purposes of the authors, but John Samuel's appearances in the Warboys court rolls from the 1580s indicate that he was frequently fined for antisocial behavior.[108]

---

[105] Ibid., sig. O2v.

[106] Ibid., sig. L1v–L2r.

[107] Ibid., sig. L2r.

[108] 1579, September, fined for having cattle in the common, 8d. 1579, September, John Bulmer drew blood from John Samuel. 1580, September, fined for hedges and ditches, 12d. and 20d. 1582, September, fined for failure to repair hedges, 12d. 1583, April, fined for throwing something into the road, 6d. 1584, March, fined for revealing the business of the jurors while he was a juror. This was the last time he served in that office. 1584–87, fined several times for breaking local ordinances regarding hedges, chickens, pigs. 1588/89, fined for reaping contrary to the ordinance, 3s. 4d. The court rolls consulted for this Samuel "biography" are as follows: Brit. Lib. Add. rolls 39783–94, 39781, 34922, 39573, and PRO SC2 179/86.

in a village with approximately seventy households,[109] there were only twenty to thirty men cited in the Warboys court rolls during the 1580s, a time when the local court was a much less important instrument of social control than it had been in the late thirteenth century.[110] Samuel's animals wandered onto neighbors' property. His hedges were repaired only in his own good time. He was quarrelsome and fiercely independent. He did agree to serve on the village jury at least three times but was not chosen to serve again after he was fined in 1584 for revealing the jurors' business.[111] The pamphlet's image of John Samuel and the image emerging from court roll evidence are not incompatible.

We cannot expect the pamphlet authors to provide us with a version of the Samuels' attitudes toward their village and their neighbors that John, Alice, and Agnes Samuel themselves would acknowledge as their own. But for the reasons outlined above, the search for a Samuel viewpoint tucked away within the Throckmorton/Pickering text is not fruitless. The Warboys pamphlet narrative will thus be used here as the basis for a reconstruction of the Samuel point of view.

Let us begin with Alice, and with her responses to the accusations against her. Alice reneged on her original confession precisely because she did not trust that confession to bring about the reconciliation Throckmorton envisioned. Alice suspected, and her suspicions were confirmed by her husband and daughter, that the label witch, once attached to her, would irreparably alienate her from her fellow villagers. Alice lacked the necessary faith that confession would indeed be followed by forgiveness and reconciliation. Unlike some African societies, or Basque villages, where guilt was usually accepted by the witch in order to bring about reconciliation, Alice's personal vision of the character of Warboys did not provide her with such a vehicle for healing.[112]

Alice reported that her husband and daughter told her that "it had been better for me to have died in the same estate I was in, then to confesse my selfe a Witch, now everie bodie will call me old Witch whilest I live."[113]

Alice did not expect a system of reconciliation to work in Warboys

---

[109] Brit. Lib. Harl. Ms. 618 temp. Elizabeth.

[110] "in this 1290 court roll, personal names are given 138 times"; Raftis (n. 20 above), p. 8.

[111] Brit. Lib. Add. roll 39791.

[112] See R. G. Willis, "Instant Millennium—the Sociology of African Witch-Cleansing Cults," in *Witchcraft Confessions and Accusations*, ed. Mary Douglas (London, 1970), p. 131; also E. E. Evans-Pritchard, *Witchcraft Oracles, and Magic among the Azande* (reprint, Oxford, 1993), pp. 41–43; Quaife (n. 87 above), p. 191.

[113] Christina Larner notes similar reactions among Scottish women accused of witchcraft but also cites one woman who accepted the label and welcomed the power it brought; *Enemies of God* (n. 87 above), p. 99. "Witches of Warboys," sig. G4v.

because that village was not, for her, the closely integrated whole that either a later romantic vision of rural life imposed on the English countryside, or that the Puritan gentry elite attempted to draw upon in their push for moral and spiritual uniformity. Mother Samuel could not trust her fellow villagers because she did not feel safely "at one" with some imagined village-wide "family." She did not trust the community to value her enough to need reconciliation. She understood Warboys to be a home shared by independent individualists, pulling in their own separate directions and guided by minimal commitments to one another.

Alice, and her husband and daughter as well, shared a vision of village life quite different from that of Throckmorton's. Theirs was embedded in generations of peasant experience. Just as village constables turned the other way and often avoided stirring up discord by refusing to enforce national statutes regulating public drunkenness or closing hours for taverns selling ale, villagers often chose the surest path to reconciliation rather than escalating conflict.[114] Informal mediation was regularly used between parties at odds with one another. Probably only a small percentage of such flare-ups ever reached even the local village court. Mutual toleration was essential in a community of individualists if disruptive chaos was to be avoided.[115]

Surely this is the reason Alice Samuel felt free to visit the Throckmorton home in the fall of 1592 after the birth of a new baby there to John and Elizabeth Pickering. In spite of the problems between herself and the Throckmorton children during the preceding three years, she expected life to go on as before. The social rituals of village life should, in her mind, continue, thereby ensuring a continuation of some form of good neighborliness and undisrupted social interaction. Such social harmony is rarely possible when one villager becomes overly concerned with the state of his neighbor's soul. For individuals such as the Samuels, one's private life must be kept private, distinct, safely apart from the public scrutiny.[116]

[114] Joan R. Kent, *The English Village Constable, 1580–1642* (Oxford, 1986), pp. 222 ff.; Ralph Houlbrooke, *Church Courts and the English People during the English Reformation, 1520–70* (Oxford, 1979), pp. 44–47; J. A. Sharpe, " 'Such Disagreement betwyx Neighbours': Litigation and Human Relations in Early Modern England," in *Disputes and Settlements: Law and Human Relations in the West*, ed. John Bossy (Cambridge, 1983), pp. 167–87.

[115] See Keith Wrightson, "Two Concepts of Order: Justices, Constables and Jurymen in Seventeenth-Century England," in *An Ungovernable People: The English and Their Law in the Seventeenth and Eighteenth Centuries*, ed. John Brewer and John Styles (London, 1980), pp. 24–25, 30.

[116] Samuel's attitude echoes through the centuries in the voice of a modern Russian rural villager who was quoted in a National Public Radio news story from September 29, 1993, as saying, "What I need is a good neighbor—one who will let me be."

Alice's attitudes may also reflect a particularly female point of view growing out of her experience of the "women's space" discussed earlier. Within a network of village women and children, a network that crossed class lines and encouraged Mother Samuel's movements into and out of the Throckmorton home to visit the children there, Alice apparently expected her relationships to continue in spite of the name-calling and outbursts of adolescent hysteria from the past. Here was a world where an ebb and flow of such social tensions must have been a regular feature of the lives of the women of Warboys. These networks were alien territory to Alice's husband, who operated in a different social and political sphere.

In that public and political sphere which was regulated in part by the local village court, John Samuel, like so many Ramsey Abbey tenants before him, was the image of the defiant individualist. The portrait surviving in Warboys court rolls confirms the image painted by the pamphlet author and belies any overly optimistic vision of village harmony. John Samuel, after all, was the one who pointed out to Robert Throckmorton that his daughters were above the age of seven and therefore should be held accountable for their own behavior. At one point he assents to his wife's observation that the Throckmorton children are simply "wanton."

The Warboys experience of the Throckmortons and Samuels thus seems the reverse of David Underdown's broad characterization of rural sociology. The clash between the Throckmortons and the Samuels is not the discordance between the village "communist" clinging to an old fashioned ideal of community harmony and cooperation, on one hand, and the Puritan gentry as individualists infecting a pastoral peace cheered by maypoles and wassails with unbridled entrepreneurialism.[117] Throckmorton, instead, attempted to draw the Samuels into a close circle of moral and social uniformity under his own authority. John Samuel had long resisted any pull from the center, as evidenced by his defiance of the village court, and he was not about to succumb to that pull when it was exerted by a newly arrived member of the gentry. His wife clearly expected the new neighbors to view her neighborly interest, perhaps even curiosity, in the same light as those of their other visitors, but when she found herself accused of witchcraft, she knew she could not count on their heartfelt forgiveness. His daughter was strong enough to resist the identity that the Throckmortons attempted to impose on her and clearheaded enough at the point of

[117] Underdown (n. 17 above), pp. 40, 42.

her death to stand up for her own reputation with at least as much determination as Robert Throckmorton had.

In conclusion, the Warboys witchcraft case has provided access to ideas about community arising from sectors of sixteenth-century rural society that are usually voiceless on this issue: yeomen who were quite probably illiterate,[118] and members of the lower gentry without political ambitions who did not entertain literary aspirations. The Warboys narrative provides a revealing glimpse into the incompatible expectations key figures in that drama held regarding their shared village. One can only assume that the social tensions within Warboys were exacerbated by the existence of these opposing blueprints for the practical functioning of community life.

This Warboys evidence fails to confirm efforts by some historians to identify the attitudes and viewpoints of the gentry and "middling sort" with one another. If Puritan preachers "spoke with particular resonance to those of the middling sort who were adopting these [acquisitive] values and abandoning the more traditional communal ones,"[119] the Warboys experience was at odds with that of other communities. First, it was the Throckmortons who were most affected by Puritan sentiment, differentiating them from the Samuels. Second, the Samuels showed no evidence that they clung to traditional communal values, but, instead, it was the Throckmorton party that seemed to adhere to some ideal of communal conformity and moral unity, an order requiring their paternalistic supervision and protection.

The Throckmorton "mentalité" coincides more closely with that described by William Hunt in his study of English Puritanism. Hunt saw the Puritan gentry as a conservative force. He cites one Puritan author's views about the obligation of the wealthy to provide interest-free loans to the poor, for example. "The implications of this social ethic are thoroughly conservative. Certainly the utopia one might extrapolate from these sermons would not look much like capitalism. . . . But a godly commonwealth would provide safeguards against misfortune."[120] Whether or not this vision was truly "conservative" in the sense that it reflected a consensus that would be recognizable

---

[118] Spufford found that only 33 percent of the yeomen in her study signed their wills, and many more women than men were illiterate; see *Contrasting Communities* (n. 10 above), p. 202.

[119] Underdown, p. 42.

[120] See Hunt (n. 1. above), pp. 137–38. Such visions certainly had medieval precedents in the ideologies expressed by some local "constitutions" such as that of fifteenth-century Wells, if not in the actual patterns of behavior revealed in local court rolls such as those of medieval Huntingdonshire; Shaw (n. 10 above), p. 179.

in medieval village court rolls is another problem, but the fact remains that those sentiments are more in tune with Robert Throckmorton's sense of obligation to his fellow villagers than to John Samuel's persistent independence. In Warboys it was Throckmorton, not Samuel, who feared the shame that would result from his failure to fulfill obligations to his community of neighbors.

If the relative success of either the Throckmorton or the Samuel vision could be indicated by continued residence in Warboys, then both families failed to translate their ideals into reality. Both families were ultimately rejected. John Samuel's abrasive personality, depicted by the pamphlet and ratified by court roll evidence, helps us to understand why the family probably failed to arouse enough sympathy and support from their other neighbors to escape hanging.[121] This negative reputation may have extended to other members of the family because the last individual bearing the Samuel surname to appear in the Warboys records was buried in 1592.[122]

Clues to the course of Robert Throckmorton's life after the executions at Huntingdon survive scattered between Warboys, his manor of Ellington, and his final home, Shoreditch in Middlesex.[123] By 1598/9 Robert had left Warboys and was most likely a resident of Ellington.[124] At about that same time, he enfeoffed Ellington to William and Edward Bedells to his own use and a certain close there to the use of "such woman as" will be Robert's wife at the time of his death.[125] It appears that the mother of the bewitched children did not survive Alice and John Samuel for very long. In the end, Warboys rejected both the Throckmortons and the Samuels.[126]

J. B. Russell has suggested that fear of the devil and an exagger-

---

[121] Note that in some areas, witchcraft accusations ended in slander prosecutions in the church courts. Mother Samuel apparently did not have enough local support to apply this strategy in her own defense against the Throckmortons. See Peter Rushton, "Women, Witchcraft and Slander in Early Modern England: Cases from the Church Courts of Durham, 1560–1675," *Northern History* 18 (1982): 116–32.

[122] The parish registers continue until 1662. Unfortunately, no Warboys court rolls survive after 1603.

[123] PRO E179/142/279; PRO B 11/161/35 Audley fol. 270v. This man is quite clearly the same man as the Robert Throckmorton from Warboys and Ellington. Legacies are left to his daughter Grace, wife of Edward Holcott, and the Ellington parish registers reveal that Grace Throckmorton married Edward Holcott in that parish in 1605. Grace is identified in the pamphlet as one of Robert's daughters.

[124] PRO E179/122/182; PRO E179/122/200, 203.

[125] PRO C142/485/94. I owe this reference to Edwin DeWindt.

[126] The Throckmorton daughters married into Huntingdonshire and Bedfordshire gentry families, but none of them left any evidence of property holding in Warboys. Robert's son Gabriel began producing children who were baptized at Ellington from the year 1604.

ated terror of his powers grow out of a sense of isolation. "The Protestant emphasis upon the lonely struggle of the isolated individual against spiritual powers meant that Faust had no recourse to a community or to the communion of saints."[127]

Even though Robert Throckmorton "won" his case against the Samuels, he did so at great cost. The fact that he left Warboys shortly after that trial and lived the last years of his life outside the county of his home manor indicates that he, too, was a man without recourse to the "imagined community" of his earlier vision. The village where he and his mother had resided, and where his children had been baptized, responded ambivalently, at best, to his attempts to shape it to his own specifications. Robert's personal conviction that he knew what was best for Mother Samuel and their Warboys neighbors violated and ultimately destroyed Alice's personal integrity and human dignity as it deprived her of life. By the time Alice and Robert faced one another in mutual incomprehension and recognized that they each represented points of view alien to the other, those differences had become irreconcilable. Villagers, both gentry and yeomen, were as yet tragically innocent of that process whereby rural society was developing "a series of superimposed cultures."[128] They still assumed, to their peril, that village neighbors would share the same language.

Fears that coalesced around the witch were one response to the tension between the need for the comforts of community and the imperfect nature of the real experience of community.[129] Such responses can be clearly attributed to the Throckmortons of Warboys. They may also explain the acquiescence of those other villagers who came to agree that Mother Samuel was, indeed, a witch and who, by their failure to defend her, facilitated the prosecutions.

---

[127] J. B. Russell, *The Prince of Darkness: Radical Evil and the Power of Good in History* (Ithaca, N.Y., 1988), p. 179.

[128] Keith Wrightson, "Aspects of Social Differentiation in Rural England, c. 1580–1660," *Journal of Peasant Studies* 5, no. 1 (1977): 35.

[129] Suggested from reading Russell, pp. 167–79.

# 10. *Witchcraft in early modern Kent: stereotypes and the background to accusations*

MALCOLM GASKILL

The study of witchcraft has been one of the best ploughed fields in the landscape of early modern social history. There is scarcely an aspect of the accusation and prosecution of witches which has not been confronted, hardly a legal archive which has not been ransacked by scholars eager to make their contribution to one of the darker chapters of Europe's past. Yet it is clear that the greater part of this research, even among English-speaking scholars, has concerned continental as distinct from English witchcraft, an imbalance attributable in the main to the towering achievements of Alan Macfarlane and Keith Thomas whose books were published in 1970 and 1971 respectively.[1] A quarter of a century later, theirs is still the dominant interpretation, but it is clear that the time is now ripe for a reappraisal of the English experience of witchcraft, especially when one considers the occasionally limited scope and overly theoretical structuring of their research.[2] Despite his chosen title, Macfarlane's survey remains essentially a study of Essex – a county sometimes mistaken for a country by social historians overawed by its bountiful records, and keen to see national resonance in the events and

---

[1] Keith Thomas, *Religion and the Decline of Magic. Studies in Popular Belief in Sixteenth- and Seventeenth-Century England* (London, 1971; 1973 edn); Alan Macfarlane, *Witchcraft in Tudor and Stuart England. A Regional and Comparative Study* (London, 1970). Although these should be seen as distinct works, Thomas and Macfarlane's relationship, as research supervisor and student respectively, fostered a harmony of interpretation.

[2] A comprehensive and updated study of witchcraft in early modern England by Dr J. A. Sharpe is, at the time of writing, in the final stages of production. See also Malcolm Gaskill, 'Witches and witchcraft accusations in England 1560–1690', in Gaskill, 'Attitudes to crime in early modern England with special reference to witchcraft, coining and murder', Ph.D. thesis, Cambridge University, 1994, ch. 2. Many of the themes of this essay are expanded there to include evidence drawn from all over England.

characteristics of the locality.[3] Furthermore, although Thomas' instincts and industry were formidable, he himself admits that his search of local archives was incomplete.[4] This chapter is based upon a primarily qualitative analysis of the prosecution of witches in the south-eastern county of Kent after 1560, and seeks to demonstrate how the anthropological framework constructed by Thomas and Macfarlane should perhaps be adjusted or applied more selectively. It is evident from the relatively unexplored Kentish material that all too often the stereotype commonly associated with English witches and their accusation fails to embrace fully the diverse, contingent and chaotic circumstances surrounding real accusations.[5]

I

First of all, let us examine the prevailing witch stereotype. Macfarlane and Thomas argued convincingly that witches in England were usually female, economically marginal, elderly and rarely had living husbands. Indeed, of the 102 women executed for witchcraft at the Home Circuit assizes between 1563 and 1682, only 32 are recorded as having had a husband alive at the time of their trials.[6] Witches were not necessarily the poorest members of the community, but in general were less well off than their accusers; they were, at least, sufficiently poor, on the one hand to warrant reliance on alms and, on the other, to be suspected of harbouring resentments against those who refused them. Accusations

---

[3] Martin Ingram has written that 'Studies of witchcraft and magic in England have given too much attention to apparently exceptional areas, especially the county of Essex, where for reasons which have not yet been fully explained the numbers of witchcraft prosecutions were unusually high', *Church Courts, Sex and Marriage in England, 1570–1640* (Cambridge, 1987), p. 96.

[4] Thomas, *Religion and the Decline of Magic*, p. 536n.

[5] The only serious study of witchcraft in Kent is Adrian Pollock, 'Regions of evil: a geography of witchcraft and social change in early modern England', Ph.D. thesis, University of Michigan, 1977. Although Dr Pollock sees a broader range of circumstances behind accusations than just conflict over alms, he upholds the broad picture of social tensions due to economic change, concluding that 'In almost all respects these characteristics are identical to Macfarlane's findings for Essex', 'Regions of evil', pp. 53–61, 164, 167–9, chs. 4–5; 'Social and economic characteristics of witchcraft accusations in sixteenth- and seventeenth-century Kent', *Archaeologia Cantiana*, 95 (1979), 37–48, quotation at 47.

[6] Thomas, *Religion and the Decline of Magic*, p. 671. This figure is taken from the abstracts of indictments printed in C. L'Estrange Ewen, *Witch Hunting and Witch Trials. The Indictments for Witchcraft from the Records of 1373 Assizes held for the Home Circuit A.D. 1559–1736* (London, 1929).

were not, we are told, made randomly, but instead were levelled at a woman with whom the victim had lately had some dealings and who probably lived nearby, particularly if she already had a reputation for witchcraft. When misfortune struck, such an individual might be identified as its cause if Providence seemed an improbable or unacceptable explanation.[7]

This functionalist model of accusation continues to influence the historical interpretation of long-term trends in English witchcraft prosecutions. It is argued that, from the later sixteenth century, declining neighbourliness and growing individualism in an expanding market economy meant that both the tendency to refuse alms and the suspicion of others within the community were increasing. The poor were disadvantaged as villagers rejected their dependants, and guilt at failing to fulfil neighbourly duties was then projected as fear of the revenge of those who had been denied charity. In a climate of religious Reformation and centralisation of criminal justice, traditional recourse to counter-magic was forbidden, and instead people were obliged to counter witchcraft in the courts. In this sense, therefore, witchcraft can be linked to a profound socio-cultural transition. However, since Macfarlane's work on witchcraft in Essex was first published, he has relocated the development of the individualism upon which his witchcraft thesis largely depends, to a period at least three centuries before the onset of witchcraft prosecutions in England.[8] This in itself represents a significant adjustment to the thesis. In any case, as evidence from Kent will hopefully demonstrate, the varied and complex realities of witch trials frequently stretch such a narrowly defined model accusation beyond its limits.[9]

Nevertheless, it is important for us to recognise that contemporaries often thought in terms of a stereotype when describing witches and their activities. Although it is true that physical appearance alone was

---

[7] Macfarlane, *Witchcraft*, pp. 30, 104–5, 110–12, 150–1, 168–76, 196–7 and *passim*; Thomas, *Religion and the Decline of Magic*, pp. 630, 652, 656–77 and *passim*.

[8] Alan Macfarlane, *The Origins of English Individualism: The Family, Property and Social Transition* (Oxford, 1978), pp. 1–2, 59–61 and *passim*.

[9] It should be noted here that most criticism of the Macfarlane/Thomas thesis to date has focused on Thomas' distinction between religion and magic; in other words, his view of early modern mentalities and beliefs. For summaries, see David D. Hall, 'Witchcraft and the limits of interpretation', *New England Quarterly*, 58 (1985), 254–61; Malcolm Gaskill, 'Witchcraft and power in early modern England: the case of Margaret Moore', in Jenny Kermode and Garthine Walker, eds., *Women, Crime and the Courts in Early Modern England* (London, 1994), pp. 125–7.

insufficient to accuse someone of witchcraft,[10] the caricature of the aged, ill-favoured and bad-tempered widow was prevalent in many portrayals of witches real and imagined. In a popular fable of 1655, a Kentish witch is described as an elderly woman with a dish-cloth around her head, and a staff in her hand, 'long nos'd, blear ey'd, crooked-neckt, wry-mouth'd, crump-shoulder'd, beettle-browed, thin-bellied, bow-legg'd, and splay-footed'. Such a description made the story instantly accessible to those who had an idea what a witch looked like, and, arguably, helped to form an image in the minds of those who did not. Sceptics noted the influence of this folkloric image on the sort of woman commonly to be seen arraigned in the courtroom. The late sixteenth-century Kentish gentle-man, Reginald Scot, described a typical defendant in a witchcraft trial as an ordinary old woman, 'lame, bleare-eied, pale, fowle, and full of wrinkles', and similarly in 1646 a minister, John Gaule, criticised those who saw a witch in 'every old woman with a wrinkled face, a furr'd brow, a hairy lip, a gobber tooth, a squint eye, a squeaking voyce, or a scolding tongue'.[11]

Recently, it has been suggested that historians have been guilty of repeating assumptions and generalisations about witchcraft taken from the work of contemporary authorities whose knowledge was far from accurate or comprehensive. Most of Reginald Scot's examples are drawn from continental sources such as Bodin, as were Henry More's for his influential work, and the Puritan minister George Gifford provided a generalised view of witchcraft in Essex which Macfarlane quoted at length in order to back up generalisations of his own concerning the same county.[12] Furthermore, popular accounts of trials, often illustrated with

---

[10] Cf. Macfarlane, *Witchcraft*, p. 158; Robert Rowland, '"Fantasticall and devilishe persons": European witch-beliefs in comparative perspective', in Bengt Ankarloo and Gustav Henningsen, eds., *Early Modern European Witchcraft. Centres and Peripheries* (Oxford, 1990), pp. 169–70.

[11] L[aurence] P[rice], *The Witch of the Wood-lands* (London, 1655); Reginald Scot, *The Discoverie of Witchcraft* (London, 1584), p. 7; John Gaule, *Select Cases of Conscience Touching Witches and Witchcraft* (London, 1646), pp. 4–5. See also Thomas Fuller, *The Profane State* (London, 1647), p. 351; Thomas Ady, *A Candle in the Dark* (London, 1655), p. 42; Francis Peck, *Desiderata Curiosa* (London, 1779), II, p. 476, quoted in Macfarlane, *Witchcraft*, p. 87.

[12] Joyce Gibson, *Hanged for Witchcraft: Elizabeth Lowys and her Successors* (Canberra, 1988), pp. 5–6, 206; Henry More, *An Antidote Against Atheisme* (London, 1653); George Gifford, *A Discourse of the Subtill Practises of Devilles by Witches and Sorcerers* (London, 1587); Macfarlane, *Witchcraft*, pp. 110–12; Alan Macfarlane, 'A Tudor anthropologist: George Gifford's *Discourse* and *Dialogue*', in Sydney Anglo, ed., *The Damned Art. Essays in the Literature of Witchcraft* (London, 1977), pp. 140–55.

woodcuts of malevolent decrepit old women, exaggerated the familiar traits of age, gender, reputation and isolation and played down details considered incongruous with received lore about witchcraft. Although Macfarlane is perhaps too ready to accept the reliability of pamphlets as historical evidence, even he concedes that 'descriptions of actual trials lay no particular emphasis on the physical stereotype of the witch', and that the familiar image mirrored reality only in a partial or distorted manner.[13]

Comparisons between first-hand legal accounts and second-hand literary versions of the same prosecution often produce discrepancies between the social characteristics of those actually tried and their sensational, popular and, therefore, saleable image. The pamphlet account of the Maidstone trials of 1652, for example, concentrates on the six Cranbrook widows whom it calls 'the most notorious', rather than the five married women and, most incongruous with the stereotype, the six *men* also arraigned at the same assizes. Indeed, only five of the eleven others are mentioned at all. But what the account lacked in comprehensive coverage it made up for in sensationalism, reporting that William Reynolds, Thomas Wilson and their wives confessed to bewitching £500 worth of cattle and nine children, including one 'whose pourtraiture in wax was found, where they had laid it, under the Threshold of a doore'. The author even suggested that the bodies of three children recently discovered at Chatham were their victims. These embellishments do not feature in the original trial documentation, and the two couples were convicted of second-degree witchcraft only.[14] It is apparent from court records that although villagers were influenced by the simple witchcraft imagery belonging to the oral tradition, and sustained by cheap print,

---

[13] Macfarlane, *Witchcraft*, pp. 81, 96, 158, 216. Some contemporaries were aware that pamphleteers gave a false image of witchcraft, see, for example, Henry Holland, *A Treatise Against Witchcraft* (Cambridge, 1590), sig. E3ᵛ; *A True Discourse. Declaring the damnable life and death of one Stubbe Peeter, a most wicked Sorcerer, who in the likenes of a Woolfe, committed many murders* (London, 1590), p. 1.

[14] H.F., *A Prodigious & Tragicall History of the Arraignment, Tryall, Confession, and Condemnation of six Witches at Maidstone, in Kent* (London, 1652), quotation at p. 6; P[ublic] R[ecord] O[ffice], ASSI 35/93/6/36–8, 41–9; 94/5. See also Ewen, *Witch Hunting and Witch Trials*, pp. 239–43 for abstracts of the original indictments. The account also failed to mention that, despite their 'notoriety', the case against three of the women was quashed by parliament; two of them were ultimately pardoned, but the executions had already taken place: PRO, ASSI 35/93/6/35; *Journals of the House of Commons*, VII, 1651–9, pp. 160, 173; C. L'Estrange Ewen, *Witchcraft and Demonianism* (London, 1933), p. 32. Sir Robert Filmer, a Kentish JP and spectator at the trials, believed the accused to be ordinary and innocent people: *An Advertisement to the Jury-Men of England, Touching Witches* (London, 1653), sig. A2 and *passim*.

they were clearly not restricted by it regarding whom they accused at law.[15] It is important to remember that neither the statute nor canon law specified who a witch should be, or how they should be known.[16] Therefore, as Bob Scribner has suggested, witch-stereotypes 'came to have a cultural life of their own among both the learned and the unlearned [who] could both believe in the broad stereotype of witchcraft, while being wholly sceptical of its particular application to their own circumstances'.[17]

The remainder of this chapter will examine what kinds of people were charged with witchcraft in sixteenth- and seventeenth-century Kent. As suggested above, the ordinary people who initiated prosecutions deployed a wider definition of a witch (and thus who might plausibly be considered to be one) than they have usually been credited with. Furthermore, given the obviously close relationship in Macfarlane and Thomas' interpretative scheme between the stereotype of the *witch* and the stereotype of the *accusation*, were a broader band of society to have been vulnerable to the charge of witchcraft, then a wider range of events and circumstances behind prosecutions might also be expected. Accordingly, one finds an array of different types of witchcraft accusation, notably – and significantly for the 'orthodox' model – between approximate social equals, and cutting across familiar patterns of gender relations.[18]

II

The idea was put forward over fifteen years ago that the high status of women in England relative to Europe meant that the intellectual frame-

---

[15] For other misleading or suspicious pamphlet accounts of witchcraft accusations, see Gaskill, 'Witches and witchcraft accusations', 46–7.

[16] On this point, see ibid., 39–41.

[17] Bob Scribner, 'Is a history of popular culture possible?', *History of European Ideas*, 10 (1989), 183–4. See also Wolfgang Behringer, *Hexenverfolgung in Bayern* (Munich, 1987), ch. 3.

[18] In all, over 200 accused witches have been traced for Kent 1560–1700 (half of which were church court cases, 1560–75). Kent witnessed a marked increase in assize prosecutions in the 1650s, accounting for 50 per cent of witches accused at the Home Circuit during the Interregnum (twenty-eight of fifty-six cases). The preponderance of ecclesiastical cases (particularly those involving *maleficium*) is highly unusual – witchcraft was the third most common offence tried at Canterbury 1559–60 – and may help to explain why the statute of 1563 was introduced: Arthur J. Willis, *Church Life in Kent being Church Court Records of the Canterbury Diocese, 1559–1565* (London, 1975), p. 73.

work supporting the concept of the female witch worked less efficiently than on the Continent. But the authors of this theory suggested not that this resulted in a larger proportion of male witches but in fewer witches altogether, and concluded that 'when accusations were made, it is hardly surprising that European stereotypes were invoked'. This interpretation was met with a reply from two historians who not only questioned why peculiarly English views about the status of women did not affect the choice of suspects, but also argued that detailed analysis of Scottish witchcraft trials revealed that 14 per cent of witches were men. In addition, only 20 per cent of all female witches whose marital status was known were widows, and overall it was suggested that evidence from Scotland 'seems to show a much greater variation amongst defendants than the stereotype would allow'.[19] More recently, interesting parallels have emerged from this side of the border. Joyce Gibson, for example, has argued of witches in Essex that 'far from being impotent with age or malicious beggars as they are often portrayed, they were people of significance in the community, and many were part of a large workforce of spinners in conflict with powerful vested interests'.[20]

Whilst this may be overstating the case a little, one of the first things that the Kent archives reveal is that by no means all of those arraigned as witches in late sixteenth- and seventeenth-century Kent were old, impecunious widows.[21] Of forty-nine women (for whom marital status is known) presented for both maleficent witchcraft and cunning magic in the Canterbury church courts between 1560 and 1575, thirty-three had husbands alive at the time of their accusation. In other words, for this particular jurisdiction and period, a female witch was twice as likely to

---

[19] Alan Anderson and Raymond Gordon, 'Witchcraft and the status of women – the case of England', *British Journal of Sociology*, 29 (1978), 181 and *passim*; J. K. Swales and Hugh V. McLachlan, 'Witchcraft and the status of women: a comment', *British Journal of Sociology*, 30 (1979), 356; Hugh V. McLachlan and J. K. Swales, 'Stereotypes and Scottish witchcraft', *Contemporary Review*, 234 (1979), 88–90, 93.

[20] Gibson, *Hanged for Witchcraft*, p. 199.

[21] Macfarlane gives the average age of an Essex witch as between 50 and 70, a calculation based on a mere fifteen women, nine of whom died from ill-treatment, and were therefore likely to have been the oldest and weakest. Moreover, the Essex data relating to gender and age seems to illustrate the stereotype unusually well when compared to continental averages: 92 per cent female defendants (against 76 per cent); and the highest percentage of witches aged over 50: 87 per cent (against 62 per cent). Although the Essex witches were usually poor, Macfarlane admits that 'No direct connexion can be drawn between poverty and accusations': Macfarlane, *Witchcraft*, pp. 150–1, 155, 161–2, quotation at p. 155; Gibson, *Hanged for Witchcraft*, pp. 205–6; Brian P. Levack, *The Witch-Hunt in Early Modern Europe* (London, 1987), pp. 124, 129.

be married as widowed. Corroborating evidence can be drawn from the secular courts of almost a century later. Between 1640 and 1660, when prosecutions in Kent were at their peak, only 30 per cent of all those accused at the county quarter sessions and assizes, for whom marital status is recorded, were widows, whereas spinsters and women specifically referred to as married comprised 48 per cent of the total. The remaining 22 per cent were men, a figure consistent with the proportion of male suspects in the period 1560–1640. Of the sample of church court defendants, 16 per cent were men.[22]

The background to witchcraft accusations was also frequently at variance with the Macfarlane/Thomas stereotype. In her study of crime in seventeenth-century Sussex, Cynthia Herrup describes a case in which a man accuses two other men and a woman of witchcraft in a normal neighbourly quarrel in which 'the accuser and accused were not exceptionally mismatched in terms of power'. Professor Herrup continues:

> In eastern Sussex the rare accusations of witchcraft stand out because of the prominence of male defendants and because of the economic and social parity of the accused and the accuser. The changes seem to express ongoing competition rather than guilt or anger born of spurned hospitality, and, as such, they seem of a kind with accusations of trespass, unlicensed alehouses, or trading without an apprenticeship.[23]

For northern England, J. A. Sharpe has argued that many prosecutions stemmed from tensions between women in competition for prominence

---

[22] The secular court statistics for 1640–60 are based on forty-eight accused witches of whom the status of only two was unspecified. Of the remaining forty-six, fourteen were named as widows, ten were men, and the rest were married and unmarried spinsters. In the period 1560–1640, six of twenty-six witches tried at the secular courts were men. In all, approximately 19 per cent of witches prosecuted in Kent at the church courts, quarter sessions and assizes between 1560 and 1660 were male. A tentative survey of Cambridgeshire and the Diocese of Ely produces a figure of 30 per cent, and continental countries range between 20 per cent and 50 per cent. Robin Briggs recently arrived at 28 per cent in a sample from Lorraine, and argues that 'over a large area of France witchcraft seems to have had no obvious link at all with gender': Levack, *Witch-Hunt*, p. 24; Carlo Ginzburg, *Ecstasies. Deciphering the Witches' Sabbath* (London, 1990), p. 311; H. C. Erik Midelfort, *Witch Hunting in Southwestern Germany 1562–1684. The Social and Intellectual Foundations* (Stanford, 1972), pp. 180–1; Robin Briggs, 'Women as victims? Witches, judges and the community', *French History*, 5 (1991), 441–2, quotation at 441.

[23] Cynthia B. Herrup, *The Common Peace. Participation and the Criminal Law in Seventeenth-Century England* (Cambridge, 1987), p. 33. For similar cases, see John Stearne, *A Confirmation and Discovery of Witchcraft* (London, 1648), pp. 34–5 (Northants.); H[istorical] M[anuscripts] C[ommission], *Salisbury MSS*, XIV (London, 1923), p. 70 (Gloucs.).

in the female realm, and evidence from the Continent certainly suggests that, far from being marginal figures, witches were more commonly active, even aggressive, personalities whose assertive behaviour led to conflicts of interest with their neighbours.[24] Arguments for the witch to be seen, not as a marginal figure, but as a competitors for power, space and resources, have been advanced for several countries, among them France, Germany, Sweden and New England.[25]

It is certainly true that many women accused of witchcraft in Kent were active and integrated in local society, rather than passive and isolated. In 1586 Joan Cason was brought before the mayor of Faversham, charged with invoking evil spirits to kill Thomas Cooke's three-year-old daughter after he had broken off her engagement to his servant.[26] Seven women and two men gave evidence, alleging that she had sworn revenge upon several of her neighbours who had then suffered misfortune. Katherine Kenwarde related how Cason had lamed her child, and had heard the witch recite the following spell:

> take the Gume of an Ivye Tree in the alleye & leye yt in the grownde & the name of the p[ar]tie uppon the Gume, that as the Gume consumyd as sholde the p[ar]tie consume in hys bodye.

Agnes Barton claimed that during a quarrel over a broken pot, Cason had told her that she would come to harm when she was least expecting it; four days later, a child which she was nursing 'was suddenlie taken sycke in the nyghte mooste straungely' and died soon after. But the most damning evidence against Cason related to her diabolic familiar, a rat, which she confessed 'came to her one nyght wyth long leane handes & a

---

[24] J. A. Sharpe, 'Witchcraft and women in seventeenth-century England: some northern evidence', *Continuity and Change*, 6 (1991), 179–99. See also Sharpe, 'Women, witchcraft and the legal process', in Kermode and Walker, eds., *Women, Crime and the Courts*, pp. 106–24. For an interpretation which places female accusers in a slightly more passive role, see Clive Holmes, 'Women: witnesses and witches', *Past and Present*, 140 (1993), 45–78, esp. 49, 54–6, 74–5.

[25] Jeanne Favret-Saada, *Deadly Words. Witchcraft in the Bocage* (Cambridge, 1990), pp. 32, 104, and *passim*; David Sabean, *Power in the Blood. Popular Culture and Village Discourse in Early Modern Germany* (Cambridge, 1984), pp. 56–8, 211; Lyndal Roper, 'Witchcraft and fantasy in early modern Germany', this volume, pp. 207–36; Bengt Ankarloo, 'Sweden; the mass burnings (1668–1676)', in Ankarloo and Henningsen, eds., *Early Modern European Witchcraft*, pp. 310–12; Carol F. Karlsen, *The Devil in the Shape of a Woman. Witchcraft in Colonial New England* (New York, 1987).

[26] The following case is drawn from *Holinshed's Chronicles of England, Scotland and Ireland*, 6 vols. (London, 1586), III, pp. 1560–1, and borough court depositions and sessions roll: K[ent] A[rchives] O[ffice], Fa/JQs 23 (bdl. 128); Fa/JQs 1 (bdl. 104).

leane face ryghte lyke her M[aste]r John Mason & dyd kysse her & the lyppes of yt was colde'. The animal made a blood-curdling noise and was apparently impossible to kill. In court, although she was acquitted on the charge of *maleficium*, a lawyer disputed over a legal technicality concerning the invocation of a spirit. His claim was upheld by the court, and, despite her vehement protestations of innocence, Joan Cason was condemned and executed.

The existence of detailed court depositions and a printed secondary account enable us to reconstruct some of the circumstances behind the trial, revealing that forces of social disparity between accuser and accused were not necessarily at work. John Waller, who related the story in *Holinshed's Chronicles*, describes the witnesses as 'all verie poore people', who soon regretted Cason's death – of which more later. We also learn not only that Thomas Cooke (whose wife was the principal witness) and Joan Cason's husband worked in the same trade (collar-making), but that Katharine Kenwarde was probably one of Cason's own kin. To cap it all, Cason may even have been slightly wealthier than those who prosecuted her, since she had recently inherited a sum of money from her master and lover, John Mason. The element of the denial of alms is entirely absent here, and the part which most closely resembles the typical chain of events described by Macfarlane and Thomas occurs when one of her accusers comes to the *witch's* house for fire and a quarrel ensues. The familiar paradigm was reversed in a dispute between neighbours of comparable social status, and most probably it was in this very similarity of social circumstance, and therefore of neighbourly competition, that this conflict has its source.

Sixty years later, such squabbles – and the serious consequences they could have – remained a part of Kentish provincial life. Indeed, in 1645 yet another witchcraft trial in Faversham attracted public attention. A cheap pamphlet records the trial before the mayor, Robert Greenstreet, of four witches, one of whom, Joan Cariden, alias Argoll or Argoe, confessed that ten years earlier in 1635, the devil first visited her 'in the shape of a blacke rugged Dog in the night time and crept into the bed [next] to her and spake to her in mumbling language'. The next night he returned and commanded her 'to deny God and to leane to him and that then he would revenge her of any one she owed ill will to'.[27] She agreed

---

[27] *The Examination, Confession, Triall and Execution of Joan Williford, Joan Cariden, Jane Hott, who were executed . . . at Faversham* (London, 1645).

to the devil's conditions, promised her soul to him, and he suckled her for the first time. She is portrayed precisely as a typical witch of the period: one of a group of deluded, poverty-stricken, old widows seeking company and sustenance from the devil.

The reality was probably somewhat different, especially regarding the reasons for Cariden's unpopularity in the community. An isolated document from 1635, which survives in the borough archives, tells of Joan Cariden's local unpopularity a decade prior to her trial for witchcraft, adding another dimension to her character which otherwise could only be assessed from the 1645 pamphlet. Although the earlier account alleged that Cariden 'doth wraile against her neighbours and saith they shall never prosper, Because she hath curst them', nowhere is witchcraft specifically mentioned.[28] As for her social standing, there are a number of clues. The 1645 account refers to Cariden ambiguously both as a widow and as William Argoe's wife, but from the 1635 report we learn also that she had a son and a daughter with whom she most probably dwelt. Overall, it is clear that she was a socially integrated, non-marginal, but – in some quarters at least – unpopular figure who sold food locally. Richard Hilton evidently held a grudge against her, for she cursed him and 'caled him puritent [i.e. Puritan] Roge for she said it was his doeings that her wheat was arested'. This last accusation is especially intriguing as it may suggest not only religious and cultural tension, but also intervention in the passage of food into the town, and may point to her unpopularity as a regrator of corn at a time of dearth. It is known, for example, that in Faversham in the early 1630s there was at least one grain riot where the kind of action allegedly taken by Hilton was common.[29] Certainly, the 1635 statement records that she was owed money, probably loans or debts for goods sold on credit. On seeking repayment from one man, Cariden claimed 'he took the tongs and hurld [them] at are [her?] and put her [out] of the house like a dog'. Also she protested that if Nathaniel Beesbedge had been mayor (as he was to be in 1637), he 'would wright her cause againe and help her to her mony of goodwife

---

[28] Public cursing by no means always led to accusations of witchcraft. Indeed, it was common to present the two offences separately against a suspect. See, for example, the case of Emme Merchante of Whitstable, who in 1572 was 'suspected to use sorcery and wytchcrafte and is a greate cursor and blasphemer of the name of Allmighty god': Thomas, *Religion and the Decline of Magic*, pp. 610–11; C[athedral,] C[ity, and] D[iocesan] R[ecord] O[ffice, Canterbury], DCb/X.1.11, f. 103ᵛ.

[29] Buchanan Sharp, *In Contempt of All Authority. Rural Artisans and Riot in the West of England, 1586–1600* (Berkeley, 1980), p. 30.

Cose'. Joan Cariden was probably resented as a creditor and retailer, as much as reviled as an evil curser and sower of discord.[30]

This conflict should perhaps also be examined against a backdrop of popular discontent with the mayoralty, and possibly of factional conflict. It is known that attacks upon urban oligarchies in the early seventeenth century were common in Kent, particularly in Faversham in the decade after 1610, and Joan Cariden's verbal assault on Mayor Greenstreet and his jurats may well have been in that tradition. Clearly dissatisfied with the administration of justice, the troublesome woman threatened to petition the lord warden of the Cinque Ports and instructed her son to 'goe and arest goodman Chillenden', and her son also said that 'he could not have noe justice of Mr Maior'. By mid-September 1635 Faversham had a new mayor, but ten years later Robert Greenstreet once again took up office, and within twelve days, intriguingly, Cariden had been thrown into gaol. Soon afterwards she was tried and executed as a witch.[31]

In general, these two cases suggest the diversity and complexity of the social environment of witchcraft accusations, and specifically how integrated and even assertive the protagonist could be. Taking this a step further, it is easy to see how in certain cases witchcraft accusations might have played a part in power struggles between different camps within the community. Annabel Gregory, for example, has demonstrated that political faction provided the dynamic for a witchcraft trial in another Cinque Port, Rye, in the early seventeenth century.[32] This, and cases from around England, indicate that witchcraft accusations could polarise communities along pre-existing fault-lines, rather than binding them together in a collective censure of a scapegoat.[33] In this regard, however,

---

[30] KAO, Fa/JQe 14; Edward Jacob, *The History of the Town and Port of Faversham* (London, 1774), p. 124.

[31] Peter Clark, 'The migrant in Kentish towns 1580–1640', in Peter Clark and Paul Slack, eds., *Crisis and Order in English Towns 1500–1800. Essays in Urban History* (London, 1972), p. 151; KAO, Fa/JQe 14. Cariden was examined for the first time on 25 September. Greenstreet would have taken up office on 13 Sept., see Jacob, *History of . . . Faversham*, p. 69.

[32] Annabel Gregory, 'Witchcraft, politics and "good neighbourhood" in early seventeenth-century Rye', *Past and Present*, 133 (1991), 33–5, 37 and *passim*. For a dramatic parallel from New England, see Paul Boyer and Stephen Nissenbaum, *Salem Possessed. The Social Origins of Witchcraft* (Cambridge, MA, 1974), pp. 37–45, 51–8, 86–109, 147.

[33] As Dr Sharpe has suggested, 'against notions of "tyranny of local opinion" or of village communities being united against the witch might be set a number of cases where reactions to witchcraft  reflected divisions rather than hegemony in local attitudes':

the Faversham cases are more suggestive than conclusive. It is true that events of 1635 show Cariden as having been more integrated in the community than the 1645 account, but if she had supporters then we can only guess at who they might have been – other traders, a possible anti-Puritan faction, Greenstreet's political opponents. And yet it remains important to accept that this theory is at least as plausible as one which automatically assigns to Cariden the role of outcast simply because she has been accused as a witch.

Other cases where the accused was not a marginal figure can be added to the above. When Dorothy Rawlins of St Dunstan's, Canterbury, appeared on a charge of *maleficium* in 1651, she was far from being an impoverished lonely figure; instead, she lived with her husband, a brewer, and sold food to local people. Mary Blyth, the wife of a rival brewer in the same parish, testified that having bought some 'seesing' (size?) from the accused, on the way home 'the pott gave a greate blowe & flew & broake and the seesing flew aboute her eares and upp unto the seeling'. She attested that Rawlins 'was a witch, if there were any in England', and other customers claimed that they had become sick after eating food bought from her. Although Rawlins was acquitted, the case shows how suspicions could develop even about a person who was well known in the community, married, and with whom her accusers had regular dealings of their own accord. Indeed, some accused witches were described as models of Christian conformity. In 1641 a gentleman, Henry Oxinden, stepped in to protect Goodwife Gilnot of Barham against the accusations of her neighbours, and spoke of a woman 'religiously disposed' and a dutiful mother who 'hath taken noe small care to have them instructed up in the feare of God'.[34]

Oxinden's intervention reinforces the impression that suspects were not necessarily universally reviled in Kent communities, and that individuals were often present who were prepared to defend them. Partly because of this, things did not always go as planned for the accuser. When John Northcliffe indicted Sibil Ferris of St Lawrence-in-Thanet

J. A. Sharpe, *Witchcraft in Seventeenth-Century Yorkshire: Accusations and Counter Measures*, Borthwick Papers, 81 (York, 1992), pp. 21–2. For other examples, see Cambridge University Library, EDR D/2/10, ff. 4ᵛ, 22, 37, 51ᵛ, 77ᵛ (Cambs., 1577); British Library, Add. MS 28223, f. 15 (Norfolk, 1600); PRO, ASSI 47/20/1/512–13; 45/11/1/90–3 (Yorks., 1651). See also Gaskill, 'Witches and witchcraft accusations', pp. 52–3.

[34] KAO, Q/SB 2/13; Q/SRc E4/111; *The Oxinden Letters, 1607–1642*, ed., Dorothy Gardiner (London, 1933), p. 222.

for *maleficium* in 1610, even though she already had a long reputation as a witch and had appeared before a church court in 1597, the magistrate, Thomas Harflete, took her side, and not only acquitted her but fined Northcliffe two shillings for scratching her face and assaulting her with a pitchfork.[35] Nor were witches always bereft of friends and family, and assistance was frequently forthcoming from less prominent figures than the likes of Oxinden or Harflete. For instance, many accused women were able to find neighbours to testify to their good name at church court hearings. In 1618 Mary Hunt of Sandwich had been spinning at a neighbour's house, when Elizabeth Clark publicly accused her of witchcraft. Offended, Hunt took her case to the Canterbury archdeacon's court, and the women who had witnessed the accusation turned up to testify to her character and bearing. Nor did Katherine Wilson and Wilman Worsiter of Ashford stand alone against the authorities when they were tried for witchcraft at Canterbury in 1651. Word reached Worsiter's husband who, working in another county at the time that his wife was accused, rushed home to raise the £40 bail for her with the assistance of Stephen Strong and John Richards, pledging that she would appear at the next sessions of the peace. Likewise, Widow Wilson was bailed by two local men – a husbandman and a labourer.[36]

Nor were such acts of communal generosity towards accused witches in Kent isolated occurrences. In 1653 alone, Anne Pottin was bailed by two local men; Richard Fosher of Brookland provided sureties for Widow Howell; and Mary Page of St Nicholas-in-Thanet was able to rely on her husband to do the same. Husbands sometimes went to even greater lengths to clear their wives' names. In 1561 a church court heard how Robert Brayne of Biddenden made diligent enquiries to discover why his 35-year-old bride was believed to be a witch, after their marriage had been objected to on these grounds, but had been unable to find any substance in the accusation. Similarly dutiful was Robert Staunton of Northfleet, whose petition resulted in a pardon for his wife in 1574, after she was convicted of bewitching a neighbour's livestock; some years later, when Ade Davie of Selling confessed to having sold her soul to the devil and bewitched her family, her husband stepped in to defend her

---

[35] KAO, QM/SI/9/9; Arthur Hussey, 'The visitations of the Archdeacon of Canterbury', *Arch. Cant.*, 27 (1905), 32; KAO, QM/SI 1610/14/12; QM/SB 989.

[36] CCDRO, DCb/PRC 39/34, ff. 52ᵛ–54ᵛ; KAO, Q/SB 2/12; Q/SRc E4/47, 50. Support could take many forms. After Katherine Fisher (see below) was charged with witchcraft in 1560, a Kenardington man was excommunicated for knowingly harbouring her: CCDRO, DCb/Y.2.24, f. 30ᵛ.

as 'a right honest bodie . . . of good parentage'. Less successful in his efforts, but equally loyal, was Thomas Sharpe of Minster, whose wife was sentenced to death in 1651 for bewitching a gelding and causing a languishing illness in a man. Sharpe petitioned magistrates for a re-trial and promised to provide evidence of his wife's good character giving assurance that he personally had 'alwaies demeaned himselfe as a Christian ought to doe'.[37]

It is evident, then, that although many witches conformed to the stereotype of the elderly woman reliant on alms, equally, many accused women in Kent emerge from the archives as altogether more potent characters, able to draw upon at least some support when they were accused. This fact alone makes a model of witchcraft, whereby an incongruous and unconforming individual was persecuted due to social and economic pressures, sometimes seem remote in its relevance. It may also help explain why so many witches, of whom no more is known than the bare details contained in an indictment, were actually acquitted – even in the sixteenth century. We need to remember that many women were significant actors in the parish, and rather than standing outside the structure of patriarchal authority – and therefore falling victim to its prejudices – were integrally involved in local networks of kinship, work and worship. As a consequence, many accused witches experienced varied currents of defence and attack emanating from both men and women in different spheres of daily life, but always inextricably bound up in very particular personal and local circumstances. Notwithstanding the argument that increasing female prominence might have put certain women at greater risk of being accused of witchcraft, a rise of prosecutions does not necessarily presuppose a crisis in gender relations. It does, however, suggest intense competition and conflict between competing households – households which comprised, naturally enough, both women and men.[38]

---

[37] KAO, Q/SRc E6/24, 38; E7/87–8; CCDRO, DCb/X.8.5, f. 87; *Calendar of the Patent Rolls, Elizabeth I, VI, 1572–1575* (London, 1973), p. 283; Scot, *Discoverie of Witchcraft*, pp. 55–7; KAO, Q/SRc E3/65–6; Q/SB 2/41. In 1606 Thomas Winter of Barham objected so strongly to a neighbour accusing his mother of witchcraft, that he took him to court to forestall future accusations: CCDRO, DCb/PRC 39/29, ff. 333ᵛ–377.

[38] As E. P. Thompson has remarked, many women occupied a central position in the market place, where they behaved not as passive adjuncts of husbands and masters, but as 'the initiators of community opinion, and the initiators of actions: *Customs in Common* (London, 1991), pp. 315–17, 322, quotation at p. 322. On crisis in gender relations, see: David Underdown, 'The taming of the scold: the enforcement of

III

However small their minority, it is important to consider the handful of men who were accused of witchcraft, maleficent and otherwise. Indeed, the husbands of accused witches were not always in a position to help their wives, as they themselves might be implicated in the charge. In 1560, for example, Robert and Katherine Fisher of Ruckinge were presented together at both the archdeaconry and consistory courts at Canterbury for using *ars magica* and incantations; and Nicholas Hardwyn of Kingsdown and his wife were accused of *maleficium*. Hardwyn, it was alleged, 'coulde saye mundayes prayer that one Seks soo cauled of the parryshe of Lynsted shoulde not lyve untyll satter daye in night'; and William Ames testified that after he fell out with Hardwyn's wife, she 'said unto me that she wolde be even w[i]t[h] me before the yeer came about And ymmediatelye I had a cowe that stode gryndinge w[i]t[h] her tethe and formynge at hyr mought as nev[er] hathe been seen hertofore as my neighbours can tell'. This indicates that both husband and wife might be seen by local people as equally active in the exercise of harmful magic, although we cannot be sure of the conflicts which lay behind suspicions that they were engaged in such practices.[39]

In the following year, however, we find a more telling case. Robert Brayne, who, as we saw above, had attempted to clear his bride's name, appeared before the ecclesiastical authorities jointly accused with his new wife of using witchcraft to kill livestock, ruin milk and beer, and cause sickness among their neighbours. Brayne was personally charged with killing James Sloman's best cow, and disabling his servant 'w[i]th a strange sycknes', after he and Sloman had fallen out whilst labouring together to repair the highway. Alice Brayne also came directly into conflict with neighbours, who were reported to be 'vexed by her p[e]rsuasion', but, as in her husband's case, this stemmed from participation in work and trade, not isolation from it. In one instance, which once again reminds us how the begging paradigm could be reversed, she declined to lend a horse to a neighbour, who then lost two bullocks; another man complained that

patriarchal authority in early modern England', in Anthony Fletcher and John Stevenson, eds., *Order and Disorder in Early Modern England* (Cambridge, 1985), pp. 116–36, esp. 119–22; Martin Ingram, '"Scolding women cucked or washed": a crisis in gender relations in early modern England?', in Kermode and Walker, eds., *Women, Crime and the Courts*, pp. 48–80, esp. p. 49.

[39] CCDRO, DCb/X.8.5, f. 23ᵛ; Y.2.24, f. 26; X.1.2, f. 1/50.

he solde her a busshell of graynes and becawse she might not have helpe soo sonne as she called to lay them upon her backe the dryncke that was made of the sayde graynes beganne to sethe abowte the tunne an w[i]thin a whyle a man might have drawen yt to the toppe of the howse at hys fingers ende

In this case, at least, the accusation makes more sense when one views the accused parties less as unpopular individuals and more as members of an unpopular household.[40] Other isolated cases strengthen this impression. In 1573 Archbishop Parker's court heard how Stephen Blusshe of Marden had encouraged a man to visit a witch who in this case happened to be Blusshe's own wife; and, some months later, a few miles away at Broomfield, William Evernden and his wife were both presented as suspected witches. In the seventeenth century such charges were more commonly heard in the secular courts, and with more serious penalties. At the Maidstone summer assizes in 1603, for instance, George and Anne Winchester confessed to having bewitched a woman to death; as already mentioned, two married couples, William Reynolds, Thomas Wilson and their wives, were indicted at the same court in 1652.[41]

But the role played by men in English witchcraft prosecutions could extend beyond mere complicity in a female crime, and although the overwhelming majority of English witches were women, 'there does not seem to have been any obvious objection to the idea of male witches', as Macfarlane himself observed.[42] Elizabethan divines were in agreement on this point. The Puritan minister Henry Holland was less concerned about 'poor doating old women (which are commonly called witches)' than the 'wicked man or woman that worketh with the devill'; and William Perkins argued that Moses' use of the feminine gender was misleading, and that, in truth, the Hebrew patriarch 'exempteth not the male'.[43] The same opinion was also current in the seventeenth century:

[40] CCDRO, DCb/X.1.3, ff. 156ᵛ–157Aᵛ.

[41] 'An unpublished record of Archbishop Parker's visitation in 1573', *Arch. Cant.*, 29 (1911), 306; CCDRO, X.1.12, ff. 52ᵛ, 132ᵛ; Ewen, *Witch Hunting and Witch Trials*, pp. 195, 239–40.

[42] Macfarlane, *Witchcraft*, p. 160; Ronald C. Sawyer, ' "Strangely handled in all her lyms": witchcraft and healing in Jacobean England', *Journal of Social History*, 22 (1989), 465. Probably the first person to be charged under the 1604 statute was a man, see HMC, *Salisbury MSS*, XVII (London, 1938), p. 36.

[43] Holland, *Treatise Against Witchcraft*, sigs. B3, E1; William Perkins, *A Discourse of the Damned Art of Witchcraft* (Cambridge, 1608), p. 168. See also Gifford, *A Discourse of the Subtill Practises of Devilles*, sig. B2. In general, see Stuart Clark, 'Protestant demonology: sin, superstition and society (c. 1520–c. 1640)', in Ankarloo and Henningsen, eds., *Early Modern European Witchcraft*, pp. 45–81.

in the 1640s, for example, learned men on either side of the witchcraft debate agreed that witchcraft was a sin like any other and as such, both sexes were vulnerable to its insinuations.[44]

These attitudes were made manifest in the Kent courts. In 1652, apart from Reynolds and Wilson, four other men were tried for maleficent witchcraft at Maidstone, a town where almost a century earlier the surgeon John Halle had railed against a different group of male suspects whom he described as 'divelishe wyches and sorcerers'. One of these earlier witches, William Winckfield, was whipped and excommunicated for necromancy by a church court and, so it was said, finally fled from the civil authorities at the introduction of the 1563 Witchcraft Act. In the early 1560s men from the parishes of Headcorn, Westwell, Otterden and Lyminge were all accused of witchcraft in the church courts, including one Kytterell, 'a sinister physicion', who had performed sorcery over a woman in labour. Visitations in the diocese of Canterbury in 1569 exposed a Westbere man as an experienced sorcerer, and one George Walcot was accused of 'the sin of witchcraft'. Similarly, in 1580 the privy council ordered that Richard Yeorke of Stoale be apprehended for 'sundry lewde and detestable practises aboute conjuracions'; a decade later, Thomas Fansome appeared before the high commission charged with practising amatory magic, principally, giving poor William Suttyll's wife 'a wrytinge or a charme to make hyr husband to love hyr'.[45] It is true that many such accusations concerned sorcery, necromancy, invocation of spirits and magical healing rather than *maleficium*, but in the eyes of the church, the distinction was less important than in the secular courts. Many entries in the ecclesiastical records fail to specify the type of witchcraft being prosecuted, and so we cannot fully assess how many men were actually accused of *maleficium*. Yet we must accept that in early modern communities, however rarely, the male witch

---

[44] Gaule, *Select Cases of Conscience*, p. 52; Stearne, *Confirmation and Discovery*, p. 12. For expressions of the same opinion, see Thomas Cooper, *The Mystery of Witch-Craft* (London, 1617), pp. 180–1; Richard Bernard, *A Guide to Grand-Jury Men* (London, 1627; 1629 edn), p. 87; Alexander Roberts, *A Treatise of Witchcraft . . . With a True Narration of the Witchcrafts which Mary Smith, wife of Henry Smith Glover, did Practice* (London, 1616), pp. 4–5.

[45] John Halle, *An Historiall Expostulation: Against the Beastlye Abusers, Both of Chyrurgerie and Physyke, in Oure Tyme* (London, 1565), ed., T. J. Pettigrew (London, 1844), pp. 7, 15 and *passim*; CCDRO, DCb/X.8.5, ff. 90ᵛ–91; X.1.2, ff. 1/35ᵛ, 1/40ᵛ; X.8.5, ff. 53, 72; Y.2.24, f. 36ᵛ; X.1.6, f. 76; X.1.4, f. 91ᵛ; Hussey, 'Visitations of the Archdeacon of Canterbury", 221; 'Peter de Sandwich', 'Some East Kent parish history', *Home Counties Magazine*, 5 (1903), 13; *Acts of the Privy Council*, n.s. XII, 1580–1581 (London, 1896), pp. 21–2; KAO, DRb/PRC 44/3, pp. 166–9.

– both helpful and harmful – was a physical as well as a theoretical reality.

Not all such men were poor and marginal figures. In 1562 an elderly woman, Joan Basden of St Paul's in Canterbury, swore before the consistory that Alderman John Twyne was a conjuror who exerted a strange coercive force over others. Twyne, she alleged, had threatened to kill her after they had argued about a debt owed to him, and had conjured up 'a black thing like a great rugged blak dogg w[hi]ch wold danse about the house, and hurle fyer'. Yet again, the roles of witch and accuser according to the Macfarlane/Thomas model would seem to have been reversed. Other accusations of witchcraft show how the socially impotent could attack figures of authority, in particular clergymen. Even after the Reformation, ministers were still seen by many as guardians of an intangible power, the potential of which might be viewed ambiguously as beneficial or malevolent. Witches accused in the church courts usually had been seeking to harness divine – as opposed to diabolical – power (remember Nicholas Hardwyn's maleficent prayer), and it may have sometimes seemed that a double standard was being observed. Moreover, it is likely that on occasion unspecified charges of witchcraft were a veil for disciplinary action against the use of traditional liturgy after the Elizabethan Settlement of 1559, and especially after the publication of the Thirty-Nine Articles of 1563. For these reasons, a clergyman might find himself under suspicion, especially if he was disliked for other reasons. In 1561 there were at least three instances of alleged clerical sorcery in Kent: the curate of Biddenden was accused of setting a bad example by burning some of his cattle in an attempt to reverse a witch's hex; a man presented for witchcraft claimed that he had learned some of his magical skills from the parish priest at Sutton; and Thomas Thompson, the vicar of Godmersham and Challock, was excommunicated for *veneficium* and incantation. To a clergyman, the consequences of such accusations might not have always been as serious as excommunication or, far worse, conviction for felony, but in many cases the damage done to his reputation in that community may well have been permanent.[46]

---

[46] CCDRO, DCb/Y.2.24, ff. 69v–70v; X.1.3, f. 156v; X.8.5, f. 72; Y.2.24, f. 54. This inversion of the stereotype can be seen in other counties, see, for example: Ewen, *Witch Hunting and Witch Trials*, p. 283; J. C. Jeaffreson, ed., *Middlesex County Records*, 4 vols. (Clerkenwell, 1886–92), I, p. 197; J. C. Cox, *Three Centuries of Derbyshire Annals*, 2 vols. (London, 1890), II, p. 90. For other cases of clerical witchcraft, see Gaskill, 'Witches and witchcraft accusations', pp. 57–9.

The accusation of men continued into the seventeenth century when, due to the growing ascendancy of the secular courts over their ecclesiastical equivalents, the penalties were more often potentially greater. The year 1617 saw the prosecution of three Kentish men under the 1604 Witchcraft Act, one of them a minister. In the village of Halden (now High Halden), Andrew Loader told justices how he witnessed the rector of the parish, William Lawse, give William Childes a conjuring book and then saw

> a Circle made with Chalke in the middle of the roome, w[hi]ch the said Chiles said that hee had made, & that it was in Compasse nine foote & a halfe, and hee told Mr Lawse that hee had gone as far as hee Could till hee had written Latine words in the Circle whereupon Mr Lawse wrot w[i]th Chalke within the said Circle three or fowre words in fowre sundry places

The rector's servant, Isaac Mungery, confirmed that the two men 'often wheare in secrett conference togethere in Mr Lawes his studdie and in other places in the house where Childs dide show Mr Lawes the seaven plannetts and divers other things'. Mungery also claimed to have seen spirits in his master's house.[47] Other cases seem equally remote from the stereotype. In the same year as Lawes was accused, the mayor and jurats of New Romney heard how when some local inhabitants voiced their suspicions about William Godfrey – a middle-aged property-owning farmer supporting a wife and children – to Thomas Bennett of Newchurch, Bennett 'did saye unto them that he thought in his Conscience that the said Godfrey was a witch'. Eight men and women came forward to give evidence against Godfrey for a variety of witch-crafts including causing lameness in lambs, leaving the devil in a house which he rented out, using familiars to attempt the abduction of a child and to kill a pig, and staining laundry with blood.[48]

The range of persons who might be implicated in witchcraft accusations extended to other family members, and it was widely held

---

[47] KAO, QM/SI 1618/2/7; QM/SB 1306–7, 1311, 1315. William Lawse obtained his MA from Cambridge in 1581, was inducted as rector of Halden in 1600 and died in 1626: J. Venn and J. A. Venn, *The Book of Matriculations and Degrees 1544–1659* (Cambridge, 1913), p. 414; *Extracts from Registers and Records: Relating to the Collation, Institution, Induction, and Composition of the Rectors of High Halden* (London, 1900), p. 11. A number of educated men were accused, see for example, Stearne, *Confirmation and Discovery*, pp. 23, 25, 32. In 1646 John Gaule asserted that many 'men of the most eminent wisdome and holinesse' had been slandered as witches: *Select Cases of Conscience*, p. 8.

[48] KAO, NR/JQp 1/30.

that witchcraft could be passed on either as a skill to family, friends and servants, or by heredity.[49] The offspring of a suspected witch were particularly at risk, and as one Jacobean minister observed, 'all who are convented upon these unlawfull actions [witchcraft] are not strucken in yeares; but some even in the flower of their youth be nuzzled up in the same, and convicted to be practizers thereof'.[50] At the bishop's court at Rochester in 1562, Alexander Goody of Tudeley told how he overheard Edmund Peyrson inform Mary Wodd that 'Fremans wedowe doythe say that thowe & thy childer bi witches', and that this was 'a Comyn Talke in Tudeley'. Again, at Canterbury in 1571, Laurence Walker and his wife accused Goodwife Champnes and her daughter of working together to bewitch their child. In 1617 when the farmer Godfrey was accused by various members of the Clarke, Barber and Ladds families, his children also fell under suspicion. William Clarke informed a magistrate that when he asked his young son to chase Godfrey's ducks from his land, the accused's daughter said 'they should repent it & that they would be quit w[i]th them for it'. Sickness among Clarke's livestock, followed by a visit to a cunning woman, convinced him that his next-door neighbours were guilty of maleficent witchcraft. Another neighbour also implicated Godfrey's adolescent son for having displayed, three years earlier, an uncanny prescience regarding some pies in his kitchen cupboard and had offered some unusual advice about a sack of flour, after which both commodities mysteriously spoiled.[51]

In this way, as suggested earlier, whole households might be ranged against one another, resulting in multiple accusations at variance with the stereotype. In 1631 John Younge's wife, Catherine, and another female relative, were tried at the summer assizes at Maidstone, where the former was sentenced to be hanged. In 1657 Stephen Allen of Goudhurst lost both wife and daughter to the hangman after they pleaded guilty to the invocation of evil spirits for maleficent purposes, and the girl even testified against her mother. Similarly, in 1566 at Wittersham, Fryswid Appes confessed that her sister was a witch, and a century later

---

[49] Norman Cohn, *Europe's Inner Demons. An Inquiry Inspired by the Great Witch-Hunt* (London, 1975), pp. 248–9. Spectators at the Maidstone trials of 1652 wanted the blood-line of the witches to be broken by fire: H.F., *Prodigious & Tragicall History of . . . six Witches at Maidstone*, p. 5. However, this connection was not – as Clive Holmes has suggested – exclusively matrilineal: 'Women, witnesses and witches', p. 51. See Perkins, *Discourse*, pp. 201–4; Bernard, *Guide to Grand-Jury Men*, pp. 206–7.

[50] Roberts, *A Treatise of Witchcraft*, p. 4.

[51] KAO, DRb/Jdl, f. 98; CCDRO, DCb/X.1.10, f. 6; KAO, NR/JQp 1/30/2, 10–12.

Katherine Huse brought her mother to the attention of the Kent magistrates for allegedly bewitching a neighbour's ring from her finger. Condemnation, as well as defence and support, therefore, could originate or be compounded from within the family, possibly serving as an outlet for domestic tensions for which no other legitimate means of expression existed.[52]

## IV

So far the intention has not been to suggest that the character of witchcraft prosecutions in Kent was intrinsically different from other counties, still less that Macfarlane and Thomas were fundamentally mistaken in their conclusions. Rather one feels that the history of English witchcraft – in Essex at least – has emphasised the model accusation at the expense of cases which fit the theory less well. One can see clearly that the process of identifying a witch could deviate markedly from the familiar progression of begging, denial, guilt, misfortune and accusation; nor did it always rely on gender or social stereotypes. In short, it is simply impossible to encapsulate the experience and meaning of witchcraft within such a narrowly conceived framework. A final observation to be made from the Kent material concerns the use and abuse of witchcraft accusations as an expression of hostility and a means to resolve local disputes – in particular, the association and conflation of the offence with a range of grievances in the community.

In the first place, a specific accusation against one person might be deflected by that individual towards another. In 1591 a church court heard how at West Farleigh, Agnes Joyner and Alice Roydon diverted the rumour that they were witches towards Joan Preble and Mary Cleeve. It was alleged that while Joyner and her husband spread vicious gossip about the two scapegoats, Rydon 'Counterfeited herself to be bewitched by them. And the same Joyner & his wife mayntayned her in that abuse.' Again, in 1617, William Lawse tried unsuccessfully to turn the tables on his servant, Isaac Mungery. Suspecting his master of witchcraft, Mungery challenged him with certain questions 'w[hi]ch he touke soe ill thatt presently he scited me uppon it to the comessaries Court to my greatt trubble and charges'. The servant, however, decided to make a civil action of the affair and went to a magistrate who released him from

---

52 Levack, *Witch-Hunt*, p. 133; Ewen, *Witch Hunting and Witch Trials*, pp. 91–2, 216–17, 249; PRO, ASSI 35/98/5/35–6; CCDRO, DCb/Z.4.12, f. 29; KAO, Q/SB 8/19.

the clutches of the ecclesiastical authorities and summoned the clergy-man Lawse instead.[53]

Formal presentment for witchcraft was often accompanied by prosecution of the same person for other offences. In April 1652 John Wills of Warehorne took Anne Pottin and John Young to court. Pottin was charged with 'entertaininge of Inmates, for livinge incontinentlie with men and being suspected to receive & keepe Fellons goodes'.[54] A note at the bottom of the recognizance recording her bail, adds the specific charge 'recevinge John Yonge who is a marryed man'. Young, a local tailor, was accused of 'dissertinge his wife: for being suspected to be lewd with other women [and] for other misdemeanures'. Both were to be indicted for evading magistrates. The outcome of the trial does not survive, but clearly John Wills was dissatisfied. In September, John Young was apprehended and imprisoned in Canterbury Castle, and early in 1653 both he and Pottin were presented by Wills for witchcraft. Of Pottin's fate the record is silent, but Young, presuming he was able to pay his gaol fees, was released when the bill against him was thrown out by the grand jury. There is nothing to suggest why Young and Pottin might have been thought to have been witches, but it would seem likely that they were engaged in an extra-marital relationship which Wills objected to. His grievance, therefore, was most likely Young's abuse of another man's wife, and his dissolute life in general, as much as a vague and unsubstantiated act of *maleficium*.[55]

Other witchcraft accusations in seventeenth-century Kent were accompanied by objections to other forms of unneighbourly conduct, such as drunkenness and other disorderly behaviour. Alice Robert of Goudhurst, for instance, was presented at a Canterbury church court in 1560 not only for witchcraft but also because she had 'Raysed Stryffe betwene Rycharde Rode and his wiffe'.[56] Others were said to have committed immoral acts. In 1563, at the same hearing as she was accused

---

[53] KAO, DRb/Pa 21, ff. 6, 55; QM/SB 1315.

[54] For a parallel case, see *APC*, n.s. XII, p. 228.

[55] KAO, Q/SRc E5/60–1; Q/SMc 1; Q/SRc E6/38, 64, 83.

[56] CCDRO, DCb/X.1.2, f. 1/63ᵛ. See also: X.1.7, f. 35ᵛ; X.1.12, f. 28. Religious nonconformity, such as failure to receive communion, also accompanied accusations. One Kentish woman was presented as a witch in part because she wore a rosary; in 1562 churchwardens at Chartham reported an Irish priest not just for fortune-telling and sorcery but for seeking to persuade people 'to contemne and despyse the religion that nowe ys set forthe': CCDRO, DCb/X.1.4, ff. 19–20ᵛ; X.1.4, f. 20ᵛ. On the Continent witchcraft was linked to offences as varied as vagrancy and rebellion: Levack, *Witch-Hunt*, pp. 137–9.

of running a brothel, a Cranbrook woman was also questioned about witchcraft. In the same decade, the necromancer Winckfield was tried by the ecclesiastical authorities 'as an adulterer, and a woorker by divilshe and magicall artes'; he was also reputed to be a notorious bigamist, having three wives living at Canterbury. Other infractions of household discipline might also compound suspicions of witchcraft. At Aldington in 1569, suspicion that Margaret Dale was a witch became a formal accusation when her neighbours learned that she was no longer living with her husband; and another accused witch, Goodwife Martyn of Warehorne, was also allegedly separated in the 1560s. Disapprobation at the adultery and sexual promiscuity of Goodwife Swayne of St John's-in-Thanet, was accompanied by a charge of witchcraft in 1582 when she was denounced for saying, 'that she can make a drink which she saith if she give it to any young man that she liketh well of, he shall be in love with her'. Likewise, Thomas Fansome, the pedlar of love charms, was also presented for seeking to interfere with the natural course of sexual relations, as well as being a nuisance and 'A longe Fornicator' living incontinently from his wife.[57]

Fansome was also condemned as a cheat who had obtained money by unscrupulous means. Disliked for similar reasons, Joan Cason, the witch hanged at Faversham in 1586, confessed not only that John Mason 'had the use hir bodie verie dishonestlie whilest she was wife to hir husband', but crucially that she had failed to make the bequests stipulated by her lover in his will. Guilt over this omission caused Cason herself to believe that the deceased Mason had sent the rat which paid frequent visits to her house, in order 'that she shoolde see hys wyll fulfylled & . . . she dothe thincke that yt was Masons soule'. Cason denied any crime 'but hir lewd life and adulterous conversation' which would seem to have been the greatest objection of her neighbours. An adulteress in the locality was undesirable, but someone who fraudulently profited from the offence was intolerable. Ill-gotten gains were also the downfall of Christopher Harrison and Margaret Baron of Saltwood, tried at the Canterbury quarter sessions in 1653 as much for their attempts to defraud 'the goode and honest persons of this comon wealth of England of theire Goods

---

[57] CCDRO, DCb/X.1.4, f. 94ᵛ; Halle, *Historiall Expostulation*, pp. 11–13; 'Some East Kent parish history', *HCM*, 5 (1903), 15; CCDRO, DCb.X.1.7, f. 48v; Hussey, 'Visitations of the Archdeacon of Canterbury', 19; KAO, DRb/PRC 44/3, pp. 85–6. Sometimes witchcraft and whoredom were associated, particularly when accusations of either were used primarily as insults. See, for example: CCDRO, DCb/X.1.7, f. 79ᵛ; 'Some East Kent parish history', *HCM*, 7 (1905), 130.

chattels and moneys', as claiming the ability to 'tell and knowe the chances and fortunes of men to come hereafter'. Although it is not recorded if Harrison was found guilty of palmistry, he was certainly punished as a vagrant and placed in the house of correction.[58] Additional charges could also be of a more serious nature. In 1641 Manly Stansall of Gillingham was charged with another man 'For practising Inchantm[en]t & Witchcraft' upon Stansall's daughter. This charge was not, however, pursued at the next assizes, and instead Stansall was convicted of a *physical* assault on the girl, and was fined and bound over to keep the peace. This case also reinforces the earlier point about conflict within the family, especially since at least four writs were issued against Stansall's wife to answer related charges at this time. Accused witches might be charged with other destructive behaviour such as arson. In 1675, when Mary Brice of Rochester was indicted for killing a woman with a broom and setting fire to property, she was also charged with bewitching a man and a woman. In a similar case in 1658, Judith Sawkins of Aylesford was condemned not just for her alleged *maleficia*, but for burning a barn by natural means.[59] Clearly, the nonconformity of the witch could comprise more than initially meets the eye.

Contributory motives for witchcraft accusations could be even more deeply embedded in a community. As already mentioned, it was the personal grudges of a neighbour and a servant which caused the rector of Halden, William Lawse, to be called before the local magistrate on a charge of witchcraft in 1617. But Lawse had not lived entirely at peace with others in the community prior to the accusation. He had quarrelled with John Whetcombe at a slaughterhouse, for instance, and Whetcombe had called him 'a skurvye shitten fellowe' for which Lawse prosecuted him. He was also frequently at law in these years over tithe disputes and may well have acquired an image as a contentious person. It would appear that one of the origins of his unpopularity was that for the past decade he had lived in a cottage without the statutory 4 acres of land, and in an inconvenient place in the village 'To the great annoyance of all the Inhabitants there'. An attempt to present Lawse for this offence resulted in failure, and soon after some of his neighbours assembled a charge of

---

[58] *Holinshed's Chronicles*, III, pp. 1560–1; KAO, Fa/JQs 23 (bdl. 128); Q/SRc E7/84; Q/SMc 1.

[59] Elizabeth Melling (ed.), *Kentish Sources, VI. Crime and Punishment* (Maidstone, 1969), p. 95; KAO, Q/SMc 1 (1640–1); J. S. Cockburn, ed., *Calendar of Assize Records. Kent Indictments, Charles I* (London, 1995), pp. 394, 399, 411, 432, 482, 502. Ewen, *Witch-Hunting and Witch Trials*, pp. 250–1, 259.

witchcraft loosely based on an event which supposedly had occurred almost a decade earlier. Although Lawse was again acquitted it is probable that his local standing was further diminished by this incident.[60]

Many prosecutions were generated by the sheer malice of personal feuds. Even if a case were thrown out of court, an accused witch would not only lose reputation, but might spend weeks or months in a noisome gaol awaiting trial – and even after acquittal if fees could not be paid. Given the appalling conditions, a protracted spell of imprisonment might even amount to a death sentence.[61] Yet, despite its importance for the history of crime, vexatious prosecution has been neglected because it is almost impossible to prove in all but a handful of cases.[62] On the whole, the safest conclusion is simply that false accusations *must* have knowingly been made because, in theory at least, vaguely defined legal provisions against witchcraft 'gave an unprecedented power to all members of the community to solve their conflicts and to take revenge for anything'.[63] Contemporaries believed that many accusations were false. Scot warned that some 'maintaine and crie out for the execution of witches, that particularlie beleeve never a whit of that which is imputed unto them'; even the witch-finder Stearne conceded as much.[64] Although Keith Thomas rightly points out that fraudulent cases 'must be recognized as essentially parasitic to the witch-beliefs, and in no way their cause', unless an individual case was directly proven to be fraudulent, it remained as serious and real as an accusation where the motive was sincere.[65]

---

[60] KAO, QM/SB 1306–7, 1311, 1315; QM/SB 1265; QM/SI 1618/2/7; CCDRO, DCb/PRC 39/32 (1613–15), ff. 12ᵛ–15; PRC 39/33, ff. 19–19ᵛ.

[61] C. L'Estrange Ewen, *Witchcraft in the Star Chamber* (n.p., 1938), p. 9; Macfarlane, *Witchcraft*, pp. 16, 60.

[62] In general, see Douglas Hay, 'Prosecution and power. Malicious prosecution in the English courts, 1750–1850', in Douglas Hay and Francis Snyder, eds., *Prosecution and Policing in Britain 1750–1850* (Oxford, 1989), pp. 343–95. See also G. R. Quaife, *Godly Zeal and Furious Rage. The Witch in Early Modern Europe* (London, 1987), ch. 10; Gaskill, 'Witches and witchcraft accusations', pp. 70–3.

[63] Gábor Klaniczay, 'Hungary: the accusations and the universe of popular magic', in Ankarloo and Henningsen, eds., *Early Modern European Witchcraft*, pp. 238–9.

[64] Scot, *Discoverie of Witchcraft*, pp. 15, 17; Stearne, *Confirmation and Discovery*, p. 34. See also Bernard, *Guide to Grand-Jury Men*, pp. 77, 194–6; Fuller, *Profane State*, p. 351; John Webster, *The Displaying of Supposed Witchcraft* (London, 1677), ch. 14. Regarding the decline of witchcraft prosecutions, 'Transparently malicious charges were frequent enough to call into doubt a crime that was easy to suspect and very hard to prove': Michael MacDonald, *Witchcraft and Hysteria in Elizabethan London* (London, 1991), p. 52.

[65] Thomas, *Religion and the Decline of Magic*, p. 646.

There are a number of cases which might be explained in this way. At the Faversham trial in 1586, described above, Joan Cason vainly asserted her innocence, and instead blamed 'diverse matters and instances of the malicious dealings of hir adversaries against hir, reciting also certeine controversies betwixt hir and them, wherein they had doone hir open wrong'. As for maleficent magic using ivy-gum, she protested sadly, it was no more than a cure for toothache. At least one contemporary observed that the evidence was weak and justice was miscarried, and perhaps the most striking indication of fraud was the regret later shown by her enemies, some of whom 'wished her alive after she was hanged, that cried out for the hangman when she was alive'. In other cases the malicious streak seems even more evident. In 1651 twenty-five parishioners at River testified against Helen Dadd of Hougham for bewitching children and livestock. The grand jury threw out all the charges against her – including one for entertaining familiar spirits – except those brought by Thomas Hogbin, yeoman, for killing his horse and his three-year-old son. She was convicted and executed, but within a matter of weeks six persons came forward to testify against Hogbin for murder. Alice Hogbin deposed that the boy had 'told herr that his Father did drive him out of his House to worke and hee sayd that hee was not well able to goe by reason of his lamenes in his backe'; another witness saw the boy struck down with a rake, whereupon his father 'did give him a kicke and a spurne with his Foote such as this inform[an]t sayth shee wold have bine loath to have given to a dogg'. Two women who secretly examined the corpse deposed that Hogbin had denied anyone access to it so as to conceal the injuries he had inflicted. If this was indeed what happened, presumably Hogbin decided to capitalise on current opinion against Helen Dadd by indicting her for murder by witchcraft.[66]

## V

Overall, one can see that whilst interpersonal disputes were often the source of witchcraft accusations, the feeling of guilt following the refusal of alms, as stressed in the model accusation, need not have played so

---

[66] Holinshed, *Chronicles*, III, pp. 1560–1; KAO, Q/SRc E3, ff. 62–3, 69–71, 75–6; E4, ff. 64, 70; Q/SB 2, f. 3; Q/SRc E4, ff. 3, 107. Despite the apparent weight of evidence against him, Hogbin was acquitted at Canterbury in 1652. In 1581 a syphilitic Kentish vicar prosecuted a woman for witchcraft against whom he was 'enviouslie bent', by which means he 'was cured or rather excused the shame of his disease': Scot, *Discoverie of Witchcraft*, pp. 5–6.

great a part. Resentment and a vengeful spirit between conflicting and competing parties of similar social status could suffice. When William Godfrey was accused, proceedings apparently followed the classic course of events: hostility and suspicion followed by misfortune, personal conviction, and, finally, by accusation. But Godfrey's social position relative to his accusers makes an explanation based on guilt seem implausible. Similar to William Lawse, tried for witchcraft in the same year, he was a middling self-sufficient landlord and householder with a family and servants. He certainly had no cause to demand anything from his neighbours and therefore gave them no reason to feel uneasy at not having fulfilled their charitable responsibilities towards him. Cases such as these seem to suggest two things: first, the operative existence of a broad scope of persons who could plausibly be accused as witches; second, the conscious or unconscious utilisation of witchcraft prosecutions by evenly matched opponents in order to break situations of deadlock, especially where patriarchal authority or superior rank could not be deployed. Accusations may also have occasionally served to redirect, even reverse, the direction in which power normally flowed in communities – between competing households as much as between feuding individuals – thereby enabling the weak to undermine the position of social superiors when conflicts arose.

In a summary of his argument, Macfarlane notes that his generalis-ations regarding strain placed upon neighbourly bonds, and the resulting accusation of witches as a reversal of guilt, are 'purely speculative and cannot be substantiated until detailed studies of the treatment of the poor and old . . . have been undertaken'.[67] Subsequently, however, the Macfarlane/Thomas framework has too often been uncritically accepted and the theoretical stereotype treated as in some way a definitive state-ment about witchcraft accusations in England. Method and result have accordingly been allowed to justify and reinforce one another, as one historian demonstrates when he unquestioningly advocates the export of 'well-established anthropological methods' to the study of witchcraft and praises the 'conceptual clarity' they produce, whilst referring to 'the now familiar generalisation that the vast majority of witches were poor, elderly women'.[68] It is clear that the experience of witchcraft in early

[67] Macfarlane, *Witchcraft*, pp. 204–7, 207n.
[68] Richard A. Horsley, 'Who were the witches? The social roles of the accused in the European witch trials', *Journal of Interdisciplinary History*, 9 (1979), 689, 694, 699–700.

modern Kent was not *necessarily* conditioned by status or gender, that accusers frequently might disregard familiar typologies, and that the prosecution of witches could reflect every sort of communal disturbance. Perhaps then, in a way, men like Godfrey and Lawse should be viewed as ordinary victims of the Witchcraft Act, rather than the exceptions to some artificially imposed rule.

In general, the value of comparative models of witchcraft prosecutions is open to question if they are used to provide ready-made answers rather than as sources of imaginative stimulation.[69] Some historians now favour a multicausal approach to the study of continental witchcraft because experience and circumstances were in fact so varied – and often the applicability of the stereotype so doubtful – even within the general 'European pattern'.[70] With this diversity in mind, there is a strong case for viewing English witchcraft as a variant of the European model rather than an exception to it – an approach which calls for comparative analysis within an early modern (as opposed to anthropological) context. The validity of Macfarlane and Thomas' comparisons to patterns of African witchcraft accusations is questionable anyway, due to differences in the economic, intellectual and legal structures of early modern European societies and their modern primitive counterparts – something Thomas himself has accepted. The final part of Macfarlane's study, moreover, in fact does more to illustrate the diversity of primitive beliefs in African countries than it does to justify the preceding interpretation of the English material.[71]

But perhaps African beliefs do have something to teach the student of

---

[69] See E. P. Thompson, 'Anthropology and the discipline of historical context', *Midland History*, 1 (1972), 43; T. G. Ashplant and Adrian Wilson, 'Present-centred history and the problem of historical knowledge', *Historical Journal*, 31 (1988), 257–60.

[70] Robin Briggs, *Communities of Belief. Cultural and Social Tension in Early Modern France* (Oxford, 1989), p. 396; Levack, *Witch-Hunt*, pp. 2–3; Marijke Gijswijt-Hofstra, 'The European witchcraft debate and the Dutch variant', *Social History*, 15 (1990), 181–94.

[71] Thompson, 'Anthropology and the discipline of historical context', 46–8; Rowland, 'Fantasticall and devilishe persons', pp. 172–6, 189; Levack, *Witch-Hunt*, pp. 234–5; Midelfort, *Witch Hunting*, p. 4; William P. Monter, *Witchcraft in France and Switzerland. The Borderlands during the Reformation* (London, 1976), pp. 10–11; Ankarloo and Henningsen, eds., *Early Modern European Witchcraft*, 'Introduction', pp. 1–2; Ginzburg, *Ecstasies*, p. 4; Keith Thomas, 'An anthropology of religion and magic, II', *Journal of Interdisciplinary History*, 6 (1975), 92–3, 108; Thomas, 'The relevance of social anthropology to the historical study of English witchcraft', in Mary Douglas, ed., *Witchcraft Confessions and Accusations* (London, 1970), pp. 55–7, 71; J. A. Sharpe, 'Witches and persecuting societies', *Journal of Historical Sociology*, 3 (1990), 78; Macfarlane, *Witchcraft*, pp. 211–36.

English witchcraft, precisely because of this very diversity. It has been argued that instead of the model accusation which tends to formularise the experience of witchcraft, evidence from Kent in the sixteenth and seventeenth centuries favours a less reductionist method of inquiry. Witches were frequently integrated and productive men and women in the local community with occupations to pursue and families to support and be supportive. At the same time, the law which enabled individuals to prosecute witches did not circumscribe who could be accused and upon what grounds. In the light of this, perhaps there can be seen a maverick principle at work, producing patterns of activity as irregular and unpredictable as human nature itself. Accordingly, one might conclude that the versatility of codes of beliefs and behaviour visible in the communities of south-east England, as much as in the tribes of Africa, have been obscured by a process of theorisation and categorisation, and that the desire to understand and predict events has sometimes compromised the ability to observe and describe them.

If one general conclusion can be drawn from this randomness, perhaps it is that the early modern mind was different not only in the belief that witches possessed occult powers, but also in that people were willing to pursue personal quarrels with a degree of persistence and ruthlessness which, though appalling to us, may have fallen within the accepted mores of the period. One can easily imagine the potentially, and even essentially, hostile character of communities in which individuals or groups might harass an enemy even unto death, and in which harmony was constantly being broken and remade.[72] As other recent studies of European witchcraft have suggested, the Kent material shows that accusations resulted from a broader range of tensions than has commonly been allowed; and yet although traumatic social and economic change in the later sixteenth century may have exacerbated these tensions, it did not necessarily lead directly to an increase in witchcraft accusations from below. The appeal of such an idea is enhanced by Macfarlane's historical relocation of the onset of individualism, referred to in the first

[72] On endemic malice, see Lawrence Stone, *The Family, Sex and Marriage in England* (London, 1977), pp. 95–9; J. S. Morrill and J. D. Walter, 'Order and disorder in the English Revolution', in Fletcher and Stevenson, eds., *Order and Disorder*, p. 154; Peter Burke, *Popular Culture in Early Modern Europe* (London, 1978), pp. 176–7; Sabean, *Power in the Blood*, pp. 31–2, 53–4. 'Hatred, jealousy, and conflicts of interest ran through peasant society. The village was no happy and harmonious *Gemeinschaft*': Robert Darnton, *The Great Cat Massacre and Other Episodes in French Cultural History* (London, 1984), p. 33.

section of this chapter. Perhaps, then, the enmity and breaches of charity that could lead to such accusations should be seen less as a product of declining standards of neighbourliness, and more as a perennial aspect of relationships within neighbourhoods.[73]

To conclude, it is conceivable that such a strong emphasis was placed upon 'neighbourliness' in the period because in reality social relations were so commonly characterised by its dark reverse side: malice – an enduring, but often latent, prickly hostility which could be channelled consciously or unconsciously into prosecutions for witchcraft. Under these circumstances it is logical to suppose that the integrated and, above all, competitive person would be as vulnerable to such a charge as would a more marginal figure in the community. This leaves many questions unanswered about exactly why there was a rise of witchcraft prosecutions in the sixteenth and seventeenth centuries, and why regional variations appear to have been so marked. But for the moment it is sufficient to observe that, in the eighteenth century, endemic hostility of the sort described here did not cease to manifest itself in the form of witchcraft trials because enlightened or humanitarian opinion prevailed at village level, still less because this hostility abated. Rather, it was that the double-edged sword of the law, which had at least made possible the rise of prosecutions in the first place, no longer permitted the physical expression of malice through this outlet.

---

[73] On the relationship of endemic malice to witchcraft accusations, see Levack, *Witch-Hunt*, pp. 118–19; Robin Briggs, 'Witchcraft and popular mentality in Lorraine, 1580–1630', in Brian Vickers, ed., *Occult and Scientific Mentalities in the Renaissance* (Cambridge, 1984), p. 342. 'Hatred, fear and violence were endemic in rural England before the Industrial Revolution, and many witchcraft accusations were simply extensions of personal hatreds and family feuds': Michael MacDonald, *Mystical Bedlam. Madness, Anxiety and Healing in Seventeenth-Century England* (Cambridge, 1981), pp. 107–11, quotation at p. 109.

I am grateful to Keith Wrightson and Cynthia Herrup for comments on an earlier draft of this chapter, and to Patrick Collinson for providing me with a number of references.

# Witchcraft in Seventeenth-Century Yorkshire: Accusations and Counter Measures

The starting point for this paper must be that the scholarly study of witchcraft in early modern England has more or less stagnated since the appearance, now more than twenty years ago, of two major works: Alan Macfarlane's analysis of Essex witchcraft, published in 1970; and Keith Thomas's magisterial study of witchcraft and associated beliefs, published in 1971.[1] The intervening years have seen a steady flow of publications on continental European, Scottish, and colonial American witchcraft and, recently, a number of works of synthesis.[2] But, apart from a few articles,[3] little of a scholarly nature has been published for some time on witchcraft in England. Thus the emphases given by Macfarlane and Thomas remain central to our understanding of witchcraft in sixteenth- and seventeenth-century England: the fundamental importance of stresses in interpersonal relations between villagers in generating witchcraft accusations; the idea that these relations were affected by a transference of guilt by richer villagers as their attitudes to the poor altered in the face of socio-economic change; the idea that the prosecution of witchcraft was at its highest in Elizabeth's reign; and the usefulness of applying anthropological concepts (and, in particular, the concepts of British functional anthropology) to historical materials relating to witchcraft. Macfarlane and Thomas's works also reiterated the notion, already present in Wallace Notestein's survey of 1911,[4] that there were marked differences between English and 'continental' witchcraft.

It would not be appropriate in a paper based on a limited amount of material relating to one region to attempt a detailed critique of the model described above. What is striking is that this model, as it has been translated into the textbook and the undergraduate seminar room, has become an orthodoxy. There is now a clear impression of the English witch: non–diabolical, functional,

almost rational, certainly a more understandable being than her continental
cousins, involved as these latter allegedly were in the perverted rites of the
sabbat and the dubious pleasures of copulation with demons. Somehow, we
seem to have developed an image of the English witch which is almost too
rational. Macfarlane, in one of his essays, commented that witchcraft accusations
demonstrate 'that overlapping with the ordinary physical world was a sphere
inhabited by strange, evil creatures, half-animal, half-demon. A world full of
"power", both good and evil'.[5] I think it is not too much of an exaggeration to
claim that our current thinking on English witchcraft has lost sight of some of
the elements hinted at in this passage: the sense of otherness implicit in
witchcraft; the sense of danger; and the sense that somehow 'power' is involved.
Perhaps the time has come to reopen the subject as an area of scholarly
investigation.

   This project would be unusually worthwhile if conducted on a regional
basis, to provide grounds for comparison with Macfarlane's work on Essex.
Such regional studies, however, are seriously hampered by a lack of the type
of source materials basic to Macfarlane's work, series of assize indictments. The
assizes were the courts where most of malefic witchcraft, as defined by the
statutes of 1563 and 1604, would be tried, yet for the years between 1563 and
1650 assize records do not survive in quantity outside of the south east, and even
there Kent is the only county other than Essex where sufficient indictments
against witchcraft survive to make a full-scale study viable.[6] Cheshire, whose
Palatinate Court of Great Sessions' records provide excellent series of indictments
and Crown Books over the relevant period did not, unfortunately, witness
many witchcraft accusations.[7] Similarly the several Welsh counties which enjoy
a good survival of appropriate records over the relevant period did not, on the
strength of preliminary investigations carried out by C. L. Ewen, experience
much by way of the indictment of witches.[8] The historian might well find much
of value in the records of such ecclesiastical courts as have yet to be examined,
as these tried lesser forms of sorcery, while there are doubtlessly occasional
references to witchcraft trials in the archives of those boroughs whose courts
were empowered to try felony, many of these archives being as yet uninvestigated.
But the long series of indictments which survive for the Home Circuit of the
assizes and for Cheshire are simply not available for most regions, for Yorkshire
certainly not before the 1640s.[9] In attempting a study of witchcraft in
seventeenth-century Yorkshire we must, therefore, turn to other materials.

   In theory witchcraft, like other forms of felony, could be tried at the quarter
sessions, but in practice (and especially after a judicial decision of 1590 reserving
'difficult', in effect capital, cases to the assize judges) it rarely figured in the work
of those courts. In Yorkshire, quarter sessions records do not survive for the East
Riding for the seventeenth century. Printed calendars of North Riding quarter
sessions records[10] provide few references to witchcraft and sorcery, the last of

these involving a gentleman named Robert Conyers, described as being resident in Guisborough, tried at the January 1657 sessions.[11] The massive and largely uncatalogued West Riding quarter sessions records are more problematic. An edition of West Riding sessions rolls for the closing years of Elizabeth I's reign reveals two cases, one involving finding lost or stolen goods by witchcraft, the other alleging that a woman had bewitched a man to death,[12] but other edited sessions records, this time for 1637–42, contain no witchcraft indictments.[13] Systematic examination of the West Riding quarter sessions records would doubtless reveal some references to witchcraft (a suspected witch was, for example, bound over at the late date of 1712)[14] but they are unlikely to have been numerous. Certainly Sarah Barbour-Mercer, whose doctoral thesis on crime in late seventeenth-century Yorkshire included extensive sampling of the West Riding quarter sessions, discovered no witchcraft cases among them.[15]

The ecclesiastical courts provide rather more references to witchcraft and associated matters. Philip Tyler, in a study of church court witchcraft cases published in 1969, showed that between 1567 and 1640 some 117 presentments were made for witchcraft and sorcery before the church courts at York. Yet these cases, while providing evidence of the widespread nature of witchcraft beliefs and practices, were concerned with less serious forms of witchcraft, and were, frequently, couched in very unspecific language. Over half simply noted the presentment of individuals for 'witchcraft' or 'charming'. Of the remainder, eighteen involved the casting or lifting of spells on animals and nineteen on humans, thirteen involved trying to find lost or stolen goods by witchcraft, and eight involved divination or fortune telling. These Yorkshire ecclesiastical court cases seem very comparable to those found in other areas.[16] To them might be added ecclesiastical cause papers relating to defamation suits prompted by accusations of witchcraft, which often reveal a pattern of tensions and accusations very similar to those revealed in the better documented assize cases.[17]

Perhaps the most valuable source materials, however, are another form of documentation generated by the assizes, the deposition. Normally taken by a justice of the peace when a crime was first complained of, the deposition provides numerous insights into the background of offences and, through the incidental comments made by witnesses, on social life more generally. Very few assize depositions survive for the seventeenth century: there are, for example, almost none for the Home Circuit, despite its good survival of indictments. For the seventeenth century, in fact, the best body of such materials survives for the Northern Circuit, which included the counties of Cumberland, Derbyshire, Northumberland, Westmorland, and Yorkshire.[18]

These depositions constitute a remarkable body of source material for the social historian and, despite their having been used in two doctoral theses,[19] they still contain much of interest for future researchers. In particular, they contain a number of sets of papers relating to witchcraft accusations. The total of these sets of papers is low: Yorkshire is the best represented county, but this only involves eighteen cases. Conversely, these materials do furnish insights into accusations which other forms of documentation, notably assize or quarter sessions indictments and the majority of church court presentments, simply do not provide. They can be supplemented by other source materials. Two well documented cases survive from Yorkshire borough courts.[20] There are also printed accounts of seventeenth-century Yorkshire witchcraft cases, notably a very detailed account of witchcraft and possession experienced by members of the Fairfax family in 1621, and a description of a similar case at Burton Agnes in the early 1660s.[21] There are other references to Yorkshire witchcraft in diaries, memoirs, and other private papers of the period, notably those of the Restoration nonconformist minister Oliver Heywood.[22] Thus, although it is impossible to provide for Yorkshire the type of statistical study of witchcraft accusations which Macfarlane conducted for Essex, materials survive which will enable us to form a more rounded impression of the qualitative aspects of the social reality of witchcraft than can be constructed from the runs of indictments upon which a quantitative survey might be based.

The absence of such statistical evidence induces caution, yet it does seem that fear of malefic witchcraft was a familiar phenomenon in Yorkshire by 1600. As we have noted, lesser forms of witchcraft were regularly presented before the Elizabethan ecclesiastical courts: indeed, at the very beginning of the reign Jane Shatter of Fishlake was presented for 'inchauntment and wychecrafte'.[23] As Elizabeth's reign progressed, witchcraft in Yorkshire began to figure among the concerns of the secular authorities. In 1583 three women, following the provisions of the 1563 witchcraft statute for causing less serious harm by witchcraft, were pilloried at Hull.[24] In 1597 the Privy Council issued a pardon to Elizabeth Melton of Collingham who had been convicted for witchcraft.[25] In 1603 a woman named Mary Panell, whose reputation for witchcraft stretched back at least to bewitching a man to death in 1593, was executed at Ledston.[26] In 1604, again at Hull, four witches (three women and one man) were executed, one of them 'confessing many things & at his death accusing divers for witchcraft'.[27] Three years earlier Marmaduke Jackson, the son of a Mr Jackson of Bishop Burton, was allegedly thrown into fits as a result of being bewitched by two women.[28] The thickening of such references around the beginning of the seventeenth century suggests a growing awareness of witchcraft as a problem.

## II

As we have suggested, recent thinking has tended to characterize the early modern English witch in a rational light as the product of the type of interpersonal disputes recorded by functional anthropologists, a marginalized figure at the mercy of social forces: thus Keith Thomas could see the witch as the victim of 'the tyranny of local opinion', while Lawrence Stone claimed that the 'only unifying bond' among early modern English villagers was 'the occasional episode of mass hysteria which bound together the majority in order to harry and persecute the local witch'.[29] Those who thought themselves to have been on the receiving end of witchcraft in the early modern period would probably have seen things very differently. To them the witch was frequently a frightening individual who could, on occasion, do harm with terrible speed and terrible effectiveness. Jane Kighly came into the house of Abraham Hobson in Idle in 1649, stroked a pig that was standing by the fire, and said that it would go mad, which it promptly did, dying half an hour later. Hobson also deposed that a fortnight after the previous Christmas he had attended 'a pig feast' where Kighly was present, and where she told him 'shee loved him and all his house', and gave him 'a little clappe on his knee'. The next day, the knee was 'like it had been nettled, & very angry', and eventually a general paralysis set in.[30] Mary Allanson of Appleton Wiske fell sick an hour after Elizabeth Lively took her hand while thanking her for alms given at Allanson's door.[31] In 1654 a Mr Francke of Rothwell fell fatally ill after Katherine Earle, with whom he had been drinking in an alehouse, gave him a blow between the shoulders. Another man deposed that his mare fell sick immediately after the same woman struck it with 'a docken stalk . . . or such like thing', and that he himself was 'very sore troubled and p[er]plexed with a paine in his neck' after she struck him there.[32] Chance meetings with suspected witches could be traumatic, as when a Leconfield man, 'driveing his draught in a laine', met Grace Darvell, a known cattle charmer.[33] Indeed, Oliver Heywood noted a general disinclination to come to his house 'for fear of witches' after his maidservant was 'distempered and strangely taken' as a result of a chance meeting with a suspected witch on her way home from the Heywood residence.[34]

Perhaps the most dramatic examples of the impact of being bewitched come from the numerous descriptions contained in these Yorkshire materials of the illnesses caused by witches. Nowhere is the discrepancy between the impression formed by the deceptively rational phraseology of indictments and that created by more descriptive sources more clearly demonstrated than in these cases. Typically, an indictment recorded that a witch bewitched somebody, who then 'languished' for a period of time before, in many cases, dying. Here, in a description of a child bewitched at Scarborough in 1651, is what 'languishing' implied:

> a woman child of about fower yeares of age that is strangely handled by fitts, namely, the hands and armes drawne together contracted, the mouth some tyme drawne together, other tymes drawne to a wonderfull widenesse, the eyes often drawne wide open and the tong rite out of the mouth (almost bitten of), looks black and the head drawes to one side, the mouth drawne

awrye, and makes noise, with trembling: and when itt is out of the fitts itt starts often as in feare.[35]

The sources are full of accounts of fits, convulsions, loss of power of speech, trances and palpitations. Some indication of what this meant for the victim can be gathered from another incident recorded by Heywood, called to Wakefield in 1665 to help with 'a young man they judged to be possessed or bewitched'. Heywood noted that 'six or seven lusty men could scarce hold him, but he was lift up off the bed with incredible violence, he had abundance of fits that day, and all his senses taken from him, was stiffe as a stone, did sing in his fits'.[36]

Most of our evidence on fits and possession comes from the second half of the seventeenth century, by which time, it might be argued, pamphlet accounts of witchcraft might have done much to educate people into ascribing certain forms of behaviour to being bewitched. It is, therefore, instructive to turn to the beginning of the century, when young Marmaduke Jackson was thought to be bewitched. Even at this date, the main elements in such cases seem to have been well established. Jackson was apparently thrown violently into the fire by an unseen force, and was also raised two yards above the ground '& turned about twise, & thrown violently upon his head, yet not hurt at all'. On falling, 'he lyeth in a dead swound half an hour except it be beside a bed then in despite of 10 men he shall be drawn under ye bed by ye heels'. He could also tell where the alleged witches were and what they were doing, and, alarmingly, 'will gallop upon his knees & hands faster yn a man can run. There is in his bones a noise like a consort of musick'. The two supposed witches had confessed to their activities, 'but the devil leaveth not from tormenting him'. Jackson's sufferings, as we have seen, set the pattern for the century.[37]

Fits became even more disturbing when the afflicted began to vomit foreign bodies. Here, as elsewhere in cases of possession, the historian is in need of medical opinion,[38] while, inevitably, a number of such cases involved fraud: John Webster, a north country clergyman – doctor who published a sceptical book on witchcraft in 1677, was convinced on this point,[39] while one witness in a Yorkshire case deposed that she had investigated the possibility that the vomiting of pins and other materials in question was simulated.[40] But, taken at their face value, the depositions describing such incidents reinforce the view that there was more to witchcraft than village tensions. Thus Elizabeth Mallory, daughter of a gentry family at Ripon, 'vomited sev[er]all strange thinges as blotting pap[er] full of pins & thred tied about & a peice of woole & pins in it and likewise two feathers & a sticke'.[41] At the other end of the social scale, John Hartley, a labourer from Baildon, recounted how his son vomited, among other things, 'a horse shoe stubb & two crooked pins', while a woman reported that the child also vomited 'two peeces of horse combe and a little p[ar]cell of strawe'.[42] Perhaps the most disturbing example of this type is provided by James Johnson, the teenage servant of a Thorne yeoman, who in 1681 passed gravel stones, some as big as a pigeon's egg, through his penis, which 'swelled to an extraordinary bigness' in the process.[43]

Another recurring feature of accounts of possession is that the sufferers regularly claimed to see their supposed tormentors in their fits, and cried out against them. Elizabeth Mallory, whose vomiting we have noted, regularly cried out against her supposed tormentors, the married couple Mary and William Waide, during her convulsions. Those attending her at one point suggested the names of various possible tormentors to her, and 'when they named W[illia]m Wayde she was paste holding, her extreamity was such, & cryed out "William Wayde, thou terrifyer"'.[44] Similarly Abraham Hartley regularly cried out against his supposed tormentor, Capp's wife, in his fits,[45] while the daughter of a gentleman named John Earnley, in the grip of a 'violent and sicke fitt', cried out that 'Anne Wilkinson was cruelly prickinge and tormenting her with pins as the s[ai]d Anne was sitting by her own fire upon a little chair'.[46] Evidence against Jennet Preston, hanged for witchcraft in 1612 at York, included accounts of how her victim, a gentleman named Thomas Lister, while on his death bed 'cryed out in great extremitie; Jennet Preston lyes heavie upon me, Preston's wife lyes heavie upon me; helpe me, helpe me: and so departed, crying out against her'.[47] We return to the point that witchcraft suspicions existed in a context of fear and drama.

Tormentors sometimes came in a non human guise, or proved themselves able to change into animal form. The daughter of Margaret Wade of Gargrave, allegedly betwitched, saw 'a great bitch with a dish in her mouth' sitting at the end of her bed, and a witness to the case reported how on one occasion the child saw three things 'like blacke dogges', two of which she identified as local women, who came to her bedside and pricked her side and head.[48] Similarly John Greenliffe, a Beverley cordwainer, claimed to see Elizabeth Roberts, a joiner's wife, in his fits, and that on one occasion she turned into a cat, and on another came 'in the likenesse of a bee' and threw his body 'from place to place', nothwithstanding the fact that there were 'five or six p[er]sons to holde him downe'.[49] It should be noted, however, that although some Yorkshire witches were clearly thought able to change into animal form, there seems to have been less concern with animal familiars than in East Anglian cases. Significantly, perhaps, the two clearest indications of such beliefs came in printed sources dealing with gentry victims of witchcraft: thus Edward Fairfax thought that Margaret Waite and the other witches afflicting his daughters had familiars, while one of the witches executed in the Corbet case confessed to having a familiar which sucked her 'witch pap'.[50]

What these accounts of bewitching, of ills inflicted, of spectral visions demonstrate is a basic consideration which it is easy to loose sight of: witchcraft was about power. As one recent writer has pointed out, early modern witchcraft was usually accomplished 'by virtue of an inexplicable power which is inherent in or possessed by the accused, perhaps manifest in a glance or a strange comment',[51] and it is interesting to note that the author of one of the most stimulating anthropological works on witchcraft, Jeanne Favret Saada, based much of her conceptualization of the subject around the idea of 'force'.[52] One suspects that such notions would have made considerable sense to the protagonists in our Yorkshire witchcraft accusations. Certainly the idea of power was there: indeed, the notion of a witch 'getting power' over her victim cropped up regularly. A witness in 1674 alleged that she heard one witch tell another that if she could induce Thomas Haigh 'to buy threepenny worth of Indicoe and look him in the face, wee shall have power enough to take his life'.[53] A cunning woman called to cure a bewitched child in Scarborough in 1651 told its mother that the suspected witch 'did gett power of the s[ai]d child in the father's arms as he was bringing itt from the fair'.[54] Oliver Heywood, in the case of the bewitched maidservant which we have already noted, thought Jaggar's wife, the alleged witch, had 'got power over her'.[55] Again, we must remind ourselves that the witch was a frightening figure, sometimes using that quality to obtain considerable power locally. Thus Edward Fairfax told how one of his daughters' tormentors

> had so powerful hand over the wealthiest neighbours that none of them refused to do anything she required; yea, they provided her with fire, and meat from their own tables; and did what else they thought to please her.[56]

Dealing with such people on a day to day basis might easily prove problematic.

This point is demonstrated by the neighbourly conflicts, the 'fallings out', which so often precipitated a witchcraft accusation. There is the fundamental difficulty that, other than in exceptional circumstances, the historian is only presented with evidence of the final breakdown in interpersonal relations. Such evidence does, however, frequently convey the menace that witches might be felt to offer. Macfarlane's work on Essex has accustomed us to one such pattern of interpersonal breakdown, when, after the refusal of alms or some other favour, a poorer villager was accused of witchcraft by a richer one after the latter experienced a misfortune: witchcraft, served, then, as an explanation for misfortune, but also a means by which the powerless could wield power. A number of such cases exist in Yorkshire,[57] but they do not seem to have been as salient as in the more economically advanced southern county. Yorkshire cases seem to have a wider range of tensions at their base, although there is a sense that commonly cases revolved around richer villagers accusing their less advantaged neighbours. Thus in 1656 Richard Jackson of Wakefield described incidents which followed George and Jennet Benton's assertion of their supposed right of way over his land. Jackson told one of his manservants to hinder the Bentons, two of the employee's teeth then being knocked out by a stone thrown by George. Jackson brought a legal action against Benton, and although settlement was made, Benton declared 'that it should be a deare day's work unto the said Rich[ard] Jackson or his before the yeare went about'. Since that time Jackson's wife had gone deaf, one of his children had fallen into fits, and he himself had fallen into a strange condition, sometimes feeling he was being pulled apart, at other times thinking he could hear the sounds of singing, dancing and music about him.[58] Another case demonstrating the passions which might be generated by landholding came in 1615, when Ann Hodgson of Easington was presented 'for swearing and cursing the whole jurie of the towne and supposed to be a charmer'. A note added that 'a jurie passing a verdict concerning some land that was hers, she out of her anger did curse them'. Once more we find the disadvantaged having recourse to such power as they thought they had, while the wording of the entry suggests that Hodgson already had a reputation as a witch.[59]

Sometimes, however, the 'falling out' defies any modern concepts of rationality. Thus Margaret Wilson described losing fifty shillings from her purse at some past point, shortly after which 'there hapned to be a great wind', after whose subsidence she met with Ann Wilkinson, 'who fell into a great rage bitterly cursing this ex[aminan]t & telling her that she had bene att a wiseman and had rais'd this wind w[hi]ch had put out her eyes'. Wilkinson cursed Wilson again, and expressed the hope that she would never thrive. Wilson was so upset that 'she fell a weeping', and with good reason: both she and her husband later sickened, her husband fatally.[60]

Such examples of hatred and malevolence between the supposed witch and her victim fit easily into models of interpersonal tension as the background to witchcraft accusations. More problematic are the ambivalences involved in exchanging gifts, or even exchanging words, with witches. Anthropologists have long been familiar with the tensions and ambiguities inherent in gift exchange,[61] and some of the instances recorded in our documentation provide further evidence on this point. It is sometimes possible to see witches gaining power over their victims by giving them a gift, notably food. One woman told in 1649 how a witch followed her son with 'an apple & a peece of bread & would not p[ar]te with him till she caused him to byte both of the apple and the bread', after which the boy began to spit blood and eventually died.[62] Another woman deposed how her child fell ill 'till he could neither go nor stand' after eating a piece of bread given to him by a woman.[63] One case involved a child falling ill after eating a prune given to her by a suspected witch, and another suspect, asked if she had given her alleged victim anything to eat, recalled on one occasion giving her, her mother, and the mother's other children 'a dish of nuts among them'.[64]

Much more commonly, however, the witch set her power into motion through words. The whole problem of how the power of words and speech was regarded in early modern England awaits further investigation. Certainly this was a period when formal cursing was seen as powerful and dangerous. Thus in one remarkable case Helen Hiley, a Wetherby widow, went down on her knees in front of her neighbour John Wood, 'and said a vengeance of God light upon the[e] Wood . . . and all thy children and I trulie pray this praier for so long as I live'.[65] It was a very short distance from this type of curse to the imprecations which so often prefaced the misfortunes which led to suspicions of witchcraft. The butcher Richard Wawne, in a series of altercations with two local women, deposed how one of them came to him when he was selling meat in Whitby market, 'and bad an ill death light on him & his goods, cursing him w[i]th many such like expressions', immediately after which one of his already depleted herd of cattle died.[66]

Yet it would seem that ambivalent comments were as likely to generate, or help confirm, witchcraft suspicions as were curses and direct threats. Showing too much solicitude for the sick, or showing too close a knowledge of their symptoms, might easily help focus suspicions of witchcraft.[67] Even apparently friendly words might hold menace: as we have seen, one man fell mortally ill after his alleged bewitcher had said to him 'you are a pretty gentleman: will you kiss mee?',[68] while a woman was bewitched after being thanked and taken by the hand when giving alms.[69] With witchcraft accusations we are obviously confronting scraps of evidence symptomatic of a whole complex of shifting social relationships and interpersonal attitudes.

It is worth pondering on where the witch's power to do such things was meant to have come from. In most cases, in these Yorkshire accusations as elsewhere, it is probable that the accused witch was simply felt to have an innate power to do ill, a power that had often been possessed for some time. Thomas Brooke of Leeds declared in 1617 that a woman he thought to be bewitching his goods had been a witch for fourteen years.[70] John Johnson of Huddersfield, who thought his daughter was being bewitched in 1652, believed that Hester France, the suspected witch, had practised her craft for twenty years.[71] Other witches were felt to have inherited their powers. Francis Ward of Kirkthorpe, one of four women who searched Margaret Morton for the witch's mark, reported that Morton 'had beene a long time suspected for a witch and that her mother & sister who are now both dead were suspected to be the like'.[72] Similarly Edward Fairfax noted of Jennitt Dibble, an old widow whom he suspected of witchcraft, that she was 'reputed a witch for many years', as were her mother, two of her aunts, two of her sisters, and some of her children.[73]

In seventeenth-century Yorkshire, as elsewhere in early modern Europe, the idea of the demonic pact and of a diabolical root to the witch's power did not figure prominently. The concern of the lower orders was with maleficium rather than with those demonological aspects of witchcraft which so exercised learned writers. Even so, ideas of the devil and the demonic pact were beginning to circulate. In 1621 Helen Fairfax in one of her early fits saw a well dressed gentleman who offered to marry her and make her queen of England, but who seemed unhappy at the mention of God. At a later point in her possession she imagined herself interviewing one of her tormentors, and asking her how she became a witch. The imaginary reply was that the woman had made a pact with a man 'like to a man of this world whom she met on the moors'.[74] Forty years later the confession of Alice Huson, as recorded by Sir Matthew Hale, included details of a pact ('he told me I should never want, if I would follow his ways') made with the devil who appeared to her 'like a black man on a horse upon the moor'.[75] Other odd remarks suggest that the notion of the devil being connected with witchcraft was not unfamiliar: a man recorded being tormented by spirits who 'advised him to worshippe the enemy'; another said a woman 'was a devill and had the devill's mark on her'; while the daughter of an alleged witch, seeing a man in pain, said to him, 'doth the devill nip the[e] in the neck? He will nip th[e] better yet'.[76] Perhaps the extent to which the concept of the demonic pact had entered the popular consciousness by the end of the century can be gauged by the rejected wooer who told the object of affections that if she continued to refuse him he would sell his soul to the devil and torment her.[77]

Whatever the popular grasp of the importance of diabolical input into their activities, it remains clear that witches were frequently regarded as frightening and powerful. The witch was capable of killing or crippling with a touch or an ambivalent phrase, she could kill cattle with a curse, and send children into terrible, incurable fits by giving them an apple or a piece of bread. Obviously, we must reiterate, behind such incidents there lurks a whole history of fears, of the building of reputations, of interpersonal tensions, a history which usually defies reconstruction. What we can examine, and what we will turn to in the next section of this paper, is what could be done, other than taking a formal accusation to court, to combat a witch's power. For these Yorkshire sources are exceptionally rich in showing how people tried to cope with the threat of witchcraft.

### III

The most efficacious way of dealing with a witch, at least in the eyes of contemporary officialdom, was to accuse her before a court of law, and a number of cases in our sample show how bewitched people gained relief after their tormentors were sucked into the legal process.[78] Conversely, the sources make clear that in many cases a formal charge was only brought in the last resort after alternative counter measures had been tried. These counter measures varied, but in the opinion of mainstream English protestantism, which included in this respect most post-Restoration nonconformists, all of them were equally reprehensible: the only remedy open to the godly was prayer. Thus, when the

servant of the Huddersfield widow Hester Spring expressed fears that she had
been bewitched, Spring replied 'she hoped she had better faith than to fear
either witch or devill', which reminds us that one position open to English
protestants was to maintain a deep scepticism over the whole issue of
witchcraft.[79] More conventionally, the mother of Margaret Wilson, confronted
by her daughter's having been reduced to tears after an altercation with the
suspected witch Ann Wilkinson, 'bad her put her trust in God, & she hoped she
could doe her no harm'.[80] As might be expected, such attitudes became more
common the higher up the social and educational scale the victim was. Thus
Elizabeth Mallory, at one stage in her afflictions, when asked who was
tormenting her, replied 'she knewe not but only trusted in God and desired
them to pray w[i]th her', which, we are told, 'this informer and the rest of the
company did accordingly'.[81] Edward Fairfax, after considering recourse to
counter magic in defence of his bewitched daughters, decided to leave 'charms,
tongs and schratchings to such that put confidence in them', deciding rather to
rely on 'the goodness of God, and invoked his help, without tempting him by
prescribing the means'.[82]

Not everybody, however, was capable of following this austere line, and,
as Fairfax's comments suggest, the temptation to resort to counter-magic, even
among the educated and the godly, could be a strong one. Oliver Heywood
was involved in a case which illustrates this point. He was called in to help when
Abraham Swift, a boy aged twelve, had 'lyen long under a strange and sad hand
of God in his body'. A doctor had been consulted, but had declared that 'it is
not a naturall distemper, that he is troubled with, but he hath had some hurt
by an evel tongue'. The doctor recommended that the parents of the boy should
'take his water and make a cake or loaf of it, with wheat meal and put in some
of his hair into it, and horse-shooe stumps, and then put it in the fire'. The boy's
mother came to Heywood and a Mr Dawson to seek advice, fearing that 'it may
be some kind of charm . . . being afraid to offend God in such a tryall'. Heywood
consulted with Dawson, and 'we both concluded it not to be any way of God,
having no foundation either in nature or divine revelation in scripture',
although he knew that according to superstition 'the witch that had hurt him
would come and discover all' if such a course of action were followed. In the
end, Heywood wrote, 'I utterly disliked it, so did her husband and she − I told
them the right way was to goe to God by fasting and prayer, they consented,
we appointed yesterday'.[83]

As the previous paragraph suggests, one of the first things which bewitched
people or their parents might do, frequently before suspicions of witchcraft had
become fully focussed, would be to call in a doctor. The outcome of such a step
was not always fruitful. Thomas Strutt of Gargrave, falling suddenly ill in 1653,
claimed to have consulted with eleven doctors, '& they were not able to give
him any ease'.[84] Joan Booth of Warmfield, consulting doctors about her sick and

possibly bewitched son, was told 'it was nothing but wormes'.[85] Others had better fortune: Margaret Wilson was ill for two years after an altercation with Ann Wilkinson, '& soe continued . . . till a Scotch phisitian came to Tollerton, who told her that she was bewitched'.[86]

The most remarkable account involving recourse to doctors, however, involved the Corbet family of Burton Agnes, one of whose daughters was seriously and inexplicably ill for about four years. From the start the girl was insistent that two women were responsible for bewitching her, but her parents refused to accept this explanation, called in doctors from Hull, York and Beverley, and at one stage sent the girl to relatives in Pickering, 'hoping that the change of air and a remote place might conduct to her health or recovery'. The daughter frequently protested that such courses were useless, 'for all the doctors and physick in the world could do no good, as long as those two women were at liberty; they would have her life, and she was contented, since she could not be believed'. Eventually her parents came round to her way of thinking, and the two women, Alice Huson and Doll Bilby, were convicted. But it had taken four years before the parents had rejected a medical explanation and accepted witchcraft as the cause of their daughter's illness. The case demonstrates how simplistic notions of the credulity of past ages should not be automatically adduced as an explanation of witchcraft accusations. Here we find an accusation was brought reluctantly and tardily after a long period of trying to cope with a difficult situation using what we would consider as 'modern', 'rational', methods.[87]

For most of the poor, especially those living in isolated parishes, doctors were too expensive or too inaccessible. Among such people recourse might well be had to the local charmers and folk medicine practitioners known as cunning men or women. Most contemporary writers on English witchcraft saw cunning folk as a major problem, and commented adversely on the willingness of the population at large to consult them. Edward Fairfax shared this view. Commenting on popular reactions to witchcraft, he wrote of persons thinking themselves bewitched

> for remedy whereof they would go to those whom they call wisemen, and these wizards teach them to burn young calves alive and the like; whereof I know that experiments have been made of the best of my neighbours, and thereby they have found help, as they reported. So little is the truth of the Christian religion known in these wild places and among this rude people.[88]

The assize depositions contain only few references to recourse to cunning folk by bewitched persons (deponents may well have been wary about talking about such matters before a magistrate) but the practice was known. Joan Jurdie, accused of witchcraft in 1605, had a reputation for being able to help bewitched persons, 'and that many of her neighbours do thinke the like of her'.[89] In 1655 a deponent told how a sick man had told her to go to 'one widow Gransley' who diagnosed witchcraft and described the circumstances of the bewitching.[90] When the daughter of John Allen of Scarborough fell ill and witchcraft was suspected in 1651, her mother was advised to 'send for one Elizabeth Hodgson, of this town, to looke or charme the s[ai]d childe'. The child began to recover but, interestingly, 'because the s[ai]d mother did tell of that cure the said child is not curable'.[91]

Although Fairfax rejected the use of cunning folk, it is noteworthy that he was willing to call in what he felt to be a legitimate adviser. Robert Pannell 'a mere stranger travelling towards York' called in on the Fairfax household, having heard of the girls' possession. He asked if he could experiment with them to see if they were bewitched, 'which', wrote Fairfax, 'I did condescend to, the rather for that the said Pannell used to serve upon juries at the assizes, being a freeholder of good estate'.[92] Indeed, it is uncertain that all gentry were as hostile to cunning people as was Fairfax: one Yorkshire gentleman, Richard Cholmeley of Brandsby, had no reservations about sending for advice to Jane Pennythorne of Sherburn 'formerly called the skylfull woman of Marshland' when he was suffering from 'a greivous fytt of the stone'.[93] Much more remarkable was Charles Atkinson, minister of Murton near York, who in the 1670s published a series of almanacs in which, along with medical advice, language teaching, and instruction in writing, he offered 'resolutions upon things lost, stole, and all temporary and horary questions'. The boundary between educated and popular attitudes to magic was more permeable than has sometimes been claimed.[94]

There were, of course, more direct forms of counter action against witches. Despite my claims that witches would be regarded as powerful people, a number of them suffered violence from persons who thought themselves to be victims of witchcraft. Oliver Heywood, indeed, noted in 1667 that three men had been hanged at York assizes for the murder of a Wakefield woman who was suspected of bewitching Nathan Dodgson.[95] Henry Cockcrofte of Heptonstall and some other men went to the house of Mary Midgley, whom Cockcrofte suspected of bewitching one of his children, and threatened and beat her until she confessed to being a witch and named two others who, she claimed, were responsible for bewitching the child.[96] In a case of 1652 we find Nicholas Baldwin of Reedness beating Elizabeth Lambe, a suspected witch, with a cane, adding in his account of the incident that 'had it not beene for my wife, because she sat down of hir knees and asked me forgiveness, I had beat her worse'. A witness added that after the incident Baldwin 'hath never since been disquieted by her', commenting further that various neighbours believed that they had lost cattle due to Lambe's witchcraft, '& that they also did beat her and was never after disquieted by her'.[97] As this case suggests, this type of counter action was unlikely to enter the historical record.

By far the most common form of violence offered to a witch, however, was scratching. It was believed that scratching a witch to draw blood of her would bring relief to the bewitched person, the logic being summed up by Richard Browne, another of Elizabeth Lambe's victims, who claimed that

> he was cruelly handled at the heart with one Elizabeth Lambe, & that she drew his heart's blood from him . . . he desired to scratch her, saying that she had drawne blood of him, & if he could draw blood of her, he hoped he should amend.[98]

This form of counter-magic was commented on by a number of contemporary writers, notably William Perkins, who singled it out for special censure,[99] and was evidently familiar in Stuart Yorkshire. Even Fairfax considered scratching the women he thought to be bewitching his children, since the practice was 'urged to me as a remedy ordained of God'.[100] Fairfax rejected scratching, but the practice was regularly recorded in depositions. Mary Dalton, on her deathbed in 1618, suspected Isabell Morris as the cause of her afflictions, and tried to scratch her when she came into the house selling bread.[101] Mary Hobson of Idle deposed in 1649 that her son, on his deathbed, accused a woman of causing his illness, '& said he intended to have drawn blood of her, if he could have but gotten to her'.[102] Susannah Keld of Skipsea, bewitched by Ann Hudson, scratched and drew blood of her, with the result that she 'presently after . . . recovered very well and lived diverse years after'.[103] So familiar was the practice that another suspected witch, Mary Sikes of Bowling, asked a woman to scratch her. When the request was refused, Sikes 'scratched her owne backe and drewe blood at everie scratch and made her back verie bloodie'. Her subsequent explanation to the examining justice that she did so because she 'hath the itch' sounds very unconvincing.[104]

As these accounts of violence and scratching suggest, one element in coping with witchcraft might well be a direct confrontation between the sufferer and the suspected witch. This could include the deployment of very direct counter magic against the witch. In 1626 Goodwife Wright was brought before the authorities in the Colony of Virginia as a suspected witch. During a discussion about witchcraft she had apparently shown a suspicious degree of knowledge about the subject: in particular, according to one witness, she recalled that when she was in service at Hull

> being one day chirninge of butter, there cam a woman to the howse who was accompted for a witch, whereuppon she by direction of her dame clapt the chirne staffe to the bottom of the chirne and clapt her hands across upon the top of it by w[hi]ch means the witch was not able to stire out of the place where she was for the space of six howers after w[hi]ch time good wiefe Wright desired her dame to aske the woman why she did not gett her gone, whereuppo[n] the witche fell downe on her knees and asked her forgiveness, and said her hand was in the chirne, and could not stire before her maide lifted up the staff of the chirne.

Another witness deposed that Wright also told how while she was at Hull her dame was sick and thought herself to be bewitched. She directed Wright that when the woman suspected of bewitching her came to the house, she was 'to take a horshwe [horseshoe] and flinge it into her dames urine, and so long as the horshwe was hott, the witch was sick at the harte'.[105]

The objective in other confrontations was to effect a reconciliation or remove the witch's influence. Thus the wife of Richard Wood of Heptonstall, another supposed victim of Mary Midgley, went to the suspected witch, 'tould her she hadd made the fault & desired her to remedie it if she could'. After some hesitation, Midgley 'at last took six pence of her and wished her to go home for the kyne should mende and desired her to take for every cow a handfull of salte and an old sickle and lay underneath them and if they amended not to come to her againe'. Later, Richard Wood met Midgley in an alehouse, and 'tould her there had beene some little fault[es] made by her since he wente from home but hee did not mention any p[ar]ticular wherein'. His circumspection obviously struck the right note, for 'shee thereuppon gave him an apple & confessed she had done him hurte divers tymes but never would doe more'.[106] Another case which we have encountered before, that of Abraham Hobson bewitched by Jane Kighly, included an incident in which Kighly, after much persuasion, was brought before Hobson as he lay near to death. She told him 'he could not passe out of the world till he asked her forgiveness', to which Hobson said he 'hoped he had made his peace with God, & told her shee was happy if shee was in as good an estate as himselfe', and accused her of bewitching him.[107]

Conversely, suspected witches could sometimes be brought before their victims in the hope that the witch would confess her offence and lift her malign influence by begging forgiveness. The problem was, of course, that asking for fogiveness in such a context was tantamount to a confession. Thus John Booth of Warmfield, 'mistrusting that . . . Margaret Morton had bewitched her child', sent for the woman, 'who asked the child forgiveness three times, & then this inform[an]t was thereby induced to believe that the said Marg[are]t had bewitched the said child'.[108] The degree of emotional stress inherent in such confrontations comes through very clearly in the case of Elizabeth Mallory, daughter of gentry parents, whose supposed tormentors, William and Mary Waide, were brought before her. William was asked by Lady Mallory, the mother of the bewitched girl, to ask her forgiveness, 'and to repeat some wordes, after hir or some other gentlmen w[hi]ch was then present', but refused to do so, on the grounds, as he explained when he was examined, that he had done nothing which needed to be forgiven. Mary 'after much intreatie being p[er]swaded to say, she had done wronge & ask her forgivenesse . . . Elizabeth stood up on her feet . . . and said she was well & walked upon the bed', despite having been paralysed until Waide spoke. Unfortunately, Mary Waide almost immediately retracted her words, and denied doing the girl wrong, upon which 'Elizabeth sayd if she denyed it I shall be ill againe, and presentlie began w[i]th her ill fitts', declaring 'she should never be well till she had confessed she had done her wronge or was carried before a justice and punished'.[109] We return again to considerations of power, fear, and fields of force, in this instance (as so often in these accounts of being bewitched) taking place in a public context before a body of observers.

As one Yorkshire case demonstrates, confrontation between the witch and her supposed victim could extend beyond the latter's death. Seventeenth-century legal opinion held that the corpses of murdered persons bled if touched by their killer.[110] So Jennet Preston, a woman from Gisburn in Craven implicated in the Lancashire trials of 1612, was brought to the body of her late master, Thomas Lister, whom she was thought to have bewitched to death.

> Preston being brought to M. Lister after hee was dead, & layd out to be wound up in his winding-sheet, the said Jennet Preston coming to touch the dead corpes, they bled fresh blood presently in the presence of all that were present: which hath ever beene held a great argument to induce a Jurie to hold him guiltie that shall be accused of murther, and had seldome, or never fayled in the tryall.

It did not fail in Preston's case, although the careful selection of a 'jurie of sufficient gentlemen of understanding', who were given instruction at the trial by a J.P. who was 'best instructed of any man of all the particular points of evidence against her' was probably also of some importance. Preston was found guilty and executed, and the account of her trial records that the presiding judge advised the jury that 'the conclusion is of more consequence than all the rest, that Jennet Preston being brought to the dead corps, they bled freshly'.[111]

In this section we have, therefore, considered the methods by which persons who thought themselves bewitched might seek to relieve themselves by means other than having recourse to formal accusation via the legal system. As we have seen, these means were varied, and, to some extent, specific to different social strata: the gentry and middling sort had recourse to prayers and doctors, the lower orders to scratching and cunning folk. Two themes emerge clearly from these witchcraft narratives. The first is the essentially confrontational nature of many of these remedies. Ever since Macfarlane focussed our attention on the issue, it has been clear that understanding witchcraft accusations in early modern England involves appreciating the importance of the interpersonal relationship between the alleged witch and her accuser. These Yorkshire materials suggest that these relationships were vital not only in the formation of the accusation, but also to those subsequent stages during which the two parties negotiated their position, often in a public or semi-public forum, the accuser or victim at least frequently being assisted by the mediation and support of friends and neighbours. Secondly, these accounts of trying to cope with witchcraft, of scratching or confronting suspected witches, of negotiating with them around the theme of forgiveness, of slowly realising that one's children were bewitched as the remedies of doctors failed, have an immediacy, a dramatic quality, equal to that so often found in the accounts of the 'falling out' that frequently precipitated a witchcraft accusation. Again, we return to the fundamental point that witchcraft accusations in early modern England were a less rational and low keyed business than we have led ourselves to believe.


IV


At the very least this paper has demonstrated how a variety of materials can be interwoven to construct a qualitative impression of witchcraft beliefs, an impression which is complementary to and at least as valid as that which might have been formed from studying a long series of indictments. These materials allow us insights into how it felt to fear that your cattle or your children were bewitched, and permit us to grasp some of the drama and immediacy of this experience. These northern materials also suggest some differences from the Essex pattern with which Macfarlane has made us familiar. Members of the Yorkshre gentry seem to have figured more prominently as victims of witchcraft than their Essex counterparts. Familiar spirits, such a feature of Essex witchcraft, and of the trials associated with Matthew Hopkins which swept across Essex and East Anglia in 1645-7, do not seem to have enjoyed similar prominence in Yorkshire. In addition, although the impression that most Yorkshire witches were socially and economically inferior to their accusers persists, the Yorkshire cases seem less closely related to wider processes of socio-economic change than do their Essex equivalents, though the point needs further investigation.

There are two other obvious areas where further research is needed. The first is the fundamental and still unresolved problem of why so many witches were women. This problem needs fuller discussion elsewhere,[112] but it is worth noting here that a large proportion of those accusing and giving evidence against witches were women. However much learned ideas about witchcraft might have owed to the patriarchal and misogynistic attitudes of male intellectuals, on a village level witchcraft seems to have been something peculiarly enmeshed in women's quarrels and the way in which they settled them. If witchcraft at an interpersonal level was about power, perhaps future investigation should direct itself towards uncovering the ways in which women, and particularly elderly, poor, and socially isolated women, were thought to wield power in a social context where their access to many forms of what contemporaries would have thought of as legitimate power was blocked.

Secondly, it is striking that many of these accusations turned on the alleged bewitching of children or adolescents. The bewitching of children is, perhaps, connected with the problem of women and witchcraft: child-care was seen primarily as a female concern, and if witchcraft was thought to be something peculiarly appropriate to female disputes, it is easy to see a logic whereby the bewitching of children would become a regular theme in accusations. But the presence of so many adolescents and young adults in these accounts of bewitching, Helen Fairfax, Elizabeth Mallory, Faith Corbet, Nathan Dodgson, James Johnson and the rest prompts a further general consideration: having accustomed ourselves to the need to analyse witchcraft accusations in terms of social stratification and gender, should we not now try to do so with the age hierarchy in mind?[113]

A final problem remains. Despite the intrinsic interest of the history of witchcraft to the inhabitants of the developed world in the late twentieth century, how large did it loom as a problem for the inhabitants of Stuart Yorkshire? The materials here do not, perhaps, allow any great assertiveness on this point. A handful of court cases and a few other scattered materials in what was England's largest county do not furnish proof of a general social fear. Yet some observations need to be made. Firstly, when somebody thought themselves to be bewitched they knew how to diagnose the problem and what the steps were that might help them alleviate it: whatever the frequency of court cases, it is evident that cultural patterns and social practices relating to witchcraft were deeply rooted and widely recognised. Secondly, our materials confirm the impression formed for other areas that alleged witches surfacing in court records often had a long standing reputation as practisers of witchcraft, even if they had never been the subject of an official complaint. And, thirdly, non-official sources, notably Oliver Heywood's writings, create an impression of a world in which witchcraft was something which was widely recognised and occasionally worried about: indeed, one night Heywood had a nightmare in which he imagined that his son John had fallen 'to the study of magick or the black art . . . I was so affrighted that I wakened and fell sweating, trembling'.[114] Heywood may have been unusual in his concern over witchcraft, and his lifetime probably comprehended the last period when such worries would be commonplace among the educated. As we shall see, however, belief in witchcraft and related superstitions were still widespread among the common people.

But in discussing the pervasiveness of witchcraft beliefs, let us turn briefly from the seventeenth century to the nineteenth. The witchcraft statutes had been repealed in 1736, and thus the types of legal records on which much of this paper has been based simply ceased to be generated. Yet well over a century after the repeal of the statutes, belief in, and fear of, witches persisted. Consider the reminiscences of J. C. Atkinson, for a long period the vicar of Danby in Cleveland. Atkinson, a keen collector of local folklore and a prolific editor of Yorkshire documents, commented in a book published in 1892 that he had

> no doubt at all of the very real and very deep-seated existence of a belief in the actuality and the power of the witch. Nay, I make no doubt whatever that the witch herself, in multitudes of instances, believed in her own power quite as firmly as any of those who learned to look

upon her with a dread . . . Fifty years ago the whole atmosphere of the folklore firmament in
this district was so surcharged with the being and the works of the witch, that one seemed able
to trace her presence and her activity in almost every nook and corner of the neighbourhood.[115]

The survival of witch beliefs into the nineteenth and twentieth centuries is a
fascinating topic which awaits further research. For our immediate purposes,
Atkinson's comments at least make it clear that levels of prosecution of witches
are a very uncertain indicator of levels of concern over witchcraft.

Indeed, it is ironical that one of the best documented quarter sessions cases
entered the historical record a few months after the repeal of the witchcraft
statutes. In various examinations taken in November 1736 witnesses described
an altercation at Baildon between Mary Hartley and Bridget Goldsbrough.
Hartley accused Goldsbrough of being a witch, of transforming herself into two
grey cats, and of bewitching her son, saying 'I wou'd have you let my barn
[bairn] alone, he works hard for his living and cannot bear to be disturbed at
night'. She elaborated the point, saying that Goldsbrough's daughter Margaret
was also a witch, and that Goldsbrough 'was riding of her son to Pendle Hill
the night before and that Margaret brought a saddle and bridle and wou'd put
the bridle into his mouth but the bitts were too large'. Mary Hartley began
scolding the Goldsbroughs in the street, joined by her husband John Hartley
'and one other John Hartley called Red John'. The three of them 'in one voice
. . . said kill them all and let them live no longer' with other 'dangerous language'
(the incident was brought to court because the Goldsbroughs wanted the
Hartleys bound over). The case demonstrates the vitality of witch beliefs among
the population in the very year when the witchcraft statute was repealed, while
the reference to Pendle Hill, which figured so prominently in the 1612
Lancashire trials, points to the durability of witchcraft traditions on a popular
level.[116]

Whatever the intensity of prosecution of malefic witchcraft in the seventeenth
century, the frequent mention of cunning folk suggests a world in which
witchcraft, charming, sorcery and occult powers were all familiar. Charmers
and cunning folk were probably the most important category of witches to
appear before the church courts, and they were also presented before secular
tribunals. A man was indicted late in the sixteenth century at the West Riding
sessions for finding stolen goods by witchcraft, four women were similarly
accused at the North Riding sessions, a man was accused before the same court
in 1606 for fortune telling, and just before the Civil Wars the York borough
sessions investigated John Arminson, a Heslington yeoman, who was consulted
by a York resident about his sick wife.[117] Another case, from 1664, which first
surfaced in the York borough sessions, but was transferred to the assizes,
demonstrated the degree of trust which could be placed in the cunning man.
Richard Redshaw was in York gaol awaiting trial for stealing money from Lord
Fairfax, and called in a cunning man named Nicholas Battersby to help identify

the real thief and locate the money.[118] Something of the cunning folks' reputation can also be inferred from Edward Fairfax's account of how 'charmers and lookers on' were discussed as he 'was in the kitchen with many of my family'. The discussion mentioned 'the names of many . . . who were thought to be skilful therein, and it was said that such as go to these charmers carry and give them a single penny'.[119]

Better documented cases give further insights into both the cunning folks' techniques and the widespread nature of their appeal. In 1651 Lancelot Milner of Nesfield told the examining magistrate how 'a man whose name hee knoweth not but p[re]tending himself to be dumbe and deafe' came to his house, and stayed there a week, 'in which tyme divers from severall p[ar]tes of the country came to enquire, the wenches what husbandes they should have, whence they should come; whether they should bee widdowes . . . some men to enquire of stolen horses, or mayres'. The man answered enquiries 'by signes in chalke, and poynting with his hand', and according to Milner, 'divers such p[er]sons so directed have tould this informer that the sayd dumbe man did directe them very truly'. The man (who, according to a passing soldier, had been born in the London area) took a penny, two pence, or a can of ale for his services, and in some instances took nothing, and, as another witnessed deposed, he 'to her knowledge demanded nothinge of any either by signes or otherwise'.[120] The activities of another cunning man, Anthony Ledgard of Heckmondwike, had been investigated two years earlier. Thomas Armitage told how, following his failure to locate wool stolen from the house of Anne Armitage, he went to Ledgard, he 'being a man comonly reputed and taken to be one who can tell where goods lost or stolne may be founde'. Ledgard commanded 'a little wench in the howse' to bring him 'an almanacke as he called it', and also consulted another book. He then told Armitage that 'he found by the plannetts that itt was of the ayre of water and saide I finde that lighes between 10 or 11 a clocke . . . in a taverne or tarnpitt covered with much wood', and continued to give further information in that vein. Ledgard obviously represented the better quality of cunning person: literate and using astrological jargon to lend authenticity to his prognoses. Yet his case provides further evidence of how cunning men and women had reputations and were sought after in times of trouble.[121] It is little wonder that John Webster should deplore 'the seeking unto witches, wizards, mutterers, murmerers, charmers, south-sayers, conjurers, cunning men and women (as we speak here in the north) and such like'.[122]

Yet these Yorkshire materials suggest a further complexity: belief in witchcraft might be widespread, but it was not monolithic, and certainly the belief that an individual woman or man was a witch might not be universal in the individual's community. Against notions of a 'tyranny of local opinion' or of village communities being united in hysteria against the witch might be set a number of cases where reactions to witchcraft accusations reflected divisions rather than hegemony in local attitudes. Edward Fairfax's attetmpt to prosecute the women he thought to be bewitching his children was defeated by their defenders in the local community, who managed to present a petition to the assize judge in support of their good character.[123] A similar petition, dating from December 1651, survives in the Northern Circuit assize records. This, to which some 200 signatures were appended, was in support of Mary Hickington, 'now a condemned prisoner in Yorke castle for witchcraft'. The petitioners declared that both she and her husband (who had previously served in the parliamentary army at Hull) were of good and honest behaviour, and that Mary was never 'in the least wise suspected to be guilty of sorcery or witchcraft or any other misdemeano[ur] not becoming a Christian'.[124] Despite our acceptance of the pervasiveness of witchcraft beliefs, such cases suggest the existence of an embryonic scepticism about witchcraft in at least some sections of local society by the mid seventeenth century: indeed, popular scepticism about witchcraft is an unexplored, if perhaps unexplorable, subject.


V


Evidence nearer the top of society is easier to uncover and of crucial importance. As Heywood's papers remind us, even among the educated, belief in witches was still a possibility. Thus we find Ralph Thoresby in 1680 taking the trouble to write down details of a sermon he had heard in which witches figured as elements in the devil's threats to mankind, and in 1692 reading Edward Fairfax's 'ingenious manuscript of witchcraft' with evident interest.[125] Others were more thoroughly sceptical. John Webster remained determinedly detached from the common people's tendency to 'perswade themselves they are bewitched, fore-spoken, blasted, fairy taken, or haunted with some evil spirit, and the like'.[126] Sir John Reresby, commenting on the trial of a suspected witch at the York assizes in 1687, distanced himself from the case, noting that 'some, that were more apt to believe those things than me, thought the evidence strong against her'.[127] But what is important is that there seems to have been no concerted official fear of witchcraft, the ingredient necessary to turn widespread popular belief into high levels of prosecution. Those in control of the Elizabethan and early Stuart church courts seemed unwilling to launch mass hunts.[128] Even the Puritan ascendancy in the 1640s and 1650s did not see a marked rise in tension over witchcraft in official circles. In the late 1650s, for example, the Puritan justice, and ex-captain of dragoons, John Pickering, found only one witch and two cunning men to add to the swearers, drunkards, unlicensed alehouse-keepers and fornicators who formed the staple of his business.[129]

Writing of early modern Lorraine, Robin Briggs has commented that one of the most surprising features of the era of the witch persecutions was that there were, given the pervasiveness of witchcraft tensions, so few accusations.[130] This study of witchcraft in seventeenth-century Yorkshire seems to support this contention. In terms of court prosecutions, even allowing for gaps in the records, Yorkshire was an area of low intensity. Yet the sheer range of sources in which witchcraft was mentioned, and the comments by educated observers on the widespread nature of witch beliefs and related superstitions on a popular level, suggest that prosecutions were a very imperfect guide to the extent of beliefs. Nonjudicial sources suggest that contemporaries had ample opportunity to know about witches. The parish registers of Pocklington, for example, record that a witch was burnt in the town's market-place in 1630, another was hanged there in 1642, while the burial of a man thought to have been bewitched to death was recorded in the following year: the inhabitants of at least one Yorkshire township, it would appear, were regularly exposed to witchcraft beliefs and accusations.[131] And, as we have tried to make clear, the experience of thinking oneself to be bewitched, or of thinking that the same fate had befallen one's children or one's cattle, was a deeply disturbing one.

But perhaps in the last resort the importance of witchcraft, and the impact of a witchcraft accusation, can best be grasped in the individual case history. In 1674, as a result of information delivered by a teenage girl named Mary Moor, suspicions of witchcraft fell on Ann Shillito, Susan Hinchcliffe, and her husband Joseph. This accusation was another which prompted a petition in support of the alleged witches, signed by fifty members of the Hinchcliffe's home parish, Denby. The petition attested to the good character of Susan Hinchcliffe, noted that 'touching the said girle who now informs, some of us could say too much concerning her, of a quite different nature', and declared the accusation 'gros and groundless (if not malitious)'. The local justices, obviously worried by the case, decided not to transfer it to the assizes but to indict it locally.[132] Their efforts, and those of the petitioners, were in vain: Oliver Heywood recorded that

> One Joseph Hincline and his wife being accused of witchcraft, and upon deposition on oath being bound to the assizes, he could not bear it but fainted, went out one thursday morning, Feb 4 1674-5 hanged himself in a wood near his house, was not found till the Lord's day, his wife dyed in her bed, spoke and acted as a Christian praying for her adversarys that falsely accused her, was buryed on Feb 4 – before he was found.[133]

Arguably the impression created by such qualitative materials provide the surest guide to the social meaning of witchcraft accusations in early modern England.

## Notes to text

1       Alan Macfarlane, *Witchcraft in Tudor and Stuart England: a Regional and Comparative Study*
        (London, 1970); Keith Thomas, *Religion and the Decline of Magic: Studies in Popular Beliefs in
        Sixteenth- and Seventeenth-Century England* (London, 1971).

2       It would be inappropriate to introduce full bibliographical details here. However, recent
        publications and recent thinking on witchcraft are discussed in four works of synthesis:
        Joseph Klaits, *Servants of Satan: the Age of the Witch Hunts* (Bloomington, Indiana, 1985);
        Brian P. Levack, *The Witch-Hunt in Early Modern Europe* (London, 1987); G. R. Quaife,
        *Godly Zeal and Furious Rage: the Witch in Early Modern Europe* (London, 1987); Geoffrey
        Scarre, *Witchcraft and Magic in Sixteenth and Seventeenth-Century Europe* (London, 1987).

3       E.g. Peter Rushton, 'Women, Witchcraft and Slander in Early Modern England: Cases from
        the Church Courts of Durham 1560-1675', *Northern History*, 18 pp. 116-32; Clive Holmes,
        'Popular Culture? Witches, Magistrates and Divines in Early Modern England', in Steven L.
        Kaplan (ed.), *Understanding Popular Culture: Europe from the Middle Ages to the Nineteenth
        Century* (Berlin, etc., 1984), David Harley, 'Historians as Demonologists: the Myth of the
        Midwife-Witch', *Social History of Medicine*, 3, pp. 1-26.

4       Wallace Notestein, *A History of Witchcraft in England from 1558 to 1718* (1911; repr. New
        York, 1965).

5       Alan Macfarlane, 'Witchcraft in Tudor and Stuart England', in J. S. Cockburn (ed.), *Crime
        in England 1550-1800* (London, 1977) p. 87.

6       The standard work on the early modern assizes is J. S. Cockburn, *A History of English Assizes,
        1558-1714* (Cambridge, 1972). The Home Circuit witchcraft cases are listed and analysed
        in C. L. Ewen, *Witch Hunting and Witch Trials: the Indictments for Witchcraft from the Records
        of 1373 Assizes held for the Home Circuit A.D. 1559-1736* (1929; repr. London, 1971). Kent
        witchcraft is currently being studied by Mr Malcolm Gaskill as one aspect of his work towards
        a Cambridge Ph.D.

7       Ewen, *Witch Hunting and Witch Trials*, p. 110; J. A. Sharpe, *Crime in Early Modern England
        1550-1750* (London, 1984) p. 55.

8       Ewen, *Witch Hunting and Witch Trials*, p. 111.

9       Yorkshire indictments along with those from other counties on the Northern Circuit form
        Public Record Office [hereafter P.R.O.] ASSI 44.

10      *Quarter Sessions Records*, ed. J. C. Atkinson (North Riding Record Society, 7 vols. 1884-90).

11      Ibid. 5 p. 259.

12      *West Riding Sessions Rolls 1597/8-1602*, ed. John Lister (Yorkshire Archaeological Society
        Record Series, 3, 1888), pp. 79, 147.

13      *West Riding Sessions Records 1611-1642* (Yorkshire Archaeological Society Record Series,
        54, 1915). This volume includes indictments for 1637-42.

14      West Yorkshire Archive Service, Quarter Sessions Records, QS1/51/2 PKT 4: I am grateful
        to Ms Caroline Martin for this reference. 1712 was, interestingly, the date of the last known
        Home Circuit indictment, the accused witch being a Hertfordshire woman named Jane
        Wenham. For another West Riding quarter sessions case, involving the destruction by
        witchcraft of £40 worth of cattle, see: *Ninth Report of the Royal Commission on Historical
        Manuscripts* (London, 1883), Part I, Appendix p. 325.

15      S. A. Barbour-Mercer, 'Prosecution and Process: Crime and the Criminal Law in late
        Seventeenth-Century Yorkshire' (unpub. University of York D.Phil. thesis, 1988) p. 135.

16      P. Tyler, 'The Church Courts at York and Witchcraft Prosecutions, 1567-1640', *Northern
        History*, 4 pp. 84-109. Essex ecclesiastical court cases are discussed extensively in Macfarlane,
        *Witchcraft in Tudor and Stuart England*.

17      Yorkshire defamation suits are discussed in J. A. Sharpe, *Defamation and Sexual Slander in Early
        Modern England: the Church Courts at York* (Borthwick Papers, 58, 1980). Slander suits

involving allegations of witchcraft were also tried at the secular courts: e.g. *Quarter Sessions Records*, ed. Atkinson, 4 p. 182, for a Malton case dating from 1640.

18   P.R.O., ASSI 45. A selection of these depositions, including many relating to witchcraft, was published in *Depositions from York Castle*, ed. J. Raine (Surtees Society, 40 1860).

19   R. A. H. Bennett, 'Enforcing the Law in Revolutionary England: Yorkshire c. 1640-c. 1660 (unpub. University of London Ph.D. thesis, 1988); Barbour-Mercer, 'Prosecution and Process'.

20   Transcripts of two borough court cases have been published: 'Alleged Witchcraft at Rossington, near Doncaster, 1605', *Gentleman's Magazine* (1857), Part 1, pp. 593-5; Joseph Brogden Baker, *The History of Scarborough from the Earliest Date* (London, 1882) pp. 481-3. The former case was noted by the antiquarian clergyman Abraham Pryme (1671-1704), who also recorded a case tried at Doncaster Borough sessions in 1623, involving a widow bewitching a yeoman's wife to death: *Ephemeris Vitae Abrahami Pryme, or, a Diary of My Own Life* (Surtees Society, 54 1869) pp. 288-9.

21   *Daemonologia: a Discourse of Witchcraft. As it was acted in the family of Mr Edward Fairfax, of Fuyston in the County of York, in the Year 1621: Along with the only two Ecologues of the same Author known to be in Existence*, ed. William Grainge (Harrogate, 1882); Matthew Hale, *A Collection of Modern Relations of Matter of Fact concerning Witches and Witchcraft upon the Persons of People* (Part 1, London, 1693) pp. 52-9. A third tract, *The most True and Wonderfull Narrative of two Women bewitched in Yorkshire . . . Also a true Relation of a young Maid not far from Luych, who being bewitched in the same manner . . . as it is attested under the hand of that most famous Phisician Doctor Henry Heers* (London, 1658) although apparently describing an authentic case, is not sufficiently detailed to be of much use.

22   *The Rev Oliver Heywood, B.A. 1630-1712. His Autobiography, Diaries, Anecdote and Event Books*, ed. J. Horsfall Turner, 4 vols. (Brighouse, 1882-5).

23   *The Royal Visitation of 1559: Act Book for the Northern Province*, ed. C. J. Kitching (Surtees Society, 187 1975) p. 65.

24   James Joseph Sheanan, *The General and Concise History and Description of the Town and Port of Kingston upon Hull* (London, 1864) p. 86.

25   *Calendar of State Papers, Domestic, 1595-7*, p. 400.

26   John Mayhall, *The Annals of Yorkshire from the earliest Period to the Present Time*, 2 vols (Leeds, 1866) 1, p. 58.

27   Hull City Archives, Bench Books, BB2, f. 359.

28   British Library, Additional MSS, 32496, f. 42v.

29   Thomas, *Religion and the Decline of Magic*, p. 526; Lawrence Stone, *The Family, Sex and Marriage in England, 1500-1800* (London, 1977) pp. 98-9.

30   P.R.O., ASSI 45/3/1/242-3.

31   Ibid. /4/1/111.

32   Ibid. /5/2/30-1.

33   Borthwick Institute of Historical Research, Cause Papers, CP H 1475.

34   Heywood, *Autobiography*, 3 p. 111.

35   Baker, *History of Scarborough*, p. 481.

36   Heywood, *Autobiography*, 1 p. 199.

37   British Library, Additional MSS, 32496, f. 42v. This type of ailment among children and adolescents may have been regarded as especially problematic in the early modern period. At the beginning of the eighteenth century, for example, a Lincolnshire doctor recorded that at the start of his career 'I cured several young children of fits, which in a small measure raised me a character': *The Family Memoirs of the Rev William Stukeley, M.D.* (Surtees Society, 73 1882) p. 47. For a more recent discussion of cases of possession, see Thomas, *Religion and the Decline of Magic*, pp. 569-88.

38   For a discussion of some of the problems as perceived by contemporaries, see David Harley,

'Mental Illness, Magical Medicine and the Devil in Northern England, 1650-1700', in Roger French and Andrew Wear (eds.), *The Medical Revolution of the Seventeenth Century* (Cambridge, 1989).

39    John Webster, the northern clergyman and doctor, discussed such cases at length in his sceptical tract on witchcraft, and declared them fraudulent: *The Displaying of Supposed Witchcraft: wherein is affirmed that there are many sorts of Deceivers and Imposters and divers Persons under a passive Delusion of Melancholy and Fancy* (London, 1677) pp. 244-65.

40    P.R.O., ASSI 45/11/1/92.

41    Ibid. 45/5/3/132.

42    Ibid. /5/5/1.

43    Ibid. /6/1/69.

44    Ibid. /5/3/132-3.

45    Ibid. /5/5/1.

46    Ibid. /9/3/94. A witness deposed how he was sent to Wilkinson's house, and found her sitting by the fire exactly as described by the girl.

47.   Thomas Potts. *The Trial of the Lancaster Witches, A.D. MDCXII*, ed. G. B. Harrison (London, 1929; repr. 1971) p. 178.

48    P.R.O., ASSI 45/5/1/36-7.

49    Ibid. /5/1/87.

50    Fairfax, *Daemonologia*, p. 32; Hale, *Collection of Modern Relations*, p. 57.

51    Richard A. Horsely, 'Who were the Witches? the Social Roles of the Accused in European Witch Trials', *The Journal of Interdisciplinary History*, 9 p. 695.

52    Jeanne Favret Saada, *Deadly Words: Witchcraft in the Bocage* (Cambridge, 1977).

53    P.R.O., ASSI 45/11/1/90.

54    Baker, *History of Scarborough*, p. 482.

55    Heywood, *Autobiography*, 3 p. 111.

56    Fairfax, *Daemonologia*, p. 34.

57    E.g., P.R.O., ASSI 45/1/5/38; /4/1/110; /5/3/133; /7/1/109.

58    Ibid. /5/3/14.

59    Borthwick Institute of Historical Research, Visitation Act Books, V 1615 CB, f. 221.

60    P.R.O., ASSI 45/9/3/9.

61    E.g., I. M. Lewis, *Social Anthropology in Perspective* (Harmondsworth, 1976), pp. 197-210. The issue is discussed further by the various essays in F. G. Bailey (ed.), *Gifts and Poison: the Politics of Reputation* (Oxford, 1971). The classic work on the subject remains Marcel Mauss, *The Gift: Form and Function of Exchange in Archaic Societies* (Paris, 1950: English edn., London, 1966).

62    P.R.O., ASSI 45/3/1/242.

63    Ibid. /4/1/131.

64    Ibid. /5/1/36; /5/3/134.

65    Borthwick Institute of Historical Research, CP H 758.

66    P.R.O., ASSI 45/7/1/109.

67    E.g. Ibid. /4/1/109-110; Borthwick Institute of Historical Research, CP H 1327; 'Alleged Witchcraft at Rossington', p. 593.

68    P.R.O. ASSI 45/5/2/31.

69    Ibid. /4/1/111.

70    Borthwick Institute of Historical Research, CP H 1296.

71    P.R.O. ASSI 45/4/2/14.

72    Ibid. /4/1/131.

73    Fairfax, *Daemonologia*, p. 32.

74    Ibid. pp. 38, 86.

75    Hale, *Modern Relations*, p. 58.

76    P.R.O., ASSI 45/5/1/32; Borthwick Institute of Historical Research, CP H 4995; P.R.O., ASSI 45/5/2/31.
77    Borthwick Institute of Historical Research, CP H 4527.
78    P.R.O., ASSI 45/5/3/133; /7/1/109; Hale, *Modern Relations*, pp. 54, 57.
79    P.R.O., ASSI 45/4/2/13. The general theological issues are discussed in Stuart Clark, 'Protestant Demonology: Sin, Superstition, and Society (c.1520-c.1630)', in Bengt Ankarloo and Gustav Henningsen (eds.), *European Witchcraft: Centres and Peripheries* (Oxford, 1990).
80    P.R.O., ASSI 45/9/3/97.
81    Ibid. /5/3/133.
82    Fairfax, *Daemonologia*, p. 89.
83    Heywood, *Autobiography*, 4 pp. 53-4. Thomas, *Religion and the Decline of Magic*, p. 648, notes that this type of counter magic was common, the rationale being that 'the witch would suffer great discomfort, usually from being unable to urinate, and thus be forced to reveal herself'.
84    P.R.O., ASSI 45/5/1/31.
85    Ibid. /4/1/131.
86    Ibid. /9/3/97.
87    Hale, *Modern Relations*, pp. 52-9, passim.
88    Fairfax, *Daemonologia*, p. 35.
89    'Alleged Witchcraft at Rossington', p. 593.
90    P.R.O., ASSI 45/5/2/30.
91    Baker, *History of Scarborough*, pp. 481-2.
92    Fairfax, *Daemonologia*, p. 80.
93    *The Memorandum Book of Richard Cholmeley of Brandsby* (North Yorkshire County Record Office Publications, 44 1988) p. 170.
94    Charles Atkinson, *Panterpe: id est Omne Delectare: or, a Pleasant Almanac for the year of our Lord 1671* (London, 1671) p. 2.
95    Heywood, *Autobiography*, 3 p. 100.
96    P.R.O., ASSI 45/1/5/38.
97    Ibid. /16/3/54-5.
98    Ibid. /16/3/56.
99    William Perkins, *A Discourse of the Damned Art of Witchcraft, so farre set forth as it is revealed in the Scriptures, and Manifest by True Experience* (Cambridge, 1608) pp. 54-5, 152, 206, 207.
100   Fairfax, *Daemonologia*, pp. 88-9.
101   Borthwick Institute of Historical Research, CP H 1327.
102   P.R.O., ASSI 45/3/1/242.
103   Ibid. /3/2/81.
104   Ibid. /3/2/134.
105   *Minutes of the Council and General Court of Colonial Virginia, 1622-1632*, ed. H. R. McIlwaine (Richmond, Virginia, 1924) p. 111. In a grateful to Dr James Horn for bringing this reference to my attention.
106   P.R.O., ASSI 45/1/5/38.
107   Ibid. /3/1/242.
108   Ibid. /4/1/131.
109   Ibid. /5/3/132-3.
110   Michael Dalton, *The Countrey Justice, containing the Practice of the Justices of the Peace out of their Sessions* (London, 1643 edn.) p. 339, specifically mentions the corps bleeding in the presence of the suspected party as proof of witchcraft. It is noteworthy that even the sceptical John Webster, in his general discussion of the issue, thought that the bleeding of corpses at the touch of a murderer was 'absolutely true de facto, and that there is something more than ordinary in it': *Displaying of Supposed Witchcraft*, p. 306.
111   Potts, *Trial of the Lancaster Witches*, pp. 179, 177, 185.

112 For an exploration of this problem, also based on Yorkshire materials, see J. A. Sharpe, 'Witchcraft and Women in Seventeenth-Century England: some Northern Evidence', *Continuity and Change*, 6 pp. 179-199. A different perspective on the topic is provided by another recent work, Marianne Hester, *Lewd Women and Wicked Witches: a Study of the Dynamics of Male Domination* (London and New York, 1992).

113 The involvement of children obviously has an international dimension, as the role of children and adolescents in such celebrated outbreaks of witch hunting as the Swedish trials of 1668-76 and the Salem trials of 1692 demonstrates.

114 Heywood, *Autobiography*, 1 p. 340.

115 J. C. Atkinson, *Forty Years in a Moorland Parish: Reminiscences and Researches in Danby in Cleveland* (London, 1892), pp. 72-3. Some late examples of witchcraft are noted in Patricia Crowther, *Witchcraft in Yorkshire* (Clapham, Yorks, 1973), chapter 5, 'Yorkshire Witches in the Nineteenth Century'.

116 Sheila Gates, 'Documentary: an Accusation of Witchcraft: 1736', *Old West Riding*, new ser., 10 pp. 17-19. I am grateful to Dr Jane Whittaker for bringing this reference to my attention.

117 *West Riding Sessions Rolls 1597/8-1602*, p. 79; York City Archives, Quarter Sessions Minute Books, F7 ff. 28-9. Abraham Pryme noted two cases from visitation records of men resorting to cunning folk, in 1682 and 1688, which suggests that there are further cases to be found in post-Restoration ecclesiastical court records: *Ephemeris Vitae Abrahami Pryme*, p. 289.

118 York City Archives, Quarter Sessions Minute Books, F8, f. 31; C. L. Ewen, *Witchcraft and Demonianism: a Concise Account derived from Sworn Depositions and Confessions obtained in the Courts of England and Wales* (London, 1933; repr., 1970), p. 401; Barbour Mercer, 'Prosecution and Process', p. 137.

119 Fairfax, *Daemonologia*, p. 42.

120 P.R.O., ASSI 45/4/2/70.

121 Ibid. /45/3/2/97.

122 Webster, *Displaying of Supposed Witchcraft*, p. 75.

123 Fairfax, *Daemonologia*, p. 127.

124 P.R.O., Northern Circuit, Prisoners' Petitions, ASSI 47/20/512-3.

125 *The Diary of Ralph Thoresby, F.R.S., Author of the Topography of Leeds* (1677-1724), ed. Joseph Hunter, 2 vols. (London, 1830), 1 pp. 70, 220.

126 Webster, *Displaying of Supposed Witchcraft*, p. 323.

127 *The Memoirs of Sir John Reresby*, ed. Andrew Browning (Glasgow, 1936), p. 446. C. L. Ewen identifies this case with that of Isabella Bowling of Leeds, a widow convicted at the assizes in 1687, but subsequently reprieved: *Witchcraft and Demonianism*, pp. 406-7.

128 Tyler, 'Church Courts at York', pp. 98, 105, 107.

129 'Justice's Note-Book of Captain John Pickering, 1656-60', ed. G. D. Lumb, *Miscellanea* (Thoresby Society, 11 1904), p. 80; *Miscellanea* (Thorseby Society, 15 1909), pp. 73, 78.

130 Robin Briggs, *Communities of Belief: Cultural and Social Tensions in Early Modern France* (Oxford, 1989), p. 22.

131 Alexander D. H. Leadman, 'Pocklington Church', *Yorkshire Archaeological Journal*, 14 pp. 115-6.

132 P.R.O., ASSI 45/11/1/93.

133 Heywood, *Autobiography*, 1 p. 362.

# 5. Shakespeare and the English Witch-Hunts: Enclosing the Maternal Body

## Deborah Willis

According to two documents among the state papers of 1590, an un-named London informer told the sheriff's office that a Mrs. Dewse had engaged the services of Robert Birche, by reputation a conjurer.[1] She sought through his magic art to revenge herself upon her enemies—the "theeves" and "villaynes" she believed were responsible for driving her husband, the Keeper of Newgate Prison, from office, "which would bee both her and her childrens undoinges." The first document names several men, among them "Mr. Younge," "Sir Rowland Heyward," and "Sye." Mrs. Dewse asked Birche to make wax images of these men and then "pricke them to the harte" to cause their death. Failing that, he was to use his art to make them die "in a damp"—that is, of typhus—as had happened in Oxford at the Black Assize of 1577, when a number of judges, jurymen, and lawyers had abruptly died of that disease. In that incident the "damp" was widely attributed to the sorcery of a bookseller, on trial for selling banned Catholic books.[2]

Birche, however, was reluctant to accommodate Mrs. Dewse. He was "lame," he said, and therefore unable to make the images. According to the second document, he even piously lectured her: "She were beste to take good heede how she dealte and whom she trusted in such mat-ters . . . . The best meanes was to pray to God that hee would turne her enemies hartes." But the angry wife was determined to make the im-ages herself, if only Birche would stand by and correct her mistakes. After several visits from Birche, Mrs. Dewse completed three pictures under his guidance. She made "one for Mr Younge & put a pynne into his harte, another for Sir Rowland Heyward & putt a pynne to his harte & another under his ribbes, & the third picture for Sye & put two pynnes into his eyes." Mrs. Dewse was apparently satisfied by the re-sults: "She thanked God that some of her pictures did work well."

Birche was paid a sum of money, sent a sugar loaf and lemons, and asked to come again "divers times."

As it happened, Mrs. Dewse had indeed placed her trust in the wrong man. Birche himself, after his very first visit, reported on their dealings to her enemy, Mr. Young—Justice Young, that is, as he is termed in the second document. Birche's subsequent visits could be considered something of a "sting" operation, as, under Young's direction, he cleverly but deviously gathered more information about Mrs. Dewse's intentions while leading her to commit the acts of sorcery on her own. The document closes with an account of the sheriff's search of her home, during which he found two pictures hidden in "a secret place" in her cupboard, "with pynnes sticked in them" just as the informant had said.

The second document is a statement taken from Birche himself after the sheriff's visit. Far from being discouraged, Mrs. Dewse now planned her revenge to extend up the social ladder to the Privy Council: she would add the sheriff, the Recorder, the Lord Chamberlain, and even the Lord Chancellor to her list of intended victims. This, apparently, was enough to prompt the sheriff to further action. She was apprehended that very day.

What happened to Mrs. Dewse? Was she charged and tried under the 1563 witchcraft statutes, which criminalized the use or practice of "anye Sorcery Enchantment Charme or Witchcrafte, to thintent . . . to hurte or destroye any person in his or her Body, Member or Goodes"?[3] If so—assuming none of her victims actually fell ill or died—she would have been subject to a one-year imprisonment, during which she would also be placed in a pillory on market day four times a year to "openly confesse" her error and offense. If her sorcery had been successful, of course, she would have been subject to the death penalty, joining the many hundreds of others—almost all women—executed for witchcraft in England between 1563 and 1736.

Her name is missing from the exhaustive lists compiled by historians of persons tried under the witchcraft statutes in this period, but other documents allow us to piece together more of Mrs. Dewse's story.[4] In the period preceding her involvement with sorcery, her husband, William Dewes, in his capacity as Keeper of Newgate, had been charged by one Humphrey Gunston of "sundry abuses and misdemeanours . . . concerninge her Majestie." Dewes, in response, had filed actions of slander against Gunston. But Gunston prevailed: the Keeper was about to be charged and bound over for trial for "treason, murder, or felony" around the time Mrs. Dewse contacted the conjurer Birche. Among Gunston's supporters were the three men targeted by Mrs. Dewse: Justice Young, a justice of the peace who frequently served as

examiner and torturer in numerous cases involving allegedly seditious
Catholics; Sir Roland Heyward, also a J.P. and twice mayor of London;
and Nicholas Sye, probably an underkeeper at Newgate Prison. These
men had petitioned the Lord Chamberlain and other officials on Gunston's behalf.

Mrs. Dewes herself mentions Gunston, naming him as one of
her husband's enemies, though the informant does not include him
among the targets of her image magic. It appears, then, that at the
time she was under investigation, her husband was on the verge of being forced out of office by the collaboration of two influential J.P.s and
a prison underkeeper, who were supporting Gunston's charges and
blocking Dewse's suits to the high officials who had formerly been his
patrons. That, at any rate, was what Mrs. Dewse believed: the "knaves"
Heyward and Young she complains, have "made the lord Chamber-
leyne that hee would not reade her husbandes peticions, and the Lord
Chauncelor who was ever her husbandes frend would do nothing for
her, & Mr Recorder whom she thought would not have bene her ene-
mie, he likewise did now (as shee heard) take his parte that should have
her husbandes office."

Was Gunston angling for Dewse's office, as Mrs. Dewse seemed to believe? Or were these men simply trying to remove from office a man
they considered corrupt? Perhaps Heyward and Young opposed Dewse
because they suspected him or his wife of Catholic sympathies—undesirable especially in a keeper at Newgate, where many suspected Catholic conspirators were held. Mrs. Dewse reportedly told Birche that by
helping her to achieve her revenge he would "greatly please God, for
one of them was that thiefe Younge who lived by robbing papists." God
apparently would be pleased that they had punished an enemy of the
Catholic church, despite their ungodly methods. Moreover, her fallback
plan, to make these men die "as they did at the assises at Oxford," was
modeled on the sorcery of a seditious Catholic bookseller.

Or were the charges against the Keeper and Mrs. Dewse entirely
made up? Perhaps Young and Heyward wanted their own man in Dewse's office for personal advantage, not for religious reasons at all; perhaps Young and Heyward cynically concocted a tale of attempted
witchcraft in order to discredit Dewse further through his wife. As is
the case in most accusations of witchcraft, we have only the accusers'
statements to go on; the accused witch can no longer speak for herself.

What is clear enough in these documents is the way a charge of
witchcraft is embedded in a larger drama of intrigue, rivalry, and revenge, of power struggle over office and retaliation for its loss. Mrs.
Dewse's case, though it involves relatively minor players, resembles a
type of politically motivated witchcraft case which historians have con-

sidered especially characteristic of the medieval period, but which continued on into the Renaissance even after lower-class witches began to be persecuted as an end in itself—exactly the type of case that Shakespeare's imagination appears to have been engaged by at the time he was writing his early history plays. In such cases a charge of witchcraft is made against someone believed to have designs against the monarch or some highly placed official. It is frequently combined with accusations of treason or conspiracy against the state. The charge of witchcraft—and perhaps also its actual practice—may emerge, in fact, from factional struggle, part of one aristocratic group's attempt to displace its rivals and remove them from power. Shakespeare's first tetralogy focuses on a number of such politically embedded witchcraft cases: Joan of Arc, Eleanor, Duchess of Gloucester, Margery Jourdain, Margaret, Queen Elizabeth, and Jane Shore are all accused—and some convicted—of witchcraft in the course of these plays.

The case of Mrs. Dewse and the cultural practices that helped produce it provide an important context for Shakespeare's construction of witchcraft and political intrigue; but Shakespeare's plays in their turn, I believe, also provide a context for "reading" the historical phenomenon of witch-hunting. I would draw attention to the suggestiveness of Shakespeare for one issue in particular: the "woman question." Why were the victims of the hunt overwhelmingly female? Why, for example, is Mrs. Dewse the object of this particular investigation and not the male conjurer whom she engaged? Why Mrs. Dewse and not the husband who paid for and apparently endorsed, however fearfully, her involvement with sorcery?

Mrs. Dewse was caught in the cross fire of a power struggle between males over which she had little control. Assuming the charges against her to be at least partly true, she probably turned to sorcery as a last resort, when her husband's attempts to defend his position had faltered. In so doing, she stepped out of place as a woman, in a sense usurping her husband's role, appropriating for herself an agency usually restricted to males. But it is unlikely that the motives behind her arrest had much to do with the perception that her behavior had violated gender norms; rather, authorities were seeking to protect highly placed state officials from a magical threat to their lives. Yet what made that magical threat believable *as* a threat? What made authorities fear Mrs. Dewse and others like her, endowing them with a frightening power?

Witches were women, I believe, because women were mothers. To any reader of feminist theory, psychoanalysis, or Shakespeare criticism, it may seem obvious to say so.[5] Yet such a claim has seldom been tested in historians' analyses of the witch-hunts. Although historians have been asking with increasing urgency why women formed the vast majority of those prosecuted under England's witchcraft statutes,[6] they have not, by and large, focused on women's roles as mothers or caretakers of small children, or considered the psychological fallout of Renaissance mothering. The mother is absent from the most influential studies of English and Scottish witchcraft, those by Alan Macfarlane, Keith Thomas, and Christina Larner.[7] With some exceptions, the same is true of studies of witchcraft in Europe and the American colonies.[8]

Mrs. Dewse was a mother, and she apparently turned to sorcery in part because of that fact: her husband's loss of office threatened to be the "undoing" of both her and her children. As mother and wife, she was dependent on her husband for economic security and social position. Mrs. Dewse's interests intersected with his and her magical acts, designed to help and avenge him, implicate her in his treasonous activities. Those acts eerily encode a nightmare version of her maternal role; the doll-like wax images to be pierced by pins suggest children over whom a controlling but monstrous mother holds the power of life and death.

In Shakespeare's first tetralogy, witches, wives, and mothers are endowed with similar nightmare powers; by both magical and nonmagical means they manipulate males and make them feel as if they have been turned back into dependent children. Like Mrs. Dewse, these women also use their powers to aid and abet "traitors" who threaten what other characters see as legitimate political authority. But whereas Mrs. Dewse's maternal role is glimpsed only briefly in the documents connected with her case, Shakespeare's plays foreground the links between the witch and the mother, making a malevolent, persecutory power associated with the maternal body a central feature of their ability to threaten order. In what follows I explore more fully the ways the first tetralogy links the witch, the mother, and the rebel; after that, I return to the witch-hunts and modern historians' intepretations of them. If the maternal plays only a minor role in the case of Mrs. Dewse, when we turn to the "mainstream" witchcraft cases taking place at the village level, a distinct and, I hope to show, undeniable connection between the witch and the mother will become clear.

I

In *1 Henry VI* Joan—French rebel against English imperial claims, base-born upstart who takes on the persona of the aristocratic military hero—is represented as a witch whose supernatural power manifests itself in exceptional physical strength and skill in combat. She would at first seem an unlikely choice for an example of the linkage between witch and mother, given her highly masculinized role. Yet the sense of triumph the English males display when Joan is captured and set off to be executed derives not just from the fact that she is a national enemy and a vulgar upstart; it also stems from her clever manipulation of male ties to the mother. Initially associating herself with "God's mother" and a miraculous heavenly power to aid the Frenchmen, she is disclosed as demonically empowered and exploitive of both French and English males in her pursuit of purely personal "glory." On the battlefield she turns the Englishmen from fierce dogs into "whelps," by implication children. The language of "turning," "whirling," and shape changing is frequently used alongside the language of bewitchment to describe her effects on the English males: she "turns" Burgundy, the French duke initially loyal to the English, back into a loyal Frenchman by her appeal to his attachment to his native land, positioning him first as the mother himself: "Look on thy country . . . / As looks the mother on her lowly babe" as it dies in her arms.[9] After appealing to Burgundy's identification with the mother, Joan uses that identification to arouse guilt, as the country France becomes the mother—more specifically, the mother's breast—which Burgundy has wounded with his sword: "Behold the wounds, the most unnatural wounds, / Which thou thyself hast given her woeful breast / . . . . One drop of blood drawn from thy country's bosom / Should grieve thee more than streams of foreign gore" (3.3.50–51, 54–55). The breast is also implicitly present later, when, as she begs her devils to continue their supernatural aid, she reminds them of her witch's teat, "where I was wont to feed you with my blood" (5.3.14). Later, Joan's father uses the breast to curse Joan after she denies her parentage: "I would the milk / Thy mother gave thee when thou suck'st her breast / Had been a little ratsbane for thy sake" (5.4.27–29). Here the breast is used in a retaliatory fashion, as if punishing Joan for her former appropriation of it—for, as it were, her fraudalent self-presentation as the nurturing breast, when all along she was a poisoning one. Her attempt to save herself from execution by a last desperate appeal to pregnancy also brings the womb into play. As she is led away to be burned at the stake, it seems clear that in her the English are punishing not only a rebel and a class upstart but also a betraying mother, in this case a phallic mother, a mother who at first seemed to have it all—breast, womb, and phallus—now reduced to futile stratagems that display only the relative powerlessness of the maternal body in the male public world.

Margaret—linked to Joan in numerous ways—is another version of the phallic mother. But whereas Joan's phallic power comes from supernatural sources, Margaret's comes from her "masculine spirit," her

potential to be a mother, and her commitment to the particular patrilineage with which she becomes associated. At the center of these plays
is a critique of the culture of aristocratic honor and the factional violence to which it gives rise, a violence Shakespeare also associates with
a problematics of "family": civil conflict is set in motion when fathers
can no longer control sons, wives, and younger brothers, and when
kings can no longer control individual patrilineages. As a "masculine"
mother in this world, Margaret comes to possess a witchlike power. She
is an object of desire in a world where fathers die prematurely; she is a
vehicle for "upstart"ambitions in a world where kings fail to rule. Later
her powers of attraction are revealed as humiliating or deadly to the
males who succumb to them—lover, husband, and son. Moreover, set
against the claims of the patrilineal family as a discrete unit are the
claims of a national "family." Viewed from this perspective, Margaret
paradoxically becomes linked to Medea, the witch-mother who kills her
own children, when her impassioned defense of her son's rights as
royal heir makes her the equally impassioned enemy of her husband's
rival's children—that is, when she authorizes the murder of "pretty
Rutland," the youngest son of her enemy York.

But it is the Duchess of York, mother of Richard III, who comes closest to the literal Medea. Her witchlike power mimics that of the real
witch Margery Jourdain (called Mother Jourdain, not incidentally),
glimpsed in 2 *Henry VI* as she raises spirits in order to prophesy the
future. Revenge and divine justice, witch's curse and godly prophecy,
merge as the words of the mother's final curse of her son seems to raise
the quasi-supernatural, ghost-filled dream that Richard has the night
before his final battle. Richard dies undermined from within as well as
without, "providentially" murdered not only by Henry of Richmond
but also by his unnerving, prophetic dream and, when he wakes, by an
inner voice that again echoes his mother's curse.

The first tetralogy thus inscribes the mother in the witch and the
witch in the mother. As the plays unfold, those terms also shift in value:
the Duchess of York's witchlike mothering makes her a hero more than
a villain in these final scenes. If at first the plays seem to substitute
mother-hunting for witch-hunting—inviting the audience to take pleasure in Richard's revenge on women while at the same time recognizing his misogyny—by the end of the tetralogy the witchy behavior of
mothers has taken on a more positive value. Whereas Margaret's
Medea-like complicity in the murder of her rival's son makes her a villain, the Duchess of York's willingness to "smother" her own son with
the words of her curse makes her the instrument of the play's restoration of order. In the interests of a national family, even participating in
the murder of one's own son can be a good thing. Richard's mother

becomes in a sense a 'white witch,' her behavior acquiring a positive value because it is deployed on behalf of this new, national family, thus making possible a partial disengagement from the fetishistic passion for "place," so closely associated with a primary narcissistic loyalty to patrilineage. Such loyalties, according to these plays, must be subordinated to other, quasi-familial ties to persons unrelated by blood or feudal contract if aristocratic civil wars are to cease. If the rhetoric of national family can all too easily be appropriated and used to mystify a state that serves only a small portion of that family—and so Shakespeare uses it for the House of Tudor and other elite interests—it is also true that this rhetoric makes possible a break from even more constricted forms of social organization and provides the play's more moving moments, in which new types of relatedness or social bonding can be glimpsed. Among such moments are those that involve the quasi-coven of mothers in *Richard III* 4.4., as Margaret teaches Queen Elizabeth and the Duchess of York, her old enemies, how to curse.

If Shakespeare at the end of this sequence opens up a space for the white witch who heals with her destructive violence, he also suggests that the national family must recognize a maternal inheritance as well as contain and redirect its destructive potential. In helping to destroy Richard, the three mothers aid the "milksop," mother-dependent Richmond; moreover, Queen Elizabeth helps Richmond consolidate his power by actively arranging his marriage to her daughter. These mothers still play a marginalized and subordinate role in this male-centered political world, but because they are outsiders they are also survivors, capable of action when the violence of masculinist honor has crippled that world. The plays do not subvert patriarchy, abandon their androcentric focus, or challenge the beliefs that informed the laws criminalizing witchcraft. But, as sons attempt to differentiate themselves from, as well as sustain a connection to, a problematic inheritance from the father, the plays do, I believe, open up a larger space within patriarchy for acknowledging an inheritance from the mother and for valorizing female solidarity and self-assertion, even when these take a violent form.

## II

Shakespeare's first tetralogy foregrounds the way witch-hunting arises in response to a political crisis deeply intertwined with a breakdown in the family; as the consequences of that breakdown play themselves out, witch-hunting becomes mother-hunting, and the need for a reevaluation of both social practices becomes evident by the tetralogy's end. The destructive potential of the witch is closely tied to that of the murdering mother, and the punishment of both figures is instrumental in the construction of a new national identity—an identity that also depends, however, on recuperating aspects of their power. In Richard's narration of his childhood history, we glimpse the way an individual subject's desire is informed and fractured by his experience within a historically specific family unit, as women in caretaking roles employ a destructive patriarchal discourse about a (third) son's (deformed) body. If Richard's narrative at first encourages the audience to participate in the substitution of mother-hunting for witch-hunting, the tetralogy goes on to make visible the ironic sequence of misrecognitions involved in such hunts: Richard's attempt to repossess a magical omnipotence associated with the mother's body through the "Elysium" of the crown is exposed as fetishistic illusion; at the same time, his attempt to silence the punitive and rejecting mother's voice through acts of dominance falters as that voice is increasingly revealed to be, on the one hand, uncannily his own, and, on the other, patriarchal and divine.

For interpreters of the witch-hunts, these plays point in useful directions. They invite us to refocus our investigations by scrutinizing those social formations most directly involved in the construction of witch-hunting subjects, to attempt to chart the steps by which such subjects adopt and redeploy a language first uttered by the mother and encountered in the intersubjective context of specific families, a language that is then transferentially reworked later in life within larger networks of social relationships. Ideally such an attempt would also include an account of the way particular individual subjects are specially positioned to affect the state apparatus, which in its turn reaches out to affect the social institutions most directly involved in the production of individual subjects.

The witch-hunts were, of course, a highly complex, multidetermined affair, involving the poor and the very poor at the village level as well as a "prosecuting class" made up of gentry-level and aristocratic judges, justices of the peace, clerics, magistrates, and kings. Low, middle, and high, peasant and elite, male and female interests intersected in fear and loathing of the witch. Alan Macfarlane and Keith Thomas have offered the most powerful analysis of witchcraft at the village level, their explanatory paradigms concentrating on social structure, economic patterns, and popular belief. Christina Larner, exploring the Scottish witch-hunts, has integrated their approach with a closer examination of the role of the state apparatus and the ruling elites. As she remarks: "Peasants left to themselves will identify individuals as witches and will resort to a variety of anti-witchcraft measures in self-defence; they cannot pursue these measures to the punishment, banishment, or official execution of even one witch, let alone a multiplicity of witches, without the administrative machinery and encouragement of their rulers."[10]

Although these historians have little or nothing to say about the relation of witch to mother, they all take up the "woman question." For Keith Thomas, the fact that most of those accused of witchcraft were women is most plausibly explained "by economic and social considerations, for it was the women who were the most dependent members of the community, and thus the most vulnerable to accusation."[11] For Alan Macfarlane, it is not women's dependence but their social position and power that made them vulnerable; they were the "co-ordinating element" in village society, and "if witchcraft . . . reflected tensions between an ideal of neighborliness and the necessities of economic and social change, women were commonly thought of as witches because they were more resistant to such change."[12] Both Thomas and Macfarlane agree that the "idea that witch-prosecutions reflected a war between the sexes must be discounted," chiefly because village-level accusers and victims were at least as likely to be female as male, if not more so.[13]

Christina Larner, while stressing the political and religious factors involved in the hunts, has also argued that the witch-hunts were sex-related, though not sex-specific. For both elite groups and the peasantry, the women who became targets of the hunts had clearly violated norms regarding appropriate behavior of women; they were angry and demanding, not meek, mild, and compliant. She disagrees with the notion that a "war between the sexes" can be discounted as an element in the hunts merely because a majority of accusers were women themselves, as Thomas and Macfarlane suggest. Larner recognizes that patriarchal beliefs and practices often have the effect of dividing women against one another; because of their dependence on men, many women attempt to distinguish themselves from and even attack women who refuse to conform to patriarchal rules.[14]

Larner's argument is a more sophisticated version of one that has surfaced in less subtle form in many appropriations of the historical witch for feminist polemic.[15] The witch is a rebel against patriarchal oppression, a transgressor of gender roles, the innocent victim of a male-authored reign of terror that functions to keep all women in their place. If it is acknowledged at all in such texts that women were participants in as well as victims of the hunts, these women are represented as lackeys of patriarchy, conservative defenders of male-defined notions of women's roles, mere cogs in the phallocentric wheel. By contrast, the witch is the heroic proto-feminist who resists patriarchal technologies for producing the female subject and contests oppressive gender norms.

Patriarchal beliefs and practices do, of course, powerfully shape witchcraft accusations. But these polemical formulations, useful as they may be in some contexts, ascribe to the participants in the hunts a monologic unity of self that directs attention away from the tensions and discontinuities within early modern constructions of the subject. As I read the hunts, the woman accused of witchcraft is a profoundly liminal and ambivalent figure, especially in the early stages of a quarrel leading to a witchcraft trial. Although she is a transgressive figure in many ways, part of her power to arouse fear in her neighbors comes from her ability to appeal to communally recognized norms. The witch's discourse is simultaneously orthodox and transgressive; her curses call upon God, not the devil, even as she pursues her "unnatural" ends. Similarly, the woman who accuses her, though frequently protecting her claim to be recognized by the community as a good wife, mother, and neighbor, may also in some respects be renegotiating the definitions of those roles and practicing a resistance strategy of her own.

In what follows I attempt to build on the work of Macfarlane, Thomas, and Larner by pursuing a trajectory suggested by the Shakespearean text.

### III

If, as Christina Larner makes clear, the impetus for the prosecution of witches ultimately came "from above," it was nevertheless primarily villagers who selected the specific individuals to be indicted for the crime and who thus played a decisive role in determining the witch's gender. And among these villagers, witch-hunting was especially women's work. Quarrels that led to accusation were significantly, though not exclusively, quarrels between older and younger women which focused on matters of feeding and child care. As a quarrel progressed, the younger woman came to see in the older one the attributes of a malevolent mother, who used her powers of suckling, feeding, and nurturing to enlist demonic aid in bringing sickness and death to the households of other mothers. For the younger woman, witch-hunting may have been a means of protecting herself from this malevolent maternal power by "enclosing" it in the witch.

The trial records analyzed by Macfarlane and Thomas reveal a profile of the witch that is remarkably similar in case after case. An older woman has a falling-out with a neighbor—in more than half the cases another woman.[16] The older woman is usually poorer, and often the falling-out has occurred after she has gone to her neighbor with a request for food or some domestic item, or for access to land. The request is denied. The woman goes away, cursing her neighbor openly, or murmuring in a sinister fashion under her breath. Later, some misfortune happens to the neighbor or her family. A child falls sick, a wife or husband dies, cattle or sheep die, a freak storm destroys the crops, the granary catches fire, the milk goes sour, the butter won't turn. The neighbor recalls the cursing of the old woman and suspects the misfortune is the product of her witchcraft.

What happens next? There are several possibilities. The neighbor might appeal to one of the local "cunning folk" to identify the witch and to procure some sort of magical protection against the witch's *maleficium*—her harmful magic. The neighbor might turn to the church or to prayer. She might also try to appease the witch in some way. But with the passage of the witchcraft statutes in 1563 she has a new option: she may appeal to the local justice of the peace, informing against the suspected witch and leading the J.P. to open an inquiry. Other informants are interviewed, and a grand jury then determines whether indictments should be handed down and a trial held. If so, the accused witch is on her way to imprisonment, execution, or possibly acquittal. The trial itself functions as a kind of countermagic, with judges and jury taking over some aspects of the role of the cunning folk, as the witch's exposure and forced confession also dissolve her magical powers.

What did it take to convict and sentence to death someone accused of witchcraft? It was not normally possible to catch the witch in the act of practicing her art; instead, the force of a gathering accumulation of circumstantial evidence determined her fate. Reports of the accused's curses, followed in a timely fashion by misfortunes, were key items in the circumstantial evidence leading to indictment. But so also were several other factors, such as observations of small animals around her home or in her vicinity (cats, weasels, ferrets, frogs, toads, "imps") and accounts of visions or dreams in which the accused appeared to the victim or the victim's relatives. By the time a woman was brought to trial, she had already developed a reputation for troublesome behavior and hostility toward her neighbors, and her suspected acts of *maleficium* had often taken place over many years. Indictment was most likely when a number of neighbors came forward to testify about the same woman— when, in other words, she was "notoriously defamed" by the "better sort" in her village community. For the death penalty to apply, her magic had to be believed to have resulted in someone's death. Once a trial was under way, the accused woman's body was examined for the devil's mark or "teat"; any unusual fleshy protuberance, especially one in a "private place," would be taken as further confirmation of the charge of witchcraft. Finally, a confession (extracted under duress, but seldom torture) would help ensure the witch's fate.

Some of the connections between the witch and the mother will already be obvious. The beliefs instrumental in conviction associate the malignant power of the witch with the maternal body. The teat which marks her as a witch, for example, is also the means by which she acquires her demonic power; it is in effect a third nipple by which she feeds her familiars, or "imps," the demonic spirits who inhabit the bodies of small animals and who help her carry out her magic. The witch, moreover, is an older woman, usually postmenopausal; beliefs about the witch may also register anxiety about the changes age brings to the female body.[17] It is as if her body encodes maternal rejection of the human child: her womb no longer fertile, her breast no longer capable of producing milk, she nevertheless can feed a counterfamily of demonic imps. Her witchcraft is frequently directed against the children of her neighbors, and almost always against domestic activities associated with feeding, nurturance, or generation. When animals rather than people are targets of the witch's magic, cattle and the milk they produce are especially likely to be affected.

Village-level witchcraft beliefs encode a fantasy of the witch as mother—a mother with two aspects. She is a nurturing mother who feeds and cares for a brood of demonic imps, but a malevolent antimother to her neighbors and their children. Over and over again in the trial records, the accused women are addressed as "Mother"—Mother Grevell, Mother Turner, Mother Dutten, Mother Devell, Mother Stile—following general village convention.[18] These women continue to be associated with the social role of mother even after they have aged and their own children are grown. But they are mothers who refuse to act like mothers. What is at stake here, however, is not their refusal to mother their own children; in a sense they are doing that by nurturing demonic imps. Rather, they refuse to play the quasi-maternal role expected of them by the larger community.

The witch's symmetrical opposite in the village community is the "gossip," a word derived from *godparent* and still related to that more specialized role. (Fairy tales in which the witch is set against the fairy godmother have an obvious relevance here.) The "gossip" is the female neighbor called in to assist at childbirth and during the "lying-in" period, who acts as midwife and helps to care for her neighbor's children, who participates in an informal village network in which women offer one another aid and advice about child care, sickness, and other areas of domestic management. These women are mothers in several senses: they "mother" one another, they mirror one another as mothers, and they act as substitute mothers for one another's children. The aid and advice they offer often involves magic; midwifery, for example, includes a range of magical techniques for helping ensure the safety of mother and child during the difficult time of childbirth. The witch is the female neighbor who brings a malevolent magic into the cultural spaces where mother and child are most at risk, introducing suspicion and fear into a community's informal network of female neighbors.[19] She uses the maternal body to betray the maternal body.

Given the fragmentary and problematic nature of the trial records, it is difficult to reconstruct the series of events that made a particular woman a target of suspicion. It is clear, however, not only that many quarrels involved women but also that the informal networks of shared mothering involved competition and conflict as well as mutual support. For example, there is the 1581 case of Cicelly Celles, an Essex woman. In one informant's statement she is seen "chiding and railing" at another woman who was engaged to replace Cicely as a wet nurse for a neighbor's child. "Thou shalt lose more by the having of it than thou shalt have for the keeping of it," Cicely reportedly threatened the woman; within a month the woman's own four-year-old daughter was dead. According to another statement, Cicely was involved in an incident with a young mother preparing to take her new baby to church. Several women, including Cicely, gathered around. After the other gossips had cooed over the baby and complimented it, Cicely uttered a dark prediction: the child would die soon and the mother would never bear another. And indeed, a short time later, the child died. (The incident recalls the christening scene in "Sleeping Beauty.") The mother, however, refused to accuse Cicely of witchcraft, instead praying God to forgive Cicely if she had "dealt in any such sort." But the husband of the woman who replaced Cicely as wet nurse was not so forbearing. He came forward to accuse Cicely in the death of his young daughter, and it was on account of the death of this child that Cicely was indicted— along with her husband—for witchcraft. Her husband was acquitted; Cicely was convicted and sentenced to death.[20]

Thomas and Macfarlane read the psychology of witchcraft accusation in the light of a conflict between "neighborliness" and "individualism." The accusers' actions, as they see it, are largely shaped by the guilt they experience after denying their neighbors' request for help— an "individualistic" transgression of traditional codes of communal sharing. Guilt manifests itself in some of the dreams and visions experienced by the accusers and their families and in the apparently psychosomatic illnesses that sometimes befall victims; it manifests itself especially in the accusers' habitual interpretation of subsequent misfortunes as retaliation for the injury to the neighbor refused aid.[21] Thomas and Macfarlane cast the accusing neighbor in the role of "individualist," as opposed to the witch, who is the defender of older norms of "neighborliness"—that is, of the norms in place before the Protestant Reformation and the sixteenth-century Poor Laws. But in the quarrels involving Cicely Celles, for example, it is difficult to see what norm of neighborliness her opponents would have felt they were violating. Rather it is Cicely herself who seems to have been out of line.[22] One can be unneighborly by demanding too much as well as by giving too little. Accusers do sometimes retrospectively come to view their actions as lacking in charity. But in many quarrels the situation is far more ambiguous.

Such cases suggest a more complex dynamic at work than Thomas and Macfarlane's formulation allows for: violating the codes of neighborliness is unlikely to be the only cause of guilt. Modern psychology and psychoanalytic theory would in any case suggest that the responses underlying victims' illnesses, visions, and interpretations of misfortune have roots in childhood.[23] Neighborliness is embedded in the child's early experiences in a family context, where quarrels over sources of nourishment and boundaries of identity first take place. Here the child learns about sharing, hierarchy, and the regulation of envy from mothers and other female caretakers, and competes for access to the mother's body (especially as symbolized by the breast) among rivals. Whatever guilt is incurred by denying a neighbor's request or violating codes of neighborliness is likely to come with a history, largely unconscious, in which the mother is both the first victim and first persecutor of the child's earliest attempts to control its environment.

Moreover, Renaissance family structure, gender norms, and popular magical beliefs worked together to make it more likely that the maternal rather than the paternal body would arouse in both men and women fears of a specifically *magical* persecution. When the child first encounters the prohibitions of her mother or other female caretakers, she is still very young and thinks magically, conflating angry wishes with destructive acts. Inevitably ambivalent about the mother who nurtures but also eludes control and thwarts the will, the child may fear that her hostile fantasies will actually destroy the mother—and that the mother may retaliate in kind. By the time the father takes over the role of prohibitor and is understood to be the ultimate power within the family and the larger social world, the child is cognitively better developed, more able to test reality; transgression against paternal authority may arouse fear of physical punishment (especially castration), but his disapproval and anger is less likely to be experienced as magically dangerous. Renaissance belief, moreover, reinforced the association of magic with the maternal body, constructing that body as especially unpredictable and difficult to control: woman was the "disorderly" sex, the site of a bewildering and often contradictory array of special dangers and powers, associated variously with her womb and its appetites, her milk and menstrual blood.

In a significant number of quarrels leading to witchcraft indictments, accusers experience symptoms of physical pain or illness shortly after the quarrels take place—what would be called today psychosomatic or hysterical symptoms. The injury to the witch uncannily reiterates itself in an injury to the accuser.[24] Accusers who fall ill in more or less direct consequence of a quarrel can be either male or female, but in either case such incidents are relatively rare. More commonly, illness or misfortune befalls some other member of the household with whom the accuser is associated: a spouse or child. In these cases retaliatory fears inform the accuser's mode of explanation rather than produce a hysterical symptom. Sickness and death are interpreted as unjust punishments, and the accuser feels persecuted. The punishment is out of proportion to the "crime" committed against the neighbor—but not, perhaps, to the unconscious fantasy that goes with it.

The accuser feels guilt and fears retaliation, I believe, not so much for violating the code of neighborliness as for injuring a body unconsciously associated with the mother of childhood. The accuser confronts in her neighbor a woman of her mother's generation. While she consciously expresses anger and perceives the older woman's request as too demanding or excessive, unconsciously she may feel that her refusal of the request injures a body with which she still feels partly fused. The misfortunes regularly attributed to the witch's malevolent magic involve the loss of things a child associates with the mother's body and believes she controls: milk, milk products, food, domestic space, babies, husbands. Having injured the source of milk, the accuser's own milk is threatened by a mother far more powerful than herself.

The witch's curse was believed to be carried out by her demonic "imps"—her children, who do her will in exchange for sucking her blood and other acts of nurturance. Imps appear with great frequency in informants' statements. They often seem to have a Janus-like aspect. On the one hand, they are extensions of the witch's malevolence, carrying illness to her victims, causing accidents, sometimes displaying hunger or nipping them. On the other hand, they make the witch herself a target of a good deal of oral greed, sucking blood not only from the "witch's tit" but from other parts of the body, leaving marks and causing the witch pain, and sometimes demanding to be fed milk, beer, or bread as well. Like children, the imps can get out of the witch's control: Elizabeth Bennet, for example, sent her imp to kill the animals of her neighbor, William Byett, but the spirit exceeded his instructions and "plagued Byett's wife to death."[25] If the imps enact the witch's destructive will, they also in a sense enact the child's rebellious resistance to the mother.

Sometimes, but by no means routinely, the witch is believed to employ wax images or doll-like figures to carry out her magic—that is, to use sorcery, like Mrs. Dewse. These images were called not only "puppets" (poppets) but also "child's babies" and "maumets" (mammets, a term for the breast-fed infant). Alice Hunt denied "having any puppets, spirits, or maumettes." Alice Manfield had an imp called "Puppet alias Mamet."[26] Employing a familiar, the witch is a mother who makes a sacrifice in order to acquire a magic power through her demonic "child." Employing image magic, the witch makes her enemy into a child, to be controlled and sacrificed.

Imps are sometimes actual animals—pets perhaps—kept by a witch or sighted in her vicinity; sometimes they are apparitions or fantasies. It is in the testimony of children, some of them children of the accused, that the demonic imps seem especially vivid. In one sense the imp is the child's "evil twin"; the child in fantasy disassociates itself from the sadistic or devouring oral impulses that threaten the mother with injury. In another sense the demonic imp is the rival child the mother appears to favor. It is difficult, of course, to tell from the statements what the child has really experienced. Has the child witnessed the mother with pets, or with creatures the mother actually treats as her familiars? Is the child reporting a fantasy or dream? Is the child merely saying what the examiner wants to hear? Some of the statements do seem believable as children's fearful fantasies of mothers they have come to distrust, and suggest a troubled family environment. Such is the case with the statements taken from Cicely Celles's two sons.[27] According to them, she fed and sheltered a rival set of demonic siblings, who threatened the sons in various ways. Henry, aged nine, described a spirit who came "one night about midnight" and took his younger brother John by "the left leg, and also by the little toe." The spirit, he said, resembled his sister, "but that it was all black." John, according to the statement,

> cried out and said, "Father, Father, come help me, there is a black thing hath me by the leg, as big as my sister": whereat his father said to his mother, "why thou whore, cannot you keep your imps from my children": whereat she presently called it away from her son, saying, "come away, come away," at which speech it did depart . . . . The next day he [Henry] told his mother he was so afraid of the thing that had his brother

by the leg that he sweat for fear, and that he could scarce get his shirt from his back: his mother answering "thou liest, thou liest, whoreson."

Henry also reported seeing his mother feed the imps "out of a black dish, each other day with milk," and carry them out to a hiding place in the roots of a crab tree near the house. One, "a black one, a he," was called Hercules or Jack, the other "a white one, a she," was Mercury, and they had "eyes like goose eyes." On the night a neighbor's maid reported a sudden but temporary illness, Henry said he heard his mother tell his father that she had sent Hercules to the maid, the father answering, "Ye are a trim fool."

Henry's story was corroborated by his brother John, though there are some discrepancies in their accounts. Taken together, the documents suggest a sadly conflict-ridden family, in which husband abuses wife, wife abuses children, and the children themselves fear further abuse from a set of rival "siblings." The cycle of conflict was undoubtedly intensified by the family's poverty, and the family is suggestively fractured along sex lines: the father protects his sons—"*my* children"— from the mother's "imps," who remind the sons of their sister. Does the mother neglect her sons while favoring a daughter as well as the alleged imps? Are the sons envious as well as afraid of the rival siblings, whom their mother feeds and sets against them? It is of course hard to draw any firm conclusions from such fragmentary evidence, but it is possible that the sons' destructive impulses toward other siblings and toward the mother who seemingly favors them are returning to haunt them in the form of fearful apparitions. These sons literally experience their mother as a witch—a witch who feeds and nourishes her brood of demonic imps while neglecting and tormenting her human children.

The revelation of the witch's teat was usually among the last pieces of evidence to be entered against the accused woman.[28] It is as if the full fantasy—of witch as malevolent mother feeding a brood of rival children— could be confronted only in the relative safety of the courtroom. Only then, in the presence of male authorities deemed to serve a power greater than that of the witch, and after a relative consensus about her danger to the community had been reached, could the ultimate source of conflict—the mother's breast—be confronted and allowed to become a target of aggression. That the witch's teat is an *extra* one seems significant here; it can be destroyed while leaving the "good" mother's body intact. The grotesque body of the witch could be punished and executed, leaving the community the maternal body in its "natural" and purified form. And since the trial was also a demonstration of the legal, paternal, and divinely sanctioned power of authority over the witch, the maternal bodies that remained—those of the female accusers—had in effect found access to an orthodox magic of the father's body far more powerful than the witch's own.

## IV

The villagers who accused women of witchcraft were intent on purging their community of a specific threat to specific individuals. The prosecuting class, however, tended to be more interested in curing the whole country; for them the witch was an abstraction, her punishment sending a message far and wide. Elite texts about witchcraft appropriate aspects of village discourse about the witch but also rewrite it. A case in point is the pamphlet containing the case of Cicely Celles, produced by one W. W., and composed almost wholly of "informations" taken by the justice of the peace, Brian Darcy, for a series of witchcraft trials in St. Osyth, Essex, during 1582. The documents are preceded by a dedicatory epistle that provides something of a frame story.[29] Dedicated to the head of the ennobled branch of the Darcy family, distant relation of Brian Darcy, it purports to show "what a pestilent people witches are, and how unworthy to live in a Christian Commonwealth." Punishing the witch with rigor, the author claims, is the most likely means to "appease the wrath of God, to obtain his blessing, to terrifie secreete offenders by open transgressors punishments, to withdraw honest natures from the corruption of evil company, to diminish the great multitude of wicked people, to increase the small number of virtuous persons, and to reforme all the detestable abuses, which the perverse witt and will of man doth dayly devise." Hanging, in fact, is too good for the witch; the penalty that suits the ordinary felon and murderer is hardly severe enough for the witch, who defies "the Lorde God to his face." To do anything less than burn the witch is to eclipse the "honour of God . . . and the glorye due to his inviolable name." The witch here is not the antimother feeding demonic imps but the servant of Satan who joins his "hellish liverie" and swears allegiance to him as to a rebellious feudal lord. The dedicatory epistle is designed to foreground Justice Darcy's heroic efforts to preserve order through his rigorous prosecution of Satan's rebellious crew.

Yet the documents that make up the rest of the pamphlet tell the story of the antimother: the case of Cicely Celles is only one of a number of others in which accusations of witchcraft arise from quarrels over sources of nourishment, milk, feeding, and child care, that record attacks on the community's children and sightings of demonic imps. Inside the enemy of God and the rebel against the state there still lurks the antimother: it is as if, despite the confident demonstration of dominance and patriarchalism expressed in the dedicatory note, the male author still finds himself vulnerable to a threat associated with this earlier figure of authority. The witch as antimother who is also a rebel and enemy of God brings us back, of course, to the central tropes of Shakespeare's first tetralogy.

This pamphlet suggests that, for governing elites as well as for peasant women and men, fantasies of maternal persecution continued to organize discourse about the witch and may have been an important factor motivating the hunts, if only one among others. To varying degrees and with varying emphases, elite discourse about the witch was also concerned with promoting a new religious orthodoxy and maintaining political order and social hierarchy; the witch is a heretic, a class upstart, a traitor, and an unruly woman as well as a malevolent mother. As Christina Larner has argued, the witch-hunts were linked to the problems experienced by the post-Reformation state as it attempted to legitimize itself in an age of religious controversy. But for the prosecuting classes such problems may have been further complicated by the sixteenth-century reconfiguration of the honor code and its consequences for male identities, a reconfiguration in which Shakespeare's first tetralogy fully participates. The honor code was undergoing a shift away from late-feudal military values and an emphasis on kinship, lineage, and local ties toward a state-centered emphasis on administrative office, learning, and the arts. This values shift, I believe, required from the male of the prosecuting class a new involvement in his psychological inheritance from the mother. He had to integrate into his masculine identity more traits that carried cultural and intrapsychic associations with her; he could not wholly disassociate himself from a primary identification with the mother, as could the late-feudal male.

The witch trials, then, may have functioned as more than a satisfying demonstration of legitimacy by a state in religious and political crisis; they may also have provided a consoling ritual for males of the prosecuting class coping with feminization. Like the younger peasant women who became accusers of the witch, the state-centered, gentry-level male felt pressure to identify with, as well as differentiate himself from, the mother; he too might fear magical retaliation from a maternal body with which he felt unconsciously fused. If Shakespeare's first tetralogy is an especially powerful evocation of the disturbing connections between the witch and the mother, such connections were also made by some of his contemporaries. I close with one last example, from *A Dialogue Concerning Witches and Witchcraft*, a pamphlet written in the form of a dialogue by the Essex clergyman George Gifford in 1593, around the time the plays making up the first tetralogy were initially being performed on the London stage. In this text Samuel, one of the speakers in the dialogue, is asked why he thinks he is bewitched. He responds: "Trust me I cannot tell, but I feare me I have, for there be two or three in our towne which I like not, but especially an old woman, I have been as careful to please her as ever I was to please mine own mother, and to give her ever anon one thing or another, and yet me thinkes she frownes at me now and then." Samuel quite explicitly—and anxiously—experiences the old woman as a mother impossible to please, suspecting her of witchcraft merely for frowning at him. Assuming that she had a counterpart in real life, here was one old woman on her way to the gallows for little more than a bad mood.

## N O T E S

1. *Calendar of State Papers Domestic—Elizabeth*, vol. 2 (1581–90) p. 644; the documents are reprinted in W. H. Hart, "Observations on Some Documents Relating to Magic in the Reign of Queen Elizabeth," *Archaeologia: or, Miscellaneous Tracts Relating to Antiquity* 40 (1866), 395–96.

2. A brief account and list of documents associated with this case can be found in George Lyman Kittredge, *Witchcraft in Old and New England* (Cambridge: Harvard University Press, 1929), pp. 89, 419–20, n. 90.

3. C. L'Estrange Ewen, *Witch Hunting and Witch Trials* (London: Kegan Paul, Trench, Trubner, 1929), p. 17. The first witchcraft statute was passed in 1542, at the end of Henry VIII's reign, then repealed in 1547 under Edward VI. According to Ewen, only one case (which resulted in a pardon) has survived from this period; see pp. 11 and 13–18 for the texts of both the 1542 and 1563 statutes.

4. John R. Dasent, ed., *Acts of the Privy Council*, n.s., 25 vols. (London: Eyre and Spottiswoode, 1897), 16:388; 17:47–48; 19:111–112. In the documents the name Dewse is spelled a variety of ways, among them Dews, Dyos, Dios, Devyes, and Devies.

5. Two essays on Shakespeare are worth special mention: Janet Adelman, " 'Born of Woman': Fantasies of Maternal Power in *Macbeth*," in *Cannibals, Witches, and Divorce: Estranging the Renaissance*, ed. Marjorie Garber (Baltimore: Johns Hopkins University Press, 1987), pp. 90–121, reprinted with revisions in Janet Adelman, *Suffocating Mothers: Fantasies of Maternal Origin in Shakespeare's Plays, "Hamlet" to "The Tempest"* (New York: Routledge, 1992); and Karen Newman, "Discovering Witches: Sorciographics," in *Fashioning Femininity and English Renaissance Drama* (Chicago: University of Chicago Press, 1991), pp. 51–70. My argument is especially indebted to Adelman's essay.

6. Some essays that take up this question include Alan Anderson and Raymond Gordon, "Witchcraft and the Status of Women—the Case of England," *British Journal of Sociology* 29 (June 1978), 171–84; and Clarke Garrett, "Women and Witches: Patterns of Analysis," *Signs: Journal of Women in Culture and Society* 3 (Winter 1977), 461–70. Both essays provoked subsequent commentary; see J. K. Swales and Hugh V. McClachlan, "Witchcraft and the Status of Women: A Comment," *British Journal of Sociology* 30 (September 1979), 349–57; Alan Anderson and Raymond Gordon, "The Uniqueness of English Witch-

craft: A Matter of Numbers?" *British Journal of Sociology* 30 (September 1979), 359–61; letters by Judith H. Balfe, Claudia Honegger, and Nelly Moia commenting on Clarke Garrett's essay, together with a reply by the author, appear in *Signs* 4 (Autumn 1978), 201–2, and *Signs* 4 (Summer 1979), 792–804.

Two books also provide lengthy treatments of the role of gender in the hunts as well as appraisals of current research. See G. R. Quaife, *Godly Zeal and Furious Rage: The Witch in Early Modern Europe* (London: Croom Helm, 1987); and Brian P. Levack, *The Witch-Hunt in Early Modern Europe* (London: Longman, 1987).

7. Alan Macfarlane, *Witchcraft in Tudor and Stuart England: A Regional and Comparative Study* (New York: Harper and Row, 1970); Keith Thomas, *Religion and the Decline of Magic* (New York: Scribner's, 1971), pp. 437–583; Christina Larner, *Enemies of God* (London: Chatto & Windus, 1981).

8. An important exception is John Demos, *Entertaining Satan: Witchcraft and the Culture of Early New England* (Oxford: Oxford University Press, 1983), esp. pp. 172–210. Although Demos's psychoanalytic assumptions are somewhat different from mine, his argument is in many respects similar to the one I offer here; I am indebted to it. In *The Devil in the Shape of a Woman: Witchcraft in Colonial New England* (New York: Norton, 1987), Carol F. Karlsen discusses motherhood in a more restricted sense; her major focus is on women and patterns of inheritance. It is perhaps significant that both of these exceptions come from studies of colonial American witchcraft, which has close affinities with English witchcraft. At the same time, because more complete records survive for many American cases, it is possible to reconstruct the relationships and family histories of participants in greater detail than in English cases. It may also be true that the role of mother is not as relevant to witch-hunting in continental Europe. There, witch-hunting was a far more virulent affair, and the social practices and psychological dynamics were significantly different from those informing the English hunts; accordingly, the profile of the typical witch was also different. Among other things, continental witch stereotypes emphasized sexual deviance.

9. *1 Henry VI* 3.3.44, 47. All quotations from Shakespeare's plays are from *The Riverside Shakespeare*, ed. G. Blakemore Evans et al. (Boston: Houghton Mifflin, 1974); subsequent citations appear in the text.

10. Larner, *Enemies of God*, p. 2.

11. Thomas, *Religion*, p. 568.

12. Macfarlane, *Witchcraft*, p. 161.

13. Thomas, *Religion*, p. 568; Macfarlane, *Witchcraft*, p. 160. Both men and women, of course, have mothers.

14. Larner addresses these issues most directly in "Witchcraft Past and Present," in *Witchcraft and Religion: The Politics of Popular Belief* (Oxford: Basil Blackwell, 1984), pp. 84–88; see esp. p. 86.

15. Some examples include Mary Daly, *Gyn/Ecology: The Meta-Ethics of Radical Feminism* (Boston: Beacon Press, 1978); Andrea Dworkin, *Woman Hating* (New York: E. P. Dutton, 1974), pp. 118–50; Robin Morgan, "The Network of the Imaginary Mother," in *Lady of the Beasts: Poems* (New York: Random House, 1970). WITCH was the acronym of a women's liberation group in the late 1960s, and the witch has continued to be a powerful symbol invoked by a wide range of feminist groups. See also Silvia Bovenschen, "The Contemporary Witch, the Historical Witch, and the Witch Myth: The Witch, Subject of the Appropriation of Nature and Object of the Domination of Nature," in *New*

*German Critique* 15 (Fall 1978), 83–119. Bovenschen describes, among other things, uses of the witch in European demonstrations by feminists; she celebrates the "anarchic" energies of the mythic impulse behind such uses while at the same time ridiculing the "rearguard" interest of "ivory tower" scholars, with their delusions of autonomy and their foot-dragging emphasis on historical accuracy. Her discussion, engaging as it is in its "bad girl" iconoclasm, reproduces the notion of an autonomous ivory tower sealed off from politics and masks the new possibilities that careful attention to historical texts can open up for feminists. But Bovenschen's point about the rearguard nature of scholars' work on witchcraft is well taken. The feminist texts I have listed are all products of the 1970s; although scholarly witchcraft studies have a long history, it was not, for the most part, until the 1980s that historians gave sustained attention to the question of gender in the witch-hunts. Larner's essay, "Witchcraft Past and Present," first appeared in 1981.

16. Macfarlane finds that as many women as men informed against witches in the 291 Essex cases he studied; about 55 percent of those who believed they had been bewitched were female (*Witchcraft*, pp. 160–61). It is possible that this figure is misleadingly low; in many cases the husband as "head of household" may have came forward to make statements on behalf of his wife, the initial or central quarrel being between her and another woman. Careful reading of the "informations" taken against the St. Osyth witches seems to bear out this observation: males testifying against a witch often are husbands of women who have quarreled with the witch or have been bewitched by her. See W. W., *A true and just Recorde, of the Information, Examination and Confession of all the Witches, taken at S. Oses in the countie of Essex: whereof some were executed, and other some entreated according to the determination of lawe* (1582; reprint Delmar, N.Y.: Scholars' Facsimiles and Reprints, 1981). In addition, George Gifford's *Dialogue Concerning Witches and Witchcraftes* (1593; reprint London: Shakespeare Association Facsimiles, 1931), makes it clear that Samuel, an accuser of witches who is one of the dialogue's main characters, is acting at the behest of his wife. It may be that many male accusers became involved in witchcraft cases in ways loosely parallel to the situation of males accused. The very small percentage of men charged with witchcraft often were the husbands or relatives of women who had already been accused of witchcraft; they suffered from guilt by association. In a similar way a quarrel between two women may have expanded to involve the males to whom they were attached.

17. Some historians have associated the behavior imputed to witches with menopause; see Quaife, *Godly Zeal*, p. 94. Reginald Scot makes a similar argument when he suggests that the fantasies of old women who think they are witches may be the result of menopause: such fantasies, "upon the stopping of their monethlie melancholike flux or issue of blood . . . must needs increase." This "weaknesse both of bodie and braine" makes them "the aptest persons to meete with such melancholike imaginations. . . . Their imaginations remaine, even when their senses are gone." Reginald Scot, *The Discoverie of Witchcraft* (1584; rpt. Carbondale: Southern Illinois University Press, 1964), pp. 65–66.

18. For some examples, see C. L'Estrange Ewen, *Witchcraft and Demonianism* (London: Heath Cranton, 1933), pp. 154, 158, 159. This highly useful book gives abstracts of depositions and confessions from a large number of English witch trials.

19. Michael Macdonald's study of the seventeenth-century physician Richard Napier provides some suggestive evidence. Napier's patients included hun-

dreds who suspected they had been bewitched. Macdonald's exploration of these cases led him to criticize Macfarlane's emphasis on quarrels over alms. He writes: "The [witchcraft] allegations Napier's clients made were occasioned by a wider range of social and personal obligations than almsgiving. The most interesting of these concerned the custom of inviting village women to assist at a childbirth. The agony of labor without anesthetic was no less intense for being familiar. . . . Nothing could make childbirth safer and easier, so contemporaries attended to reducing the fear it provoked. . . . When birth was at hand, village women were invited to attend. The importance contemporaries attached to these displays of feminine solidarity is plain. The law prevented midwives from delivering babies without other women present; women whose travails had been marred by strife were said to have consequently gone mad. Mary Aussoppe became anxious and utterly depressed after a disgruntled neighbor cursed her during her labor. The woman burst into the house, fell to her knees, and "prayed unto God that . . . the plague of God light upon her, and all the plagues in hell light upon her." Five of Napier's clients thought that women whom they had not invited to their deliveries had bewitched them: "Participation in this feminine rite was an essential duty and privilege of village women, and omitted neighbors had reason to be angry." Michael Macdonald, *Mystical Bedlam: Madness, Anxiety, and Healing in Seventeenth-Century England* (Cambridge: Cambridge University Press, 1981), pp. 108–9.

20. For abstracts of the documents connected to this case, see Ewen, *Witchcraft*, pp. 155, 162–63. See also W. W., *A true and iust Recorde*, C8–D4ff.

21. Macfarlane, *Witchcraft*, pp. 196–98; Thomas, *Religion*, 553–69.

22. In other cases quarrels begin when the witch is caught stealing wood; when she wants to buy wheat at too low a price; when she refuses to help heal a child whose illness she is believed to have caused.

23. A thoroughgoing psychoanalytic account of the role of childhood experience in the construction of witch-hunting lies outside the scope of this essay. But among psychoanalytic approaches the work of Melanie Klein and those who have built on her theories seems especially promising. Klein's central preoccupations seem highly relevant to the witch-hunts: she focuses, among other things, on persecutory anxiety and retaliatory fears as they arise within the early mother-child relationship. For an overview of her work, see Hanna Segal, *Introduction to the Work of Melanie Klein* (London: Hogarth Press, 1973), and R. D. Hinshelwood, *A Dictionary of Kleinian Thought* (London: Free Association Books, 1991); for an appraisal of her work by a feminist psychoanalyst as well as a selection of significant writings, see *The Selected Melanie Klein*, ed. Juliet Mitchell (New York: Free Press, 1987); for one attempt to adapt Klein's thought for social theory, see C. Fred Alford, *Melanie Klein and Critical Social Theory* (New Haven: Yale University Press, 1989). Of course, Klein's theories cannot be applied to the witch-hunts without also taking into account the historically specific aspects of early modern subject formation and family life.

24. Margery Stanton, for example, indicted as a witch, was blamed for the illnesses that followed her quarrels with numerous neighbors. Thomas Prat, after some angry words, "raced her face with a needle. 'What,' quoth she, 'have you a flea there?" The next night he was "grievously tormented in his limbs" (the limbs, presumably, with which he scratched her). In another incident, she was denied milk by the wife of Robert Cornell and defecated outside the door of the house in departing, presumably as a gesture of contempt. The next day the wife was "taken sick with a great swelling." See Ewen, *Witchcraft*, pp. 151–52.

25. Ewen, *Witchcraft,* pp. 144, 145, 149, 157–58, 159, 160, 167.

26. Ibid., pp. 158, 159. Ewen discusses "puppets" in his introduction (p. 79).

27. Their statements, from which the quotations in this discussion are taken, may be found in W. W., *A true and just Recorde,* pp. D–D2.

28. According to Ewen, the belief in the witch's teat was a peculiarly English variation on the notion of the devil's mark, the sign of the witch's servitude to the devil, rather like the liveries worn by servants identifying them with their feudal masters. The belief in the witch's teat, moreover, did not become widespread in England until the mid-sixteenth century—in other words, around the time witch-hunting began in earnest. See Ewen, *Witchcraft,* pp. 63, 73–74.

29. W. W., *A true and just Recorde,* pp. A3–6.

*Folklore* vol. 97:i, 1986

# Ghost and Witch in the Sixteenth and Seventeenth Centuries

GILLIAN BENNETT

IN the huge amount of scholarship surrounding the figure of the sixteenth and seventeenth century witch, there is one curious aspect still left unexplored: that is, the mutual influence of the concepts of ghost and witch.

Historians charting the development of the witch crazes have often been concerned with the basis of folklore out of which the stereotype of the witch arose—either to affirm its importance (Kittredge, Lea, Cohn)[1] or to deny it (Peters).[2] But, as far as I am aware, in all the folkloristic material there has been little or no direct consideration of the traditional figure of the ghost. For instance, Keith Thomas gives a cogent account of ghost belief in the medieval and early modern period, but he treats it in a separate section as an "allied belief" and does not integrate it into his main line of reasoning.[3]

As might be expected, folklorists are more aware of the links between the two,[4] but even here the tendency, even in historical works, is to keep to certain well defined classes of supernatural creatures and exclude consideration of others for convenience' sake.

In the literature of the period, however, no such clear-cut picture emerges. A view of the English literature of the supernatural from the late sixteenth to the early eighteenth—the age of maximum belief in both creatures—shows that, in this country at least, the two were so closely allied that for over a hundred years they constituted virtually a single subject. This close connectedness has important repercussions for historians of the witch persecutions and especially for folklorists interested in the historical tradition of the ghost.

The literature of the period shows that ghost and witch were for people of early modern times not merely 'allied beliefs' but intrinsic parts of a single system. One was seldom mentioned without the other, as in this passage from *Religio Medici*:

It is a riddle to me . . . how so many learned heads should so far forget their Metaphysicke, and destroy the ladder and scale of creatures, as to question the existence of Spirits. For my part, I have ever believed, and now do know, that there are witches: they that doubt of these, doe not only denie them, but Spirits: and are obliquely and upon consequence a sort not of Infidels, but Atheists. Those that confute their incredulity desire to see apparitions, shall questionless never behold any, nor have the power to be so much as Witches; the Devil hath them already in a heresie as capital as Witchcraft; and to appear to them were but to convert them.[5]

In this passage the fit between ghosts and witches is so neat as to constitute virtual synonymity. After introducing the topic of spirits, Browne moves in the next sentence and without apparent change of topic to witches and in the one after that to apparitions, explaining that sceptics wishing to see apparitions cannot even be witches. The Devil will not waste his time appearing to them—whether *to* witches or *as* apparitions, this statement leaves ambiguous, and the confusion between the two is complete.

In this system, apparitions are essential evidence for the existence of witches, witches for devils, devils for Satan, and Satan for God, because all are part of the supernatural hierarchy which tops the Great Chain of Being. The system as a whole stands or falls on the strength of its parts. It was simply not possible in theory or in practice to separate out one supernatural creature for belief or disbelief. To paraphrase John Donne, each was not 'an island, entire of itself, but a part of the continent, a piece of the main.'[6] In discussions of the period, the whole supernatural edifice, both of entities and effects, is customarily listed together as evidence for one of its parts, and the whole edifice taken as evidence of the existence of God. The extract from a sermon preached by Isaac Barrow, the teacher of Newton, is typical:

I may adjoin to the former sorts of extraordinary actions, some other sorts, the consideration of which . . . may serve our main design; those which . . . concern apparitions from another world . . .; concerning spirits haunting persons and places . . .; concerning visions made unto persons of special eminency and influence . . . concerning presignifications of future events by dreams; concerning the power of enchantments . . . concerning all sorts of intercourse and confederacy . . . with bad spirits . . .

Now if the truth and reality of these things (any or all of them) infering the existence of powers invisible . . . be admitted, it will at least . . . confer much to the belief of the Supreme Divinity.[7]

Not only did the system as a whole work together, and by the appearance— empirically verified time and again—of apparitions and evil spirits, witches and their familiars, provide evidence for the higher order Beings, but it appears that it worked as an organized instrument of social control.

Keith Thomas[8] and others[9] argue most effectively that witch persecutions fluctuated as social order and provisions for the poor declined or improved, the witch acting not only as a barometer of the stability of social mores, but as means of social control. In his treatment of ghosts, Thomas is equally persuasive in his argument that 'ghosts [too] were a sanction for general standards.'[10] In his work on threatening figures, John Widdowson has demonstrated that the use of ghosts, witches, bogeys, elementals and other supernatural entities as means of child-control is not a modern phenomenon but 'has long been part of oral tradition in many cultures.'[11] The same system is demonstrated in Gomme's *Handbook of Folklore* which, under the heading of 'Goblindom,' lists a wide range of creatures from goblin proper to will-o'-the-wisps and apparitions pertaining to set locations.[12] Again, Wirt Sikes's *British Goblins* discusses a wider variety of creatures than his title implies, approaching witch traditions very closely in his instances of spectral flight.[13] In *Teutonic Mythology* Jacob Grimm forges links between the witch and the wild hunt, between older elvish traditions of the Frau Holda type and witch beliefs, and between witches, household spirits and ghosts (in particular the poltergeist).[14]

These figures of threat were partially assimilated in the early modern period and the distinction between classes of supernatural creature seems to have been particularly hard to maintain, the relationship between elemental and familiar, elemental and ghost, apparition and witch being especially close. In many cases the effects of a supernatural visitation were the same whatever the class of visitor. Witches, imps and ghosts were all responsible for twitching bedclothes off the insomniac, buffeting the sceptical, and causing madness. Both imps and witches could turn the heads of cattle awry, and the witch could cause poltergeist-like effects, as could household spirits, and devils unaided by witches. Poltergeists, though often accompanied by spectres and attributed variously to possession, demons, or spirits, were a frequent accompaniment of witchcraft. For example, what is now considered the classic account of poltergeist infestation—the case of the Drummer of Tedworth—was regarded by contemporaries as a case of witchcraft, and the drummer was found guilty of and transported for that offence. Ghost beliefs were always thus closely linked with witchcraft, for 'a person who was troubled by a poltergeist or spectre might well blame a malevolent neighbour for the intrusion.'[15] Not only that, but the appearance of the spectre of the 'malevolent neighbour' was often evidence enough for an indictment on a charge of witchcraft. This 'spectral evidence,' doubts about which were among the chief reasons for the recantation of the Salem jurors, had been widely accepted previously both in old and New England.[16]

Again, traditions of both witch and ghost depended on a fascination with death and the horrors of the dead body. Compare, for example, this graphic description of the · ghost of a murdered man with the details of the accusations against Dame Alice Kyteler in Ireland in 1324:

> . . . all they are able to effect, if they have been murdered, is to commonly appear near the very place where their body lies, and to seem as if they sunk down, or vanished in the same; or else to appear in the posture of a murdered person, with mangled and bloody wounds, and hair dishevelled.[17]

Dame Alice was alleged to have used the brain and clouts of unbaptized infants and the hair and nails of corpses, boiled together in the skull of a beheaded robber. Again, Norman Cohn lists similarly disgusting practices as being put to the charge of Waldensians and other heretical sects, whose persecution paved the way for the trial of witchcraft.[18] Indeed, the term 'necromancy' itself had the double meaning of witchcraft and the calling up of the dead.

Nor can the contemporary learned literature on ghost and witch beliefs be easily separated into distinct classes. The principal sources for the study of late sixteenth and seventeenth century ideas of the ghost in England are the works of Lavater,[19] Scot,[20] Le Loyer,[21] Taillepied,[22] Webster,[23] Glanvil,[24] Bovet,[25] Sinclair,[26] Baxter,[27] Kirk,[28] Aubrey,[29] and Beaumont,[30] whose works span the period 1572 to 1705. Of these twelve, half[31] are primarily works devoted to the discussion of witchcraft. Even as late as the early years of the eighteenth century, discussions of ghosts found their way into the literature of the witch, Francis Hutchinson's great *An Historical Essay concerning Witchcraft* (1718)[32] having a sermon 'concerning Good and Evil Angells' [i.e. ghosts] appended to it; and Jaques De Daillon's *A Treatise of Spirits* (1723)[33] being forced to consider the question of the appearance of the ghost of Samuel to King Saul, as an integral part of his attack on the possibility of witchcraft. As late as 1725, Bourne's *Antiquitates Vulgares*[34] deals with the whole range of supernatural entities and effects as examples of superstitions the populace need freeing from. The British Library catalogue cites no vernacular books on the supernatural before Lavater's of 1572, nine years after the enactment of Elizabeth's Witchcraft Act of 1563. By the time of Hutchinson and De Daillon, James's Act of 1604 was seldom used and was to be repealed in 1736. After this time there is a gap of almost a century before serious books on the supernatural begin to be published again.[35] If no more than circumstantial evidence, this does strongly suggest the relatedness of ghost and witch in the minds of people of the early modern period.

It is particularly important that the historian of the folklore of ghosts should recognize this relatedness, for as R. A. Bowyer says:

> While the modern 'ghost' appears in a psychological vacuum, terrifyingly isolated from our normal, everyday experience, the medieval 'ghost' or 'spirit' appears as an integral part of an immense and ordered spiritual world which includes not merely tormented sinners and devils, but also guardian angels and benevolent saints.[36]

What goes for the medieval world applies equally to the early centuries of the modern world. Brian Easlea ably demonstrates this in his discussion of the scientific revolution of 1450 to 1750, showing that this orderly magical world crumbled only slowly and reluctantly, and was not replaced until philosophers could offer an equally orderly mechanical world.[37]

The close relationship of ghost and witch in philosophical and theological writing of the sixteenth and seventeenth centuries is inevitable in the context of this world view. In particular, works in defence of witches stand or fall by how much of the total supernatural system the writers feel they can afford to repudiate. If too little, like Weyer and Montaigne on the continent and Gifford and Webster in England, then the writer's position is obviously inconsistent. Why deny one part and affirm another part of a unified organic whole? The only possible way the witches could be effectively defended was to undermine the *whole* edifice—witch, devil, familiar, housesprite, ghost and all—proving not that witchcraft *did not* happen, but that it *could not* happen. To defend the witches, a writer had to attack the whole concept of the supernatural; it was not enough merely to attempt to prove there were no such things as witches, for the evidence for witches was overwhelming. He had, rather, to take a thoroughgoing rationalistic stance and argue that whatever the 'evidence' it still was just not possible, and therefore, everybody, including the witches themselves, had to be mistaken. Only a mind of entrenched scepticism could even approach the problem. A mind that could dismiss the weight of evidence for the existence of witches would have no trouble doubting the evidence for ghosts or any other uncanny phenomenon. Scot and Bekker, the most courageous of the defenders of witches, therefore attacked, as far as they dared, the supernatural system as a whole. Scot left corners of it untouched; Bekker, none. Scot escaped with contumely; Bekker was deprived of his living and excluded from communion.

In turn, those who believed in witches simply insisted on the unity and common sense of the received philosophy, avouched for by religion and the empirical evidence supplied in the visions and apparitions commonly known to be part of the experience of sober and honest people. Thus it is that a large part of the evidence about ghost belief in the early modern period is to be found in the treatises on witchcraft. How long this close connection was to hold together in conservative minds is evidenced by the fact that, as late as 1768, John Wesley could write:

> It is true likewise that the English in general, and indeed most of the men of learning in Europe, have given up all accounts of witches and apparitions, as mere old wives fables. I am sorry for it; and I willingly take this opportunity of entering my solemn protest against this violent compliment which so many that believe in the Bible pay to those who do not believe . . .
> They well know (whether Christians know it or not), that the giving up of witchcraft is, in effect, giving up the Bible.[38]

Since the Reformation, ghost and witch had formed an even closer association than merely that of connected links in a single supernatural order. By definitional changes, the homely ghost came for a while to be considered—like witches—as one of the works of the Devil. The manner in which this came about—well documented in continental works translated into English during the period—is instructive to folklorists and to any who would meddle with received tradition.

Perhaps the bitterest argument between Catholics and Reformers in the second phase of the Reformation was over the existence of Purgatory. It was in pursuit of this disagreement that a controversy arose over the existence of ghosts. Catholic divines needed the concept of the ghost because the existence of disembodied spirits of the dead was vital evidence for the existence of Purgatory. The reasoning was that if the soul of the departed went straight to Heaven or straight to Hell, as Protestant doctrine taught, then ghosts could not exist. The Blessed would not want to leave Heaven; the Damned would not be allowed to leave Hell. That ghosts were seen and heard by reputable people was therefore crucial in the argument against Protestant doctrine.

The Protestant divines were put in an awkward position. Argument demanded that they should reject the notion of the supernatural, but logic and empiricism both demanded that it should be kept. To defeat the Catholic argument it was necessary for them to discredit all known examples of ghostly visitations, yet this could not simply be done. As defenders of the witches were to find, it was virtually impossible to take out any single strand in the nexus of supernatural belief without threatening the whole structure. Secondly, the belief in ghosts rested on a long folklore tradition, and thirdly, the ghost had previously held an important position in religious tradition as the creature in the supernatural hierarchy most easily attested by everyday experience. More importantly still, there were examples of ghostly apparitions in the Bible, most notably the appearance of Samuel to Saul through the mediumship of the witch of Endor. All this evidence had either to be rejected or reinterpreted. For logical reasons it could not be rejected. As a member of the hierarchy of supernatural creatures mentioned in the Bible and the works of the Christian Fathers, the ghost was vouched for on the highest authority. If the Bible and the Fathers could not be taken as authoritative on this matter, they could not be relied on in others. There was no logical place at which to put scepticism aside, and the whole edifice of religion was therefore threatened.

The answer to the dilemma was first to discredit as much of the evidence as possible and then to redefine the remainder. This process of redefinition was quite simple, intellectually satisfying and incapable of being refuted on empirical grounds. If the ghost could not be a departed soul, and yet if it obviously existed, then it had to be another type of supernatural creature masquerading as the spirit of the dead. It could be an angel sent from God to warn or comfort, or it could be a devil sent from Satan to alarm, confuse, deceive or entrap. The second of these hypotheses was more likely because God was Truth and would not lightly deceive the Faithful. Furthermore there was a precedent for such beliefs. Early legends of the Saints and Fathers frequently told of devils masquerading in forms other than their own.[39] This scheme also had the bonus that it removed one creature from the hierarchy of the supernatural yet left the structure as a whole untouched.

This approach can be seen most clearly in Ludowig Lavater's *Of Ghostes and Spirites Walking by Nyght* (1572). The first part of the book is given to undermining as much as possible of the empirical evidence for ghosts, by systematically listing all possible causes of deception and mistake; the second part to reinterpreting the Biblical and patrisitic references to ghosts. In Book 1 chapters 11-19, Lavater discusses the core of veridical folklore he cannot dispose of by logic, admitting that 'daily experience techeth us that spirits do appear to men,'[40] but insists that such experiences are not what people imagine them to be.

I pray you what are they? To conclude in a few words: If it be not a vayne persuasion proceeding through weaknesses of the senses, through feare, or suchlike cause, or if it be not the decyte of men, or some natural thing; it is either a good or evill Angell, or some other forewarning sent by God.[41]

The shift in the classification of the ghost spread confusion because not only did it undermine established belief systems, but it also left people unable to interpret their experiences. Their life and salvation depended on guessing correctly whether the ghostly visitations to which they were accustomed were from Angels or Devils, but there was no way of telling them apart.

The common people were not the only ones to be confused; the clergy appear to be no better informed. Throughout the period the matter is still in dispute and no settled pattern of belief emerges. There are Protestant philosophers and divines who believe in ghosts as spirits of the dead, and there are Catholic scholars who utilize the notion that ghosts are, or can be, devils in disguise. The debates of the post-Reformation period, in fact, upset traditional patterns of thought without replacing them with anything as intelligible.

The unsettled, and unsettling, nature of the theory of ghosts can be seen in the work of Father Noel Taillepied. *A Treatise of Ghosts* (1588) begins confidently enough. The first ninety pages run through such traditional concepts as ghosts who demand revenge, burial or absolution, mysterious footsteps, omens of death, spirits in houses and mines, second sight, phantom funerals and mysterious warnings. Obviously here he is dealing with a folklore so secure in the public mind that no theory can disrupt it. The same list of phenomena is to be found in Lavater, Book 1 chapters 11-19, and constitutes the core of veridical experience he cannot argue away. Similar descriptions are to be found in Kirk and Aubrey. Reginald Scot also adumbrates a similar list of commonly held supernatural beliefs in order to scorn the gullibility of the age. Scot's sneers make it plain that all this is a matter of established folkloric traditions:

And as among faint-hearted people; namely women, children and sick-folks they usually swarmed; so among strong bodies and good stomachs they never used to appear.[42]

The words 'used' and 'usually' indicate an accepted tradition, and the ascription of those beliefs to 'women, children and sick-folks' is a slur folklorists have learned to recognize as a reliable guide to the presence of folklore.

In the first ninety pages of *A Treatise of Ghosts,* then, Taillepied feels he is on strong ground. However, he begins to flounder when he has to deal with poltergeist and other unpleasant phenomena that call for reinterpretation according to recent theory. It is interesting to note the influence of Reformist thought even on an orthodox Catholic like Father Taillepied. There is a clear confusion in the latter part of the treatise between ghost and devil, and this is exacerbated by having, for theological reasons, to insist that God is responsible for all occurrences. So we read that God 'permits' that certain places and people 'should be plagued and haunted by evil spirits,' but that 'Disembodied Spirits, however, more often manifest themselves in their own proper mortal likeness.'[43] Poltergeists are discussed in a chapter dealing with 'Daemons,' referred to as 'spirits,' and their power of malice and injury is seen as derived from God:

It is well-known that spirits often contrive to render a man's nights sick and helpless by their malice . . . perilously molesting men and women, even sometimes, if God permits, endangering life and limb.[44]

The confusion obviously arises out of trying to graft new theories on to old traditions, and also because the divines can offer for the common people's use no useful criteria for distinguishing between ghosts, devils and angels. Taillepied spends two chapters on this problem but can only lamely suggest that the percipient should be guided by the appearance and discourse of the apparition, then promptly contradicts himself by saying that the Devil can assume the shapes of the departed.[45]

For historians of witchcraft the onset of definitional changes and its repercussions on the concept of the ghost may be important, for these things must have significantly added to the fear and proliferation of devils that created the psychological conditions for the witch persecutions. Whereas before there had been the forces of good and evil, and below them, most influencing daily life, amoral elemental creatures and morally neutral ghosts, after the Reformation these lower-order creatures became assimilated into the higher orders. The balance of fear in the supernatural world was drastically revised, the forces of evil and danger now outnumbering those of good by about three to one. In addition, the supernatural creature for which there was best evidence was now no longer the harmless ghost, but (possibly) an evil spirit out to entrap the unwary. And where before the ghosts had behaved according to a strict code of haunting—seeking revenge, preventing injustice, revealing sin and secrets—the devils were subject to no such well-understood conventions. Charles Lamb put this well when he wrote:

once the invisible world was supposed to be open, and the *lawless* agency of bad spirits assumed, what measures of probability, of decency, of fitness, or proportion—of that which distinguished the likely from the palpably absurd—could they have to guide them in the rejection or admission of any particular testimony?[46] [My emphasis]

The potential for terror is clear enough, but what perhaps made it worse was that the transmogrification of ghost into devil was never fully completed, never became fully assimilated into the folklore tradition. This left a situation in which fear was exacerbated by confusion. Not being able to punish the supernatural creatures who had thus betrayed them to evil, it is not surprising that the populace was ready to persecute the mortal creatures they imagined had likewise betrayed them.

In considering the onset of witch persecutions in England, Keith Thomas notes that:

Few cases of misfortune are known to have been blamed upon witches before the mid sixteenth century, even though the legal machinery, both ecclesiastical and secular, undoubtedly existed for their prosecution.

He links their emergence to the second phase of the Reformation and the consequent deprivation of the populace of their traditional rites for exorcising evil spirits and evil magic:

Before the Reformation the Catholic church had provided an elaborate repertoire of ritual precautions designed to ward off evil spirits and malevolent magic . . . After the Reformation . . . Protestant preachers denied that such aids could have any effect. They reaffirmed the power of evil, but left believers disarmed before the old enemy.[47]

Though Thomas does not point this out, more than any other factor it was the Reformers' rejection of the traditional idea of the ghost that caused this alarming vacuum, and through Lavater these theories were introduced into educated clerical thought by 1572, and from there would percolate into the popular mind through sermons and homilies.

Put together, then, the effects of the banishment—or rather redefinition—of the ghost do cast additional light on the onset of witch persecutions.

Though the redefinition of the ghost was less radical, perhaps, in England than on the continent, and continental writers are our chief sources for the process, it is still plain that the doctrine had its influence here. Purgatory was denied in No. LXXII of the Thirty-nine Articles, which also forbids exorcism. The position of the clergy was generally that ghosts were either hallucinations or devils in disguise;[48] the quotation from Browne which started this discussion shows plainly that ghosts were thought to be sent from Satan; the relics of the theory can be found in Hutchinson's treatment of ghosts as 'Good or Evil Angells'[49] and in Defoe's tripartite classification of apparitions as either good or evil angels or the souls of the departed.[50] The ghost in fact had not been eliminated from the Protestant mind, merely transformed into a creature even more frightful. This, at one move, both alarmingly altered the balance of fear in the supernatural world, and left the people with no way of dealing with that world on its own terms. Moreover, it is possible that the terrible fear of judgement fostered by the new Protestantism with its graphic descriptions of Hell-fire anaesthetized people's minds to the mental and (even in England) physical torments of the accused witches, hardening people's hearts towards their sufferings, and making them indifferent to the means used to procure confessions. As Jean Bodin wrote:

Whatever punishments we can order against witches . . . is very little in comparison with . . . the eternal agonies which are prepared for them.[51]

If consideration of the long and close association of ghost and witch may prove useful to historians of witchcraft, it has even more to offer—in a cautionary way—to historians of the folklore of ghosts. Principally it would suggest some wariness about the main source books for ghost lore of the sixteenth and seventeenth centuries. Many of these are also source books for witch belief, and we must ask ourselves in what context these texts came to be compiled. In particular closer attention should be given to the work of Glanvil, Bovet and Sinclair in the late seventeenth century.

Glanvil's *Sadducismus Triumphatus* of 1682, Bovet's *Pandaemonium* of 1684, and Sinclair's *Satan's Invisible World Discovered* of 1685, are the most influential compilations of supernatural lore and legends of their day. They are, too, with Aubrey, the writers most often quoted by folklorists of the occult, more or less relied on as guides to seventeenth century ghost lore. How far their reliability matches their popularity, however, merits some consideration. It has to be asked whether these works are collections of folklore or polemics.

In aim they are definitely polemical: their purpose is explicitly to give both logical and empirical proof of the existence of witches to an increasingly sceptical world. Writing at a time when the 1604 Witchcraft Act was seldom invoked and belief in witches was lessening its hold on the minds at least of the educated elite, Glanvil, Bovet and Sinclair were fighting a rearguard action against the atheistic materialism of philosophers like Hobbes, using the old weapon of fear of witchcraft. That Glanvil, at least, feared that the battle was already lost can be seen from his title. In an earlier treatise he had written:

those that deny the being of Witches, do it not out of ignorance of those Heads of Argument, of which they have probably heard a thousand times; but from an apprehension that such a belief is absurd, and the thing impossible. And upon these presumptions they condemn all demonstrations of this nature, and are hardened against conviction.[52]

Accounts of apparitions and other ghostly phenomena are not the central concern of the books; they are included solely as strong empirical evidence for the existence of witchcraft and, through witchcraft, of God. In a letter to Glanvil, Dr. Henry More summed up the position well:

I look upon it as a special Piece of Providence that there are ever and anon such fresh examples of Apparitions and Witchcrafts as may rub up and awaken their benumbed and lethargic Mindes into a suspicion at least, if not an assurance, that there are other intelligent Beings besides those that are clad in heavy Earth or Clay: In this, I say, methinks the Divine Providence does plainly outwit the Powers of the Dark Kingdom, in permitting wicked men and women and vagrant spirits of that Kingdom to make Leagues or Covenants one with another, the Confessions of Witches against their own Lives being so palpable an Evidence, (beside the miraculous feats they play) that there are bad Spirits, which will necessarily open the Door to the belief that there are good ones, and lastly that there is a God.[53]

Their interest in ghosts, then, was 'investigative' in the sense that they were concerned primarily about the truth of the beliefs and experiences they recorded, and their value as evidence for a fixed point of view; it was not folkloristic in any sense of the term. Their motive was religious zeal and the maintenance of the cultural status quo, and their material was therefore no doubt selected to serve those purposes. If their work is representative of popular ghost belief then it is accidentally so, for that is not its aim. In addition they are collections for which certain sorts of material were actively sought: Glanvil's group would neither be offered nor accept material which did not fit their preconceptions. The stories were collected from self-selected informants drawn from a limited group of educated, upper-class people known to the collectors, and may not have been representative of the 'folk' at large. One cannot suppose, therefore, that their collections today would be considered to have much value as folklore. They would, perhaps, be adequate for indicating trends in the content of supernatural beliefs in the period, in conjunction with writers more inclined to antiquarian pursuits, such as Kirk and Aubrey, but it would surely be unwise to rely on them as the sole source for any particular belief or narrative. Furthermore, they never indicate how the beliefs they list formed a system and were acted upon or reacted to by their contemporaries. One of the major drawbacks of this is that there can be no way of assessing how far the fear and confusion sown by the Reformation redefinition of the ghost affected the way the average seventeenth century man or woman *felt* about ghosts. It may be that even where the content of ghost stories seems to have remained constant from pre-sixteenth century times, the emotion they evoked significantly changed. This is where a genuinely folkloristic study of seventeenth century beliefs would have been so useful. Without one, scholars should be wary of using data from Glanvil, Bovet and Sinclair as evidence of a continuing tradition of ghosts.

Unfortunately it has been the usual practice to quote stories from these sources verbatim and to treat them as if they were thoroughly reliable.[54] Even more importantly, perhaps, there is good reason to think that the later influential writer, Francis Grose, based the totality of his first chapter of 'popular superstitions' on Glanvil.[55] This chapter, which deals with 'Apparitions,' not only contains constant references to Glanvil and quotes no fewer than five of Glanvil's 'Relations' directly, but on examination reads suspiciously like a witty paraphrase of Glanvil's collection. As if this were not bad enough, Ellis's important edition of Brand's *Popular Antiquities*,[56] a book which in turn updates Bourne's *Antiquitates Vulgares* of 1725, replaces the original Bourne entries on ghosts and apparitions with very extensive quotation from Grose's section on apparitions.[57] It becomes rather strikingly obvious that not only may our ideas about seventeenth century ghost lore be mistaken, but that the ghost lore of the eighteenth and early nineteenth century might be misrepresented by our major sources.

Finally one must consider how far the close association of ghost and witch for a century and a half may have affected ordinary people's reaction to the ghost. At this distance of time and without genuinely contemporary folkloristic works to guide us, this can only be speculation. Two points do, however, seem to be worth making. First, it seems highly probable that the transmutation of the morally neutral ghost into the servant of a higher, moral power (usually the Power of Evil) would lead not only to short-term confusion but to a longer-lasting fear of ghosts, ghouls and things that go bump in the night. Even where the surface detail of supernatural tales shows little change throughout the period, it seems hardly possible that attitudes to those stories should not have undergone some mutation. Secondly, the more folkloristically-minded writers of the period, Kirk and Aubrey, apparently betray little fear of such occult phenomena. In so far as their work is based on traditional lore, it is likely that they reflect the attitude to that lore. Later texts, however, do not reveal that same mixture of acceptance, credulity and freedom from fear. It is possible, therefore, that the close connection of witch and ghost in the investigative literature of the seventeenth century, prepared for by the redefinition of the ghost in the sixteenth, in turn paved the way for the Gothic horrors of the nineteenth century and still influences our attitudes towards the supernatural today.[58]

The trend in the literature of the occult between the mid-sixteenth century and the end of the second decade of the eighteenth is clear. The period begins with a flux of books, largely theoretical and abstract, in which the folk-concept of the ghost is taken up by leading men of ideas and examined for its usefulness in contemporary religious disputes. These texts, mainly the product of Catholic versus Reformist theological argument, are useful to the folklorist in that they reveal that foundation of supernatural belief which is so entrenched as to be considered irrefutable. These are the texts, however, that spearheaded changes of attitude towards and definition of the ghost. Definitional changes of ghost into devil contributed their measure to that most disgraceful episode of European and American history—the witch crazes. Simultaneously the attitudinal changes which resulted in the original redefinition and the long and close association of ghost and witch in clerical and lay mind alike caused confusion which makes it difficult for the historian of ideas now to piece together the seventeenth century attitude to the humble ghost. (As a consequence of later writers' reliance on these texts of the late seventeenth century, it now is also difficult to assess the nature of the beliefs of the eighteenth and early nineteenth centuries.) In addition, perhaps it is this confusion and terror which has left the twentieth century its legacy of fear of the supernatural.

Surely this makes the study of the historical interrelationship of ghost and witch worth pursuing by historian and folklorist alike?

*The Centre for English Cultural Tradition and Language,*
*University of Sheffield, S10 2TN*

### NOTES

1. George Lyman Kittredge, *Witchcraft in Old and New England* (New York, 1929); H. C. Lee, *Materials Towards a History of Witchcraft* (New York, 1957); Norman Cohn, *Europe's Inner Demons* (St. Albans, 1976) and the shorter version of his thesis, contained in Norman Cohn, 'The Myth of Satan and his Human Servants,' in Mary Douglas (ed.), *Witchcraft: Accusations and Confessions* (London, 1970), pp. 3-16.

2. Edward Peters, *The Magician, the Witch and the Law* (Philadelphia, 1978).

3. Keith Thomas, *Religion and the Decline of Magic* (Letchworth, 1971), p. 586.

4. See especially: James Steven Stallybrass (ed. and translator), Jacob Grimm's *Teutonic Mythology* (London, 1900); Andrew Lang, *Cock Lane and Common Sense* (London, 1894). Theo Brown's recent *The Fate of the Dead: A Study in Folk Eschatology in the West Country after the Reformation* (Ipswich/Cambridge, 1979) is also good from this point of view in the early chapters.

5. Sir Thomas Browne, *Religio Medici, The Works of Sir Thomas Browne* (London, 1928), Vol. 1, p. 38.

6. John Donne, *Devotions* XIII.

7. Isaac Barrow, *Theological Works* (1830 ed.) Vol. IV, pp. 480-2.

8. Keith Thomas, 'The Relevance of Social Anthropology to the Historical Study of English Witchcraft,' in Mary Douglas (ed.), *op. cit.*, pp. 47-80.

9. See: Marvin Harris, *Cows, Pigs, Wars and Witches* (Glasgow, 1977); Brian Easlea, *Witch-hunting, Magic and the New Philosophy* (Brighton, 1980); Alan MacFarlane, *Witchcraft in Tudor and Stewart England: A Regional and Comparative Study* (London, 1970); Kittredge, *op. cit.*,

10. Thomas (1971), p. 602.

11. J. D. A. Widdowson, 'Aspects of Traditional Verbal Control: Threats and Threatening Figures in Newfoundland Folklore,' unpublished Ph.D. Thesis (Memorial University of Newfoundland), p. 6.

12. Sir George Lawrence Gomme, *The Handbook of Folklore* (London, 1890), chapter 5, pp. 30-38.

13. Wirt Sikes, *British Goblins* (Wakefield, 1973), first published London, 1880, pp. 152-164.

14. Grimm, Vol. 3, p. 1053; pp. 1062-3; pp. 919-950; and pp. 510-514.

15. Thomas (1971), p. 594.

16. Kittredge, pp. 221-5 and pp. 363-6.

17. Reginald Scot, *'A Discourse Concerning Devils and Spirits'* (Appendix to: *The Discoverie of Witchcraft*, 3rd ed. London, 1665), Book 2, p. 46.

18. Cohn (1976), pp. 15-59.

19. Ludowig (Lewes) Lavater, *Of Ghostes and Spirites Walking by Nyght,* 1572 (reprinted Oxford, 1929).

20. Reginald Scot, *The Discoverie of Witchcraft* (London, 1584).

21. Pierre Le Loyer, *Livres des Spectres en Apparitions et Visions d'Esprits, Anges et Demons se montrans sensiblement aux Hommes* (Angers, 1586), translated as, *A Treatise of Specters* (London, 1605).

22. Fr. Noel Taillepied, *A Treatise of Ghosts,* translated and edited by Montague Summers (London, 1705). First published in Paris, 1588.

23. John Webster, *The Displaying of Supposed Witchcraft* (London, 1677).

24. Joseph Glanvil, *Sadducisimus Triumphatus* (London, 1682).

25. Richard Bovet, *Pandaemonium: Or the Devil's Cloister,* 1684 (reprinted Aldington, 1951).

26. George Sinclair, *Satan's Invisible World Discovered,* 1685 (reprinted Gainsville, Florida, 1969).

27. Richard Baxter, *The Certainty of the World of Spirits fully evinced,* 1691 (reprinted London, 1840).

28. Kirk, *The Secret Commonwealth of Elves, Fauns and Fairies,* 1691 (reprinted Stirling, 1933).

29. John Aubrey, *Miscellanies* (London, 1696).

30. John Beaumont, *An Historical, Physiological and Theological Treatise of Spirits, Apparitions, Witchcrafts and Other Magical Practices* (London, 1705).

31. That is: Scot, Webster, Glanvil, Bovet, Sinclair, Baxter.

32. Francis Hutchinson, *An Historical Essay concerning Witchcraft* (London, 1718).

33. Jacques De Daillon (Comte du Lude), *A Treatise of Spirits* (London, 1723).

34. Henry Bourne, *Antiquitates Vulgares,* 1725 (reprinted New York, 1977).

35. See: John Ferrier, *An Essay Towards a Theory of Apparitions* (London, 1812). Samuel Hibbert Ware, *Sketches of the Philosophy of Apparitions* (Edinburgh, 1825). John Abercrombie, *An Enquiry concerning the Intellectual Powers* (London, 1830).

36. Richard Bowyer, 'The Role of the Ghost Story in Medieval Christianity,' in H. R. E. Davidson and W. M. S. Russell (eds.), *The Folklore of Ghosts* (Bury St. Edmunds, 1981), p. 177.

37. Easlea, *op. cit.*

38. Wesley Journal, May 25th 1768, quoted in Christina Hole, *A Mirror of Witchcraft* (London, 1957), pp. 32-3.

39. See Lea, pp. 61-8, and Kittredge, pp. 174-184.

40. Lavater, Initial chapter summary, no pagination.

41. Lavater, p. 160.

42. Scot, p. 16

43. Taillepied, pp. 99-100.

44. Taillepied, p. 106.

45. Taillepied, p. 130.

46. Charles Lamb, *The Essays of Elia,* quoted in Gustav Jahoda, *The Psychology of Superstition* (London, 1969), p. 98.

47. Thomas (1970), p. 58.

48. See Brown (1979), p. 19.

49. Hutchinson, 'A Sermon concerning Good and Evil Angells.'

50. Andrew Moreton (alias of Daniel Defoe), *The Secrets of the Invisible World Disclosed* (London, 1729). p. 3.

51. Quoted in Easlea, p. 18.

52. Joseph Glanvil (1675), 'Against Modern Sadducism,' in *Essays on Several Important Subjects in Philosophy and Religion* (facsimile ed. Freiderich Frommann Jerlag, 1970), p. 3.

53. Quoted in Glanvil (1682), p. 16.

54. For example, R. C. Finucane in *Appearances of the Dead: A Cultural History of Ghosts* (London, 1982). Though well aware of the polemical intent of Glanvil, Bovet and Sinclair, Finucane still quotes their narratives as illustration of popular belief.

55. Francis Grose, *A Provincial Glossary with a collection of Local Proverbs and Popular Superstitions* (2nd ed., London, 1790), pp. 5-11.

56. John Brand, *Observations on the Popular Antiquities* (London, 1913).

57. See Brand, pp. 625-634.

58. And see Bowyer, p. 191: 'It was perhaps this change in the church's position which fostered our modern concept of the 'ghost'—a word which has come to mean not the diversity of medieval apparitions . . . but rather one specific type of apparition—the sinister revenant of an unknown outsider who represents a vague threat to our world-view, who is laid by no prayers or ceremonies.'

꒜

# Desire and Its Deformities: Fantasies of Witchcraft in the English Civil War

*Diane Purkiss*
University of Reading
Reading, England

As a contemporary pamphlet tells it, some soldiers searching for food before the first battle of Newbury had a strange encounter with an old woman, spotted in the act of crossing a river on a raft. The old woman was not merely floating on the raft, but manipulating it unnaturally. Somehow she was able to turn it from side to side, changing direction at will, oblivious of the current, ignoring the laws of nature. Her power over the water terrified the soldiers, and they immediately concluded it was supernatural. Worse was to follow. The soldiers struggled to kill the old woman, who proved impervious to their efforts. After shooting at her:

> One [s]et his carbine close unto her breast, where discharging, the bullet back rebounded like a ball, and narrowly he missed it in his face that was the shooter; this so enraged the gentlemen, that one drew out his sword and manfully run at her with all the force his strength had power to make, but it prevailed no more than did the shot, the woman still though speechless, yet in a most contemptible way of scorn, still laughing at them which did the more exhaust their fury against her life.

At last, one soldier remembered a method of dealing with a body reinforced by magic:

> yet one among the rest had learned that piercing or drawing blood forth from the veins that cross the temples of the head, it would prevail against the strongest sorcery, and quell the force of witchcraft, which was allowed for trial; the woman hearing this, knew then the devil had left her and her power was gone, wherefore she began aloud to cry, and roar, tearing her hair and making piteous

*Journal of Medieval and Early Modern Studies 27:1, Winter 1997.*
*Copyright © by Duke University Press / 97 / $2.00*

moan, which in these words expressed were "And is it come to pass that I must die indeed? Why then his excellency the Earl of Essex shall be fortunate and win the field."[1]

With this gratifying disclosure, the witch proves that Satan is on the king's side: the earl of Essex was a leading parliamentarian general at Newbury. Since her magical armor has been unlocked by the act of piercing her at a particular spot, her body is no longer invulnerable. So she is shot and sinks to the bottom of the river. Her initial invulnerability and subsequent collapse can be allegorized as a story of the decline of royalist military fortunes, and they partake in particular of the logic of siege. Both cities and castles under siege are often compared to the female body, just as Petrarchan poetry borrowed the language of war to describe seduction.[2] Here, after artillery has failed, a sneak attack on the body's weak point causes its defenses to collapse.

Yet the besieged human body is not quite like a town: once conquered, there can be no rebuilding. The soldiers who killed the witch were themselves soon to be besieged bodies, soon to be forced to assume the same iron-hard defensiveness and confident fearlessness that she assumed. But they would be forced to assume these postures by nature, as a function of their masculinity, their godliness, their salvation in both physical and spiritual senses. (In the Civil War, as in other wars, to run away was to betray one's fellows to the slaughter of a rout.) The witch's bizarre doubling of the ideal soldier's posture of ironclad defense, her body's power to repel shot and sword, replicates the very identity her murderers wished to claim. As long as she is so defensively arrayed, she is their opponent. And so it also follows that like any other military opponent, she must be divested of her defenses and destroyed, so that her destroyers can be safe.

Offered as a story before the battle, the witch of Newbury's story can only have been told *after* the battle. It makes sense only in the context of that battle, since Newbury was a particularly frightful and frightening experience for parliamentarian soldiers. Fright, as Freud rightly notes, differs from fear and anxiety in that it involves surprise, the subject at a loss as to how to protect himself against it or master it. "Many men were killed on both sides," says the ardently parliamentarian newsbook account,

> but god be praised wee won the field of them. . . . The fight was long and terrible, some talke of thousands slaine on the kings side; I viewed the field, and cannot guesse above 500, but this the townsmen informed us, that they carried 60 cart loads of dead

and wounded men into the Towne before I came to view the place, and much crying there was for Surgeons as never was the like heard.[3]

As never was the like heard: the pamphlet lamely tries to record fright, the moment when the subject is challenged by an experience so unprecedented that it is threatening, an undoing of the known.

The nakedness of relatively new recruits to the horrors of battle was exacerbated by the unleashing of new weapons of unprecedented destructive power. Cannon played an especially large role at Newbury, and John Milton was not alone in thinking it an invention of the devil. Captain Gwynne described its consequences when he saw "a whole file of men, six deep, with their heads struck off with one cannon shot of ours." The tendency of cannon to dismember was recalled with a mixture of horror and relish in George Lauder's ballad, *The Scottish Soldier*: "to see legs and arms torn ragged fly / And bodies gasping all dismembered lie." Colonel Slingsby, similarly, saw "legs and arms flying apace" when cannon fired point-blank at infantry, while Sergeant Henry Foster, another parliamentarian, recalled that "they did some execution amongst us at the first, and were somewhat dreadful when men's bowels and brains flew in our faces."[4] As if this were not enough to unsettle, there was another alarming incident in which the parliamentarians were surprised on the second day of the Newbury battle:

> Colonel Hurry . . . made after us, but such was the cowardice of our horse . . . that upon a weake assault of the enemy they ran away, rode quite thorow our foot in a narrow lane, prest many of them downe under their horses feet, and for the present utterly routed us, which caused the enemy to fall on with great eagernesse and resolution, but God be praised our Foot got over into the fields out of the lane, lined the hedges with Musketiers, and killed them like Dogs.[5]

This providential turning of the tide replicates the story of the witch, successful right up to the moment when she is unmasked — or uncased — as vulnerable.

It is apparent that the story of the witch of Newbury is a fantasy story, a story that expresses and manages the terrible anxieties created by war and battle and the assumption of military identity. Throughout the Civil War, as I will try to show in this essay, those anxieties, and the others produced by the national cataclysm, found an outlet in the manufacture and circulation of stories about witches, so that the figure of the witch was constantly caught up in and reshaped by the swirling, ceaselessly changing discourses of the politics and persons of the Civil War era.[6] This essay will focus on one particular kind of fantasy, the fantasy produced by and from the stresses the Civil War produced for combatant men and also for noncombatant spectators. I shall be arguing that the crisis in masculinity produced by the experience of battle and the ever-present threat of war and of concomitant loss of control over one's own life issued forth in violent fantasies and violent deeds, some using the figure of the witch as a condensed, displaced image of all there was to fear. By destroying her, men could feel, as the soldiers at Newbury felt, that they were restoring normality and thus restoring their own gender identities as well.[7] I will be looking at the recurrence of this fantasy in a number of different contexts, but I shall be focusing at length on one man's stories, stories which allow us to see how public issues were vivified by personal investments, or self-fashioning. These are the stories told by England's self-appointed Witch-Finder General, the notorious Matthew Hopkins. I will be suggesting that, although as far as we know Hopkins was not a combatant, his fantasies are best understood in the context of Civil War anxieties about masculinity and its preservation.[8]

Matthew Hopkins was, however, just one of those able to use the figure of the witch to understand their position in the Civil War years. The witch proved to be a figure so labile that diverse and even opposed meanings could attach to her, making her immensely useful to the factious polemicists of the Civil War era. The persistent connections between witchcraft and civil war are less surprising when we recall the pervasive influence of Lucan's *Pharsalia* as a literary model for understanding the strife. In Lucan's text, the witch Erictho is a potent source of subversive energy, assisting the rebellious to achieve their aims by supernatural if not by natural means. Lucan's text can only have been known directly by the better sort, yet the same narrative structures are repeated in seventeenth-century popular newsbooks, perhaps because Lucan had influenced pre–Civil War dramas like *Macbeth* and *Sophonisba*, which likewise connect witchcraft with illegitimate rule. Many commentators interpreted the proliferation of witch-trials as a sign of disorder.[9] On the royalist side, the text "rebellion is as the sin of witchcraft" (1 Samuel 25.23) was frequently quoted, while the royalist newspaper *Mercurius Aulicus* observed that witchcraft is "an usuall attendant on former rebellions."[10] James Howell, while wearing his royalist hat, remarked that we have also multitudes of *witches* among us, for in Essex and Suffolk there were above two hundred indicted within these two years, and above the one half of them executed. More, I may well say, than ever this Island bred since the Creation, I speak it with horror. God guard us from the Devil, for I think he was never so busy upon any part of the Earth that was enlightened with the beams of Christianity; nor do I wonder at it, for there's never a Cross left to fright him away.[11]

*The Parliamentary Journal* responded irritably that "it is the ordinary mirth of the malignants of this city to discourse of the association of witches in the associated counties, but by this they shall understand the truth of the old proverb, which is that where God hath his church, the Devill hath his Chappel."[12] More ambiguously, a pamphlet entitled *Signes and Wonders from Heaven* bundles witches together with monsters and thunderstorms to argue that

the Lord decreed a separation between the King and his parliament before the wars began in England for the sins of the whole nation. That the Lord is angry with us every one; for our sin, doth appear in this; . . . have not a crew of wicked Witches, together with the Devils assistance done many mischiefes in Norfolke, Suffolke, Essex, and other parts of our Kingdome, whereof some were executed at Chenfford in Essex last to the number of fourteen?[13]

For others it was belief in witches and witch-prosecutions which represented the intellectual and social disorder of the Civil War years.[14] For Sir Robert Filmer, the fact that parliament had the upper hand was a sign that popular ideas had got quite above themselves. In his *Advertisement to the Jury-men of England*, Filmer scouted popular witch beliefs in robust terms: "To have nothing but the publique faith of the present Age, is none of the best evidence." From an entirely different and far more godly perspective, Thomas Ady located belief in witchcraft in an ungodly and outdated reliance on inappropriate worship and ritual of the kind parliament was seeking to reform.[15] Both Filmer and Ady agreed in finding witch-beliefs plebeian and superstitious, but differed in assigning causes, each blaming his opponents. Similarly, *The Moderate Intelligencer*, a parliamentarian journal, questioned Hopkins's activities in East Anglia, scornfully inquiring "whence is it that the Devills should choose to be conversant with silly women that know not their right hands from their left, is the great wonder. . . . They will meddle with none but poor old women, as appears by what we received this day from Bury."[16]

Both sides also used the figure of the witch as a propaganda weapon, trying to build up an association between prominent enemy figures and witchcraft. Two examples, one from each side, are Oliver Cromwell and Prince Rupert. The imagery surrounding Rupert was more luridly imaginative than that surrounding Cromwell. *Signes and Wonders From Heaven* reports that the Norfolk witches' arrest, like the death of the witch of Newbury, would impede royalists, since the witches had been working for Rupert:

> It is likewise certified by many of good quality and worth that at
> the last Assizes in Norfolke there were 40 witches arraigned for
> their lives, and 20 executed: and that they have done very much
> harme in that countrey, and have prophesied of the downfall of
> the King and his army, and that Prince Robert [Rupert] shall be
> no longer shot-free: with many strange and unheard-of things that
> shall come to passe.[17]

James More of Halesworth, admitting to making a covenant with the devil, said he returned his imp to his sister Mary Everard, "to send with others to Prince Rupert." There were a number of satirical portrayals of Prince Rupert's dog, Boy, as a familiar. "Certainly he is some Lapland Lady," said one none-too-serious account, "who by nature was once a handsome white woman, and now by art is become a handsome white Dogge, and hath vowed to follow the Prince to preserve him from mischiefe." Among his other gifts, Boy can find hidden treasure: the Oxford plate, which could not be found by parliament. Like the witch of Newbury, the dog is proof against attack: "once I gave him a very hearty stroke, with a confiding Dagger, but it slided off his skin as if it had been Armour of proofe nointed over with Quicksilver." He also catches bullets aimed at Rupert in his mouth. "He prophesies as well as my lady Davis, or Mother Shipton," concludes the pamphlet. Neither Boy nor Eleanor Davies could have felt complimented.[18] This reads like a joke about preoccupations with occult significances on the parliamentarian side, rather than as a serious account of such preoccupations; it shows too that the figure of the witch could retain, in royalist hands, some of the comic suggestion of hicks and ignoramuses that it acquired in the 1630s.[19]

276

Cromwell too was likened to a witch, often metaphorically rather than literally. When Denzil Holles described Cromwell as a witch working to overthrow the realm, he was using witchcraft as a metaphor for a secret plot: "your Sabbaths, when you have laid by your assumed shapes, with which you have cozened the world, and resumed your own; imparting to each other and both of you to your fellow-witches."[20] This metaphor of the witch as spy, plotter, or secret agent also surfaces in the account of the witch of Newbury as an agent sent to blow up the magazine of the earl of Essex.[21] An eighteenth-century historiographical tradition depicted Cromwell making a pact with the devil before the battle of Worcester, to run for seven years. Cromwell was also associated with a witch in a post-Restoration pamphlet, *The English Devil, or Cromwell and his Monstrous Witch discovered at Whitehall*. The witch, "disguised" as a prophetess, is given the role of suggesting regicide to the Council of State. Dimly recognizable as Elizabeth Poole, who in fact made herself unpopular with the Council by urging them *not* to kill Charles, this represents a woman with occult powers as secrecy or duplicity.[22] Whereas the reference to Eleanor Davies in the pamphlet about Rupert is primarily intended to ridicule, the reference to Poole belittles her supernatural claims, while associating her with treachery and regicide. These ideas could be taken up with frightening literalism by soldiers or prosecutors with the power to harm those on whom their eye fell.

In the summer of 1645, *The Parliaments Post* reported that "There is an infection in wickednesse; and the spirit of the Cavillers because it could not prevaile with our men, hath met with some of our women, and it hath turned them into Witches."[23] Elegantly equating weakness with femininity, and thus expressing through the figure of the witch terror of the feminization of the army and its consequent vulnerability, this statement encapsulates relations between Civil War witch-trials and the war itself. War creates a number of anxieties about gender and masculinity. We have already seen the anxiety around masculinity adopting defensive positions, not giving way or opening up, in the case of the witch of Newbury. This genders the correctly military and male body as closed, hard, tight, and paradoxically, at one with the similarly disposed bodies of other men. For instance, Donald Lupton's *A warre-like treatise on the pike* found it natural to link effeminacy and cowardice. During the siege of Devizes a message arrow struck just in front of Sir Jacob Astley, slicing past his genitalia: "You rogues," he quipped, "you missed your aim." Jokingly, he equated penetration and defeat with emasculation.[24] At the same time, battle itself presented not merely an image of death, but an image of engulfment: "the air was so darkened with smoke of powder that for a quarter of an hour together (I dare say) there was no light seen, but what the fire of the volleys gave . . . 'twas the greatest storm that I ever saw, in which I thought I knew not wither to go, nor what to do," wrote Richard Atkyns, a bemused combatant.[25] "In the fire, smoke and confusion of that day I knew not for my soul wither to incline," wrote Sir Arthur Trevor of the rout at Marston Moor,

> The runaways on both sides were so many, so breathless, so speechless, and so full of fears that I should not have taken them for men, but by their very motions which still served them well: not a man of them being able to give me the least hint where the Prince was to be found.[26]

Loss of sight is accompanied by a terrifying, dizzying loss of self, an *abysme* into which disappear all agency, all power of decision-making, self-fashioning, and action. The identity, carefully stiffened to meet the onslaught, suddenly and in fright dissolves into the darkened air.

Yet war also arouses the desire to escape the self, to avoid literal death by the figurative death of flight. The tension between these two powerful impulses shakes assumptions that the self is natural and inevitable, unseating notions of the naturalness of the hard masculine body. To put this in more technical terms, war unleashes the death drive in a series of aggressive and repetitive acts which menace the identity of the perpetrator, who can always envisage himself as victim. The death drive is the desire not to be, to dissolve, to disappear, but it is also the desire to thwart the desire. The ego responds to the phenomena of fragmentation, destruction, decay by assuring itself that life can be preserved.[27] Death is always implicated in attempts at pleasure. Whenever the subject constructs a fantasy of wholeness and security gained by an appropriation of the beloved, modeled along the lines of the infant-mother dyad, he also risks a return to a pre-birth stasis or ination, a loss of self—that is, a form of death. The finding of a love-object is always a finding of the lost maternal body. Hence another connection between the death drive and femininity emerges: the return to a prior state involves the maternal body as the real material body lost at birth, the fictional phallic mother whose body represents a lost unity, as a figure of the dust to which the human being must return; hence a female figure alone offers ways of representing and also appearing—at least in fantasy—to manage the death drive and to control and satisfy it.[28] Paradoxically, then, the lost mother is actually the model for the tight, hard body assumed to be the acme of masculinity by the discourses of war. Yet that same maternal body can also be understood as engulfing and formless, and hence threatening, when it seems to be on the point of swallowing up the ego, now itself understood as the locus of tight integrity. This oscillating imagery of firmness and swallowing vagueness is characteristic of representations of witches.[29] Consequently, it is not surprising that murdering or trying and executing a witch was one possible fantasy resolution of the intolerable pressures placed on the death drive by the war.

In its complex relation to the body of the mother and hence to femininity, the workings of the death drive recall Kristeva's notion of abjection. Kristeva understands abjection as a response to the constant threat of the mother's return and reabsorption of the ego, a return represented through chaos, pollution, dirt, and disorder.[30] War is a prolific producer of all four; and, in particular, the spectacle of dismembered and disordered bodies, living and dead, creates acute anxieties, and not only because the corpse represents death. In representing the end of life, it must also represent the beginning, the mother. Most of all, however, the very disruptive effects of war itself on the life of the individual and the nation impact on the ego to generate fears of further engulfment and chaos, setting abjection in motion. Both aggressive actions and violent repudiations are produced by these psychic pressures.[31] Freud's theory of the death-drive is a negotiation of a desperately problematic historical moment, the moment of the rise of fascism. Kristeva develops his theory further to provide an analysis of that same moment, as does her follower Klaus Theweleit. Their analyses give new vitality to Freud's theory by demonstrating its purchase on the historical particularity which produced it, and yet their writings seem to allow that theory to be applied to other situations in which violence is unleashed and licensed on a wide scale.

One instance of the effect of such pressures is the systematic iconoclasm of the 1640s. In Suffolk, William Dowsing led a campaign which destroyed decorations in one hundred fifty Suffolk churches. Though not a combatant, Dowsing believed his activities had a direct relation to the course of the war: he thought Fairfax was given victory at Nantwich because on that day images were destroyed at Orford, Snape, and Saxmundham. Like those who unmasked the witches who had enchanted Prince Rupert, Dowsing had removed the protective carapace of one side and thus strengthened the other.[32] King-breaking, Margaret Aston claims, was lumped with thing-breaking by royalist historians, but the same was also true of parliamentarians in the sense that there was an effort to make something new by cleansing, by destruction.[33] All this applies also to the parliamentary soldiers at Newbury, and to Hopkins, whose zeal came from the same impulse to obliterate whatever might hold England back.

Iconoclasm also resembled atrocities, and was often described as if it were an atrocity; it offered the same chance to organize the self by attacking the helplessly mysterious and powerful: soldiers attacking a figure of Christ might have been attacking any feminized target:

> another said "here is Christ," and swore that he would rip up his bowels: which they accordingly did, as far as the figures were capable thereof, besides many other villanies. And not content therwith, finding another statue of Christ in the frontispiece of the South-gate, they discharged against it forty shot at the least, triumphing much, when they did hit it in the head or face.[34]

Iconoclasm and the removal of witches were sometimes linked:

> The late lamentable Warres began, yet God was good to us in discovering many secret treacheries. . . . And many superstitious reliques were abolished, which neither we nor our godly fathers (as ye have heard) were able to beare. Since which time, ye knew, many witches have been discovered by their own confessions, and executed; many glorious victories obtained (beyond any man's expectation) and places of strength yielded, above seventy in eight moneths space.[35]

After Naseby, some victorious parliamentarian troops came across a party of women, said to be camp-followers. They slashed at the women's heads and faces, with such ferocity that some of them later died of their wounds. According to one story, they were seen as whores; another account says they were assumed to be Irish because they understood no English (they were Welsh).[36] But there is yet another Other that the women might have represented to the soldiers. Attacking the women's faces and heads is reminiscent of the most common and most thoroughly masculinized method of dealing with a witch, scoring above the breath, or scratching.[37] This is used by the soldiers at Newbury to great effect: it is piercing the witch's temples that allows the soldiers to kill her. It may even be that the troops at Naseby had heard about the events at Newbury. A very similar episode occurred during the Irish uprising of 1641, where a Scottish settler attacked an Irishwoman in reprisal for what he claimed were attacks on his own family. Grany ny

Mullan told the story: John Erwyn led a party of Scots soldiers to Edward O'Mullan's house on Sunday, 2 February 1642. He drew his sword,

> and wounded the said Mary Mullen in her head, and forehead, and cut her fingers, at which time she cried out, "Dear John, do not kill me, for I never offended you," repeating this to him two or three times, whereupon he thrust her under the right breast and she gave up the ghost. . . . And after a time the said Erwyn took a mighty lump of fire and put it on the said Mary Mullen's breast, expecting she was still living.[38]

Mary's words sound like the excuses of women accused of witchcraft by violent neighbors. Particularly telling is the test to see if Mary is really dead; it sounds as if Erwyn expects Mary to be impervious to weapons. Alternatively, he may not really have believed she was a witch, but may have intended to insult her by comparing her with one. In England, "witch" was a standard term of abuse, like "whore."[39] Erwyn may have intended to mark Mary as a witch, to convey to her and to himself his notion of how an unruly woman might be mastered. As a settler, Erwyn was also symbolically mastering the rebellion itself, and hence the Irish, then as now apt to be figured by their colonial rulers as repositories of the primitive, the superstitious, and hence the feminine. More than one early modern colonizer compared the Irish to Circe, a figure combining femininity, seductively uncontained sexuality, and witchcraft.[40] Just as the parliamentarian soldiers saw the witch of Newbury and other witches as responsible for royalist successes, so those fighting the Irish saw witches as involved in making their jobs harder. When a large storm blew up in early summer of 1641, men and officers "attributed this hurrikan to the divelish skill of some Irish witches." Similarly, Ann Fanshawe describes seeing an apparition during a sojourn in Ireland; she and her husband "concluded the cause to be the great superstition of the Irish, and the want of that knowing faith which should defend them from the power of the Devill, which he exercises among them very much."[41] The soldiers at Naseby may not have cared whether the women were whores, witches, Irish, or all three; they may not have made especially sharp distinctions between these groups. What all three represented was the kind of feminized chaos which as soldiers they must control, contain, and even deny in order to assert their own identities.

An even more egregious case of violence and aggression among soldiers taking a woman as witch as object comes from Warminster. Anne Warberton was attacked by a group of soliders there, as she described

upon the feast day of thannunciation of the Blessed Virgin Mary
last past [25 March 1643/4] was two yeares sithence one George
Long of Warminster came to the house of yor peticoner and two
souldiers in Armes with him and the said Long and one of the
souldiers required the peticoner to open her dore who answered
she would not unless he was an officer. Then the said Long said he
was as good as any officer whatsoever and ymediately by force
broke downe a windowe leafe w[hi]ch fell into the house upon a
paile of water whereby both window leafe and paile of water fell
upon yor peticoner and her child w[hi]ch dod so bruise the child
that it fell sick and shortly after dyed. Yet not being contented they
also broke up the dore and entered the house by force and then the
said Long fell to byting pinching and scratching of yor peticoner
saying and swearing in most execrable and ignominious manner
shee was a witch and therfore hee would have her blood which he
drawed from her in great abundance for w[hi]ch abuse hee was
bound over to answer at a generall Sessions at [th]e Devizes but
while yor peticoner went for a bill of indictment the said Long ran
away from the Devizes and hath not answered the Law.[42]

In Wiltshire the Civil War was grim: the county changed hands several times
with bitter fighting until the final triumph of parliament in 1645. This may
have been the occasion for many acts of violence. The Civil War often
enabled behavior ordinarily open to censure; like other wars, it both placed
intolerable strain on male identity and allowed it full and destructive rein.
Both interpretations—the psychic and the opportunistic—are also possible
for Matthew Hopkins's activities in East Anglia, also characterized by
repeated acts of seemingly incomprehensible aggression. And yet the English Civil War did not "cause" the witchcraft prosecutions of the 1640s and
1650s. In Europe there was a commonsense inverse relationship between
really intensive warfare and witchcraft prosecutions in the courts. Warfare
left no time for orderly prosecutions. However, this does not take account of
soldiers taking the law into their own hands, as they did in the English Civil
War.[43] The anxieties produced by the war and revolution could sometimes
be relieved via witch-discourses, and conversely these anxieties reshaped the
fantasy of witchcraft.

There was no special reason why a witchcraze of vast proportions should
have started in Essex rather than in Wiltshire or Hertfordshire.[44] What

started it, and then facilitated it at every turn, was the presence of Matthew Hopkins. The depositions collected from plaintiffs closely resemble those from other witch-trials, recapitulating popular preoccupations with food preparation, the household economy, family tensions, and the stresses and strains imposed by pregnancy, childbirth, and maternity.[45] Once the prosecutions did start, however, Hopkins's fantasies and the local depositions he collected were tinted by the particularities of the locale, the historical moment, the man himself. As far as we know, Hopkins was not a soldier, yet his fantasies seem motivated by similar anxieties about the fragility of masculine identity. Though not literally involved in war, Hopkins may nevertheless have seen the witch-hunt as analogous to war, because of the discursive context which understood witches to be part of the war effort. His partner, John Stearne, wrote of witch-hunting as a way of fighting spiritual battles in language which recalls the New Model Army's understanding of its literal military activities as metaphorically spiritual: "And so going ever well-armed against these rulers of darknesse, devills and evil spirits, furnished with the heavenly furniture and spirituall weapons, of which the Apostle speaketh, Eph. 6.14.18, and being thus qualified, and armed, to trust in God only, who will keepe thee under the shadow of his wings, Psal. 91."[46] As a godly soldier facing danger, Hopkins uses the same narratives and metaphors as the soldiers at Newbury and Naseby, and experiences the same terrors.

There is a local and possibly unreliable tradition that Hopkins "as a childe" "tooke affrighte at an apparition of the Devill, which he saw in the night."[47] Though not authenticated, this story is believable in the light of the fantasies that Hopkins was to produce, fantasies that resemble godly nightmares. As the child of a godly vicar, whose will insists firmly on salvation through faith alone, Hopkins was part of a godly discourse that could terrify through its vehement insistence on the gap between election and damnation.[48] Although all his biographers have seen Hopkins as marked by this lineage, Hopkins himself frequently invented alternative ancestries for himself, possibly grounded in family legend, but betokening a wish to make something, or perhaps to make something different of his patronymic. He told William Lilly that he came from a line of schoolmasters in Suffolk, "who had composed for the psalms of King David"; there was indeed a John Hopkins, an English hymn-writer, a different godly father, perhaps, from his own—one less terrifying, more obviously a maker himself. By contrast, Hopkins told Lady Jane Whorwood that he was really named Hopequins and was the grandson of an English Catholic diplomat, Richard Hopequins.[49] Lady Jane was a royalist, so this may have been designed to create an identity acceptable to her, as well as to Hopkins. But it may also have given him subtle pleasure to represent himself in a way not approved by his father. Self-fashioning involves the death of the father in the refusal to replicate his social identity; there is even a kind of murderousness in the obliteration of the father.

Hopkins first appears as a witness in the 1645 pamphlet account of the Essex witch-trial, in which, as well as featuring as a witness to the principal confession, he also offers, more unusually, an account of strange goings-on to supplement the witches' confessions and depositions of *maleficium*. It is these narratives that bring us closest to the mind of Matthew Hopkins, since they offer an opportunity to analyze his own witch-stories, and since they are markedly different from standard popular accounts of local *maleficium* without direct recourse to the theorists of demonology. The first such story goes like this:

> And this informant further saith, That going from the House of the said Mr Edwards to his own house, about nine or ten of the clock that night, with his Greyhound with him, he saw the Greyhound suddenly give a jumpe, and ran as shee had been in a full course after an hare; and that, when this informant made haste to see what his greyhound so eagerly pursued, he espied a white thing about the bignesse of a kitlyn, and the greyhound standing aloofe from it; and that by and by the said white impe or kitlyn daunced about the said greyhound, and by all likelihood bit off a piece of the flesh of the shoulder of the said greyhound, for the greyhound came shrieking and crying to this informant, with a piece of flesh torne from her shoulder.[50]

Though told by a young man, this is a little boy's story and a frightened little boy's at that. It parallels stories told by other little boys anxious to make an impression as heroic battlers against evildoers. The presence of the greyhound points to the influence of Edmund Robinson's deposition in the 1633/4 Lancashire case, which Hopkins could have heard about in childhood.[51] But it is also influenced by the folktales which gave rise to this story, in which witches in hare-form cannot be coursed by dogs.[52] Both Robinson's dog and Hopkins's are bitches, too. It is interesting that Hopkins begins with a story told by a known faker; Edmund Robinson eventually confessed to making his story up to escape trouble at home. Did Hopkins know that

Edmund Robinson had confessed to inventing his story? Or were the witches discredited in parliamentarian eyes, having been saved by the efforts of the king and the Laudian bishops? Whether or not Hopkins knew of Robinson's use of the greyhound motif, his own story stars a dog in a rather different role. In Robinson's story, the greyhound, too, was a witch; Hopkins sets up a neater, less ambiguous opposition between kitten and dog, where the dog is not only victim, but silent witness to the demon's presence by her unnatural behavior (the dog did do something in the night?). Is the dog a figure for deformed nature, then, and thus for other, wider anxieties? The dog confirms this by the testimony of her torn shoulder, a wound with a tongue to cry out against evildoers, made to speak by Hopkins's probing of it, his giving it a voice. The torn flesh of the greyhound is in fact doubly unnatural (cat bites dog). Does it also represent, at a deeper level, a deeper wound? It is, after all, a wounded *female* body which becomes the principal evidence for witchcraft here. The wound does not merely signify castration, but may also represent that maternal body which must be hastily abjected, that which threatens masculinity by its Medusan and apotropaic woundedness. The femininity of the wound, which is not only a wounding but a tearing, an emphasized act of violence and violation, both challenges and paradoxically reinforces Hopkins's masculinity, which unlike the wound can really speak, can remain in control by talking. At the same time, it may represent not only the *maleficium* of the witch, but her power to make a visible difference. Hence, the witch's familiar is also the deformer of a society made unnatural by false religion, the creator of disorder threatening to identity and therefore violently repressed. Like a cannonade, she turns what had been known into a torn and mangled landscape of what can never be known again, woundedness, deformity, symbolic death.

There are idiosyncrasies which may open up the singularity of Hopkins. The kitlyn, or kitten, dances. Is this a dead metaphor, merely meaning evasion of the hunting dog? Or does it point to forbidden, ungodly, even alluring dancing, dancing in a round, perhaps resembling un-godly church festivals? Is this the point at which Hopkins's father's voice is heard, connecting the ungodly with the Satanic? Oddly, too, the story is not very useful in establishing the validity of Hopkins's methods of witch-hunting. It climaxes not with the discovery of the familiar (as one might expect from Hopkins) but in the discovery of the wound in the greyhound's shoulder. This alone excites real interest, real feeling. Hopkins emerges from this story as a man who wants to talk about wounds, rather than a man who wants to talk about familiars. And yet this is not the end of the Hopkins story. It continues, as follows:

> And this Informant further saith, That coming into his own yard
> that night, he espied a black thing, proportioned like a cat, onely
> it was thrice as big, sitting on a strawberry bed, and fixing the eyes
> on this Informant, and when he went towards it, it leaped over
> the pale towards this Informant, as he thought; but ran quite
> through the yard, with his greyhound after it, to a great gate,
> which was underset with a paire of tumbrell strings, and did
> throw the said gate wide open, and then vanished; and the said
> greyhound returned againe to this informant, shaking and
> trembling exceedingly. (3)

The greyhound, duly feminized again, is now opposed even more violently
to her demonic foe, who takes on the characteristics Hopkins formerly gave
to the wounded dog. The black cat of uncertain size has invaded the bounds
of Hopkins's garden, as the white kitlyn broke the greyhound's skin. The
cat's mastery of bounds are also manifest in its ability to open the gate, and
its uneasy sexualization may be signified by its position on a strawberry bed,
often a signifier of female sexuality. Here the strawberries suggest both the
domestic (and significantly, the food-producing element of it) that the beast
has invaded, the order that has been scattered. But they might also remind
us of the wound in the greyhound's shoulder: red, soft, crushed. The cat's
gender, not specified, is ambiguous; it is both associated with the crushed
strawberries and also their macho conquerer. Most importantly of all for
Hopkins's later career, the cat is the owner of the gaze, the one who can look
at "this Informant," fixing its eyes, getting him in its sights. This fixing, effective look contrasts with the cat's own slipperiness, its blackness, its power to
slip away. While in witch-stories told by witches themselves, the familiar
often takes on the qualities of a child, in Hopkins's account the familiar is
the feminine other. Such figurations bring with them a fear of engulfment
manifest in the shadiness (in both senses) of Hopkins's apparitions: as John
Stearne put it, "the secresie of the grounds of witchcraft is so close and hidden, as being one of the greatest workes of darknesse committed this day
under the Sunne: for that naturall causes may arise very strong, and many
may cunningly counterfeit outward appearances, and witnesses may feign
their accusations out of malice."[55]

At this point it becomes important to notice where we are. Manningtree, where Hopkins lived and where his career began, is a curious place in the mid–seventeenth century because it is both a center of activity and geographically marginal. It was a center of activity because it was a port and shipbuilding dockyard—Manningtree sent ships against the Armada—and it was peripheral because the Tendring Hundred is literally on the edge of Essex, and Manningtree and Mistley were themselves surrounded by the great and misty sea-marshes. The marshes and the Stour River were sites of a trade boom, but also of illegal activities. There was extensive smuggling up the Stour River, and over the marshes.[54] The marshes and the river represent opportunities for secret enterprises, for a form of self-fashioning, wealth creation, business, which is neither sanctioned nor scrutinized by the authorities; as such they might seem a masculine, even a macho space, or at any rate a space prodigal of opportunities for machismo. This might seem exemplary to a man like Hopkins, so eager to fashion himself, or it might have seemed an occasion for renewed suspicion, for the full force of surveillance and the law. When we take into account the other associations of the marshes and the Stour valley, this explanation becomes more likely.

Folktales from the East Anglian area prior to the drainage of fens and marshes stress the division between arable land and marsh. Regarded as unhealthy because of the miasmas associated with them, in these stories marshes are given over to the supernatural activities of boggarts, hags, and witches.[55] The Stour Valley is the site of the appearance of two strange green children, who materialize in a pit and require green food; the story is told by Camden as part of his description of the Stour valley.[56] These stories and their production are part of an index of beliefs and practices which a godly man like Hopkins would have seen as superstition. As Stuart Clark has shown, for the godly, superstition was not supernatural belief, but irrelevant or excess worship, or the correct form of worship applied to the wrong deity. As such, as another East Anglian, John Gaule, argued, witchcraft in the sense of evil magic and a pact with the devil was the *telos* of superstition.[57] They needed to be cleared up, their human contents made visible, reordered, re-educated. The marshes were outside the law of church as well as state, and in local legends they take on a feminine aspect, lawless, silent, pervasively misty. It was against this backward, maternal background that the towns and their inhabitants defined themselves, just as the godly defined themselves against backward, hazy superstition. Perhaps this exacerbated the tendency to separate violently from the mother, as well as the fear of being sucked back into her, of losing one's way, and hence one's self.

This was further exacerbated by fear of another kind of engulfment.

Essex was one of the areas which quickly declared for parliament, to the delight of its godly inhabitants. But throughout 1645 and 1646, the royalist army was trying to break into East Anglia, and the whole territory was under threat of turning into a battlefield. The eventual siege of Colchester was one of the most bitter campaigns of the war. Although Hopkins's activities predate the real military crisis, godly folk in Essex had heard of events in other counties, and knew (or feared) what might occur. For John Stearne, as we have seen, the war against witches was another way of fighting the Civil War. What with one thing and another, the psychic pressures on a man like Hopkins and on his masculine identity reached nearly intolerable levels in the mid-1640s, with the result that he produced a spate of fantasies to alleviate them.

Hopkins's fantasies had another purpose, too. They were part of his ruthless self-fashioning, a process which enabled him to flee not only his parents, and perhaps especially the femininity which for him came to represent and equate with sin, but also to flee from his family, to prove his masculine identity by exerting his will over society, by making a place for himself among the better sort, and also by piling up at least some personal wealth.[58] Hopkins's self-fashioning as powerful Witch-Finder General is evident in his own account of his first encounter with witches in his self-defense, written some two years after the 1645 pamphlet I have been citing. This account explains how he became involved in the process of discovery, and differs in tone and substance from his reported trial depositions:

> The Discoverer never travelled far for it, but in March 1644, he had some seven or eight of that horrible sect of witches living in the town where he lived, a towne in Essex called Manningtree, with divers other adjacent witches of other towns, who every six weeks in the night (being alwayes on the Friday night) had their meeting close by his house, and had their severall solmne sacrifices there offered to the Devill, one of which this discoverer heard speaking to her Imps one night, and bid them goe to another Witch, who was thereupon apprehended, and searched by women who had for many yeares knowne the Devills marks, and found to have three teats about her, which honest women have not: so upon command from the Justice, they were to keep her from sleep two or three nights, expecting in that time to see her familiars, which the fourth night she called in by their severall names, and told them what shapes a quarter of an houre before they came in, there being ten of us in the roome.[59]

288

This is not a private story, but an ordered, shaped fantasy, smoothed out for public consumption, partaking of godly and even elite discourses and not simply of depositions and folktales. And yet some of the psychic content is the same as that in his earlier, less structured stories. "Close by his house," says the anecdote. Closeness is the source of the "experience" Hopkins valorizes. Yet Hopkins turns this problematic closeness into valuable experience: threatened with engulfment, with darkness, the marshes, the night, the neighbors, he responds by establishing the ineluctable distance of the interrogator, the investigator, the finder. Again, Hopkins overhears what the witch says: overhearing is emblematic both of a problematic and frightening closeness and of an effort at distance. Yet distance threatens to collapse into identity: the people of East Anglian towns and villages called Hopkins in as a consultant, just as in less godly days or among less godly company they might have called in the local cunning man to finger the witch. Since for the godly (like John Stearne) a cunning person was culpable as a malicious witch, Hopkins opened himself to identification as supernaturally gifted when exposing such gifts in others.[60] This interpretation may have occurred to no one but him, since there is no evidence for the tradition that he was himself swum as a witch and convicted (reported in *Hudibras*), but the first question in *The Discovery of Witches* is a refutation of the idea that he must be "the greatest Witch, Sorcerer and Wizzard himselfe, else he could not doe it."[61] Hopkins was of course aiming at a far more godly kind of identity, perhaps even at an *imitatio Christi*. Perhaps in a spirit of competitive envy, Gaule wrote that "country People talke already and that more frequently, more affectedly, of the infallibel and wonderfull power of the witchfinders, then they doe of God, or Christ, or the Gospell preached."[62]

We can now begin to understand the fantasy for which Hopkins has been remembered by our own culture, the fantasy that witches had sexual relations with devils.[63] Nineteenth-century art and writing teach us to take sadistic pleasure in the victimization of a beautiful, wild-eyed, young victim tortured, accused, forced to confess to exciting obscenities.[64] We therefore assume too easily that Hopkins saw it that way, but in that case his penchant for elderly victims is hard to explain. Hopkins stripped his victims, but not erotically; he exposes their eroticism, but not to unveil a concomitant desire of his own.[65] Rather, horror seems to have swallowed eroticism. It was to avoid the erotic and its entanglement that he got pleasure from seeing the elderly witch naked and hearing her disclose her sexual relations with the devil. Were the elderly women Hopkins victimized desired by him for their power to reduce desire, needed because powerless to arouse? Far from seeking otherwise forbidden pleasures, Hopkins seems to have sought to distance himself from the eroticized female body by conjuring it up in a repulsive form. This tactic, common also to more straightforwardly anerotic medieval texts urging a life of celibacy, involved the disclosure of the mutability of the erotic female body, its vulnerability to age. Hopkins's fantasy is in a line which includes Villon's "She Who Was The Beautiful Helmetmaker's Wife," a poem in which an object of desire articulates under interrogation the tragic transience of her desirability in comparison with the permanence of her own desires.

Rather than being a desiring subject, Hopkins strives to be without desire. As his later, manicured version of the story shows, he becomes the successful investigator, the one who knows and discloses the secret world and words of women, who knows their bodies, too. Nakedness was in any case not a way of gratifying curiosity, but a public signifier, or rather a public loss of a public signifier. During the war, prisoners were often stripped of their clothes. This was partly an act of simple robbery, but it also served to remove signs of class, status, gender, identity, individuality. When the prisoners at Barthomley Church at Christmas 1643 were stripped stark naked by their royalist slaughterers, the stripping signified death, for like death it took from the victims the identity and respect that they had laboriously created, leaving them exposed as nothing but vulnerable, mortal flesh.[66] Similarly, Hopkins's stripping of his suspects was not merely a humiliation, but a signification of their loss of public identity and respect, a way of teaching them the godly lesson that worldly things pass, leaving the body's nakedness to symbolize the visibility of the soul to God. As they lost their identities, Hopkins created his. Like God, he could see their essential nakedness, their truth. Hopkins appropriates what had been a proto-Enlightenment discourse (the witchmark) for his own more directly misogynistic and psychosexually motivated fantasy.[67] The witchmark becomes a way to know a woman's body, to make it speak of what it has done. But it is not enough. She must also be naked, and naked, made to speak. This desire for absolute nakedness, and hence for absolute disgust, is channeled through discourses of Puritan confession and testimony, discourses of confession as a cutting open of what was problematically hard and solid.[68] So Hopkins dissolves away his own sexuality by constant encounters with what short-circuits it. He thus drives himself ever further from the messy world of the engulfing body. In Hopkins's world, if something needs to be confronted, it is the portability and exchangeability of the disclosed female body and its value as payment. Hopkins is taking a merchant-class view of desire; for him confession to sex with the devil is confession to using the body as (the only) means of payment for services rendered. This is not peculiar to him; it is registered in Margaret Johnson's apparently voluntary confession in the Lancashire trial of 1633/4.[69] Hopkins echoes Johnson in seeing the offer of sex as the only recourse of a poor woman who hopes to attract a man of wealth and taste.

It is thus that social and godly order is overturned rather than supported by the commodification of the female body, for that commodification can allow women to "sell" their way out of their just place in the hierarchy.[70] Having done so, they impinge upon and threaten Hopkins, as is clear from another of his stories:

> 29 were condemned at once, 4 brought 25 miles to be hanged, where this Discoverer lives, for sending the Devil like a Beare to kill him in his garden, so by seeing diverse of the mens [*sic*] Papps, and trying ways with hundreds of them, he gained this experience, and for aught he knowes any man else many find them as well as he and his company, if they had the same skill and experience.[71]

The witches sent a devil to kill Hopkins personally, we now learn for the first time; this cannot be the cat or the kitlyn of Hopkins's original depositions, and his role in the story has changed since he made them. In accordance with his general psychic pattern, his fractured and deeply unstable masculine identity is now shored up with a new self-image, that of hero. A cat does not sound like much of a threat; to have faced down a bear sounds far more heroic. What Theweleit calls "fragmented armour" seems relevant: Hopkins's persona is dependent on meeting and vanquishing foes, on triumph.[72] Yet this is not just a psychic dependency; it is also a role he is enjoying, one that he can act out to gain social rewards. Here, his self-representation as hero and defender of the just is invested with the pleasure of success.

Heroism is also uppermost in Hopkins's understanding of his role as interrogator. Godly preachers and congregations did not see interrogation and confession in quite the secular light in which they appear to us. Rather than forcing an unwilling admission from a suspect in violation of their personal integrity and civil liberties, Puritan ministers and preachers frequently saw themselves as desperately trying to break through a personhood which was simply an encrustation of sin over the true, God-given soul. Stearne explains that watching is "not to use violence, or extremity to force them to confesse, but onely the keeping is, first, to see whether any of their spirits, or familiars come to or neere them":

> that Godly Divines and others might discourse with them, and idle persons be kept from them, for if any of their society come to them . . . they will never confesse; . . . But if honest godly people discourse with them, laying the hainousness of their sins to them, and in what condition they are in without Repentance, and telling them the subtleties of the Devill, and the mercies of god, these wayes will bring them to Confession without extremity, it will make them breake into Confession hoping for mercy.[73]

Though using the same discourse as Henry Goodcole a few decades earlier, Stearne has moved on from Goodcole's position; or rather, the epistemology of confession and truth have become even more debatable in the aftermath of a civil war characterized by the spread of rumors, cryptographs and disinformation, the movement of agents and double agents in disguise, the emergence of plot and counterplot, the battles in which each side tried to deflect fire by impersonating the other.[74] This theatrical war, which ironically saw the closure of the only institution likely safely to canalize the uncertainties thus created—the theatre itself—necessarily problematized identities even as it licensed their recovery by brutal and illicit means. The delicate cryptograph, so complex in decipherment, had to be roughly seized and exposed. Paradoxically, epistemological difficulty, as all good postmodernists know, can lead not to paralyzed skepticism but to a willingness to cast caution to the winds and to seize on any possibility, no matter how ruinous. The war, in other words, corrupted not only the practice of interrogating the accused but also the discourses in which this might be explained or justified.

And yet Hopkins's voice should not be allowed to be or seem the only one, or even the dominant one, in creating witch fictions, for it was one voice among others eager to heal or anaesthetize the wounds of the Civil War by the psychic pleasures involved in the witch's identification and destruction. If Hopkins was particularly motivated, he was not unusual in his desires, however deformed they may appear. The soldiers at Newbury and Naseby and in Wiltshire and Ireland were acting on similar psychic orders, desperately trying to maintain their own identities intact and sustain the fiction of masculinity in the face of intolerable pressures. It has often been remarked that the Civil War was relatively free of atrocities. Perhaps this is partially because its tensions were discharged elsewhere, off the field, against the ambiguous, shadowy figure of the witch. Admittedly there were plenty of early modern wars in which violence selected its objects almost at random, or in which private prosecution of witches was supplemented by the military murder of civilians. The multiplicity of potentialities for violence created by violence itself must never be underrated. Nonetheless, we should not fail to notice the peculiarity and particularity of the Civil War. Nor should we overlook attacks on witches, whether judicially sanctioned or not, among its death toll. Perhaps it was not a war without an enemy after all.

ॐ

## Notes

I am grateful to Miranda Chaytor, Ivan Dowling, David Harley, and Nigel Smith for advice and help, to Jim Sharpe for lending me his own forthcoming study of Matthew Hopkins, and to David Aers and Michael Cornett for their patience and kindness. For seventeenth-century works cited in the notes place of publication is London unless otherwise stated. Pamphlets for which no author is cited are anonymously written.

1  *A most certain, strange and true discovery of a witch, being taken by some of the parliament forces* (1643). The witch of Newbury was said by the parliamentarian newspaper *Mercurius Civicus* of 21–28 September 1643 to be a royalist agent sent to destroy the magazine of the earl of Essex (p. 140).

2  Peter Stallybrass and Ann Rosalind Jones, "The Politics of *Astrophil and Stella*," *Studies in English Literature* 24 (1984): 53–68.

3  *A true relation of the late battel neere Newbery* (1643), 5.

4  Captain John Gwynne, *Military Memoirs of the Great Civil War* (London, 1822), 42; *The Cavalier Songs and Ballads of England from 1642 to 1684*, ed. Charles MacKay (London, 1863), 125; Henry Slingsby, *Original Memoirs Written During the Great War*, ed. Sir Walter Scott (London, 1806), 23; Sergeant Henry Foster, *A True and Exact Relation of the Marchings of the Two Regiments of the Trained bands of the City of London* (1643), repr. *Bibliotheca Gloucesterinsis*, ed. James Washbourne, 2 vols. (Gloucester, 1828), 1:267. For further discussion of reactions to such events, see Charles Carlton, *Going to the Wars: The Experience of British Civil Wars, 1638–1651* (London: Routledge, 1992), 139; and Carlton, "The Impact of the Fighting," in *The Impact of the English Civil War*, ed. John Morrill (London: Collins and Brown, 1991), 25.

5  *A True Relation*, 5–6.

6  There are surprisingly few discussions of the figure of the witch in a Civil War context, and even the Hopkins trials have been neglected as atypical of English witchcraft, though Jim Sharpe offers a corrective view in his forthcoming book.

7  There was an upsurge in prosecutions all over England in the 1640s. For witchcraft cases 1640–60 outside East Anglia, see PRO ASSI 45, which contains a number of

records from the Northern Circuit; these are partially and somewhat inaccurately transcribed in James Raine, ed., *Depositions from York Castle*, Surtees Society, vol. 40 (London, 1860). Pamphlet accounts include *An account of the trial, confession, and condemnation of six witches at Maidstone at the assizes held there . . . to which is added The trial, examination, and execution of three witches executed at Faversham* (1645); *The Divel's Delusions or a faithful relation of John Palmer and Elizabeth Knott, two notorious witches lately condemned at the sessions of Oyer and Terminer in St Albans* (1649); Mary Moor, *Wonderful News from the North, or a True Relation of the Sad and grieving Torments Inflicted upon the Bodies of three children of Mr George Muschamp* (1650); *A Prodigious and Tragicall history of the Arraignment, trial, confession and condemnation of six witches at Madistone in Kent* (1652); F. H., *An Account of the trial, confession and condemnation of six witches, at Maidstone . . . at the assizes held there July 1652* (1653); *The Tryall and examination of Mrs Joan Peterson for her supposed witchcraft and poisoning of the Lady Powel at Chelsea* (1652); *The Witch of Wapping, or an exact and Perfect Relation of the Life and Devilish Practices of Joan Peterson* (1652); *A Declaration in Answer to Several Lying pamphlets Concerning the Witch of Wapping, showing the bloody plot and wicked conspiracy of one Abraham Vandenbemde, Thomas Crompton, Thomas Collet, and others* (1652); Edmond Bower, *Dr Lambe's Darling and Dr Lambe Revived: or witchcraft condemned in Anne Bodenham* (1653). For a peak in witchcraft cases in the West of England in the 1650s, see Janet Thompson, *Wives, Widows, Witches, and Bitches: Women in Seventeenth-Century Devon* (Frankfurt: Lang, 1992), 67–75.

8    Records of the Hopkins cases include the following: in manuscript, Cambridge University Library Ely, Assize Depositions Michaelmas 1647, EDR 12/20, 12/3, and E12 1647; British Library, MS Add. 27402, fols. 104–21; in printed form, *A True and Exact Relation of the Several Informations, Examinations, and Confessions of the late witches arraigned and executed in the county of Essex* (1645); *A True Relation of the Arraignment of eighteene Witches that were tried, convicted and condemned, as a sessions holden in St Edmonds-bury in Suffolke . . . the 27 day of August 1645* (1645); John Davenport, *The Witches of Huntingdon, their Examinations and Confessions exactly taken by his Majesties Justices of the Peace for that County* (1645); *The Lawes Against Witches and Conjuration, And some breif notes and observations for the discovery of Witches . . . , also the Confession of Mother Lakeland, who was arraigned and condemned for a witch at Ipswich in Suffolk* (1645).

9    For Lucan's influence, see Nigel Smith, *Literature and the English Civil War* (New Haven: Yale University Press, 1992), 203–11; and on Lucan and witchcraft, see Diane Purkiss, *The Witch in History* (London: Routledge, 1996), chap. 8. For this notion in learned demonological texts in general, see Stuart Clark, "Inversion, Misrule, and the Meaning of Witchcraft," *Past and Present* 87 (1980): 98–127.

10    10–17 August 1645.

11    *Epistolae Ho-Elianiae: The Familiar Letters of James Howell*, ed. J. Jacobs (London, 1890), 506, 3 Feb 1646, addressed to Endymion Porter, a Catholic at the queen's court in exile; see also pp. 511, 515, and 547.

12    11–17 July 1645. The Association Counties is a reference to the East Anglian counties that had gone over to parliament in a body.

13  *Signes and Wonders From Heaven, With a True Relation of a Monster borne in Ratcliffe Highway* (1645), 2–3.

14  This was especially true in reports of witch-prosecutions in Scotland, which were generally hostile to the use of torture and implicitly or explicitly contrasted this with the less tyrannical rule of England. See for instance *Mercurius Politicus*, 28 October–4 November, which is especially unkeen on the use of torture.

15  Robert Filmer, *An Advertisement to the Jury-men of England touching witches* (1653), prefatory epistle, sig. A2r. Thomas Ady, *A Candle in the Dark, or a treatise concerning the nature of witches and witchcraft* (1656).

16  *The Moderate Intelligencer*, 4–11 September 1645. The reference is probably to the trials at Bury-St. Edmunds, described in *A True Relation of the Arraignment of eighteene Witches that were tried, convicted and condemned, as a sessions holden in St Edmondsbury in Suffolke . . . the 27 day of August 1645* (1645).

17  *Signes and Wonders From Heaven*, 7.

18  This derogatory reference to Davies suggests that this is a roylist satire, despite appearances, for she had prophesied the deaths of Buckingham and of the king, and hence was particularly disliked by royalists. For Eleanor Davies' prophecies, see *The Prophetic Writings of Lady Eleanor Davies*, ed. Esther S. Cope (Oxford: Oxford University Press, 1996). "Mother Shipton" was a fictional woman prophet invented during the Civil War, but purporting to be ancient.

19  *Signes and Wonders from Heaven*, 4; Richard Deacon, *Matthew Hopkins: Witchfinder General* (London, Frederick Muller, 1976), 139–140; *Observations Upon Prince Rupert's White Dogge Called Boy* (1643), 4–9. For Rupert's other remarkable qualities, see also *Prince Rupert's Disguises* (1642); and *A Dog's Elegy* (1644). On the witch as comic figure, see Purkiss, *The Witch in History*, chaps. 8 and 9.

20  In his *Memoirs* Holles mentions the "sabbaths" held by Cromwell and St. John, where they "imparted to your fellow witches the bottom of your designs, the policy of your actings, the turn of your contrviances, all your falsehoods, vilanies and cruelties with your full intention to ruin three kingdoms." *The Memoirs of Denzil Lord Holles, Baron of Ifield*, ed. John Toland (1699), 237.

21  Ady gives another instance: one of the "poor women that was hanged as a witch at Berry assizes in the yeare 1645 did send her imp into the Army to kill the parliamentary soldiers and another sent her imps into the army to kill the king's soldiers" (*A Candle in the Dark*, 65).

22  S. Everard, "Oliver Cromwell and Black Magic," *Occult Review* (April 1936): 84–92; *The English devil, or Cromwell and his monstrous witch discovered at Whitehall* (1660). Elizabeth Poole's actual address to the Council of State can be found in *An Alarum of War* (1647). For a discussion of Poole, see my doctoral thesis, *Gender, Power, and the Body: Milton and Seventeenth-Century Women's Writing* (University of Oxford, 1991). Cromwell's own position in relation to witchcraft was ambiguous. Huntingdon, site of a large Hopkins-related trial in 1646, was the home of Cromwell, and the master of Huntingdon Grammar, Thomas Beard, was the godly author of *The Theater of Gods Judgements*, which took a strong line about witches. Yet Cromwell also stopped a major persecution in Scotland. See Christopher Hill, *God's Englishman* (Harmondsworth: Penguin, 1975), 250.

23 *The Parliaments Post* 13, 29 July–5 August 1645.

24 Donald Lupton, *A warre-like treatise on the pike* (1642), 35; and *Memoirs of Colonel John Birch* (Camden Soceity, 1873), 92; both in Carlton, *Going to the Wars*, 47–48, 106. I discuss these issues more fully in *Gender and Politics in the English Civil War*, Cambridge University Press, forthcoming.

25 *The Vindication of Richard Atkyns, Esquire* (1669), 32.

26 Quoted by Carlton, *Going to the Wars*, 130, 143.

27 Sigmund Freud, *Beyond the Pleasure Principle* (1920), in *The Pelican Freud Library, Volume 11: On Metapsychology and the Theory of Psychoanalysis*, trans. James Strachey (Harmondsworth: Penguin, 1984), 269–337.

28 Two useful analyses of the negotiation of the death drive via a female figure are Elisabeth Bronfen, *Over Her Dead Body: Death, Femininity, and the Aesthetic* (Manchester: Manchester University Press, 1992); and Klaus Theweleit, *Male Fantasies, Volume I: Women, Bodies, Floods, History*, trans. Stephen Conway with Erica Carter and Chris Turner (Cambridge: Polity, 1987).

29 See *The Witch in History*, chap. 6.

30 Julia Kristeva, *Powers of Horror*, trans. Leon S. Roudiez (New York: Columbia University Press, 1982).

31 My thinking on this question has been influenced by work on more recent wars, especially the First World War: see in particular Joanna Bourke, *Dismembering the Male: Men's Bodies, Britain, and the Great War* (London: Reaktion, 1996).

32 On Dowsing's career, see Margaret Aston, *England's Iconoclasts* (Oxford: Clarendon, 1989), 75 ff.; and John Morrill, "William Dowsing, the Beaurocratic Puritan," in *Public Duty and Private Conscience in Seventeenth-Century England*, ed. John Morrill, Paul Slack, and Daniel Woolf (Oxford: Oxford University Press, 1992), esp. 206.

33 Aston, 77.

34 *The copy of a letter sent to an honourable Lord, by Doctor Paske* (1642), repr. *Mercurius Rusticus, or the Countries Complaints of the barbarous out-rages committed by the Sectaries*, ed. Bruno Ryves, repr. of 1646 ed., 3 vols. (1685), 2:119–20; hence a royalist source. There was iconoclasm in the areas of Essex where Hopkins began his career: at St. Mary's Church, Lawford, near Manningtree, the carved heads of the saints were hacked off during the 1640s (E. Auston, *Historic Notes on Twenty-Four Villages in the Tendring Hundred* (Colchester: E. Auston, 1951), 4.

35 B. Hubbard, *Sermo Secularis* (1648), 19.

36 Carlton, *Going to the Wars*, 143. See also "The Impact of the Fighting," 28; and Barbara Donagan's account of the intellectual background of the rules of war, "Atrocity, War Crime, and Treason in the English Civil War," *American Historical Review* 99 (1994): 1137–66.

37 See *The Witch in History*, chap. 5.

38 Mary Agnes Hickson, *Ireland in the Seventeenth Century, or the Irish Massacres of 1641-2*, 2 vols. (London, 1884), 1:152; deposition dated 25 May 1653.

39 Peter Rushton, "Women, Witchcraft, and Slander in Early Modern England: Cases from the Church Courts at Durham, 1560–1675," *Northern History* 18 (1982): 116–32.

40 Claire Carroll, "Representations of Women in Some Early Modern English Tracts on

the Colonisation of Ireland," *Albion* 25 (1993): 391. I am grateful to Lisa Jardine for suggesting the relevance of the Irish question to witchcraft.

41 Turner, letter of 8 May 1642, in Thomas Fitzpatrick, *The Bloody Bridge and Other Papers Relating to the Insurrections of 1641* (Dublin: Sealy, Bryant, and Walker, 1903), 127; and Ann Fanshawe, *Memoirs*, ed. John Loftis (Oxford: Clarendon Press, 1979), 125. For a similar pattern of beliefs about New World natives, see *The Witch in History*, chap. 10. Both Old English and ethnic Irish tended to prefer to settle witchcraft cases without recourse to the courts; Ireland as a result had no witchcraze; see Elwyn C. Lapoint, "Irish Immunity to Witch-Hunting, 1534–1711," *Eire-Ireland* 22 (1992): 76–93; and Robin Gillespie, "Women and Crime in Seventeenth-Century Ireland," in *Women in Early Modern Ireland*, ed. Margaret MacCurtain and Mary O'Dowd (Edinburgh: Edinburgh University Press, 1991), 45–46.

42 "The humble peticon of Anne the wife of John Warberton of Warminster Bricklayer," Warminster Quarter Sessions, 14 and 15 July 1646, in B. Howard Cunnington, ed., *Records of the County of Wilts* (Devizes: G. Simpson and Co., 1932), 154.

43 Robin Briggs, *Witches and Neighbours: The Social and Cultural Context of European Witchcraft* (London: HarperCollins, 1996), 308.

44 Cases based in Manningtree began in the winter of 1644, and the first confession was recorded March 1645. Trials began in Chelmsford in July. Hunt spread into Suffolk just over the border from the Tendring Hundred, and also into Norfolk, Cambridgeshire, Northamptonshire, and Bedfordshire. Trials also took place in Great Yarmouth, Aldeburgh, Stowmarket, King's Lynn, and the Isle of Ely.

45 See my article "Women's Stories of Witchcraft: The House, the Body, the Child," *Gender and History* 7 (winter 1995): 408–32; Jim Sharpe also points to the unexceptional nature of many of the Hopkins trial materials in his forthcoming book on the history of witchcraft; I am grateful to him for allowing me to consult his manuscript in preparation.

46 Stearne, *A Confirmation and Discovery of Witchcraft* (1648), 3.

47 Deacon, *Matthew Hopkins*, 39, citing a manuscript, which is not identified, from the Essex County Record Office. The meager biographical facts assembled by Deacon and others are as follows: Hopkins was born c. 1619–22, making him in his early twenties at the beginning of his activities. His mother, Marie Hopkins, was possibly a Huguenot refugee. A manuscript now lost allegedly said Hopkins was a lawyer "of but little note" (Deacon, 13–14). Since there is no record of him at the Inns of Court or in other court records, he may have worked as a legal clerk, possibly for a ship-owner in Mistley. The Suffolk Record Office contains a conveyance of a tenement in Bramford, only just outside Ipswich, dated 1641, bearing Hopkins's signature as a witness, which may imply a role as a lawyer's clerk. Hopkins allegedly told Lady Jane Whorley that he had studied maritime law in Amsterdam. It is generally agreed that he did spend some time in the Netherlands, possibly with his Huguenot connections, but some suggest that this may mean the Essex village of Little Holland, and in that case it may be relevant that Brian Darcy, the chief justice in the St. Osyth case of 1582, was briefly owner of the manor there ( J. Yelloly Watson, *The Tendring Hundred in the Olden Time* [Colchester, 1877], 69). Hopkins knew that other great self-fashioner of the Civil War years, William Lilly. Hopkins was not hanged as a witch, but died of a

consumption: "he died peaceably at Manningtree, after a long sicknesse of a Consumption, as many of his generation had done before him, without any trouble of conscience for what he had done, as was falsely reported of him" (Stearne, *Confirmation and Discovery of Witchcraft*, 61). He was buried on 12 August 1647 at Mistley.

48   Hopkins's father was the Vicar of Great Wenham. He uses Puritan discourse in his extant will: "I shalbe receved to Mercy only through the Righteousnesse & Merritts of the Lorde Jesus Christ my Saviour." John Stearne says of Hopkins that "he was the son of a godly minister, and therefore without doubt within the covenant" (Stearne, 61)

49   Deacon, *Matthew Hopkins*, 37, 61.

50   *A True and Exact Relation of the Several Informations, Examinations, and Confessions of the late witches arraigned and executed in the county of Essex* (1645), 3. There is a slightly inaccurate transcription of this pamphlet in Peter Haining, *The Witchcraft Papers* (Secaucus, N.J.: University Books, 1974).

51   The fullest text of Edmund Robinson's confession is in John Webster, *The Displaying of Supposed Witchcraft*, 347, but the numerous transcriptions of it testify to the wide circulation of the story (e.g., BL MS Harleian 6854, fol. 26v; Bodleian MS Dodsworth 61, fols. 45–47v; Bodleian MS Rawlinson D.399, fols. 211–12v; BL MS Add. 36674, fols. 193, 196).

52   Katherine Briggs, *A Dictionary of British Folktales*, 4 vols. (London: Routledge and Kegan Paul, 1970–71), cites several instances of witches transforming themselves into hares (2:626-27, 699).

53   *A Confirmation and Discovery of Witchcraft* (1648), 34. John Stearne was Hopkins's principal associate. He was gentry; Stearne was still paying hearth tax in Manningtree in 1666, despite apparently moving to Lawshall in 1648. In his writings, Stearne was heavily influenced by William Perkins's godly and influential *Discourse of the Damned Art of Witchcraft* (1608), but he also borrowed at length from Richard Bernard, *A Guide to Grand Jurymen* (1627, repr. 1629); these may have been among Hopkins's intellectual antecedents, too, but there is little trace of their influence in his writings.

54   On the area, see P. Morant, *The History and Antiquities of the County of Essex* (London, 1816); Watson, *Tendring Hundred*; William Andrews, *Bygone Essex* (Colchester, 1892); and Auston, *Twenty-four Villages*.

55   See M. C. Balfour, "Legends of the Lincolnshire Cars," *Folklore* 11 (1891): 145–418; and W. H. Barrett and R. P. Gar‧‧d, *East Anglian Folklore and Other Tales* (London: Routledge and Kegan Paul, 1976).

56   William Camden, *Remaines Concerning Britain*, trans. Philemon Holland, 5th ed. (1637), 345. The original source is medieval: the *Chronicon Anglicarum*, by Ralph of Coggeshall.

57   Stuart Clark, "The Rational Witch-Finder: Conscience, Demonological Naturalism, and Popular Superstition," in *Science, Culture, and Popular Belief*, ed. Stephen Pumfrey, Paolo L. Rossi, and Maurice Slawinski (Manchester: Manchester University Press, 1991), 235, 237; and John Gaule, *Select Cases of Conscience Touching Witches and Witchcraft* (1646), 63–64.

58   Deacon claims Hopkins made as much as £23 from Stowmarket and £15 from King's Lynn, with promises for more after the next sessions. His inn bill was also paid in Stowmarket. But he only got £6 in Aldeburgh—£2 from each visit, three visits—

suggesting that the rate was decidedly variable (*Matthew Hopkins*, 73). Hopkins himself denies that he made much money: *The Discovery of Witches* (1647), 5–6.

59  Hopkins, *Discovery of Witches*, 1.

60  Stearne writes of the exchangeability of godly and satanic idenitities: "many of these witches have made outward shows, as if they had been Saints on earth, and so were taken by some; as one of Catowth in Huntingtonshire, . . . by their carriage seemed to be very religious people, and would constantly repair to all sermons neer them; yet notwithstanding all their shews of religion, there appeared some of these probabilities, wherby they were suspected" (*Confirmation and Discovery of Witchcraft*, 39).

61  Hudibras 2.3, 139 ff., *The Poetical Works of Samuel Butler*, ed. Robert Bell (London, 1862); Hopkins, *Discovery of Witches*, 1.

62  Gaule, *Select Cases of Conscience*, 93.

63  A fairly typical confession of this is that of Thomazine Ratcliffe of Shellie, Suffolke, who confessed "that it was malice that had brought her to that she was come to, meaning Witchcraft; for she confessed, that soone after ther husbands decease, above twenty yeares before her confession, there came one in the likenesse of a man, into bed to her, which spoke with a hollow, shrill voyce, and told her, he would be a loving husband to her, if she would consent to him, which she said, she did, and then he told her, he would revenge her of all her enemies, and that she should never miss anything, in which she said, she found him a lyer, but said, that Satan often tempted her to banning, swearing and cursing, which shee confessed shee did use a long time, and that many times it fell out accordingly, and that she, falling out with one Martins wife, who had a child drowned, for that she called her witch, saying, shee was the cause of the childs drowning, she bad her goe home and look to the rest, lest she lose more, and one died suddenly after" (Stearne, *Confirmation and Discovery of Witchcraft*, 22).

64  See for instance Bram Djikstra, *Idols of Perversity: Fantasies of Feminine Evil in Fin-de-Siècle Culture* (Oxford: Oxford University Press, 1986).

65  Nor did they desire him, as Stearne mischeviously reports: "Then said Mr Hopkin, in what manner and likenesse came he to you? shee said, like a tall, proper, blackhaired gentleman, a properer man then you selfe, and being asked which she had rather lie withall, shee said the Devill" (p. 15).

66  For the massacre at Barthomley, see Thomas Malbon, *A breefe and true relacon of all suche passages & Things as happened . . . in Namptwich*, in *Tracts Relating to the Civil War in Cheshire*, ed. James Hall, *Lancashire and Cheshire Record Society* 19 (1889): 94–97.

67  For the witchmark as a proto-Enlightenment sign, see *The Witch in History*, chap. 9, which recounts William Harvey's involvement int the 1633/4 case.

68  On confession, see John Bossy, "The Social History of Confession in the Age of the Reformation," *Transactions of the Royal Historical Society* 5th series, 25 (1975): 21–38; and Michel Foucault, *The History of Sexuality, Volume I*, trans. Robert Hurley (Harmondsworth: Penguin, 1985).

69  For Johnson's confession, see *Calender of State Papers Domestic* (1634), 141. Similarly, Gaule mentions the devil's "marriage" to his votaries, and reports that Hopkins said he used the *Book of Common Prayer* to do it, meaning the Laudian prayerbook.

70  I am referring to Luce Irigaray's celebrated essay, "Women on the Market," in *This Sex*

Which Is Not One, trans. Catherine Porter (Ithaca: Cornell University Press, 1985), 179–92, and suggesting that feminists have underestimated the subversiveness of the female body as commodity.

71  *Discovery of Witches*, 3.

72  Klaus Theweleit, *Male Fantasies, Volume 2. Male Bodies: Psychoanalysing the White Terror*, trans. Chris Turner and Erica Carter (Cambridge: Polity, 1989), 206 f.

73  Stearne, *Confirmation and Discovery of Witchcraft*, 14.

74  Henry Goodcole was Elizabeth Sawyer's confessor, and wrote *The Wonderful Discovery of Elizabeth Sawyer A Witch* (1621).

*Chapter Six*

# Witchcraft and power in early modern England: the case of Margaret Moore

## Malcolm Gaskill

A witch-hunt, instigated by Matthew Hopkins, the self-appointed Witchfinder-General, took place in East Anglia in the years 1645–7, and claimed the lives of around two hundred women and men.[1] This chapter examines the case of just one victim of the trials, in the light of some of the ideas which have emerged from historical studies of witchcraft in early modern England. Typically, these studies have sought to explain the rise and fall of prosecutions between about 1560 and 1680, among which the most popular explanation remains, in short, that the deterioration of social cohesion in communities raised fears of innocent villagers using witchcraft against those who denied them traditional charity. It will be suggested here that because witchcraft accusations arose from a wide variety of inter-personal conflicts, and because some accused witches believed in their own magical powers, in certain cases individuals might be seen to play out struggles in an imaginary supernatural arena. This chapter does not seek ecological causes for witchcraft accusations. Instead, it explores the possible meaning of a single supernatural occurrence in the broader context of popular beliefs and mentalities, with a view to understanding how ordinary people might perceive power – its limitations and its extension – in an extraordinary manner.

## I

The model of the rise of English witchcraft prosecutions constructed over two decades ago by K. Thomas and A. Macfarlane, connects a small-scale dynamic of tension and accusation in local communities with the larger dynamic of long-term change in social relations in the country as a whole.

It is argued that in the second half of the sixteenth and first half of the seventeenth centuries, social and economic pressures caused English villagers to abandon their charitable obligations to the poor of the parish, thereby opening a gulf of misunderstanding and suspicion between neighbours at the lower end of the social order. Guilt produced by this abdication of responsibility thereafter manifested itself as a defensive fear of the magical revenge of those who had been denied charity. These dispossessed persons were usually elderly widows, often with a reputation for using cunning magic or *maleficium*. Accusations usually focused on specific misfortunes suffered after disagreement with a likely suspect – frequently involving the refusal of alms – which subsequently might be attributed to acts of witchcraft.[2]

Since then, historians have demonstrated that social and economic pressures could also lead to witchcraft accusations between competitors more intimately connected socially. Cynthia Herrup has suggested of witchcraft accusations in Sussex that "the accuser and accused were not exceptionally mismatched in terms of power", reflecting "ongoing competition rather than guilt or anger born of spurned hospitality".[3] Similarly, J. A. Sharpe has interpreted seventeenth-century Yorkshire witchcraft depositions in terms of tensions between women vying for prominence in female spheres of activity.[4] Many women (and men) accused of witchcraft elsewhere deviate from the stereotype of the poor, marginal figure, and instead appear to have been vocal and active members of the community whose very integration, rather than their isolation, brought them into conflict with their neighbours. Research into the background to pre-Civil War witchcraft prosecutions in Kent and Sussex (which superficially fit the Macfarlane–Thomas model) has revealed pre-existing conflicts based on local religious and political factionalism,[5] and in other instances, quarrels ending in allegations of *maleficium* stemmed from disputed ownership of land.[6] Similar arguments for the witch as a competitor for influence, space and material resources have also been advanced for Europe and the New World.[7]

However, both models outlined above, although correct to seek the causes of witchcraft accusations in social tensions, tend to neglect the participation of the witch in a shared culture of popular beliefs. In the 1920s a British anthropologist, M. Murray, argued that the witch-hunts of the sixteenth and seventeenth centuries represented the mass persecution of devotees of a widespread pagan fertility cult.[8] While this explanation is highly implausible, the compounded effect of functionalist refutations of her claims has been to strip witchcraft of any kind of reality as a belief in the mind of the accused, presenting it as a paranoid and oppressive dogma existing solely in the mind of the accuser.[9] Accordingly, all witches have been categorized as the passive and innocent victims of persecuting mentalities and impersonal economic tensions, and confessions of involvement with the black art have been presented as the products of inquisitorial duress or mental illness. After all, in anthropological terms, it is dysfunctional to accuse oneself of a capital crime.

Objections to this approach have formed the mainstay of criticism of Thomas & Macfarlane's work on witchcraft. It has been argued that magic cannot be understood outside complete systems of thought and belief, and that objective assessments of events made outside the mental and cultural context within which they took place have robbed them of their true meaning.[10] This meaning, H. Geertz has argued, stemmed "not so much from empirical testing but from the fact that a particular notion is set within a general pattern of cultural concepts".[11] Another critique levels the more direct charge that Thomas' work "was conducted within a specific framework of assumptions, and therefore could not produce any modification of the framework nor any test of the assumptions". In short, it is argued that the anthropological theories which underpinned *Religion and the decline of magic* must be seen as the product of modern mentalities, and, therefore, that the historical presentation of pre-industrial beliefs was essentially a "present-centred" exercise.[12]

Arguably, the study of witchcraft would benefit from a more self-consciously past-centred approach which seeks to insert the speech and action contained in recorded accusations back into the fluid structure of mentalities that shaped them. This raises a number of methodological difficulties, not least of which is the comparative sparseness of suitable evidence. Printed literary accounts are usually too sensational to be reliable, and most legal records are terse. One can say with certainty that the belief that diabolical power could be harnessed by humans to cause harm was widely held at all social levels, and that change in élite attitudes (given the currency of popular superstitions at least into the nineteenth century) caused the decline of formal witchcraft prosecutions. Applied to the basic details offered by a typical assize indictment, such knowledge merely confirms the established fact that people occasionally blamed naturally occurring misfortunes on the supernatural power of neighbours and sought redress at law. Detailed depositions provide greater insight in that they contain information about the relative standing of accused and accusers and often describe some of the circumstances preceding an accusation. However, in terms of mentalities, even depositions usually enable historians to do little more than illustrate recognized witch-beliefs in practice, confirming what is already known, without significantly penetrating the membrane that separates modern and early modern mental worlds.

Ideally, instead of accounts of supernatural interpretations of natural happenings, such as languishing illnesses, one requires firsthand descriptions of supernatural occurrences to which the modern reader cannot immediately ascribe a natural explanation. As R. Darnton has suggested, "by picking at the document where it is most opaque, we may be able to unravel an alien system of meaning".[13] Since accusers rarely offer more than an unproven equation between suspicion and misfortune, the opacity to which Darnton refers is mainly to be found in witches' confessions, for it is there that the witch might acknowledge and describe his or her own power, and indicate how and why it was acquired. Neither is it adequate always to ascribe such confessions to insanity – a dismissive present-centred reflex, precluding the need for further inquiry. Where possible, the claims made by witches should not be interpreted in terms of our own knowledge and experience, but treated instead as reflecting a facet of a thought-structure unique unto itself.[14] As one historian of German witchcraft prosecutions has argued, depositions need to be understood "as mental productions with an organization that is in itself significant".[15] In these terms, confessions of witchcraft constitute valuable and intriguing raw material for understanding an aspect of early modern mentalities that no longer occupies a place in the way the western world views its condition. In England, such admissions of guilt were not common outside of the 1645–7 trials, but in the few which do exist it is possible to see signs of a dynamic meeting between belief and behaviour.

So what did witchcraft represent in the early modern mind? Although it is difficult to separate élite and popular attitudes regarding magic, in the eyes of the authorities witchcraft was seen as an offence against religious and secular order, and both "white" and maleficent witchcraft were condemned as, at best, sacrilegious and superstitious, and, at worst, physically destructive.[16] More than any other sort of nonconformity, witchcraft could be held up by moralists to illustrate the ideal of religious and secular conformity because it displayed this ideal in its most inverted and corrupted form.[17] But in daily life witchcraft also posed a real and immediate threat to the health and property of individuals at all social levels. To ordinary people, given that many relied on magic in their daily lives, witchcraft could be both evil and beneficial; therefore, its deviant or criminal aspects were largely restricted to its destructive manifestations. Indeed, one could say that the only characteristic shared by cunning magic and maleficent witchcraft in the popular mind was the exercise, or the imagined exercise, of supernatural power by persons who were otherwise relatively powerless in terms of wealth and social status – particularly women. As J. A. Sharpe reminds us, witchcraft was "an explanation for misfortune, but also a means by which the powerless could wield power".[18]

In later sixteenth- and seventeenth-century England, opportunities to live according to individual preference were rare, and for most people the pattern of life was determined by adverse economic conditions over which they had little or no control: population increase; land hunger; inflation; dearth; and, as a result, competition for power, space and resources. Under such harsh conditions, it is easy to imagine that an atmosphere of fear and insecurity might form the backdrop to the daily life of many communities, and that charity and good neighbourliness existed as unrealized Christian ideals as much as they faithfully mirrored social relations in the period.[19] In many instances of conflict, often between close neighbours, and especially where disputants were too poor to engage in protracted litigation, impotence prevailed and a tense state of deadlock emerged. Equally, for many, life was a struggle not only with other people, but with the impersonal obstacles put up by the social and economic environment: poverty, disease and mortality. Women were particularly powerless, and therefore resorted to (or were believed to resort to) other means of overcoming hardship and opposition; the use of words to compensate for the lack of more direct female power, for example, has been suggested.[20]

In such straitened circumstances, personal frustration and despair encouraged the belief in some individuals that magical power might be harnessed as a means of extending the boundaries of terrestrial power. This is a familiar explanation of sorcery and cunning magic, where a consensus of belief usually existed between witch and client, but it is less commonly encountered in discussions of *maleficium* or diabolic communion because the witch trials have been inextricably linked to the history of persecuting societies – an approach which mutes any agency on the part of the witch. However, belief in an act of harmful magic was also *potentially* shared by accused and accuser alike. Viewed together, a physical world marked by hardship, and a mental world which permitted the possibility of witchcraft, provided fertile psychological ground either for delusion and desire in the witch, and/or paranoia and hostility on the part of the witch's victim.

Struggles with neighbours and nature alike could be elevated to an imaginary, supernatural plane, and ultimately resolved (on the part of a victim) in the material world of the criminal legal process. In this way, a dramatic paradigm was applied to real life, and depositions containing accusations and confessions might be seen, in modern terms, to overlay reality with fantasy as a conscious or subconscious means of influencing a court. Such documents constitute, then, a real and powerful "fiction in the archives".[21]

## II

The lives of ordinary individuals in early modern England flicker for a moment before the eyes of historians fumbling in the darkness of the past, and then disappear as quickly as they appeared. The life of Margaret Moore is a case in point.[22] She lived in the first half of the seventeenth century in Sutton, a comparatively large village in the hundred of Witchford in the south-western corner of the Isle of Ely, Cambridgeshire. Then, as now, Sutton was dominated by a central street, at the eastern end of which stood the parish church, and behind which the village sloped away to the south, overlooking a large expanse of fenland towards the village of Haddenham. Until the eighteenth century this lowland was flooded, but elsewhere rich arable land was to be found, and Sutton was noted for its cherry orchards.[23] Moore had a husband, who may not have been present at the time she was accused of witchcraft, but was almost certainly still alive (she is consistently referred to as the wife of Robert Moore). At some point in her life she had four children, three of whom died in infancy – a fact which, it will be argued, is crucial to a proper understanding of the story. Various clues from the surviving documentation suggest that she was poor, although she was probably not among the poorest since she kept animals.[24] At present, this is virtually all that is known of her for certain prior to her apprehension as a witch in May 1647.[25]

Some time before this date, in the parish of Witchford just over three miles to the east of Sutton, three farmers suffered misfortunes which were attributed to the witchcraft of Margaret Moore. Thomas Maynes and John Foster both lost cattle, and Thomas Nix fell sick and died. According to Matthew Hopkins' associate, John Stearne, who mentions Moore specifically in his memoir of the witch-hunt, her murdered victim (presumably Nix) sold her a pig for 2s 2d but she paid him only the two shillings. Soon after coming to her door one day, either to collect the debt or reclaim the pig, he became ill and, thinking of his debtor Moore, summoned her, pleading that "he could not depart this life, untill hee had spoken with her". At first, she refused to go but finally was forced to attend by Nix's friends just prior to his death.[26] It is unusual that the approximate date of the bewitchings is not stated either in the depositions or in Stearne's account, and both narratives accordingly give the impression of a rapid transition from crime to apprehension, examination and trial. However, there are good reasons for believing that these events occurred as much as a decade earlier; e.g., the will of a Thomas Nyx, husbandman of Witchford, was proved at the consistory court at this time.[27] Witchcraft prosecutions occurring so long after the fact were by no means unusual, and may reflect the gradual accretion of suspicions and feelings of hostility against an individual over a period of time. By the time well nursed grudges spilled over into formal accusations, a long litany of alleged offences might be stored in the collective memory of the community.

If either Maynes or Fisher, or the family and friends of Thomas Nix, gave evidence against Moore, it does not survive. What is certain is that, some time after the alleged bewitchings, she was apprehended and examined informally by two gentlemen of Sutton, Benjamin Wyne and Perry Jetherell, before whom she confessed herself to be a witch and guilty of the charges laid against her. On 26 May 1647, Wyne and Jetherell then appeared with Moore before the magistrate at Haddenham, Lieutenant-Colonel Thomas Castell, where they deposed their evidence and were jointly bound to present a bill of indictment against Moore at the next assizes. Moore appeared before Castell on the same day, repeated her confession, expressing regret for what she had done, and was committed to Ely gaol pending trial.[28] Stearne concluded his summary of the case by saying that she wept at her trial, confessed her witchcraft a third time, and was condemned.[29]

From the Ely archives and Stearne's account, in 1646 and 1647 twenty persons from the Isle are known to have been prosecuted for maleficent witchcraft, of which two-thirds were women. Over half of this number lived in Sutton and its two neighbouring parishes, Stretham and Haddenham. It is certain that Hopkins and Stearne were active in Cambridgeshire at this time, and it is logical to suppose from this fact, and the content of the various surviving depositions, that they were involved with most, if not all, of these accusations.[30] In two cases Stearne appeared in person to give evidence.[31] In the last eleven days of May 1647, seven women and four men (four from Sutton; four from Stretham; three from Haddenham), most of whom confessed, were examined by Castell,[32] and at least nine of their number were committed to Ely gaol.[33] By the middle of September, there were twelve witches at Ely: seven men and five women.[34]

One is tempted to think that these patterns were formed by more than a witch panic, and that in Moore's case, specifically, relations between her family, the Sutton gentlemen, the magistrates of Haddenham and the Witchford farmers would be a significant factor.[35] Close examination of subsidy assessments, parish registers, wills and church court and manorial records would probably offer more information here, and politics – local and national – doubtless played an important rôle in forming the tensions which lay behind the events of May 1647. The Jetherell family, for example, were lessees of the manor of Sutton under the dean and chapter of the diocese of Ely, and from 1624 were involved in disputes with local people over rights of common in the fen. Drainage and enclosure provided a major source of discontent and disorder in the parish, leading to the withholding of fines, and the petitioning of Parliament by the poorer inhabitants on more than one occasion in the 1640s. In 1649 it was alleged that, four years earlier, seven petitioners were gaoled to prevent them going to fight the King's army,[36] and, indeed, fen drainage has been strongly linked to Civil War allegiance.[37] It has also been suggested that many of the witches accused by Hopkins were believed to be royalist informers (the capture of the King followed only days after Moore's apprehension). This theory could account for the disproportionate number of men accused, the outlandish nature of the confessions, and the relatively high social status of some of the accusers, but it cannot be adequately substantiated.[38]

The various details and possible connections assembled here are inconclusive, and serve only to provide background to the predicament in which Margaret Moore found herself in 1647, and to indicate the direction in which future studies of fenland witchcraft prosecutions in the seventeenth century might lie. For the present, our interest is solely with Margaret Moore, why she confessed to being a witch and what coded meanings might lay hidden in the account of what she was reported to have said.

The first witness, Benjamin Wyne, deposed that Moore had told him that she had surrendered her soul to the Devil "because shee would save the life of on[e] of hir Children which upon the Contract he would save & to doe for hir what she should Command". A familiar spirit named Annis was sent to her, which she allowed to suckle before sending it to bewitch Thomas Nix who died soon afterwards. Jetherell elaborated on this story, relating that Moore had confessed that one night, soon after the death of her three children, the following strange and poignant event had occurred:

> she herd a voyce Calling to hir after this Manner, Mother Mother to
> which the said Margeret answered sweet Children where are you
> what would you have with me & thay demanded of hir drincke
> w[hi]ch the said Margeret Answered that she had noe drincke then
> theire Came a voyce which the said Margeret Conceaved to be hir
> third Child & demanded of hir hir soule, otherwise she would take
> a-way the life of hir 4th Child which was the only Child she had left
> to which voyce the said Margeret made answer that rather then shee
> would lose hir last Child she would Consent unto the giving a-way
> of hir soule & then a spirit in the liknes of a naked Child appeared
> unto hir & suckt upon hir Body.[39]

Moore herself confessed before the magistrate that "she hard ye voyce of
hir Children whoe had formerly died Calling unto hir in these words
mother mother good sweet mother lett me In". She arose at once to open
the door, and although she could see no one, the voice continued, "good
mother give me some drincke", to which she answered that "she had noe
drincke but water". She closed the door, returned to her bed, but the
voice started again, closer to the bedside this time: "mother mother Give
me yo[u]r soule & I will save the life of yo[u]r 4[th] Child w[hi]ch is now
livinge w[i]th yow". Moore immediately agreed, sealed the covenant and
then suckled her two spirits, Annis and Margaret, which she sent to
Witchford to kill Thomas Nix, three of Thomas Maynes' bullocks and
John Foster's cow. She ended by saying that she had perfomed many other
acts of witchcraft, and that she was very sorry for all she had done.[40]

If Hopkins' and Stearne's motivations (and those of their clients) seem
obscure, knowledge of their methods is perhaps more enlightening for
explaining Moore's confession. Illegal torture, such as sleep deprivation
followed by leading questioning (a favourite method of Hopkins and
Stearne), cannot be ruled out in the case of Moore and the other Sutton
witches.[41] One contemporary described these methods:

> Having Taken the suspected Witch, shee is placed in the middle of a
> room upon a stool, or Table, crosse legg'd, or in some other uneasie
> posture, to which if she submits not, she is bound with cords, there
> is she watcht & kept without meat or sleep for the space of 24
> hours.[42]

Hopkins denied that this was a means of extracting confessions (adding that forced confessions were worthless for establishing guilt), and argued that "they being kept awake would be more the active to cal their Imps in open view the sooner to their helpe".[43] But Hopkins and Stearne contrived to justify this practice, in modern times extremes of fatigue have proved to be a highly effective means of extracting the most outlandish confessions from detainees without recourse to physical force.[44]

Conspiracy and malice against individuals cannot be ruled out as motivations for the accusations, especially when one considers that Moore's case was not isolated. On the same day that Moore was examined and committed, two other accused witches from Sutton, John Bonham and William Watson (Bonham's wife having been taken into custody five days earlier), also confessed and were sent to Ely for trial.[45] It is perhaps significant that the depositions for the three Sutton witches taken on this day consisted solely of the accused's confession and Wyne's brief and unsubstantiated information. The Bonhams were certainly unpopular in Sutton, and were prosecuted (unsuccessfully) at least twice for the suspected murder of their son – in 1636 and 1662; witchcraft was not mentioned in either prosecution.[46] Watson's and Bonham's confessions were relatively simple in content, and did not specify what the suspects had to gain from their diabolical pact. Both confessed that the Devil appeared to them as a large mouse and a mole respectively, and both fed their familiar on blood pricked from a finger, before it set off to inflict damage on local livestock. But the case of Margaret Moore is different. Accusations made against her may well have been malicious, but, as with the other cases, this is very difficult to demonstrate. Of greater interest than the sincerity of the accusers, is the style and content of Moore's confession, because it concerns imagined power, and therefore has implications for the way in which an ordinary person might view his or her place in the world.[47]

## III

Even if Margaret Moore was the victim of torture, there are grounds for thinking that her story was not concocted by her tormentors, but constructed in her own mind from desire, emotion, experience and belief. Neither did the story necessarily originate at the time of her examination: long before that she could have believed that she had actually seen the spirits and given her soul to the Devil, thereby making her testimony a faithful account of an experience which, when challenged by her neighbours, she confessed out of a sense of remorse. In Continental trials, it was common for the suspect's adherence to a confession to last only as long as the torture under which it was extracted.[48] Moore, however, confessed three times before different audiences: to Wyne and Jetherell; to Castell; and to an assize court, suggesting the possibility of genuine belief in her own guilt. It is possible that accumulated vocalized suspicions, rumours and accusations of witchcraft suggested to her that she actually possessed the powers attributed to her by others. In criminological terms, "primary deviation" might have been succeeded by "secondary deviation" occurring when a suspect begins to accept his or her own allotted rôle as a social deviant.[49] In this circular fashion, Moore could have assumed the mantle of witch laid out for her by neighbours suspicious of her conversation and behaviour.

Regardless of the influence exerted by her neighbours, delusions of the kind described by her would have have been understandable considering the loss of three children and her natural concern for the life of the last surviving child.[50] A modern study of hallucinations experienced by the bereaved revealed that almost half the subjects studied experienced visions of the dead, while their mental state remained otherwise normal. Moreover, it is apparently common for such persons to believe in the objective reality of what they have witnessed, and to feel comforted by the experience.[51] Illusion and delusion deserve to be seen in the context of contemporary beliefs, since apparitions and fantasies, such as those experienced by Moore, were formed in an area between universal human anxieties and aspirations on the one hand, and specific cultural traits on the other.[52] Even if her experience can be attributed to psychological behaviour recurrent over the centuries, it remains an important event historically because of the specific form of the vision, and the manner in which she interpreted and described it.[53]

The same recommendation would apply if Moore's vision was, in fact, a dream. It was common in this period for the sources of dreams to be identified as carnal, divine or diabolic, and for their content to be interpreted in one of three ways: as an excursion of the soul into the spirit world; as a symbol; or as an apparition – a real encounter with a spirit.[55] Social anthropology provides an interesting parallel here: in his famous study of modern African witchcraft, Evans-Pritchard offered the following insight:

> It must be remembered that a bad dream is not a symbol of witchcraft but an actual experience of it. In waking life a man knows that he has been bewitched only by experiencing a subsequent misfortune or by oracular revelation, but in dreams he actually sees witches

and may even converse with them. We may say that Azande see witchcraft in a dream rather than that they dream of witchcraft.[56]

Many sixteenth- and seventeenth-century sources include references to persons who suffered nightmares attributed to the malign practices of witches.[57] But, as Moore's case might suggest, dreams of witchcraft could also invade the sleep of the witch, and therefore a functionalist assessment (such as that of Evans-Pritchard) could be extended to allow for a greater consensus of belief between accuser and accused. Some studies of early modern witchcraft have even described opponents playing out conflicts at the dream level, with both witch and victim dreaming their respective rôles.[58]

Boundaries separating the physical and the metaphysical, the natural and the supernatural, were drawn differently in the seventeenth-century mind,[59] and it has been argued that because the material world limits the possibilities open to the individual (in a way that the dream world does not), it is understandable that our ancestors were slow to dismiss the dream experience as an illusion. As one student of the subject has expressed it: "if the waking world has certain advantages of solidity and continuity, its social opportunities are terribly restricted".[60] If Moore's communion with the spirits of her children was indeed a dream – and it is no accident that this and similar visitations in other depositions occurred at night in the bed chamber – then considering her desperate condition, it may well have been an event of fundamental importance in her life, a perceived chance to enter an overlapping sphere between the worlds of life and death to alter the course of her fate.[61]

Seen in the context of prescientific mentalities in general, and her viewpoint in particular, Moore's witchcraft becomes just another form of power: defensive and offensive magic employed by a woman with limited command of the resources of the natural world for the benefit of her family. The power to inflict *maleficium* might even be seen as a skill towards which some men and women actually aspired.[62] Whatever misfortunes the farmers of Witchford might have seen fit to explain by witchcraft, arguably Moore was fighting her own battle with adversity, and her words can be interpreted as reflecting her desire to conquer it. Although in many ways it is true that this explanation simply takes refuge in traditional functionalism, it does at least return a greater measure of human agency to the equation, and the individual actions that constitute a witchcraft accusation can be seen to have been determined by personal belief and choice, rather than generalized patterns of behaviour shaped by impersonal forces. In other words, Moore could have been accused of witchcraft not simply because she looked and behaved according to a popular stereotype (the classic anthropological reduction), but because, for her own reasons, she herself believed that she was a witch.

There are obvious parallels between her case and the Faust myth: a transaction with the Devil in which the soul could be exchanged for material gain. This familiar fictional paradigm pervaded high literature, cheap print and folklore throughout medieval and early modern England,[63] but is less commonly encountered in real English witchcraft trials.[64] Faustian temptation played a part in the Lancashire trials of 1634, during which one suspect confessed that she was "in greate passion & anger & discontented & w[i]thall oppressed w[i]th some want", and the Devil appeared and offered her all she needed in return for her soul.[65] Overall though, the East Anglian examinations of the mid-1640s are unusual for the explicit presence of the Devil, and his offers of assistance to the poor, financial and otherwise.[66] Adam Sabie, for example, one of the suspects from Haddenham, confessed that a spirit had visited him in the form of a child and had comforted him with the words: "ffeare not Sabie for I am thy God" and then told him to go to Lady Sandys' house where he would be given £20 – a substantial sum to a poor fenman.[67] This pattern appears in the examination of suspects in other counties. In the Suffolk trials of 1645, one man was offered a deal by the Devil "he beinge at plowgh curseinge &c"; another was promised an annual income of £14 in return for his soul.[68]

These confessions, forced or voluntary, took the form that they did because it was (and remains) common for poor or otherwise oppressed people to fantasize about the reversal of their predicament – Margaret Moore's specific fantasy, as we have seen, concerned resisting the domination of death and poverty.[69] As one anthropologist has written: "Witchcraft is in many respects the classical resort of vulnerable subordinate groups who have little or no safe, open opportunity to challenge a form of domination that angers them".[70] In Moore's case though, as in many cases from the 1640s, the deployment of witchcraft by the poor and vulnerable person to resist domination serves constructive, personal ends at the expense of harm caused to others, not just causing harm for purposes of revenge. It is especially noticeable in Moore's confession (and in others similar to hers) that the story turns from a description of personal powerlessness to a situation where the witch is issuing commands, at the precise moment the diabolical compact is sealed. Furthermore, it must be significant that one of

Moore's familiar spirits shares her name, suggesting a more powerful alter ego, a supernatural version of herself, able to perform her will on earth in a way that she could not otherwise manage (the familiar of one of the other Sutton witches, John Bonham was named John).[71] In context, surrendering her soul for the sake of her child can be equated with a metaphysical extension of the principle of laying down life for love, and therefore represents an extension of power, whereby the soul is reified in an imaginary sphere as something with which she is able to bargain.

★ ★ ★

This study has not sought to explain the events which occurred at Sutton in 1647, still less to establish a new model of witchcraft prosecutions in early modern England as a whole. Rather, it has offered one interpretation among the many required to accommodate the wide variety of circumstances behind individual accusations – variety that more schematic interpretations can overlook. To this extent, neither argument nor example are intended to be in any way typical. On the other hand, an attempt has been made to readdress the more general problem of the functional value of witchcraft, by looking at a case where both accuser and accused offer their views on, first, the potency of magic and, secondly, the occasions on which such magic might have been used. Each of these areas of thought has an important implication for the long-term history of mentalities as a whole, and of witchcraft specifically. In the first place, participants in this drama demonstrate explicitly that they inhabit the same mental universe, a universe in which the boundary between the realms of the natural and supernatural was yet to be fixed. Secondly, it is possible to see that witchcraft accusations might be explained in terms of developing social and economic competition, without tying the dynamic to any particular aspect of this change. Together, these conclusions suggest that, until such time as developments in religious and scientific attitudes "disenchanted" the world, and mounting pressure of population against resources was relieved by more favourable economic conditions, overlap between the material and invisible worlds would continue to offer not only a means of explaining misfortune – as for Margaret Moore's accusers – but also a potential source of power with which the weak might seek to free themselves from the constraints of daily life and take control of their destinies.

314

## Notes

1. There is no satisfactory account of this unique event. R. Deacon, *Matthew Hopkins: witch finder general* (London, 1976) has many failings, including an unawareness of the existence of the Ely records upon which this essay is based. M. Summers, *The discovery of witches. A study of Master Matthew Hopkins* (London, 1928), also skims over the Ely trials.

2. K. Thomas, *Religion and the decline of magic* (London, 1971; 1988 edn); A. Macfarlane, *Witchcraft in Tudor and Stuart England. A regional and comparative study* (London, 1970).

3. C. B. Herrup, *The common peace. Participation and the criminal law in seventeenth-century England* (Cambridge, 1987), p. 33.

4. J. A. Sharpe, Witchcraft and women in seventeenth-century England: some northern evidence, *Continuity and Change*, 6, 1991, pp. 179–99. For a continental parallel, see L. Roper, Witchcraft and fantasy in early modern Germany, *History Workshop Journal*, 32, 1991, pp. 19–43.

5. A. Gregory, Witchcraft, politics and "good neighbourhood" in early seventeenth-century Rye, *Past & Present*, **133**, 1991, pp. 31–66; M. Gaskill, Witchcraft in Tudor and Stuart Kent: stereotypes and the background to accusations, in *Witchcraft in early modern Europe: studies in culture and belief*, eds J. Barry, *et al.* (Cambridge, 1995).

6. For examples of witchcraft accusations connected to disputes over borders and land ownership in Yorkshire (1615), Sussex (1617), and Kent (1617), see J. A. Sharpe, *Witchcraft in seventeenth-century Yorkshire: accusations and counter measures*, Borthwick Papers, 81 (York, 1992), p. 9; Herrup, *Common peace*, p. 32; Kent RO, NR/JQ p1/30.

7. B. Ankarloo, Sweden: the mass burnings (1668–1676), in *Early modern European witchcraft. centres and peripheries*, eds B. Ankarloo & G. Henningsen (Oxford, 1990), pp. 310–12; G. R. Quaife, *Godly zeal and furious rage. The witch in early modern Europe* (London, 1987), p. 90; J. Favret-Saada, *Deadly words: witchcraft in the Bocage* (Cambridge, 1990), pp. 32, 104 and *passim*; D. Sabean, *Power in the blood. Popular culture and village discourse in early modern Germany* (Cambridge, 1984), pp. 56–8, 211; C. F. Karlsen, *The devil in the shape of a woman: witchcraft in colonial New England* (New York, 1987).

8. M. Murray, *The witch cult in western Europe* (Oxford, 1921).

9. Witch-hunts have even been portrayed as planned campaigns waged by a ruling class determined to enforce conformity. For a recent extreme recitation of this thesis, see J. Oplinger, *The politics of demonology. The European witchcraze and the mass production of deviance* (London & Toronto, 1990).

10. It should be remembered that, at the time of its publication, Murray's thesis was a refreshing antidote to the nineteenth-century "rationalist" view which utterly disregarded the belief aspect, preferring to see magic as nothing more than a symbol of ignorance and delusion. Cf. Thomas, *Religion and the decline of*

*magic*, p. 615.

11. E.g., H. Geertz, An anthropology of religion and magic, I, *Journal of Interdisciplinary History*, VI, 1975, pp. 71–89, esp. 72–7, quotation p. 84; T. G. Ashplant & A. Wilson, Present-centred history and the problem of historical knowledge, *Historical Journal*, 31, 1988, pp. 257–60; C. Ginzburg, *Ecstasies. Deciphering the witches' sabbath* (London, 1990), pp. 3–6; C. Ginzburg, *The night battles. Witchcraft and agrarian cults in the sixteenth and seventeenth centuries* (Baltimore, 1983), see p. xiii for a partial resurrection of Murray. E. Le Roy Ladurie distinguishes between two historiographical models: the "archaic"' model of belief from below, and the "modern" model of witchcraft as a criminal practice defined by the state. Between the two, he argues, "an impoverishment is observable". *Jasmin's witch* (London, 1987), pp. 18–19.

12. Ashplant & Wilson, Present-centred history, pp. 253–74, quotation p. 260. See also E. P. Thompson, Anthropology and the discipline of historical context, *Midland History*, I (1972), pp. 41–55.

13. R. Darnton, *The great cat massacre and other episodes in French cultural history* (London, 1984), p. 13.

14. Useful on this this point are: L. Lévy-Bruhl, *The notebooks on primitive mentality* (London, 1975), p. 43; M. Foucault, *The order of things. An archaeology of the human sciences* (London, 1970), e.g., p. xv. On the other hand, past mentalities should not be artificially "defamiliarized". E. Muir, Introduction: observing trifles, in *Microhistory and the lost peoples of Europe*, eds E. Muir & G. Ruggiero (Baltimore, 1991), p. xiii.

15. Roper, Witchcraft and fantasy, pp. 21–2.

16. Some accounts are misleading on the question of the relationship between educated and popular witchcraft beliefs, for example, G. Scarre, *Witchcraft and magic in sixteenth- and seventeenth-century Europe*, (London, 1987), p. 48. The relationship is much more profitably explored in more dynamic terms, that is, beliefs demonstrated through actions. C. Holmes, Popular culture? Witches, magistrates and divines in early modern England, in *Understanding popular culture. Europe from the middle ages to the nineteenth century*, ed. S. L. Kaplan (Berlin, 1984), pp. 85–111. See also S. Clark, Protestant demonology: sin, superstition, and society (c. 1520–c. 1630), in Ankarloo & Henningsen (1990), p. 62.

17. See C. Larner, *Enemies of God: the witch-hunt in Scotland* (London, 1981); S. Clark, Inversion, misrule and and the meaning of witchcraft, *Past & Present*, 87 (1980), pp. 98–127.

18. Sharpe, *Witchcraft in seventeenth-century Yorkshire*, p. 8.

19. L. Stone, *The family, sex and marriage in England 1500–1800* (London, 1977), pp. 95, 98; Sabean, *Power in the blood*, pp. 31–2, 53–4; Gaskill, Witchcraft in Tudor and Stuart Kent, in J. Barry *et al.*, forthcoming.

20. See for example, C. Z. Wiener, Sex roles and crime in late Elizabethan Hertfordshire, *Journal of Social History*, 8, 1975, pp. 46–9; D. E. Underdown, The taming of the scold: the enforcement of patriarchal authority in early modern

England, in *Order and disorder in early modern England*, eds A. Fletcher & J. Stevenson (Cambridge, 1985), pp. 116–36; J. A. Sharpe, *Defamation and sexual slander in early modern England: the church courts at York*, Borthwick Papers, 58 (York, 1980).

21. N. Z. Davis, *Fiction in the archives. Pardon tales and their tellers in sixteenth-century France* (Stanford, 1987).

22. The following profile, and subsequent discussion, is based on a deposition to be found in the assize files of the Ely Diocesan Records, E12 1647/14, in the Cambridge University Library [Camb UL]. An imperfect transcript is to be found in *East Anglian notes and queries*, XIII (1909), pp. 277–8.

23. *Victoria County History, Cambridgeshire* [*VCH*], IV, p. 159. An approximate esti-mate of the size of the parish in the first half of the seventeenth century can be made from a church seating plan, made in 1614 after a pew-dispute, which names 329 inhabitants: Camb UL, EDR, B/2/35, ff. 207–10v.

24. In 1673 a Robert Moore of Sutton made a will, in which he was styled "yeo-man" and bequeathed several acres of copyhold land. There was, however, more than one man of this name in Sutton. See Cambs RO, Ely Consistory Wills, C32, ff. 219v.–20; P148/1/2 (21/4/1639, 22/1/1643).

25. The parish register of Sutton indicates that on 10 May 1641, Robert Moore married Margaret Holland. This name cannot be found elsewhere in the Sutton register, but there was a Holland family in nearby Stretham, to whom a daughter, Margaret, was born 17 July 1586. This is probably too early to be Moore, but it is interesting that the the verso of the 1647 deposition gives her parish as Stretham rather than Sutton. Cambs RO, P148/1/2 (Sutton, 1621–54); Transcript of Stretham parish register, p. 10. Camb UL, EDR, E12 1647/12.

26. J. Stearne, *A confirmation and discovery of witchcraft* (London, 1648), p. 21.

27. Cambs RO, Ely Consistory Court Wills, Thomas Nyx, (19 Feb. 1636/7). A suspect examined soon after Moore, Adam Sabie of Haddenham, specified that he was last visited by a spirit in 1636. Camb UL, EDR, E12 1647/17v. Also in 1636 a Sutton couple, later charged with witchcraft, were accused for the first time of the murder of their son (see p. 135). If events did take place then, it would mean that Moore's children came from an earlier marriage, given that she married Robert Moore in 1641.

28. According to one source, the trial took place at Ely on Wednesday 22 Septem-ber 1647, where 17 cases were heard, 13 of which concerned witchcraft (eight women, five men). See *East Anglian notes and queries*, p. 277.

29. Stearne, *Confirmation and discovery of witchcraft*, p. 22.

30. There is no evidence that Stearne personally supervised any part of Moore's examination, but other depositions indicate that he was nearby at the time. Hopkins himself probably oversaw the Ely campaign from outside the county after the spring of 1646. Deacon, *Matthew Hopkins*, pp. 173–4; Summers, *Discovery of witches*, p. 45.

31. Robert Ellis of Stretham (30 May 1647), and Adam Sabie of Haddenham (1 June 1647). Camb UL, EDR, E12 1647/17-18.

32. Castell was assisted in the committals of 26 May by John Towers JP, who also lived at Haddenham.

33. A gaol calendar from September 1647 survives. In order of committal, the nine suspects were: Bridget Bonham, John Bonham, William Watson, Margaret Moore, Robert Ellis, Thomasine Reade, Elizabeth Foote, Adam Sabie and Joan Salter. (Between July and September another three suspected witches from Ely and Wisbech were committed), Camb UL, EDR, E12 1647/23. The other two Witchford suspects for whom depositions survive, but no entry in the gaol calendar, were Dorothy Ellis of Stretham and Joan Briggs of Haddenham, EDR, E12 1647/10, 15.

34. Camb UL, EDR, E12 1647/23.

35. The practice of witch-hunting in England, from above as it were, was rare, and here was probably only facilitated by the Civil War. The clergyman, John Gaule, who criticized Hopkins, wrote that witch-hunting was "a trade never taken up in England till this". However, Hopkins claimed that he never entered a village unless it was by invitation, and indeed, Gaule lamented that the people of the countryside admired "the infallible and wonderfull power of the Witchfinders". Macfarlane argues that, since they did not always appear as witnesses, witchfinding depended on widespread support, but Deacon denies that "persons other than Hopkins in any way encouraged or influenced this campaign against witches". J. Gaule, *Select cases of conscience touching witches and witchcrafts* (London, 1646), pp. 6, 93; M. Hopkins, *The discovery of witches* (London, 1647), p. 10; Thomas *Religion and the decline of magic*, pp. 544–5; Macfarlane, *Witchcraft*, ch. 9, esp. pp. 137–8, 140–41; Deacon, *Matthew Hopkins*, p. 87.

36. *VCH*, IV, pp. 159, 161; H. C. Darby, *The draining of the fens*, (Cambridge, second edn 1956), pp. 49–64; K. Lindley, *Fenland riots and the English revolution* (London, 1982), pp. 40, 60, 64, 142–3; C. Holmes, Drainers and fenmen: the problem of popular political consciousness in the seventeenth century, in Fletcher & Stevenson (1985), p. 194; Camb UL, Palmer Papers, B/70 (transcript of Chancery proceedings, 1622–3); House of Lords RO, Main Papers [1649]. Petition of divers poor inhabitants of the parish of Sutton. For a summary of the 1649 petition, see Historical Manuscripts Commission, *Seventh Report, Part 1* (London, 1879), p. 75.

37. Lindley, *Fenland riots and the English revolution*, p. 142 and *passim*.

38. However, the evidence for this which does exist is tantalizing, see Deacon, *Matthew Hopkins*, pp. 14–15, 106–8, 164–5, 180–91, 196–7. Religion may also have been significant. Sutton was noted for its nonconformity and clerical absenteeism, and contained several Quaker households. *VCH*, IV, p. 159. For evidence of clerical shortcomings at Sutton in 1638, see also W. M. Palmer, *Episcopal visitation returns for Cambridgeshire . . . 1638–1665* (Cambridge,

1930), pp. 53–4. It is noteworthy that in one month in 1633 no less than 26 presentations for falling asleep during divine service were made. M. Cross, *The church and local society in the diocese of Ely, c. 1630–c. 1730*, PhD thesis, University of Cambridge, 1991, p. 63.

39. Camb UL, EDR, E12 1647/14. None of the three children were found in the parish register under the name of Moore, suggesting either Civil War under-registration, that they died before they could be christened or that they were christened elsewhere.

40. Camb UL, EDR, E12 1647/14v.

41. On confessions extracted by Hopkins and others, see Thomas, *Religion and the decline of magic*, pp. 617–20. Macfarlane asserts that one should not discount the effectiveness of "indirect pressures" for eliciting confession: subtle persuasion, intimidation, threats and promises, directed at the suspect by neighbours, clergy and magistrates. Macfarlane, *Witchcraft*, p. 20.

42. Gaule, *Select cases of conscience*, p. 78.

43. Hopkins, *Discovery of witches*, pp. 5, 7.

44. See, for example, A. Koestler, *Darkness at noon* (London, 1940).

45. Both Bonham and Watson appeared among the list of poor petitioners in the 1620s, cf. Camb UL, Palmer Papers, B/70.

46. Camb UL, EDR, E9/1/20 (1636); E45 Quarter Sessions Files, 1662 (unnumbered); E42 Fragments (unnumbered). Evidently, the Bonhams were acquitted of witchcraft in 1647.

47. Roper makes the point that, in spite of the stereotyped form of confessions, witches added their own personal inflections, and constructed their own narratives; Witchcraft and fantasy, pp. 24–6. For a historian who is more pessimistic – where judicial sources are concerned – of the ability to "unsnarl ordinary beliefs from the manipulative processes in which they were embedded", see R. C. Sawyer, "Strangely Handled In All Her Lyms": witchcraft and healing in Jacobean England, *Journal of Social History*, 22 (1989), pp. 462–3.

48. B. P. Levack, *The witch-hunt in early modern Europe* (London, 1987), pp. 13, 16.

49. E. Lemert, *Human deviance. Social problems and social control* (New Jersey, 1972), ch. 3. See also R. Muchembled, *Les derniers bûchers* (Paris, 1981), cited by Ladurie, who writes of the confessional witch: "At first, she is unaware of the character attributed to her. She does not notice that she is maleficent. Then, gradually, she yields to this circumstance". *Jasmin's witch*, p. 18.

50. The emotionally charged issue of the lives of children could provide the key to other accusations in 1647; one of the Haddenham witches confessed that although she agreed to signing a pact with the Devil, she refused to surrender the life of her child. Camb UL, EDR, E12 1647/11v. (T. Read, Haddenham, 29 May 1647). In the early seventeenth century a high proportion of the cases of "disturbing grief" encountered by the physician Richard Napier were bereaved mothers; see M. MacDonald, *Mystical bedlam. Madness, anxiety, and healing in seventeenth-century England* (Cambridge, 1981), p. 82.

51. W. D. Rees, The hallucinations of widowhood, *British Medical Journal*, 4, 1971, pp. 37–41; E. Parish, *Hallucinations and illusions. A study of the fallacies of perception* (London, 1897), p. 36; W. F. Matchett, Repeated hallucinatory experiences as a part of the mourning process among Hopi Indian women, *Psychiatry*, 35, 1971, pp. 185–94. See also J. Wertheimer, Some hypotheses about the genesis of visual hallucinations in dementia, in *Delusions and hallucinations in old age*, eds C. Katona & R. Levy (London, 1992), pp. 201–208, esp. p. 207, where it is stated that visions of the bereaved manifest "the hallucinatory realization of the desire to rediscover the departed, and fantasized ambiguity of the absent presence".

52. E. R. Dodds, *The Greeks and the irrational* (Berkeley, 1951), pp. 103–4, 116–17.

53. On the difficulty of separating universal and specific components of mentalities, see G. E. R. Lloyd, *Demystifying mentalities* (Cambridge, 1990), pp. 135–6.

54. For a seventeenth-century ballad where, in different circumstances, starving children calling for food and drink haunt the dreams of the woman responsible for their death, see *The midwife's maid's lamentation, in Newgate* (London, 1693), in *The Pepys ballads*, 8 vols, ed. H. E. Rollins (Cambridge, MA, 1929–32), VII, pp. 14–16.

55. Thomas, *Religion and the decline of magic*, pp. 151–3, 176, 286, 768–9; A. Macfarlane, *The family life of Ralph Josselin, a seventeenth-century clergyman* (Cambridge, 1970), p. 183n; H. J. Rose, *Primitive culture in Greece* (London, 1925), pp. 151–2. The ancient Greeks did not speak of "having" dreams, but of "seeing" them. Dodds, *Greeks and the irrational*, p. 105. Visions in early modern England were also described as waking dreams: in the 1680s Francis North explained the confessions by witches in these terms. R. North, *The lives of the Norths*, ed. A. Jessopp, 3 vols (London, 1890), III, p. 152. On the symbolic meaning of dreams, see Macfarlane, *Family life of Ralph Josselin*, ch. 12; P. Burke, L'histoire sociale des rêves, *Annales Economies, Societés, Civilisations*, 2 (1973), pp. 329–42.

56. E. E. Evans-Pritchard, *Witchcraft, oracles and magic among the Azande*, abridged edn (Oxford, 1976), p. 230.

57. For some sixteenth-century examples of this, see C. L'Estrange Ewen, *Witchcraft and demonianism* (London, 1933), pp. 70, 75–6.

58. Ginzburg, *Night battles*; Ladurie, *Jasmin's witch*, pp. 50, 60. See also G. Henningsen, *The witches' advocate: Basque witchcraft and the Spanish Inquisition (1609–1619)* (Nevada, 1980), which describes the dream aspect of sorcery and counter-sorcery in the Basque country in the early seventeenth century. On witchcraft fantasies, dreams and confessions, see Levack, *Witch-hunt*, pp. 16–18.

59. Macfarlane writes of "reciprocity": associations of thought and event which "worked across the artificial boundaries demarcating the social, physical and spiritual worlds". *Family life of Ralph Josselin*, p. 195.

60. Dodds, *Greeks and the irrational*, p. 102.

61. D. H. Lawrence once wrote:"When anything threatens us from the world of death, then a dream may become so vivid that it arouses the actual soul. And when a dream is so intense that it arouses the soul – then we must attend to it". *Fantasia of the unconscious* (London, 1923; Penguin edn, 1971), p. 165.

62. In 1632 an Essex woman was presented before the archdeacon's court for wishing herself to be a witch so as to be revenged on a neighbour with whom she had previously fought in the street. Macfarlane, *Witchcraft*, p. 286.

63. For a seventeenth-century broadside ballad which describes the power fantasy of a poor man and his subsequent temptation by the Devil, see *The Roxburghe Ballads*, 8 vols eds W. Chappell & J. W. Ebsworth (London & Hertford, 1871–95), II, pp. 222–8. See also *A true relation of the most inhumane and bloody murther* (London, 1609). In 1655 Essex clergyman Ralph Josselin noted that an acquaintance had claimed to have signed a diabolical pact to satisfy his craving for money. A. Macfarlane (ed.), *The diary of Ralph Josselin 1661–1683* (Oxford, 1976), p. 347. A similar tale was related by Lawrence Southerne in *Fearefull newes from Coventry, or, a true relation and lamentable story of one Thomas Holt . . . who through covetousnesse and immoderate love of money, sold himselfe to the devill* (London, 1642).

64. On this theme generally, see Thomas, *Religion and the decline of magic*, pp. 564–5. In one late sixteenth-century trial, a witch was reputed to have refused to renounce her allegience to the Devil, because he had served her well for the past 30 years. H. More, *An antidote against atheisme* (London, 1653), p. 111.

65. BL, Add. MS 36,674, f. 196.

66. For a fuller discussion of the place of the Devil in these trials, see J. A. Sharpe, The devil in East Anglia: the Matthew Hopkins trials reconsidered, in J. Barry *et al.*

67. Camb UL, EDR, E12 1647/17v.

68. BL, Add. MS 27,402, ff. 108v., 120. For other examples and a discussion of poverty as a motivation for witchcraft, see Thomas, *Religion and the decline of magic*, pp. 620–24.

69. The 1649 petition suggests that this was a time of high mortality, unemployment, and poverty in Sutton, and called for redress for its inhabitants "soe they may not all perish by famine in time of plentie as many allreddie doe". House of Lords RO, Main Papers [1649]. Petition of divers poor inhabitants of . . . Sutton.

70. J. C. Scott, *Domination and the arts of resistance. Hidden transcripts* (Yale, 1990), pp. 36–44.

71. In the 1660s a poor Lancashire woman confessed to having been a witch since her mother died 30 years earlier. The mother had nothing to bequeath, and so left her daughters a pair of familiars. T. Heywood (ed.), *The Moore Rental*, Chetham Society, Old Series, II (1847), pp. 59–60.

# 9. The devil in East Anglia: the Matthew Hopkins trials reconsidered

## JIM SHARPE

The East Anglian witchcraft trials of 1645–7 constitute one of the most remarkable episodes in the history of the European witchcraze. Despite the survival of a large body of relevant source material,[1] there are sufficient gaps in the records to make it unlikely that the full story of what happened during this outbreak of witch hunting will ever be completely reconstructed. Let us remind ourselves, however, of the main outlines. Over the winter of 1644–5 Matthew Hopkins, an obscure petty gentleman living at Manningtree in north-east Essex, became worried about witches in his neighbourhood. His worries bore fruit in the

[1] There is an extensive body of material, both manuscript and printed, relating to the East Anglian trials of 1645–7. The most important manuscript sources are: indictments and gaol delivery roll relating to prosecution of witches at the Essex assizes, Summer 1645, PRO ASSI 35/86/1/7–13, 19, 32–3, 41–3, 46, 51–6, 58–64, 66–73, 78–80, 82–91, 98; a large body of what appear to be notes taken from depositions relating to the investigation of witchcraft in 1645 in Suffolk, written in a mid-seventeenth-century hand, British Library Additional MSS 27402 ff. 104–21; and sets of depositions relating to the examination of seventeen witches held in the Isle of Ely's gaol delivery records, Michaelmas 1647, Cambridge University Library, EDR E.12. Printed sources include: *A True and Exact Relation of the severall Informations, Examinations, and Confessions of the late Witches arraigned . . . and condemned at the late Sessions holden at Chelmsford before the Right Honorable Robert, Earle of Warwicke, and severall of his Majesties Justices of the Peace, the 29 of July, 1645* (London, 1645); *A True Relation of the Arraignment of eighteene Witches at St. Edmondsbury, 27th August 1645* (London, 1645); John Davenport, *The Witches of Huntingdon, their Examinations and Confessions* (London, 1646). Both of the main protagonists in the trials put their thoughts on their activities into print: Matthew Hopkins, *The Discovery of Witches* (London, 1647); John Stearne, *A Confirmation and Discovery of Witchcraft* (London, 1648). The 1645–7 trials have not been the subject of a full-scale scholarly study, although references to many of the relevant sources can be found in Richard Deacon, *Matthew Hopkins: Witch Finder General* (London, 1976), while Essex's contribution is discussed in Alan Macfarlane, 'The witch-finding movement of 1645 in Essex', in Macfarlane, *Witchcraft in Tudor and Stuart England: a Regional and Comparative Study* (London, 1970), ch. 9.

prosecution of thirty-six witches, of whom perhaps nineteen were executed, at the summer 1645 assizes in Essex. Accusations spread rapidly over the Suffolk border, and we know of 117 witches who were examined or tried in that county. A stray reference[2] suggests that another forty were tried at the Norfolk assizes, while it seems that a further six were tried (and five subsequently executed) at the Great Yarmouth borough sessions.[3] Further trials (we have no way of calculating their total, although they were probably not numerous) occurred in Cambridgeshire, Huntingdonshire, Bedfordshire and Northamptonshire during 1645–6, while a body of depositions in the records of the Isle of Ely assizes reveals that a further seventeen suspected witches were examined there in 1646–7. Altogether we have references to some 240 alleged witches who came before the authorities during this episode, over 200 of them between July and December 1645.

In terms of statistics, then, these trials represent a major witch panic, comparable with those experienced in a number of continental outbreaks. Indeed, there were few continental crazes which witnessed the prosecution (frequently followed by execution) of 200 witches over a six-month period. Yet these East Anglian trials have been regarded also as remarkable for a number of other reasons. With the presence of Matthew Hopkins, and his associate John Stearne, we have, unusually for England, if not 'professional' witch hunters, certainly two men who were interested in hunting witches, and who were to come to claim expertise in this activity.[4] Also, in the sleep deprivation and other forms of pressure used in the interrogation of suspects, there was something approximating to the torture and inquisitorial procedures so familiar in European trials. And lastly, many of those accused were suspected not merely of *maleficium*, doing harm through witchcraft, but also of keeping and consorting with evil spirits. What we can reconstruct of

---

[2] *Signs and Wonders from Heaven. With a true Relation of a Monster borne in Ratcliffe Highway* (London, 1645), p. 4.

[3] J. G. Nall, *Great Yarmouth and Lowestoft* (London, 1867), p. 92 n. 2. Wallace Notestein, *A History of Witchcraft in England from 1558 to 1718* (1911: reprinted New York, 1965), p. 181 n. 50, regards this total as more reliable than the figure of sixteen which has frequently been cited.

[4] It is this emphasis on Hopkins' role in 1645–7 which has allowed me to use the term 'the Matthew Hopkins trials' as a convenient shorthand to describe the East Anglian trials of those years. This is not to deny that Hopkins was frequently operating with the active cooperation of local people who evidently held suspicions of witchcraft against their neighbours. For some observations on this point see Macfarlane, *Witchcraft*, pp. 137–8.

pre-trial depositions demonstrates that many of those who were examined confessed to keeping familiars, allowing to suck their blood, making pacts with the devil and (less frequently) having sexual intercourse with him.

It is this last issue which creates the greatest problems. The Matthew Hopkins trials offer a challenge to the standard interpretation of English witchcraft. English witch beliefs, let us remind ourselves, according to this interpretation, were not meant to be much concerned with the devil or his works, and witches were rarely thought to make pacts with the devil, and almost never to have sexual intercourse with him. What witches were meant to do usually was to inflict harm on their neighbours or their goods. Suspicion that they had done so, as Macfarlane demonstrated more than twenty years ago, normally followed neighbourly tensions or arguments which made English witchcraft accusations explicable more readily in terms of twentieth-century social anthropology than early modern demonology. The confessions and indictments of 1645–7 sit uncomfortably with such views, and, understandably, historians of English witchcraft have tended firstly to stress the peculiarities of these trials, and secondly to attribute those peculiarities to the presence of Hopkins. In 1933 Ewen suggested that the demonic aspects of the Essex and Suffolk trials were connected with 'Master Hopkins' reading of some continental authority'.[5] Later researchers have reached much the same conclusion. Macfarlane, for example, likewise attributed the peculiarities of the 1645 Essex trials to 'the influence of continental ideas, perhaps mediated through Matthew Hopkins'.[6] We are tempted, therefore, to write off the Hopkins trials as an aberration, in which 'continental ideas' temporarily sullied the English witch's normal image as 'a curiously tame and homely creature':[7] it is no accident that Keith Thomas should describe the Hopkins prosecutions as 'highly untypical'.[8]

While not wishing to get too deeply into what a 'typical' English witchcraft prosecution was like, and while accepting that the context of

---

[5] C. L. Ewen, *Witchcraft and Demonianism: a Concise Account derived from sworn Depositions and Confessions obtained in the Courts of England and Wales* (London, 1933), p. 52.

[6] Macfarlane, *Witchcraft*, p. 139.

[7] Alan Macfarlane, *The Culture of Capitalism* (Oxford, 1987), p. 110.

[8] Keith Thomas, 'The relevance of social anthropology to the historical study of English witchcraft', in Mary Douglas, ed., *Witchcraft Confessions and Accusations* (London, 1970), p. 50.

1645–7 was exceptional, it nevertheless seems to me that the Matthew Hopkins trials are too important to be written off as an aberration. Records relating to them do, after all, provide evidence of the largest single sample we have of English witches, and it would be unhelpful to dismiss their apparently unusual features as untypical and probably generated by Matthew Hopkins' alleged familiarity with continental witch beliefs. What I intend to do in this chapter is to examine the records of these trials, and analyse the alleged witches, what they were meant to have done, and what were the beliefs about them. The outcome of this exercise, it is to be hoped, will be not only to reassess the significance of the Hopkins trials, but also to demonstrate that they suggest that we need to make some modifications to the current orthodoxy about witchcraft in early modern England.

Any discussion of the typicality of the Hopkins trials ought to begin with a consideration of who the witches tried were, and what they were supposed to have done. Firstly, it is obvious that the traditional stereotype of the witch did not break down. During the Hopkins period, of 184 witches whose sex can be determined, 161, or 87.5 per cent, were women. This is a slightly lower female participation rate than that found by Macfarlane in his study of Essex witchcraft,[9] but hardly sufficiently so to suggest a breakdown in gender stereotypes about malefic witchcraft.

Similarly, although detailed research on this point has still to be undertaken, most of those accused seem to have come from the poorer elements of village and small-town society.[10] There were exceptions, but the trials under consideration here do not seem to have brought about that erosion of the social stereotype of the witch that occurred, for example, in some of the larger German persecutions.[11] Intriguingly, however, there were a few exceptions. A contemporary newsletter mentioned 'a

---

[9] Macfarlane, *Witchcraft*, p. 160, notes that only 23 of the 291 persons accused of witchcraft at the Essex assizes in the period of his study were men, making 92 per cent of this sample female.

[10] Records from the unusually well documented Suffolk parish of Framlingham, for example, which was the home of possibly as many as sixteen suspected witches in 1645, demonstrate that suspects were drawn from the local poor, while their accusers and witnesses against them were usually persons of at least some substance: Suffolk Record Office, FC 101/E2/26 (Framlingham Churchwardens' Accounts, 1642–6); FC 101/G7/1–2 (Framlingham Overseers of the Poor Accounts, 1640, 1645).

[11] H. C. Erik Midelfort, *Witch-Hunting in Southwestern Germany, 1562–1684: The Social and Intellectual Foundations* (Stanford, CA, 1972), pp. 137, 150.

parson's wife' named Weight among the early Essex accused, although no further reference has been found to her.[12] John Stearne noted 'one Henry Carre of Ratlesden, in Suffolke, who I have heard was a scholler fit for Cambridge (if not a Cambridge scholler) and was well educated' who died in gaol before trial.[13] Mother Lakeland, burned at Ipswich in 1645 for killing her husband by witchcraft, clearly had good social connections and had been thought of as a godly and respectable woman.[14] Perhaps the best documented of these socially exceptional witches was John Lowes, vicar of Brandeston in Suffolk. Although the tradition that Lowes had popish leanings is probably unfounded, it is clear that he was, as a later note in the Brandeston parish register put it, 'a contentious man', who had been prosecuted for barratry, and who had already aroused his flock's suspicion that he was a witch. Lowes had been instituted to his living in 1596, and was an octogenarian when he was swum in the castle ditch at Framlingham, subsequently being subjected to sleep deprivation for several nights and being run around the room in which he was kept until he was breathless.[15]

Lowes was also unusual in the type of harm he was meant to have caused. Some of the witnesses against him testified that he had inflicted the normal damage attributed to witches: the death of a child after an altercation with its father, or the killing of numerous cattle. Yet one witness, Daniel Rayner, also claimed that Lowes had confessed to using a familiar to do all the harm he could between Great Yarmouth and Winterton, while Hopkins testified that Lowes had admitted using a familiar to sink a ship off Landguard Fort, near Harwich. There are few other indications that the witches in our sample were thought to have inflicted unusual harm. Anne West was alleged to have sunk Thomas Turner's hoy and drowned him. Walter Maye claimed that Ann Dewsburowe fell out with his maidservant, and twice sank a boat that was carrying her. A Suffolk woman confessed that the devil told her to blast corn, while Thomasine Reade, one of the Isle of Ely accused, sent

[12] Notestein, *History of Witchcraft*, p. 174, citing *A Diary or an Exact Journal* (24–31 July 1645).

[13] Stearne, *Confirmation and Discovery*, p. 25.

[14] *The Lawes against Witches and Coniuration. And some brief Notes and Observations for the Discovery of Witches . . . Also the Confession of Mother Lakeland, who was arraigned and condemned for a Witch at Ipswich in Suffolke* (London, 1645), pp. 7–8.

[15] Relevant details are given in Deacon, 'The extraordinary case of John Lowes', in *Matthew Hopkins*, ch. 9. A note on the case, apparently dating from the early eighteenth century but incorporating the memories of persons present in 1645, survives in the parish register for Brandeston: Suffolk Record Office, FC 105/D1/1.

an imp to 'destroy the corn that groweth in Hillbrow field'. In another Ely case, Henry Freeman claimed that after an altercation Peter Burbush caused his mill to fall down.[16]

For the most part, however, the harm inflicted was similar to that which had formed the basis for English witchcraft prosecutions over the previous eighty years, namely minor matters, like bewitching a cow so that it gave 'naughty milk of two of her teats and since hath dried upp',[17] and more serious accusations like causing the death or sickness of cattle and human beings. The source materials surviving for the Hopkins period permit us to reconstruct 110 narratives of witchcraft suspicions: these include 36 incidents where the targets of the witch's wrath were adult humans, 56 children, 53 cattle, and 9 inanimate objects, ranging, as we have seen, from a mill which was demolished to beer which refused to brew.[18] These figures can be compared with those for the Home Circuit of the assizes between 1610 and 1659, when of 192 indictments for witchcraft alleging harm to persons or property, 61 involved adults, 44 children, 29 animals, and 2 other forms of property.[19] Thus the East Anglian trials of 1645–7 seem to demonstrate an unusual emphasis on the killing of children and cattle. The youth of witches' human victims in the Hopkins trials becomes more marked when it is realised that a large number of those classified here as adults were servants, so often in the front line of altercations with suspected witches, many of whom must have been in or barely out of their teens. It may be that in these trials, as in the rather different contexts of Mora in Sweden or Salem in Massachusetts, the misfortunes of children and adolescents played a crucial role in fuelling a large-scale witch panic.

Many of the witches and witnesses, again along very familiar lines, testified how witchcraft fears followed an altercation, or 'falling out' as they most frequently put it. Many of these incidents involved those tensions following a refusal to give goods which so often precipitated a witchcraft accusation. Margaret Benet, a Suffolk witch, told how she sent her imp to afflict Goody Gunshaw 'and that because she refused to let her

---

[16] BL Add. MSS 27402, f. 114v; *A True and Exact Relation*, pp. 4–5; Cambridge University Library, EDR 12/19; BL Add. MSS 27402, f. 118; Cambridge UL, EDR 12/11, 12/2.

[17] BL Add. MSS 27402, f. 110.

[18] Ibid., f. 117v.

[19] These calculations are based on the details of Home Circuit assize indictments given in C. L. Ewen, *Witch Hunting and Witch Trials* (London, 1929), pp. 200–52, augmented by additional information on Essex cases given in Macfarlane, *Witchcraft*, pp. 265–70.

have half a pint of butter'. Mary Bush, obviously a very poor woman, simply sent her imp to anyone who refused her relief. A woman witness deposed how a child in her master's house was stricken and died the day after Mary Edwards came to her house and was given 'some milk but not so much as she desired, and she went away mumblinge'. In another case a servant told how mother Palmer came to her master's house and asked for beer. Refused it, 'she went away thretning . . . she might want a cup of beere her selfe ear longe', from which moment no beer could be brewed successfully in that household. Susan Cocke of St Osyth in Essex sent her imps to torment the servant of John Turner after he refused to give her a sack of woodchips.[20]

A number of other bases for 'falling out' were recorded, although, as might be imagined, these were too varied to allow categorisation. Mary Sexton told how a dog came to her, and asked 'if she would revenge her self of the constables that had carried her to Ipswitch upon [a] misdemeanor'. Elizabeth Clarke, one of the first Essex witches to be examined, was thought to have killed the couple in whose favour her landlord, Richard Caley, had turned her out of her tenancy. Elizabeth Chandler, one of the Huntingdonshire accused, claimed she desired revenge on goodwife Darnell, 'having received some hard usage from the said goodwife Darnell, by causing her to be duckt'. Francis Moore told how 'one William Foster, some sixteen years since, would have hanged two of her children, for offering to take a piece of bread', and how she subsequently cursed him and caused his death. Two witches, one in Essex and one in the Isle of Ely, were thought to have used their powers against parish officers who tried to press their sons into the army.[21] The tensions underlying a witchcraft accusation in the Hopkins period could, therefore, be very varied: indeed, one witch, Elizabeth Weed of Catworth in Huntingdonshire, recalled sending an imp to kill a child, adding 'she wisht him to doe the same when she was angrie, but doth not well remember for what'.[22] In general, however, the impression in 1645–7, as was usually the case, was that members of the community with limited access to other forms of power were suspected of using witchcraft to revenge themselves on those who had offended them.

This being so, it is hardly surprising that another familiar theme to

[20] BL Add. MSS 27402, ff. 115, 114v, 116v, 117v; *A True and Exact Relation*, p. 29. Cf. the examples given in Stearne, *Confirmation and Discovery*, p. 36.

[21] BL Add. MSS 27402, f. 121v; *A True and Exact Relation*, pp. 21–2; *Witches of Huntingdon*, pp. 7, 8; *A True and Exact Relation*, p. 25; Cambridge UL, EDR 12/1.

[22] *Witches of Huntingdon*, p. 2.

surface in these trials is the frequency with which suspects had a long-established reputation for witchcraft. A witness deposed of a Suffolk witch that 'the parents of this woman and this woman have been formerly counted and commonly reputed for a witch'. John Abrahams claimed of Peter Burbush of Ely that 'he hath bin com[m]only reputed a witch & his mother before him'. In another Ely case, an alleged victim accused Joan Briggs of being a witch 'because they have had many fallens out & the s[ai]d Jone hath used many threatning speeches ag[ains]t this informant she having been a woman that hath a long tyme been suspected for a witch'. A fuller denunciation was made by one of the witnesses against Anne Morrice of Upwell: 'she hath bin a long tyme accompted a witche and her mother before her, and that shee is a com[m]on curser, and that by reporte of her neighbours much harme and damage hath befallen such as had difference with her'.Voicing such suspicions too vociferously could, of course, bring trouble down upon the accuser: Dorothy Ellis, another of the Isle of Ely accused, confessed to laming John Gotobed by witchcraft 'because he cald this ex[aminate] old witch & flung stones att this ex[aminate]'.[23]

On one level, then, the witchcraft detected in the East Anglian outbreak of 1645–7 was hardly atypical: most of those accused of witchcraft were women from the lower orders; many of them had a long-standing reputation for practising witchcraft. Their *maleficium*, overwhelmingly involving harm to children, adult humans and cattle, followed the pattern long familiar in England and most of the occasions when this harm was inflicted followed altercations, 'fallings out', between the witch and a neighbour in which those disputes over loans, alms or favours delineated by Macfarlane constituted a recurrent theme. Thus the alleged atypicality of the Hopkins trials lay not in these areas, but rather in the high profile which the devil enjoyed in the witches' account of their activities: John Stearne, indeed, after recounting a number of such cases, declared 'if I should goe to pen all of these sorts, then I should have no end, or at least too big a volume'.[24] Stearne's opinion is confirmed when we find that of our 110 witchcraft narratives, 63 involve accounts of the witch's meeting with the devil in one form or another (as we shall see, the varied nature of those forms raises a number of interesting issues). These cases obviously challenge the accepted interpretation of English

---

[23]  BL Add. MSS 27402, f. 110; Cambridge UL, EDR 12/2, 12/10, 12/1, 12/15.
[24]  Stearne, *Confirmation and Discovery*, p. 32.

witchcraft as non-diabolical, and obviously need some serious attention before we can dismiss them as untypical.

In fact, these accounts of dealings with the devil open up a rich seam of contemporary beliefs about him. Witches under examination confessed to meeting him for the first time in a number of different circumstances. Susan Marchant, a Suffolk witch, told how the devil first came to her when she was 'milking off a cow and singing off a psalme, and asked her why she singe psalmes as she was a damned creature', from which time she received familiars. The devil came to Priscilla Collet and tempted her to do away with herself or her children 'or else she sho'd always continue poore'; she did, in fact, subsequently try to kill one of her children, although it was rescued by another. Some first saw the devil, as demonologists warned their readers people would, when they were riven by despair or anger. The devil first came to Abigail Briggs a month after her husband died, and she told how he came 'to her shop and lay heavy upon her', and spoke to her 'in the voyce of her husband'. Similarly, the devil appeared to Mary Skipper shortly after her husband's death, and told her 'if she would make a covenant w[i]th him he wold pay her debts'. Mary Beckett recounted how the devil came to her 'and told her her sins weare so great that there was no heaven for her'. The devil first appeared to Ann Moats 'after she had beene cursinge of her husband and her childering'. Mary Wyard was offered material temptations when the devil told her that 'there weare soame witches had gold ringes on theyr fingers'.[25]

At the first meeting, or shortly after it, the devil began to try to convince the witch to enter into a covenant with him. He usually offered revenge or, as the case of Mary Wyard suggests, material wealth. Abigail Briggs, according to John Stearne's evidence, said the devil told her she would be revenged on her enemies, but [as was so often the case] 'she s[ai]d she found Satan a liar'. Elizabeth Richmond told how the devil 'came to her & imbraced her and asked her to love him & trust in him & would defend her & curse her enemies'. Elizabeth Hobard confessed that the devil came to her thirty years previously, that he took blood of her against her will, and 'at the same time she covenanted w[i]th him that he shold have her body and soule and wold avenge her of those that angered her', adding that 'he would furnish her w[i]th money but never p[er]formed it'. Similarly, the devil promised Ann Usher that if she denied Christ she would get richer, but he brought her nothing. Elizabeth

---

25 BL Add. MSS 27402, ff. 110v, 111v, 114, 121, 117, 117v.

Currey, a widow of Riseley in Bedfordshire, confessed that the devil 'had the use of her body, and lay heavie upon her, and that through her wilfulnesse, and poverty, with desire of revenge, she denied God, and Christ, and sealed it with her blood'.[26]

The motif of the devil taking a few drops of blood to seal the covenant between him and the witch, and sometimes making a writing, runs through these narratives. Even more unexpectedly, as this last case suggests, there are fairly frequent references to sexual liaisons between the devil and the witch. In a practically unique case, Ellen Driver of Framlingham in Suffolk, aged 60, confessed that many years previously 'the devill appeared to her like a man & that she was married to him . . . and that he had lived with her 3 years and that she had 2 children by him in that time w[hi]ch weare changelinges . . . after she was married he had the use of her but was cold, and inioyned her before marriage to deny God and Christ'. Most of those who confessed to having intercourse with the devil found the experience an odd and not entirely pleasurable one. As we have seen, Elizabeth Currey felt the devil 'lay heavie upon her', while Ellen Driver felt him physically cold. These notions, strikingly similar to those attributed by continental writers to witches who had copulated with the devil, were echoed by other alleged witches. The devil came two or three times a week to widow Bush of Barton, 'but she said he was colder than a man, and heavier, and could not performe nature as a man'. The devil constantly had the use of Mary Skipper's body after she made a covenant with him, 'but she felt him always cold'. Other cases were less clear cut, and sometimes involved the devil in an animal shape. Alice Marsh, a Suffolk witch, claimed that the devil came to her in the shape of a rat, and desired her soul, 'but she wold not give it to him but she gave him hir body & after this he had the use of her body and so dep[ar]ted'. Margaret Bayle, also from Suffolk, told how 'when she was at work she felt a thing come upon her legs and so into her secret p[ar]tes and nipped her in that secret part where her markes weare found'. Ann Usher, probably a relative of Bayle's, simply 'felt 2 things like butterflies in her secret p[ar]tes'.[27]

These last cases introduce a major complication: the devil appeared in a variety of shapes. Frequently, of course, he was of human appearance:

[26] BL Add. MSS 27402, ff. 114, 108, 107, 117v; Stearne, *Confirmation and Discovery*, p. 31.
[27] BL Add. MSS 27402, f. 116v; Stearne, *Confirmation and Discovery*, pp. 28–9; BL Add. MSS 27402. ff. 121v, 108, 117.

'in the shadow of a man'; 'a handsome young gentleman with yellow hayre and black cloathes'; 'in the shape of a proper gentleman, with a laced band, having the whole proportion of a man'; 'in the likeness of a man called Daniel the Prophet'. Even with the devil in his human shape, however, there might be problems. Some of these East Anglian villagers knew that the devil was meant to have a cloven foot. Ellen Driver of Framlingham recounted that while she was in bed with the devil 'she felt his feet and they weare cloven'. Margaret Wyard, in the very act of making a covenant with the devil, 'observed he had a cloven foot'. Even more alarming was the experience of the Huntingdonshire witch Jane Wallis, who noticed the ugly feet of a man she met, 'and then she was very fearfull of him for that he would seem sometimes to be tall and sometimes lesse, and suddenly vanished away'. Others told how the devil might appear in animal form. As Joan Salter was going from the house of one of the witnesses giving evidence against her 'a black horse came to hir & crept betwixt her legges & carried hir over the green to hir own house, w[hi]ch this inform[an]t beleaveth to be the divell in the likeness of a horse'. The devil came to one of the Isle of Ely witches in 'the likness of a great mouse', to a Suffolk witch in the 'shape of a crabfish'. Mary Scrutton, another Suffolk witch, reported seeing the devil variously in the shape of a cat, a bear, or a man.[28]

With such confessions we plunge directly into the problem of the interplay between educated (or 'continental') ideas on the devil's role in witchcraft, and those of the populace. As we have seen, some of our East Anglian witches encountered the devil of the learned demonologists: appearing in the shape of a man (sometimes a handsome young gentleman, but sometimes with a cloven foot); offering wealth or the power to revenge wrongs; making a covenant, often sealed with the witch's blood, in which the witch renounced God and Christ; a covenant which was often followed by sexual relations between the devil and the witch, relations which were often unsatisfactory ('he was colder than a man, and heavier, and could not perform nature as a man'). Such a pattern would have been recognisable to continental writers of witchcraft tracts like Bodin or Remy, or to English ones like William Perkins, and there is every likelihood that their pervasiveness in 1645–7 owed much to the

---

[28] BL Add. MSS 27402, f. 110v, 117v; *A True and Exact Relation*, pp. 1–2; Stearne, *Confirmation and Discovery*, p. 30; BL Add. MSS 27402, f. 116; *Witches of Huntingdon*, p. 12; Cambridge UL, EDR 12/20, 12/16; BL Add. MSS 27402, ff. 111, 116v.

investigative techniques of Hopkins, Stearne and their associates. But what are we to make of witches confessing to seeing the devil in the shape of a cat, a black horse, a crabfish, or a 'great mouse', and what are we to make of Ann Usher, experiencing not the cold and unsatisfactory embraces of a humanoid devil, but rather the sensation of '2 things like butterflies in her secret p[ar]tes'? Here we are encountering, surely, not the devil of the learned demonologists, but rather something very like the animal familiars that had long been a staple of English witch beliefs. As Macfarlane noted, if English witches wanted a link with the devil 'it was not through weekly or monthly meetings with him, but rather by keeping a small domestic pet, thought to be her "imp" or "familiar"'.[29] Whatever was untypical in the Hopkins trials, the familiar was not: indeed, the very first pamphlet generated by an English witchcraft trial, published in 1566, depicted a witch called Mother Waterhouse having a familiar, called Sathan, in the shape of a cat. This familiar performed acts of vengeance for her in return for drops of her blood.[30]

The familiar presents a key area in English witchcraft beliefs which is, sadly, as yet under-researched. At the very least, as the case of Mother Waterhouse suggests, the widespread belief in familiars takes us away from a model of witchcraft which is based on village *maleficium* into one where something very like a diabolical element is present. And if trial records of 1645–7 furnish us with considerable evidence about popular beliefs about the devil, even more do they provide insights into the folklore of familiars, or 'imps' as they were more often referred to in the documentation in question. Of the 110 narratives, 78 involve familiars. They came in numerous animal guises: mice, dogs, chickens, rabbits, turkey-cocks, a rat, a polecat. They were given names: indeed, Macfarlane's observation that 'even in witchcraft, the English obsession with pet-keeping emerged', may well suggest an interesting line of approach.[31] Many witches claimed that their familiars were passed on to them after the covenant was sealed, although others received them from their mother,[32] grandmother,[33] or friends.[34] Witches occasionally used their familiars in unison to create harm, or shared or borrowed them,

---

[29] Macfarlane, *Culture of Capitalism*, p. 109.
[30] *The Examination and Confession of certaine Wytches at Chensforde in the Countie of Essex before the Quenes Majesties Judges, the XXVI daye of July Anno 1566* (London, 1566), reprinted in Barbara Rosen. *Witchcraft* (London, 1969), pp. 72–82.
[31] Macfarlane, *Culture of Capitalism*, p. 109.
[32] BL Add. MSS 27402, f. 115v.
[33] Ibid., ff. 110, 121.    [34] Ibid., f. 115.

while Margery Sparham, a Suffolk witch, told how she sent two of her three imps 'after her husband beeinge a soldier to p[ro]tect him'.[35] Most female witches confessed that they allowed their familiars to suck blood from them through teats in their genitalia, and the Hopkins materials contain rich details about the resultant witches' marks. Indeed, one of the most graphic images furnished by the documentation comes from Margaret Wyard, who confessed that she had seven imps, but only five teats, so that 'when they come to suck they fight like pigs with a sow'.[36] One suspects that Wyard did not owe this particular image to continental notions foisted upon her by Matthew Hopkins.

So how should we regard the supposed untypicality of the Matthew Hopkins trials? Obviously, the context was untypical: the disruption, both administrative and psychological, of three years of war on local society provided a unique context for an English witchcraze. Moreover, the presence of Hopkins and Stearne as catalysts was a novel feature in English trials. But, at the risk of overstating my case, I would contend that in the actual content of the witch beliefs that surfaced in the course of the trials, there was much more which was familiar than unfamiliar. As we have seen, the alleged witches, and the harm which they were meant to have done, were firmly in the English mainstream. The wealth of information about, for example, familiars, is remarkable, but then we are looking at a remarkably rich body of documentation. The presence of the devil is unusually marked, but even here, as we have seen, English beliefs were still, to a large extent, conflating the devil of the learned demonologists and the neo-diabolical familiars of English witchcraft tradition, thus demonstrating that the issue is a more complex one than the straightforward imposition of learned beliefs on the populace. The Hopkins trials, perhaps, do not so much confront us with the unusual, but rather furnish us with unusually rich evidence of an ever-developing body of beliefs about witchcraft.

The exact relationship between popular beliefs and the demonological input of Hopkins, Stearne and other interested parties remains, and is likely to remain, problematic. Clearly there is enough uniformity (the sealing of the covenant with a few drops of blood, the devil's limitations as a lover) in the accounts given by confessing witches to suggest that what they said owed much to the leading questions of their interrogators. It is probable that a broad cultural vocabulary of diabolic beliefs was

---

[35] Ibid., f. 120v.    [36] Ibid., f. 117v.

being focused in the process of interrogation. Yet it is likewise clear that the populace did possess a repertoire of beliefs about the devil, and that what appeared in the witches' confessions was not simply 'imposed'. Similarly, the exact position on the continuum between popular and learned beliefs of the familiar so often alluded to in 1645–7 is uncertain. The existence of familiars (not least because of their obvious connection with that most certain proof that a person was a witch, the witch's mark) was obviously something which witch hunters had an interest in establishing. Even so, after eighty years of their presence in accounts of English witch trials, it seems likely that, by 1645, they had entered the popular consciousness as an element in witchcraft beliefs.[37]

Doubtless, however, this popular consciousness had been sharpened, not least in Puritan East Anglia, by the experience of listening to sermons in which the devil and his works figured prominently. The degree to which sermons were attended, how much attention to their content was given by those who did attend, and how much of that content was internalised and affected subsequent behaviour or subsequent patterns of belief, remains unclear. Even so, the statements of some of those participating in the Hopkins trials, whether as accused, accusers, witnesses or assistants to Hopkins and Stearne, demonstrates that at least some of the middling and lower sorts of Essex, Suffolk and the Isle of Ely had acquired a basic awareness of the threat offered to the godly commonwealth by the devil. Two more immediate factors were also at work. The point awaits further investigation, but it is probable that the parliamentarian propaganda of 1642–5, in both print and sermon, was tending to view the struggle against the royalists in increasingly apocalyptic terms, and was coming increasingly to employ the rhetorical device of describing royalists as agents of the devil.[38] And, more concretely, a number of clergy were actively involved in the search for witches. Three were active in the early Essex investigations,[39] while others were involved in Suffolk.[40] More remarkably, the Special Commission of Oyer and Terminer sent to try witches in that latter county in 1645 included two divines, Samuel Fairclough and Edmund

---

[37] Belief in familiars, indeed, predated the witchcraft statutes: Ewen, *Witchcraft and Demonianism*, p. 73. cites a Yorkshire case of 1510 as the first occasion when familiars (in this instance bees) sucked blood from their owner.

[38] I am grateful to Peter Lake for suggesting this point to me.

[39] Macfarlane, *Witchcraft*, p. 137.

[40] E.g. BL Add. MSS 27402, ff. 111, 115v.

Calamy, both of whom had local connections. It should be noted, however, that the exact impact of these two worthies on the rhythm and content of accusations remains elusive.[41]

Similarly, examination of the works published by Hopkins and Stearne makes it difficult to accept that they were responsible, in any simple way, for the promotion of 'continental' ideas. Hopkins' tract, apart from a reference to James VI's views on the validity of the swimming test[42] demonstrates little by way of any acquaintance with learned writings on witchcraft. Indeed, he explicitly denied that his skill in witch hunting was founded on 'profound learning, or from much reading of learned authors concerning that subject', attributing it rather to 'experience, which though it be meanly esteemed of; yet the surest and safest way to judge by'.[43] Stearne's rather longer publication presents more complexities. It is evident that he was familiar with the Warboys case of 1593, the Lancashire trials of 1612, and the bewitching of Francis Manners, earl of Rutland, in 1618–19,[44] while he also alludes to Thomas Cooper's *Mystery of Witchcraft* of 1617.[45] As G. L. Kittredge demonstrates in 1929, he also made heavy and unacknowledged use ('enormous plagiarism' is Kittredge's phrase) of Richard Bernard's *Guide to Grand Jury Men*, first published in 1627.[46] Bernard's marginal references suggest that he was familiar with the works of Bodin and Del Rio, but 'continental' notions do not figure prominently in his work, far more attention being devoted to the 1612 Lancashire trials and other English cases.[47] Thus even what we can reconstruct of the intellectual

---

[41] Notestein, *History of Witchcraft*, pp. 177–8. I am grateful to Keith Thomas for informing me of Fairclough's involvement in the Suffolk trials. It should be noted, however, that of the two sermons he preached before the Commission's sitting, one confirmed the existence of witchcraft, but the second stressed 'the hainousness of the sins of those, who would violently prosecute, or unduly endeavour to convict any person, except plain convincing evidence could be brought', which suggests a somewhat guarded attitude: Samuel Clark, *The Lives of Sundry Eminent Persons in this Later Age* (London, 1683), p. 172. In any case, Fairclough's sermons in Suffolk in late August cannot have affected earlier investigations in that county or Essex. Fairclough was, indeed, almost certainly the 'Master Fairecloth . . . an able orthodox divine' whom Stearne records as being invoked by a Haverhill witch apparently in hopes of clearing her name: *Confirmation and Discovery*, p. 54.

[42] Hopkins, *Discovery of Witches*, p. 6.     [43] Ibid., p. 1.

[44] Stearne, *Confirmation and Discovery*, p. 11.

[45] Ibid., p. 26.

[46] G. L. Kittredge, *Witchcraft in Old and New England* (1929: repr. New York, 1959), pp. 273, 564 n. 146.

[47] Richard Bernard, *A Guide to Grand Jury Men: Divided into Two Books* (London, 1627). The demonic pact and related matters are discussed in Book 2, chapters 3–7.

background of Hopkins' and Stearne's views on witchcraft reflects the mainstream of English Protestant writing rather than continental publications, while for Stearne, as for Hopkins, the actual experience of witch hunting seems to have been a greater influence in forming a view of what witches did than reading demonological tracts.

What this evidence from 1645–7 demonstrates (and what, I think, has impeded our proper appreciation of the Hopkins episode) is that the notion of a polarity between a 'learned', 'continental', and 'demonological' set of beliefs held by the elite and a popular concern with witchcraft which centred on *maleficium* is a gross oversimplification.[48] Obviously, at certain points in the Hopkins trials it is possible to see confessions coming through under pressure from Hopkins and Stearne giving details of the diabolical pact which may well reflect the accused's thoughts being moulded by continental notions. A much more common impression, however, is that of a jumble of popular and 'educated' beliefs which were mobilised into an agitated interaction by the conditions of a mass witch hunt. So we have not just the devil of the demonologists, but also a devil as imagined by the population at large. As Clive Holmes has pointed out, whatever input Hopkins may have had into confessions giving details about the devil, these confessions were not stereotyped.[49] There were, of course, some common themes: the devil's appearance at moments of stress, the taking of blood when the covenant was sealed, the unsatisfactory aspects of the devil as a lover. But close reading of the confessions reveals a host of variations and the insertion of elements which owed little to learned demonology. And there remains the problem which many witnesses and confessing witches had in distinguishing between the devil and the animal familiar. We therefore have the sense not of the imposition of ideas about the devil's role in witchcraft, but rather of a wide range of ideas being allowed to run free, and being allowed to enter the historical record, due to an unusual set of circumstances.

Even the presence of the devil in these East Anglian trials may not have been so novel a feature as has been thought. I would suggest that there is a serious gap in our knowledge here, and that the folklore of the devil in early modern England is a subject which needs to be more

---

[48] This point has been made by Clive Holmes, 'Popular culture? Witches, magistrates and divines in early modern England', in Steven L. Kaplan, ed., *Understanding Popular Culture: Europe from the Middle Ages to the Nineteenth Century* (Berlin, 1984), pp. 85–110.

[49] Ibid., p. 101.

thoroughly researched.[50] Even on a superficial level, however, one comes across constant indications that the devil featured fairly prominently in people's consciousness in the first half of the seventeenth century. The case-books of the astrological physician Richard Napier contained numerous references to clients who were convinced of the threat offered to them by the devil and his agents.[51] In 1608 Roger Houlte of Bury found himself the defendant in an ecclesiastical court defamation suit for saying of some women that 'they are all witches, they have given theire selves to the devill'.[52] In 1621, Helen Fairfax, the daughter of a Yorkshire gentleman, in the course of a fit imagined one of the women whom she thought to be bewitching her confessing to making a pact with the devil 'like to a man of this world whom she met on the moors'.[53] In 1638 Jane Moxie, a young woman from Lympstone in Devon, among other thoughts on witchcraft, allegedly held that witches met with the devil once a year on a hill on midsummer eve.[54] In 1641 a Chester man found himself in trouble for drinking healths to the devil.[55] Late medieval sources demonstrate that the devil was already a familiar figure, and that the notion of the demonic pact was well established.[56] Arguably the image of the devil, and of the satanic pact, was not such a novelty in 1645 as has been claimed: even the suggestions of the sabbat that appeared in some of the Essex trials of 1645 were, to say the least, no stronger than those found in the Lancashire witch scare of 1633.[57]

Mention of the Lancashire episode of 1633 moves us to a final

[50] Some indication of the value to historians of folkloristic approaches to witchcraft can be gleaned from K. M. Briggs, *Pale Hecate's Team: An Examination of the Beliefs on Witchcraft and Magic among Shakespeare's Contemporaries and his Immediate Successors* (London, 1962).

[51] Michael MacDonald, *Mystical Bedlam: Madness, Anxiety and Healing in Seventeenth-Century England* (Cambridge, 1981), p. 175.

[52] Cheshire Record Office, Consistory Court Papers, EDC5 (1608) 11.

[53] *Daemonologie: a Discourse on Witchcraft. As it was acted in the Family of Mr. Edward Fairfax, of Fuyston in the County of York, in the Year 1621; along with the only two Eclogues of the same Author known to be in Existence*, ed., William Grange (Harrogate, 1882), p. 86.

[54] Devon Record Office, Quarter Sessions Rolls, Box 41, Bapt. 1638, docs. 52, 56–7. I am grateful to Mary Wolffe for bringing this reference to my attention.

[55] Cheshire Record Office, EDC5 (1641) 9.

[56] See Kittredge, *Witchcraft in Old and New England*, pp. 239–43.

[57] See the materials collected in Ewen, *Witchcraft and Demonianism*, pp. 244–51. Although the notion of the sabbat (a meeting of thirty or forty witches, to which they were conveyed by their familiars, and at which the devil might be present) was stronger than in the Essex cases, and sexual intercourse between witches and the devil or their familiars in human form was mentioned, this incident also demonstrated a conflation of the devil and animal familiars.

contention: that the Hopkins trials might well benefit from being studied on a comparative basis with other major outbreaks of witch hunting. Comparisons with the large-scale German and Scottish trials might well help deepen our understanding of the variables involved. More value, however, might be found in looking at other serious outbreaks which occurred more or less unexpectedly in areas which, like England in 1645, had not been experiencing high levels of witchcraft prosecution: the Swedish trials of 1668–76; the Salem trials of 1692; and (to move geographically and chronologically nearer to 1645), the above-mentioned Lancashire incident of 1633, this last an elusive and ill-documented example of a potential large-scale outbreak which was nipped in the bud by a sceptical officialdom. In all these outbreaks, as in East Anglia in 1645, a large-scale witch hunt developed against a background of apparently low levels of tension over witchcraft, and in all of them the dynamics of the interaction between popular and official attitudes to witchcraft, and of new and old beliefs on the subject, were marked. The Hopkins trials, starting as they did in Essex, where witchcraft indictments had been low in the 1630s, remind us of the gap between the pervasiveness and richness of witch beliefs and what entered the historical record.

# 12. Witchcraft repealed

## IAN BOSTRIDGE

### I

For a long time now, the study of witchcraft has been afflicted with a tenacious and commonsensical historical assumption: that some time around 1700, probably before, and almost certainly in league with something like 'rationality', 'science' or 'rationalisation', witchcraft disappeared off the intellectual map.[1] The period between widespread educated credulity around 1670 and the triumph of confident jeering scepticism some time in the eighteenth century has been largely ignored.[2]

[1] For example, W. E. H. Lecky, *A History of England in the Eighteenth Century*, 7 vols. (1878), I, pp. 266–7; Lecky, *History of the Rise and Influence of the Spirit of Rationalism in Europe*, 2nd edn, 2 vols. (1865), I, pp. 1–150; H. T. Buckle, *The History of Civilisation in England*, new edn, 3 vols. (1871), III, p. 363; H. C. Lea, *A History of the Inquisition of the Middle Ages* (New York, 1955); Lea, *Materials Towards a History of Witchcraft*, ed., A. C. Howland, 3 vols. (New York, 1957); Wallace Notestein, *A History of Witchcraft in England from 1558 to 1718* (Washington, 1911), especially pp. 313–33, and tribute to Lecky, p. ix; G. L. Burr, ed., *The Witchpersecutions . . .* (Philadelphia, 1897); K. V. Thomas, *Religion and the Decline of Magic* (Harmondsworth, 1973), especially chs. 18, 22; Brian Easlea, *Witch Hunting, Magic and the New Philosophy* (Brighton, 1980); Barbara Shapiro, *Probability and Certainty in Seventeenth-Century England* (Princeton, 1983), ch. 6; Brian Levack, *The Witch-hunt in Early Modern Europe* (1987), esp. pp. 217–24; E. W. Monter, 'The historiography of European witchcraft: progress and prospects', *Journal of Interdisciplinary History*, 2 (1972), and his more recent brief review article, 'European witchcraft: a moment of synthesis?', *Historical Journal*, 31 (1988).

[2] For the 1670s see, for example, Henry More, Joseph Glanvill and Robert Boyle, shoring up religion with authenticated supernatural narratives. See Joseph Glanvill, *Some Philosophical Considerations touching Witchcraft* (1676); Robert Boyle to Joseph Glanvill in *The Works of the Honourable Robert Boyle*, ed., Birch, 6 vols. (1772), VI, p. 58 (18 Sept. 1677) and pp. 59–60 (10 Feb. 1678). For confident ridicule see, for example, Robert Halsband, ed., *The Complete Letters of Lady Mary Wortley Montagu* (Oxford, 1967), III, pp. 187–9, letters to Lady Bute and Sir James Steuart, 8 Nov. and 14 Nov. 1758.

Elsewhere I have tried to present a history of belief in this period which goes beyond joining the dots.[3] But any account, provisionally entitled 'The Decline of the Belief in Witchcraft in England', is beset with problems of definition and conceptual confusion (for instance, how is a belief historically manifested?). A few pointers must suffice in this brief chapter, which is not to say that the grander effort is not worth making. If we can understand the relationship between writing, action and belief in a marginal but defining area like witchcraft, we will have achieved a great deal both in terms of reassessing historical monsters like 'the Enlightenment' and in providing a model for understanding similar problems in other periods.

The relationship between these variables – writing, action and belief – is, however, complex. We should not confuse the business of the prosecution of witches in England – the history of persecution – with either the 'discourse of witchcraft' (narrowly and unproblematically defined as a body of texts) or the belief in witchcraft (often parlously psychologistic, individualistic and awkwardly placed for historical analysis). There is no universally valid connection between these three, although they can overlap: for instance, the belief of an individual is often if not always conditioned by the discursive resources available to that individual.

Peaks of prosecuting zeal in the late sixteenth and mid-seventeenth centuries were extraordinary events, perhaps 'epidemics' (which we might indeed want to treat psychologistically) and were followed by long periods of piecemeal, or routine, 'endemic' prosecution of witches at a lower 'sustainable' rate. From the viewpoint of 1700, the possibility of another bout of witchcraft persecution was not safely dead and buried as those with hindsight may assume. Moreover, the discourse of witchcraft – the public elaboration of witchcraft's place in the order of things – has no self-evident dependence on the intensity of prosecution. That this discourse needed a high, or even a moderate level of active participation, prosecution or conviction to thrive or survive is not self-evident. It may be so. It may not be so. It cannot simply be assumed.

This chapter tried to do its work without these assumptions. If we start by refusing to take the fact or chronology of 'the decline of witchcraft' for granted we can look afresh at the eighteenth-century evidence. That evidence does not point to witchcraft retaining its seventeenth-century

---

[3] Ian Bostridge, 'Debates about witchcraft in England, 1650–1736', Oxford D.Phil thesis (1991).

virulence into the eighteenth century, but it does indicate a different story from the familiar tale of intellectual redundancy. Witchcraft theory was startlingly persistent. The body of ideas built around the threat of the witch was remarkably resilient. There are no new eighteenth-century witch-finder generals to be unearthed, but we can find strongly held beliefs and strong commitments operating even in an ideologically inauspicious climate. As a body of ideas, witchcraft had a currency and a certain viability in the eighteenth century, despite the absence of widespread or legitimate persecution. By 1736, the year of the repeal of the British witchcraft legislation, witchcraft theory was isolated and much ridiculed in print and, doubtless, coffee-house. But behind closed doors, we cannot be so sure; and witchcraft theory was certainly *not*, to borrow a phrase from Dr Johnson, 'beyond the need for rational confutation'. That it is today should not mislead us into assuming that this sweeping brand of modern scepticism came into the world confident and fully armed.

By showing the political and religious crannies in which witchcraft theory could lurk in 1736, I hope to give credence to two related notions: that the demise of the witchcraft debate between members of the elite who wanted to be taken seriously had political and ideological rather than purely intellectual occasions; and that the ideological colouring which witchcraft acquired in the early eighteenth century was a double-edged affair, both ensuring the demise of witchcraft as a mainstream discourse, and paradoxically ensuring its survival and occasional reemergence at the fringes, as long as the ideological framework of the *ancien régime* remained in force.

This exploration of the repeal of witchcraft legislation in the British parliament will eventually form part of an attempt to write a synoptic account of the decline or transformation of witchcraft as an intellectual category; but it also stands as a simple exercise in historical reclamation. The repeal of the witchcraft legislation of England and Scotland in 1736 is still seen as an afterthought;[4] it has never been deemed worthy of explanation. This chapter will start by asking why repeal happened, and why it happened in March 1736. It will then look at the opposition to repeal and identify the interests – political, religious and national – which motivated the admittedly small number of outright opponents. But any account of 1736 needs to start with a brief sketch of the seventeenth- and

---

[4] See, for example, Paul Langford, *A Polite and Commercial People: England 1727–1783* (Oxford, 1989), p. 282.

eighteenth-century background and an inoculation against the familiar answers of the prevailing historical model.

## II

In the seventeenth century, witchcraft was a handy ideological tool with a real intellectual appeal, a wide constituency and a capacity to be moulded to serve new and varied interests. During the 1640s, to be sure, witchcraft prosecution had acquired a dangerous association with disorder, notably through the witch 'craze' initiated and sustained by the 'witch-finder general' Matthew Hopkins. Consequently, at the Restoration it was easy to ridicule the persecution of witches as the chosen pursuit of lunatic sectaries.[5] Nevertheless, witchcraft was not easily to be marginalised or driven to the fanatical fringe. The discourse of witchcraft had not spent its force by 1660, and a wide range of intellectuals subsequently maintained its necessity as a piece of Christian orthodoxy. One author among them even placed it at the centre of a response to fanaticism. The excluded Laudian cleric, Meric Casaubon, writing after his own restoration, saw the virtues of preserving traditional supernatural beliefs, bringing them to the aid of the whole process of a miraculously guaranteed and sacred Restoration. The supernatural elements of the old intellectual order – including witchcraft – had to be respected if the restored social, political and ecclesiastical order was to capture hearts and minds. Moreover, supernatural aspects of the orthodox world view, from royal divinity to miracles and diabolical intercourse with human beings were all of a piece. There could be no picking and choosing. All had to be retained and refurbished.[6]

Of course, the late-seventeenth-century affinity between witchcraft belief and dissent or religious radicalism cannot be entirely gainsaid. Witch hunting, the gruesome practical instantiation of the belief in witchcraft, is a feature mainly of dissenting circles by the 1690s, from Salem to the affair of the 'Surey Demoniack'. Men like Casaubon were not, as far as is known, great witch-finders, but witchcraft remained an entrenched part of their intellectual agenda for reasons of religion and statecraft combined. This only confirms the point made in opening, that

[5] Samuel Butler, *Hudibras*, ed., J. Wilders (Oxford, 1967), part 2, canto 3.

[6] Meric Casaubon, *Of Credulity and Incredulity in Things Natural and Civil*, 2nd edn (1672), for example, pp. 7, 29, 36, 164–5, 186–7, 199. See Bostridge, 'Debates', pp. 114–25.

belief and discourse have to be methodologically disentangled from the process of persecution.

This is not to say that there were not established clerics in the British Isles busy persecuting witches – but many of them were Scottish. To these activists, witchcraft was more than a theoretical buttress of church and state. The campaign against witchcraft, with all its heady rhetoric, played a symbolic role in Scottish opposition to English intellectual and religious colonisation of their kingdom. This is particularly evident in covenanting attacks on the variety of English infidelities, religious and political, from the 1650s on. For many Scots, the English were both leaguers with the devil and an impediment to godly resistance to witchcraft, makers of diabolical pacts and breakers of solemn leagues and covenants.[7] The Renfrew witch trial of 1696–7 was an occasion for Scots to worry about English interference in Scottish concerns. As one individual put it: 'the proceeding of the Government in another Nation', Scotland, is not to be 'Judged and Censured' by English *Esprits forts.* English responses to Scottish prosecution of witches in fact show no rising tide of scepticism south of the border.[8] Indeed, publication of Francis Hutchinson's major sceptical work on witchcraft, *An Historical Essay concerning Witchcraft* (1718), first planned in the first decade of the eighteenth century, was delayed over ten years by the English ecclesiastical hierarchy's reluctance to offend Scottish sensibilities around the time of the union of the two kingdoms.[9] The belief in the validity of laws against witches remained a feature of Scottish intellectual life long after the union.[10] As we shall see, the slight parliamentary resistance to the repeal of 1736 derived from Scottish opposition to Walpole. In itself, the Scottish example demonstrates the continuing and

---

[7] *The Scotch Presbyterian Eloquence* (1692), for example, pp. 45–6, 50, 55, 58–9, 66, 100, 107; Alexander Shields, *A Hind Let Loose* (n.p., 1687), pp. 324, 368; Edward Gee, *The Divine Right and Original of the Civill Magistrate from God* (1658), pp. 220–4; Bostridge, 'Debates', pp. 141–5.

[8] Bodleian MSS Locke b4 d107, Robert Wylie to William Hamilton, 16 June 1697; see also the sermon preached by James Hutchisone before the Commissioners of Justiciary appointed for the trial of the Renfrew witches in 1697, printed in *Scottish Historical Review* (1910); reports in *The Flying Post* (266, 267, 283, 285, 297, 308), *Lloyd's News* (64), *The Protestant Mercury* (130, 131, 134, 137, 141, 149, 150, 153, 154, 162), *The Post Boy* (275), and *The Foreign Post* (9).

[9] See BL Sloane MS 4040, f. 302, Francis Hutchinson to Hans Sloane, 4 Feb. 1706.

[10] Alexander Carlyle, *Autobiography* (1800), ed., J. H. Burton (1910), introduction, for the Associate Presbytery's judgement in 1743; David Hume to William Mure, MP for Renfrewshire, 14 Nov. 1742 in *The Letters of David Hume*, ed., J. Y. T. Greig, 2 vols. (Oxford, 1932), I, p. 44.

powerful appeal of the rhetoric of witchcraft as a means of organising political and religious perceptions.

There was no one historical moment at which witchcraft ceased to be a serious subject of educated concern in England, but neither is there a single perspective from which we can trace the 'decline of witchcraft belief' as if it were a piece of natural history. The reason for concentrating on the repeal of the laws about witchcraft in this essay is partly formal and partly a matter of perspective. We seek to explain an undoubted event in the history of witchcraft, and to do so without all the unwarranted assumptions we have unpicked hitherto. But focusing on one historical moment between the 1690s and 1736 can help us prepare for repeal by letting us understand how and why the climate of the debate had frozen out those who were zealous for prosecution. My necessarily brief account of that moment is particularly schematised because it pivots about one individual, Daniel Defoe. The intention is not to privilege Defoe's point of view, as if he were some sort of historical world soul, but rather to show the process of discursive transformation through the history of an individual, and to explain a conundrum. Supernaturalism and the occult are important features of Defoe's work, fictional, quasi-fictional and non-fictional alike. He was a man educated firmly within a dissenting tradition which treasured supernaturalism in its heart.[11] The conundrum is Defoe's apparent volte-fact on the issue of the existence of witchcraft. In 1711, at the height of the 'rage of party', and as a writer in the interest of Harley's moderate and eirenic Tory ministry, Defoe wrote an article in his *Review* which thoroughly endorsed belief in witchcraft as a piece of Christian orthodoxy. Yet in the 1720s he produced works pursuing a far more ambiguous line.[12] Analysis suggests that in 1711 support for witchcraft belief was calculated to appeal to the sort of cross-party coalition which Harley and,

---

[11] For example, Daniel Defoe, *Robinson Crusoe* (1719) (Oxford, 1981), esp. pp. 133, 78–9, 153–5; Defoe, 'A vision of the angelick world', in *Serious Reflections of Robinson Crusoe, Romances and Narratives by Daniel Defoe*, ed., Aitken (1899); Defoe, *A Journal of the Plague Year* (1722) (Harmondsworth, 1966), esp. pp. 124, 204, 205, 252; Defoe, *The Storm* (1704); Defoe, *The Fortunate Mistress* (1724) (Oxford, 1981), esp. pp. 220, 289; Defoe, *Moll Flanders* (1722) (Penguin, 1989), esp. pp. 65, 257–8, 268. Defoe was educated at Newington Green Academy under the supervision of Charles Morton, later cosignatory to the preface to Cotton Mather, *Memorable Providences Relating to Witchcraft* (1689). See also Charles Morton, *Compendium Physicae*, ed., S. E. Morison (Boston, 1940), esp. pp. 4, 161, 87, 195.

[12] *Review*, VIII: 90, 20 Oct. 1711; Daniel Defoe, *A Political History of the Devil, As Well Ancient as Modern* (1726); Defoe, *A System of Magick* (1727); Defoe, *Essay on the History and Reality of Apparitions* (1727).

by extension, Defoe, his agent, were trying to construct. In October 1711, it was a non-party issue, secular cum religious, which could embody a vision of a broad Christian commonwealth defined negatively against the image of depravity and deviance, the witch. This is a role the diabolical trafficker had played in Meric Casaubon's world view, and it was to form part of the medical controversialist Richard Boulton's stillborn defence of traditional belief in the 1720s.[13]

However, in 1712, during the contentious trial and pardon of the supposed witch, Jane Wenham, the issue of witchcraft itself became politicised in a welter of pamphlets for and against the conviction, pamphlets which revelled in the rhetoric of party conflict; yet again the Whig and Tory hobbyhorses of priestcraft and the church in danger were trotted out. What is more, during the course of the period between Defoe's *Review* article and the works on the occult he published in the 1720s, his Harleian vision of non-party Christian government evaporated. Party rule triumphed in Defoe's eyes. Witchcraft thus lost much of its use in Defoe's scheme of things. It reemerged, parodically inverted, as a metaphor for party conflict and party rule themselves. In Defoe's history of the devil, witches properly speaking were no longer needed because diabolism (factional rule incarnate) reigned at the very seat of power.[14]

This analysis of witchcraft during and after the 'rage of party', focused on discursive transformation – indeed, *inversion* in a very strict sense – in the work of one individual, Daniel Defoe, could be extended. Initially the bipartisan theory of witchcraft was an intellectual resource for all. Then, seized upon in the party struggle, it became increasingly perceived as the intellectual property of a discredited clique of highflyers and Tory extremists. The witch had been a focal point for a quasi-religious conception of political authority, a mixture of the anti-sacerdotal and anti-regal qualities analogous to and a diabolical inversion of that paramount exemplum of the mixed person, the king himself. The crime of witchcraft embodied the amphibian nature of political authority in the highflying scheme of things, as an offence which blended together civil and religious apostasy. The belief in it was beginning to be perceived as wrongheaded, and as having a dangerous potential for raising

---

[13] Richard Boulton, . . . *A Vindication of a Compleat History of Magick* . . . (1722).

[14] For example, Francis Bragge, *A Full and Impartial Account of the Discovery of Sorcery and Witchcraft, Practis'd by Jane Wenham* (1712); *A Full Confutation of Witchcraft* . . . (1712); Defoe, *A Political History of the Devil*, pp. 388–9.

uncomfortable issues and civil disturbance. Having then become associated with the losers in the political struggle, belief in witchcraft came to be seen as fit matter for ridicule.[15] What might be called the last witchcraft debate took place in the years around 1720 between the future bishop of Down and Connor, Francis Hutchinson, and the eccentric physician, Richard Boulton. Hutchinson pointed out the dangerous religious factionalism and potential for popular ferment which witchcraft belief involved. Boulton's forlorn attempt to resurrect the vision of a unified Christian community defining itself against the enemies of society harks back to Defoe and Casaubon. In retrospect, it was a plain anachronism.[16]

By the 1720s the ideological foundations of witchcraft had slipped. The metaphysical underpinnings and an ontology alive with spiritual activity remained intact but irrelevant or at most mildly embarrassing for sceptics like Hutchinson who wriggled out of the contradictions which the rejection of witchcraft and the necessity of spirits at work in the world seemed to entail. One need only consider John Locke's remarks on spirits, scattered through a variety of his works, to see that witchcraft was not ruled out by the new epistemology. Locke's conception of human understanding could be used, as Boulton used it, in support of belief in witches.[17] In general it was not. The reasons were ideological. Witchcraft belief was not exterminated by new forms of reasoning about the material world. The metaphysics and the epistemology to support such beliefs remained intact. But in political terms, we can see why witchcraft theory could have had little appeal for those wedded to Lockean

---

[15] See, for example, Anthony Collins, *A Discourse of Free-Thinking* (1713), p. 30; White Kennett, *The Witchcraft of the present Rebellion* (1715); Joseph Addison, *The Drummer* (1716), prologue and p. 47; *A Seasonable Apology for Father Dominick, Chaplain to Prince Prettyman the Catholick . . . In which are occasionally inserted some weighty Arguments for calling a General Council of the Nonjuring Doctors, for the further Propagation of Ceremonies, Unity, Dissention, and Anathemas; and for the better improvement of Exorcism and March-Beer* (1723), pp. 7ff., 14, 28; Thomas Gordon, *The Humourist* (1725), dedication and p. 74.

[16] Francis Hutchinson, *An Historical Essay Concerning Witchcraft* (1718), esp. p. 181; Boulton, *Vindication*, pp. 117, 155, ix, v, xii, 82.

[17] See Richard Boulton, *A Complete History of Magick, Sorcery, and Witchcraft* (1715), frontispiece and preface; Philip van Limborch to John Locke, *Correspondence of John Locke*, ed., de Beer (Oxford, 1976– ), IV, pp. 295–8, 17/27 and 21/31 July 1691; John Locke to Nicolas Thoinard, *Correspondence . . .* , II, p. 454, 14 Oct. 1681; John Locke, *An Essay Concerning Human Understanding*, Bohn's edn (1885), I, p. 425, sect. 5; p. 443, sect. 31; II, p. 124, sect. 23; Locke, 'Some thoughts concerning education', in *The Works of John Locke*, 10 vols. (1823), IX, pp. 6, 205, 182–3; Locke, 'A discourse of miracles', in *Works* (1823), IX, p. 264.

ideals such as the confirmed separation between secular and religious jurisdiction.[18]

Having reassessed the credibility of witchcraft theory up to 1736, we can turn to the question of repeal. The circumstances of repeal can tell us how much further the marginalisation of witchcraft had gone by 1736; an analysis of those circumstances can tell us how marginalisation was occurring and amplify the ideological tale we have already told.

## III

Religious controversy broke out with renewed vigour in the 1730s after a decade of relative stability presided over by Walpole's 'Pope', Edmund Gibson, bishop of London. Gibson himself sensed in parliament 'an evil spirit . . . working against Churchmen and Church matters'. He had wished to revive the jurisdiction of ecclesiastical courts, and commit the execution of laws against vice and irreligion to the ecclesiastical hierarchy, and spoke in a letter to Walpole of being 'tossed about and insulted by people of almost all denominations, many of whom were known to stand very well with the Court'. As Hervey noted in his *Memoirs*, the 1735–6 session of the new parliament devoted its chief discussions to 'Church matters'. An attempt to repeal the Test and Corporation Acts was followed, most disastrously for Edmund Gibson, by the furore over the Mortmain and Quakers' Tithe Bills, which led to his final break with Robert Walpole. As in the years preceding the Hanoverian succession, accusations of priestcraft and irreligion were bandied and anathemas hurled.[19]

This anti-clerical temper was not a mere whim of elements within the House of Commons. It extended throughout the elite, with the hubbub surrounding the nomination of the supposedly deistical Dr Rundle to the see of Gloucester; the abuse and criticism newly directed at Bishop Gibson's own magnum opus, the *Codex Juris Ecclesiae Anglicanae* of 1713 which had given theoretical form to attacks on ecclesiastical jurisdiction; and the controversy on the nature of heresy between James Foster, a dissenting lecturer, and Henry Stebbing, a high church divine.

---

[18] On which see Richard Ashcraft, *Revolutionary Politics and Locke's 'Two Treatises of Government'* (Princeton, 1986), pp. 496–7.

[19] Norman Sykes, *Edmund Gibson* (Oxford, 1926), pp. 122–82 and esp. 148–9; J. Hervey, *Memoirs of the Reign of George II*, ed., J. W. Croker, 2 vols. (1848), II, p. 87; see also Stephen Taylor, 'Sir Robert Walpole, the Church of England, and the Quakers' Tithe Bill of 1736', *Historical Journal*, 28 (1985).

All this added to the sense of religious ferment. The uproar ended in the political arena with Gibson's withdrawal from the charmed circle of power, and in the contemplative realm with William Warburton's *Alliance between Church and State* of 1736 which set out new rules of engagement.[20]

Witchcraft disappeared from serious discourse in the period following the extinction of the rage of party; and it is my contention that a period of parallel and intense religious controversy two decades later revived the issue, in attenuated form. The context for the repeal of the witchcraft legislation is not a putative judicial spirit of reform, but rather a half-decade or more of ecclesiastical upset.[21] The religious set-tos just outlined were exactly the sort of thing which Walpole had sought to avoid through Gibson's management of the church. Having wanted to move away from the sectarianism of the last years of Anne, Walpole had ended up with a prelate who some saw as being bent upon imitating William Laud. The repeal of the witchcraft act in early 1736 might have been seen as an indication that such high-church pretensions were being expelled from the body politic in their most absurd form. But can we get any further than this in relating the measure to the hither and thither of political manoeuvre?

The problem with the 1736 repeal is that it seems to emerge out of nowhere. The ideology of witchcraft lost credibility and usefulness in the wake of its adoption by Tory factionalism, and the ensuing Whig ascendancy, but the process by which this ideological transformation became a root-and-branch change in mentality is more difficult to judge. By the time of the Jew Bill, in 1753, when images of witchcraft were

---

[20] M. Foster, *Examination of the Scheme of Church Power laid down in the Codex* (1735). See, for example, H. Stebbing, *A letter to Mr Foster on the subject of Heresy* (1735); J. Foster, *An answer to Dr Stebbing's Letter on the subject of Heresy, a letter* (1735). Stebbing possibly contributed *The Case of the Hertfordshire Witchcraft Considered* to the Wenham debate, but see Notestein, *A History of Witchcraft*, p. 374; J. C. D. Clark, *English Society 1688–1832* (Cambridge, 1985), pp. 137–41; Langford, *A Polite and Commercial People*, pp. 38–44. But, for a caveat as to Warburton's significance see Stephen Taylor, 'William Warburton and the alliance of church and state', *Journal of Ecclesiastical History*, 43 (1992).

[21] Although the House of Lords, agreeing on 24 Feb. 1735/6 to meet in committee on the 26th to discuss the bill for the repeal of the witchcraft act, did suggest 'that the Judges do then attend', *Journal of the House of Lords*, 9 Geo II, 1735/6. On motives and means for eighteenth-century legislation see Joanna Innes, 'Parliament and the shaping of eighteenth-century English social policy', *Transactions of the Royal Historical Society*, 5th ser., 40 (1990), esp. 77–8 (on the role of judges and law officers); 82 (on anti-Walpolean moves for law reform); 89 (on the role of the executive in generating or directing legislation).

deployed in the satirical print (whether as an implicit condemnation of the absurd highflying fanaticism of those who opposed Jewish naturalisation, or as a reminder of the diabolical motivation of the Jewish lobby, we cannot be sure) we know that belief in witchcraft was eccentric, its use in propaganda a reworking of the rhetorical deposits of the generations.[22] The year 1736 is a different matter. What is more, the precise purpose of the bill is unclear because of the paucity of surviving parliamentary evidence. There are no official records of any parliamentary debate beyond the bare outline provided by the journals of the houses. Government involvement in the initiation of the bill is, as so often, difficult to fathom.[23] Any account must be tentative and rely on the accumulation of anecdote or the extrapolation of motive. Despite all these problems, it certainly seems worth asking why the witchcraft act was repealed in 1736, whether there was opposition, and from whom.

The bill's sponsors included John Crosse, described by Horace Walpole as 'a very good friend to my brother' and a fairly representative Old Whig, and John Conduitt, who served as master of the mint from 1727 until his death ten years later. A frequent speaker for the government in the house, he opposed the repeal of the Septennial Act, that coping stone of Whig stability, in the 1735/6 session. What makes Conduitt's sponsorship of repeal more interesting is that he was Sir Isaac Newton's nephew by marriage, his chosen successor at the Mint, and the guardian of the Newtonian tradition. Conduitt's involvement in the repeal of the witchcraft act may well have enhanced the identification of Newtonianism as the ideology of a sound and rational Whig settlement which purged the nation of antique superstition. The bill was presented to the Commons and delivered to the Lords by Conduitt; Crosse chaired the committee of the whole house which considered the bill before third reading.

The third and final sponsor, Alderman George Heathcote, was 'one of the most frequent and violent speakers for the opposition'. Heathcote was, according to Lord Egmont, 'a republican Whig', who in March

---

[22] See *Catalogue of Prints and Drawings in the British Museum*, Division 1, 'Political and personal satires', 3 vols. (1870– ), for example, 3270, 'All the world in a hurry, or the road from London to Oxford' (1753), 3214, 'The gypsy's triumph' (1753). But cf. [Adam Fitz-Adam], *The World*, 34, 23 Aug. 1753: 'it is shrewdly suspected that the same people who imagined their religion to be at stake by the repeal of the one [the Witchcraft Act], are at present under the most terrible consternation at the passing of the other [the Jew Bill]'.

[23] See Innes, 'Parliament and the shaping of eighteenth-century English social policy', p. 85, on paucity of records; p. 89, on obscurity of motive.

1731 participated in the anti-clerical assault by moving the motion to prevent the translation of bishops. Even more significantly, in the year of the repeal of the witchcraft act, he spoke in favour of the repeal of the Test Act. He did not oppose the government out of sheer spite, and on several occasions voted with the ministry.[24]

These are a mixed lot, but if we are looking for a common thread, the sponsors of repeal might be seen as representative of an emerging 'coalition' between some ministerial and opposition whigs in reaction to the revived highflying favoured by Gibson, and his attempts to advance ecclesiastical influence. The same groups formulated and supported the schemes concerning Quaker tithes and mortmain which drove Gibson from influence. The Quaker tithes bill was read for the first time in the Commons a week before the new Witchcraft Act received royal assent; and the day after the third reading of the witch bill, a motion for the repeal of the test laws was lost in the Commons. According to Stephen Taylor, at this stage in his career 'Walpole probably hoped that debate on religious issues, by appealing to ideology, would emphasize the differences between opposition whigs [who supported some measure of relief for the Quakers] and Tories [who did not]'.[25] Repeal of the witchcraft legislation may have played a symbolic role in indicating the increasingly, though not definitively, secular nature of the state, legislation less liable to offend or inconvenience than the repeal of the test and corporation acts. It is striking that when those latter measures were under threat again, in the 1820s, witchcraft emerged once more as an issue.[26] But while repeal of the witchcraft legislation may have formed a fairly uncontentious part of the response to feelings that the state was in danger – no-one was suggesting that Gibson was a proselytising believer in witchcraft – there was some opposition, and it is important to analyse its motivation.

The historian chancing upon a stray parliamentary opponent of the

---

[24] Romney Sedgwick, *The House of Commons 1715–1754*, 2 vols. (1970), under name of member; *Journal of the House of Commons*, 9 Geo II, 1735/6. For the continued association between the Newtonian tradition and the rout of superstition and witch beliefs in particular, see Hogarth's execrably punning 'Frontis-Piss' of 1763, engraved by LaCave; Samuel Ireland, *Graphic Illustrations of Hogarth* (1794–99), 2 vols., I, pp. 175–6.

[25] Taylor, 'Sir Robert Walpole', 58.

[26] Within the framework of the *ancien régime*, the test and witchcraft continued to be somehow perceived as bound together, see *Antipas: a solemn appeal to the Archbishops and Bishops with reference to several Bills . . . especially that concerning Witchcraft and Sorcery* (1821), opposing the repeal of the Irish witchcraft legislation.

witchcraft repeal in 1736 might be forgiven for experiencing incredulity closely followed by a conviction that the individual concerned must have been singularly eccentric. For the traditionalist, who sees repeal as the progressive and inevitable result of a communal 'loss of belief' in the late seventeenth century, this is self-evidently so. Any opposition was, in the event, wide of the mark. The contemporary mood suggests the same: two parliamentary journals, Edward Harley's and Thomas Wilson's, allude to repeal with no hint of real controversy.[27] In a historical account which charts a different course, the loner could instead be a key to unlock yet more of the ideological secret history of the expulsion of witchcraft from public affairs. Unusual certainly, in his willingness to raise the issue in parliament, he is a man with a history and with interests which, however marginalised, might be profitably analysed rather than rejected out of hand as mere lunacy. The eccentric in question was the brother of the earl of Mar, rebel leader of 1715 – James Erskine, Lord Grange.

The received account of Erskine's stand on sorcery is utterly contemptuous and dismissive:

[Erskine] contracted such a violent aversion at Sir Robert Walpole, that having, by intrigue and hypocrisy, secured a majority of the district of burghs of which Stirling is the chief, he threw up his seat as a Judge in the Court of Session, was elected member for that district, and went to London to attend Parliament, and to overturn Sir Robert Walpole, not merely in his own opinion, but also in the opinion of many who were dupes to his cunning, and his pretensions to abilities that he had not. But his first appearance in the House of Commons undeceived his sanguine friends, and silenced him for ever. He chose to make his maiden speech on the Witches Bill, as it was called; and being learned in daemonologia, with books on which subject his library was filled, he made a long canting speech that set the House in a titter of laughter, and convinced Sir Robert that he had no need of any extraordinary armour against this champion of the house of Mar. The truth was, that the man had neither learning nor ability. He was no lawyer, and he was a bad speaker. He had been raised on the shoulders of his brother, the Earl of Mar, in the end of the Queen's reign, but had never distinguished himself. In the General Assembly, which many

---

[27] C. L. S. Linnell, ed., *The Diaries of Thomas Wilson, D.D., 1731–7 and 1750, son of Bishop Wilson of Sodor and Man* (1964), entry for Thursday, 26 Feb. 1735/6; Edward Harley, Cambridge University Library MS Add. 6851 (Parliamentary Journal for 1734–51), entry for 22 Jan. 1735/6, f. 30.

gentlemen afterwards made a school of popular eloquence, and where he took the high-flying side that he might annoy Government, his appearances were but rare and unimpressive; but as he was understood to be a great plotter, he was supposed to reserve himself for some greater occasions.[28]

This anecdote is alluded to in Keith Thomas' *Religion and the Decline of Magic*, setting a seal on the accepted model of the decline of witchcraft; but by unpicking it in detail we can build up a very different picture of Erskine.[29] To view the 1736 repeal as a dotting of i's evades the need for explanation; in the same way, to label Erskine's opposition as mere eccentricity is to dismiss his actions as inexplicably bizarre. They may have been, but they deserve a rational examination first. We need to explore the motivation of his stand in this particular instance, to relate it to his other political actions, unwinding the tangled mess of his political career to understand why Erskine, undoubtedly capable of shrewd behaviour, could have been so spectacularly off course.

We can start by reconstructing Erskine's intellectual formation and milieu. Only thus can his opposition to the 'Witches Bill' be understood. His desire to 'overturn Sir Robert Walpole' and 'annoy Government', his relationship to the earl of Mar and his reputation as a 'great plotter' will all have their part to play. For the purposes of this chapter, however, the vital recognition is that Erskine's ideological affiliations in the years between 1715 and 1745 are a link between two important features of the discourse of witchcraft up to 1715 as outlined above. A Scot and a 'highflyer', it will emerge that Erskine's opposition to the repeal was indeed part of a more general attack on Walpole; but one which drew its consistency from a concern for Scottish rights and Scottish religion, and a related anxiety about the spiritual standing of the 'Robinocracy'.

Erskine's diary reveals that in his youth he was far from being the sort of convinced Presbyterian we have earlier implicated in the defence of witchcraft belief and prosecution. In the late 1690s he had condemned Scots Calvinists as 'narrow spirited and prejudiced creatures' and affected 'a great esteem for John le Clerc at Amsterdam' reckoning him 'one who had shook off these prejudices and thought freely'.[30] In

---

[28]  Carlyle, *Autobiography*, p. 10.

[29]  Thomas, *Religion and the Decline of Magic*, p. 694.

[30]  James Erskine, Lord Grange, *Extracts from the Diary of a Senator of the College of Justice* (Edinburgh, 1843), p. 83. These are extracts from the MS listed in HMC, *Report on the Manuscripts of the Earl of Mar and Kellie* (1904), marked 'Memoirs VI'. Most of it relates to Erskine's religious experiences.

1708, Erskine might have been over such youthful freethinking, but remained ironically dismissive of the supposed virtues of clerical government: 'It is a good thing that now both Church and high Kirk join in their principles as to screwing up the power of the clergy; which I hope will teach people that Church and Kirk are at the bottom of the same kidney, and that neither ought to be too much indulged or trusted to.'[31]

By this time Erskine was a successful lawyer, well on the way to influence. Snugly ensconced in the bosom of the Stuart establishment he was successively member of the faculty of advocates (1705), lord of session (1707) and, finally, lord justice clerk (1710). In the years around 1707 he was as keen on the union as any Scotsman on the make, despite the caveats:

> I'm much affraid that there may still be a great deall of uneasyness about it. [But] I'm sure it is in the power of the Government and Parliament of Brittain to make the Union not only durable, but most acceptable and advantagious to this country, *as I expect it shall.* [my emphasis]

An ardent pragmatist, he was full of scorn for the 'fury and impertinence of biggots on either side'.[32]

The death of Queen Anne and the ensuing rebellion were turning points in Erskine's career. In 1714 he was dismissed from his post. In 1715 his brother Mar led the Jacobite uprising, and the family estates were consequently sequestered. In subsequent decades Erskine did his best, in his own words, 'to preserve from ruine the forfeited famillys of my friends and relations'. Having been a student companion of Walpole's Scottish agent, Islay, Erskine thought he had a sure route back into the confidence of the government. He had been disappointed, his family slighted, as he made clear in a letter of 1733:

> Such has long been their way, to profess great friendship to me and the familly . . . and much readyness to do us good, and seemingly to propose better for us than we do for ourselves; but when it came to the execution, to prevent the doing of it by shifts, tricks, and lies . . . Why should we sit still and let them trick us into poverty, contempt, and insignificancy?[33]

---

[31] Letter to his brother Mar, 29 Jan. 1708 in HMC, *Mar and Kellie*, p. 426.
[32] Ibid.
[33] 'Letters of Lord Grange', in *The Miscellany of the Spalding Club*, III (Aberdeen, 1846), pp. 1–71.

In the same period, after 1715, Erskine's religious leanings were transformed. By the 1720s he was the very model of a Kirk man, active in the affairs of the General Assembly, well-known for 'strengthening the hands of the zealous orthodox ministers'. 'It verie much refreshes me', wrote one correspondent, 'to find any, especially of your high station, that often live at the greatest distance from God, fill'd with just and clear apprehensions of true religion, and the decayed and languishing state thereof in this dead and withered time.' Indeed, the decayed and languishing state of religion, in its broad and narrow senses, became a theme of Erskine's opposition to Walpole's regime. He complained of the great man's 'openly rediculing all vertue and uprightness'; of the 'geddyness and corruption of our age'; and an addiction to 'lewd and idle Diversions'. He gave his friend Robert Wodrow a picture of Queen Caroline continually 'bantering and scolding the narrou principles of the Church of Scotland'.[34]

This last remark alerts us to the framework within which this spleen and religious anxiety were exercised. From 1715 on Erskine was moving towards a thoroughgoing defence of Scots rights and Scots particularity, in both politics and religion. We need not, as so many of Erskine's enemies did, stoop to accusations of hypocrisy.[35] To start with, family and personal honour were legitimately bound up with national honour in the case of a family as prominent as Erskine's: 'poverty, contempt, and insignificancy' was the threatened fate not only of the Erskines, but of the whole kingdom under the new dispensation. Walpole and his crew were 'these oppressors of the familly we belong to, *and* enemys of Britain'. Religion and politics were bound up together, too, as Erskine's attitude to the Simson affair acutely demonstrates.[36]

John Simson was a notorious Scottish theologian, prosecuted in the General Assembly of the Kirk for teaching unsound doctrine. The case created uproar and became one of the *causes célèbres* of eighteenth-century Scottish ecclesiastical politics. Erskine, deeply involved in the prosecution of the deistical Simson, was convinced that the affair was being used by the Walpole administration as part of an attack on Scottish rights and integrity:

[34] John Wylie to Erskine, pp. 1–71, 8 May 1721, HMC, *Mar and Kellie*, p. 521; Andrew Darling, minister at Kintoul, to Erskine, 3 Feb. 1724; HMC, *Mar and Kellie*, p. 525; 'Letters of Lord Grange', pp. 56, 57; *The History and Proceedings of the House of Commons . . .* , 1742, IX, p. 93, 5 Mar. 1735; Robert Wodrow, *Analecta*, ed., M. Leishman, 4 vols. (Glasgow, 1842), IV, p. 146.

[35] See Wodrow, *Analecta*, III, pp. 510, 306.    [36] 'Letters of Lord Grange', p. 47.

ther seems to be a designe, at some Assembly, to throu up him [Simson], or some other bone of contention, to break and divide us: That when our Assemblys break upon this or other points, they will be prohibited by the King, and either Commissions, or some other select meetings, called by the King's writ, will have the management of Church affairs.[37]

For Erskine, as for so many others before the '45, the religious and state affairs of Scotland were of a piece, and seemed increasingly under threat from English interference. The unionist careerist, sceptical of temperament, came to believe, under the pressure of a variety of events, that the balance of the 1707 settlement was being unbalanced by the actions of a corrupt and irreligious ministry. It is within this context that we have to locate Erskine's opposition to the witch bill, taking him as seriously as his friend Robert Wodrow did:

> that person hath made a bold appearance for the truth; and if any suspect him as forming a designe to manage a party among the Ministry, and to affect leading and dictating to them, such, in my opinion, have acted a very imprudent part at this time in supporting Mr Simson so much, since by this method they have given that eminent person a handle (wer he seeking one) to recommend himself to the affections of all in Scotland, who have a concern for the purity of doctrine, and preventing error in this Church.[38]

Before outlining the sequence of events which may have led to Erskine's speech of 1736, Erskine's relation to the discourses of witchcraft outlined in the first part of this chapter needs to be charted. First of all, Erskine's personal beliefs, his inner and inaccessible convictions, are debatable; but it is worth noting that from the 1720s to his death he was unambiguously supernaturalist in religion, both in matters of the operation of divine grace and the ministrations of the devil and his agents.[39] Secondly, Erskine's early if temperate enthusiasm for the Anglo-Scottish union does place him initially outside the orbit of the Presbyterian knot who saw true witchcraft belief as a mark of Scottish rectitude as against English infidelity; but, his increasing suspicion of the English government and concern for Scottish identity and honour make his visible support for the Jacobean witchcraft

---

[37] For Simson see *DNB*; *Analecta*, IV, p. 144.
[38] *Analecta*, III, p. 511.
[39] See, for example, *Analecta*, III, pp. 207, 410; II, pp. 47, 86–7, 171, 255, 323, 379.

legislation an ideological manoeuvre within an identifiable tradition.[40] Finally, Erskine was, as our opening anecdote has it, a 'highflyer': hot for the rights of the Kirk; for the power of the General Assembly; for the restriction of lay intrusion into clerical privileges. His refusal to distinguish between the religious and political well-being of his nation has been noted. Despite the doctrinal chasm which separated such Calvinist highflyers north of the border from highflyers and non-jurors in England, there is an affinity in their common attitude to the proper relationship between the sacred and secular domains, an affinity which was reflected in the resilience of the discourse of witchcraft within both groups. This makes it all the more striking that Erskine was, in his latter years, an associate of John Wesley, whose public condemnation of the repeal of the witchcraft act reflected his own highflying roots as well as his Scriptural fundamentalism.[41]

The attack on Scottish rights reached its apogee in 1734 during the election of the representative Scottish peers; troops were used to overawe the electors. Members of the Whig opposition – Chesterfield and Carteret – approached the dismissed peers in the wake of the election, and proposed that steps should be taken to force the ministry to account for the apparent malpractice. The peers engaged two men as their chief advisers, Dundas and the lawyer, James Erskine of Grange. Erskine was heavily involved in opposition manoeuvres, and the government started to move against him, introducing a bill to prevent Scottish lords of session like himself from being elected to the House of Commons. He quit his employment to secure his seat.[42]

Having been alienated from the mainstream of Westminster politics, 'represented as a hypocrite, and pretender to religion . . . as divisive and factious', in anger of 'lossing his friends at London', political crisis now pushed Erskine back into the centre of affairs.[43] The period which

---

[40] For the distance between the pre-1715 Erskine and, for example, Robert Wylie, an opponent of union and proponent of legislation against witches (see n. 8 above), see HMC, *Mar and Kellie*, p. 273, Erskine to Mar, 20 Aug. 1706.

[41] HMC, *Report on the Laing Manuscripts*, 2 vols. (1914, 1925). II, p. 348. For Wesley see, for example, Henry Moore, *The Life of the Reverend John Wesley* (Leeds, 1825), p. 323 and *The Journal of the Reverend John Wesley*, Everyman edn, iii, p. 412, entry for 4 July 1770.

[42] See *Arniston Memoirs: Three Centuries of a Scottish House 1571–1838*, ed.. G. W. T. Omond (Edinburgh, 1887), pp. 82–3; Erskine's speech against the manipulated election in *The History and Proceedings of the House of Commons*, IX, pp. 69–71; Pulteney to Erskine, 24 Feb. and 22 Mar. 1734 and Earl of Stair to Erskine, 20 Mar. 1734, all in HMC, *Mar and Kellie*, pp. 531–4.

[43] *Analecta*, III, pp. 306, 510.

followed the failure of Walpole's Excise scheme was one of threatening instability for the ministry, in its relations with Scotland as elsewhere. In 1735 Dundas, Erskine's colleague, gave his son an apocalyptic vision of a 'struggle for the sinking liberty of our country [Scotland] till God in his providence interpose to save us'. Erskine himself declared that 'the opposition to Sir Robert Walpole and Ilay is stronger and more rooted than, perhaps, it was to any ministry since the Revolution . . . high church, whig and dissenter, closely united in it, and all their own disputes buryed in this common pressure'.[44] It was in the midst of this turmoil that Erskine chose to speak against the new witchcraft legislation. We have seen how in 1711 the Harleyite Daniel Defoe sought to bury disputes and appeal to 'high church, whig and dissenter' by writing in support of an orthodox belief in witchcraft. Whatever Erskine's hopes as to the likely appeal of witchcraft belief to disaffected Tories, his speech against repeal must be seen primarily as that of a Scottish member, concerned for Scottish particularity in government and religion, and for the maintenance of orthodoxy in the kingdom as a whole (a favourite Scottish theme since the 1630s).[45] In the 1730s Erskine was still a supporter of the union between England and 'North Britain', joining with the Whig opposition to espouse the complaints of England as well as his own nation. He used English grievances as a lever to effect common relief: '[Walpole] makes bold schemes against our libertys, as was most certainly his excyse scheme which he pushed like a mad man after England.' But he had a particular concern for English invasion of Scottish prerogatives, complaining that 'in England, nothing is made of our Act of Settlement, and all pouer is undoubtedly in the hands of the Supream Court [sc. Parliament]'. Religion could be a target for an irreligious, scheming, Anglicising ministry, with Walpole and Islay seeking 'our breaking in pieces' and making 'Mr S[imson] an instrument to tear and rent us'.[46] In the year following repeal, Erskine was still pursuing Scottish interests, speaking in the debate on the Porteous riots, and opposing the bill of pains and penalties against the city of Edinburgh.

Erskine's behaviour seems less eccentric in such a context. His behaviour shows a specifically Scottish tradition trying to operate in an

---

[44] *Arniston Memoirs*, p. 81, Dundas to his son at Utrecht, 6 Feb. 1735; 'Letters of Lord Grange', p. 44. By late 1736, Thomas Wilson was convinced that 'Scotland and England are ripe for Rebellion', see his journal p. 178, entry for 24 Oct. 1736.

[45] See Conrad Russell, *The Causes of the English Civil War* (Oxford, 1990), pp. 118–22 on 'Scottish imperial' policy in the 1630s and 1640s.

[46] *Analecta*, IV, p. 144.

English arena. What is more, Erskine was no dolt. The worthy Wodrow eulogised him; Pulteney and other members of the opposition wooed him; Walpole feared him enough to frame legislation to exclude him from the House of Commons. What remains to be explained is the chasm between the sponsors of repeal, with their negative manoeuvre to paper over the cracks in the Whig coalition; and Erskine, with his positive gesture, via witchcraft, to the ranks of outraged Scottish and, perhaps, English orthodoxy. The chronology is unfortunately lost to us – we cannot know precisely when Erskine spoke, in response to what, or whether his intervention elicited or followed the amendment which extended the new legislation to Scotland. But Erskine's decision to speak against the 'Witches Bill' was a miscalculation because he mistook the complexion of the House of Commons, and the shift in the status of English discourse about witchcraft which had followed 1712–14. He was playing by Scottish rules. That anecdotal 'titter of laughter' may indeed have ended Erskine's career as a serious politician, but it did not silence him nor can it be denied that Erskine had his reasons for responding to the repeal. The development of his religious and political stance pushed him closer to a position which earlier Scots had adopted, where belief in witchcraft became for Erskine, as it had been for them, a matter of national pride, a symbol of independence, and an act of resistance to a deistical and irreligious English ministry. It may well be that repeal, calculated from one angle to define a common whiggish rationalism, was also intended to split the opposition, or at least to expose the likes of Erskine to a salutary dose of ridicule. It may be that Erskine hoped to carry disaffected Tories and dissenters with him.[47] We can be sure that 'his sanguine friends', the anti-Walpolean Whigs with whom he had joined forces, were disappointed. The paucity of opposition to repeal within the House of Commons does not tell us much about the beliefs of individual members, the residual prejudices and sentiments of Tory or Scottish members. But the fact that only Erskine was bold enough, or misguided enough, to brave the giggling and scorn of the house, tells us something about the triumph of polite and 'rational' discourse, and the rising blushes which must have stifled any budding expressions of a belief in the power of witches. Nursing for so long his Scottish resentments, smarting from English abuse, Erskine confused the English and Scottish contexts of opposition and his attacks were brushed aside as uncouth nonsense.

[47] Cf. Stephen Taylor at n. 25.

IV

James Erskine evidently saw the repeal of the witchcraft act as part of a more general assault upon the citadels of fidelity. He worried about the credentials of English bishops, 'none of them being firm to any set of doctrinall principles, they are much dispised'. One of his particular *bêtes noirs* was Benjamin Hoadly: 'Bangor, nou Sarum, is sunk into a hackney writer.'[48] Hoadly's reputedly deistical *Plain Account of the Nature and End of the Sacrament of the Lord's Supper*, appeared in 1735. The issue of Hoadly's freethinking in the *Plain Account* was the starting point for the only extant pamphlet straightforwardly opposing the repeal of the witchcraft act, written in the form of an address to the sponsoring members, and attached to a reissue of an anonymous work, *The Witch of Endor: Or a Plea for the Divine Administration by the Agency of Good and Evil Spirits* (original date uncertain, but some time in the early years of the century). It manifested many of the same concerns as Erskine and may help us to understand latent prejudices which remained, for the most part, unexpressed.

This *Address* recapitulates many of the old arguments about witchcraft, but it focuses on the threat of freethinking which the repeal of the witchcraft legislation represented: 'the design being to secure some of the *Outworks* of *Religion*, and to regain a Parcel of Ground, which *bold* Infidelity hath invaded'. The author uses heavy sarcasm and addresses the House of Commons with heavy irony: 'I dare not entertain the least Thought, Gentlemen, that you have any of the *Freethinking* Qualities, that are so prevalent, at this Time of Day . . . ' While implying that the arguments against a proper belief in witchcraft are irredeemably vulgar, the product of ignorance and raillery, the author wryly exempts his distinguished audience: 'It would be inexcusable to trouble you any longer, *Gentlemen*, with this Way and Manner of *decrying Witchcraft*; and I'll venture of Prophesy [!], *such* sort of Arguing will not be made use of in your *own Learned Debates* upon the same subject.'[49]

It is Francis Hutchinson, now bishop of Down and Connor, author of

---

[48] *Analecta*, IV, p. 146.
[49] *The Witch of Endor* (1736), pp. xlv, xliii. Cf. footnote on p. v which mocks the Commons' contempt for the authority of Coke's *Pleas of the Crown*, 'which I don't doubt, but your Worships have consulted, and pity'd *his* Understanding and Knowledge too'. At one point the mockery verges on the insulting: 'When the *Gospel* of Christ was Preaching, (which ever condemns Witchcraft, and *Sorcery* . . . however you, our *Representatives*, shall please to determine the Affair *within Doors* . . . '), p. xi.

the definitive sceptical work, *An Historical Essay concerning Witchcraft* (1718), whom the pamphleteer wants to discredit. He paints him as a vulgarian, free and easy with fantastical stories about the contortions and wonders which may be achieved (implausibly) by nature alone, without the intrusion of the supernatural. Hutchinson's book bandies tales about showmen and charlatans, so many indeed that his opponent, with a nod and a wink, can 'profess . . . [that] I am perfectly Ignorant whence our Right Reverend, got all this KNOWLEDGE, or where his SOBER AUTHORS are to be met with'. The pamphleteer shows his opponents playing with dangerous vulgarity and outrageous freethinking, mounting a disturbingly plebeian, if episcopal, threat to traditional orthodoxy. It is to the service of this scheme that the author of the *Address* bends his urbane and witty tone, punning and cracking jokes about the Gin Act, the other 'spiritual' crisis of 1736.[50]

The intellectual and theological argument pursued in tandem with this drollery is one which unmasks the central contradiction in Hutchinson's discourse, between the denial of witchcraft on the one hand, and the assertion, on the other, that, as Hutchinson put it, 'the sober belief of good and bad Spirits is an Essential Part of every good Christian's Faith'. How can this assertion and this denial be squared? Or, as our author has it: '[it is] inconsistent with such a Belief, that all Communications should be reckoned Imaginary, and that the Intellectual World should not serve the Purposes of an Almighty Being, in rewarding or punishing according to the Divine Appointment'. The author is keen in associating the 'Fundamental Part of the Statute' with the 'Protestant Religion and Interest', which 'as 'tis grounded on the Holy Scriptures, so it stands, and I hope, will ever stand, supported by the Legislature'. His definition of witchcraft is a broad one – 'any sort of Communication with, or Operations upon the Intellectual, and Corporeal World' – and having cited the Bible, and Hutchinson himself, on the necessity of spiritual ministration and depredation, he asks how the legislature can possibly be considering what he calls an 'absolute Repeal'. This last phrase suggests the possibility that the witchcraft legislation could have been revised so as to minimise prosecution, while retaining its ideological and defining function, in both religion and statecraft; a contemporary nod to the conceptual distinction between ideology and persecution. But then, the author is adamant that, as 'an Offence capital immediately against the Divine Majesty', witchcraft deserves to be punished. The association

---

[50] *The Witch of Endor*, pp. xxv–xxvi, xxxiii. Cf. *The Hyp-Doctor*, no. 285, 23 Mar. 1736.

between orthodox belief in witchcraft and the maintenance of true religion culminates in this passage:

> [I] must believe, that, in the *Preamble* of your Bill (which I have not seen) you have taken all possible Care to guard against the Suggestions of a *censorious* Age; by *supporting* the *Christian Doctrine*, and declaring to the World, (as Bishop *Hutchinson* does) *That the* sober *Belief of Good and Bad Spirits is an* essential *Part of every good Christian's Faith.*[51]

There is also a social threat lurking behind this legislation, which points back to the condemnation of Hutchinson as a dangerous truckler with plebeians and freethinkers: 'However, it must be said, the *contrary* Temper [i.e. freethinking] is too obvious amongst us *without Doors*; and this has induc'd me to trouble you in such a Manner . . . ' The author poses as a hard-nosed realist who can tell the honourable members about affairs in the outside world, 'however *merry* you may have made your-selves about SPIRITS in St *Stephen's* Chapel'. Witchcraft belief is an important buttress of orthodox religion, which parliament neglects at its peril.

The postscript alludes to a very different sort of pressure from without doors, 'your *Electors* . . . [and] *Thousands* besides' who require an answer to these objections. There is a tension, between this manipulation of public opinion, and the author's almost paranoid fear of the licentious mob: 'I now hear what I have to offer, comes *too late*, and there seems no other *Reason* possibly to be assign'd for it, but, that my unknown *Printer sides* with the *Majority*, in *procrastinating* the birth of this little Pamphlet.' That this charge reached the light of day hardly indicates particular interest on the part of the threateningly *anonymous* artisan; but fear of the plebeian is in evidence, in both mysterious particularity (the printer) and threatening mass (the '*Majority*').[52]

Earlier, however, the author makes an assessment of the balance of clerical opinion which is very different:

> [witchcraft can be considered as] an Affair purely of a *Religious Nature*, abstracted from the *Civil Punishment* [again the distinction between persecution and ideology]; and, if I might ask; what, if the *Concurrence* of an *English Convocation* had been had, in making such a *General Repeal*?

Witchcraft is evidently a Tory issue, and the cherished belief of a silent majority of the English clergy. The author manages to bind up witchcraft

---

[51] *The Witch of Endor*, pp. viii, xxviii, v.     [52] Ibid., pp. xliii, xlix–l, xliii.

with another recognisably Tory grievance, the disappearance of a sitting convocation. This involved the entrusting of the nation's spiritual interest to parliament. In the pamphlet as a whole, the author asks the legislators to exercise their spiritual responsibilities with care. In this particular passage, he asserts that were the clergy to have a say, as would be proper in a consideration 'abstracted from the *Civil Punishment*', the matter would stand very differently.[53]

So we can identify this address as thoroughly Tory in ideology: siding with the ordinary clergy, as against two bishops, but fearing the mob; crying out that the church is in danger, and condemning the licence of the modern majority. This reading of the text allows us to define the sense in which those who supported the old witchcraft legislation felt embattled; and to catch the authentic but silent meaning of the constituency – marginalised, embarrassed, ridiculed – from which its author emerged. It was a constituency Erskine's 'long canting speech' in the Commons failed either to find or arouse.

V

It is misleading, therefore, to make the repeal of the Jacobean legislation against witchcraft a mere footnote to the history of rationalism. Repeal did not emerge from out of nowhere as an afterthought, a process of mopping-up in a struggle against superstition that had been won some time 'between the Restoration and the Revolution'. It had a context and a meaning, both to some extent recoverable. Erskine and our anonymous pamphleteer represent an identifiable nexus of concerns which can be seen at work long before 1736, and did not suddenly die a death either on the stroke of midnight, 31 December 1699, or when George II put his signature to the act of repeal.[54]

Neither was repeal an undifferentiated and simple, nor a solely English process. The parliamentary procedure of discussion and amendment resulted not in a simple repeal as had been envisaged by the bill's

---

[53] Ibid., p. xxvii. Compare the pamphleteer's concern for convocation, with that of Erskine and his predecessors – like Robert Wylie – for the continued existence and dignity of the General Assembly of the Scottish church. Highflying in Scotland and England was being bound up with the issue of witchcraft.

[54] Buckle, *The History of Civilisation*, III, p. 363: 'the destruction of the old notions respecting witchcraft . . . was effected, so far as the educated classes are concerned, between the Restoration and the Revolution'.

sponsors, but in a new witchcraft act which punished imposture, the pretended 'use or exercise [of] any kind of Witchcraft, Sorcery, Inchantment, or Conjuration'. The Lords' consideration of the bill also ensured the extension of the new legislation to Scotland; an afterthought which is a neat example of the insensitivity to the affairs of North Britain about which the likes of Erskine complained. The late measures against imposture had an ideological function, serving to underline the new reading of the Old Testament injunctions against witchcraft which those who wished to ditch the prosecution of witches had long favoured.[55]

The 1736 legislation was itself repealed in the 1950–1 session of parliament with the intention of preventing possible prosecutions of well-meaning spiritualists. Chuter Ede, home secretary, was whiggish in every sense, asserting that 'this Measure is a considerable advance in the direction of religious Toleration'. Another member, Lieutenant-Commander Thompson, saw the measure in a more engagingly eccentric light, making a speech which encapsulates many of the false conceptions besetting the historian of witchcraft:

If, as I hope, the House gives a Second Reading to this Bill today we shall be doing rather a remarkable thing. I do not speak as a Spiritualist, but in my view we shall be reaffirming an outlook and a point of view very necessary in an increasingly material age. In 1735 [*sic*] the Witchcraft Act brought to an end officially what had, in fact, been at an end for some years – the belief in the reality of witchcraft. Witchcraft had been practised from the very beginning of time; during the 16th and 17th centuries there was tremendous activity in England and on the Continent, but with the dawn of the 'age of reason', so called, belief in the reality of witchcraft faded . . . By 1735 the official view was that these powers no longer existed, whether they were good or evil, and we have been committed to a sort of official scepticism ever since that day . . . [this bill will] reaffirm that we honestly admit that there are powers given to some people in the community which enable them to do things which, for 215 years, we have not believed were physically possible.

This passage sums up many historical misconceptions, unwittingly hints

---

[55] For amendments see *Journal of the House of Lords*, 26 Feb. 1735/6 and *Journal of the House of Commons*, 4 Mar. 1735/6. On the 'proper' reading of the scriptural injunctions against witchcraft, see *The Witchcraft of the Scriptures: A Sermon Preach'd on a Special Occasion. By Ph.S LL.D* (1736), esp. pp. 19, 22, 24, and Joseph Juxon, *A Sermon upon Witchcraft* (1736).

at a truer perspective, and suggests unexpected continuities in the history of witchcraft legislation.[56]

This chapter set out by questioning the cogency of vague notions according to which belief in the reality of witchcraft 'faded' in the wake of a nebulous 'age of reason', some time around 1700. As an intellectual assumption about the genealogy of our own beliefs, this position runs very deep, as Lieutenant-Commander Thompson's remarks show. Once the assumption has been questioned, and we ask whether witchcraft might not have been a serious issue in 1700 and beyond, our whole perspective on this issue shifts radically.

As we have seen, the 1735–6 act did not commit everyone to scepticism as regards the existence of these powers, 'good or evil'. Even after 1736, apologists for the old attitudes continued to speak out; but their fate was increasingly to be marginalised and ridiculed. The repeal of the Jacobean legislation set the seal on an elite consensus that convictions of witches for real sorcery were unsafe. This was, then, a confirmation of an 'official view' in force since the end of the 'rage of party'. It is here that Thompson's remarks point towards the perspective canvassed in this essay: the history of the fate of the elite discourse of witchcraft is largely the history of an official point of view and its trans-formations, transformations effected both by specific, and contingent, political events, and by longer-term shifts in the structure of ideology.

Finally, of course, 215 years on, witchcraft legislation was once more being used to fight bigger battles to defend spiritual values 'in an increasingly material age'. The witchcraft issue had its various uses in the seventeenth, the eighteenth, the nineteenth, and even the twentieth centuries. And writing about witchcraft today, no doubt, has its uses too.[57]

---

[56] *Hansard*, 5th ser., vol. 481, session 1950–51, cols. 1486, 1467 (1 Dec. 1950). On 20 June 1950, Charles Botham had been convicted on three counts of false pretences. He had also been charged with two counts of conjuration under the 1735/6 act, but these were not considered by the court.

[57] 14 and 15 Geo. 6. ch. 33. *Fraudulent Mediums Act, 1951.* (An Act to repeal the Witchcraft Act, 1735, and to make in substitution for certain provisions of section four of the Vagrancy Act, 1824, express provision for the punishment of persons who fraudulently purport to act as spiritualistic mediums or to exercise powers of telepathy, clairvoyance, or other similar powers. 22 June 1951.) For recent, non-historical, debate about witchcraft see 'Propaganda, fantasy and lies blur reports of ritual abuse', *The Guardian*, 10 Sept. 1990; 'Save poor little witch girl; drugged child rape victim's nightmare in lair of Satan', *News of the World*, 6 May 1990; 'I sacrificed my babies to Satan', *Sunday Mirror*, 25 Mar. 1990; 'Witch story to believe?', *The Spectator*, 24 Mar. 1990; 'Root out Satanists . . . Mrs Thatcher last night vowed to rid Britain of devil worship orgies involving the sexual abuse of children', *The Sun*, 14 Mar. 1990.

# 12

## The fear of the King is death: James VI and the witches of East Lothian

### P. G. MAXWELL-STUART

On 1 September 1589, Anne of Denmark set sail for Scotland from Copenhagen and got as far as Elsinore. For the next six days North Sea storms drove the flotilla back and forth until, on 7 September, it was forced to put in at Mardø on the Norwegian coast. The succeeding five weeks are a story of leaking vessels, continuing storms, further attempts to reach Scotland, and finally the Princess's decision to weather it out in Oslo while some of her ships made their way back to Copenhagen. On 8 October, King James wrote to Anne in French, apparently the language they had in common, and then in the second half of the month — sources differ about the precise date — set sail himself for Norway to fetch back his bride. He, too, was subjected to storms but eventually came to Oslo where he and Anne were married on 23 November. They stayed there until 22 December when they left and made their way by stages into Denmark. Once there, they were married again in Kronborg on 21 January and stayed in Denmark until 21 April. Upon setting to sea on their homeward voyage they were attended yet again by storms but arrived safely in Leith on 1 May, thus ending their Scandinavian adventure.[1]

Scotland managed to survive the King's prolonged absence, and he seems happy to have been away, for it is noticeable how rarely he attempted to contact his Council. A month after his arrival in Norway there was no news from him, nor week by week after that until a message arrived at Leith on 15 December to say that James would be absent until the spring. Even so, communications were still being sent to Oslo long after the King had left.[2] The round of royal engagements during this period included a prolonged visit to Tycho Brahe's home at Uraniborg where James noticed a picture of George Buchanan, his former tutor, and a lengthy conversation with the leading Danish theologian of the day, Niels Hemmingsen. The principal subject of their discussion appears to have been predestination.[3] But while the King was enjoying an extended break from his fraught and dangerous existence in Scotland, Peder Munk, the Danish admiral who had been in charge of Anne's flotilla, was eager to clear himself of any accusations of negligence consequent upon the embarrassments of the previous winter. A court case brought by him against Christofer Valkendorf, the governor of Copenhagen and the man responsible for keeping the Royal Navy in repair, threw up charges of witchcraft against several named women who were supposed to have raised the storms which delayed Princess Anne; and one of them, Ane Koldings, may have gone on trial in Copenhagen two days before James and Anne left for Scotland. In spite of this, however, the general consensus of those involved with the earlier voyages was that the problems they had encountered were entirely natural.[4]

In Scotland, meanwhile, there was absolutely nothing to suggest an upsurge of potentially treasonable witchcraft. On 28 April 1590, Meg Dow was put on trial for witchcraft and infanticide, found guilty, and later executed; on 7 May, the Haddington Synod had begun to investigate a complaint of witchcraft (first raised the previous September) against Agnes Sampson; on 22 July, Lady Fowlis and Hector Munro were finally tried on charges of witchcraft and murder going back as far as 1577; and several witches were arraigned in Edinburgh on charges relating to the Laird of Wardhouse. The matter of these trials involved the murder of children and adults, poison, personal abuse, elf-shot, sorcery, devilish incantations, and consultation with witches – nothing in the least unusual, and none of it touched the King or Queen at all.[5] Early in November 1590, however, all that changed. The Bailiff Depute of Tranent in East Lothian, David Seton, became suspicious of his maid, Gellie Duncan, who was frequently absent overnight from his house. She had a reputation as a remarkable healer and this, although harmless in itself, might always be liable to trigger a suspicion of witchcraft. After torture, applied by Seton, and the discovery of a witch's mark on her throat, Gellie Duncan was put in prison, where she began to tell a tale which soon involved a large number of others, both men and women. Two names quickly surfaced as particularly significant, those of Richard Graham and Francis Stewart, Earl of Bothwell; and two confessions transformed the investigation from local to national interest. First, it was alleged that a group of Scottish witches had deliberately sought to delay or destroy the King and Queen on their homeward journey and also made later attempts to kill the King by means of witchcraft and poison. Secondly, it was said that these treasonable attempts had been made at the request of the Earl of Bothwell.

Now, the trials of 1590–91 have been the subject of comment before, and two points have been repeated so often that they are in danger of turning into received wisdom. The first is that although a belief in witches was common in Scotland before the King's visit to Scandinavia, witchcraft was treated with a degree of scepticism, and penalties for its practice were not always inflicted according to the rigour demanded by statute law; but while James was in Denmark, he came into contact with Continental theories about witchcraft and upon his return home began to have them applied with a certain degree of ferocity. Torture, it is suggested, was used in witchcraft cases for the first time, and investigators started to look for the apparatus of the witch-mark, the *Sabbat*, flying through the air, and the Satanic pact, all of which characterised Continental theory but none of which had played a part hitherto in Scottish opinion. This proposition, I shall maintain, is broadly mistaken and has little evidence to support it.[6]

The second is that these East Lothian trials were similar in nature to an earlier type of witch-trial, 'in which the accusation of witchcraft was used, sometimes cynically, as a means to convict, or make popular the conviction of, a particular person'.[7] This, too, is somewhat dubious.[8]

Let us take first the suggestion about Denmark as a turning-point. As Larner has pointed out, there is no evidence that James was interested in witchcraft before 1590.[9] There are no books on the subject in the list we have of his library, nor was Buchanan in the least sympathetic to occult studies. Indeed, in his astronomical poem, *Sphaera*, he warns of the dangers of astrological prophecy and magic. Nor were there many books on witchcraft printed in or imported into Scotland: we know only of two. Alchemy was much more popular.[10] In c.1580, James may have been present at a performance of Montgomerie's *Flyting* which contains humorous scenes of elves and fairies and witches. Certainly he knew the work, for he quotes from it in an essay on poetic skills, written in 1584. If Montgomerie could use the subject for Court entertainment, it follows that James must have known enough about it to appreciate the plot, and the likelihood that he was entertained by it suggests he did not find witchcraft frightening at this stage.[11]

Nor would the situation in Scotland have particularly encouraged untoward fear. Certainly it is true that the Act of 1563 forbade anyone to use witchcraft, sorcery, or necromancy, to claim any powers thereby or knowledge thereof, or to seek help, response, or consultation of anyone claiming to be a witch, the penalty for both witch and client being death. But the wording of the statute treats the reality of witchcraft with a reticent scepticism, calling it 'a heavy and abominable superstition' and referring to witches as abusers of the people. So, as Legge points out, it is curious that all subsequent witch-trials in Scotland should have been founded on an enactment which seems to have been aimed at nothing worse than the fraudulent assumption of 'supernatural power'.[12] It is also true that the Act was not always enforced to the letter, the General Assembly of the Kirk, for example, on 12 August 1573, ordering merely that witches do penance in sackcloth. But the Satanic pact was known in Scotland at least as early as 1552 when a reference to it appears in a catechism,[13] and in none of the extant papers relating to the East Lothian witches (or, indeed, to any others at this date) is there any suggestion that they were attending anything like a Continental *Sabbat* or that they travelled thither by flying through the air. What, therefore, might James have learned from his Danish experience?

The Danish Church's attitude to witchcraft before and after the Reformation remained more or less unchanged. Ecclesiastics were not particularly interested in witchcraft, although some priests were known to practise it, and so they did not busy themselves unduly with fighting the phenomenon unless it was linked in some way with harmful magic (*maleficium*).[14] Denmark, in fact, seems to have regarded cunning folk and maleficent witches more or less as two separate species. Its two key witchcraft statutes of 1547 and 1576 declared: (i) that no evidence obtained from a dishonest person could form the basis wherefrom a third party might be convicted, and that torture could not be employed until after the final sentence; and (ii) that no one convicted by a jury could be executed until an appeal had been heard.[15] Neither of these is typical of Continental practice. It is also important to note that Danish trials almost invariably concerned themselves with specific offences committed by sorcery, and they scarcely bothered with the notion either of the *Sabbat* or of the Satanic pact.[16] Two of the characteristic features of Continental theory were therefore little regarded in Denmark.

Now, while James was there, he had a lengthy conversation with Niels Hemmingsen. Could this have made a difference to his attitude to witchcraft? Hemmingsen was the most important Danish Reformation theologian of his day, with an international reputation. He wrote a book on magic and related subjects, *Admiratio de Superstitionibus Magicis Vitandis*, published in Copenhagen in 1575, but although (as one might expect) he accepted the reality of the existence of witches and sorcerers who were able to effect *maleficium* against both people and animals, he was not very sure whether witches could fly through the air and absolutely denied the reality of the *Sabbat*: 'statuendum est illusionem diabolorum esse'. Hemmingsen's influence on the next generation of Danish clergy was immense and, in the words of Johansen, 'as there was no other Danish source where the vicars could read about these subjects, it must be regarded as unlikely that they would have described the organisational side of the witch-system from the pulpit'.[17] Had James and Hemmingsen talked about or touched upon witchcraft, therefore, it is most unlikely that Hemmingsen would have said anything to convert James to standard Continental witch-theory. But in any case, if the surviving minutes of their discussion give an accurate account of what was said, it is clear the subject never arose at all. So it is difficult to see how James could have been influenced in this regard by his Danish experience.[18]

That leaves Norway as a source for consideration. James was there for nearly two months. Could he have picked up Continental theory during those eight weeks? From 1536 Norway was considered by Denmark to be a Danish province. After the Reformation, the priests were gradually replaced by Lutheran pastors, many of them Danish, trained in both Germany and Denmark. Some of these, at least, followed quite closely the concepts of witchcraft and demonology common elsewhere on the Continent, and a set of circumstances peculiar to Stavanger in 1584 led the local Bishop to obtain passage of a law that all forms of witchcraft – in other words, cunningness as well as malefice – should be punishable by death. Torture, however, was forbidden and a right of appeal allowed. Moreover, this legislation applied only to Bergen and Stavanger, and was not extended to the rest of Norway until 1593. What is more, it was never introduced into Denmark. In Norway, moreover, in the last decades of the sixteenth century, several women were acquitted of the charge of witchcraft after they had sworn a co-oath, that is, an oath to a person's innocence sworn by the accused together with twelve, six, or three others.[19] The situation, therefore, is not quite the same as that of Denmark, although we might perhaps ask whether it was those pastors who had studied in Germany (as opposed to Denmark) who waged war more fiercely against witches and sought to explain their existence by notions they had picked up abroad. Nevertheless, the Danish account of James's journey through Norway gives no indication that he or his hosts concerned themselves with witchcraft. If anything, the King was more interested in theology, the kind of topic he took up later with Hemmingsen.

The evidence relating to James's stay in Denmark, then, does not suggest that he absorbed or even discussed Continental theories of witchcraft and demonology. It is possible he did so in Norway, but there is no evidence to support that notion and in consequence we must question whether he came into contact with the subject at all in either country.

Had he done so, and had he been profoundly affected by it, we should expect to see some sign of that influence when he returned to Scotland. Such signs, however, are missing, as the schedule of royal events suggests. May was preoccupied with Anne's coronation, her state entry into Edinburgh, and entertainment of the Danes who had come to Scotland with her. In the second week of June, the Earl of Worcester arrived bearing official messages from the English Court. He stayed for about a week.[20] On 4 July,

a woman from Lübeck arrived with a prophecy for James, that he was the
'prince of the north' of whom noble deeds were foretold. Robert Bowes
wrote to Burghley that

> she had sought the King of Scots at Elsinore, but coming after his departure
> took her voyage hither. She brings a Latin letter ... [and] she had conference
> with the Queen in her own language, 'having no other tongue than the
> Dutch' [i.e. German] ... The King and country think her a witch; yet he is
> purposed to hear her.[21]

Bowes describes her as a 'gentlewoman'. It would be interesting to know
whether the Latin letter was her own or entrusted to her by someone else.
But she was obviously respectable, which probably played a part in her gaining an audience with the Queen. James may have thought she was a witch,
but his curiosity and eagerness to listen to her clearly stem from the contents of the letter and her announcement that he was destined to be a great
prince, rather than from any special interest in witchcraft.

Throughout May, June and July the women arrested in Copenhagen
were examined and put on trial. Ane Koldings was tortured: the others may
or may not have been. One hanged herself in prison.[22] On 25 June, Burghley received word from Copenhagen that a witch (probably Ane Koldings)
had been burned for bewitching Princess Anne's attempted voyage to Scotland the previous autumn. No news of this, however, appears to have
reached Scotland until 23 July.[23] In August there was a little flurry of witch-
activity in Scotland: an excommunication, one or two trials for witchcraft,
in one of which the panel was acquitted of all charges. But nothing in any
of them would have been of especial interest to James.[24]

Still, this does not mean to say that the King's existence was entirely
tranquil. Papists, Jesuits, pirates, and quarrelsome Scottish lords, took up
much of his attention on his return as, one may note, they did that of the
kirk. Robert Bruce's sermons in St Giles's, for example, in 1589 and 1590,
are much occupied with the threat posed by papistry and when he talks of
the Devil, the context makes it clear that he is referring to Catholic activity
in Scotland.[25] But of immediate interest, in view of the later witch-trials,
must be James's relationship with the Earl of Bothwell between May and
November 1590. We can follow the course of it in *CSPS*. In the middle of
May they are in amity, then Bothwell takes the huff and departs from Court.
In June he returns, quarrels, and departs again. This time the King is irritated. In July Bothwell is involved in Court intrigue, prepares to leave Scot-
land for Germany, but stays and is reported to be very friendly with the
Chancellor and to have been reconciled with the Master of Glamis. In
August he is lodged overnight in Edinburgh Castle. In September he is

appointed Lord Lieutenant of the Borders. In October he and the King are blowing somewhat cold, and by the end of the month Bothwell is said to be at Kelso on local business.[26] The important point to note is that none of this is serious enough to engender in the King a desire to destroy Bothwell politically or personally. So when Bothwell's name turned up in the East Lothian witchcraft investigations, as it did very quickly, the King may have been irritated or even angered, but not necessarily to the point where he would want to go as far as engineering Bothwell's death.

By 11 November, Richard Graham and other witches had been arrested and lodged in the Edinburgh Tolbooth.[27] Thereafter, investigations proceeded apace. As we have seen, this sequence of events was triggered by a local incident – David Seton's suspicions about the behaviour of his maid, Gellie Duncan. Gellie confessed that she had heard Bothwell's name in connection with Agnes Sampson at a convention of witches in Prestonpans. She also said that the King, too, had been named, but after a fashion she did not fully recollect; and that Agnes Sampson had said, 'The King is going to see his wife, but I shall be there before them.' Some of these details were confirmed by Donald Robinson and Janet Straton, two more of the accused.[28] Agnes, questioned by William Schaw, the Master of the King's Works, and John Geddie, confessed to a number of different witch-conventions including the latest (and subsequently most notorious) at North Berwick on 31 October 1590.[29] According to the pamphlet, *Newes From Scotland*, published in London in 1591 and giving an apparently reliable account of events, Agnes was further examined by the King himself both before and after torture. She told him details of the meeting at North Berwick, including the Devil's expressed rage at the King of Scotland. She also drew him on one side and 'declared unto him the very words which passed between the King's Majesty and his Queen at Oslo in Norway the first night of their marriage, with their answer each to other'.[30] It is hardly surprising that James was mightily disturbed. The anecdote raises interesting questions. How did she know what was said? James and Anne almost certainly exchanged remarks in French, the language they had in common. Did Agnes repeat them to James in French, or did she use a Scots translation? Either would have seemed extraordinary, but the former perhaps even more so. What is the connection between this episode and the cryptic remark attributed to her by Gellie Duncan, that when the King arrived in Scandinavia to meet Princess Anne, she would be there before them?

Altogether Agnes Sampson was accused of 102 articles and confessed to 58 which included the usual cures, raising of storms, attempted magical murder, and trafficking with the Devil.[31] But both from her testimony and from that of the other witches, it emerged most damagingly that there had been three separate attempts to kill the King and Queen. First, cats had been bewitched and thrown into the sea at Leith and Prestonpans with a view to raising a storm and thus delaying the Queen's journey to Scotland and drowning both her and her company.[31] Secondly, a picture of James was made from wax and passed from witch to witch to be enchanted. Donald Robinson describes the process clearly. At a convention in Acheson's Haven at which there were more than twenty people present,

> Agnes Sampson brought the picture to the field. She delivered it to Barbara Napier. From Barbara it was given to Euphemia MacCalyean. From Euphemia to Meg Begton of Spilmourford. It passed through eight or nine women. At last it came to Robert Greirson. From him to the Devil. They spoke all 'James the Sixth' amongst them, handling the picture. The Devil was like a man. Agnes Samson said there would be both gold and silver and victuals gotten from my lord Bothwell.[33]

Thirdly, a toad was hung up by its heels, 'dripping between three oyster shells and nine stones, cooking slowly for three nights'. The poison thus extracted was to be dropped, along with other magical items, on some pathway along which the King would walk; or placed on a ceiling so that it might fall on the King's head or body. The object, clearly stated, was to kill the King,[34] and curiously enough, Agnes seems to have had indirect access to James's bedchamber. *Newes From Scotland* tells us that she required a piece of the King's dirty linen whereby to work this magic, 'which she practised to obtain by means of one John Kers who being attendant in his Majesty's chamber, desired him for old acquaintance between them, to help her to one or a piece of cloth as is aforesaid'.[35] Kers in fact refused, but it is an interesting question how the two people became acquainted at all. The answer is likely to involve magical consultation. Item 31 of Agnes's dittay informs us that she cured the late Robert Kerse in Dalkeith. He was gravely tormented by both witchcraft and disease which had been laid upon him when he was in Dumfries by a Westland warlock, and Agnes assumed the sickness herself until Robert Kerse recovered.[36] Was this Robert Kerse a relation of John Kers, and did Agnes make her request to John in the knowledge that he was under a family obligation to her? We are also told by Melville that Richard Graham was a Westland man.[37] Is there any connection between him and the male witch who tormented Robert Kerse? The possibilities of interconnection between the parties need to be pursued further.

The evidence of intent to kill the King might well be worrying, but it depends how seriously the King took it. In the cases of Gellie Duncan and a male witch, John Fian, he seems to have been more curious than alarmed. Gellie was supposed to have played the jew's harp at the convention of

North Berwick, and James had her brought to play the same tune to him. Fian, too, was fetched into the King's presence, on 24 December, to demonstrate magical frenzy, which he did to remarkable effect.[38] James was probably also aware that several of the witches contradicted themselves, admitting – presumably after the pain or fear of torture had diminished – that their former testimonies had been 'false and feigned'.[39] To be sure, any reservations the King may have had did not interfere with the judicial procedures: nor could they have been allowed to do so. These witches were deeply involved in treason. So Agnes Sampson was duly executed on 28 January 1591, and when, soon after, certain witches escaped and fled into England, David Seton of Tranent was despatched to get them back.[40] But James's behaviour so far does not strike one as that of a man in a panic, although what must have lodged in the King was Agnes Sampson's apparent knowledge of the private conversation between himself and the Queen on their wedding-night in Oslo. If nothing else about this witch-investigation was frightening (as opposed to worrying), that point surely was. But the person who may have frightened him thereby was Agnes Sampson, not the Earl of Bothwell, and she was easy to kill. Had Bothwell been shown, at this stage, to be much more than a suspicious irritant?

The principal witness against him was proving to be somewhat unreliable. Richard Graham, a witch well known to Bothwell and to several of the East Lothian witches, had been warded in the Edinburgh Tolbooth since at least 11 November 1590. This did not please him at all. He sent a letter to William Schaw, Master of the King's Works – an interesting comment on his acquaintance with important people – to give to James himself. A précis of its contents, signed by Schaw and Durham of Duntarvie, runs as follows:

> In the first part of this bill he declared his hard handling in the Tolbooth and want of entertainment in meat and clothing against conditions made to him.
>
> He declared that conditions were made that he should be warded in the castle of Stirling and entertained, himself and a servant, honestly for his surety against his jewels.
>
> He desired, saying that he had kept conditions to them in saying that which he was desired or promised, that they would keep conditions to him in warding and entertainment in clothing and meat as is above said.
>
> This bill was publicly read at the Master [of] Household's table before the Master of Works presented the same to the King's Majesty.[41]

This is an extraordinary document. It suggests, unmistakably, that there was some kind of arrangement made between Graham and a person or persons unknown to deliver a certain story in relation to the matters under investigation. The story he was telling is fairly obvious, but was it true, either in part or in whole? Had the arrangement he mentions existed from the start, or did Graham become involved later on? Who was manipulating the evidence in this business, and how deeply was Bothwell engaged?

That he was engaged to some degree there is no doubt. For while it is true that Bothwell's name does not appear in the official dittays of John Fian, Agnes Sampson, Barbara Napier, Euphemia MacCalyean or *Newes From Scotland*, it does crop up frequently in the manuscript records. Gellie Duncan, for example, confessed that she had heard he had promised Agnes Sampson gold, silver and food for herself and her children; and Donald Robinson said more or less the same – Bothwell was paying them to bewitch a picture intended to destroy the King. Moreover, a connection is well established between Bothwell and Richard Graham. Graham is supposed to have said that Bothwell sent him money on several occasions during his imprisonment,[42] and in the account of the dittay against Bothwell and the decision of the jury at his trial, which is dated 10 August 1593, details are given of alleged meetings between the two men in Edinburgh and Crichton on various occasions since 1582. According to Graham's depositions these occasions numbered twenty. Bothwell admitted four and flatly denied two.[43]

But how far can anyone rely on what Graham is reported as having said? His letter to James is not the only indication that something mysterious was afoot. A document entitled 'Certain infallible reasons wherefore of law nor practice Richard Graham's depositions cannot make faith against my lord Bothwell' lists twelve points supported by marginal notes referring to legal sources. The body of the paper is scribbled and nearly illegible, with a title clearly written in a different hand, but out of the scrawl one can gather the main thrust of this *aide-mémoire*, which is (a) that Graham's testimony is unsupported by other witnesses; (b) that he was not sworn to tell the truth; (c) that he had been subject to threats; (d) that he was a depraved individual whose evidence should therefore not be believed.[44] It has the look of a hasty memorandum drawn up by one of Bothwell's defence advocates. We know that all three were dissatisfied by the contradictions in Graham's depositions and that they made other submissions to the court which suggested that Graham's evidence was not admissible.[45] In addition, Barbara Napier wrote to Bothwell, perhaps in April 1591, urging him 'to stand fast, showing that his enemies had devised his dittay'.[46] This letter was opened and read by several people before being burned, but its contents were conveyed by Robert Bruce to the King. Bruce may, of course, have given the King a tendentious version, but James would have added this information to that store of impressions he had started to form of the reality or otherwise of Bothwell's guilt.

The fact of the matter is, James at this stage seems to have been in two minds about the whole affair, even though he himself had sent for Graham and listened to what he had to say.[47] An accumulation of small points in 1591 hints at his uncertainties. He was eager to know what the Queen thought about how things were going and, according to Robert Bowes, the English ambassador, 'seems to look for advice from her'.[48] Most tellingly, he wrote to Maitland, 'the rest of the inferior witches, off at the nail with them' – that is, they are completely confused. Nevertheless, he wanted Graham kept in prison with 'his ordinary allowance' while he considered further what he should do about his evidence.[49] As for Bothwell, the King listened to the Earl's impassioned self-defence and found himself no further resolved. But he was eager to see justice done and to preserve Bothwell's children from any consequences attendant upon their father's being found guilty. On the other hand (an important clue to his state of mind), he remarked that he 'will be loath to be the instrument that the Devil or any necromancer shall be found true in their answers'.[50] Bothwell was now lodged in Edinburgh Castle (17 April) – scarcely surprising in view of the seriousness of the charges against him. His trial was set for 6 May, but by 5 May the King was saying that 'the evidence against Bothwell for conspiring his death was so weak as the assize of the nobility would hardly be satisfied to declare him guilty'.[51]

His wavering is understandable. He was being told from various quarters not only that the evidence against Bothwell was deeply flawed, but also that it was questionable whether that evidence was admissible in a court of law. This presented such a problem that James had to assemble the Lords of Session and other lawyers to determine what the answer might be.[52] The King was also under pressure from the kirk. On 6 June, Robert Bruce urged him in a sermon to 'execute justice upon malefactors, although it should be with the hazard of his life'.[53] The remark may have been general, but the political circumstances made its import clear, although James seems to have wondered whether it would not be better for Bothwell to take himself into exile and thus solve the problem.[54] The trial and condemnation of Euphemia MacCalyean on 8 June did nothing to help.

At this critical juncture, however, when the King was increasingly nervous about the extent of the witchcraft in East Lothian and the evident desire of a large number of witches to kill him and the Queen, and when his mind towards Bothwell seems to have been somewhat divided, a novel figure suddenly appeared with the evident aim of dispelling the King's irresolution. On 14 June a witch called Kennedy, who came from Reddon in

Roxburghshire and had recently been in England, had a private audience with the King and told him that Graham was right and that the Earl was indeed guilty of trying to engineer the King's death by witchcraft.[55] The result was enough to tip the tremulous scales. To be sure, James still hesitated to set the Earl at liberty, but on 19 June, uncomfortably aware that he was being in some measure manipulated, he remarked waspishly that 'he would not have so many kings in this realm, neither should Bothwell be delivered in time and manner as they had promised'.[56] Nevertheless, arrangements were made to release Bothwell on bail and grant him liberty on certain stipulated conditions. These included the requirement that he go at once into exile overseas. Robert Bowes observed in a letter to Burghley, 'thus Bothwell has found the King's mind more resolute than he or others looked for'.[57]

On 21 June, Bothwell was informed of the King's decision. That night he broke out of the Castle and fled south; and at once he was proclaimed traitor, with his possessions and estates declared forfeit.[58] From this point, the effect wrought by Kennedy starts to become more evident. Relations between James and Bothwell rapidly deteriorated and it is obvious that the two men had become frightened of one another. Each fed the other's fear and thus Bothwell's downward spiral into ruin began in earnest. The nobility, as one might expect, split into faction. James and Bothwell pursued each other round the south and east of Scotland and into the Borders until, on 27 December, while James was at Holyrood, Bothwell and his supporters broke in and tried to seize the King's person.[59] The raid was unsuccessful, but it destroyed whatever lingering doubts the King may have had about Bothwell's intention to kill him. In January 1592, he instructed the Scottish ambassador in England to tell Elizabeth that 'some of our most unnatural subjects [have been] led by the abominable author who betrays himself guilty of that sorcery and witchcraft devised against our own person'.[60] Bothwell's subsequent behaviour, wilder and less predictable with each passing month, served only to confirm this conviction.

His eventual trial in August 1593, however, resulted in an acquittal, largely because he had excellent defence advocates and the jury and court were packed with his supporters. But was the Earl actually innocent? The whole episode, from Princess Anne's attempts to reach Scotland in 1589 to this theatrical judicial performance in 1593, is in need of thorough investigation.[61] Nevertheless it is clear that, far from being a political assize to which witchcraft had been added in order to stimulate prejudice against the accused, the trial was about witchcraft rather than anything else. In essence it was no different from any other Scottish trial – no Continental theories in evidence – in which a witch was accused of murder or attempted murder by magical means. The difference in this and the other East Lothian cases is that the intended victims apparently included the King and Queen, and this point strikes one as odd. These witches were principally healers of the sick, raisers of storms, and murderers of unwanted relatives. Why should they suddenly venture into potentially fatal high politics? For what reason, and *cui bono*? Bothwell himself blamed the Chancellor, Maitland, and it is interesting to note that Maitland seems to have known Richard Graham. On one occasion Bothwell met him at the Chancellor's house. The three men went riding and during the course of their excursion, Graham showed the others an enchanted stick, so Maitland cannot have been in any doubt about Graham's status as a student of magic.[62] But one cannot start to blame Maitland on the strength of Bothwell's word alone. Here is another point for further investigation, along with the further question, if there was some kind of conspiracy against the Earl of Bothwell, was it planned from the start or did someone take advantage of the witchcraft investigations to involve Bothwell to his possible destruction? One may ask further whether this was not the cause treason was added to a series of witchcraft trials – to add a fatal prejudice against the accused. If Bothwell were actually guilty of consorting with witches, he would fall (technically) under the provisions of the Act of 1563, although had he done no more than consult witches, or practise witchcraft himself, it would have been difficult to cause a man of his standing more than some temporary embarrassment. He was, when all was said and done, the King's cousin. But if his consultation and practice had involved the King and Queen, that would be treason and the case would be transformed.[63]

Should that be so, the most intriguing question is, who did the adding? To that there is, unfortunately, no immediate answer. But one can be in no doubt that both the King and Bothwell were being manipulated. Someone was playing on their fear of each other for his own ends, and in the end he was successful. The extent to which the King became afraid is a matter for further investigation. The examinations of 1590–91 uncovered an extensive and organised body of witches operating in East Lothian. As the extent of this became clearer; as the realisation that a large number of women was routinely exercising maleficent as well as beneficent power within a few miles of Edinburgh became obvious; and as the knowledge that these people forming a coherent, regulated group numbering at least 100 persons, probably more, had ventured into the realm of politics and treason, lodged in the King's consciousness, one can see how his initial relative insouciance could turn into something like panic. Conspiracies against him by nobles might be frightening, but they had happened before and were composed of human beings with human motives and human power. They

did not represent a combination of factors unknown. The East Lothian
witches, on the other hand, did and in consequence the suggestion that they
and their master, Satan, were allied with the increasingly unstable Earl of
Bothwell might well have been enough to play ruinously upon the King's
unhappy nerves.

Out of this fear came his book, *Daemonologie*, published in 1597 but
obviously planned and prepared some time before. A manuscript of it survives, in the margin of which appear three sets of initials, EM, RG and BN,
each set accompanying, so to speak, a descriptive phrase in the text. EM
may well refer to Euphemia MacCalyean, her phrase being, 'rich and wordly
wise'; BN, 'given over to the pleasures of the flesh', could be Barbara
Napier; and RG, 'fat or corpulent', may be plausibly identified as Richard
Graham.[64] The presence of these three sets of initials, if they have been correctly attributed, will therefore suggest that the *Daemonologie* was directly
inspired by the events of 1590–93. Indeed, the book may have been
intended as an accompaniment to the *Newes from Scotland* which appeared in
1591;[65] and in as far as it can be read as a political as well as a demonological work[66] – the intellectual offspring from a war of nerves conducted
between the King and an unknown puppet-master – one must acknowledge
that it had a long-term, widespread, potentially insidious influence stretching far beyond the local, transient turmoil which produced it.[67] If Kings are
afraid, the rest of the body politic suffers too.

*Notes*

1  The sequence of events is laid out in B. Liisberg, *Vesten for Sø og Østen for Hav* (Copenhagen, 1909), 9–15. Copenhagen GkS 2586, fos. 8v–21v. T. Riis, *Should Auld Acquaintance Be Forgot* (Odense, 1988), 1: 264–5. All dates in this chapter are given in the New
   Style.

2  *CSPS*, 10: 195, 197, 198, 204, 212, 216. D. Moysie, *Memoirs of the Affairs of Scotland*
   (Edinburgh, 1830), 81. *CSPS*, 10: 223, 241, 847–8.

3  Riis, *Acquaintance*, p. 121. *CSPS*, 10: 281.

4  Liisberg, *Vesten for Sø*, 21–2, 95. Riis, *Acquaintance*, 266, and n. 16. James himself proclaimed to the people of Scotland in October 1589 that 'the contrarious winds stayed
   [the Queen]' and that 'she was stayed from coming through the contrarious tempests of
   winds and ... her ships were not able to perfect their voyage through the great hurt they
   had received', in G.V.P. Akrigg, ed., *Letters of James VI* (Berkeley 1984), 98. Cf. W.
   Murdin, ed., *Collection of State Papers, 1571–1596* (1759), 637.

5  SRO, JC26/2/27. Pitcairn, *Criminal Trials in Scotland*, 1.1–2 (Edinburgh, 1833), 1.2:
   186. J. Kirk, ed., *The Records of the Synod of Lothian and Tweeddale* (Edinburgh, 1977), 12,
   22. Pitcairn, *Trials* 1.2: 191–204. *CSPS*, 10: 365.

6  'It is quite clear that James encountered the witch theory while in Denmark', A. H.
   Williamson, *Scottish National Consciousness in the Age of James VI* (Edinburgh, 1979), 61.
   Cf. C. Larner, *Enemies of God* (Oxford, 1983), 69, 198; E. J. Cowan, 'The darker vision
   in the Scottish Renaissance', in I. B. Cowan and D. Shaw, eds, *The Renaissance and Refor-
   mation in Scotland* (Edinburgh, 1983), 127, and T. D. Whyte, *Scotland Before the Industrial
   Revolution* (1995), 226. The suggestion had actually been made a long time before by F.
   Legge, in 'Witchcraft in Scotland', *SR*, 18 (1891), 261. One should bear in mind that

this is supposed to refer only to Lowland witchcraft. Highland witchcraft was quite different and neither its beliefs nor its practices played any part in the Lowland situation. For a good example of a case in 1588/89, see J. G. Campbell, *Witchcraft and Second Sight in the Highlands and Islands* (Glasgow, 1902), 27–30.

7  Larner, *Witchcraft and Religion* (1984), 10. Cf. Whyte, *Scotland*, 226.

8  One may also note that Cowan's particular claim that Bothwell was not implicated until April 1591 is actually wrong; 'Darker vision', 130.

9  Larner, *Witchcraft and Religion*, 8.

10  G. F. Warner, 'The library of James VI in the hand of Peter Young, his tutor, 1573–1583', in *Miscellany of the Scottish History Society* (Edinburgh 1893), 1: ix–lxxv. The only two books on occult subjects are the *Poimander* attributed to Hermes Trismegistus, and Agrippa's *De Vanitate Scientiarum*, which is actually a repudiation of his own former interest in them. I. D. MacFarlane, *Buchanan* (1981), 527–31. The *Sphaera* was published in Paris in 1585. For the animadversions therein against magic and astrology, see Book 5.42sq. M. A. Bald, 'Vernacular books imported into Scotland, 1500 to 1625', *SHR*, 23 (1926), 260–1.

11  J. Simpson: '"The weird sisters wandering": burlesque witchery in Montgomery's Flyting', *Folklore* 106 (1995), 9, 10–11, 17.

12  *SR*, 18 (1891), 260.

13  'For without doubt, all witches, necromancers and suchlike, work by operation of the Devil under a pact, condition, bond or obligation of service and honour to be made to him', T. G. Law, ed., *The Catechism of John Hamilton* (Oxford, 1884), 50.

14  K. S. Jensen, *Trolddom i Danmark, 1500–1588* (Copenhagen. 1982), 30. Cf. *Idem*, 'Med trolddom som saadan, var ikke noget kirken specielt focuserede paa', 27; and J. C. V. Johansen, 'Faith, Superstition, and Witchcraft in Reformation Scandinavia', in O. P. Grell, ed., *The Scandinavian Reformation* (Cambridge, 1995), 187–8, 211.

15  J. C. V. Johansen, 'Denmark, the sociology of accusations', in B. Ankarloo and G. Henningsen, eds, *Early Modern European Witchcraft: Centres and Peripheries* (Oxford, 1990), 340–1.

16  G. Henningsen, 'Witchcraft in Denmark', *Folklore*, 93 (1982), 134.

17  Johansen, 'Denmark', 362–3. Jensen, *Trolddom*, 20–5. He regarded witchcraft as a denial of God and a pact made with the Devil. H. E. Naess, *Med Bål og Brann* (Stavanger, 1984), 93.

18  See the brief comment in Copenhagen GkS, 2586, fol. 22, and *CSPS*, 10: 281. It is true that in his *Daemonologie* James cited Hemmingsen as an authority on witchcraft, but the most likely explanation for this lies in the existence of Hemmingsen's book on magic rather than in any conversation with the King himself.

19  Naess, *Med Bål og Brann*, 109, and 'Norway, the criminological context', in Ankarloo and Henningsen, *Early Modern European Witchcraft*, 368, 373–5. Johansen, 'Faith, superstition, and witchcraft', 195, 200, 205.

20  Moysie gives a useful summary of these and other preoccupations at the time; *Memoirs*, 83–5.

21  *CSPS*, 10: 348. There is no warrant in the sources for Cowan's use of the word 'crazed' to describe her 'Darker vision', 129.

22  Liisberg, *Vesten for Sø*, 46, 50, 54, 55, 59, 60–1.

23  R. B. Wernham, ed., *List and Analysis of State Papers: Foreign, Elizabeth* (1964), 1 (Aug. 1598–June 1590): no. 752. *CSPS*, 10: 365.

24  *Register of the Privy Council*, Appendix, 14: 373 (Neving MacGhie). Pitcairn, *Trials*, 1.2: 206–9, the trials of Jonett Grant, Bessie Roy, William Leslie, and Violat Auchinleck.

25  *Sermons Preached in the Kirk of Edinburgh* (Edinburgh, 1591), 171, 202–3, 308, 317. In a list of things he considers wrong with contemporary Scotland, he makes no mention of witchcraft, *ibid.*, 288. See also *Acts and Proceedings of the Kirk of Scotland*, part 2 (Edinburgh, 1840).

0036-9330/96/03096/152 $2.00 in USA
© 1996 Scottish Medical Journal

Scot Med J 1996; 41: 152-158

# THE BARGARRAN WITCHCRAFT TRIAL — A PSYCHIATRIC REASSESSMENT

*S. W. McDonald, A. Thom\*, A. Thom#,*

Laboratory of Human Anatomy, University of Glasgow. \*Gartnavel Royal Hospital, Glasgow. #Parkhead Hospital, Glasgow.

*Abstract: In 1697, seven people were condemned at Paisley for using witchcraft to torment Christian Shaw, daughter of the laird of Bargarran. For seven months, Christian had bizarre seizures during which she claimed to see the Devil and her tormentors assaulting her. She also exhibited pica and said that the foreign material had been forced into her mouth by her invisible assailants. The notable Glasgow physician, Matthew Brisbane, was consulted and gave evidence at the trial; he could find no natural explanation for the pica. It is likely that Christian had a dissociative (conversion) disorder after being cursed by a servant. Christian recovered and later married the minister of Kilmaurs. After his untimely death, she established a highly successful spinning business which lead to the Paisley cotton industry.*

Keywords: Bargarran, witchcraft, Renfrewshire, Matthew Brisbane, dissociative disorder, pica, non-epileptic seizures.

Three hundred years ago, one of the last trials for witchcraft in Scotland took place at Paisley and six people were hanged and burned. The case centred around the supposed possession of Christian Shaw, the 11 year old daughter of John Shaw, laird of Bargarran. In this article, we retell the story and consider whether Christian's condition can be explained by modern psychiatry. Excellent overviews of the celebrated case of Bargarran's Daughter were given by John Millar in his *"History of the Witches of Renfrewshire"* and by Robert Chambers in *"The Domestic Annals of Scotland"*.

Bargarran was a modest estate in the parish of Erskine on the south side of the Clyde. The small mansion house, occupied by John Shaw and his wife, Christian McGilchrist, and their children, belonged to an earlier period and was, with adjacent ancillary buildings, surrounded by a semi-defensive wall. Christian was said to be lively and "well-inclined" and seems to have had a normal childhood up to the time of the events to be described.

The troubles started on Monday, 17th August 1696 when Christian reported to her mother that Catherine Campbell, a servant girl, had stolen some milk. Campbell swore at Christian with oaths of terrible violence, calling the curse of God upon her and hoping her soul would be dragged through Hell. The following Saturday, these words were to have terrible repercussions.

On the Friday of the same week, in the early morning, a malicious, ignorant old woman, Agnes Naismith, who lived in the neighbourhood, appeared at Bargarran House. She frequently threatened people and it was believed that deaths had followed. When she arrived at Bargarran, she found Christian and her little sister playing in the courtyard. 'She asked how the young lady and the young child did, and how old the suckling child was; to which Christian replied, *"What do I know?"* Agnes then asked, how herself did, and how old she was; to which she answered she was well and in the eleventh year of her age.'

The next day, the Saturday, shortly after going to bed, Christian suddenly awoke shouting *"Help! Help!"* and immediately sprang up into the air with enormous force, astonishing her parents and others in the room. She was put back to bed but

remained stiff and appeared unconscious for half an hour. For the next forty-eight hours, she was restless and complained of violent pains throughout her body and, if she fell asleep, she immediately awoke again crying in terror *"Help! help!"*

For eight days, Christian had violent seizures in which the pain localised in her left side and in which she was "often so bent and rigid that she stood like a bow on her feet and neck at once," and lost the power of speech. There seemed to be a short period of delirium as the fits came and went and they were interspersed by short intervals in which she seemed perfectly well. A doctor, John Johnstone, and an apothecary, John White, a relation of the Shaws, were called from Paisley but their bleedings and medications had no effect.

Presently Christian's condition changed and she appeared to fight against an invisible enemy. Her abdomen rose and fell, with a motion like that of a pair of bellows, and her whole body shook alarmingly. In these fits, she started to denounce Catherine Campbell and Agnes Naismith, claiming that they were cutting the sides of her body even though they were actually elsewhere. It was at this crisis, two months after the start of the symptoms, that Christian's parents took her to see the eminent Glasgow physician Matthew Brisbane.

For the eight days in which Christian remained in Glasgow

**Fig. 1** Bargarran House - *by kind permission of the Keeper of Special Collections, Glasgow University Library*

**BARGARRAN HOUSE.**

Correspondence and requests for reprints to: Stuart W. McDonald, Laboratory of Human Anatomy, University of Glasgow, Glasgow, G12 8QQ.

152

Fig. 2 Title page of "A Relation of the Diabolical Practices of the Witches of the Sheriffdom of Renfrew in the Kingdom of Scotland" — *by kind permission of the Keeper of Special Collections, Glasgow University Library*

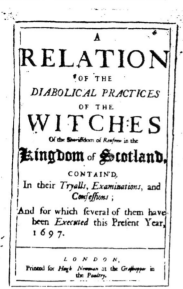

A

**RELATION**

OF THE

*DIABOLICAL PRACTICES*

OF THE

**WITCHES**

Of the Sheriffdom of Renfrew in the

**Kingdom of Scotland.**

CONTAIN'D,

In their *Tryalls, Examinations,* and
*Confessions* ;

And for which several of them have
been *Executed* this Present Year,
1 6 9 7.

L O N D O N,

Printed for Hugh Newman at the Grashopper in
the Poultry.

after consulting Brisbane and for eight days after her return home, she was well. The fits then returned with increased violence. She would become stiff as a corpse and be senseless and motionless. Her tongue would stick out to a great length and her teeth would close on it. At other times her tongue was drawn far back into her mouth.

The parents decided to take her back to Dr Brisbane but, as they were going, there was a new development in Christian's condition. From time to time, she spat or took from her mouth balls of hair of various colours, which she claimed had been forced down her throat by her assailants. There were large quantities of hair, some of it was curly and some of it was plaited or knotted. Soon other material was to appear from her mouth. She also had fainting fits every quarter of an hour. During this visit to Glasgow, as well consulting Dr Brisbane, Christian was also seen by an apothecary Henry Marshall. Dr Brisbane's medical evidence was to be an important document in condemning seven people to be burned for witchcraft.

### Reports of Matthew Brisbane and Henry Marshall reproduced from: *A History of the Witches of Renfrewshire*

"The subscribed attestations of Dr Matthew Brisbane, Physician, and Mr Henry Marshall, Apothecary in Glasgow, did influence the belief of an extraordinary cause of these events. "

"The doctor, on the 31 December 1696, tells, that at first sight, when he was brought to the girl she appeared so brisk in motion, so florid in colour, so chearful, and in a word every way healthful, that he could hardly be persuaded she had need of a physician; but within ten minutes he found himself obliged to alter his thoughts, for she rose from her seat, and advertised she was instantly to be seized with a fit, according whereunto he observed a considerable distension in the left hypochondre, which in a trace falling, she was forthwith taken with horrid convulsive motions and heavy groans at first; which afterwards as soon as she was able to frame words, turned into an expostulatory mourning against some women; particularly Campbell and Naesmith. Yet he thought these symptoms were reducible to the freaks of hypochondriac melancholy, and therefore put her in such a course proper (i.e. appropriate treatment) against that kind of malady. Upon which being freed for some time: he was alarmed that the child was returned to town worse than ever for having his assistance.

"He was then frequently with her, and observed her narrowly, so that he was confident she had no visible correspondent to subminister hair, straw, coal, cinders, hay, and such like trash unto her; all which upon several occasions he saw her put out of her mouth without being wet; nay rather as they had been dried with artifice, and actually hot above the natural warmth of the body; sometimes after severe fits, and other times without trouble when discoursing with him. When she had only light convulsive motions, but to a high degree, such rigidity of the whole body, as we call *tetivo* (tetanus), she did not fancy as at other times, she saw these persons already named about her; but the upcasting of the trash above-mentioned, did no sooner cease, than in all her fits, when she was able to speak any, she always cried out they were pricking or pinching her. He saw her also when free of fits suddenly seized with dumbness, etc. And this he solemnly declares himself to have seen and handled, and were it not for the hay, straw etc he should not despair to reduce the other symptoms to their proper classes, in the catalogue of human diseases.

"Mr Marshall the apothecary concurs with the doctor; and gives some particular instances of his own observation; and among the rest, that the girl having fallen headlong on the ground, as (if) she had been thrown down with violence, fell a reasoning very distinctly thus: "Katie what ails thee at me, I am sure I never did thee wrong; come let us agree, let there be no more difference betwixt us, let us shake hands together (putting forth her hand said, well Katie, I cannot help it, ye will not gree with me ". And immediately she cried, fell into a swoon, and out of that into a rage, wherein she continued without intermission for about half an hour, and perfectly recovered. Then she told him that she saw Katie Campbell, Nancy Naismith, etc and many more; Campbell was going to thrust a sword into her side, which made her so desirous to be agreed with her; and when the girl told him this, she instantly fell into another fit as formerly, in which she continued another half hour, etc. . . .dated 1st Jan, 1697 "

As well as the items pulled from her mouth in the presence of Dr Brisbane, on other occasions Christian regurgitated small sticks of candle-fir (a type of fir which burns like a candle), stable-dung mixed with hay, hens' feathers, gravel, a whole gallnut and egg-shells. The Laird of Kellie witnessed Christian's fits and during one of them he gave her a sore pinch in the arm to which Christian seemed totally insensitive. During her fits, she sometimes tried to reason with the invisible Catherine Campbell, pleading for a return to their old friendship and quoting much Scripture. Witnesses were surprised at the child's command of the Scriptures. In an old account of the case, the narrator says, "We doubt not that the Lord did, by his good spirit, graciously afford her a more than ordinary measure of assistance. " Interestingly, the account also tells that Christian's fits became worse if there was talk about religion and that, if someone prayed with her, she initially did a lot of loud talking, whistling, singing and roaring, to drown the voice of the person

153

383

praying but usually subsequently quietened down.

John Millar in his *"History of the Witches of Renfrewshire"* gives an account of some of Christian's dialogue with the invisible entities; the speech is said to have been written down as well as could be remembered around the time of the events. The following extract gives a flavour of such a conversation with Catherine Campbell:

*"Thou sittest there with a stick in thy hand to put in my mouth, but through God's strength thou shall not get leave: thou art permitted to torment me, but I trust in God thou shalt never get my life, though it is my life thou designest " (And at that time calling for a Bible and candle), said; "Come near me Katie and I'll let thee see where a godly man was given up to Satan to be tormented, but God kept his life in his own hand; and so I trust in God thou shalt never get my life, and all that thou shall be permitted to do unto me, I hope through God's mercy shall turn to my advantage. This man was robbed of all, and tormented in body, and had nothing left him but an ill wife. Come near me, Katie, and I'll read it to thee" And reading that passage of Job, when she came to the place where his wife said to him, "Curse God and die!" the damsel considering these words a little, said; "O! what a wife this has been, that bids her goodman curse God and die? she who should have been a comfort to him in his trouble, turned to cross to him. "Then, after reading of the chapter to the end, she looks toward the foot of the bed and said; "Now, Katie, what thinkest thou of that? Thou seest for all the power the Devil got over Job, he gained no ground on him; and I hope he shall gain as little on me. Thy master the Devil deceives thee; he is a bad master whom thou servest, and thou shalt find it to thy smart, except thou repent before thou die. There is no repentance to be had after death. I 'll let thee see, Katie, there is no repentance in hell." And turning over the book, citing Luke, Chap xvi, near the latter end thereof, and reading the same over, said; "Katie, thou seest there is no repentance in hell, for this rich man besought Abraham to testify to his five brethren, that they come not to the place of torment, where he was, but repent and turn to the Lord, for there was no winning out, if once they come there; now, Katie, thou heard this, what thinkest thou of it?"*

Before leaving Glasgow for the second time, she started to mention four other people as being among her tormentors. These were Alexander and James Anderson and two others whose names she did not know.

Following her return to Bargarran about 12th December, Christian was well for around a week before her fits became worse than ever. The Devil appeared to her in various forms and threatened to devour her. Her face and body would become dreadfully contorted and she would point to where her tormentors were standing and could not understand why no-one else could see them. Agnes Naismith, whom Christian accused of being one of her tormentors came in the flesh to visit the girl and spoke kindly to her, praying that God would soon restore her health. Thereafter, Christian believed that Agnes Naismith had ceased to be among her tormentors and that she actually protected her from the rest. Catherine Campbell was less benevolent, cursing Christian and hoping that the Devil would never let her get better for all the trouble she had brought on her. Shortly afterwards, Campbell was imprisoned and from that time Christian seemed to stop regarding her as a tormentor. It was claimed that a ball of hair was found in her pocket and was burnt on a fire and from that time on the child ceased to regurgitate hair.

By now public attention was starting to focus on Bargarran and it was becoming generally held that Christian Shaw was the victim of witches colluding with the Devil. Representatives

of the Presbytery were sent to Bargarran to lend all possible spiritual help. One evening, Christian was reported to have been carried, laughing wildly, and with unaccountable motion through the bedroom and hall and down the long winding stairs to the outer gate. Witnesses claimed *". . . her feet did not touch the ground, so far as anyone was able to discern"*. At the gate she was rigid and, on being brought back, said she felt as if she had been carried on a swing. The next evening, in a similar episode, she appeared to be carried to the top of the house and then back down to the outer gate where she lay as if dead. She said that some men and women had been trying to throw her in the well so that everyone would think that she had drowned herself. On a third occasion, Christian went into the cellar where a minister who tried to restrain her said he felt as if someone was pulling her back from his arms. It was said that on several occasions she spoke of things of which she had no means of knowing, but which were found to be true. This phenomenon was regarded as a sign of possession. She said that someone spoke over her head and distinctly gave her the information.

Some of incidents, which seem to have been regarded as supernatural at the time, have a distinct atmosphere of deceit. An entry for 21st January in *"The History of the Witches of Renfrewshire"*, says that Christian's fits again altered and started with her making heavy sighs, groans and hideous cries and saying that cats, ravens, owls and horses were pushing her down in the bed. Her mother and another woman declared that when they took Christian out of the bed, they saw something about the size of a cat moving under the bedclothes.

John Millar's book also reports that sometimes she cried out in pain because of violent blows from her invisible tormentors and that bystanders distinctly heard them.

One night, Christian was sitting with several people including her parents when she cried out that something was wounding her thigh. Her mother found that her folding knife was open in her pocket. Her uncle closed the knife and put in back in her pocket and presently she suddenly cried out as before that the knife was cutting her thigh. The uncle searched the pocket and found that the knife was opened again. Christian said it had been unfolded by her tormentors and it is said that those present could not account for its having been opened.

According to the contemporary narrative, on 18th February *"She being in a light-headed fit, said the Devil now appeared to her in the shape of a man; whereupon being struck in great fear and consternation, she was desired to pray in an audible voice: "The Lord rebuke thee, Satan!" which trying to do, she presently lost the power of her speech, her teeth being set, and her tongue drawn back into her throat; and attempting it again, she was immediately seized by another severe fit, in which, her eyes being twisted almost round, she fell down as one dead, struggling with her feet and hands, and, getting up again suddenly, was hurried violently to and fro through the room, deaf and blind, yet was speaking to some invisible creature about her, saying: "With the Lord's strength, thou shalt neither put straw nor sticks into my mouth." After this she cried in a pitiful manner: "The bee hath stung me." Then, presently sitting down, and untying her stockings, she put her hand to that part which had been nipped or pinched; upon which the spectators discerned the lively marks of nails, deeply imprinted on that same part of her leg. When she came to herself, she declared that something spoke to her as if it were over her head, and told her it was Mr M. in a neighbouring parish (naming the place) that had appeared to her, and pinched her leg in the likeness of a bee."*

Another time, while addressing an invisible assailant, she suddenly asked the entity where she had got her red sleeves.

There was a ripping sound and Christian was suddenly holding two pieces of red cloth. It seemed as if they had been torn from a witch's arms and astonished those present in the room, who were certain that there had been no such cloth there beforehand.

The case was referred by the Presbytery to the Privy Council who set up a special commission, chaired by Lord Blantyre, the principal man in the parish. The commissioners came to Bargarran on 5th February 1697. Catherine Campbell, Agnes Naismith, a man called Anderson and his daughter Elizabeth, Margaret Fulton, James Lindsay and a Highland beggar, were all accused of being among Christian's tormentors. Each was confronted with the girl and when they touched her, she fell into fits; this did not happen when she was touched by others. When blindfolded, she could still recognise that the Highland beggar had touched her. Three other people were also implicated.

A boy in the neighbourhood, Thomas Lindsay, who used to say charms for a halfpenny, was called in and quickly confessed to being in league with the Devil and bearing his marks. Elizabeth Anderson also confessed to attending meetings with the Devil and said that her father and the Highland beggar were involved in tormenting Christian Shaw. The plan to torment Christian had been devised at a meeting with the Devil in the orchard at Bargarran House. Two other women were also accused, Margaret Lang and her daughter Martha Semple. Margaret Lang had a better background than the others and was a midwife. Hearing that she had been accused she came to Bargarran to plead her innocence. At first Christian did not accuse Maggie further. However, a ball of hair was found under the chair where she had been sitting. Christian declared that this was a charm which prevented her from saying that Mrs Lang was indeed one of her tormentors. The two women were later to be pricked to detect the Devil's marks, insensitive areas of skin; it seems that no such areas were found on Martha Semple.

During these proceedings, the Presbytery held a fast in Erskine parish with special services in the church. Christian was present throughout the day but nothing happened to her. On 28th March, Christian recovered her former health and had no further fits or hallucinations.

Presently the case was compiled and seven people were summoned to appear at an assize in Paisley. The Lord Advocate was prosecutor and, as was customary in Scotland, an advocate was appointed to represent the accused. A new commission had been appointed to judge the case; it was composed of several persons of honour with special knowledge and experience. The charges were for several murders including children and a minister and for tormenting several people, particularly Christian Shaw. Reading, the account of the charges and the confessions, there is a distinct impression that the confessions may have been forced as they show general agreement about a conspiracy with the Devil to torment Christian Shaw and others and describe the Devil as a dark man whom they met several times, once in the orchard at Bargarran House. The reports that the defendants bore the marks of the Devil suggests that they had been pricked.

The minister who was said to have been murdered was John Hardie, minister of Dumbarton who died in November, 1696. He had been ordained in March 1693 and died unmarried. The Bargarran witches were said to have met one night in his manse garden. The basis of the belief that Rev Hardie and some children had been murdered is not clear; it seems more likely that they suffered sad and untimely deaths from natural causes.

For twenty hours, witnesses were carefully questioned and the jury took six hours to reach the verdict that the defendants were guilty. In his address to the jury, the Lord Advocate, Sir James Steuart, claimed that all the instances of clairvoyance and of flying locomotion were completely proven. He had no doubt about the murders and torments carried out by the accused. He stressed that the Devil's marks had been found on the witches and pointed out the many coincidences between what Christian Shaw alleged and what the accused confessed.

On 10th June 1697, a gibbet and fire were prepared on the Gallow Green of Paisley. This was the scene of the execution of six of the condemned, including Maggie Lang. Each was strangled on a gibbet for a few minutes and was then thrown on the flames. A seventh victim, John Reid, was found hanged in his cell by his handkerchief attached to a nail in the wall; he was believed to have been strangled by the Devil. A horse-shoe in the cross-roads at the intersection of Maxwellton Street and George Street in Paisley is said to mark the place where the witches' ashes were buried.

Further information about those who died has been obtained from Poll Tax Records of 1695:

**Margaret Lang**, wife of William Semple, cottar in Cartympen in Orbistoune's lands, Parish of Erskine.

**John Lindsay**, cottar in Barloch of Bargarran, Parish of Erskine.

**James Lindsay**, cottar in Billboe in Orbistoune's lands, Parish of Erskine.

**John Reid**, smith in the Laird of Hapland's lands, Parish of Inchinnan.

**Catherine Campbell, Margaret Fulton and Agnes Naismith** do not appear in these rolls. It is thought that Catherine Campbell may have become a servant to the Laird of Bargarran at Whitsun 1696, that Margaret Fulton may have been a resident of Dumbarton and that Agnes Naismith may have lived in Kilpatrick across the Clyde from Bargarran.

Christian Shaw seems to have suffered no recurrences of her condition after her symptoms ceased on 28th March, while the enquiries of the commission were still in progress. She later became Mrs Miller, wife of the minister of Kilmaurs in Ayrshire, whom she married in 1718. Rev John Miller died in 1721 on a visit to his wife's family and was buried at Erskine. Christian learned the techniques of spinning thread and, in the early 1720s, she and the Shaw family set up a mill producing Bargarran thread. The product became famous in its day and brought good prices. It had a special mark which bore the arms of the Shaw family, "azure, three covered cups *or*".

Fig. 3 Arms of the Shaws of Bargarran and trade-mark of Bargarran thread, produced by Christian Shaw and her family.

A spool of Lady Bargarran's thread is preserved in the Scottish Museum of Antiquities. The Bargarran business paved the way for, but was absorbed by, the Paisley spinning industry.

## Psychiatric assessment
### Comments on history

This is an 11 year old prepubertal girl of well-to-do parents. Christian is assumed to be normal developmentally and to have no significant medical or psychiatric history, including sexual abuse. There is no evidence of premorbid personality dysfunction and is described as lively and well-inclined. She seems to have suffered no longterm sequelae after this seven month episode. No drug history is available including substances administered by the physicians.

### 17th August 1697

Christian suffers acute stress after Catherine Campbell's anger was displaced onto Christian. This may have caused her to feel guilty and at fault. Apart from the visit of Agnes Naismith, there is no history of events in the five days between the verbal attack and the onset of illness (eg. personality change, head injury, infection, further confrontation). There is also no information about the parents' mental state or whether there is any marital stress, important considerations when dealing with ill health in a child. Misidentifications, visual hallucinations and peculiar time distortions often occur to children who have experienced single intense, unexpected shocks.

The prodromal period of Christian's illness appears to be when she awakes with night terrors and remains restless for the next eight days complaining of nonspecific symptoms. Accounts indicate there were episodes of opisthotonus and aphonia. Bleeding and treatment by a doctor and an apothecary from Paisley fail. Christian then develops acute delirium, convulsions and visual hallucinations. Anaemia or, more likely, the psychological stress induced by the treatment, may have precipitated further seizures. Tongue-biting, incontinence and self-injury can occur in conversion non-epileptic seizures as well as in epilepsy. It is claimed that the tolerance of pain conferred by dissociation can account for substantial self-injury including bony fractures. Non-epileptic seizures (NES) are less likely to lead to discrete gaps in memory that are characteristic of complex partial seizures. NES are usually of longer seizure duration and vocalisations are associated with emotional content. There is also more frequent crying, yelling and use of profanity in NES.

### October 1696

Around the time of the consultation with Matthew Brisbane, Christian develops generalised seizures associated with pica. Patients with pica may have a false or craving appetite and deliberately ingest a bizarre selection of foods and non-food items. It is more common in women and may be associated with iron-deficiency anaemia. During seizures, Christian quotes scriptures and names those she implicates in witchcraft. There is no mention of her cognitive state although she seems to be aware of her surroundings, with her vocalisations influenced by the attention and subsequent reactive behaviour of her carers.

On presentation to Dr Brisbane, Christian is noted to be well. Five minutes into the consultation she develops convulsions, heavy groanings and murmurings against two women. She had announced the oncoming event previously, a feature more common in pseudoseizures than in epilepsy.

### 12th December 1696

For one week, Christian remains symptom-free, then develops fits, visual hallucinations and bizarre behaviour resembling trance disorder. She appears to sleepwalk for a considerable distance (with dim light and tired carers, this is the most likely explanation for her moving across the ground). Her behaviour confirmed existing beliefs of witchcraft within the parish.

### February 1697

Christian falls into fits whenever any of the alleged perpetrators touch her. When blind-folded she is only able to positively identify the Highland beggar by his touch. There is no mystery in this as his smell, clothes and manner would differentiate him from local people. Thomas Lindsay confesses to being in league with the Devil, however, it would seem that he was a young, impressionable boy. Elizabeth Anderson also testifies that there is no note of her level of intelligence nor of the methods used to obtain her confession, although its nature suggests it was extracted under duress.

156

386

More interestingly, when Maggie Lang, a lady of superior character, challenges Christian, she is initially unwilling to identify her as a perpetrator. A ball of hair is taken as evidence that Maggie made Christian initially silent. It would seem that Christian, who was now of special significance to the townspeople, was believed implicitly with alternative explanations discounted.

**18th February 1697**

Christian is delirious and visually hallucinating, witnessing the Devil appearing in human form. She experiences tactile hallucinations and seizure activity is noted. Her self-injurious behaviour has religious significance attached to it. A degree of suggestibility of her carers and manipulative behaviour by Christian is demonstrated on several occasions, particularly when supernatural significance is given to a simple conjuring trick with two pieces of red cloth.

**28th March 1697**

Christian becomes symptom free. A new commission is appointed. Its members are honourable, experienced and less likely to be controversial in a case of notoriety. Crimes are attributed to the defendants which seem unrelated to the case and with no evidence proffered other than supposed confessions. The Lord Advocate instructed the jury in forceful terms as to the decision expected. In particular, his evidence was based on Christian's bizarre behaviour and the coincidences between what Christian stated and the confessions obtained from the accused.

**10th June 1697**

Six people executed and one suicide.

## Diagnoses

While the story is bizarre, modern psychiatry could certainly explain Christian Shaw's condition. Because of the incomplete history and the inability to examine the patient, diagnosis can only be tentative but the following would be likely. The definitions are those given in the appropriate classification.

**F44 (ICD 10) Dissociative disorder/ 300.11 (DSM IV) Conversion Disorder** with mixed presentation (which encompasses NES). Following the DSM IV classification, diagnosis of "300.11 Conversion disorder" is dependent on the following:

A  One or more symptoms or deficits affecting voluntary motor or sensory function that suggest a neurological or other medical condition.

B  Psychological factors are judged to be associated with the symptom or deficit because the initiation or exacerbation of the symptom or deficit is preceded by conflicts or other stresses.

C  The symptom or deficit is not intentionally produced or feigned (as in factious disorder or malingering).

D  The symptom or deficit cannot, after appropriate investigation, be fully explained by a general medical condition, or by the direct effects of a substance, or as a culturally sanctioned behaviour or experience.

E  The symptom or deficit causes clinically significant distress or impairment in social, occupational, or other important areas of functioning or warrants medical evaluation.

F  The symptom or deficit is not limited to pain or sexual dysfunction, does not occur exclusively during the course of a somatisation disorder, and is not better accounted for by another mental disorder.

**F44.3 (ICD 10) Trance and possession disorder.**

Disorder is which there is a temporary loss of the sense of personal identity and full awareness of surroundings.

**Pica of infancy and childhood.**

Persistent eating of non-nutritive substances (such as soil, paint chippings etc.). It may occur as one of many symptoms that are part of a more widespread psychiatric disorder or as a relatively isolated psychopathological behaviour (F98.3, ICD 10).

**G40.0 (ICD 10) Localisation-related (focal) (partial) idiopathic epilepsy and epileptic syndromes with seizures of localised onset.**

Benign childhood epilepsy with centrotemporal EEG spikes. Childhood epilepsy with occipital EEG paroxysms.

**F23 (ICD 10) Acute and transient psychotic disorder.**

A heterogeneous group of disorders characterised by the acute onset of psychotic symptoms such as delusions, hallucinations and perceptual disturbances, and by the severe disruption of ordinary behaviour. Acute onset is defined as a crescendo development of a clearly abnormal clinical picture in about two weeks or less. For these disorders there is no evidence of organic causation. Perplexity and puzzlement are often present but disorientation for time, place and person is not persistent or severe enough to justify a diagnosis of organically caused delirium. Complete recovery usually occurs within a few months, often within a few weeks or even days. If the disorder persists, a change in classification will be necessary. The disorder may or may not be associated with acute stress, defined as unusually stressful events preceding the onset by one to two weeks.

Christian's age would mitigate against diagnosing personality disorder as this does not fully develop until the age of eighteen.

## Investigations and treatment

If Christian were to be seen today, in order to diagnose an organic disorder, there would be a full range of haematological investigations including serum prolactin, and a 24 hour EEG. A CT scan would be helpful. Full thyroid investigations would be carried out if merited by the clinical picture. Hypocalcaemia secondary to anxiety-based hyperventilation would not be of sufficient severity to account for the opisthotonus. Assuming normal renal function, it would be unlikely that significant hypercalcaemia would result from pica involving eggshells.

In modern psychiatry, initial investigation would be a mental state examination, with a history from both parents and any other significant carer. Educational assessment would be important along with information about her friendships, religious teaching and her interaction with siblings. Information would be corroborated with the patient's general practitioner and with her school. A psychometric assessment would also be warranted at the beginning and end of the episode to elucidate any cognitive decline. Due to the severity of these symptoms, she would most likely be admitted to a child in-patient unit for observation and would be detainable under Section 25 (1) Mental Health (Scotland) Act 1984.

Treatment may consist of individual work for Christian and family work, possibly marital counselling, and minimal use of sedative drugs until the diagnosis was clarified. A social work colleague may be involved as a co-worker for the family and to offer practical advice. Liaison with the school would be important to ensure that Christian would not fall behind with schoolwork and also to guide the teachers how to deal with Christian on her return. When her symptoms resolved she would be followed-up at psychiatric out-patients and thereafter by her general practitioner.

157

## Biographical note
## Dr Matthew Brisbane

Matthew Brisbane was a very successful and well respected Scottish medic of the later half of the 1600s and was the city of Glasgow's physician in the last two decades of the century. He was the son of the manse of Erskine in Renfrewshire, where his father Matthew had succeeded his own father, William, as minister. William Brisbane was minister of Erskine from 1592 to c1640-2 and his son held the charge from 1642 to 1648. The Brisbanes were well connected and were a scion of the family of the Brisbanes of nearby Bishopton, believed to be descendants of one William Brisbane who was chancellor of Scotland in 1332. In addition, Rev Matthew Brisbane's wife, the mother of the physician, was the youngest daughter of John Napier of Merchiston, the famous inventor of logarithms. The main Brisbane line also had property in Ayrshire, the estate of Brisbane at Largs, and later the family resided there as Brisbane of that ilk. Last century, one of their descendants, Sir Thomas Brisbane, was to become famous as the Governor of New South Wales in Australia and the city of Brisbane is named after him.

Little is known of Matthew Brisbane's early career but he received a classical education at the College of Glasgow and was awarded the degree of M.D from the University of Utrecht in the Netherlands in 1661; his thesis was entitled *"De Catalepsi"*. At this time there was little opportunity for studying medicine in the Scottish universities and presumably his choice of the Netherlands was related to its being a country whose religion was reformed and, therefore, sympathetic to a Scottish presbyterian.

Clearly Matthew Brisbane was well-respected. There is a record in the Glasgow City Accounts for 1682 that he was the town physician and was paid the same salary as the surgeon, John Robisoune, and the stone-cutter, Evir McNeill. Each received £66 13s 4d. Scots. About 1684, he was entered in the roll of the Glasgow Faculty of Physicians and Surgeons. His name appears on a list of *"The names of such worthie persons as have gifted books to the Chierurgions Librarie in Glasgow"*. He also held office in the University, being Dean of Faculty in 1675-76 and Rector in 1677-81. Matthew Brisbane died in 1699.

A pamphlet entitled *"A relation of the diabolical practices of the witches of the Sheriffdom of Renfrew in the Kingdom of Scotland contained in their tryalls, examinations, and confessions; and for which several of them have been executed this present year 1697."* contains a horrific section in its preface in which the trial of the witches by pricking is described in fearsome detail. It makes clear that Dr Brisbane had at first disbelieved that witches bore the mark of the devil but it seems that he was called to witness the pricking of two of the women and shown the evidence. A three-inch long needle was inserted at the top of the vertebrae in one victim and into the lower abdomen a hands-breadth below the ribs in Margaret Lang; neither woman, the writer claims, felt pain or bled.

ACKNOWLEDGEMENT: The authors are grateful for the kind assistance of the staff at the Glasgow University Library.

**BIBLIOGRAPHY**
**Bargarran witchcraft trial and Dr Matthew Brisbane.**
Anderson, W. The Scottish Nation. A. Fullarton and Co., London 1863.
Chambers, R. Domestic Annals of Scotland. W. & R. Chambers, Edinburgh 1861
Clark, S. Paisley: A History. Mainstream Publishing Co. (Edinburgh) Ltd., Edinburgh 1988
Duncan, A. Memorials of the Faculty of Physicians and Surgeons of Glasgow 1599-1850. James Maclehose and Sons, Glasgow 1896.
Gardner, A. A History of the Witches of Renfrewshire (New Edition). Alexander Gardner, Paisley 1877.
Innes Smith, R. W. English-Speaking Students of Medicine at the University of Leyden. Oliver and Boyd, Edinburgh 1932.
Lang, A. History of Scotland. William Blackwood and Sons, Edinburgh 1907.
Larner, C., Lee, C. H. and McLachlan, H. V. A Source-Book of Scottish Witchcraft. University of Glasgow 1977.
Metcalfe, W. M. A History of Paisley 600 - 1908. Alexander Gardner, Paisley 1909.
Millar, John. A History of the Witches of Renfrewshire. John Millar, Paisley 1809.
Scott, H. Fasti Ecclesiae Scoticanae. Oliver and Boyd, Edinburgh 1920.
"T. P." A Relation of the Diabolical Practices of the Witches of the Sheriffdom of Renfrew in the Kingdom of Scotland. Hugh Newman at the Grashopper in the Poultry, London 1697.
**Psychiatric assessment.**
Alper, K. Nonepileptic seizures. Neurologic Clinics 12 153-173, 1994.
Diagnostic and Statistical Manual of Mental Disorders, 4th Ed., American Psychiatric Association, Washington D. C. 1994.
Hare, E. The history of "nervous disorders" from 1600 to 1840, and a comparison with modern views. British Journal of Psychiatry; 159: 37-45, 1991.
Hornstein, N. L. and Putnam, F. W. Clinical phenomenology of child and adolescent dissociative disorders. American Academy of Child and Adolescent Psychiatry; 31: 1077-1085, 1992.
International Classification of Diseases and Related Health Problems, 10th Ed., World Health Organisation, Geneva 1992.
Mace, C. J. Hysterical conversion I: a history. British Journal of Psychiatry; 161: 369-377, 1992.
Mace, C. J. Hysterical conversion II: a critique. British Journal of Psychiatry; 161: 378-389, 1992.
Parry-Jones, B. and Parry-Jones, W. L. Pica: symptom or eating disorder? A historical assessment. British Journal of Psychiatry; 160: 341 - 354,1992.
Small, G. W., Propper, M. W., Randolphs, E. T. and Eth, S. Mass hysteria among student performers: social relationship as a symptom predictor. American Journal of Psychiatry; 148: 1200- 1205, 1991.
Terr, L. C. Childhood traumas: an outline and overview. American Journal of Psychiatry; 148: 10-20. 1991.

158

# IRISH IMMUNITY TO
# WITCH-HUNTING, 1534–1711

ELWYN C. LAPOINT

AS DIFFICULT as it often is to explain events which occurred in a society distant in time from our own, it is even more difficult to explain nonevents —expected developments which failed to materialize.[1] Early modern Ireland failed to mount any sustained campaign against suspected witches. There were no serial chain-reaction witch-hunts comparable to the virulent purges that took place contemporaneously in other European societies. This is surprising, given the prevalence and scale of witchcraft prosecutions elsewhere in Europe at the time. During the early modern period, European trials resulted in the execution of some 60,000 condemned witches.[2] Even England, with its relatively moderate record of witchcraft prosecutions, executed perhaps 500 to 1,000 witches.[3]

Ireland, however, proved a notable exception to this pattern. Despite the fact that the Irish were then subject to the English crown and derived their 1586 witchcraft statute from England, very few witch trials occurred in Ireland during the early modern era. From the beginning of Tudor

1   I would like to express my appreciation to the Northwest Institute of Advanced Studies, Eastern Washington University, for the grant which enabled me to conduct research in Ireland, and to Trinity College Library, the National Library and National Archives, the Royal Irish Academy, the Dublin Institute for Advanced Studies, Archbishop Marsh's Library, and the Archives of the Department of Irish Folklore of University College, Dublin, for access to their several collections. Finally, I want to thank Larry Beason, John Ross, Martin Seedorf and Deborah Lapoint for their helpful comments on earlier drafts of this paper, as well as Roxann Dempsey and Theresa Gardea for preparing the ts.

2   Brian P. Levack, *The Witch-Hunt in Early Modern Europe* (London: Longman, 1987), p. 21.

3   Christina Larner, *Witchcraft and Religion: The Politics of Popular Belief*, ed. A. Macfarlane (Oxford: Basil Blackwell, 1984), p. 72, suggests the lower figure. Keith Thomas, *Religion and the Decline of Magic* (New York: Charles Scribner's Sons, 1971), p. 450, following Ewen, gives the larger number.

rule to Ireland's last known witch trial in 1711, no more than nine proceedings against witchcraft are attested.[4] Of this number, only three are known to have resulted in the execution of the accused, although it is probable that a fourth case had a similar outcome. During these two centuries there was but one mass trial, the Island Magee affair in 1711, and, while the seven women codefendants in the case were eventually found guilty of witchcraft, none was hanged.[5] As sensational as certain features of this incident proved to be, it was self-contained, a local matter, and led to no further prosecutions. Ireland produced no large scale chain-reaction hunts comparable, say, to the 1645 Essex witch-finding movement or the Salem witch-hunt of 1692.[6]

By the standards of contemporary continental society, and even those of neighboring England, early modern Ireland exhibited a remarkably low level of antiwitchcraft jural activity. What accounts for the dearth of Irish prosecutions? What is responsible for the country's singular immunity to the epidemic witch-craze that swept Europe during the period? The questions are worth exploring not only for what may be revealed about Ireland, but also for what we may discover about the dynamics of witch-hunting in early modern Europe.

Ireland's resistance to witch-panics has attracted the notice of historians, but proposed explanations do not satisfactorily account for the country's invulnerability. Christina Larner, for example, claims that Ireland was among those European nations that "acquired the persecution late."[7] Apart from skirting the issue of the frequency of cases entirely, this proposal is inconsistent with the historical evidence. The first and most famous of all Irish witchcraft cases, the trial of the confederates of Dame Alice

4  St. John D. Seymour, *Irish Witchcraft and Demonology* (1913; rept. New York: Causeway Books, 1973), *passim*.

5  *Ibid.*, p. 221. See also Samuel McSkimin, *The History and Antiquities of the County of the Town of Carrickfergus*, new ed. (Belfast: Mullan and Son, James Cleeland, Davidson and M'Cormack, 1909), p. 74.

6  On the 1645 Essex witch-finding movement, see Alan Macfarlane, *Witchcraft in Tudor and Stuart England* (New York: Harper and Row, 1970), pp. 135–42. The Salem witch-hunt is covered in many sources, but one of the best recent treatments appears in Paul Boyer and Stephen Nissenbaum, *Salem Possessed: The Social Origins of Witchcraft* (Cambridge, Mass: Harvard University Press, 1974).

7  Larner, *Witchcraft and Religion*, p. 4.

Kyteler, took place in Kilkenny in 1324.[8] Occurring well before the early modern witch-craze, the Kyteler case was fully typical of the politically motivated European sorcery trials of its time.[9] In addition scattered references to witchcraft proceedings appear in Irish records for both the sixteenth and seventeenth centuries — the very period during which the great continental hunts occurred.[10] Presumed cultural lag, therefore, cannot explain the scarcity of Irish witch trials.

Neither can this scarcity be explained by the geographic factors invoked by Rossell Hope Robbins.[11] Geographic marginality does not necessarily guarantee cultural isolation. There is no convincing evidence that a geographic position on the outskirts of Europe spared any society from a witch-hunt. Certainly, Scandinavia, Poland, and even Russia were not immune to witch-scares during the early modern period.[12] Neither were the British Isles, as the major Scottish and English hunts attest. And, if peripheral location were indeed an effective immunizing factor, we should face a considerable challenge in accounting for the witch trials of colonial America.

Contrary to Robbins's depiction of insular isolation, however, Ireland

8 Key sources include: Thomas Wright, ed., *A Contemporary Narrative of the Proceedings Against Dame Alice Kyteler, Prosecuted for Sorcery in 1324*, by Richard Ledrede, Bishop of Ossory, Camden Society Series No. I 24 (1843; rept., New York; AMS Press, 1968); John T. Gilbert, ed., *Chartularies of St. Mary's Abbey, Dublin: With the Register of its House at Dunbrody, and Annals of Ireland* (1844; rept., Weisbaden, Germany: Kraus Reprint, 1965), pp. 362–64; V. Rev. Richard Butler, ed., *The Annals of Ireland by Friar John Clyn, and Thady Dowling, Together with the Annals of Ross* (Dublin: Irish Archaelogical Society, 1849), pp. 16–17; Rev. William Carrigan, *The History and Antiquities of the Diocese of Ossory*, vol. I (Dublin: Sealy, Bryers and Walker, 1905), pp. 45–57; Anne Neary, "The Origins and Character of the Kilkenny Witchcraft Case of 1324," *Proceedings of the Royal Irish Academy, Section C*, 83, C, 13 (Dublin: Royal Irish Academy, 1983), 333–50; William Renwick Riddell, "The First Execution for Witchcraft in Ireland," *Journal of Criminal Law and Criminology and Police Science*, 7, 6 (1917), 828–37; and Norman Cohn, *Europe's Inner Demons: An Enquiry Inspired by the Great Witch-Hunt* (New York: Meridian Books, 1975), pp. 198–204. See also Seymour, *Irish Witchcraft*, pp. 25–51.

9 Richard Kieckhefer, *European Witch Trials: Their Foundations in Popular and Learned Culture, 1300–1500* (Berkeley: University of California Press, 1976), pp. 13–14. See also Neary, "Kilkenny Witchcraft Case," 333–50.

10 Seymour, *Irish Witchcraft, passim.*

11 Rossell Hope Robbins, *The Encyclopedia of Witchcraft and Demonology* (New York: Crown, 1959), p. 275.

12 Levack, *Witch-Hunt in Early Modern Europe*, pp. 187–201.

clearly did participate in the intellectual and cultural currents elsewhere associated with witch-purges. That the English civil and ecclesiastical authorities in Ireland were conversant with contemporary Protestant theories of witchcraft is clear from the records they have left. [13] As for the Roman Catholic clergy who served the Anglo-Irish and Gaelic Irish populations, synodal decrees, ecclesiastical correspondence and other documents indicate that they were well versed in Counter-Reformation theology and demonology. [14] This should scarcely surprise us, since their clerical education was of necessity received in continental seminaries.

If cultural lag and geographic isolation were not responsible for protecting Ireland from witch-panics, perhaps the religious loyalties of the population provide an answer. So argues Brian Levack. [15] Taking a cue from H. R. Trevor-Roper, [16] who some years ago demonstrated the link between religious conflict and continental purges, Levack maintains that "religiously homogeneous or monolithic states generally experienced only occasional witch-hunts and relatively low numbers of executions." [17] Curiously, he includes Ireland among his religiously homogeneous societies, because the population "remained predominantly Catholic." [18] Despite the allegiance of most of the ethnic Irish to Roman Catholicism, however, the ruling English elite was largely Protestant, as was the Scottish immigrant population. The predictable result was that, throughout the period in question, Irish society was racked by profound religious conflicts. [19] As Trevor-

13  See: Margaret T. Hodgen, *Early Anthropology in the Sixteenth and Seventeenth Centuries* (Philadelphia: University of Pennsylvania Press, 1964), p. 366; David Beers Quinn, *The Elizabethans and the Irish* (Ithaca: Cornell University Press, 1966), pp. 28–29, 84–87; Henry Morley, ed., *Ireland under Elizabeth and James the First: Described by Edmund Spenser, by Sir John Davies, and by Fynes Moryson* (London: George Routledge and Sons, 1890), p. 37; and Edward MacLysaght, *Irish Life in the Seventeenth Century* (Dublin: Irish Academic Press, 1979), pp. 300–11.

14  See V. Rev. Laurence F. Renehan, *Collections of Irish Church History*, vol. I, *Irish Archbishops*, ed. Rev. D. McCarthy (Dublin: C. M. Warren 1861), pp. 159–61, 433, 500–1; as well as two books by Patrick J. Corish, *The Catholic Community in the Seventeenth and Eighteenth Centuries* (Dublin: Helicon, 1981), pp. 49–51, 65–67, and *The Irish Catholic Experience: A Historical Survey* (Wilmington, Delaware: Michael Glazier, 1985), pp. 91–122.

15  Levack, *Witch-Hunt in Early Modern Europe*, pp. 106–7.

16  Hugh R. Trevor-Roper, *The European Witch-Craze of the Sixteenth and Seventeenth Centuries* (London: Penguin Books, 1969), pp. 67–70, 82–83, 88–90.

17  Levack, *Witch-Hunt in Early Modern Europe*, p. 106.

18  *Ibid.*, p. 107.

19  Brendan Fitzpatrick, *Seventeenth Century Ireland: The War of Religions* (Dublin: Gill and Macmillian, 1988), *passim*.

Roper notes, elsewhere in Europe such conflicts generally set the stage for epidemics of witch-hunting.[20] But not in Ireland. Why not?

To answer that question, we must examine closely the social and cultural preconditions underlying witch-panics in early modern Europe.[21] We may take for granted that some form of interpersonal or intercommunal conflict found expression in witchcraft prosecutions. Witchcraft regularly comprised the idiom of social conflict in premodern and early modern societies, and witchcraft accusations characteristically furnished the rhetoric through which conflict was expressed. But social dissension alone was not a sufficient condition for epidemic purges. In addition to general social unrest and interpersonal discord, several other predisposing factors proved absolutely necessary.

First was an implicit belief in witchcraft and its destructive capacity. In early modern Europe this belief entailed more than the ubiquitous notion of *maleficium* or injury wrought through occult agency. The early modern witch was more than mere sorcerer. He or, more often, she was a diabolist and demonolater as well.[22] The witch had formed an irrevocable pact with Satan whose intercession enabled her to work her mischief. Before this prevailing belief in diabolical witchcraft could inspire widespread prosecutions, however, it had first to be translated into law. Another prerequisite for witch-hunting, then, was the existence of applicable statutes or legal codes. Moreover, large-scale purges depended on the presence of legal authorities who possessed the will and the means to enforce the available codes vigorously.

Finally, and critically, jural witch-hunters required a ready source of accusations in order to prosecute. Given the clandestine nature of the crime, such attestations to the invisible workings of witchcraft were pivotal to the legal process. In turn, an ample supply of accusations depended on a climate of popular opinion that was tolerant of or at least acquiescent before the juridical juggernaut that drove the witch trials. Therefore, in addition to the social conflicts that fostered them, early modern witch-hunts required stern laws and zealous lawyers, a supportive ideology and, above all, a reliable supply of accusations.[23] Of all these factors, it was the last-mentioned,

20  Trevor-Roper, *European Witch-Craze*, pp. 64–73, 82–83, 88–90.

21  See Levack, *Witch-Hunt in Early Modern Europe*, pp. 147–52.

22  See: Thomas, *Religion and the Decline of Magic*, pp. 435–49, 493–501; Cohn, *Europe's Inner Demons*, pp. 180–205, 225–38, 251–55; Larner, *Witchcraft and Religion*, pp. 3–5, 10, 32, 38, 44, 55, 76–77, 80–82; and Levack, *Witch-Hunt in Early Modern Europe*, pp. 7–18, 27–40.

23  Levack, *Witch-Hunt in Early Modern Europe*, pp. 147–52.

a steady stream of witchcraft accusations, that sixteenth and seventeenth century Ireland so conspicuously lacked.

There was certainly no shortage of witch-beliefs. At various provincial synods during the seventeenth century, the resident Catholic clergy inveighed against the manifold superstitions of the Irish populace, including in their enumerations witchcraft, sorcery, and divination through demonic invocation.[24] Likewise, visiting Elizabethan English clerics, including the Catholic William Good and the Protestant Meredith Hanmer, commented on Irish credulity, instancing beliefs in such homely forms of supernatural mischief as the bewitchment of cattle and horses.[25] The rural folk feared occult interference with livestock as well as dairy operations. They also guarded their houses with horseshoes.[26] Folk anxieties about supernatural malevolence were not new. The seventeenth-century synodal harangues against popular superstition recall the sixth- or seventh-century Irish penitentials, specifically the *Synodus I S. Patricii*, which sets a penance for credence in witches.[27] Apparently then, witch-beliefs were current in early medieval Ireland. As if to confirm the fact, early works of Irish heroic and mythological literature, such as the eighth-century *Táin Bó Cuailnge*,[28] describe the calamitous effects of curses and black magic, while the roughly contemporaneous Brehon law tracts contain provisions against maleficent sorcery.[29] And, writing in the twelfth century, Giraldus Cambrensis depicts Ireland as a land of miracles, magic and baneful curses.[30] And if the native Irish entertained persistent beliefs in sorcery, it need scarcely be added that the new immigrant populations of English and Scottish settlers brought with them to Ireland their own vigorous traditions concerning the injurious

24  Renehan, *Irish Archbishops*, pp. 161, 502; Corish, *Catholic Community*, p. 50.

25  Quinn, *Elizabethans and the Irish*, pp. 85-86. See also Reginald Scot, *The Discoverie of Witchcraft* (1584; rept. New York: Dover, 1972), pp. 36-37.

26  MacLysaght, *Irish Life in the Seventeenth Century*, p. 178.

27  Ludwig Bieler, ed., *The Irish Penitentials* (Dublin: Dublin Institute for Advanced Studies, 1963), pp. 56-57. See also Michael Richter, *Medieval Ireland: The Enduring Tradition* (New York: St. Martin's Press, 1988), pp. 75-77.

28  Thomas Kinsella, trans., *The Tain* (Mountrath, Portlaoise, Ireland: The Dolmen Press, 1969), pp. 7-8, 61, 132-3, and *passim*.

29  See *Ancient Laws of Ireland*, 5 vols. (Dublin: Alexander Thom, 1865-1901), especially vols. I (1865), p. 203, and V (1901), p. 295; also Fergus Kelly, *A Guide to Early Irish Law* (Dublin: Dublin Institute for Advanced Studies, 1988), pp. 44, 74, 128.

30  Gerald of Wales, *The History and Topography of Ireland* (Harmondsworth: Penguin Books, 1982), pp. 68-72, 81, 89-90.

effects of occult malevolence.[31]

The English, moreover, introduced their legislation against witchcraft to Ireland. As part of a general effort to complete the Tudor conquest and extend English statute law throughout the island,[32] the Irish Parliament enacted Queen Elizabeth's statute against witchcraft in 1586, twenty-three years after the bill had been adopted in England.[33] Although the Irish legislators never replaced this law with the harsher 1604 act of King James I,[34] the earlier Elizabethan statute proved perfectly adequate to try the few accused witches who were brought before Irish courts during the seventeenth century and the opening years of the eighteenth. Those same few cases — among them, the 1606 proceeding against the Protestant minister John Aston; the trial of Florence Newton, the witch of Youghal, in 1661; and the Island Magee mass trial of 1711 — demonstrate that judges serving on the Irish bench were prepared to prosecute suspected wizards to the full extent of the law.[35]

31 For English beliefs, consult Thomas, *Religion and the Decline of Magic*, pp. 435–49, 493–501; and Macfarlane, *Witchcraft in Tudor and Stuart England*, pp. 3–5, 14–20, 178–198. For Scottish witch beliefs, see Christina Larner, *Enemies of God: The Witch-hunt in Scotland* (Oxford: Basil Blackwell, 1981), pp. 134–191, *passim*; as well as Larner, *Witchcraft and Religion*, pp. 3–26, 69–78.

32 On English statute law in Tudor and Stuart Ireland, see Alfred Gaston Donaldson, *Some Comparative Aspects of Irish Law* (Durham, N.C.: Duke University Press, 1957), pp. 7–8, 10–11; Nicholas P. Canny, *The Elizabethan Conquest of Ireland; A Pattern Established* (New York: Barnes and Noble, 1976), pp. 33, 52–60, and *passim*; J. C. Beckett, *The Making of Modern Ireland: 1603–1923*, new ed. (London: Faber and Faber, 1981), pp. 34–35; and Margaret MacCurtain, *Tudor and Stuart Ireland* (Dublin: Gill and Macmillan, 1972), pp. 45–46, 58–59, 69–71.

33 The Elizabethan witchcraft statute, passed by the Irish Parliament in 1586, appears in *The Statutes at Large, Passed in the Parliaments Held in Ireland* (Dublin: George Grierson, Printer, 1786), pp. 403–405. See also Seymour, *Irish Witchcraft*, pp. 61–65; and Robbins, *Encyclopedia of Witchcraft and Demonology*, p. 275.

34 Seymour, *Irish Witchcraft*, pp. 65–66; Robbins, *Encyclopedia of Witchcraft and Demonology*, p. 275.

35 The principal source on the trial of Florence Newton is Joseph Glanvill, *Saducismus Triumphatus: Or, Full and Plain Evidence Concerning Witches and Apparitions* (1689; rept., Gainesville, Florida: Scholars' Facsimiles and Reprints, 1966), pp. 372–87. All subsequent accounts of this trial, including Francis Bragge's treatment in *Witchcraft Farther Display'd* (London: E. Curll, 1712), rely on Glanvill. He, in turn, apparently based his discussion on a set of trial notes prepared by the presiding judge, Sir William Aston; at least this is what Seymour concludes (see his *Irish Witchcraft*, pp. 130–31, although Glanvill seems to have regarded Aston as a notary or trial record-keeper (see *Saducismus Triumphatus*, p. 386). On the Newton Trial, see also Seymour, *Irish Witchcraft*, pp. 105–31, and James F. Fuller, "Trial of Florence Newton for Witchcraft in Cork, 1661," *Journal of the Cork Historical and Archaeological Society*, X, Second

Of the several preconditions that made possible the virulent forms of witch-hunting known to early modern Europe, Ireland was amply endowed with both relevant law and resolute lawyers. The Irish folk, moreover, credited the existence of maleficent witchcraft, as did the immigrant English and Scottish settlers. What was missing, as has already been noted, was a plentiful source of accusations to set the judicial machinery in motion.

Under the inquisitorial legal procedure that then prevailed on the Continent, a steady stream of accusations could be expected automatically as a predictable byproduct of the confessions extracted from accused witches under torture.[36] But the English legal system was not inquisitorial, and English authorities did not officially condone the use of torture in witchcraft cases.[37] While those suspected of occult acts of *maleficium* occasionally confessed and even implicated their supposed accomplices in diabolical sorcery, court authorities had to rely primarily on charges lodged by the alleged victims of witchcraft or by their neighbors and relations, by the very people, in short, who would later testify against the accused at their trials. Court reliance on volunteered witchcraft accusations was as essential to Irish proceedings as it was to those held in England itself. After all, the English legal system had been effectively established throughout Ireland after the Elizabethan conquest,[38] while in the early Stuart years all new judges recruited to serve on the Irish bench were either themselves English or were at least English-trained.[39]

Even in the absence of judicial torture, volunteered accusations proved sufficient to trigger virulent hunts in England and New England.[40] But in Ireland the supply of accusations largely failed. The very few witchcraft

Series (1904), 174–83. On the Island Magee trial see McSkimin, *History and Antiquities of Carrickfergus*, pp. 73–74. General coverage of Irish cases will be found in Seymour, *Irish Witchcraft*; Robbins, *Encyclopedia of Witchcraft and Demonology*, pp. 275–76, 294–95, 329–30; and, briefly, in Levack, *Witch-Hunt in Early Modern Europe*, pp. 185–86.

36  See Trevor-Roper, *European Witch-Craze*, pp. 46–47; Cohn, *Europe's Inner Demons*, pp. 22–23, 225–26; and Levack, *Witch-Hunt in Early Modern Europe*, pp. 67–77.

37  On this point, see Levack, *Witch-Hunt in Early Modern Europe*, pp. 67, 183–84; Macfarlane, *Witchcraft in Tudor and Stuart England*, p. 20; Robbins, *Encyclopedia of Witchcraft and Demonology*, pp. 508–9; Thomas, *Religion and The Decline of Magic*, p. 517; and Trevor-Roper, *European Witch-Craze*, p. 47.

38  Beckett, *Making of Modern Ireland*, pp. 34–35; Canny, *Elizabethan Conquest of Ireland*, pp. 33, 54, and *passim*; MacCurtain, *Tudor and Stuart Ireland*, pp. 69–71.

39  Donaldson, *Comparative Aspects of Irish Law*, p. 10.

40  Macfarlane, *Witchcraft in Tudor and Stuart England*, pp. 135–42; Boyer and Nissenbaum, *Salem Possessed*, pp. 1–21.

cases reported from Ireland for the early modern period serve only to underscore the imperviousness of the ethnic Irish community to legalized witch-hunting. For, wherever information on provenience is available, it appears that those cases had their origins in English or Scottish immigrant communities.[41] The principals in these proceedings — both the accused and those who testified against them — hailed from such settler communities as Youghal and Island Magee, near Carrickfergus in Antrim.[42] Furthermore, the cases were tried according to English law in courts presided over by judges recruited from the English bar.

Most importantly, the trials were culturally British and reflected the witchcraft beliefs of their English or Scottish instigators. Nowhere is this more evident than in the trial of Florence Newton at the Cork Assizes in September, 1661.[43] This case originated in the English settler community of Youghal, site of Sir Walter Raleigh's Irish estate.[44] In every particular the Newton trial was faithful to English precedent in both the magical beliefs expressed by witnesses and the trial procedure employed by the court. Indeed, Joseph Glanvill in his *Saducismus Triumphatus* cites this case as fully typical of English witchcraft proceedings of the time.[45] To begin with, Florence Newton resembled most accused witches in being an indigent, elderly woman.[46] In fact, it was her begging that first attracted the negative attention of her Youghal neighbors.

Denied charity, Gammer Newton resorted to cursing, a response that typically gave rise to suspicions of witchcraft in English communities. When a servant girl, who once had denied her, subsequently fell victim to convulsive fits, Florence Newton was accused of bewitching the maid. At her trial, the old woman was charged with having "overlooked" the afflicted

41 Seymour, *Irish Witchcraft*, pp. 105-31, 171-72, 200-21.

42 For Youghal, see A. R. Orme, "Youghal, County Cork – Growth, Decay, Resurgence", *Irish Geography*, V, (1964–1968), 121–49; Rev. Samuel Hayman, *Guide to Youghal, Ardmore, and the Blackwater* (Youghal: John Lindsay, 1860), pp. 24–25, 30. On Island Magee and its environs, see McSkimin, *History and Antiquities of Carrickfergus*.

43 Glanvill, *Saducismus Triumphatus*, pp. 372-87.

44 Orme, "Youghal, County Cork," 121–49; Hayman, *Guide to Youghal*, pp. 24–25, 30.

45 Glanvill, *Saducismus Triumphatus*, pp. 372-87.

46 On the Newton trial, see Glanvill, *Saducismus Triumphatus*, pp. 372-87; and Seymour, *Irish Witchcraft*, pp. 105-31. On women's place in contemporary English witchcraft proceedings and related beliefs, see Macfarlane, *Witchcraft in Tudor and Stuart England*, pp. 150-51, 160, and 230; Thomas, *Religion and the Decline of Magic*, p. 520; and Larner, *Witchcraft and Religion*, p. 85.

servant, of bewitching her with a kiss, of consorting with a familiar spirit in the form of a greyhound, and of an inability to recite correctly the Lord's Prayer, a feat which any good Christian — but no real witch — should be able to do.

These themes — the cursing, the victim's seizure, overlooking with a malevolent eye, the animal familiar, and, finally, the inability to repeat the Lord's Prayer — all typify English trials and English beliefs of the period.[47] This could only be expected, of course, given the English origins of the settler community in which the case arose. Likewise, Ireland's last witchcraft trial reflected the cultural provenience of its protagonists who, in this instance, belonged to Ulster's Scottish Presbyterian population. It was among members of this immigrant population residing in the Antrim coastal parish of Island Magee that rumors of witchcraft proliferated early in 1711.[48]

As had happened in the Florence Newton case, the Island Magee incident began with the violent seizures of a young person, eighteen-year-old Mary Dunbar. During her convulsions Mary exhibited such strength that she could scarcely be restrained by several muscular adult men. She choked on her own tongue, vomited up sundry objects — including feathers, cotton, yarn, pins, and buttons — and alternately raved or fell mute. When vocal, she complained of bodily pains inflicted by spectral tormentors.[49] Mary Dunbar's symptoms, however startling, were not unprecedented. They had been encountered before in Mary Longdon, the servant girl allegedly bewitched by Florence Newton.[50] Similar symptoms had also been reported for Christine, or Christian, Shaw, the victim in a recent Scottish witchcraft case, who suffered spasms in which she too swallowed her own tongue and, on occasion, disgorged pins, bones, feathers, egg shells and other matter.[51] Indeed, dramatic seizures of this sort were a recurrent element in early modern witchcraft cases throughout Scotland, England, and New

47  See Thomas, *Religion and the Decline of Magic*, pp. 435-49, 493-501; Macfarlane, *Witchcraft in Tudor and Stuart England*; pp. 3-5, 14-20, 178-98; and also Boyer and Nissenbaum, *Salem Possessed*, pp. 1-21.

48  Seymour, *Irish Witchcraft*, p. 207; Robbins, *Encyclopedia of Witchcraft and Demonology*, p. 329.

49  Mary Dunbar's symptoms are described in McSkimin, *History and Antiquities of Carrickfergus*, pp. 73-74, as well as in Seymour, *Irish Witchcraft*, pp. 208-19.

50  Glanvill, *Saducismus Triumphatus*, pp. 373-83; Seymour, *Irish Witchcraft*, pp.109-22.

51  This case, the Paisley episode of 1697, is reported in Larner, *Enemies of God*, pp. 163-65, and in Robbins, *Encyclopedia of Witchcraft and Demonology*, p. 39.

England.[52] So common were these transports that they could be viewed as a diagnostic feature of the prevailing witchcraft syndrome of contemporary English-speaking societies.

The remedy for such afflictions was culturally ordained as well; the cure lay in English law. Once the witch was in custody, the means were at hand to check her power and bring relief to her possessed victims. Here, again, the Island Magee case conformed to pattern. Recovering from the second of her convulsive attacks, Mary Dunbar identified several local women as her tormentors. As a result of her accusations, seven women, all of whom were themselves Presbyterian, were arrested, questioned, and eventually placed on trial for witchcraft. The trial, which occurred in Carrickfergus on March 31, 1711, lasted no more than a few hours. As if to underscore the communal nature of the case, several Presbyterian clergymen testified as witnesses.[53] The victim herself did not, as she was temporarily struck speechless and remained so throughout the trial. Nonetheless, the seven accused were duly convicted and sentenced to one year's imprisonment punctuated by four appearances in the pillory.[54]

The Island Magee affair proved to be the final witchcraft trial held in Ireland. In its exogenous cultural roots, however, it resembled the cases which had preceded it. Strikingly, all documented Irish witchcraft cases whose demographic origins can be traced derive from English or Scottish settler communities. And yet these immigrant communities represented only a minority of Ireland's population at the time. The vast bulk of that population, over three quarters of the total figure of 1.5 to 2 million, consisted of the Gaelic or ethnic Irish.[55] But of any possible actions against witches

52  On Scotland, see Larner, *Enemies of God*, pp. 110, 165. For England, refer to Macfarlane, *Witchcraft in Tudor and Stuart England*, pp. 183–84, and to Thomas, *Religion and the Decline of Magic*, p. 489. New England examples are given in John Putnam Demos, *Entertaining Satan: Witchcraft and the Culture of Early New England* (New York: Oxford University Press, 1982), pp. 7–9, 99–111; Carol F. Karlsen, *The Devil in the Shape of a Woman: Witchcraft in Colonial New England* (New York: Vintage Books, 1987), pp. 10–11, 134–36; and Marion L. Starkey, *The Devil in Massachusetts: A Modern Enquiry into the Salem Witch Trials* (1949; Garden City, NY: Anchor Books, 1969), pp. 39–48, among others. See also Robbins, *Encyclopedia of Witchcraft and Demonology*, pp. 68–69, 227–29, 385–86, 527–30, and *passim*.

53  McSkimin, *History and Antiquities of Carrickfergus*, p. 74; Seymour, *Irish Witchcraft*, p. 214.

54  McSkimin, *History and Antiquities of Carrickfergus*, p. 74; Seymour, *Irish Witchcraft*, p. 221.

55  R. A. Butlin, "Land and People, c. 1600," *A New History of Ireland*, vol. III, *Early Modern Ireland, 1534–1691*, ed. T. W. Moody, F. X. Martin, and F. J. Byrne (Oxford: Oxford University Press, 1976), p. 148; R. F. Foster, *Modern Ireland 1600–1972* (New York: Penguin Books, 1988), pp. 14, 130.

taken by members of this majority population, we know nothing. There is absolutely no evidence that the native Irish ever referred witchcraft accusations to their English governors. Significantly, even the notorious Kyteler case of 1324 involved members of the Anglo-Norman community and not the ethnic Irish.[56] As far as extant case law in the surviving historical record is concerned, Irish witchcraft is not Irish at all; it is, instead, thoroughly and prototypically English.

Moreover, throughout the early modern era the English authorities in Ireland could spare little time for witchcraft prosecutions. They were preoccupied with the serious business of completing the conquest, coping with recusancy and civil unrest, and extending crown control throughout the country.[57] Even in comparatively settled times, British jurists evinced an overriding concern with public order and with those political crimes that posed a threat to the crown. We may cite as an example the legal reports and correspondence of Sir John Davies, solicitor-general and later attorney-general for Ireland under James I.[58] During the first decade of that Stuart monarch's reign, Davies served as a justice of assize, touring Ireland to conduct court inquiries into a variety of offenses. In his correspondence with the earl of Salisbury, Davies alludes to numerous cases of rebellion and recusancy, intercommunal theft, and residual observance of the legally nullified Irish customs of tanistry and gavelkind.[59] All these matters are either overtly political in character or possess clear political implications. In none of Davies's reports, however, does witchcraft figure as an important concern.

If Davies's views are typical of his contemporaries on the Irish bench, and the evidence would suggest that they are, then we may conclude that the English jurists then serving in Ireland manifested greater interest in political offenses against public order than in private crimes such as witchcraft. This legal focus on public order would help to account for the fact

56  Carrigan, *History and Antiquities of Ossory*, pp. 49–50.

57  See Fitzpatrick, *Seventeenth Century Ireland, passim*; and MacCurtain, *Tudor and Stuart Ireland*, pp. 44–46, 54–59, 69–71, 89, 114, and *passim*.

58  Sir John Davies, *State Papers on Ireland* (1604-5-1610) and *Le primer report des cases et matters en ley resolues & adiuges en les courts del roy en Ireland* (London: Printed for the Company of Stationers, 1628). See, too, Davies in Morley, ed., *Ireland Under Elizabeth and James the First*, pp. 334–36, and also Richard Bagwell, *Ireland Under the Stuarts*, vol. I (London: The Holland Press, 1963), pp. 91–96.

59  Davies's correspondence with the earl of Salisbury appears in his *State Papers on Ireland* (1604-5-1610), see especially pp. 137, 141, 169, 191, 195, 206 and *passim*.

that, even in immigrant settler communities, witchcraft prosecutions were relatively rare throughout the period in question.

The political conditions that so preoccupied English judges on the Irish bench are likewise directly relevant to understanding why the historical record for early modern Ireland reveals no instances of witchcraft prosecutions triggered by Gaelic Irish accusations. Given the fragmentary nature of the documentation for the period, it is of course possible that, as Levack suggests,[60] such proceedings may have occurred without leaving a trace in surviving judicial reports. Yet, since no other documentation in the correspondence, diaries or pamphlet literature of the era, of Irish accusations survives and since, moreover, there is some documentary evidence of jural actions triggered by settler suspicions, we may infer that the ethnic Irish simply did not refer witchcraft accusations to the courts.

If, as seems likely, this indeed proves to be the case, then it would take us some distance toward explaining the dearth of witchcraft prosecutions in Ireland. The Irish formed the great majority of the national population.[61] Without a steady flow of accusations from them to initiate individual or mass trials, it is difficult to conceive how any court proceedings could have escalated into a chain-reaction hunt. And, without popular support from members of the Gaelic Irish community, it would have been impossible to sustain any such hunt for very long. Yet, this raises another question. If the native Irish entertained vigorous witch-beliefs, and we know that they did, then why did they not translate those beliefs into public accusations of suspected witches? As suggested above, contemporary political conditions provide the answer to this question.

Throughout the early modern era the Irish were a subject people. In the wake of the Elizabethan conquest, indigenous Irish leadership was effectively neutralized and the Irish Brehon code supplanted by English statute law. In the Irish law courts not only the statutes, but also the judges themselves and the very language employed in court proceedings were English. To the Gaelic-speaking Irish, these courts and the laws they administered represented an alien institution, as incomprehensible as it was pernicious. The harsh treatment meted out to recusants as well as recalcitrant Irish leaders must have convinced the predominantly Roman Catholic Irish of the hostility of the English courts and Protestant officialdom. Of the

60 Levack, *Witch-Hunt in Early Modern Europe*, p. 185.
61 Butlin, "Land and People," p. 148; Foster, *Modern Ireland*, pp. 14, 130.

flagrant contempt in which the English held the Irish and their customs, the contemporary literature provides numerous examples.[62] There was little reason, therefore, for the Irish to entrust their witchcraft suspicions to essentially foreign and unsympathetic courts. No Irish accuser could be certain of mobilizing effective legal support for his charges in this alien milieu.[63] Since the Irish Catholic clergy themselves railed against lay witchcraft superstitions,[64] the Irish laity would have had little cause to suppose that Protestant English jurists would exhibit greater tolerance of their disclosures concerning what were, after all, spiritual crimes.

More is involved here, however, than an understandable reluctance to pursue unpredictable channels of legal recourse. Any potential accuser would have risked retaliation from the Irish community itself should he betray a member of that community to the English authorities. The correspondence of Sir John Davies sheds light on this point. In his letters to the earl of Salisbury, Davies vents his frustration at the difficulty encountered by the justices of assize in persuading the Irish citizenry to cooperate with the courts against their compatriots.[65] In Monaghan, for example, Davies observes that "the poor people seemed very unwilling to be sworn of the juries, alledging [sic], that if they condemned any man, his friends in revenge would rob, or burn, or kill them for it."[66] Although the trials in question did not involve witchcraft, this example clearly illustrates the hazards faced by any native Irishman who dared to break ranks and traduce his fellows to crown officials. Moreover, the Monaghan sessions should not be considered unique or viewed as an isolated case of popular resistance to crown law. On the contrary, one can readily find other instances of Irish noncooperation with the English legal authorities. To illustrate, during the reign of Henry VIII, the Irish clans of the Wicklow Hills interfered with the king's judges whenever the latter attempted to ride their circuits beyond the Pale.[67] And much later, at the height of Jacobean concern over

---

62 See, for example, Quinn, *Elizabethans and the Irish*, pp. 68-69, 135-36; Hodgen, *Early Anthropology*, pp. 364-66, and Morley, ed., *Ireland Under Elizabeth and James the First*, pp. 37-39, 426, 430.

63 For a twentieth-century ethnographic parallel, see Basil Sansom, "When Witches are not Named," in *The Allocation of Responsibility*, ed. M. Gluckman (Manchester: Manchester University Press, 1972), pp. 193-226.

64 Renehan, *Irish Archbishops*, pp. 161, 433, 502; Corish, *Catholic Community*, pp. 49-51.

65 Davies, *State Papers on Ireland*, pp. 136-37.

66 *Ibid.*, p. 137.

67 John P. Prendergast, *The Cromwellian Settlement of Ireland* (Dublin: Mellifont Press, 1922), p. 27.

recusancy in 1616, Irish Catholic jurors obstructed grand jury proceedings in Cavan and elsewhere by refusing to find against their coreligionists for failing to attend Reformed church services. As a consequence, the recalitrant jurors were themselves penalized with heavy fines and imprisonment.[68]

The examples just cited bring up a final factor which should be mentioned in this connection. Assuming that these episodes of grassroots opposition to English law bespeak a general unwillingness to accommodate established authority, we must consider the likelihood that the Irish refrained from referring witchcraft accusations to the courts precisely because they viewed those courts as an instrument of foreign oppression. The failure to cooperate with alien rulers and imposed institutions is a widespread phenomenon in peasant societies of the type represented by early modern Ireland. In such societies, agrarian disaffection with dominant elites sometimes erupts in open defiance and rebellion, but it often takes a subtler shape in the covert modes of evasion that James Scott has labeled *"everyday* forms of peasant resistance."[69] Among the most pervasive of these tacit forms of resistance is the purposeful circumvention of government courts and magistrates.

If, for political reasons, the early modern Irish withheld their complaints from English authorities, then we may well ask what alternative weapons against witchcraft they did employ. Traditional avenues of legal redress were no longer available, as Brehon law had been effectively suppressed by the first decade of the seventeenth century.[70] Moreover, the early modern historical record contains no evidence of vigilantism against witches. Apparently, therefore, the Irish of this period did not resort to extralegal means of retaliation. Of course, it must be admitted that, if such retaliatory episodes had occurred, they might well have escaped official notice and thus never have left any trace in the documentary record. As we have seen, however, there is evidence that the Irish relied on ritual to ward off supernatural malevolence. Houses were protected from evil spirits by horseshoes nailed on the threshold, and May Eve cattle drives were organized to shield

68 *Ibid.*, pp. 50–51. See also Bagwell, *Ireland Under the Stuarts, I:* 150; and Fitzpatrick, *Seventeenth Century Ireland*, p. 34.

69 James C. Scott, "Weapons of the Weak: Everyday Struggle, Meaning and Deeds," in *Peasants and Peasant Societies*, 2nd ed., ed. T. Thanin (Oxford: Basil Blackwell, 1987), p. 343.

70 Beckett, *Making of Modern Ireland*, pp. 34–35; MacLysaght, *Irish Life in the Seventeenth Century*, p. 118.

livestock from witches.[71] That popular magical measures of this sort had little to do with orthodox Catholicism is evident from the disapproval formally expressed by the clergy at ecclesiastical synods.[72] If magical prophylaxis proved ineffectual, the Irish sought relief through recourse to holy relics and various other ritual remedies. One monastic account of the early seventeenth century, for example, tells of a County Kilkenny woman who had fallen victim to sorcerous spells and was cured by indirect contact with a fragment of the holy cross.[73] Such examples of magical protection and healing, drawn from contemporary records, strongly suggest that ritual praxis provided early modern Irish society with its principal techniques for combating maleficent witchcraft.

The ethnic Irish seem to have preferred ritual solutions over legal solutions to witchcraft. Their neglect of jural alternatives contributed directly to the low incidence of witchcraft prosecutions in early modern Ireland. Given the numerical preponderance of the Gaelic Irish in the national population, their refusal to refer witchcraft accusations to the courts necessarily resulted in a dearth of witch trials. In the absence of wholesale accusations lodged by members of this ethnic community, no large-scale witch-hunts could be mounted or sustained.

The reasons for Irish avoidance of the judicial process are not difficult to discover. Under the precarious political conditions in which the Gaelic Irish then found themselves, their reluctance to prosecute witches in England's Irish courts becomes perfectly understandable. From the English judges on the bench they could have expected only a response that was at best disinterested or disdainful, and at worst openly hostile to Irish concerns. Moreover, the English legal system itself constituted an instrument of foreign domination. Imposed on the Irish people against their will, English law stood as a reminder of their disenfranchisement. Despite persistent Irish efforts to resist objectionable government laws and policies, English conquest and colonization ultimately spelled the end of Gaelic civil institutions. Yet, if Gaelic Ireland was to be denied its own legal and political forms, the Irish could at

71  On the ritual use of horseshoes, see MacLysaght, *Irish Life in the Seventeenth Century*, p. 178. May Eve cattle drives are discussed in Quinn, *Elizabethans and the Irish*, pp. 85-86.

72  Renehan, *Irish Archbishops*, pp. 161, 433, 502; Corish, *Catholic Community*, pp. 37-38, 49-51, 65-71; Corish, *Irish Catholic Experience*, pp. 107-8, 116-18.

73  Quoted in Seymour, *Irish Witchcraft*, pp. 79-80.

least withhold support from the alien arrangements that had replaced them. Viewed from this larger political perspective, the absence of Irish witchcraft accusations signifies more than just a prudent avoidance of problematic legal resources. It represents an expression of Irish passive resistance to the English authorities – a protest against the ruling order and the judicial system on which it depended.

*— Eastern Washington University*

COVER

Aside from the opening index issue, ÉIRE-IRELAND'S covers for the 1992 volume will present paintings from the O'Malley Collection now on loan to the Irish Museum of Modern Art at the Royal Hospital, Kilmainham, in Dublin. Given to the Irish American Cultural Institute in 1979 by Helen Hooker O'Malley Roelofs, this important collection of paintings is currently featured in an exhibition at the IMOMA which will continue until October 11, 1992. The O'Malley family's longstanding association with the arts in Ireland is also recalled in the annual presentation, by the Irish American Cultural Institute, of the O'Malley Award for the visual arts.

This issue's cover reproduces *Composition* by Mainie Jellett (1897-1944). Although her life was brief, Jellett became Ireland's leading exponent of cubism, having studied in Paris with André Lhote and Albert Gleizes. This colorful, rhythmic, but severely linear *Composition* dates from Jellett's studio work in the early 1930's. Jellett's talks on painting and the modern movement were collected in *The Artist's Vision* (1958), with an introduction by Gleizes. Notably, Yale University Press has just issued Bruce Arnold's *Mainie Jellett and the Modern Movement in Ireland*, which delineates both the character or her painting and her contributions to modern Irish art. ÉIRE-IRELAND is pleased to display this painting by Jellett and could not have done so without the help of An Músaem na Nua Ealaíne and, particularly, of Ruth Ferguson.

IRISH IMMUNITY TO WITCH-HUNTING, 1534-1711

*The Eighteenth Century,* vol. 34, no. 3, 1993

# "LIKE IMAGES MADE BLACK WITH THE LIGHTNING": DISCOURSE AND THE BODY IN COLONIAL WITCHCRAFT

## Michael Clark

Signs appeared in many forms to the Colonial Puritans, though seldom so dramatically as in a case reported by Increase Mather in his *Essay for the Recording of Illustrious Providences* (Boston, 1684). Some years earlier in England, Mather writes, a doctor was examining a woman thought to be possessed by evil spirits when

> She was to the amazement of all Spectators, pricked and miserably beaten by an invisible hand; so as that her body from head to foot was wounded, as if she had been whipped with Thorns. Sometimes a perfect sign of the Cross was imprinted on her skin; Sometimes the usual configurations whereby Astronomers denote the Caelestial Bodies, such as ♉ and their Conjunctions, and oppositions by ♂♀ and the Characters used by Chymists △☉ &c. (in which Sciences, though that be not usual for those of her Sex, she was versed) These Characters would remain for several Weeks after the invisible hand had violently impressed them on her body . . . . (197)

Even in a book filled with what Increase's son Cotton would later call the "wonders of the invisible world," this scene stands out. Rising up before the eyes of the helpless doctor, the welts on the poor woman's skin spell out a brutal parody of the Puritans' faith in a "crucified phrase."[1] The spiritual significance of the Passion is demonically inverted as the flesh is made word, and the sign of the cross returned to the body as the invisible world of spirits breaks across into the visible world around us.

Since the crucifixion, most Puritans believed that the division between those realms had remained secure; the days of miracles, visions, and incarnation were over. What remained of the presence of that Spirit in this world were only signs that, like the scars slowly healing from the late revelation Mather describes, merely bore the imprint of that presence as a promise of things to come. For over half a century, Colonial Puritans had lived in the light of that promise, looking forward to the realization of God's plan on the rocky soil of New England. But the barrier between the visible and invisible worlds complicated the relationship between signs and the wonders they would unveil. That relation was sealed by faith but obscured by the ontological difference between flesh and spirit and by the typological deferral of their union to the last day. Only in language did the Puritans find some relief from this desperate paradox, and we often find that desperation registered in their obsessive concern with the semiotic minutiae of phonetics, grammar, and what the Colonial poet Edward Taylor described as the "quill-slabbered draughts" of the written word.

It should not be surprising, then, that Mather dwells on a case in which written signs literally embody a relation between the flesh and the spirit. Nor should we be surprised to see that case reported in a book published near the end of the seventeenth century, when Puritans' anxieties about their place in this world and the next had been compounded by theological disputes, political confusion, and an increasingly diverse and secularized population in the Colonies. So Mather observes at one point that thunder and lightning had not caused much harm "for many years after the *English* did first settle in these *American Desarts*. But that of later years fatal and fearful slaughters have in that way been made amongst us, is most certain. And there are many who have in this respect been as Brands plucked out of the burning, when the Lord hath overthrown others as God overthrew *Sodom* and *Gomorrah*" (72-73). "Such solemn works of Providence ought not to be forgotten," he adds, and he goes on to list a number of "Remarkables" in which balls of fire fall from the sky, coins melt in the purse of their amazed owners (76), men are struck dead where they stand—and left standing "like Images made black with the Lightning" (75, 98)—cats killed, cows addled, pigs singed (85), and rooms filled with smoke "smelling like Brimstone" (85; see 81, 77, et passim).

Such events were seldom forgotten and quickly became the stuff of folklore and legend. But Mather's admonishment to remember them as "works of Providence" urges his reader to go beyond mere curiosity and aspire to understanding and vision. In what amounts to a cosmological weather report, with isobars and coldfronts replaced by divine judgment and God's wrath, Mather embeds the popular anecdotes about thunder and lightning in a narrative of revelation and merciful intervention. It is God's mercy that saves the group standing next to their neighbor smoldering in his shoes, and the spiritual significance of Richard Goldsmith being blasted by lightning just after renouncing his sins and uttering the phrase "blessed be the Lord" is undeniable in Mather's account, if somewhat ambivalent (82).

When Mather's scrupulous fidelity to his sources inhibits his imposing such interpretations, his disappointment is almost palpable, as in the story of John Phillips. On June 23, 1666, the hapless Phillips, whose son had been struck by lightning eight years earlier, saw his house destroyed in a thunder storm. One of the survivors told Mather that "he saw the house full of Smoke, and perceived a grievous smell of Brimstone, and saw the fire ly scattered." However, Mather reports, "though whether that fire came from Heaven or was violently hurled out of the Hearth, he can give no account." But Mather quickly recovers from his narrator's unfortunate lapse into secular uncertainty and cheerily adds that, although he believed all of the people in the house killed, "it pleased God to revive most of them. Only three of them were mortally wounded with Heavens Arrows," Phillips' wife and another of his sons among them (77-78).

Mather treats the capacity to see God's will in these disasters as a mark of faith and humility. Although not a sure sign of election, that ability is an indication of membership in the visible community of Puritan believers, and Mather's stories position the narrators within that community at the same time that they link the natural phenomena to their preternatural significance. Begging the reader's leave to indulge in some "Theological Improvement" of these tragic stories, Mather observes that "There are Wonders in the Works of Creation as well as Providence, the reason whereof the most knowing amongst Mortals, are not able to comprehend" (99-100). How can we hope to understand the strange case of the man who breaks out in a sweat at the sight of a cat (101), or the one who "would fall into a *Syncope* if either a Calves-head or a Cabbage were brought near him" and who, Mather adds, bore the marks of those terrible totems on his body, "imprinted there by the Imagination of his Longing Mother" (102)? Some would claim that "an *occult Quality* is the cause of this strange operation," Mather says, but such an argument "is only a Fig-leaf whereby our common Philosophers seek to hide their own ignorance" (100). It is God who directs the lightning, and it is his voice we hear in the thunder. So Mather concludes the first half of his book with a story about a "prophane Man" and his wife, who were riding through a storm one day. The man trembles at every thunderclap and wonders that his wife can remain so calm. Are you not afraid, he asks, and she replies no, not at all, "for I know it is the voice of my Heavenly Father; and should a Child be afraid to hear his Fathers voice? At the which the Man was amazed," Mather says, "concluding with himself, these *Puritans* have a divine principle in them, which the World seeth not, that they should have peace and serenity in their Souls when others are filled with dismal fears and horrors" (134).

Puritan poets used their poetry to establish similar connections among one's place in this world and the next, personal identity as a

child of God, and membership in the Puritan community of visible
saints.[2] Language did for the Puritan poet what lightning does in
Mather's tales, stripping this world of its apparent solidity and leaving
in its place an image that could direct our vision beyond the limits of
everyday life to the transcendent glory of what Taylor called simply
"things to come." Yet in Mather's *Essay*, there is little of the security
and joy that Taylor projected through his meiotic representation of
worldly beauty in his *Meditations*, or that Anne Bradstreet postponed
past the humiliating limits of her present state in "Contemplations."
The world does not give up its earthly weight so easily as words. The
membrane between sound and sense is more permeable, at least in
the poet's hand, than that separating flesh and spirit. When *that*
barrier was crossed, the effect was devastating, as horrible as the stench
of blackened flesh, as palpable as the grotesque contortions of the
possessed.

   Spirit had once inhabited flesh in the miracle of the Incarnation,
but the Crucifixion had severed them irrevocably, leaving us only the
metaphorical signs through which we recall that miracle in our time.
As Thomas Hooker reminded the Colonists, those signs are born out
of the Passion, and in them Christ's agony on the Cross is writ small
in the torturous confrontations where men and women struggle with
their spiritual fate.[3] That is why Mather is drawn to scenes of horror
and despair rather than reassurance when portraying his remarkable
providences; why witches, rather than saints, occupy so many of his
pages; and it is why odors from the fires of hell, rather than the
perfumes of heaven, linger after the wonders have passed. For the
sudden eruptions of the spiritual world around us signalled not only
the immanent transcendence of their difference. They marked a
judgment against the sin that had separated the spirit from the flesh,
and the closure of the typological narrative in which that separation
had been sustained through the scriptural figures and historical
parallels that measured it. So a decade after Increase Mather recorded his *Illustrious Providences*, his son Cotton would describe the
outbreak of witchcraft at Salem not only as a collapse of the barrier
between flesh and spirit but also as a horrible realization of the signs
by which the final union of flesh and spirit had been at once foretold
and postponed:

> Such is the descent of the Devil at this day upon our selves, that I may truly tell you,
> *The Walls of the whole World are broken down!* The usual *Walls of* defence about mankind
> have such a Gap made in them, that the very *Devils* are broke in upon us, to seduce
> the *Souls*, torment the *Bodies*, sully the *Credits*, and consume the *Estates* of our
> Neighbours, with Impressions both as *real* and as *furious*, as if the *Invisible* World were
> becoming *Incarnate*, on purpose for the vexing of us. (80)

Behold, Sinners, behold and *wonder*, lest you *perish*: the very *Devils* are walking about our Streets, with lengthened *Chains*, making a dreadful Noise in our Ears, and *Brimstone* even without a Metaphor, is making an hellish and horrid stench in our Nostrils. (95)

In his depiction of this scene, Mather portrays witchcraft phenomena as a breakdown in the delicate metaphorical balance between the visible and invisible worlds. That portrayal extends his father's fascination with the spectacle of writing and visible signs into a more subtle understanding of the way those signs negotiated our relation to each of those worlds. In fact, Mather's *Wonders* begins with a negotiation between Satan and God over access rights to the visible realm:

The Devil is called in 1. *Pet* 5, 8. *Your Adversary*. This is a Law-term; and it notes *An Adversary at Law*. The Devil cannot come at us, except in some sence according to *Law*; but sometimes he does procure sad things to be inflicted, according to the *Law* of the eternal King upon us. . . . There is a Court somewhere kept; a Court of Spirits, where the Devil enters all sorts of Complaints against us all; he charges us with manifold *sins* against the Lord our God: *There* he loads us with heavy *Imputations* of Hypocrisie, Iniquity, Disobedience; whereupon he urges, *Lord, let 'em now have the death, which is their wages, paid unto 'em!* If our *Advocate* in the Heavens do not now take off his Libels; the Devil, then, with a Concession of God, *comes down*, as a *destroyer* upon us. Having first been an Attorney, to bespeak that the Judgments of Heaven may be ordered for us, he then also pleads, that he may be the *Executioner* of those Judgments; and the God of Heaven sometimes after a sort, signs a Warrant for this *Destroying Angel*, to do what has been *desired* to be done for the *destroying of men*. (48-49)

The use of a courtroom scene to stage a debate about the relation between the spiritual and corporeal worlds was no accident, of course. Mather wrote *Wonders of the Invisible World* in part as a defense of the legal practices of the Salem judges, who had been criticized for accepting testimony about spiritual torments that were invisible to all but a few of the afflicted. Nevertheless, Mather's association of law and theology in the negotiation of spiritual presence in the physical world was more than strategic. It also reflected the long and often contentious struggle between the courts and the Church over the right to define and hence to prosecute the phenomena of witchcraft. By the time Mather wrote, this struggle had generated three distinct forms of discourse about witchcraft.[4] The oldest is that of folk superstition, where witchcraft is restricted mostly to manipulations of the natural world and is clearly derived from ancient fertility rituals. Those rituals were fully integrated into the life of the community and usually regulated by informal social pressure, but by 1258, Alexander IV issued a papal bull that insisted on distinguishing between witchcraft as superstition and witchcraft as heresy (bull dated 13 December 1258). Alexander said that inquisitors against heretical pravity could not sit in judgment over crimes '*de divinationibus et sortilegiis*', except when "*manifeste haeresim saperent.*"[5] If heresy was not manifest in a particular case, then the witch was usually remanded to a secular authority for trial as a criminal rather than as a heretic, though in 1541 Nicholas V gave inquisitors the power to arrogate to "themselves cases involving simple superstition," and they did that often.

The determining factor in deciding whether a witch would be tried as a heretic or a criminal seemed to be the relation between the inquisitor and the judge or magistrate in each locale (Ginzburg, 177, n. 31). Either way, the trial or examination provided the occasion for authorities to impose more formal schema onto the superstitious beliefs and practices of the people. Between the 13th and 15th centuries, Ginzburg says, "demonologists, judges, and inquisitors" repeatedly and systematically imposed an "inquisitorial schema" onto the "generic superstitions" of the folk through treatises, sermons, woodcuts, etc. (xv, xviii). Distinctions among superstition, heresy, and crime persisted, but according to Monter ("Pedestal"), by the end of the 15th century that imposition had transformed the public perception of witchcraft into a diabolical schema that combined, though often uneasily, the forms of superstition and heresy. With the publication of the *Malleus maleficarum* (*The Hammer of Witches*) in 1490, the prosecution of witchcraft as heresy was codified into an elaborate formal procedure with explicit instructions on the diabolical dimension of folk superstitions and how to find it.[6]

The *Malleus* had tremendous influence on Continental attitudes towards witchcraft throughout the sixteenth century. It also seems to have determined the treatment of witchcraft in England as well, since witchcraft was generally treated there as an ecclesiastical offense in the first third of the sixteenth century. When the first English statute directly addressing witchcraft was enacted in 1542, however, it defined witchcraft in legal terms as the visible and physical offense of *maleficium* rather than as heresy. The statute declared it a capital offense to use magic to afflict anyone "in his body, members, or goodes" but left matters of the soul and power over the spirit to less worldly authorities. Nevertheless, upon the repeal of all the Henrician statutes in 1547, the Church assumed virtually complete power over witchcraft prosecutions, and when a new witchcraft statute was issued in 1563, it defined witchcraft as the invocation of evil spirits, even in the absence of worldly *maleficium*.

The supremacy of the Church in matters dealing with witchcraft was never so secure in England as on the Continent. The *Malleus* was not translated into English until 1584, and in that same year Reginald Scot's *Discovery of Witchcraft* also appeared. Scot bitterly attacked the *Malleus* for what he saw as its uncritical acceptance of a spiritual dimension in all witchcraft phenomena and specifically for the authors' assumption that spirits could take on physical forms. King James I responded to Scot with his *Daemonologie* (1597), in which he condemned Scot's skepticism and defended the possibility of spirits assuming a corporeal image. In 1604, a new statute brought English law into line with the Continental tradition. Penalties for *maleficium* were increased, and trafficking with the spiritual world was condemned under a sweeping proscription against anyone who would "consult, covenant with entertaine employ feede or rewarde any evil and wicked spirit to or for any intent or purpose."[7]

The statute of 1604 remained in effect until 1736 and served as the basis for the statutes passed in Massachusetts Bay (1641) and Connecticut (1642). Those Colonial laws were less specific and focussed on the theological definition of witchcraft as a heretical contact with the spiritual world: "If any man or woman be a witch (that is hath or consulteth with a familiar spirit) They shall be put to death" (Weisman 13). As Richard Weisman has pointed out, however, in practice the Colonial courts handled witchcraft much as the courts in England did—that is, as *maleficium* rather than heresy.[8] In Massachusetts, for example, more than ninety-five percent of witchcraft accusations involved criminal charges of bodily harm or property damage. Furthermore, the adversarial nature of British legal practice (as opposed to inquisitional techniques) and a more general resistance to the Continental union of legal and theological authority as inherently "foreign" to English thought made it even more difficult to associate heresy and *maleficium* as prosecutable offenses (see Weisman 12-14). Under British and Colonial law, it was simply easier to prosecute witchcraft as a criminal attack on the visible body than as the spiritual possession of an invisible soul.[9]

It would seem, then, that Satan's case for a warrant to cross over from the world of spirits onto the soil of New England was lost in the Colonial courts even before it was argued to God. But in fact, traditional distinctions between ecclesiastical and legal authority were based on the same ontological distinctions between the visible and invisible worlds that were being contested by witchcraft in New England, as Cotton Mather has shown. The provenance of those authorities, as well as the relation between them and their jurisdiction over the popular realm of superstition and rumor, depended on a connection between the body and the spirit that was not always apparent, and never self-evident. That connection had to be produced each time the power of the Law or the Church was enacted as a concrete social practice, either in a trial and execution, or in the admonitory rhetoric of a jeremiad. It was the production of that connection through discourse, not its "discovery" in some anterior realm of the law or spirit, that actually constituted witchcraft in Colonial New England and authorized the extension of legal and ecclesiastical authority to the body of the accused.

This necessity of linking body to spirit underlies all manifestations of witchcraft in the Colonies, and it confounds materialist explanations of the phenomena that attempt to divorce the material and spiritual dimensions of witchcraft. For the Colonial Puritans, witchcraft existed on the border between the spiritual and material realms, and the relation between those realms was established, sustained, and regulated through an array of systematic discursive practices. Those practices can be specified in terms of concrete social relations, to be sure, but their aims and operative principles were derived from the semiotic relationship between corporeal signs and their spiritual significance, rather than from the abstract prescriptions of theological dogma or the material conditions that supported it. As Mather told his readers, the fate of the body in this world and the next would be inscribed in the flesh, since it was the body that was the instrument and expression of the power that controlled it. This emphasis on the production and interpretation of the flesh as sign led the Colonial Puritans to understand witchcraft primarily as a discursive event that was regulated less by ecclesiastical doctrine and legal statutes and more by the rhetorical practices that determined the place of the individual in the symbolic order of language.[10]

Elsewhere in his *Essay* Mather reports two other cases that make the discursive nature of witchcraft and possession clear because they emphasize the rhetorical strategies used to join the flesh and the spirit. The first deals with the affliction of Elizabeth Knapp of Groton, Massachusetts. In the fall of 1671, Knapp suddenly was afflicted with fits of bizarre behavior, weeping and laughing for no apparent reason. Then, in November, Elizabeth's tongue "for many hours together was drawn like a semicircle up to the roof of her Mouth, not to be removed, though some tried with their fingers to do it . . . and now a *Daemon* began manifestly to speak in her" (140). The affliction of organs of speech was quite common in cases of possession. Psycho-historians have compared such contortions to contemporary cases of hysteria, and no doubt would have diagnosed Elizabeth that way had they been there. Mather, however, is most interested in the contradictions associated with the production of speech in this situation. "Many words were uttered wherein are the *Labial Letters*, without any motion of her Lips, which was a clear demonstration that the voice was not her own. Sometimes Words were spoken seeming to proceed out of her throat, when her Mouth was shut. Sometimes with her Mouth wide open, without the use of any of the Organs of speech" (140).

Here Mather is maddeningly reticent about what was actually said because his interest is focused on the production of discourse rather than its "content." A similar interest is apparent in his report concerning the possession of Ann Cole of Hartford in 1662. In Ann's fits, her tongue was "improved by a *Dæmon* to express things which she her self knew nothing of," and in a "*Dutch-tone*" at that. Even more remarkably, Ann's discourse contains a debate among the demons about how they will afflict her, "mentioning sundry wayes they should take for that end, particularly that they would afflict her Body, spoil her Name, etc." (136).[11] When the debate is finished, the demons confound her language so that "she may tell no more tales."

All of these examples show that witchcraft and possession existed in Colonial New England principally as discursive events occurring in a narrative context that determined the significance of the symptoms and the fate of those accused of causing the afflictions. The afflictions in these cases are horribly physical (though somewhat tame compared to many others), but in the cases of both Ann and Elizabeth the physical afflictions are pointedly limited to the organs of speech. Far from being simply a material phenomenon, a physical act embedded in the economic and social hierarchies of the time, these cases hinge upon the possibility of a disjunction between the body and the voice that is conceivable only in rhetorical terms. Rather than determining the significance of the discourse that flows from their lips, the physical bodies of Ann and Elizabeth—with all their specificity of age, sex, and class—simply serve as arenas in which a purely discursive struggle is waged for control of the voice, for the position of speaker or subject in relation to the words that are uttered. Weisman and other social historians are undoubtedly correct to claim that witches and their victims were "produced" by specific tensions among social and institutional forces in their communities. But as these cases make clear, what was really "produced" was discourse, and the identities and social relations that discourse constituted and sustained. When evil spirits "appeared" to the Puritans, they manifested themselves as disruptions within the normal discursive patterns of the colonists' lives, and the language of the trials was all directed by a desire to restore that discursive regularity and the stable social relations associated with it.

The discourse produced in these trials may easily be categorized into the popular, legal, and theological forms noted above, since witchcraft appears in these cases variously as superstition, crime, and heresy. The popular belief in the magical power of the witch to cause harm to others through black magic or *maleficium* is evident in Elizabeth Knapp's claim that one of her neighbors appeared to her during a fit and "was the cause of her Affliction" (141). Similarly, Ann Cole's accusation of Greensmith "as active in the mischiefs done and designed" (137) testifies to the element of *maleficium* in her case, and the fact that Cole's afflictions ceased when the suspected witches "were either executed or fled" graphically demonstrates the function of the witch's prosecution as a scapegoat ritual that served to rid the community of undesirable elements.

As many historians have noted, such popular superstitions—and their concomitant social functions—antedate considerably the theological and legal treatment of witchcraft and possess a logic of their own. Though the example of Greensmith is too abbreviated to tell us much about those superstitions, most scholars agree that the magical power attributed to the witch in such accusations usually derives from ancient fertility rituals and the array of pantheistic beliefs endemic to most agrarian societies and those on the frontier of a wilderness. This ancient ritualistic source is suggested by the claim discussed below that the devil appeared to an accused witch "in the form of a Deer or Fawn," as well as by the woman's use of the explicit sexual motif of fornication with the Devil.

Anthropologists have also long considered witchcraft accusations and trials to be a social mechanism by which a community can establish and enforce a sense of "normalcy" in the behavior of its members. That social function is evident in the cases of Elizabeth Knapp and Ann Cole, which show those mechanisms at work in the local context of witchcraft accusations. Cole claimed that she was being tortured by the specter of a woman named Greensmith, whom Mather describes as "lewd and ignorant" and who was already imprisoned on suspicion for witchcraft (137). The woman is therefore already isolated from the community on several levels: literally separated from the others by the prison walls, morally stigmatized by her lewdness, and, a more complicated notion, alienated culturally (or what I will discuss below as "conversationally") by her "ignorance." Her presence in the community is therefore socially disruptive, as is suggested by the temper of her response to Mr. Hain, when "her rage was such that she could have torn him in pieces." The effects of that disruption are expressed in the accusation of witchcraft, and her execution restores order to Ann Cole's body and, by extension, the body of the community as well.

The social motives behind the persecution of such alienated individuals is particularly vivid in contrast with Elizabeth Knapp's case. When Knapp accuses someone of *maleficium*, the accusation is discounted because the accused is "a very sincere, holy Woman" whose "friends" advise her to visit the witch. This observation is a clear indication of the holy woman's connections with the community—she has friends—and of her spirit of what Cotton Mather might call "neighborly love," demonstrated by her visit to Elizabeth. This "gracious" woman prays with the afflicted, who soon realizes that the Devil has tricked her into believing evil "of her good Neighbour without any cause" (141).

The criminal dimension of these two cases is abbreviated in Mather's report, but tragically important. Most obviously, it accounts for the imprisonment and execution of the woman Greensmith, but the legal procedures associated with those events are evoked in several other ways. Before she is executed, Greensmith is subjected to an examination, further evidence is adduced, and a legal confession is extracted that authorizes the execution: "Upon this Confession, with other concurrent Evidence, the Woman was Executed" (138). The distinction between superstitious and legal procedures is all the more apparent in Mather's remarks about the witches who escaped. The popular superstition that a witch would float because the "pure" element of water would reject her evilness is comically discounted by Mather's description of the crowd's eagerness to experiment with the procedure: a local skeptic is thrown into the water and sinks, while the accused witches flee under the realization that "an Halter would choak them, though the Water would not" (139). "This was no legal Evidence against the suspected persons," Mather adds, so "Whether this experiment were lawful, or rather Superstitious and Magical, we shall . . . enquire afterwards" (139).

The theological dimension of these cases is certainly the thematic focus of Mather's account, and in his narrative he subordinates the legal and superstitious dimensions to it. The first thing we find out about Ann Cole is that she is "accounted a person of real Piety and Integrity" (135), and he directly attributes her fits to a "Daemon." Her affliction is eventually attributed to a woman whose power to harm Ann comes from her "familiarity with the Devil," which includes sexual union, attendance at a sabbat, and the promise to "go with him when he called" though without a formal covenant. Similarly Mather tells us that the Devil spoke through Elizabeth Knapp, blaspheming and insulting the pastor Mr. Willard, and that he was chased from her body through prayer (141). Each of these claims draws upon a theological schema that is quite distinct from the elements of crime and superstition, though obviously related to them in Mather's narrative, and it is clear that they impose a demonic causality upon the events that is not, strictly speaking, necessary to our understanding them within the law or folk tradition. For example, Ann Cole's fits could be the result of *maleficium,* quite apart from her piety or the question of demonic possession, and Greensmith's execution depends on legal principles of evidence despite the fact that her confession involves a blatant act of heresy.

One need not invoke precise distinctions among legal, theological, and ritual schema to explain the outcomes of these two cases, of course. The different social status of the women accused by Cole and Knapp easily predict their fates. Yet in both cases the connection between the social conditions of the people involved and the consequences of the accusations are mediated by conversations in which the identity and guilt of the interlocutors are negotiated through various discursive strategies that ground the abstract categories of theology, the law, and superstitious belief within a specific situation. In Knapp's case, for example, witchcraft ceases to exist when the accused prays with her accuser. The change in their relation—victim and witch become friend and neighbor—is brought about by a change in the discourse that links them, the change from accusation to prayer. The accused woman in this case is no doubt exonerated because of her prior integration into the social community, but that exoneration takes place in and through the discursive act of prayer.

Greensmith, on the other hand, never has a chance. Her prosecution simply reinforces a judgment that society had already made. Morally corrupt, intellectually deficient, and physically segregated from the community, Greensmith is a natural—that is to say, a "normal"—target for an accusation. It is all the more remarkable, then, that Greensmith is subjected to a discursive make-over just as complete, and just as successful, as the good woman accused by Knapp. Greensmith's identity as a witch—and the existence of witchcraft in this case—has to be constituted through discursive rituals, even though the outcome of those rituals may be predetermined by her marginal social position.[12]

It would be possible, of course, to explain the discursive basis or narrative form of these afflictions simply as a consequence of the crucial role language played in the Puritan's sense of the relation between the visible and the invisible world, as I have suggested above. The issue is not only theological, however, for the legal examination of the accused witches proceeds along very similar lines, and it turns upon an identical struggle to determine the speaker of a discourse produced in the course of the examination. Elizabeth Knapp's accusation of "her good Neighbor," for example, can be ignored once the words are attributed to Satan's ruse, in which he tormented her in the shape of others "and then told her it was not he but they that did it," a claim repeated in her accusation (141-42). The validity of the accusation depends, in short, on the "authority" of the speaker, who is not necessarily identical to the "person" from whose lips the words are uttered.

This point is made inversely but even more dramatically in the examination of Greensmith. That examination consists of two scenes in which an utterance is presented apart from its association with the speaker, much as the language issues from Elizabeth's mouth without her active speech. Then a debate ensues in which the examiners attempt to link the body of Greensmith with the utterance that issues from her lips, either as its subject or its object. This process begins when "several worthy persons"—three men—"wrote the intelligible sayings expressed by Ann Cole" when she accuses Greensmith. Later, two of the men read what they wrote in the presence of Greensmith and the local Magistrate, and Greensmith confesses to the deeds described "in this preternatural Discourse." The men ask her if she has made an express covenant with the devil—important for the legal conviction of a witch—and Greensmith denies it, saying she only promised the devil "to go with him when he called."

The questioning continues the next day, with more satisfying results:

> She then acknowledged, that though when Mr. Hains began to read what he had taken down in Writing, her rage was such that she could have torn him in pieces, and was as resolved as might be to deny her guilt (as she had done before) yet after he had read awhile, she was (to use her own expression) as if her flesh had been pulled from her bones, and so could not deny any longer: She likewise declared, that the Devil first appeared to her in the form of a deer or fawn . . . and that by degrees he became very familiar, and at last would talk with her. Moreover, she said that the Devil had frequently the carnal knowledge of her Body. And that the witches had Meetings at a place not far from her house . . . . Upon this Confession, with other concurrent Evidence, the Woman was Executed. (138)

Greensmith's examination and trial consist of two separate scenes, both of which turn upon her being associated with a particular discursive position. The first day, Greensmith willingly occupies the passive role of the object of discourse as it is represented to her by the transcript the men are reading: she admits to being the person addressed by Cole's accusation and to promising to answer if Satan calls. The actual situation, in which the two men are reading a written transcript of Greensmith's statement back to her, simply stages the passive role represented in the transcript itself, and the circumstances of their reading to her are ignored. On the second day, however, when the men begin to read to her, Greensmith becomes enraged: "when Mr. *Hains* began to read what he had taken down in Writing, her rage was such that she could have torn him in pieces, and was as resolved as might be to deny her guilt." Yet, as he reads, her immedi-

ate bodily presence in the actual scene seems to dissolve, and with it
her resistance to the role they would have her play in the demonic
discourse: "after he had read awhile, she was (to use her own expression) as if her flesh had been pulled from her bones, and so could not
deny any longer." Greensmith goes on to confess to a relation with
the Devil in a narrative that moves from a paganistic scene of bestial
spirits to the purely demonic motif of fornicating with the Devil and
attending a sabbat, all, significantly, through the mediating event of
conversation: "by degrees he [the Devil] became very familiar, and at
last would talk with her."

"Talking with her" is exactly what the examiners have been doing,
of course, and the outcome of that conversation granted them a fatal
power over Greensmith's body just as her demonic interlocutor acquired a carnal knowledge of it through their talk. In most cases, as
here, that power was derived from those properties of the spoken word
that made it possible to transcend ontological boundaries between
flesh and spirit and to translate the body into an image of demonic
presence that becomes a target for legal authority. That translation
positioned the body of the individual as a subject within a discursive
structure that determined her identity as a witch, someone who could
communicate with the spiritual world and invoke its power for her
own ends. To assume that position, however, the physical person who
stood before her neighbors and the judge had to be replaced by an
imaginary body that could shed its corporeality at will, passing from
the streets of New England to the sabbath grounds of the covenantal
meetings and the devil's bed. We have already seen this happen in
Greensmith's confession, where she testified to the sensation of her
flesh melting away, then to a conversation with the devil, and finally
to fornication between her now imaginary body and the demonic
spirit. Her examiners press their questions upon Greensmith, swimming her in words with all the urgency of the curious crowds who
bound the accused and dunked them in ponds to see if they would
float.

Less systematic examples of such translations abound in accounts
of witchcraft, where witches confess to leaving their corporeal bodies
at home to attend covens, and victims testify to being tormented by
the specters—that is, life-like images—of the accused even while their
physical bodies are imprisoned. It is only after the body of a woman
is supplanted by the incorporeal image of the witch that she can be
subjected to the law of discourse. Like any abstract system of social
organization, the Law reaches the members of that community only
through the subordination of the body to the sign, an inscription of
the word in flesh. And although the effects of this signifying act were

usually less dramatic than blasting the flesh with a bolt of lightning, the consequences for the victim were often the same.

This subjection of the body to the order of discourse is governed by the same kinds of social practices that regulate behavior of all sorts, whether that regulation consists of the formal systems of law and theology or the more informal but nonetheless powerful disciplinary practices of folk customs and superstition. Each of those discursive systems also possesses its own system of rules as well as a specific and usually unique social space in which it exercises its authority, though the examples discussed above testify to the difficulty of always distinguishing the borders of the church, the courtroom, and the parlor when witchcraft is concerned. Despite the many differences among these discursive systems, however, they all have the same objective: the "discovery" of witchcraft through the representation of the accused as a witch. When successful, this conversion produced not only a verbal confession but also an affective transformation of the body into a form that could cross the boundary between flesh and spirit and embody the symbolically transgressive threat of witchcraft and demonic possession. That transgression is dramatically evident in the manifestation of somatic symptoms that literally shape the flesh into symbols or otherwise distort our image of the body and its normal biological functions, and it underlies the more common reports of dismembered bodies, books signed in blood, and spectral images of corporeal shapes that violate the physical limits of space and time. The specter, the criminal, and the heretic thus share a strange and dangerous cultural space in Colonial New England where the flesh joined the word and so fell under its jurisdiction.

The discursive history of Colonial America that would map that liminal space has yet to be written. The spectacularly strange phenomena reported in examples such as those discussed above have, however, generated considerable curiosity among psychologists and psycho-historians about the psychic mechanisms powerful enough to mold the flesh in their image, and some of these discussions of witchcraft as hysterical symptom begin to address the same issues of corporeal signification that preoccupied the Puritans. George M. Beard was the first to propose a link between demonic possession and hysteria in the Salem witchcraft controversy. In *The Psychology of the Salem Witchcraft Excitement,* Beard claimed that "The basis of the Salem witchcraft trials was composed of trance, insanity, and hysteria, and it was ignorance of the phenomena of trance, insanity, and hysteria that made those trials possible" (14; see also 10, 28). The association of witchcraft and insanity has a long history—Montaigne insisted that witches were out of their right minds, and most of the skeptical works follow his lead—but Beard's account is exceptionally astute in its portrayal of witchcraft as the product of medical confusion and theological dogma.

The most famous psychoanalytic essay on the topic of witchcraft is Freud's "A Seventeenth-Century Demonological Neurosis" (1923; *G.S.* 10, 409-45; *S.E.* 19, 69-105). There Freud suggests that at least some fantasies about making pacts with the Devil may have their origins in a neurotic attachment to the father that yields narcissistic transferences on inverted father-figures. This insight informs the detailed and insightful analysis of Knapp's case by John Demos in his recent work *Entertaining Satan,* which also notes the prominence of oral symptoms. Demos accounts for the fixation on the organs of speech as a defensive reaction to a narcissistic imbalance resulting from the disintegration of Knapp's ego and a partial regression to the oral stage:

> Her "speechlessness," for example, may be understood as a signal instance of compromise between unconscious aims and defenses. The need for life-giving sustenance is too admixed with angry, "biting" impulses; the wish to take in quickly becomes the wish to devour. As a result, the apparatus of "oral" interaction is temporarily shut down. . . . Her sense of being strangled is a somatic epitome of the *defensive* process—the repression needed to hold herself back. (122; see 99-131)

Demos' painstaking reconstruction of the biographical context behind Knapp's historical symptoms is crucial to any reading of Mather's report, but Demos' interpretation of Knapp's behavior differs significantly from the one I propose above in its emphasis on the somatic basis of oral fixations. As the preceding analysis suggests, I am more interested in the rhetorical character of her symptom than its somatic base. The fixation of Knapp's symptoms on the lips, mouth, and tongue is, indeed, crucial to understanding their significance, but not necessarily because their biological function is associated with a specific stage of development. Rather, the lips and tongue mark the threshold of the body and its relation to others, not only in the physical sense of occupying a corporeal edge or rim separating the outside from the inside, but more importantly as the bodily site of speech. The pathology of Knapp's affliction may have more to do with a disturbance of the intersubjective relations associated with the symbolic order of language than the somatic dislocations Demos describes.

While this suggestion does not contradict the brilliant and detailed historical analysis of Knapp's biographical situation that Demos offers, it does impute a constitutive role for language in the formation and maintenance of subjective identity that is incompatible with the ego psychology underlying Demos' analysis of the witchcraft phenomena. Although not directly concerned with linguistic disturbances in his own essay, Freud himself did note the pervasive presence of totemic attitudes toward language in folk superstitions when he reports on two written pacts that the painter in the case signed and then retrieved from the Devil through the intercession of the Virgin Mary. More specifically, many of the linguistic disturbances reported by Mather have also figured prominently in medical and psychoanalytic approaches to hysteria not directly associated with witchcraft. In *Hysteria*, for example, Abse argues that all hysterical symptoms represent a failure to resolve an emotional conflict symbolically. Abse says that the "degradation of word language," as in glossolalia and other linguistic disturbances associated with hysteria, represents "a halfway house between the loss of valid word language and motor automatisms" (295). If the hysteria progresses, Abse says, it will result in "a release of motor automatisms in an ecstatic crisis" (294). Treatment of such automatisms therefore must proceed from the "preliminary retranslation of hysterical somatic symptoms to word-language," which may involve actual words or "the laryngeal apparatus" itself (145), as it does in Knapp's case.

The relevance of Abse's remarks to the cases reported by Mather is obvious, but Abse's argument becomes especially trenchant in light of Lacan's account of the individual's relation to the symbolic order. Lacan began his career as a medical psychiatrist in the 1920s studying schizophrenics whose physical symptoms bear a remarkable resemblance to those of the afflicted girls in Massachusetts. As he became increasingly interested in Freud's work, however, Lacan came to understand the formation of an individual's sense of self as the product of his assimilation into a social order not only structured by but constituted within the signifying chain of language. Although Lacan recognizes the crucial importance of biological needs to the early life of the infant, he also insists that each individual is born into a pre-existent cultural system that he calls simply "the Symbolic." Individuals assume their place in that symbolic order by passing through a developmental phase that Freud identified as the Oedipal crisis but that Lacan redefines as a transition through "the Imaginary" to the Symbolic.·

That transition takes place in two stages, both of which are relevant to phenomena of witchcraft reported in Colonial New England. The first stage Lacan describes as the "mirror stage," a point at which the child comes to identify with some image of bodily coherence: a mirror-image, a sibling or companion of the same age, etc. This imaginary identity is only transitory, however, because it is fraught with the ambivalence and instability inherent in the narcissistic identification of the self with an other. Eventually, the child must assume another kind of identity, one that is established in relation to the symbolic order that governs social relations. To do that, the child's sense of self must be divorced from the image of the body and transferred to the signifying system that makes up the Symbolic. Lacan refers to this as the individual's assuming a place as subject in the symbolic order, and that place is marked, literally, by signifiers: the child begins to recognize a name as its own and soon progresses to more subtle and complex relations with pronouns, shifters, and other deictic terms.

At this point, the body's relation to imaginary others is supplanted by the signifier that marks the place of the individual as subject in the symbolic order. This transference of the child's sense of self from the imaginary body to the signifier occurs, Lacan says, when the child recognizes that parts of that body can be separated from the imaginary whole and function within the social network as his or her representatives. Lacan claims that this recognition is what Freud discovered as "castration," and he goes on to argue that what Freud described as the cultural function of the phallus is in fact the fundamental property of all signifiers: i.e., it marks the social identity of an individual as male or female precisely at the moment of Oedipal anxiety when the child recognizes the possibility of its detachment from the body. The individual's position in the symbolic order consequently depends on a sense of lack, and Lacan says that most social relations, especially those based on speech, are motivated by a desire to overcome this sense of lack and restore that imaginary sense of wholeness.[13] Thus Lacan argues that speech addressed from one individual to another is always oriented toward a "third" position that represents an unattainable ideal of absolute totality and coherence that motivates symbolic relations but is always excluded from them. In Freudian terms, this "third" is the Father who intervenes between Mother and Child in the Oedipal triangle. In Lacanian terms, it is the Name of the Father or the Symbolic Other, a counterpart to the imaginary other, but whose relation to the individual is always one of absence and lack. In more specific terms, as Louis Althusser has explained, this "third" is any transcendent source of identity and authority: God or Christ in a Christian society, or more simply the Law in contemporary secular cultures.[14]

Even this brief characterization of Lacan's central premise may suggest how the etiology of abnormal bodily functions in cases of witchcraft and possession might best be described in terms of Lacanian neurosis: i.e., as a disruption of the individual's relation to the signifiers that mark his or her place in the symbolic order. This explanation accounts for the curious prevalence of disturbances to organs of speech that I noted above, such as the tortured body of Ann Cole, lying rigid beneath the gaze of her minister and doctor, while demons speak to them through her mouth and deliberate "sundry wayes . . . that they would affiict her Body, spoil her Name, etc." Similarly, the images of broken and dismembered bodies that abound in the confessions of witchcraft and affliction gathered in Colonial Massachusetts are obvious manifestations of what Lacan called the *corps morcelé*, i.e., fantasized images of broken bodies. These images indicate the disintegrating ego and eroding sense of self characteristic of neurotic fantasy, as Demos points out, but Lacan helps us understand the specifically linguistic character of that disintegration—and, as a corollary, the linguistic character of the *re*integration of the accused as a witch in the examination.

As we saw in the case of Greensmith's confession, such disintegration of the bodily image could be brought about by forcing the accused to conform to a subjective identity not her own—i.e., confessing to "being" a witch. It was usually followed by the accused compensating for the disintegration by assuming an imaginary body and so projecting her "self" into a fantasmatic scene—as Greensmith does when she reports copulating with the Devil. Following such confessions, the tension and anxiety stemming from this identity crisis are resolved as the accused then assumes a symbolic position in the discourse of the Law—her words constitute her guilt—and that assumption links legal discourse to the body in a literal and often fatal bond. Greensmith's sense that her physical body is dissolving, its recomposition as the imaginary body of Satan's lover, and its ultimate subjection to the symbolic authority of the Law, reflect the neurotic anxiety inherent in the formation of the subject as described by Lacan or, in this case, the "reformation" of that subject as a confessed witch.

In every aspect of these cases, despite the social and economic conditions that resulted in those specific people occupying those specific rooms at that time, who those people were, what they did in those rooms, what it meant, and where it led was governed by the purely discursive relations established and contested through conversation, confession, and prayer. Her "identity" was constituted through those discourses, which existed independently of any particular individual. Had the blasphemous words that issued forth through the rigid lips of Elizabeth Knapp been attributed to Knapp herself, for example, she may well have been identified as being a witch rather than the victim of possession. Similarly, Greensmith's confession essentially consists of her repeating a description of her sabbaticals that was spoken by her accusers, written down, and then read to her. The discourse that convicts her is thus three times removed from the circumstances in which it originally occurred and from the individual who originally uttered it, whose position Greensmith assumes when she admits that the words are "hers" and confesses to being a witch. Through this discursive elision of the differences between real and imaginary conversations, Greensmith's physical existence as a Colonial woman has been supplanted by the "body" of the witch, and it is *that* body which is hanged.

## NOTES

1. The theological argument behind the Puritan plain style insisted on stripping language of its worldly "body" in the double sense of references to physical imagery and of the materiality of the signifier itself. Divested of its double materiality, the word was supposed to yield up its spiritual significance more immediately. This rhetorical principle was at times compared to the crucifixion of Christ, when his spirituality was revealed as the body died. I have traced this analogy in "'The Crucified Phrase': Sign and Desire in Puritan Semiology," *Early American Literature* 13:3 (1978/9):278-93.

2. I have studied these themes in "The Honeyed Knot of Puritan Aesthetics," *Puritan Poets and Poetics: Seventeenth-Century American Poetry in Theory and Practice*, ed. Peter White (University Park, 1985), 67-83. See also Ivy Schweitzer, *The Work of Self-Representation: Lyric Poetry in Colonial New England* (Chapel Hill, 1991), for an analysis of how this attitude toward language affected the Puritan poet's effort to represent a "self" in the text. William J. Scheick, *Design in Puritan American Literature* (Lexington, 1992) discusses similar issues in Puritan poetics but reaches quite different conclusions about the nature of the text and the self.

3. For a discussion of Hooker's sermon on this point, see "'The Crucified Phrase.'"

4. Most historians of witchcraft follow this tripartite division of discourses on witchcraft, which was first proposed by J. Hansen in *Zauberwahn, Inquisition und Hexenprozess im Mittelalter und die Enstehung der grossen Hexenverfolgung* (Munich and Leipzig, 1900). The most influential contemporary history informed by this distinction is Keith Thomas' *Religion and the Decline of Magic: Studies in Popular Beliefs in Sixteenth and Seventeenth Century England* (London, 1971). Much of the brief historical summary that follows is based on Thomas; Alan Macfarlane, *Witchcraft in Tudor and Stuart England* (London, 1970); and, to a lesser extent, George Lyman Kittredge, *Witchcraft in Old and New England* (1926; rpt. New York, 1956).

5. Quoted in J. Hansen, *Quellen und Untersuchungen zur Geschite des Hexenwahns und der Hexenverfolgung im Mittelalter* (Bonn, 1901).

6. The *Malleus maleficarum* was written by James Sprenger and Henry Kramer, German Dominicans, and published with the papal bull by Innocent VIII, who appointed them Inquisitors of the Germanic countries. See *Malleus maleficarum*, trans. Rev. Montague Summers (1928; rpt. London, 1969). Carlo Ginzburg discusses the relation between local authorities in *The Night Battles: Witchcraft and Agrarian Cults in the Sixteenth and Seventeenth Centuries*, trans. John and Anne Tedeschi (Baltimore, 1983).

7. Quoted in Richard Weisman, *Witchcraft, Magic, and Religion in 17th-Century Massachusetts* (Amherst, 1984), 12. The statute of 1604 was based on an Act passed in March 1563 "agaynst Conjuracions Inchantments and Witchecraftes." That act was motivated in large part by a desire to contain the threat of treason that had emerged in the guise of various magical practices at the time. See Macfarlane, 14, and Kittredge, 255-61.

8. In fact, several of the indictments issued in the Salem trials invoke the statute of 1604 rather than the Colonial laws, but as Weisman notes, that may be simply the result of the recent arrival of a public attorney trained in England (13).

9. There are several excellent accounts of the Salem trials. The most detailed general account is John Demos, *Entertaining Satan: Witchcraft and the Culture of Early New England* (New York, 1982). For a detailed chronological account of the trials themselves see Enders A. Robinson, *The Devil Discovered: Salem Witchcraft 1692* (New York, 1991). The most important analysis of the role of gender in Colonial witchcraft is Carol F. Karlsen, *The Devil in the Shape of a Woman: Witchcraft in Colonial New England* (New York, 1987), but see also Selma R. Williams and Pamela Williams Adelman, *Riding the Nightmare: Women and Witchcraft from the Old World to Colonial Salem* (1978; rpt. New York, 1992). Weisman's *Witchcraft, Magic, and Religion* provides an incisive analysis of the relation between theological and legal issues involved in Colonial witchcraft, and the standard economic analysis of the Salem controversy is Paul Boyer and Stephen Nissenbaum's *Salem Possessed: The Social Origins of Witchcraft* (Cambridge, Mass., 1974). The entire transcripts of the Salem trials have been edited by Boyer and Nissenbaum: see *The Salem Witchcraft Papers: Verbatim Transcripts of the Legal Documents of the Salem Witchcraft Outbreak of 1692*, 3 vols. (New York, 1977).

10. Jack Goody makes a similar point in *The Logic of Writing and the Organization of Society* (New York, 1986). Defending his interest in the processes of communication rather than just their material causes, Goody says he has tried "to shift some of the weight that has often been placed on the means and relations of production to the means and relations of communication" (175). Dividing analysis into "materialist" or "ideological" factors "smacks of by-gone debates, long since by-passed. Who nowadays would think of the intellectual products of the human hand and mind, such as writing, as being purely internal or external, as relating only to matter or to ideas?" (176).

11. Cotton Mather expresses a similar anxiety about the destruction of his name in his *Diary*. Noting the scandalous rumors that he had abused a young woman afflicted with witchcraft whom he had observed, Margaret Rule, Mather observes that "her Tormentors . . . made themselves Masters of her Tongue so far, that shee began in her fits to complain that I threatened her and molested her. . . . I was putt upon some Agonies" as a result of these accusations, Mather says, but he found consolation "in the Resignation of my Name unto the Lord; content that if Hee had no further service for my *Name*, it should bee torn to pieces with all the Reproches in the world" (I, 178). Here "Name" is simply a synecdoche for his reputation, of course, but the physical image of ripping his name to pieces recalls the Puritans' emphasis on the materiality of the signifier and, of course, on its close connection to the body.

As we will see in the case of Greensmith, the fear of one's flesh being pulled from the bone and ripped apart by demons was a common motif in the folk superstitions about witchcraft. This fear obviously derives from anxiety about what Demos describes as the disintegration of the ego (see n.11 above), and the motif in its various forms reflects the *corps morcelé* described by Lacan, which I discuss below.

12. Karlsen adds an important caveat to generalizations about the marginal status of women accused of witchcraft. While many were poor and otherwise disenfranchised from the community of their accusers, others were quite secure, if not wealthy, and some had long family histories where they lived. What distinguishes the accused more consistently is their violation of socially acceptable levels of wealth, aggression, or, occasionally, litigiousness. A widow who inherited her husband's estate and insisted on managing it herself rather than immediately turning it over to her sons, for example, might be especially vulnerable precisely because she had more wealth and power than the community thought appropriate for an unmarried woman. See Karlsen, esp. Chapters two and three.

13. The semiotic function of the phallus as described by Lacan may help explain its prominence in popular superstitions about witchcraft. If the phallus does represent that

very possibility of "separation" between the signifier and the signified—that is, if the phallus marks our anxiety about that separation and the consequent determination of a semiotic realm somewhere "between" the objective world and the world of the spirit—that would explain why so many stories about witches focus on the loss of a penis and the quest for its retrieval.

Several of those stories are collected in the *Malleus maleficarum* (Part II, Chapter 7). One of the more interesting accounts describes a witch who collected male organs and would "put them in a bird's nest, or shut them up in a box, where they move themselves like living members, and eat oats and corn." One man who was missing his penis came to the witch and asked her to give it back. She told him to climb a nearby tree, where he would find a nest with several members in it, and to select one he wanted. Unfortunately, when he tried to take the biggest one she told him that he could not have it because it belonged to a parish priest (121). I must thank my friend Jim Calderwood for pointing out this story to me, though he professes to have no special interest in the topic.

14. As noted above, Freud claimed that the Devil often occupied the role of the Father in neurotic fantasies, and in "A Seventeenth-Century Demonological Neurosis" he generalizes that position to include any authoritative figure, including God. Lacan's description of that position in rhetorical terms allows us to explore the function of the Father apart from speculation about the specific person who occupies the role in any particular case. So, for example, it is unnecessary to prove that Greensmith associated her examiners and the Devil with her father to demonstrate the fact that the examiners and the Devil function in similar ways when they talk to her. It is the functional parallels that determine what happens in these conversations, not any idiosyncratic association an individual might make on the basis of her personal history.

# Tituba's Story

BERNARD ROSENTHAL

CENTRAL to our popular understanding of events in seven-teenth-century Salem is the contrived image of Samuel Parris's slave Tituba driving a circle of girls into a frenzy that would later lead to charges of witchcraft.[1] Despite the fictional nature of that characterization, Tituba's actual confession of witchcraft is historically significant, for it confirmed witchcraft activity in the community.[2] Although not the only slave caught up in the 1692 episode, Tituba has a unique role in the litera-ture about Salem, for her story has taken on nothing short of mythical dimensions. As in the originary myth of the Fall, a woman, here a dark-skinned one, has carried the burden of having introduced sin and loss.

As the events of 1692 unfolded, interest in Tituba receded. New charges, new confessions, and a new cast of participants emerged to catch the interest of the community. Following the record of circumstances surrounding her admission of guilt, very little contemporary commentary appeared on Tituba, the most significant being assertions that her confessions were prompted by beatings from her master, the Reverend Parris, and that she herself was afflicted by witches.[3]

---

[1] For a discussion of Tituba's magic and storytelling, see my *Salem Story: Reading the Witch Trials of 1692* (Cambridge: Cambridge University Press, 1993), pp. 10–14.

[2] *The Salem Witchcraft Papers: Verbatim Transcripts of the Legal Documents of the Salem Witchcraft Outbreak of 1692*, ed. Paul Boyer and Stephen Nissenbaum, 3 vols. (New York: Da Capo Press, 1977), 3:358.

[3] On the claim that Parris beat Tituba, see Robert Calef, *More Wonders of the Invisi-ble World* (1700), in *Narratives of the Witchcraft Cases, 1648–1706*, ed. George Lin-coln Burr (New York: Charles Scribner's Sons, 1914), p. 343; for Tituba herself claim-ing affliction, see John Hale, *A Modest Inquiry into the Nature of Witchcraft* (1702), in *Narratives of the Witchcraft Cases*, p. 415. Both conclusions are carried forth in the first major history of New England, Daniel Neal's *History of New-England*, 2 vols. (London, 1720), 1:496–97.

Subsequent early narratives, such as those by eighteenth-century historians Daniel Neal and Thomas Hutchinson, made no reference to the voodoo or storytelling that would come to be associated with Tituba; nor did they mention a circle of girls.[4] Neal, however, emphasized that through her confession and through her participation in making a "witch cake" to identify the tormentors of the afflicted, Tituba was influential in setting the witchcraft episode in motion. Thus Neal launched a tradition that placed Sarah Good's significance in supporting claims of witchcraft at a remove. Good, prior to Tituba's confession, had named Sarah Osborne as a witch.[5]

In 1828, another Neal, John, wrote the first novel about the Salem witch trials, and therein the Tituba legend begins to assume its future shape. In *Rachel Dyer*, Neal depicts the slave as "a woman of diabolical power."[6] Three years later, the Reverend Charles W. Upham essentially followed Daniel Neal's account when he issued *Lectures on Witchcraft, Comprising a History of the Delusion in Salem in 1692*. Upham does not mention her name, but he clearly has Tituba in mind when he refers to an old Indian woman.[7] Had Upham never written another word on the subject, our view of Salem would be much different than it is. But he expanded his study, revised his tale, and in 1867 published the most influential book ever written on the Salem witch trials, *Salem Witchcraft*.

Upham was a skilled historian, but in *Salem Witchcraft* he introduced some myths that would become facts for future narra-

---

[4]Neal, *History of New-England*, 1:496–97; Thomas Hutchinson, *The History of the Colony and Province of Massachusetts-Bay* (1764), ed. Laurence Shaw Mayo, 3 vols. (Cambridge: Harvard University Press, 1936), 2:20. Citations here are to the descriptions of Tituba by Neal and Hutchinson.

[5]Neal, *History of New-England*, 1:496–97. Whether Tituba helped make the "witch cake" is unclear. See my *Salem Story*, pp. 25–27. It is not my intention to shift blame from Tituba to Sarah Good; no scapegoat can account for the chaotic complexity of the witchcraft episode. Neal, of course, was not the first to consider Tituba's confession as precipitating subsequent events. John Hale had done so in 1702 with his *Modest Inquiry*, p. 415.

[6]John Neal, *Rachel Dyer* (Portland, 1828), p. 75.

[7]Charles W. Upham, *Lectures on Witchcraft, Comprising a History of the Delusion in Salem in 1692* (Boston, 1832), p. 22. I cite the second edition, but the first edition of 1831 is identical in its treatment of Tituba.

tors. In particular, he ascribed to Tituba a new role in the witchcraft episode.[8] He did so by introducing two narrative elements: that Parris's slaves had imported provocatory tales from their homeland; and that Tituba had met with a circle of girls and "inflamed" their imaginations with those tales. Stopping short of John Neal's fictionalized Tituba, Upham characterizes the slave woman as superstitious rather than as a practitioner of black magic. The line between those two attributes would blur as new accounts of events in Salem emerged over time.

Where Upham found evidence for his new interpretation is unknown. J. W. DeForest had suggested nothing of this role for Tituba in his novel *Witching Times*, serialized a decade earlier, beginning in 1856.[9] Around 1850 G. P. R. [George Payne Rainsford] James, the British writer and acquaintance of Nathaniel Hawthorne, wrote a tale about the Salem episode, but he made no reference to voodoo or a circle of girls.[10] Even Hale's account of 1702, which argues that the fortune-telling practiced by some girls had the effect of precipitating the witchcraft incident, in no way ties the activity to meetings in the Parris house, to John Indian, another Parris slave traditionally associated with Tituba, to Tituba, nor to the original girls involved, Betty Parris and Abigail Williams.[11] Indeed, I have found no written historical or fictional record in America to support Upham's assertions about Tituba.

A story by British writer Elizabeth Gaskell entitled "Lois the Witch," however, offers some intriguing possibilities not found in American sources. Published in 1859, Gaskell's tale follows an eighteen-year-old girl sent from England to Salem, where she is to stay with relatives because her parents have died. In Lois's new home lives an old Indian woman named Nattee. At

---

[8]*Salem Witchcraft; with An Account of Salem Village, and a History of Opinions on Witchcraft and Kindred Subjects*, 2 vols. (1867; reprinted, Williamstown, Mass.: Corner House Publishers, 1971), 2:2–3.

[9]*Putnam's Magazine*, vols. 8–9, 1856–57.

[10]G. P. R. James, *Christian Lacy: A Tale of the Salem Witchcraft* [ca. 1850]. I have been unable to ascertain whether the story was ever published. The manuscript, nineteen handwritten pages, is found in the holdings of the University of Arizona.

[11]Hale, *A Modest Inquiry*, pp. 132–133.

another household, clearly modeled after Samuel Parris's, a minister named Tappau dwells with his wife, two young girls, and an Indian servant named Hota, who eventually confesses to witchcraft after being beaten.

While neither Indian woman precisely accounts for the prospective myth of Tituba, each manifests an aspect of it. Lois's cousin Faith, who knows that Hota is innocent, nonetheless affirms that the Indian "has done harm enough with her charms and her sorcery on Pastor Tappau's girls" to be hanged.[12] Telling frightening stories to trembling girls, however, is the province of Nattee, whose description strikingly resembles future depictions of Tituba:

> Nattee, the old Indian servant, would occasionally make Lois's blood run cold as she and Faith and Prudence listened to the wild stories she told them of the wizards of her race. It was often in the kitchen, in the darkening evening, while some cooking process was going on, that the old Indian crone, sitting on her haunches by the bright red wood embers which sent up no flame, but a lurid light reversing the shadows of all the faces around, told her weird stories while they were awaiting the rising of the dough, perchance, out of which the household bread had to be made. There ran through these stories always a ghastly, unexpressed suggestion of some human sacrifice being needed to complete the success of any incantation to the Evil One; and the poor old creature, herself believing and shuddering as she narrated her tale in broken English, took a strange, unconscious pleasure in her power over her hearers—young girls of the oppressing race, which had brought her down into a state little differing from slavery, and reduced her people to outcasts on the hunting-grounds which had belonged to her fathers.[13]

As far as I have been able to determine, Nattee and Hota's magical dabblings as well as their connections to and influences on the girls are original to Gaskell.

---

[12] Elizabeth Gaskell, "Lois the Witch," in *Cousin Phillis and Other Tales*, ed. Angus Easson (Oxford: Oxford University Press, 1981), p. 165. I am indebted to Philip Rogers for calling "Lois the Witch" to my attention.

[13] Gaskell, "Lois the Witch," pp. 126–27. On an Indian woman telling stories in the "kitchen," see especially Marion Starkey's popularly influential *The Devil in Massachusetts: A Modern Enquiry into the Salem Witch Trials* (1949; reprinted, New York: Anchor Books, 1969), pp. 30–31.

Of course Gaskell may herself have been influenced by Neal's *Rachel Dyer*. Certainly, she was acquainted with a variety of sources. Her recent editor, Angus Easson, is probably correct that she dipped into Upham's *Lectures,* even though much of her scene setting for the witch trials has its origins elsewhere.[14] But Gaskell's probable use of Upham creates a striking irony. The British storyteller reads the American historian and embellishes his tale to create a fictional role for Tituba and a circle of girls. A decade later, Upham incorporates that fiction into his history, establishes an enduring myth, and the generations that follow subscribe to a tale told by a nineteenth-century American historian that may indeed have been invented by a nineteenth-century British novelist.

The Tituba myth does not, however, spring solely from Upham's *Salem Witchcraft.* Future writers would make another crucial alteration: they would shift her racial identity. This metamorphosis has been splendidly chronicled by Chadwick Hansen in a March 1974 *New England Quarterly* essay tracing Tituba's transformation from Indian, to half Indian and half "Negro," to "Negro."[15] Although some commentators have continued to view Tituba as an Indian and although her racial malleability has not been a simple function of linear time, the direction of change has nonetheless certainly been from Indian to half-breed to "Negro" to black. The latter designation, which postdates Hansen's study, culminates in the brilliantly imaginative depiction by Maryse Condé in her novel *Moi, Tituba, Sorcière . . . Noir de Salem,* published in 1986 and translated into English in 1992 as *I, Tituba, Black Witch of Salem.*[16]

[14] Gaskell, "Lois the Witch," p. 358. I am indebted to Dean DeFino for his insights into Gaskell's use of Upham's *Lectures.*

[15] Chadwick Hansen, "The Metamorphosis of Tituba, or Why American Intellectuals Can't Tell an Indian Witch from a Negro," *New England Quarterly* 47 (1974): 3–12. I use the term "Negro" to be faithful to the sources and to indicate an older usage that then shifts as we come into the later twentieth century.

[16] Maryse Condé, *Moi, Tituba, Sorcière . . . Noir de Salem* (Paris: Mercure de France, 1986); *I, Tituba, Black Witch of Salem,* trans. Richard Philcox (Charlottesville: University Press of Virginia, 1992).

In the face of this noteworthy trend, a basic point should be clarified: no matter how *we* choose to define Tituba's race, her contemporaries were clear about racial classifications. The Puritans made unambiguous distinctions between Indians and "Negroes." There were among those caught up in the Salem witch trials people of African descent: a woman named Mary Black, described by her contemporaries as a "Negro"; a woman named Candy, similarly designated a "Negro," a self-proclaimed native of Barbados.[17] Tituba was classified as an Indian, not just once but repeatedly. Indeed, in the space of thirteen pages of the *Salem Witchcraft Papers*, Tituba is described as an Indian no less than fifteen times, an attribution that also emerges elsewhere in the collection of contemporary documents.[18] This hard evidence is important, for it bears directly on the current propensity to refashion Tituba from a passive Indian unleashing forces she could not control into a woman of African descent actively shaping events.

This desire to empower Tituba emerges in 1964 with Ann Petry's novel *Tituba of Salem Village*.[19] Still an Indian, Petry's Tituba is transformed from a passive victim into an assertive woman who, functioning in a world where magic appears to be a reality, uses its power to counteract fear and oppression. Selma R. and Pamela J. Williams embraced that point of view in their 1978 *Riding the Night Mare: Women & Witchcraft*, where they portray Tituba as having "outraged the Puritans by daring to introduce several young girls to the forbidden art of foretelling the future."[20] Condé's *I, Tituba*, a powerful, comic, tragic story of New World oppression, centers itself on Tituba's defiance and retribution. Her confession becomes an act of "revenge," a decision to "unleash the storm" that would engulf her oppressors.[21] Caught in the web falsely spun years ago by Charles Upham, Condé's tale further complicates the myth by

[17]*Salem Witchcraft Papers*, 1:113–14, 179–81.

[18]*Salem Witchcraft Papers*, 3:745–57.

[19]Ann Petry, *Tituba of Salem Village* (New York: Harper Trophy, 1964).

[20]Selma R. and Pamela J. Williams, *Riding the Night Mare: Women & Witchcraft* (New York: Atheneum, 1978), p. 147.

[21]Condé, *I, Tituba*, p. 93.

portraying Tituba as the daughter of an African woman raped by a white sailor while being transported into slavery.

Condé's novel, too complex for detailed analysis here, draws the mythic Tituba into the service of a new master. But those despising Tituba and those celebrating her all ultimately return to the same invented narrative. And to challenge the regnant version of the myth is to hazard rhetorical retribution. As Angela Davis writes in her foreword to *I, Tituba*:

> There are those who dispute [Tituba's] African descent, countering that she was Indian, perhaps hoping to stir up enmity between black and Native American women as we seek to recreate our respective histories.[22]

Davis's allegation emerges from her commitment to bring "suppressed cultural histories" to light, but in this moment of pursuing her own ethnic identity, she unwittingly participates in a battle to reclaim not history but myth. The more contested Tituba becomes, it seems, the more thoroughly is Upham's codification enshrined.

Yet, the contemporary interest reflected in Davis's gloss suggests a broader and potentially rewarding concern with recovering the historical Tituba. Despite its methodological problem of depending too heavily on etymology, Elaine G. Breslaw's *Tituba, Reluctant Witch of Salem* is the most intriguing scholarly attempt to date to place Tituba.[23] Breslaw's ambitious search is grounded in the all but ubiquitous assumption that Parris brought Tituba from Barbados. Indeed, it is hard to find scholars, myself included, who have not gone into print accepting as fact what Richard B. Trask has been wise enough to question: "Tradition holds that Tituba and John [John Indian, almost always identified as Tituba's husband] were acquired by Parris when in the Barbados, though no direct proof of this exists."[24]

[22]Angela Davis, foreword to Condé's *I, Tituba*, p. xii.

[23]Elaine G. Breslaw, *Tituba, Reluctant Witch of Salem* (New York and London: New York University Press, 1996).

[24]Richard B. Trask, *"The Devil Hath Been Raised": A Documentary History of the Salem Village Witchcraft Outbreak of March 1692* (Danvers, Mass.: Yeoman Press, 1997), p. 131.

The case for identifying Tituba as Barbadian is purely circumstantial. Mustered as evidence is Parris's prior residence in Barbados, although there is no record that he brought slaves or servants with him when he returned to New England.[25] Others have argued that John Hales's reference to Tituba's "own Country" and hers, in a response to a question posed by her examiner on 1 March 1692, to her "owne Country" must hearken back to Barbados.[26] In 1692, however, the meaning of the word "country" was less restrictive than it is today, as in the following definition from the *Oxford English Dictionary:* "A tract or expanse of land of undefined extent; a region, district." Clarifying usage, the OED goes on to note that "Two adjoining parishes might be spoken of as different countries."

Of course, while we cannot prove the traditional assumption that Tituba came from Barbados, neither can we disprove it. Studies like Breslaw's, including one by Peter Charles Hoffer, nonetheless risk an elaborate tautology, since their central arguments are firmly entrenched in the unproven premise of Tituba's Barbadian heritage. Still, since the Barbadian connection remains plausible, studies depending on it continue to be potentially productive, even while essentially speculative. In other words, if Tituba did hail from Barbados, Breslaw may have made a stunning discovery: she has located "the name 'Tattuba' for a slave girl in a 1676 deed" which refers to a person in Barbados who she argues is Tituba.[27] The vagaries of seventeenth-century orthography coupled with Parris's ties to Barbados raise tantalizing possibilities.

But since Breslaw knows that Tituba's contemporaries uniformly characterized her as an Indian, Tattuba must also be identified as such even though the Barbadian slave culture was largely African. To accomplish her goal, Breslaw relies primarily on an etymological analysis of the name Tattuba, at the end

[25]The best biographical treatment of Parris is Larry Gragg's *A Quest for Security: The Life of Samuel Parris, 1653–1720* (New York: Greenwood Press, 1990). Gragg, as with most others, assumes that Tituba came from Barbados, but he offers no evidence to support the claim, other than a reference to Tituba's "own Country" (p. 113).

[26]Hale, *A Modest Inquiry,* p. 414, *Salem Witchcraft Papers,* 3:752.

[27]Breslaw, *Tituba, Reluctant Witch,* p. 22.

of which she concludes that it is a Spanish derivative of an Arawak name. Despite this happy conclusion, a sticky issue remains: the name Tattuba appears on a list of "Negroes" identified as slaves. Here Breslaw makes a reasonable case that the term "Negro" "was intended to connote the condition of enslavement and not necessarily color or ethnicity." In seeking to establish Tituba's identity, however, Breslaw never departs from the received opinion that the slave woman was, "of course, responsible for initiating the panic and help[ing] to maintain the acute sense of diabolical invasion."[28] The validity of that view is implicitly reconsidered in a recent study by Peter Hoffer entitled *The Devil's Disciples: Makers of the Salem Witchcraft Trials.*

In pondering the crucial question of why Tituba escaped the gallows, Hoffer argues that she was acquitted. His evidence is the word "Ignoramus" written on the reverse of Tituba's bill of indictment, which indicates that she was cleared of charges brought before a grand jury on 9 May 1692.[29] With evidence so compelling and witchcraft scholars aplenty, Hoffer did well to take this second look.[30] But Hoffer, like others before him, has been victimized by a misplaced faith in the accuracy of the Boyer and Nissenbaum edition of *The Salem Witchcraft Pa-*

---

[28]Breslaw, *Tituba, Reluctant Witch*, pp. 13, 24–25, 31, 178. For an illuminating study of the redefinition of Indians as Negroes in early New England, see Ruth Wallis Herndon and Ella Wilcox Sekatau, *Ethnohistory* 44 (Summer 1997): 433–62.

[29]Peter Charles Hoffer, *The Devil's Disciples: Makers of the Salem Witchcraft Trials* (Baltimore: Johns Hopkins University Press, 1996), pp. 154–55, 258–59 n. 4.

[30]To assume that other scholars have not been aware of the "Ignoramus" notation is, however, an oversimplification. The term does not always predict a happy fate, as we see in the case of George Jacobs, Sr. Two indictments of him survive: one lists no verdict; the other is marked "Ignoramus." He was hanged. Other "Ignoramuses," though accompanied by different indictments that return true bills, appear in the cases of John Proctor, John Willard, and Wilmott Reed. All were hanged. Such matters require investigation not yet adequately performed. (See *Salem Witchcraft Papers*, 2:477–79, 2:679, 3:832, 3:712.)

In the case of Tituba's "Ignoramus," most scholars probably assumed incorrectly, as I did, that the notation was entered when people were being cleared in the January 1693 trials. This is a point I never made in print, because I thought it obvious given Tituba's continuation in jail.

*pers.* Errors abound: most minor; some not so minor. The one Hoffer encountered is not minor. An examination of the manuscript referring to Tituba's court appearance reveals that the date was 9 May 1693, not 1692.[31]

Hoffer's assumption that Tituba was "cleared by an Ipswich grand jury on May 9" 1692 does not prevent him from concluding that if not for Tituba, "there would have been no witchcraft crisis in Salem."[32] A grand jury's finding Tituba not guilty and her being responsible, by means of confession, for provoking the crisis are not mutually exclusive, but the two propositions do not comfortably converge. The mythic power of Tituba as scapegoat overwhelms even the idea that people in her own day did not believe her. However, the apparent paradox need not be explored, since it stems from a textual error.

But a textual error cannot address the more startling claim that Hoffer makes. Tituba, according to Hoffer, was an African brought in slavery to the New World. Hoffer is the first scholar published by a university press—a prestigious one at that—to support the contention that Tituba was a "Negro."[33] The odds against him are enormous. To cite Breslaw again, "Nowhere in the seventeenth-century records is there so much as a hint that she was of even partial African descent."[34] Hoffer, who has also familiarized himself with the records, is undeterred.[35]

---

[31] The error resides in the WPA edition Boyer and Nissenbaum reproduced without systematic verification of the manuscript transcriptions. Like Hoffer, I was lured by my faith in *The Salem Witchcraft Papers* and erroneously asserted that a witchcraft case, Tituba's, had been addressed outside of the court of Oyer and Terminer (see my *Salem Story,* pp. 27–29). A more reliable edition, although it only covers events in March, is Trask's *The Devil Hath Been Raised.* His 1997 edition corrects errors in the 1992 edition. For some, though by no means all, of the textual difficulties in *The Salem Witchcraft Papers,* see Trask and my *Salem Story,* p. 235 n. 25, p. 240 n. 47, p. 241 n. 6, p. 242 n. 12, and p. 254 nn. 38, 39.

[32] Hoffer, *Devil's Disciples,* pp. 154, xviii.

[33] John Demos, in his "Underlying Themes in the Witchcraft of Seventeenth-Century New England," *American Historical Review* 75 (1970): 1316, refers to Tituba as a "Negro," but this appears to be a slip, and it is certainly not a point that he argues.

[34] Breslaw, *Tituba, Reluctant Witch,* p. xxi.

[35] Hoffer, *Devil's Disciples,* pp. 205–10.

Like Breslaw, Hoffer rests his case on an etymological analysis, although the two scholars reach radically different conclusions. Hoffer identifies Tituba's name as "a Yoruba name."[36] Even if the attribution were correct, we do not know how she received her name nor the original spelling of it. In a quick survey of *The Salem Witchcraft Papers,* I counted more than forty occurrences of Tituba's name, only thirteen of which carried the "uba" ending needed for the etymological argument. On the other hand, Tituba's owner, Parris, whose authority in such a matter should be primary, renders her name "Tituba"; perhaps his lead has influenced the spelling we use today.[37]

Even under the best of circumstances, Hoffer takes his argument too far. In an age of haphazard orthography, there can be no basis for attributing an individual's heritage to three letters ("uba") in a name. Moreover, what was to prevent a white owner from naming his female slave simply according to his fancy? How many slaves named Cassandra or Caesar had Greek or Roman origins? Slave masters who could rape women with impunity could surely name them as they chose.

Hoffer admits that "When we only have the name, there is only a great deal of speculation and the danger of unwarranted invention." But he resists his own admonition. Against overwhelming contemporary evidence, he insists that Tituba is an African, an African brought to the colonies in the slave trade. Other than her name, however, he offers no evidence. Her ubiquitous identification as an Indian in her own time, Hoffer speculates, may have resulted from her marriage to an Indian.[38] Yet this speculation is not supported, for no evidence appears in Hoffer's study that it was customary to redefine the woman's ethnicity in seventeenth-century New England "interracial" marriages. In fact, there is no evidence that Tituba and John were married, or even cohabiting, although almost every

[36]Hoffer, *Devil's Disciples,* pp. 2–3.

[37]On her arrest warrant, her name is spelled "titibe" and on the bill of indictment "Tittapa" (see *Salem Witchcraft Papers,* 3:745, 755).

[38]Hoffer, *Devil's Disciples,* pp. 217 n. 6, 5–8, 210.

scholar assumes, without proof, that a conjugal relationship existed.[39]

Of course one could speculate that a designation of Indian also encompassed the West Indies, but the case of the slave Candy, the Barbadian who was identified as a "Negro," seems to refute that theory.[40] Tituba, residing in a community that habitually made clear distinctions between Indians and "Negroes," was never labeled a "Negro." In the end, even Hoffer is troubled by the case of Candy. After pages and pages of treating Tituba's "Africanness" as a fact, he reluctantly concedes, "I cannot be sure."[41]

His faint demurrer notwithstanding, in Hoffer's hands the myth of Tituba has metamorphosed from tentative hints that she might be a "Negro" into a scholar's argument that she was. As a cultural icon, apparently, Tituba has not been sufficiently useful as the Indian her contemporaries knew her to be. Here I can only speculate about why that might be so. Branded the instigator of the crisis as early as 1702,[42] characterized in popular

[39]The earliest reference to a marriage between the two is Neal's *History of New-England*, 1:496. Chadwick Hansen writes that "they are always referred to as man and wife in the documents," but I have been unable to find any such reference ("The Metamorphosis of Tituba," p. 7).

In the surviving documents related to the witchcraft cases, women were usually identified by marital status: as wives, widows, or single women. Tituba is not identified by any marital status. For example, in the arrest warrant for Tituba and Sarah Osborne, dated 29 February 1691/92, Osborne is identified as "the wife of Alexa' Osburne," while Tituba is identified as "an Indian Woman servant, of mr. Sam'l parris" (*Salem Witchcraft Papers*, 3:745). Of course, servant status may have overtaken marital. The burden of proof, however, remains with those who claim that Tituba and John were married.

[40]In an intriguing study, Matti Rissanen offers a linguistic analysis of speech patterns from the Salem judicial proceedings and concludes that Tituba's ethnicity differs from Candy's. See "'Candy no Witch, Barbados': Salem Witchcraft Trials as Evidence of Early American English," *Language in Time and Space: Studies in Honour of Wolfgang Viereck on the Occasion of His Sixtieth Birthday*, ed. Heinrich Ramisch and Kenneth Wynne (Stuttgart: Franz Steiner, 1997), pp. 183–93.

[41]Hoffer, *Devil's Disciples*, p. 209.

[42]Hale, *A Modest Inquiry*, p. 415. Hale writes: "And the success of Tituba's confession encouraged those in Authority to examine others that were suspected, and the event was, that more confessed themselves guilty of the Crimes they were suspected for. And thus was this matter driven on."

culture and even traditional scholarship as a woman who practiced voodoo and cast children into spells, Tituba has been col-
lectively imagined as the dark outsider, the intruder who could
be blamed for the community's troubles. The romanticized Indian of the nineteenth century having been virtually eliminated
or removed to reservations, the feared "Negro" survived. In
popular culture's unrelenting effort to shape history by elevat-
ing heroes and punishing villains, an identity was forged for
Tituba, and it is not at all surprising that that identity should be
racialized, that Tituba should be classed with others like her
who inspired fear. Now fixed in popular imagination as a black
woman, Tituba retains her usefulness only if she remains so, for
only through her blackness can a new generation, seeking to reverse the sins of the past, reinterpret and empower her, convert
her from a trouble-making victim into a noble woman powerfully resisting oppression. In her new incarnation, then, Tituba
can reflect contemporary political vision rather than the stereotypes of previous generations. What, after all, is history, Ralph
Waldo Emerson reminded us, "but a fable agreed upon."[43] Perhaps it might be.

What magic politics and art will next work on Tituba remains
to be seen. For those who insist on hard evidence, however, the
facts are few. She lived in the household of the Reverend
Samuel Parris. Her prior whereabouts are not known. Her culture defined her as an Indian. Her contemporaries offered no
verifiable clues about her age. She was accused of witchcraft
and confessed. She claimed to have been beaten and to have
been herself afflicted by witches. From the beginning of March
1692 until she was brought to a court of General Jail Delivery
on 9 May 1693, she presumably languished in prison. Exactly
when she was released and whether she was ever reunited with
John Indian—or whether she had reason to be—is also not
known. Beyond those simple facts lies the realm of fictional
narrative and historical speculation. It is in that realm that

---

[43]Emerson cites Napoleon for the now-famous rhetorical question. See *The Complete Works of Ralph Waldo Emerson*, The Centenary Edition, 12 vols., ed. Edward
Waldo Emerson (Boston and New York: Houghton Mifflin, 1903), 2:9.

Tituba has long abided. In our periodic visits to her over the centuries, we have learned less about her than we have of ourselves. As we redefine ourselves in the future, we may expect our conversation with Tituba to continue.

Bernard Rosenthal, *Professor of English at the State University of New York, Binghamton, is the author of* SALEM STORY: READING THE WITCH TRIALS OF 1692.

The Historical Journal. 40. 2 (1997), pp. 331–358
Copyright © 1997 Cambridge University Press

# SPECTRAL EVIDENCE, NON-SPECTRAL ACTS OF WITCHCRAFT, AND CONFESSION AT SALEM IN 1692*

WENDEL D. CRAKER

*University of Georgia*

ABSTRACT. *It is commonly asserted that people were hanged at Salem on charges of spectral appearance; and the way to avoid hanging was to confess. Non-spectral acts of witchcraft are regarded as inconsequential to the outcome of the trials. Yet it was the non-spectral acts which provided the one magnet that attracted attention from the court. No one charged only with spectral appearance was even tried. The reprieves granted to confessors were the last decisions the court was allowed to make. This profile provides evidence that the standard claims about the court of oyer and terminer's use of evidence are the reverse of what actually happened, and highlights a number of patterns that have gone unremarked, requiring fresh interpretations.*

The Salem witchcraft episode of 1692 was a baroque manifestation, with a multitude of contorted configurations and florid descriptions that defy any standard, comprehensive retelling. After three hundred years, it still reflects a turbulence in society that is difficult to tame into normal channels of rational discourse. The subject matter itself carries an esoteric aura that feeds popular fantasy, and impedes scientific efforts to unravel the data of what happened, when, and how. There is an emotional content in the original documents that is difficult to recapture in rational descriptive discourse. Partly because of these esoteric and emotive elements, the fads of Salem scholarship have often perpetuated misunderstandings that have told us more about the predilections of the period in which they were produced than they have about the original event.

## I

One unresolved difficulty concerns how to interpret the roles played by the various types of evidence presented to the court of oyer and terminer as it conducted the trials. Standard interpretations fail to reflect the bases upon

* The original study, of which this is an extension, was under the direction of Barry Schwartz. Thanks also to Fred Bates, Robert Bogue, Dwight Freshley, Sandy Martin, and Ira Robinson for dialogue and commentary. Richard Weisman provided critical comments on an earlier draft of this argument. Larry Gragg's comments have shaped the outcome, and the argument is sharpened by responses of anonymous referees. The article grew, in part, out of participation in the 'Perspectives on Witchcraft' conference, a tercentenary observance of the Salem witchcraft trials, held in Salem, MA, June 1992, sponsored by Salem State College, the Essex Institute, et al. An abbreviated form of this argument was presented at the New England Historical Association, Waltham, Massachusetts, 23 Apr. 1994.

which selection for trial and execution occurred. It is the thesis of this study that there has been a general misunderstanding of the rules used by the court in making its selections which continues to hamper development of an adequate theoretical base upon which to build a satisfactory critical understanding.

Three major types of evidence were present in the proceedings – spectral evidence, non-spectral acts of malefic witchcraft, and confession. Definitions are as follows:

*Spectral evidence* refers to the common belief that, when a person had made covenant with the devil, he was given permission to assume that person's appearance in spectral form in order to recruit others, and to otherwise carry out his nefarious deeds. Ubiquitous and sensational, testimony concerning the spectral appearance of the alleged witches dominated the preliminary hearings and was a factor in the trials themselves. A special coterie of accusers had developed, first at Salem, then another at Andover, claiming the power to see the alleged spectres. Testimony concerning spectral appearance was limited to these self-selected groups who were enabled by a 'special sight' to see what to others was invisible. It is doubtful that anyone was accused who was not charged with having appeared in spectral form.

In contrast to allegations of spectral appearance were charges that the persons accused had engaged in what is here described as *non-spectral acts of malefic witchcraft*, which sprang from the malice and ill-will of neighbour against neighbour.[1] The concept was deeply embedded in the culture that some individuals, through the devil's arts, could obtain magical powers by which to cast spells, pronounce curses, and cause accident, storms, sickness and death. Such persons were alleged to have power to foretell the future, and to perform supernatural feats of strength.[2] The use of poppets and potions, sometimes described as 'object magic', is here considered as part of this more general category of non-spectral acts of witchcraft. There were, in fact, people who claimed these kinds of powers. While the appearance of spectres was limited to those few bewitched individuals who had been given a 'special sight', the non-spectral acts of malefic witchcraft were openly visible to anyone who observed the misfortunes of life, and chose to put a diabolic construction upon them. After accusations of spectral appearance had been made by members of this select group, which was said to be 'bewitched', ordinary people from the community stepped forward with additional accusations of non-spectral acts of witchcraft against thirty of them. Twenty-seven of the thirty were named during the Salem phase of accusation (late February to early June 1692). Three were named during the Andover phase (mid-July to mid-September 1692).

The third type of evidence was that of *confession*. By confessing, the individuals acknowledged having made a covenant with Satan, thus confirming the

---

[1] The phrase *non-spectral acts of malefic witchcraft* is a somewhat cumbersome way of making the distinction, but is utilized here to make explicit the difference in concepts involved. Weisman (see note 5) called it 'ordinary witchcraft', but I have chosen to retain in the designation both the distinction between spectral and non-spectral acts, and the distinction between black magic that springs from a malefic spirit, and so-called white magic that could be used for benevolent purposes.

[2] Samuel G. Drake, *The witchcraft delusion in New England* (3 vols., New York, 1970), I, 37–46.

accusations that had been made against them. Roughly one third of those charged admitted complicity with the devil (50 out of 156). However, forty-three of the fifty confessions on record came during the later Andover phase of the accusations. Only seven confessions had been forthcoming during the earlier Salem phase. This flurry of confessions toward the end of the proceedings reflected a change in the dynamic of the accusations that should not be read back into the Salem stage of events.

The purpose of this discussion is to examine how these forms of evidence entered into the selection of individuals for trial and execution. One hundred and fifty-six persons were indicted before and during the active life of the court of oyer and terminer. But then, as now, the process of indictment was separate from that of trial. Of the one hundred and fifty-six persons handed over to the court by the local magistrates, twenty-eight were brought to trial, and twenty were executed.[3] While everyone indicted was potentially at risk, it was only these twenty-eight persons who were placed immediately at risk, for it was only the court which could determine guilt, and pronounce judgment. The question to be explored is whether it is possible to discover a relationship between the types of evidence with which a prisoner had been charged and the selection process for trial and subsequent execution.

Determination of the court's method of procedure has been made more difficult by the fact that the records of the trials themselves have been lost. All that remain are secondary sources.[4] But the record of the persons called for trial, and the disposition of each case has been known and remained constant for over three hundred years. What is critical to our understanding is not the popular conversation that surrounded the trials, but the basis upon which the court selected those persons to be tried, and the principles upon which judgment was declared. And enough information remains to examine those issues.

Standard explanations have affirmed that individuals were hanged on the basis of spectral evidence alone, that confession was the surest way to avoid trial, and that non-spectral acts of witchcraft entered only marginally into the court's decisions because they provided no clear link of a covenant with Satan. Documentation for these generalizations will be provided as the skein of the argument develops. That argument will demonstrate that not one person was even called to trial, much less hanged, on the basis of spectral evidence alone. The single magnet that most notably attracted the court's attention was the charge of non-spectral acts of malefic witchcraft. And because of the court's early preoccupation with persons charged with non-spectral acts of witchcraft,

---

[3] Technically, Giles Corey was not tried because he refused to plead to the charges. However, in calling for the English expedient of pressing with weights to compel a plea, the court, in effect, sentenced him to death, and for the purposes of this summary he is included in the totals without footnoting the exception every time it occurs.

[4] Charles W. Upham, *Salem witchcraft* (2 vols., New York, 1867), II, 256, 462–3. Paul Boyer and Stephen Nissenbaum, *Salem possessed: the social origins of witchcraft* (Cambridge, MA, 1974), p. 7, n. 16.

confession was not even formally considered by the court until the last set of trials (17 September 1692). When it did finally turn to prisoners who had confessed, it continued its practice of convicting all those whom it tried, but faltered at their execution. The reprieves it then granted were the last decisions the court of oyer and terminer was allowed to make. Thus confession, arguably, became the issue upon which the court foundered.

## II

Warrant for these arguments is drawn from a chronological listing of the one hundred and fifty-six persons indicted before and during the active life of the court of oyer and terminer. This master list is then sorted into three tables that name the persons who bore only charges of spectral appearance, those who were charged with non-spectral acts of malefic witchcraft, and those who are on record as having confessed. A fourth table provides a chronological list of the trials.

The master list is a compilation from five different sources, utilizing lists prepared by Boyer and Nissenbaum, Weisman, Godbeer, the Danvers Archival Center, and Robinson.[5] No attempt has been made to reconcile differences in those lists. There are, and probably always will be, gaps in our knowledge about persons, dates, and charges. But together they form a composite of what is currently known. Their presentation in tabular form makes it possible to see where there is strongest agreement, and where judgments vary. For the most part, the chronological order used in these tables is an adaptation of an original alphabetical listing by the authors. Only Robinson also utilized the chronological format. The sequence here follows an earlier version limited to the lists from Boyer and Nissenbaum, and Weisman.[6]

[5] Paul Boyer and Stephen Nissenbaum, *Salem-Village witchcraft: a documentary record of local conflict in New England* (Belmont, CA, 1972); Richard Weisman, *Witchcraft, magic, and religion in 17th-century Massachusetts* (Amherst, MA, 1984); Richard Godbeer, *The devil's dominion: magic and religion in early New England* (Cambridge, 1992); Danvers Archival Center, Richard Trask, Dir. (Danvers, MA: unpublished, compiled 1992); Enders Robinson, *Salem witchcraft and Hawthorne's 'House of Seven Gables'* (Bowie, MD, 1992).

[6] Wendel D. Craker, *Cotton Mather's wrangle with the devil: a sociological analysis of the fantastic* (Ann Arbor, 1990). The question is legitimately raised about why the perspective on the court's use of evidence discussed first in this dissertation, and elaborated in the accompanying article, has not been uncovered by earlier researchers dealing with the Salem material. An answer to that question can only be speculative in nature. What can be noted with greater certainty are the two methodological steps included in this research which have not been previously reported. The first is the compilation of the chronological chart appearing as an appendix to this discussion. Developments outlined in the text could not have been so sharply defined without conversion of these earlier alphabetical listings to the chronological format. The second methodological contribution is a more rigorous separation of indictment from trial. Authors vary in the degree to which they even recognize that such a distinction was possible; but few, if any, have made the separation an integral part of their argument. Often descriptions of the 'dynamic' of the trials include testimony taken at the indictments of people who were never brought to trial. The choices made by the court of oyer and terminer become dramatically clear only after separating the chronological chart into the kinds of evidence used against particular prisoners. Tables 1–3 provide the demonstration of those distinctions. I was surprised that no one had taken these two critical

However, once the lists are tabulated, there arises the question of how those results fit into the documentary record of the trials which has been used to support the standard explanations described above. Significantly helpful in this re-examination of the court's use of evidence is Cotton Mather's discussion in *The wonders of the invisible world*.[7] It was late in the summer of 1692 that he conceived the idea of writing a defence of the court of oyer and terminer to counteract the mounting criticism of the trials. He was urged forward in that task by both Chief Justice Wm Stoughton and Governor Wm Phips. The tract that he put together was derived from a disparate set of sources, including a couple of his own sermons, reflections on conditions in the colony, and descriptions of similar episodes in Europe. But the central purpose was the publication of transcripts from several of the trials, designed to show the carefulness with which the court had acted, and the justice of the outcome.

However, *Wonders* was not completed until 11 October 1692, three and one-half weeks after the last of the trials had been conducted (17 September 1692), so it came too late to affect the further course of the trials. Yet from that belated effort have derived two serious misunderstandings of Mather's role in the events. The impassioned language with which he defended the court has caused him to be mistakenly perceived as one of the chief fomenters of the witchcraft episode.[8] Moreover, since the court is commonly regarded as having acted rashly, his defence is frequently considered as an attempt to provide a cover for the excesses of that body.[9] However, it will be argued that beneath his florid rhetoric, Mather provides a more compelling account of the actual course followed by the court than is provided by those who dismiss his argument as self-serving by the court and the clergy.

Cotton Mather's review of the rules governing evidence in witchcraft trials is the most thorough discussion available. Utilizing three English authors,

---

steps earlier. It would appear that the Salem episode is an apt illustration of the principle that the way an event is framed sets limits to what can be seen. One can only surmise that the standard interpretations discussed in the text, or other theoretical blinders, have kept scholars from asking the kinds of questions that did, in this instance, lead to the explorations presented here. Salem scholarship did not really begin until the mid-nineteenth century, and when it did, it arose as a reaction of abhorrence that such an event could have occurred. It turned the original rage on its head, and tended to demonize the perpetrators of the trials in a manner similar to the way the colonists had demonized the accused witches. It was in that period that stereotypical assumptions about the use of spectral appearance and confession became a part of the 'received understanding' concerning the trials. It was not until the mid-twentieth century that scholars began to sort through the impact of that visceral reaction on contemporary understandings of the episode. Stereotypes about the court's use of evidence appear to this writer as among those vestiges of the earlier reaction which have not yet been put aside.

[7] Cotton Mather, *The wonders of the invisible world* (Boston, 1693). Citations in this article are from the reprint appearing in Drake, *The witchcraft delusion*.

[8] The role of principal instigator of the witchcraft episode was assigned to Cotton Mather by Upham, *Salem witchcraft*, and the designation remains firmly in place in popular understanding. A more balanced view of Mather's role is succinctly stated in Kenneth Silverman's, *Selected letters of Cotton Mather* (Baton Rouge, LA, 1971), pp. 31,32.

[9] Weisman, *Witchcraft, magic, and religion*, pp. 170, 171.

William Perkins, John Gaule, and Richard Bernard,[10] Mather discussed how the various kinds of evidence were weighted to bring a conviction in court. With a straight-faced seriousness which defies comprehension by a contemporary reader he summarized their discussions of the relative merits of the range of superstitions that comprised the common folklore of witchcraft. Quoting Perkins, he noted first of all that ' *There* are *Presumptions*, which do at least probably and conjecturally note one to be a *Witch*. These give occasion to Examine, yet they are no sufficient Causes of Conviction '.[11] In a letter to Judge Richards, Cotton Mather utilized this concept of 'presumptive evidence', and relegated spectral appearance to that category.[12] If such evidence were true, Mather elsewhere argues, 'Providence at the same time [would] have brought into our hands, these more evident and sensible things whereupon a man is esteemed a criminal'.[13] What Mather described as 'evident and sensible things' we would describe as empirical evidence. The admission of spectral evidence at the indictments served the principle of presumptive evidence similar to a grand jury's inquiry into probable cause. In the early stages it was regarded as a valid means for procedure. The key question was whether it was, in the end, allowed to stand by itself.

Perkins went on to describe two forms of evidence that were deemed sufficient to warrant a conviction. One was 'the free and voluntary Confession of the Crime, made by the party suspected and accused ... ' The other was:

The Testimony of two Witnesses, of good and honest Report, avouching before the Magistrate, upon their own Knowledge ... that the party accused hath made a League with the Devil, *or hath done some known practices of witchcraft*. And, all Arguments that do necessarily prove either of these ... (emphasis added).[14]

A 'known practice of witchcraft' would include 'any action or work which necessarily infers a Covenant made, as, that he hath used enchantments, divined things before they come to pass (etc.) ... ' Feats that could only be accomplished by super-human assistance also fall into the same category.[15]

By this formula, spectral evidence could be used to indict, but not to convict. For this, either confession or evidence of non-spectral acts of witchcraft would be required. But the confession must be credible, and the testimony concerning non-spectral acts of witchcraft must be by at least two persons of good character, and must either expressly or inferentially reflect actions accomplished with the aid of Satan. Within these hedges the court could and, in fact, should proceed. It is the argument of this study that these distinctions do, indeed, make an aptly significant overlay when applied to the actions of the court of oyer and terminer.

However, to support the common view, it is necessary to argue that the court ignored these distinctions. Weisman, for instance, comments about the role of

[10] Richard Bernard, *A guide to grand-jury men* (London, 1627); John Gaule, *Select cases of conscience concerning witchcraft* (London, 1646); William Perkins, *A discourse of the damned art of witchcraft* (London, 1631).    [11] Drake, *Witchcraft delusion*, I, 37, 38.
[12] Silverman, *Selected letters*, p. 36.    [13] Drake, *Witchcraft delusion*, I, p. 35.
[14] Ibid. I, 41.    [15] Ibid. I, 41-2, 44.

Increase and Cotton Mather (father and son) in defending the court. Speaking of Cotton Mather's account in *Wonders*, he correctly notes that 'Mather's work presented a version of the Salem trials that articulated the standpoint of the magistrates.' But he asserts that this version fraudulently 'represented judicial policy as if it had never deviated from the ecclesiastical recommendations'. Yet, from Weisman's own research it is possible to demonstrate that the court did keep the letter of ecclesiastical recommendations, however much one may want to argue that the passions of the day violated their spirit.[16]

## III

There follow four tables that list the persons charged only with spectral appearance; those that also carried the charge of non-spectral acts of witchcraft; those who confessed; and a chronological listing of the trials. Together, these tables provide a different way of viewing the dynamic of the trials from that portrayed by standard assumptions. They call for a rethinking of some of the traditions most deeply embedded in Salem scholarship, and open the door to fresh theorizing about the forces at work in what remains an enigmatic episode in colonial history.

The largest sub-set of prisoners was that group of seventy-nine persons who were charged only with spectral appearance. These persons were not charged with non-spectral acts of witchcraft, nor did they confess. This was one-half of the total accused. Fifty-two were from the Salem phase, and twenty-seven from the Andover period. Table 1 demonstrates that not one of them was called by the court to answer charges. Not only did the court ignore this group, but so have most authors since.

The standard claims assert that the court condemned people on the basis of spectral appearance alone, and that it targeted those intransigent prisoners who maintained their innocence. Nearly everyone recognizes the presence of non-spectral evidence in the trial of Bridget Bishop, who became the first convicted witch at Salem. But it is common to dismiss the presence of such evidence in later trials as inconsequential, if present at all. Hansen explicitly states that 'of all the hundred or so then in prison there was this kind of evidence *only* against Bridget Bishop' (emphasis in the original). Yet, in a later work he includes description of non-spectral evidence gathered against three others (Martha Carrier, who was already imprisoned at the time of Bishop's trial, Mary Parker, and Samuel Wardwell, who were added later). But Hansen does not seem to realize the impact the inclusion of this evidence has on his earlier argument, for he supports his prior comments about spectral evidence

---

[16] Weisman, *Witchcraft, magic, and religion*, p. 171. In Appendix C of the same volume (pp. 208–216) Weisman notes with an asterisk those whom his research found to be charged with non-spectral acts of witchcraft, a category which he describes as ordinary witchcraft. This includes all of those hanged, with the exception of Mary Parker. That exception is discussed more fully in the text, and note i in the Masterlist.

Table 1. *Chronological chart of accusations of spectral appearance*[a]

| No. | Name | Age | B, | W, | G, | D, | R | Init Chrg | Date Conf | Ord Wtch | Date Trial | Final Result |
|-----|------|-----|----|----|----|----|----|-----------|-----------|----------|------------|--------------|
| SALEM | | | | | | | | | | | | |
| 003 | Sarah Osborne | 50 | B, | W, | G, | D, | R | 2/29 | | | | DIED |
| 008 | John Lee | | B, | W, | G | | | 4/01 | | | | ? |
| 009 | Sarah Cloyce | 51 | B, | W, | G, | D, | R | 4/04 | | | | SCJ |
| 016 | Neh. Abbot, Jr[b] | 29 | B, | W, | G, | D, | R | 4/21 | | | | ? |
| 017 | Edward Bishop, Jr | 44 | B, | W, | G, | D, | R | 4/21 | | | | ESC |
| 018 | Sarah Bishop | 41 | B, | W, | G, | D, | R | 4/21 | | | | ESC |
| 019 | Mary Black (slave) | | B, | W, | G, | D, | R | 4/21 | | | | SCJ |
| 021 | Mary English | 40 | B, | W, | G, | D, | R | 4/21 | | | | ESC |
| 022 | William Hobbs | 50 | B, | W, | G, | D, | R | 4/21 | | | | SCJ |
| 026 | Thomas Dyer | | | | | D, | R | 4/27 | | | | ? |
| 027 | Sam. Passanauton[c] | | | | | D, | R | 4/28 | | | | ? |
| 028 | Thatcher (female slave) | | | | | D, | R | ? | | | | ? |
| 034 | Sarah Murrill | 14 | B, | W, | | D, | R | 4/30 | | | | SCJ |
| 035 | Mary Morey | | B, | W, | G | | | 5/? | | | | SCJ |
| 036 | Mary Cox | | | | | D, | R | 5/? | | | | ? |
| 037 | Bethia Carter, Sr | 47 | B, | W, | G, | D, | R | 5/07 | | | | ? |
| 038 | Bethia Carter, Jr | 21 | | W, | G, | D, | R | 5/07 | | | | ? |
| 040 | Ann Sears | 71 | B, | W, | G, | D, | R | 5/07 | | | | SCJ |
| 041 | Elizabeth Colson | 15 | B, | W, | G, | D, | R | 5/10 | | | | ESC |
| 047 | Thomas Hardy | | | | G, | | R | 5/13 | | | | ? |
| 048 | Abigail Somes | 37 | B, | W, | G, | D, | R | 5/13 | | | | SCJ |
| 049 | Dan Andrew | 48 | B, | W, | G, | D, | R | 5/14 | | | | ESC |
| 050 | Sarah Buckley | 70 | B, | W, | G, | D, | R | 5/14 | | | | SCJ |
| 051 | Tom Farrer | 75 | B, | W, | G, | D, | R | 5/14 | | | | SCJ |
| 052 | Elizabeth Hart | 65 | B, | W, | G, | D, | R | 5/14 | | | | SCJ |
| 053 | George Jacobs, Jr | 50 | B, | W, | G, | D, | R | 5/14 | | | | ESC |
| 054 | Rebecca Jacobs | 46 | B, | W, | G, | D, | R | 5/14 | | | | SCJ |
| 055 | Mary Witheridge | 27 | B, | W, | G, | D, | R | 5/14 | | | | SCJ |
| 056 | Mehitabel Downing | 40 | | | G, | D, | R | 5/15 | | | | SCJ |
| 058 | Sarah Bassett | 35 | B, | W, | G, | D, | R | 5/21 | | | | SCJ |
| 059 | Sarah Proctor | 15 | B, | W, | G, | D, | R | 5/21 | | | | SCJ |
| 060 | Susanna Roots | 70 | B, | W, | G, | D, | R | 5/21 | | | | SCJ |
| 061 | Mary De Rich | 35 | B, | W, | G, | D, | R | 5/23 | | | | SCJ |
| 062 | Sarah Pease | | B, | W, | G, | D, | R | 5/23 | | | | SCJ |
| 063 | Benjamin Proctor | 33 | B, | W, | G, | D, | R | 5/23 | | | | SCJ |
| 064 | Jerson Toothaker | | B, | W, | G | | | 5/24 | | | | SCJ |
| 065 | Arthur Abbot | 53 | B, | | G, | D, | R | 5/28 | | | | SCJ |
| 066 | Capt. John Alden | 69 | B, | W, | G, | D, | R | 5/28 | | | | ESC |
| 068 | Elizabeth Cary | 42 | B, | W, | G, | D, | R | 5/28 | | | | ESC |
| 069 | Capt. John Flood | 55 | B, | W, | G, | D, | R | 5/28 | | | | ? |
| 070 | Elizabeth Fosdick | 32 | B, | W, | G, | D, | R | 5/28 | | | | ? |
| 072 | William Proctor | 17 | B, | W, | G, | D, | R | 5/28 | | | | SCJ |
| 074 | Sarah Rice | 61 | B, | W, | G, | D, | R | 5/28 | | | | ? |
| 076 | Margaret Toothaker | 9 | B, | | G, | D, | R | 5/28 | | | | SCJ |
| 077 | Elizabeth Paine | 53 | B, | W, | G, | D, | R | 5/30 | | | | ? |
| 079 | Sarah Churchill | 20 | | | G, | | R | 6/01 | | | | AFFL |

452

Table 1. *Cont.*

| No. | Name | Age | Source B. | W, | G, | D, | R | Init Chrg | Date Conf | Ord Wtch | Date Trial | Final Result |
|-----|------|-----|----|----|----|----|---|-----------|-----------|----------|------------|--------------|
| 080 | Mary Ireson | 32 | B, | W, | G, | D, | R | 6/04 | | | | SCJ |
| 082 | Ann Doliver | 29 | B, | W, | G, | D, | R | 6/06 | | | | SCJ |
| 084 | Sarah Bibber | | | | G | | | ? | | | | AFFL |
| 085 | Mercy Lewis | | | | G | | | ? | | | | AFFL |
| 086 | Susanna Sheldon | | | | G | | | ? | | | | AFFL |
| 087 | Elizabeth Scargen | | | | | D, | R | 7/? | | | | ? |
| **ANDOVER** | | | | | | | | | | | | |
| 097 | Mary Green | 34 | B, | W, | G, | D, | R | 7/30 | | | | ? |
| 099 | Mary Post | 28 | B, | W, | G, | D, | R | 8/02 | | | | SCJ |
| 100 | Mary Clarke | 53 | B, | W, | G, | D, | R | 8/03 | | | | SCJ |
| 101 | John Howard | 48 | B, | W, | G, | D, | R | 8/05 | | | | ? |
| 102 | John Jackson, Sr | 50 | B, | W, | G, | D, | R | 8/05 | | | | SCJ |
| 105 | Daniel Eames | 29 | | | | D, | R | 8/09 | | | | ? |
| 111 | Sarah Parker | 22 | | | G, | D, | R | 8/15 | | | | SCJ |
| 112 | Frances Hutchins | 75 | B, | W, | G, | D, | R | 8/18 | | | | ? |
| 113 | Ruth Wilford | 17 | B, | W, | G, | D, | R | 8/18 | | | | ? |
| 122 | Abigail Johnson | 10 | B, | W, | G, | D, | R | 8/29 | | | | SCJ |
| 129 | Eliz. Dicer | | B, | W, | G, | D, | R | 9/03 | | | | ? |
| 130 | Marg. Prince | 62 | B, | W, | G, | D, | R | 9/03 | | | | ? |
| 131 | Mary Colson | 41 | | W, | G, | D, | R | 9/05 | | | | SCJ |
| 132 | Joseph Emons | | B, | W, | G, | D, | R | 9/05 | | | | SCJ |
| 133 | Nicholas Frost | | B, | W, | G, | D, | R | 9/05 | | | | ? |
| 134 | Jane Lilly | 48 | B, | W, | G, | D, | R | 9/05 | | | | SCJ |
| 135 | Mary Taylor | 40 | | W, | G, | D, | R | 9/05 | | | | SCJ |
| 138 | Dane (male slave) | | | | | D, | R | 9/07 | | | | ? |
| 142 | Eunice Fry | 51 | B, | W, | G, | D, | R | 9/07 | | | | SCJ |
| 144 | Reb. Johnson, Jr | 17 | | | | D, | R | 9/07 | | | | SCJ |
| 146 | Henry Salter | 65 | B, | W, | G, | D, | R | 9/07 | | | | ? |
| 147 | John Sawdy, Jr | 13 | B, | W, | G, | D, | R | 9/07 | | | | ? |
| 149 | Joanna Tyler | 11 | | | G, | D, | R | 9/07 | | | | SCJ |
| 151 | Mary Tyler | 40 | | | | D, | R | 9/07 | | | | SCJ |
| 154 | Hannah Carroll | | B, | W, | G, | D, | R | 9/10 | | | | ? |
| 155 | Sarah (Davis) Cole | 42 | B, | | G, | D, | R | 9/10 | | | | SCJ |
| 156 | Joan Peney | 72 | B, | W, | G, | D, | R | 9/13 | | | | ? |

[a] This is a chronological list of persons charged only with spectral appearance during the Salem witchcraft episode. They neither were charged with non-spectral acts of witchcraft, nor did they confess. This list is extracted from the Master List of the accused at the end of this article. Since the focus of this inquiry is on the use that the court of oyer and terminer made of the three forms of evidence presented in the trials, only those who were accused before the last action of the court on 22 September 1692 are included in this list. The significance of this chart is in the information not present. Among those who were not charged with non-spectral acts of witchcraft, and who did not confess, there was not a single person who was called before the court of oyer and terminer for trial. However much weight the court may have given to spectral evidence when it appeared in conjunction with other types of evidence, the court was meticulously careful to consider only those who also bore charges of non-spectral acts of witchcraft, or who had confessed. For a key to the headings, see Master List.

[b] See note e, Master List.     [c] See note g, Master List.

with a footnote in his later article.[17] Similarly, Weisman affirms that in the second set of trials the five accused were condemned on the basis of spectral evidence, and this policy was not altered in the subsequent sessions.[18] And Weisman, too, lets this affirmation stand despite the fact that in an appendix to his work he demonstrates that nineteen of the twenty who were executed had been charged with what he calls 'ordinary witchcraft'. Mary Parker was the only exception in Weisman's list, and as noted above, Hansen cites testimony that would place her among those charged with non-spectral acts of witchcraft.[19] Even more recently, Godbeer asserts the reliance of the court on spectral evidence in the remark, 'Indeed, were it not for confessions and the afflicted girls' testimony, there would have been very few, if any, convictions in 1692'. His comments are based, not so much on the complete absence of non-spectral evidence as on its limited presence, and its alleged irrelevance to the purposes of the court.[20] Conclusions such as those cited by Hansen, Weisman, and Godbeer have gone largely uncontested.

Given the presuppositions just enumerated, there is an anomaly in the make-up of the set of prisoners listed in Table 1. This is the one group of those indicted for witchcraft which was cited only for spectral appearance, and which opted not to use the alleged cover of confession – thus combining both of the features which are generally supposed to have most put a prisoner at risk. Yet this group was completely overlooked by the court, even though it comprised the largest set of prisoners which was available for trial.

Once the pervasive role of spectral appearance in bringing people to indictment is granted, it disappears altogether as a factor in selecting individual prisoners for trial. Not one of these confessed, not one was charged with non-spectral acts of witchcraft, and not one was tried. These figures compellingly illustrate the principles to which Mather appealed in the rules of evidence, and the meticulous care that the court demonstrated in following those rules. Those charged only with spectral appearance were not called to trial because they bore no corollary charge of non-spectral acts of witchcraft or confession. They languished in prison, a few escaped, some died, but none were required to face the court. There simply is no statistical basis for the popular generalization that people were hanged on charges of spectral appearance alone.

Table 2 takes up the question of whether the court of oyer and terminer did, in fact, ignore the testimony concerning non-spectral acts of witchcraft. With the weight accorded to spectral appearance the significance of non-spectral acts of witchcraft has often been set aside as inconsequential. Once again, an observation by Weisman illustrates the point: 'The popular [non-spectral] testimony could be disqualified with little or no inconvenience to the court and

[17] Chadwick Hansen, *Witchcraft at Salem* (New York, 1969), p. 123; and Hansen, 'Andover witchcraft and the causes of the Salem witchcraft trials', in Howard Kerr and Charles L. Crow, eds., *The occult in America: new historical perspectives* (Urbana and Chicago, 1983), pp. 38–57.

[18] Weisman, *Witchcraft, magic, and religion*, p. 153.

[19] Hansen, 'Andover witchcraft', pp. 41–50.      [20] Godbeer, *The devil's dominion*, p. 216.

Table 2. *Chronological chart of accusations of non-spectral acts of witchcraft*[a]

| No. | Name | Age | B. | W. | G. | D. | R | Init Chrg | Date Conf | Ord Wtch | Date Trial | Final Result |
|-----|------|-----|----|----|----|----|----|-----------|-----------|----------|------------|--------------|
| 002 | Sarah Good | 38 | B. | W. | G. | D. | R | 2/29 | | X | 6/29 | EXEC |
| 004 | Martha Corey | 65 | B. | W. | G. | D. | R | 3/19 | | X | 9/09 | EXEC |
| 006 | Rebecca Nurse | 70 | B. | W. | G. | D. | R | 3/23 | | X | 6/29 | EXEC |
| 007 | Rachel Clinton[b] | 63 | B. | W. | G. | D. | R | 3/29 | | X | | SCJ |
| 010 | Elizabeth Proctor[c] | 41 | B. | W. | G. | D. | R | 4/04 | | X | 8/05 | RPRV |
| 011 | John Proctor | 60 | B. | W. | G. | D. | R | 4/11 | | X | 8/05 | EXEC |
| 012 | Bridget Bishop | 60 | B. | W. | G. | D. | R | 4/18 | | X | 6/02 | EXEC |
| 013 | Giles Corey[d] | 80 | B. | W. | G. | D. | R | 4/18 | | X | 9/17 | EXEC |
| 015 | Abigail Hobbs[e] | 22 | B. | W. | G. | D. | R | 4/18 | 4/18 | X | 9/17 | RPRV |
| 020 | Mary Easty | 51 | B. | W. | G. | D. | R | 4/21 | | X | 9/09 | EXEC |
| 024 | Sarah Wilds | 65 | B. | W. | G. | D. | R | 4/21 | | X | 6/29 | EXEC |
| 025 | Mary Bradbury[f] | 75 | B. | W. | G. | D. | R | 4/26 | | X | 9/09 | ESC |
| 029 | George Burroughs | 41 | B. | W. | G. | D. | R | 4/30 | | X | 8/05 | EXEC |
| 030 | Lydia Dustin[b] | 65 | B. | W. | G. | D. | R | 4/30 | | X | | DIED |
| 031 | Philip English | 41 | B. | W. | G. | D. | R | 4/30 | | X | | ESC |
| 032 | Dorcas Hoar[e] | 60 | B. | W. | G. | D. | R | 4/30 | 9/21 | X | 9/09 | RPRV |
| 033 | Susanna Martin | 66 | B. | W. | G. | D. | R | 4/30 | | X | 6/29 | EXEC |
| 039 | Sarah Dustin[b] | 39 | B. | W. | G. | D. | R | 5/07 | | X | | SCJ |
| 042 | George Jacobs, Sr | 76 | B. | W. | G. | D. | R | 5/10 | | X | 8/05 | EXEC |
| 044 | John Willard | 33 | B. | W. | G. | D. | R | 5/10 | | X | 8/05 | EXEC |
| 045 | Alice Parker | | B. | W. | G. | D. | R | 5/12 | | X | 9/09 | EXEC |
| 046 | Ann Pudeator | 65 | B. | W. | G. | D. | R | 5/12 | | X | 9/09 | EXEC |
| 057 | Roger Toothaker | 58 | B. | W. | G. | D. | R | 5/18 | | X | | DIED |
| 067 | Martha Carrier | 38 | B. | W. | G. | D. | R | 5/28 | | X | 8/05 | EXEC |
| 071 | Elizabeth How | 54 | B. | W. | G. | D. | R | 5/28 | | X | 6/29 | EXEC |
| 073 | Wilmot Reed | 55 | B. | W. | G. | D. | R | 5/28 | | X | 9/17 | EXEC |
| 081 | Job Tukey[b] | 27 | B. | W. | G. | D. | R | 6/04 | | X | | SCJ |
| 104 | Margaret Scott | 72 | B. | W. | G. | D. | R | 8/05 | | X | 9/17 | EXEC |
| 109 | Samuel Wardwell[e] | 49 | B. | W. | G. | D. | R | 8/15 | 9/01 | X | 9/17 | EXEC |
| 126 | Mary Parker[g] | 55 | B. | W. | G. | D. | R | 9/01 | | X | 9/17 | EXEC |

[a] This is a chronological list of persons charged with non-spectral acts of witchcraft during the course of the Salem witch trials. The information is extracted from the Master List of the accused at the end of this article. Since the focus of this inquiry is on the use that the court of oyer and terminer made of the three forms of evidence presented in the trials, only those who were accused before the last action of the court on 22 September 1692 are included in this list. This list is indebted to Weisman (*Witchcraft, magic, and religion*, pp. 208–16). Twenty-nine names in his Appendix C are marked by an asterisk, indicating that non-spectral acts of witchcraft were charged against them. Mary Parker is the single exception, and the basis of her inclusion is discussed in the text. The most significant information on this chart is the indication that every person who was put to death during the Salem witchcraft trials bore charges of non-spectral acts of witchcraft in their indictment. Twenty-four of the thirty persons so charged were brought to trial. For a key to the headings, see Master List.

[b] See note a, Master List.    [c] See note b, Master List.
[d] See note c, Master List.    [e] See note d, Master List.
[f] See note f, Master List.    [g] See note i, Master List, and p. 342 in the text.

with few misgivings by the clergy'. Even more expressly, Godbeer affirms, 'Because these witnesses [to non-spectral acts of witchcraft] did not interpret witch incidents in diabolical terms, their evidence was of little use to the court'.[21] Yet Table 2 suggests that the court took a different view.

Of the one hundred and fifty-six accused before the demise of the court thirty were charged with such non-spectral acts. Twenty-seven, named at Salem, were already in custody when the court was appointed. Three others were added in the Andover phase of accusations. Twenty-four of the twenty-eight persons tried were from this group of thirty. No one was called for trial from the Salem phase who had not been charged with non-spectral acts of witchcraft. Without exception, the twenty persons put to death had borne charges of non-spectral acts.

Mary Parker has already been noted as the only one among this number who is not so identified in Weisman's table. However, her indictment, after citing Martha Sprague's testimony concerning spectral affliction, also speaks of 'Sundry other acts of witchcraft by the said Mary Parker'. Affidavits by John Bullock, John Westgate, and Samuel Shattock contain evidence that is non-spectral in nature.[22] Shattock was one of the most damaging witnesses against Bridget Bishop, and his testimony, together with the corroborating evidence offered by Westgate and Bullock, meets the criteria for conviction described by Perkins.[23] Despite the omission by Weisman it seems clear that Mary Parker's trial, too, included charges of non-spectral acts of witchcraft. Clearly, it would be hard to explain why the court would have allowed her to stand as a single exception to an otherwise uniform practice.

Thus, the smallest subset of prisoners (twenty percent) accounted for eighty-five percent of the trials, and one hundred percent of the executions. Of the six persons charged with non-spectral acts of witchcraft who were *not* called to trial, Philip English escaped, and Roger Toothaker died in prison. The other four were held over for disposition by the superior court of judicature for reasons that remain obscure.[24] Still, it can be confidently affirmed that non-spectral acts of witchcraft provided the one charge that most surely drew the court's attention. The court devoted itself exclusively to persons with those charges as long as individuals with viable cases remained on the docket. Six of the ten last cases heard by the court in its final sitting still carried charges of non-spectral acts of witchcraft. However much spectral evidence may have served as a predisposition to judgment, the court's nearly exclusive interest in this sub-set of prisoners requires an acknowledgment that has not been accorded it.

[21] Weisman, *Witchcraft, magic, and religion*, p. 150; Godbeer, *The devil's dominion*, p. 216.
[22] *Records of Salem witchcraft: copied from the original documents* (2 vols., New York, 1969), II, 153–60.    [23] Drake, *Witchcraft delusion*, I, 41.
[24] These exceptions are a reminder of lacunae in the records, but they do not seriously undermine the argument that the court of oyer and terminer regarded its task as requiring that those charged with non-spectral acts of witchcraft be tried, and that it turned its attention to other prisoners only after it had examined those available with such charges. See note a in the Master List.

There was, however, an ambiguity at the heart of both spectral and non-spectral evidence. Under the puritan rubric it was necessary to establish that the accused had made a covenant with the devil. While spectral appearance was most commonly taken as evidence of a covenant with the devil, it was acknowledged that under some circumstances the devil might also be permitted to impersonate innocent people. Such a 'juggle' would be in keeping with his duplicitous nature, and might even be used by Satan to bring a halt to the proceedings. If the guilty could no longer be distinguished from the innocent, the task of judgment would be hopelessly complicated.[25] Controversy over whether the devil could represent innocent people in spectral form was a thread that ran through the proceedings. This ambivalence about the validity of spectral testimony certainly added tension to the proceedings, which were already overwrought with fear and anxiety.

Yet Weisman and Godbeer are correct in noting a hesitation implicit in testimony concerning non-spectral acts of witchcraft as well. Magic arts for the performance of such non-spectral acts were commonly practised, and did not, in the eyes of many, necessarily constitute a deliberate covenant with the devil. The line of distinction between benevolent and malevolent witchcraft was not as sharply distinguishable as the terms suggest, and the shading from relatively innocent or neutral acts into those malefic acts that demonstrated a 'trafficking' with Satan, only added to the consternation of those charged with evaluating evidence and making judgment.

Complicating matters further, some elements of divination were even undertaken by the accusers – as in Mary Sibley's resort to a 'witches cake' to find out who was tormenting Elizabeth Parris and Abigail Williams – a practice which Parris castigated as 'a going to the Devil for help against the Devil'.[26] Nevertheless, by its actions the court demonstrated the significance it attached to non-spectral evidence by dealing only with persons so charged as long as triable cases were present.

But because of the ambiguities associated with both spectral and non-spectral evidence a third possibility was pursued. On the face of it, the third option appeared ideal. The accused persons themselves might give evidence. Through severe cross-examination the accused might reveal his/her complicity with the devil by self-contradiction or confusion. Or, the accused might offer voluntary confession. As Perkins remarked, what need would there be then for further testimony?[27] Both badgering and pressures to confess were applied at the preliminary hearings, and the subsequent trials. But badgering did not always work, and even confession, when it was offered, required caution, and corroborating evidence. Even so, out of the one hundred and fifty-six indictments, there were fifty confessors, three of whom were also charged with non-spectral acts of malefic witchcraft (Abigail Hobbs, Dorcas Hoar, Samuel Wardwell). However, it will be demonstrated that what appeared to be the

---

[25] Drake, *Witchcraft delusion*, I, 19.
[27] Drake, *Witchcraft delusion*, I, 41.

[26] Upham, *Salem witchcraft*, II, 95, 96.

Table 3. *Chronological chart of confessions*[a]

| No. | Name | Age | B, | W, | G, | D, | R | Init Chrg | Date Conf | Ord Wtch | Date Trial | Final Result |
|-----|------|-----|----|----|----|----|---|-----------|-----------|----------|------------|--------------|
| | | | | | Source | | | | | | | |
| SALEM | | | | | | | | | | | | |
| 001 | Tituba (slave) | | B, | W, | G, | D, | R | 2/29 | 2/29 | | | SCJ |
| 005 | Dorcas Good | 4 | B, | W, | G, | D, | R | 3/23 | 3/23 | | | SCJ |
| 014 | Mary Warren | 20 | B, | W, | G, | | R | 4/18 | 4/21 | | | AFFL |
| 015 | Abigail Hobbs[b] | 22 | B, | W, | G, | D, | R | 4/18 | 4/18 | X | 9/17 | RPRV |
| 023 | Del. Hobbs | | B, | W, | G, | D, | R | 4/21 | 4/22 | | | SCJ |
| 032 | Dorcas Hoar[b] | 60 | B, | W, | G, | D, | R | 4/30 | 9/21 | X | 9/09 | RPRV |
| 043 | Margaret Jacobs | 16 | B, | W, | G, | D, | R | 5/10 | 8/? | | | SCJ |
| 075 | Mary Toothaker | 47 | B, | W, | G, | D, | R | 5/28 | 7/30 | | | SCJ |
| 078 | Candy (slave) | | B, | W, | G, | D, | R | 6/01 | 6/01 | | | SCJ |
| 083 | Margaret Hawkes | | B, | W, | G, | D, | R | 7/01 | 7/? | | | SCJ |
| ANDOVER | | | | | | | | | | | | |
| 088 | Ann Foster | 72 | B, | W, | G, | D, | R | 7/15 | 7/15 | | 9/17 | RPRV |
| 089 | Mary Lacy, Jr | 18 | B, | W, | G, | D, | R | 7/19 | 7/21 | | | SCJ |
| 090 | Mary Lacy, Sr | 40 | B, | W, | G, | D, | R | 7/19 | 7/21 | | 9/17 | RPRV |
| 091 | Andrew Carrier | 15 | B, | W, | G, | D, | R | 7/21 | 7/23 | | | SCJ |
| 092 | Richard Carrier | 18 | B, | W, | G, | D, | R | 7/21 | 7/22 | | | SCJ |
| 093 | Thomas Carrier | 10 | B, | W, | G, | D, | R | 7/21 | 7/21 | | | SCJ |
| 094 | Martha Emerson | 24 | B, | W, | G, | D, | R | 7/22 | 7/23 | | | SCJ |
| 095 | Mary Bridges, Sr | 48 | B, | W, | G, | D, | R | 7/28 | ? | | | SCJ |
| 096 | Hannah Bromage | 60 | B, | W, | G, | D, | R | 7/30 | 7/30 | | | SCJ |
| 098 | Rebecca Eames | 51 | B, | W, | G, | D, | R | 8/01 | 8/19 | | 9/17 | RPRV |
| 103 | John Jackson, Jr | 22 | B, | W, | G, | D, | R | 8/05 | ? | | | SCJ |
| 106 | Sarah Carrier | 7 | B, | W, | G, | D, | R | 8/10 | 8/11 | | | SCJ |
| 107 | Eliz. Johnson, Jr | 22 | B, | W, | G, | D, | R | 8/10 | 8/11 | | | SCJ |
| 108 | Abig. Faulkner, Sr | 40 | B, | W, | G, | D, | R | 8/11 | ? | | 9/17 | RPRV |
| 109 | Samuel Wardwell[b] | 49 | B, | W, | G, | D, | R | 8/15 | 9/01 | X | 9/17 | EXEC |
| 110 | Edward Farrington | 30 | B, | W, | G, | D, | R | 8/15 | 9/17 | | | ? |
| 114 | Wm Barker, Sr | 46 | B, | W, | G, | D, | R | 8/29 | 8/29 | | | SCJ |
| 115 | Mary Barker | 13 | B, | W, | G, | D, | R | 8/29 | 8/29 | | | SCJ |
| 116 | Mary Bridges, Jr | 13 | | W, | G, | D, | R | 8/25 | 8/25 | | | SCJ |
| 117 | Sarah Bridges | 17 | B, | W, | G, | D, | R | 8/25 | 8/25 | | | SCJ |
| 118 | Mary Marston | 27 | B, | W, | G, | D, | R | 8/29 | 8/29 | | | SCJ |
| 119 | Susanna Post | 31 | B, | W, | G, | D, | R | 8/25 | 8/25 | | | SCJ |
| 120 | Hannah Post | 26 | B, | W, | G, | D, | R | 8/25 | 8/25 | | | SCJ |
| 121 | William Barker, Jr | 14 | B, | W, | G, | D, | R | 8/29 | ? | | | SCJ |
| 123 | Eliz. Johnson, Sr | 51 | B, | W, | G, | D, | R | 8/29 | 8/30 | | | SCJ |
| 124 | Stephen Johnson | 13 | B, | W, | G, | D, | R | 8/30 | 9/01 | | | SCJ |
| 125 | Sarah Hawkes | 21 | B, | W, | G, | D, | R | 9/01 | 9/01 | | | SCJ |
| 127 | Mercy Wardwell | 18 | B, | W, | G, | D, | R | 9/01 | 9/01 | | | SCJ |
| 128 | Sarah Wardwell | 42 | B, | W, | G, | D, | R | 9/01 | 9/01 | | | SCJ |
| 136 | Abigail Barker | 36 | B, | W. | G, | D. | R | 9/07 | ? | | | SCJ |
| 137 | Deliverance Dane | 37 | B, | W. | G, | D. | R | 9/07 | ? | | | SCJ |
| 139 | Joseph Draper | 21 | B, | W. | G, | D. | R | 9/07 | 9/? | | | SCJ |
| 140 | Abig. Faulkner, Jr | 9 | B, | W, | G, | D. | R | 9/07 | 9/17 | | | SCJ |
| 141 | Dorothy Faulkner | 12 | B, | W, | G, | D, | R | 9/07 | 9/17 | | | SCJ |
| 143 | Reb. Johnson, Sr | 40 | B, | W, | G, | D. | R | 9/07 | ? | | | SCJ |

Table 3. *Cont.*

| No. | Name | Age | Source | | | | | Init Chrg | Date Conf | Ord Wtch | Date Trial | Final Result |
|---|---|---|---|---|---|---|---|---|---|---|---|---|
| | | | B. | W. | G. | D. | R | | | | | |
| 145 | Mary Osgood | 55 | B. | W. | G. | D. | R | 9/07 | ? | | | SCJ |
| 148 | Hanna Tyler | 14 | B. | W. | | D. | R | 9/07 | 9/16 | | | SCJ |
| 150 | Martha Tyler | 11 | B. | W. | G. | D. | R | 9/07 | 9/16 | | | SCJ |
| 152 | Sarah Wilson, Sr | 44 | B. | W. | G. | D. | R | 9/07 | 9/17 | | | SCJ |
| 153 | Sarah Wilson, Jr | 14 | B. | W. | G. | D. | R | 9/07 | 9/? | | | SCJ |

[a] This is a chronological list of those persons who confessed during the course of the Salem witchcraft trials. This list is extracted from the Master List of the accused at the end of this article. Since the focus of this inquiry is on the use that the court of oyer and terminer made of the three forms of evidence presented in the trials, only those who were accused before the last action of the court on 22 September 1692 are included in this list. For a key to the headings, see Master List. This table demonstrates that the court of oyer and terminer heard no cases including confession until 17 September 1692, and these were the last cases heard by the court. When all cases including charges of non-spectral acts of witchcraft were completed, the court turned to confession as the corollary testimony required to confirm charges of spectral appearance. In hesitating at the point of hanging those who had confessed, the court had no other direction to turn by which to complete its work. In its hesitation public support for its actions was weakened, allowing the governor and council to step in and cancel its proceedings. Confession was the issue upon which the court foundered.

[b] See note d, Master List.

ideal solution for the ambiguity in the first two types of evidence turned out to be the most controversial approach of all.

Arguments related to confession are more complex than those related to spectral evidence and non-spectral acts of witchcraft. The assertion that confessors were spared can be traced to Robert Calef, a Boston merchant who was a persistent critic of both Increase and Cotton Mather following the trials. His book, *More wonders of the invisible world*, was written as a specific counter-statement to what he considered Cotton Mather's credulous account. In a single-paragraph summary of the Salem trials he observed: 'Though the confessing Witches were many; yet not one of them that confessed their own guilt, and abode by their Confession were put to Death'.[28]

Following the assumptions implicit in Calef, it has frequently been asserted that confession, rather than being the surest form of evidence, was the surest way of escaping the wrath of the court. On the surface the argument appears valid. After all, only six confessors were brought to trial, and the only one of them who was put to death was Samuel Wardwell, who, as Calef indicated, had renounced his confession. Arguing back from Calef's observation, Hansen observes that the majority of those executed could have saved their lives by

[28] Robert Calef, *More wonders of the invisible world* (London, 1700), reprinted in Drake, *Witchcraft delusion*, citation in III, 54–5.

459

lying because after the first execution 'it became obvious to everyone that persons who confessed, like Tituba and Dorcas Good, were not being brought to trial'.[29] It is common to treat this attitude toward confession as though it had early become a settled issue. At a 1992 conference in Salem marking the tercentennial anniversary of the trials the statement was made that among the first three accused, Tituba confessed and was not tried, while Sarah Good held to her innocence and was hanged, thus setting the stage for the pattern to follow. The simple logic of that observation was later included in a broadcast on the trials aired by the Canadian Broadcasting Corporation, which had covered the Salem conference.[30]

Yet Tituba and Sarah Good could not have served the prototypical pattern implied. Seventy-nine persons had been indicted at Salem by 1 June (including twenty-one of the twenty-eight who would be tried, and seventeen of the twenty who would be put to death). Since the court of oyer and terminer did not begin its work until 2 June these people had been indicted before *anybody* was tried. They could not have been comparing fates, for there had been no fates to compare.

Similarly, Hansen's argument about confession, cited above, flies in the face of reason.[31] With seventy-nine prisoners to choose from when Bishop was selected for trial, how would 'everyone' immediately discern that it was Tituba and Dorcas Good who made the critical difference, and not any of the other seventy-six who had been passed over for trial?

Assertions about the court's use of confession are dogmatic when compared to the paucity of evidence. Weisman declares, 'In a decision virtually without precedent for capital offenders in Massachusetts Bay, the magistrates chose to exempt confessors from execution. *While the precise date of introduction of the policy is unknown* ... etc.' (emphasis added). Despite the strong assertion, a little later he adds, 'The judicial improvisation on confessions may well constitute the most enigmatic feature of the entire proceedings, *particularly since the magistrates appear not to have disclosed grounds for the policy even to contemporaries*' (emphasis added).[32] Far-reaching consequences have been ascribed to a policy decision that remains undocumented except for hearsay evidence in the popular conversation that surrounded the trials.

In order to understand the role of confession in the proceedings it will be helpful to look more closely at the chronological chart of the confessors. Table 3 lists the fifty individuals whose confessions have been recorded. At the time the court began building its docket only five confessions had been offered. One of these was that of a four year old girl (Dorcas Good), and the other four presented the ambiguity of having served both as accusers and accused (Tituba, Abigail Hobbs, Deliverance Hobbs, Mary Warren). Moreover, Deliverance Hobbs demonstrated evidence of mental instability that would

---

[29] Hansen, *Witchcraft at Salem*, pp. 87–8.
[30] CBC IDEAS, Toronto. Ontario. Canada. David Wilson. producer. The programme was broadcast shortly before Christmas, 1992.     [31] Hansen, *Witchcraft at Salem*, pp. 87–8.
[32] Weisman, *Witchcraft, magic, and religion*, pp. 157, 158.

have made prosecution difficult. Why should a prosecutor have begun with such questionable cases when there was present a pool of prisoners against whom had been offered solid evidence of non-spectral acts of malefic witchcraft, as required by ecclesiastical and criminal law?

Upon the trial of Bridget Bishop the accusers at Salem fell silent. A six week lull in accusations set in while the court and clergy reflected on what had occurred in the first trial, and charges were brought against a second set of five prisoners. It was after their conviction and before their execution that accusations began again, this time at Andover. The first persons named were Ann Foster, her daughter Mary Lacey, Sr, and her granddaughter Mary Lacey, Jr. They immediately confessed, and implicated the five victims about to be hanged as having been present at the same witches sabbats as they (the confessors) had attended. This news ran like wild-fire through the colony. Cotton Mather described it as a remarkable providence, vindicating the judgment of the court, which had experienced criticism in its handling of the trials involving the five victims scheduled for execution.[33] After that, both accusations and confessions proliferated at a rapid rate. Twelve confessions came in the period between the July and August trials, with thirty-two additional confessions between the August and September trials. It is this remarkable upsurge right at the end of the active life of the court which is the most notable feature of the confessions. Although interest in confession had been present from the start, it was not until this dramatic proliferation of confessions at the very end that response to the confessions became a pressing problem. Confessors were, in fact, brought to trial as their numbers increased and the remaining number of those charged with non-spectral acts was reduced.

Table 4 provides a chronological outline of the trials, demonstrating both the charges preferred, and sentences carried out. It provides a ready reference by which to compare the observations of the first three tables with the outcomes in the trials themselves.

During the first four sets of trials (2 June, 29 June, 5 August, 9 September 1692) the court devoted itself exclusively to prisoners from Salem who had been indicted before the court was named, and who bore charges of non-spectral acts of witchcraft. Questions about confession had risen around the preliminary hearings, and some of the judges may have let their personal persuasions be known. But the court itself had not formally ruled about the use to be made of confessions in the trials. Rather than controlling events through the early course of the summer, intense speculation about confession arose only in their last stages.

At the last trial (17 September 1692), six of the ten prisoners tried still bore charges of non-spectral acts of witchcraft, continuing the court's emphasis on the significance of that type of evidence. However, two of the six charged with non-spectral acts of witchcraft had also confessed. The four additional confessors were brought to trial simply on the basis of their confession to the

---

[33] Silverman, *Selected letters*, pp. 40, 41.

Table 4. *Chronological chart of the trials*[a]

| No. | Name | Age | Phase | Init Chrg | Date Conf | Ord Wtch | Date Trial | Final Result |
|---|---|---|---|---|---|---|---|---|
| 2 June 1692 | | | | | | | | |
| 012 | Bridget Bishop | 60 | Salem | 4/18 | | X | 6/02 | EXEC |
| 29 June 1692 | | | | | | | | |
| 002 | Sarah Good | 38 | Salem | 2/29 | | X | 6/29 | EXEC |
| 006 | Rebecca Nurse | 70 | Salem | 3/23 | | X | 6/29 | EXEC |
| 024 | Sarah Wilds | 65 | Salem | 4/21 | | X | 6/29 | EXEC |
| 033 | Susanna Martin | 66 | Salem | 4/30 | | X | 6/29 | EXEC |
| 071 | Elizabeth How | 54 | Salem | 5/28 | | X | 6/29 | EXEC |
| 5 August 1692 | | | | | | | | |
| 010 | Elizabeth Proctor | 41 | Salem | 4/04 | | X | 8/05 | RPRV |
| 011 | John Proctor | 60 | Salem | 4/11 | | X | 8/05 | EXEC |
| 029 | George Burroughs | 41 | Salem | 4/30 | | X | 8/05 | EXEC |
| 042 | George Jacobs, Sr | 76 | Salem | 5/10 | | X | 8/05 | EXEC |
| 044 | John Willard | 33 | Salem | 5/10 | | X | 8/05 | EXEC |
| 067 | Martha Carrier | 38 | Salem | 5/28 | | X | 8/05 | EXEC |
| 9 September 1692 | | | | | | | | |
| 004 | Martha Corey | 65 | Salem | 3/19 | | X | 9/09 | EXEC |
| 020 | Mary Easty | 51 | Salem | 4/21 | | X | 9/09 | EXEC |
| 025 | Mary Bradbury | 75 | Salem | 4/26 | | X | 9/09 | ESC |
| 032 | Dorcas Hoar | 60 | Salem | 4/30 | 9/21 | X | 9/09 | RPRV |
| 045 | Alice Parker | | Salem | 5/12 | | X | 9/09 | EXEC |
| 046 | Ann Pudeator | 65 | Salem | 5/12 | | X | 9/09 | EXEC |
| 17 September 1692 | | | | | | | | |
| 013 | Giles Corey[b] | 80 | Salem | 4/1 | | X | 9/17 | EXEC |
| 015 | Abigail Hobbs | 22 | Salem | 4/18 | 4/18 | X | 9/17 | RPRV |
| 073 | Wilmot Reed | 55 | Salem | 5/28 | | X | 9/17 | EXEC |
| 104 | Margaret Scott | 72 | Andover | 8/05 | | X | 9/17 | EXEC |
| 109 | Samuel Wardwell | 49 | Andover | 8/15 | 9/01 | X | 9/17 | EXEC |
| 126 | Mary Parker | 55 | Andover | 9/01 | | X | 9/17 | EXEC |
| 088 | Ann Foster | 72 | Andover | 7/15 | 7/15 | | 9/17 | RPRV |
| 090 | Mary Lacy, Sr | 40 | Andover | 7/19 | 7/21 | | 9/17 | RPRV |
| 098 | Rebecca Eames | 51 | Andover | 8/01 | 8/19 | | 9/17 | RPRV |
| 108 | Abig. Faulkner, Sr | 40 | Andover | 8/11 | ? | | 9/17 | RPRV |

[a] This is a chronological listing of those persons who were called before the court of oyer and terminer to answer to their indictments. For a key to the headings, see Master List.

[b] See n. 3 above, and note c, Master List.

charges of spectral appearance. There were several firsts at this set of trials. It was the first time that anyone from the Andover accusations was tried. It was the first time that anyone who had confessed was tried. And it was the first time that anyone had been reprieved for reasons other than pregnancy. Each of these firsts demonstrates how abruptly things changed when the court had finished its work with those accused at the Salem phase, and turned to those accused at Andover.

It has already been established that spectral evidence was not allowed to stand by itself as evidence before the court. It is apparent, then, that when triable prisoners charged with non-spectral acts of witchcraft were no longer present on the docket, the court turned to confessors for the necessary corollary evidence to secure conviction in order to carry forward the task which it still regarded as unfinished. This transition by the court provides added reason to recognize that it was deliberately working within the guidelines laid down by Perkins. Once again, the actions of the court confirm the care with which the rules of evidence were being followed.

Among those who confessed before trial, all who were tried appeared at the 17 September 1692 sitting of the court. (Dorcas Hoar did not confess until after conviction, and only shortly before her scheduled execution, set for 22 September.) Though condemning the confessors, because of mounting public controversy the court was unable to bring them to execution. Before the court could meet again the governor first delayed the October sitting, and then the council disbanded the court altogether. Thus the reprieves to confessors granted by the court were the last pattern of sentencing to appear. Once reprieve for confession had been offered, it could not have been repeated, for there were no further trials. Far from providing options of choice throughout the summer, the decisions concerning confessors were the last decisions the court was allowed to make.

## IV

Surprisingly, the juxtaposition between the court's first hearing of confessions, and its last sitting in official capacity, has been passed over without comment. But it would seem to be a more significant coincidence of events than the much touted, though imperfectly understood, failure of the court to hang any of the confessors. Chronologically, it was the court's inability to carry forward the execution of the confessors which brought about the end that Calef most desired – the demise of the court. Following those reprieves, not only was no one else hanged – none were even tried by the court of oyer and terminer. It is unfortunate that Calef's cryptic remark has set the tone for discussion since, obscuring the complex dynamic that underlay the choices of the court.

The substance of the argument presented here agrees with the thesis set forth in another recent study of the court's actions. Just as the court of oyer and terminer has been described as hanging innocent people on the basis of spectral evidence, so have the constables been described as being opportunistic in seizing the goods of accused witches for personal gain. David Brown has demonstrated that, in this matter as well, the legal system meticulously followed the guidelines set forth in English and New English law.[34] If the system

[34] David Brown, 'The forfeitures at Salem, 1692', *The William and Mary Quarterly*, 3rd series, 1 (1993), pp. 85–111.

of magistracy was one that was following protocol in such careful detail, then commonly accepted presuppositions of a system out of control surely misdirect the focus of research. Interestingly enough, the conclusions of both Brown and this argument rest not on new evidence, but on uncluttering misunderstandings attached to the evidence that has been there from the beginning. The failure has not been in the evidence, but in the clarity with which the evidence has been read.

The argument set forth here has been designed to demonstrate that the court performed a much more finely tuned balancing act than is generally recognized. It tried no one based solely on spectral evidence; it hanged no one who had not been charged with what in that day was considered empirical evidence; and its formal consideration of confession came last in the trials and became the issue upon which the court foundered. When the court, in its own day, answered criticism for violating protocols, it is evident that it literally spoke the truth – even though the truth did not succeed in its attempt to shield the colony from what Cotton Mather called a 'heartquake'.[35]

But understanding that does not, of itself, move the scholar closer to a theoretical understanding of why the Salem episode broke with such force upon the colony, nor why it overflowed the elaborate protective barriers raised by the colony's officials until it overtook the innocent caught in its path. That the victims of the Salem trials suffered from malice is abundantly clear. But the question remains, 'Whose malice?' Over the years focus has shifted from the clergy, to the accusers, and to the courts.[36] But none of the conclusions offered are either comprehensive or compelling. The same can be said for attempts to explain the episode by impersonal forces such as mercantile capitalism, misogyny, or classical understandings of deviance.[37]

It is acknowledged that this study, of itself, does little to advance theoretical understanding of the Salem episode. All that has been done here has been to demonstrate that the court moved with caution and within established guidelines. If its actions are to be viewed as deliberate deception to cover its own malice, then the court moved more cannily than it is generally given credit for. If the court, itself, was self-deceived, then the source of that self-deception remains to be more adequately explained.[38]

[35] Drake, *Witchcraft delusion*, I, 78.

[36] Upham, *Salem witchcraft*, cites the puritan clergy, and Cotton Mather in particular. Marion Starkey, *The devil in Massachusetts* (New York, 1950) cites the set of accusers. Weisman, *Witchcraft, magic, and religion*, explains the episode in terms of judicial activism.

[37] Boyer and Nissenbaum, *Salem possessed*, cite the rise of mercantile capitalism as the cause of Salem conflict. John Demos, *Entertaining Satan: witchcraft and the culture of New England* (Oxford, 1982) and Carol Karlsen, *The devil in the shape of a woman* (New York, 1987), each in a different way, takes note of the role of misogyny in the events. Kai Erikson, *Wayward puritans: a study in the sociology of deviance* (New York, 1966) applied classical deviance theory to that period of colonial history.

[38] I am, of course, indebted to the intellectual efforts of those who have provided the corpus of work upon which this analysis is based. But if theoretical assumptions have kept scholars from seeing the 'hard facts' incorporated in this study, it is also true that the changed perspectives these facts call for should influence the theoretical presuppositions with which the episode is now addressed. For a discussion of theoretical implications that could be used to explain this change in perspective see Craker, *Cotton Mather's wrangle with the devil*.

The participants of that day were as perplexed about the causes after it was over as they had been during the process of events. Ann Putnam and Samuel Sewall each offered public confession in church some years after the trials. Cotton Mather recorded some later episodes of self-reflection in his diary. In each instance it is clear that they struggled with their complicity in an event that had obviously gone wrong. But they remained puzzled about how it had gone wrong.[39]

Some time after the trials Calef seized on a turn of the phrase in Mather's defence of the court to make it appear that he admitted the court had proceeded on insufficient evidence. The response to that charge, though appearing anonymously, clearly has the stamp of Mather's hand. It provides the most succinct statement of the official attitude that can be found in the literature:

What was done in the dark Time of our Troubles from the *Invisible World*, all honest Men believe, they did in Conscience of the *Oath* of God upon them, and they followed unto the best of their Understanding, as we are informed, the Precedents of *England* and *Scotland*, and *other Nations* on such dark and doleful Occasion. When they found the Matter beyond the Reach of Mortals, they stopt.[40]

And so, the evidence shows, they did. When the 'more evident and sensible' testimony of non-spectral acts of witchcraft was completed, when spectral appearance and confession were all that was left to judge, the judgment stopped.

But the debate about those judgments has not stopped. Nor will it until analysis is offered that more adequately reflects the perceived reality to which the Salem episode was a response. Clarifying the use the court made of the evidence presented to it will alleviate distortions, and opens the door to a more accurate understanding of the complex interplay of forces at work in the event.

### Master list: chronological chart of accusations

The following is a chronological list of persons accused of witchcraft by some form of legal documentation that remains in the record. This list is a composite of lists compiled by Paul Boyer and Stephen Nissenbaum (B), Richard Weisman (W), Richard Godbeer (G), The Danvers Archival Center (D), and Enders Robinson (R). Each differs in some respects from the others, and no attempt has been made to reconcile those differences. The surviving documentation comes from a variety of sources that can be classified as follows: formal complaint; warrant for arrest; the arrest itself; examination; or record of imprisonment.

The chronological format provides a picture of the flow of events in tabular form. The records are fragmented, and establishment of dates is sometimes

---

[39] Ann Putnam's confession is found in Upham, *Witchcraft delusion*, II, 510. That of Samuel Sewall in *The diary of Samuel Sewall* (New York, 1973), I, 366, 367. Cotton Mather's after-reflections can be found in *The diary of Cotton Mather* (New York, 1957), I, 153, 154, 216.

[40] Drake, *Witchcraft delusion*, III, 122 n. 122.

difficult. The source lists themselves, while agreeing on names, may differ on dates. Generally the earlier of the dates listed has been chosen for inclusion here. Where dates are unclear, secondary factors may suggest one place in the chronology as more appropriate than another. Names for which no dates have been traced are placed at the end of the chronology, though some may well have appeared earlier in the accusations. Clearly there is work still to be done to provide a complete list with standard criteria for inclusion.

## Key to the headings

*No.*   The number shows approximately where in the sequence action against this person was initiated. Information is not complete enough in all cases to assign the number with certainty, but the exact placement is seldom critical to the argument.
*Source*   Which of the source lists include this name.
*Chrg.* (Charge)   The date is that of the initial formal action on record. Where there are question marks, the placement is made on the basis of secondary information that suggests the most likely period for the initial arraignment.
*Conf.* (Confession)   This column is filled only if the individual is recorded as having made a confession. Generally the information is drawn from the indictments. In a few cases, the confession is known through supplementary testimony. Where it is known, the date is that of the first confession. Some of the accused offered confession on more than one occasion.
*Ord. Wtch.* (Ordinary Witchcraft)   This column is filled only if the individual is recorded as having been charged with non-spectral acts of witchcraft.
*Trial*   This column is filled only if the person named went to trial. The date is that on which the trial opened.
*Result*   Several different results occurred that are noted according to the following formula:

AFFL:   Confessed, but then returned to the accusing group as one of the afflicted.
EXEC:   Were executed subsequent to trial.
ESC:   Fled from prison either before or after trial.
DIED:   Died in prison.
RPRV:   Were reprieved following conviction, but still were held in custody.
SCJ:   The case was settled by the Superior Court of Judicature, or by writ of the governor.
?   No further information about the disposition of this case has been found.

Interspersed with the chronological list of accusations is a notation of the trials and executions that were taking place within the same time frame.

| No. | Name | Age | Source B, W, G, D, R | Init Chrg | Date Conf | Ord Wtch | Date Trial | Final Result |
|---|---|---|---|---|---|---|---|---|
| SALEM | | | | | | | | |
| 001 | Tituba (slave) | | B, W, G, D, R | 2/29 | 2/29 | | | SCJ |
| 002 | Sarah Good | 38 | B, W, G, D, R | 2/29 | | X | 6/29 | EXEC |
| 003 | Sarah Osborne | 50 | B, W, G, D, R | 2/29 | | | | DIED |

| No. | Name | Age | Source B. W. G. D. R | | | | | Init Chrg | Date Conf | Ord Wtch | Date Trial | Final Result |
|---|---|---|---|---|---|---|---|---|---|---|---|---|
| 004 | Martha Corey | 65 | B. | W. | G, | D, | R | 3/19 | | X | 9/09 | EXEC |
| 005 | Dorcas Good | 4 | B, | W, | G, | D, | R | 3/23 | 3/23 | | | SCJ |
| 006 | Rebecca Nurse | 70 | B, | W, | G, | D, | R | 3/23 | | X | 6/29 | EXEC |
| 007 | Rachel Clinton[a] | 63 | B, | W, | G, | D, | R | 3/29 | | X | | SCJ |
| 008 | John Lee | | B, | W, | G | | | 4/01 | | | | ? |
| 009 | Sarah Cloyce | 51 | B, | W, | G, | D, | R | 4/04 | | | | SCJ |
| 010 | Elizabeth Proctor[b] | 41 | B, | W, | G, | D, | R | 4/04 | | X | 8/05 | RPRV |
| 011 | John Proctor | 60 | B, | W, | G, | D, | R | 4/11 | | X | 8/05 | EXEC |
| 012 | Bridget Bishop | 60 | B, | W, | G, | D, | R | 4/18 | | X | 6/02 | EXEC |
| 013 | Giles Corey[c] | 80 | B, | W, | G, | D, | R | 4/18 | | X | 9/17 | EXEC |
| 014 | Mary Warren | 20 | B, | W, | G, | | R | 4/18 | 4/21 | | | AFFL |
| 015 | Abigail Hobbs[d] | 22 | B, | W, | G, | D, | R | 4/18 | 4/18 | X | 9/17 | RPRV |
| 016 | Neh. Abbot, Jr[e] | 29 | B, | W, | G, | D, | R | 4/21 | | | | ? |
| 017 | Edward Bishop, Jr | 44 | B, | W, | G, | D, | R | 4/21 | | | | ESC |
| 018 | Sarah Bishop | 41 | B, | W, | G, | D, | R | 4/21 | | | | ESC |
| 019 | Mary Black (slave) | | B, | W, | G, | D, | R | 4/21 | | | | SCJ |
| 020 | Mary Easty | 51 | B, | W, | G, | D, | R | 4/21 | | X | 9/09 | EXEC |
| 021 | Mary English | 40 | B, | W, | G, | D, | R | 4/21 | | | | ESC |
| 022 | William Hobbs | 50 | B, | W, | G, | D, | R | 4/21 | | | | SCJ |
| 023 | Del. Hobbs | | B, | W, | G, | D, | R | 4/21 | 4/22 | | | SCJ |
| 024 | Sarah Wilds | 65 | B, | W, | G, | D, | R | 4/21 | | X | 6/29 | EXEC |
| 025 | Mary Bradbury[f] | 75 | B, | W, | G, | D, | R | 4/26 | | X | 9/09 | ESC |
| 026 | Thomas Dyer | | | | | D, | R | 4/27 | | | | ? |
| 027 | Sam. Passanauton[g] | | | | | D, | R | 4/28 | | | | ? |
| 028 | Thatcher (female slave) | | | | | D, | R | ? | | | | ? |
| 029 | George Burroughs | 41 | B, | W, | G, | D, | R | 4/30 | | X | 8/05 | EXEC |
| 030 | Lydia Dustin[a] | 65 | B, | W, | G, | D, | R | 4/30 | | X | | DIED |
| 031 | Philip English | 41 | B, | W, | G, | D, | R | 4/30 | | X | | ESC |
| 032 | Dorcas Hoar[d] | 60 | B, | W, | G, | D, | R | 4/30 | 9/21 | X | 9/09 | RPRV |
| 033 | Susanna Martin | 66 | B, | W, | G, | D, | R | 4/30 | | X | 6/29 | EXEC |
| 034 | Sarah Murrill | 14 | B, | W, | | D, | R | 4/30 | | | | SCJ |
| 035 | Mary Morey | | B, | W, | G | | | 5/? | | | | SCJ |
| 036 | Mary Cox | | | | | D, | R | 5/? | | | | ? |
| 037 | Bethia Carter, Sr | 47 | B, | W, | G, | D, | R | 5/07 | | | | ? |
| 038 | Bethia Carter, Jr | 21 | | W, | G, | D, | R | 5/07 | | | | ? |
| 039 | Sarah Dustin | 39 | B, | W, | G, | D, | R | 5/07 | | X | | SCJ |
| 040 | Ann Sears | 71 | B, | W, | G, | D, | R | 5/07 | | | | SCJ |
| 041 | Elizabeth Colson | 15 | B, | W, | G, | D, | R | 5/10 | | | | ESC |
| 042 | George Jacobs, Sr | 76 | B, | W, | G, | D, | R | 5/10 | | X | 8/05 | EXEC |
| 043 | Margaret Jacobs | 16 | B, | W, | G, | D, | R | 5/10 | 8/? | | | SCJ |
| 044 | John Willard | 33 | B, | W, | G, | D, | R | 5/10 | | X | 8/05 | EXEC |
| 045 | Alice Parker | | B, | W, | G, | D, | R | 5/12 | | X | 9/09 | EXEC |
| 046 | Ann Pudeator | 65 | B, | W, | G, | D, | R | 5/12 | | X | 9/09 | EXEC |
| 047 | Thomas Hardy | | | | G, | | R | 5/13 | | | | ? |
| 048 | Abigail Somes | 37 | B, | W, | G, | D, | R | 5/13 | | | | SCJ |
| 049 | Dan Andrew | 48 | B, | W, | G, | D, | R | 5/14 | | | | ESC |
| 050 | Sarah Buckley | 70 | B, | W, | G, | D, | R | 5/14 | | | | SCJ |
| 051 | Tom Farrer | 75 | B, | W, | G, | D, | R | 5/14 | | | | SCJ |
| 052 | Elizabeth Hart | 65 | B, | W, | G, | D, | R | 5/14 | | | | SCJ |

| No. | Name | Age | Source B, W, G, D, R | | | | | Init Chrg | Date Conf | Ord Wtch | Date Trial | Final Result |
|-----|------|-----|----|----|----|----|----|------|------|------|------|--------|
| 053 | George Jacobs, Jr | 50 | B, | W, | G, | D, | R | 5/14 | | | | ESC |
| 054 | Rebecca Jacobs | 46 | B, | W, | G, | D, | R | 5/14 | | | | SCJ |
| 055 | Mary Witheridge | 27 | B, | W, | G, | D, | R | 5/14 | | | | SCJ |
| 056 | Mehitabel Downing | 40 | | | G, | D, | R | 5/15 | | | | SCJ |
| 057 | Roger Toothaker | 58 | B, | W, | G, | D, | R | 5/18 | | X | | DIED |
| 058 | Sarah Bassett | 35 | B, | W, | G, | D, | R | 5/21 | | | | SCJ |
| 059 | Sarah Proctor | 15 | B, | W, | G, | D, | R | 5/21 | | | | SCJ |
| 060 | Susanna Roots | 70 | B, | W, | G, | D, | R | 5/21 | | | | SCJ |
| 061 | Mary De Rich | 35 | B, | W, | G, | D, | R | 5/23 | | | | SCJ |
| 062 | Sarah Pease | | B, | W, | G, | D, | R | 5/23 | | | | SCJ |
| 063 | Benjamin Proctor | 33 | B, | W, | G, | D, | R | 5/23 | | | | SCJ |
| 064 | Jerson Toothaker | | B, | W, | G | | | 5/24 | | | | SCJ |
| 065 | Arthur Abbot | 53 | B, | | G, | D, | R | 5/28 | | | | SCJ |
| 066 | Capt. John Alden | 69 | B, | W, | G, | D, | R | 5/28 | | | | ESC |
| 067 | Martha Carrier | 38 | B, | W, | G, | D, | R | 5/28 | | X | 8/05 | EXEC |
| 068 | Elizabeth Cary | 42 | B, | W, | G, | D, | R | 5/28 | | | | ESC |
| 069 | Capt. John Flood | 55 | B, | W, | G, | D, | R | 5/28 | | | | ? |
| 070 | Elizabeth Fosdick | 32 | B, | W, | G, | D, | R | 5/28 | | | | ? |
| 071 | Elizabeth How | 54 | B, | W, | G, | D, | R | 5/28 | | X | 6/29 | EXEC |
| 072 | William Proctor | 17 | B, | W, | G, | D, | R | 5/28 | | | | SCJ |
| 073 | Wilmot Reed | 55 | B, | W, | G, | D, | R | 5/28 | | X | 9/17 | EXEC |
| 074 | Sarah Rice | 61 | B, | W, | G, | D, | R | 5/28 | | | | ? |
| 075 | Mary Toothaker | 47 | B, | W, | G, | D, | R | 5/28 | 7/30 | | | SCJ |
| 076 | Margaret Toothaker | 9 | B, | | G, | D, | R | 5/28 | | | | SCJ |
| 077 | Elizabeth Paine | 53 | B, | W, | G, | D, | R | 5/30 | | | | ? |
| 078 | Candy (slave) | | B, | W, | G, | D, | R | 6/01 | 6/01 | | | SCJ |
| 079 | Sarah Churchill | 20 | | | G, | | R | 6/01 | | | | AFFL |

*First Trial*: 2 June 1692: Bridget Bishop (012)

| No. | Name | Age | Source B, W, G, D, R | | | | | Init Chrg | Date Conf | Ord Wtch | Date Trial | Final Result |
|-----|------|-----|----|----|----|----|----|------|------|------|------|--------|
| 080 | Mary Ireson | 32 | B, | W, | G, | D, | R | 6/04 | | | | SCJ |
| 081 | Job Tukey[a] | 27 | B, | W, | G, | D, | R | 6/04 | | X | | SCJ |
| 082 | Ann Doliver | 29 | B, | W, | G, | D, | R | 6/06 | | | | SCJ |

*First Execution*: 10 June 1692: Bridget Bishop (012)

*Second Trial*: 29 June 1692: Sarah Good (002), Elizabeth How (071), Susannah Martin (033), Rebecca Nurse (006), Sarah Wilds (024)

| No. | Name | Age | Source B, W, G, D, R | | | | | Init Chrg | Date Conf | Ord Wtch | Date Trial | Final Result |
|-----|------|-----|----|----|----|----|----|------|------|------|------|--------|
| 083 | Margaret Hawkes | | B, | W, | G, | D, | R | 7/01 | 7/? | | | SCJ |
| 084 | Sarah Bibber | | | | G | | | ? | | | | AFFL |
| 085 | Mercy Lewis | | | | G | | | ? | | | | AFFL |
| 086 | Susannah Sheldon | | | | G | | | ? | | | | AFFL |
| 087 | Elizabeth Scargen | | | | | D, | R | 7/? | | | | ? |

## ANDOVER

| No. | Name | Age | Source B, W, G, D, R | | | | | Init Chrg | Date Conf | Ord Wtch | Date Trial | Final Result |
|-----|------|-----|----|----|----|----|----|------|------|------|------|--------|
| 088 | Ann Foster | 72 | B, | W, | G, | D, | R | 7/15 | 7/15 | | 9/17 | RPRV |

*Second Execution*: 19 July 1692: Sarah Good (002), Elizabeth How (071), Susannah Martin (033), Rebecca Nurse (006), Sarah Wilds (024)

| No. | Name | Age | Source B, W, G, D, R | | | | | Init Chrg | Date Conf | Ord Wtch | Date Trial | Final Result |
|-----|------|-----|----|----|----|----|----|------|------|------|------|--------|
| 089 | Mary Lacy, Jr | 18 | B, | W, | G, | D, | R | 7/19 | 7/21 | | | SCJ |
| 090 | Mary Lacy, Sr | 40 | B, | W, | G, | D, | R | 7/19 | 7/21 | | 9/17 | RPRV |
| 091 | Andrew Carrier | 15 | B, | W, | G, | D, | R | 7/21 | 7/23 | | | SCJ |
| 092 | Richard Carrier | 18 | B, | W, | G, | D, | R | 7/21 | 7/22 | | | SCJ |
| 093 | Thomas Carrier | 10 | B, | W, | G, | D, | R | 7/21 | 7/21 | | | SCJ |

| No. | Name | Age | Source B, W, G, D, R | | | | | Init Chrg | Date Conf | Ord Wtch | Date Trial | Final Result |
|---|---|---|---|---|---|---|---|---|---|---|---|---|
| 094 | Martha Emerson | 24 | B, | W, | G, | D, | R | 7/22 | 7/23 | | | SCJ |
| 095 | Mary Bridges, Sr | 48 | B, | W, | G, | D, | R | 7/28 | ? | | | SCJ |
| 096 | Hannah Bromage | 60 | B, | W, | G, | D, | R | 7/30 | 7/30 | | | SCJ |
| 097 | Mary Green | 34 | B, | W, | G, | D, | R | 7/30 | | | | ? |
| 098 | Rebecca Eames | 51 | B, | W, | G, | D, | R | 8/01 | 8/19 | | 9/17 | RPRV |
| 099 | Mary Post | 28 | B, | W, | G, | D, | R | 8/02 | | | | SCJ |
| 100 | Mary Clarke | 53 | B, | W, | G, | D, | R | 8/03 | | | | SCJ |

*Third Trial*: 5 Aug. 1692: George Burroughs (029), Martha Carrier (067), George Jacobs, Jr (042), Elizabeth Proctor (010), John Proctor (011), John Willard (044).

| No. | Name | Age | Source B, W, G, D, R | | | | | Init Chrg | Date Conf | Ord Wtch | Date Trial | Final Result |
|---|---|---|---|---|---|---|---|---|---|---|---|---|
| 101 | John Howard | 48 | B, | W, | G, | D, | R | 8/05 | | | | ? |
| 102 | John Jackson, Sr | 50 | B, | W, | G, | D, | R | 8/05 | | | | SCJ |
| 103 | John Jackson, Jr | 22 | B, | W, | G, | D, | R | 8/05 | ? | | | SCJ |
| 104 | Margaret Scott | 72 | B, | W, | G, | D, | R | 8/05 | | X | 9/17 | EXEC |
| 105 | Daniel Eames | 29 | | | | D, | R | 8/09 | | | | ? |
| 106 | Sarah Carrier | 7 | B, | W, | G, | D, | R | 8/10 | 8/11 | | | SCJ |
| 107 | Eliz. Johnson, Jr | 22 | B, | W, | G, | D, | R | 8/10 | 8/11 | | | SCJ |
| 108 | Ab. Faulkner, Sr[h] | 40 | B, | W, | G, | D, | R | 8/11 | ? | | 9/17 | RPRV |
| 109 | Samuel Wardwell[d] | 49 | B, | W, | G, | D, | R | 8/15 | 9/01 | X | 9/17 | EXEC |
| 110 | Edward Farrington | 30 | B, | W, | G, | D, | R | 8/15 | 9/17 | | | ? |
| 111 | Sarah Parker | 22 | | | G, | D, | R | 8/15 | – | | | SCJ |
| 112 | Frances Hutchins | 75 | B, | W, | G, | D, | R | 8/18 | | | | ? |
| 113 | Ruth Wilford | 17 | B, | W, | G, | D, | R | 8/18 | | | | ? |

*Third Execution*: 19 Aug. 1692: George Burroughs (029), Martha Carrier (067), George Jacobs, Jr (042), John Proctor (011), John Willard (044).

| No. | Name | Age | Source B, W, G, D, R | | | | | Init Chrg | Date Conf | Ord Wtch | Date Trial | Final Result |
|---|---|---|---|---|---|---|---|---|---|---|---|---|
| 114 | Wm Barker, Sr | 46 | B, | W, | G, | D, | R | 8/29 | 8/29 | | | SCJ |
| 115 | Mary Barker | 13 | B, | W, | G, | D, | R | 8/29 | 8/29 | | | SCJ |
| 116 | Mary Bridges, Jr | 13 | | W, | G, | D, | R | 8/25 | 8/25 | | | SCJ |
| 117 | Sarah Bridges | 17 | B, | W, | G, | D, | R | 8/25 | 8/25 | | | SCJ |
| 118 | Mary Marston | 27 | B, | W, | G, | D, | R | 8/29 | 8/29 | | | SCJ |
| 119 | Susanna Post | 31 | B, | W, | G, | D, | R | 8/25 | 8/25 | | | SCJ |
| 120 | Hannah Post | 26 | B, | W, | G, | D, | R | 8/25 | 8/25 | | | SCJ |
| 121 | William Barker, Jr | 14 | B, | W, | G, | D, | R | 8/29 | ? | | | SCJ |
| 122 | Abigail Johnson | 10 | B, | W, | G, | D, | R | 8/29 | | | | SCJ |
| 123 | Eliz. Johnson, Sr | 51 | B, | W, | G, | D, | R | 8/29 | 8/30 | | | SCJ |
| 124 | Stephen Johnson | 13 | B, | W, | G, | D, | R | 8/30 | 9/01 | | | SCJ |
| 125 | Sarah Hawkes | 21 | B, | W, | G, | D, | R | 9/01 | 9/01 | | | SCJ |
| 126 | Mary Parker[i] | 55 | B, | W, | G, | D, | R | 9/01 | | X | 9/17 | EXEC |
| 127 | Mercy Wardwell | 18 | B, | W, | G, | D, | R | 9/01 | 9/01 | | | SCJ |
| 128 | Sarah Wardwell | 42 | B, | W, | G, | D, | R | 9/01 | 9/01 | | | SCJ |
| 129 | Eliz. Dicer | | B, | W, | G, | D, | R | 9/03 | | | | ? |
| 130 | Marg. Prince | 62 | B, | W, | G, | D, | R | 9/03 | | | | ? |
| 131 | Mary Colson | 41 | | W, | G, | D, | R | 9/05 | | | | SCJ |
| 132 | Joseph Emons | | B, | W, | G, | D, | R | 9/05 | | | | SCJ |
| 133 | Nicholas Frost | | B, | W, | G, | D, | R | 9/05 | | | | ? |
| 134 | Jane Lilly | 48 | B, | W, | G, | D, | R | 9/05 | | | | SCJ |
| 135 | Mary Taylor | 40 | | W, | G, | D, | R | 9/05 | | | | SCJ |
| 136 | Abigail Barker | 36 | B, | W, | G, | D, | R | 9/07 | ? | | | SCJ |
| 137 | Deliverance Dane | 37 | B, | W, | G, | D, | R | 9/07 | ? | | | SCJ |

| No. | Name | Age | B | W | G | D | R | Init Chrg | Date Conf | Ord Wtch | Date Trial | Final Result |
|---|---|---|---|---|---|---|---|---|---|---|---|---|
| 138 | Dane (male slave) | | | | | D | R | 9/07 | | | | ? |
| 139 | Joseph Draper | 21 | B | W | G | D | R | 9/07 | 9/? | | | SCJ |
| 140 | Abig. Faulkner, Jr | 9 | B | W | G | D | R | 9/07 | 9/17 | | | SCJ |
| 141 | Dorothy Faulkner | 12 | B | W | G | D | R | 9/07 | 9/17 | | | SCJ |
| 142 | Eunice Fry | 51 | B | W | G | D | R | 9/07 | | | | SCJ |
| 143 | Reb. Johnson, Sr | 40 | B | W | G | D | R | 9/07 | ? | | | SCJ |
| 144 | Reb. Johnson, Jr | 17 | | | | D | R | 9/07 | | | | SCJ |
| 145 | Mary Osgood | 55 | B | W | G | D | R | 9/07 | ? | | | SCJ |
| 146 | Henry Salter | 65 | B | W | G | D | R | 9/07 | | | | ? |
| 147 | John Sawdy, Jr | 13 | B | W | G | D | R | 9/07 | | | | ? |
| 148 | Hanna Tyler | 14 | B | W | | D | R | 9/07 | 9/16 | | | SCJ |
| 149 | Joanna Tyler | 11 | | | G | D | R | 9/07 | | | | SCJ |
| 150 | Martha Tyler | 11 | B | W | G | D | R | 9/07 | 9/16 | | | SCJ |
| 151 | Mary Tyler | 40 | | | | D | R | 9/07 | | | | SCJ |
| 152 | Sarah Wilson, Sr | 44 | B | W | G | D | R | 9/07 | 9/17 | | | SCJ |
| 153 | Sarah Wilson, Jr | 14 | B | W | G | D | R | 9/07 | 9/? | | | SCJ |

*Fourth Trial*: 9 Sept. 1692: Mary Bradbury (025), Martha Corey (004), Mary Easty (020), D. Hoar (032), Alice Parker (045), Ann Pudeator (046).

| No. | Name | Age | B | W | G | D | R | Init Chrg | Date Conf | Ord Wtch | Date Trial | Final Result |
|---|---|---|---|---|---|---|---|---|---|---|---|---|
| 154 | Hannah Carroll | | B | W | G | D | R | 9/10 | | | | ? |
| 155 | Sarah (Davis) Cole | 42 | B | | G | D | R | 9/10 | | | | SCJ |
| 156 | Joan Peney | 72 | B | W | G | D | R | 9/13 | | | | ? |

*Fifth Trial*: 17 Sept. 1692: Abigail Hobbs (022), Wilmot Reed (073), [Giles Corey refused to plead] (013), Rebecca Eames (098), Abigail Faulkner (108), Ann Foster (088), Mary Lacey, Sr (090), Mary Parker (126), Margaret Scott (104), Samuel Wardwell (109).

*Fourth Execution*: 19 Sept. 1692: Giles Corey pressed to death.

*Fifth Execution*: 22 Sept. 1692: Martha Corey (004), Mary Easty (020), Dorcas Hoar (032), Alice Parker (045), Ann Pudeator (046), Mary Parker (126), Margaret Scott (104), Samuel Wardwell (109).

| No. | Name | Age | B | W | G | D | R | Init Chrg | Date Conf | Ord Wtch | Date Trial | Final Result |
|---|---|---|---|---|---|---|---|---|---|---|---|---|
| 157 | Sarah (Aslet) Cole | 30 | B | W | G | D | R | 10/01 | | | | SCJ |
| 158 | Phoebe Day | 39 | | | G | D | R | 10/? | | | | ? |
| 159 | Mary Roe | 34 | | | | D | R | 10/? | | | | ? |
| 160 | Rachel Vinson | 62 | | | G | D | R | 10/? | | | | ? |
| 161 | Rebecca Dike | 41 | B | W | G | D | R | 11/05 | | | | ? |
| 162 | Esther Elwell | 53 | B | W | G | D | R | 11/05 | | | | ? |
| 163 | Abigail Roe | 15 | B | W | G | D | R | 11/05 | | | | ? |
| 164 | John Durrant | 44 | | | | D | R | ? | | | | DIED |
| 165 | Henry Somers | | | | | D | R | ? | | | | ? |
| 166 | Edward Wooland | | | | | D | R | ? | | | | ? |
| 167 | Mary Watkins[j] | | | | | | R | ? | | | | ? |

[a] Rachel Clinton, Lydia Dustin, Sarah Dustin, and Job Tukey are the only persons charged with non-spectral acts of witchcraft who might have been tried by the court of oyer and terminer but were not. It is unclear why the court passed over these persons, but any number of circumstances could have contributed to that choice without cancelling the underlying principle that those bearing charges of non-spectral acts of witchcraft were the first to be tried. Job Tukey was tried by the superior court of

judicature on 10 Jan. 1693 (Upham, *Salem witchcraft*, II, 349). Lydia and Sarah Dustin were tried on 31 Jan. 1693. All were acquitted, though Lydia Dustin died in prison before paying her prison charges. Calef seems to have confused Lydia and Sarah Dustin in his account (Drake, *Witchcraft delusion*, III, 127–8).

ᵇ Elizabeth Proctor was reprieved when found to be pregnant. She was the only one who had not confessed who was reprieved.

ᶜ Technically, Giles Corey was not tried because he refused to plead to the charges. But in ordering that he be pressed with weights, the court, in effect, sentenced him to death, and he is included as among those tried.

ᵈ The dilemma of the court is aptly illustrated in its treatment of the three instances that combined charges of non-spectral acts of witchcraft with confession. Abigail Hobbs, Dorcas Hoar, and Samuel Wardwell confessed under very different circumstances. Abigail Hobbs confessed at the time of her indictment, and subsequently testified against others. In this, she served as a prototype for others who would confess after her. Dorcas Hoar maintained her innocence through her trial, and confessed only hours before her scheduled execution on 22 Sept. 1692. John Hale interceded on her behalf and she was granted a one month reprieve, but was eventually released by the superior court of judicature. Hoar was the only one who literally 'saved her life through confession'. Samuel Wardwell had a reputation as a 'cunning man' well before the trials. He confessed at the time of his indictment. By later withdrawing his confession the charges of non-spectral acts of witchcraft still stood against him, and he was condemned and hanged as the others who were so charged.

ᵉ Nehemia Abbot, Jr is apparently the only one accused against whom charges were later withdrawn by the accusing young women.

ᶠ Mary Bradbury was the only prisoner to escape after conviction. The others who fled did so either before their arrest, or after their indictment but before being called for trial. The Danvers Archival Center and Robinson place the date of her arrest as 28 or 29 June, rather than 26 April as listed by Boyer and Weisman.

ᵍ Samuel Passanauton: the only American Indian named on the list.

ʰ Abigail Faulkner's confession is ambivalent, seeming both to admit and deny complicity with the devil in the same statement. Given the court's predisposition to judgment, this listing assumes that the judges gave greater weight to the confession than to the denial (*RSW*, II, 131).

ⁱ Mary Parker is the only one among the executed who is not identified by Weisman (*Witchcraft, magic, and religion*, pp. 208–16) as having been charged with non-spectral acts of witchcraft. See text, p. 342, for discussion.

ʲ Mary Watkins is listed by Calef as having been sold into Virginia (Drake, *Witchcraft delusion*, II, 129). Robinson (*Salem witchcraft*, p. 357) describes her as a young white woman who was sold into slavery sometime after 11 Aug. 1693 to pay for her imprisonment.

## Notes on exceptions to the lists

The following individuals appear on one or more of the lists cited above, but were omitted from this list for the following reasons:

(1) Martha Sparks is listed by B, W, and G; but Robinson describes her as having been imprisoned by Lt. Gov. Thomas Danforth in Nov. 1691, which would have placed her before the Salem trials. She remained imprisoned until 6 Dec. 1692.

(2) Arthur Abbot is listed by Boyer and Nissenbaum as Nehemia Abbot, Sr.

471

(3) Sarah Davis, listed by Godbeer, is the unmarried name of Sarah (Davis) Rice, also listed by Godbeer.

(4) Rachel Hatfield, listed by Godbeer, is the unmarried name of Rachel (Hatfield) Clinton, also listed by Godbeer.

(5) Robinson lists 'Three or four men' imprisoned at Ipswich with no further data.

(6) Robinson lists four infant children who were imprisoned with their mothers. Two of them died under prison conditions. The mothers were: Sarah Good (child died), Elizabeth Scargen (child died), Sarah Wardwell, and Rebecca Dike. The children, indeed, innocently suffered as a result of the witchcraft trials, but are omitted here because they were not subject to court action, except as left in the care of their mothers.

# New England Witch-Hunting and the Politics
# of Reason in the Early Republic

### PHILIP GOULD

S INCE its appearance during the height of the McCarthy era,
Arthur Miller's *The Crucible* (1953) has been read as a
scathing commentary on postwar American political culture. Indeed, the author himself was far from subtle in suggesting the
way in which the Salem witchcraft trials provided a historical
metaphor for a contemporary crisis: "In the countries of the
Communist ideology, all resistance of any import is linked to the
totally malign capitalist succubi, and in America any man who is
not reactionary in his views is open to the charge of alliance with
Red hell." The ease with which Puritan witch-hunting was appropriated for ideological purposes during the 1950s was not, of
course, restricted to literary texts. One notable historian, Marion
Starkey, referred to the "delusion" of 1692 as "an allegory of our
times." Granted the sophistication that historical distance provides, we now rather easily recognize how postwar political anxieties impinged on the historical record of seventeenth-century
New England.[1] Such impositions were not characteristic of the
1950s alone, however. They are also readily discovered in the
early American republic.

I would like to thank Dale M. Bauer, Sargent Bush, Jr., and Charles L. Cohen, who
each read earlier versions of this essay and offered unique insights and suggestions.

[1] Arthur Miller, *The Crucible* (New York: Viking, 1981), p. 34; Marion L. Starkey, *The
Devil in Massachusetts: A Modern Enquiry into the Salem Witch Trials* (New York: Alfred A. Knopf, 1949), pp. ix–x. More recent historical scholarship on Salem is not, of
course, colored by postwar politics and has addressed the subject of witch-hunting in
diverse and compelling ways. See, e.g., Paul Boyer and Stephen Nissenbaum, *Salem Possessed: The Social Origins of Witchcraft* (Cambridge: Harvard University Press, 1974);
John P. Demos, *Entertaining Satan: Witchcraft and the Culture of Early New England*
(New York: Oxford University Press, 1982); Carol Karlsen, *The Devil in the Shape of a
Woman: Witchcraft in Colonial New England* (New York: Norton, 1987); Larry P. Gragg,

Between the 1790s and 1830s, both historical and literary treatments of Puritan witch-hunting, particularly the infamous episode at Salem, were saturated with words such as "bigotry" and "superstition," or "zeal," "delusion," and "infatuation." As much a product of the period in which it was written as the period being written about, this language of irrationality reflected the political and social anxieties rampant in the early republic. These anxieties derived from both the rise of modern political parties and the gradual democratization of politics. If such trends led to "witch-hunts," such as the Federalists' passage of the Alien and Sedition Acts in 1798, they also produced the first truly popular political campaigns during the 1820s and 1830s, Jacksonian spectacles the zealous excesses of which conservatives viewed with horror. In the midst of this uneasy transition to modern politics, historical and literary writers, both traditionally responsible for inculcating virtue in republican citizens, turned to Salem for proof of the dangers inherent in the people's unbridled "passions." The success of the writers' mission, however, was complicated not only by a shifting political environment but also by emerging literary trends as well. By excavating and analyzing such complications, we can develop a more sophisticated historical and literary understanding of the genre of witchcraft writing, and by viewing a number of early texts—the anonymous *The Witch of New England* (1824) and James Nelson Barker's *The Tragedy of Superstition* (1824), as well as John Neal's *Rachel Dyer* (1828) and John Greenleaf Whittier's *Legends of New England* (1831)—in their own terms, we can take proper measure of their value beyond the usual standard that has been applied, namely, the degree to which they influenced Hawthorne's subsequent treatment of the subject.

---

*A Quest for Security: The Life of Samuel Parris* (New York: Greenwood Press, 1990); and Richard Godbeer, *The Devil's Dominion: Magic and Religion in Early New England* (Cambridge: Cambridge University Press, 1992).

Recently, Bernard Rosenthal has traced the legacy of Salem into modern times. My focus is confined to the early national era, and in my argument about witch-hunting as a political metaphor, I differ from Rosenthal, who sees Salem as a metaphor of persecution. See *Salem Story: Reading the Witch Trials of 1692* (Cambridge: Cambridge University Press, 1993).

I

Late eighteenth-century Americans conceived of a republic in both behavioral and institutional terms. As many scholars over the last thirty years have shown, the political culture of the Revolutionary era derived in part from the classical theory that the very existence of a republic depended largely upon the people's devotion to the public good.[2] "Virtue" described the full expression of civic personality, which rulers and people realized principally through public service and the call to arms. While many American Revolutionaries admired the institutional "balance" of the English constitution (the one, the few, and the many expressed by the Crown, Lords, and Commons), they embraced as well a political world view that was essentially corporate, consensual, and hierarchical. The bane of republican stability were factions, which openly contended for particular "interests" at the expense of the common good.

Powerful and outspoken, English opposition writer Henry St. John, Lord Bolingbroke, whose writings later influenced American Revolutionaries, excoriated the host of power-seeking stock-jobbers and financiers who flocked to the Walpole administration. These sycophants, dubbed the Court, Bolingbroke contrasted with the people at large, or the Country. "Faction is to party," he began an analogy, "what the superlative is to the positive: party is a political evil, and faction is the worst of all parties."[3] Factions theoretically demonstrated the "basest passions," in the clutches of which "men were unwilling to sacrifice their immediate desires for the corporate good."[4] As Daniel Walker Howe has shown, Common Sense philosophy also influenced this conservative politicization of faculty psychology. As in the

---

[2]The historiography on republicanism is vast, and over the past twenty-five years, it has sustained challenges as well as new syntheses. The original triumvirate of texts on republicanism and American political culture is Bernard Bailyn's *The Ideological Origins of the American Revolution* (Cambridge: Harvard University Press, 1967), Gordon Wood's *The Creation of the American Republic, 1776–87* (Chapel Hill: University of North Carolina Press, 1969), and J. G. A. Pocock's *The Machiavellian Moment: Florentine Political Thought and the Atlantic Republican Tradition* (Princeton: Princeton University Press, 1975). Because of the nature of my argument and practical considerations of space, I will not treat competing views.

[3]Quoted by Bailyn, in *Ideological Origins*, p. 151, n. 12.

[4]Wood, *Creation of the American Republic*, p. 59.

state itself, the individual's faculties were arranged in a hierarchy ideally governed by reason: "Left to themselves, the lower powers [of mechanical and appetitive impulses] would escape control and wreak havoc. An unregulated faculty—whether pride, licentiousness, or some other appetite or emotion—was called a 'passion.'"[5]

The Revolutionary settlement of 1787–88 significantly recast the danger of factions. In the tenth *Federalist Paper*, of course, James Madison had theorized that factions could be controlled only, not eliminated. But if the new formulation, as Gordon Wood has persuasively argued, emphasized the institutional means by which the emerging union could limit the danger of tyrannical majorities in the states, it did not abandon traditional assumptions about civic virtue and the common good.[6] Ronald P. Formisano similarly has claimed that "The period from the 1780s to the 1820s possessed almost a split personality: intensely passionate in partisan conviction but inhibited by antipartisan assumptions about the nature of politics and society."[7] Others have extended this line of argument to the development of the second American party system between the 1820s and 1840. During this era, American Whigs drew upon republicanism's longstanding fears of conspiracy to denounce the demagogic threat of "King Andrew," while Democrats played upon republican suspicions of "moneyed interests" to attack Whig plans for government-supported business enterprises, particularly the National Bank. Whigs actually tried to turn their apparent lack of "party" organization into a virtue. Similarly, the Democrats fashioned themselves the Bolingbrokean "Country"—"the tribune or sentinel of the people in defense of the republic"[8]— which was a deft maneuver, since they were the group *in* power until 1840. Histori-

[5]Daniel Walker Howe, *The Political Culture of the American Whigs* (Chicago: University of Chicago Press, 1979), p. 29.

[6]Wood makes the cogent point that during the Constitutional debates of the late 1780s, it was actually the Antifederalists who embraced what we call a "modern" understanding of pluralist, interest-group politics. See his *The Radicalism of the American Revolution* (New York: Vintage, 1991), pp. 243–70.

[7]Ronald P. Formisano, *The Transformation of Political Culture: Massachusetts Parties, 1790s–1840s* (New York: Oxford University Press, 1983), p. 10.

[8]Major Wilson, "Republicanism and the Idea of Party in the Jacksonian Period," *Journal of the Early Republic* 8 (Winter 1988): 419–42, 423.

ans thus have described the 1820s as a "watershed decade" characterized by a "fluid character" and a capacity for "blending" premodern and modern styles.[9] Even though political parties selfishly appropriated—and often redefined—premodern political assumptions, the rhetoric of republicanism endured.[10]

Embedded in the conservative strain of this rhetoric was a lament about the very nature of democracy itself. From the 1790s to the 1830s, the specter of Jeffersonian and, later, Jacksonian democracy haunted Federalists, disenchanted National Republicans, and Whigs, who continued to embrace a republican ideal of a consensual and hierarchical order. Facing expanding electorates and parvenu political leaders, these political conservatives often employed the language of premodern politics to forestall what they envisioned to be social and political chaos. In their writings, "reason" and "passions" became the code-words for hierarchical order and democratic anarchy. "National passions," John Adams argued, were dangerous things: "This national attachment to an elective first magistrate, where there is no competition is very great; but where there is a competition, the passions of his party, are inflamed by it, into a more ardent enthusiasm."[11] Benjamin Rush considered democracy a kind of disease: "anarchia," as he called it, "a species of insanity," which was characterized by "[t]he excess of the passion for liberty."[12]

Appalled by Jeffersonian deism and egalitarianism, New England divines warned of "the propensities and passions peculiar

[9]Formisano, *Transformation*, pp. 15–16; Richard P. McCormick, *The Second American Party System: Party Formation in the Jacksonian Era* (New York: Norton, 1966), p. 12; and Wilson, "Idea of Party," p. 431.

[10]Most historians of this subject note the self-serving nature of this partisan appropriation of republican ideology. See, esp., Marc W. Kruman, "The Second American Party System and the Transformation of Revolutionary Republicanism," *Journal of the Early Republic* 12 (Winter 1992): 509–37.

[11]John Adams, *Discourses on Davila: A Series of Papers on Political History Written in the Year 1790, and then Published in the Gazette of the United States* (Boston: Russell and Cutler, 1805), p. 57.

[12]Benjamin Rush, "Influence of the American Revolution," in *The Selected Writings of Benjamin Rush* (New York: Philosophical Library, 1947), p. 333, quoted by Melvin Yazawa in *From Colonies to Commonwealth: Familial Ideology and the Beginnings of the American Republic* (Baltimore: Johns Hopkins University Press, 1985), p. 152, and Kenneth Silverman, *A Cultural History of the American Revolution* (1967; reprinted, New York: Columbia University Press, 1987), p. 512.

to human nature . . . [the] destructive courses of error and delusion"; the masses' "strong delusions," John Smalley observed, had fueled "the boasted experiment of liberty and revolutions."[13] Rulers, of course, could be seduced too. Mercy Otis Warren advocated "the control of reason" to prevent ambitious authorities from becoming tyrants.[14] The language of George Washington's "Farewell Address" (1796) is quite pointed in this regard. Factions, he announced, were engineered by "ambitious, corrupted, *or* deluded citizens" (italics mine) who "gild[ed]" their motives in the cant of patriotism."[15] Factions thus commingled deluded sincerity and designing calculation.

For many conservative New Englanders, the French Revolution confirmed their worst fears. High Federalists like Timothy Dwight and Noah Webster called the Reign of Terror a "dance of Jacobin phrenzy" and "a whirlwind, a tornado of passions."[16] In "The Revolution in France" (1794) Webster scrupulously analyzed the theoretical distinction between "superstition" and "enthusiasm," but in the end he concluded simply enough that both foibles produced the same disastrous results. What struck Webster as the most darkly ironic feature of the French Revolution was that, as deists, the Jacobins had turned reason itself into a deity to be fanatically worshiped. "But I will meet your philosophy upon your own ground," he challenged the Jacobins (and their Jeffersonian supporters), "and demonstrate, by the very decrees which demolish the ancient superstition, that you yourselves are the most bigotted men in existence." What he called "the mad rancor of party and faction" described only the worst

[13]Stephen Peabody, "A Sermon Delivered at Concord Before the Honourable General Court of the State of New Hampshire at the Annual Election," in *Political Sermons of the American Founding Era, 1730–1805*, ed. Ellis Sandoz (Indianapolis: Liberty Press, 1991), p. 1332, and John Smalley, "On the Evils of a Weak Government," in *Political Sermons*, p. 1444.

[14]Mercy Otis Warren, *History of the Rise, Progress, and Termination of the American Revolution* (1805), ed. Lester Cohen, 2 vols. (Indianapolis: Liberty Press, 1988), 1:3.

[15]George Washington, "Farewell Address," in *The Speeches, Addresses and Messages of the Several Presidents of the United States* (Philadelphia: Robert Desilver, 1825), pp. 109–10.

[16]Timothy Dwight, "The Duty of Americans, at the Present Crisis," in *Political Sermons*, p. 1382, and Noah Webster, "The Revolution in France," in *Political Sermons*, p. 1298.

instance of the inevitable pitfalls of democracy, and, in this respect, the abundance of words like "superstition," "enthusiasm," and "bigotry" throughout his narrative provide a political glossary for later narratives about Salem.[17]

The politics of faculty psychology sounded well into the early antebellum era. In "The Duties of an American Citizen" (1825), Francis Wayland, the pastor of Boston's First Baptist Church, struck the chord in earnest: if the people's "decisions become the dictates of passion and venality, rather than of reason and of right," he admonished, "that moment are our liberties at an end; and glad to escape the despotism of millions, we shall flee to the despotism of one."[18] Emma Willard, the founder of the Troy Female Seminary, included Washington's "Farewell Address" as one of three documents worth reprinting (the others were the Declaration of Independence and the Constitution) in the appendix to the first edition of her *History of the United States* (1828). Willard praised Washington for his "paternal anxiety" to instill "those maxims of virtue and prudence, from which [America's] prosperous condition had arisen. . . . Americans should learn [them] in youth, and practice [them] in later life."[19]

## II

To early national history writers, the tragedy at Salem was a decidedly political event. The episode of 1692 took on the quality of a "tornado," a "fury," or a "furious volcano."[20] Certainly Puritan sources, such as Cotton Mather and Robert Calef, offered evidence of social and political disorder,[21] but early nationals de-

---

[17]Webster, "Revolution in France," pp. 1254, 1264.

[18]Francis Wayland, *The Duties of an American Citizen* (Boston: James Loring, 1825), p. 37.

[19]Emma Willard, *History of the United States, or Republic of America* (New York: White, Gallaher, and White, 1828), p. xl.

[20]Jedidiah Morse and Elijah Parish, *A Compendious History of New England* (London: William Burton, 1808), p. 165; Hannah Adams, *A Summary History of New England* (Dedham: H. Mann and J. H. Adams, 1799), p. 163; Epaphras Hoyt, *Antiquarian Researches: Comprising a History of the Indian Wars* (Greenfield, Mass.: Ansel Phelps, 1824), p. 175.

[21]Cotton Mather, *The Wonders of the Invisible World* (1693) (Amherst, Wis.: Amherst Press, 1862), p. 91; Robert Calef, *More Wonders of the Invisible World* (1700) (Bainbridge, N.Y.: York Mail-Print, 1972), pp. 152–53.

veloped it into the episode's central theme and specifically asked their readers to apply its lessons to contemporary times. The Unitarian minister Charles Wentworth Upham, for example, concluded his *Lectures on Witchcraft* (1832) with the exhortation that "whenever a community gives way to its passions . . . and casts off the restraints of reason, there is a delusion. . . . It would be wiser to direct our ridicule and reproaches to the delusions of our own times, rather than to those of a previous age, and it becomes us to treat with charity and mercy the failings of our predecessors, at least until we have ceased to imitate and repeat them."[22]

In this same vein, Abiel Abbot reminded his readers that "[t]his delusion [of witch-hunting] is not confined to religious subjects." He argued that "There seems founded deep in human nature passions, which often prevail over the understanding, an enthusiasm, a frenzy which hears not the voice of reason."[23] Compare Abbot's final summation of the contemporary relevance of ancestral history with that of Charles Goodrich, one of the most popular historians of the antebellum era. Abbot asked,

Have not many been seen in a frenzy on politics, assembled and full of tumult, like the Ephesians, crying out, great is their cause? but they know not why, or wherefore; they will drag this man to death, and that they will raise on their shoulders, but they know not why they kill the one, and extol the other. It is the same spirit that pervades the quack in all professions, and by which his deceptions are so successful.

For Goodrich, reason also provided the only remedy:

Now, whenever we see a community divided into parties, and agitated by some general excitement—when we feel ourselves borne along on one side or the other, by the popular tide, let us inquire whether we are not acting under the influence of a delusion, which a few years, perhaps a few months, or days, may dispel and expose. Nor, at such a time, let us regard our sincerity . . . or the seeming . . . certainty of our reason-

---

[22]Charles Wentworth Upham, *Lectures on Witchcraft, Comprising a History of the Delusion in Salem in 1692*, 2d ed. (Boston: Carter and Hendee, 1832), pp. 277–78.

[23]Abiel Abbot, *History of Andover from Its Settlement to 1829* (Andover: Flagg and Gould, 1829), pp. 172–73.

ings, as furnishing an absolute assurance that, after all, we do not mistake, and that our opponents are right.[24]

At the mercy of political "quacks" and the "popular tide" (a metaphor, we might note, for an inevitable force of nature), the republic appears caught in an endless cycle of deluded majorities manipulated by skillful demagogues.

The era's sectarian hostility between orthodox Calvinists and Unitarians over the meaning of Puritan history was nowhere more visible than in the historiographic, literary, and legal battles between the orthodox minister Jedidiah Morse and the liberal Hannah Adams. If Morse, along with Elijah Parish, struggled more assiduously than did Adams to protect the Puritans from contemporary ridicule (suggesting, for example, that colonial New England's belief in witchcraft was an English inheritance derived from authorities such as Joseph Glanvil and Mathew Hale), both he and Adams still agreed that the episode instanced the perilous fragility of the people. Morse lamented that "a terror of the public mind . . . was driving the people to the most desperate conduct," while Adams observed that the "strength of prejudice" and "the force of imagination" produced a "gloom and horror" that "in some respects appeared more replete with calamity, than even the devastations of war." For Adams and others, the real "tragedy" of Salem occurred when "profligate characters" began to accuse those "of superior rank and character"—the "most respectable families" and the "best people" such as Governor Phips's wife.[25]

In examining the events at Salem, early national elites were really considering their own waning political authority. As they meditated upon a "delusion," in the midst of which established hierarchies had suddenly collapsed, they understandably obsessed about its causes. How had the "pillars of civil government [been] shaken"?[26] What struck so many as particularly perverse

---

[24]Charles Goodrich, *A History of the United States of America* (Hartford: H. F. Sumner, 1833), pp. 173, 162.

[25]Morse, *Compendious History*, pp. 170, 165; Adams, *Summary History*, pp. 160, 162, 164–65.

[26]David Ramsay, *History of the United States* (Philadelphia: Matthew Carey, 1818), p. 90.

about the Salem witch trials was the political power temporarily wielded by the disenfranchised—young girls like Elizabeth Parris and Abigail Williams, along with Tituba, Samuel Parris's West Indian slave, and dozens more Puritan women. Men like Morse and Charles Goodrich shuddered over these outsiders' ability to shape political events. Goodrich proclaimed that when "[c]hildren of not more than twelve years of age were permitted to give their testimony [and] Indians were called to tell their stories of wonder, and women of nocturnal frights," then "the counsels of the age were unheard [and] wisdom was confounded." Native Americans were to blame as well. Morse argued that the Puritan fathers, frightfully isolated in the New England wilderness, were vulnerable to local legends of the fireside which "furnished fuel for approaching terrors."[27] In this manner, early national history writing codified the civic and political importance of reason *and* the stereotypes underwriting the period's disenfranchisement of women and people of color. Puritan leaders were criticized chiefly for their credulity rather than their wickedness, a formula that vindicated the ruling elite's right to rule as the very corollary of the demonstration that it had not ruled well enough.

Cotton Mather bore the brunt of this criticism.[28] In addition to the charges about Mather's credulity, the Unitarians marshaled republican ideology to wage their attack on the divine.[29] Charles Wentworth Upham's *Lectures on Witchcraft*, for example, arouses Whiggish fears of conspiracy by portraying Mather as a calculating and overly ambitious demagogue, one who, as Upham says, showed "an inordinate love of temporal power and distinction." At George Burroughs's execution, Mather issued an "artful declamation" against the former Salem minister which

[27]Goodrich, *History of the USA*, p. 123; Morse, *Compendious History*, p. 168.

[28]See, e.g., Ramsay, *History of the United States*, p. 92, and Joseph Felt, *The Annals of Salem*, 2d ed. (Salem: W. & S. B. Ives, 1845), p. 484. On Mather's modern reputation, see David Levin, *In Defense of Historical Literature: Essays on American History, Autobiography, Drama, and Fiction* (New York: Hill and Wang, 1967), pp. 35–36. Albert B. Cook recently has provided a further context for the injury done to Mather for his role in the Salem proceedings; see "Damaging the Mathers: London Receives the News from Salem," *New England Quarterly* 65 (June 1992): 302–8,

[29]Lawrence Buell, *New England Literary Culture: From Revolution to Renaissance* (New York: Cambridge University Press, 1986), pp. 218–24.

"had the intended effect upon the fanatical multitude." Burroughs's dead body was thus "trampled down by the mob." Echoing Robert Calef, Upham insists that Mather and the leading ministers were "ambitious of spiritual influence and domination," a political power-play that could be engineered only "by carrying the people to the greatest extreme of credulity, fanaticism, and superstition." Like any "ambitious and grasping" leader, Mather "was anxious to have the support of all parties at the same time."[30] Hence Upham's exhortation to read Salem as a political trope, one in which the designing and the deluded together brought down the foundations of order in commonwealths as well as republics.

## III

The early republic's literary representations of witch-hunting were no less politicized than its histories. Just as Upham had taken up the subject of witchcraft as a means to "check the prevalence of fanaticism,"[31] the anonymously written *The Witch of New England* (1824) and Whittier's *Legends of New England* (1831) dramatize for contemporary audiences the political ramifications of irrationality. In *The Witch of New England* these dangers originate on the margins of society. Much of the plot of the novel is propelled by the town "hag" (a word Cotton Mather used to describe Martha Carrier) who preys upon Puritan Connecticut's "universally prevalent" fears of witchcraft. By playing the role of a witch, Annie Brown successfully intimidates Minister Bradley ("the dark, superstitious but well meaning clergyman"), his daughter Agnes, and, indeed, the entire body politic. "Over common minds," the narrator concludes, "she invariably obtained an influence and stern mastery that she seldom relinquished, and often used with heartless and unrelenting disdain."[32] The real devil in *The Witch of New England* is a distinctly political one.

[30]Upham, *Lectures on Witchcraft*, pp. 103–4, 106, 111.
[31]Upham, *Lectures on Witchcraft*, pp. iv–v.
[32]*The Witch of New England: A Romance* (Philadelphia: Carey and Lea, 1824), pp. 36, 33, 98.

The novel's oscillations between sportive and serious gothic effects reflect its attempt to mock Puritan superstition while simultaneously illustrating that the people's reckless passions are no laughing matter. As Annie gradually gains control over the community, her characterization gathers seriousness, and the novel leaves behind its farcical elements. At one moment, Annie stands high on a mountain and laughs at a funeral procession below (of a child she has kidnapped and murdered), her perch symbolic, it would seem, of her newfound political power.

In *The Witch*, as in the period's histories, gender and race serve to heighten the dramatic effect of the politics of irrationality. Annie and a Native American character, Samoset, are doubled as demagogues who manipulate "superstition" as the means for self-promotion. Like Annie, Samoset possesses a "sagacity and cunning [that] often induced the ignorant and superstitious savages to yield to him the deference and obedience, held to be due to the favorite of their gods." Several parallel scenes in the novel—the Native American war council, the Puritan witch trials, and the Puritan persecution of Quakerism—convey the sense that the colonials are no more immune to the dangers of zealotry than those in a state of nature. Both are easily brought "to a pitch of enthusiasm bordering upon insanity."[33] The net result of this equivalence is a host of racial and political ironies. As the Puritans zealously aim to purge the "other" from community, they are themselves represented as distinctly alien. This kind of zeal, it would appear, has no place in the contemporary political environment.

John Greenleaf Whittier stages the social and political consequences of superstition in "The Haunted House." Whittier's active political life as a Whig reformer and his disdain for Jacksonian democracy have often been noted.[34] Whatever sympathy he

---

[33]*The Witch of New England*, p. 168.

[34]Whittier edited the pro-Clay *American Manufacturer* in 1828 and was elected as a Whig to the Massachusetts legislature in 1835. Like all good Whigs, he called the Democrats "Tories"; certainly, the support Jackson drew from Southern slaveholders contributed to Whittier's disdain. See Lewis Leary, *John Greenleaf Whittier* (New York: Twayne, 1961), p. 27; Edward Wagenknecht, *John Greenleaf Whittier: A Portrait in Paradox* (New York: Oxford University Press, 1967), pp. 51–53; John B. Pickard, ed., *The Letters of John Greenleaf Whittier*, 3 vols. (Cambridge: Harvard University Press, 1975), 1:159.

initially allows for his dispossessed protagonist, Alice Knight, Whittier stresses the "fierce passions" of the "enraged Pythoness." Like Annie Brown, her mistreatment inspires a desire for revenge that, in turn, creates a new kind of *political* power founded on her ability to manipulate the "credulity and fears of her neighbors." The victim in Whittier's tale is Adam McOrne, who refuses Knight's son as a suitor for his daughter. McOrne's roots in the Scottish Highlands make him a fitting parallel to the outback Puritans, and as Alice terrorizes his home by populating it with "imaginary demons," he is "shaken by the controlling superstitions of the time."[35] Paralyzed by his irrational fears, McOrne is enslaved, his will incapacitated.

All of the tale's gothic effects—its wonders of the invisible world—are explained as the tale draws to an end. Such a closure contains the fantastic, tames it, by quietly inviting readers to measure their *own* capacity for reason against that of McOrne, who, rather ironically, ends up "laughing, heartily as before, at the superstitions and credulity of his [Puritan] neighbors." Whiggishly, Whittier allies the forces of delusion and the dangers of conspiracy. McOrne's servants, we finally learn, had been in cahoots with Alice: they "had been persuaded by [Alice] to aid her in the strange transactions—partly from an innate love of mischief, and partly from a pique against the worthy Scotchman, whose irritable temperament had more than once discovered itself in the unceremonious collision of his cane with the heads and shoulders of his domestics."[36] Literary convention and political ideology converge as early American gothic envelops national concerns. Just as in *The Witch of New England*, the stock figure of the town "hag" is invested with political significance as she manipulates the lower orders to disrupt established hierarchies, violating class distinctions as well as gendered ones. Again, we feel Morse and Goodrich shudder.

Republican fears were so widespread in the early national period that even some Democrats were infected. James Nelson

---

[35]John Greenleaf Whittier, "The Haunted House," *Legends of New England* (1831) (Gainesville, Fla.: Scholars Facsimiles and Reprints, 1965), pp. 58–59, 66.

[36]Whittier, "The Haunted House," p. 74.

Barker certainly expressed them in his historical drama about Puritanism, *The Tragedy of Superstition* (1824), a work that contemporary playwright and theatre historian William Dunlap considered "an honour to the dramatic literature of the country."[37] Barker's loyalty to the Democratic Party was, on the surface, striking. Veteran of the War of 1812 and later mayor of Philadelphia, he was a member of Philadelphia's "Democratic Young Men," an organization that helped oversee Andrew Jackson's 1828 campaign in that city. Proud beneficiary of the spoils system, Barker was a Jackson appointee (to the post of Collector of the Port of Philadelphia) and later a Van Buren one as well.[38] Those few critics who have turned their attention to *The Tragedy of Superstition* have tended to historicize it simply by revealing Barker's familiarity with Puritan sources; they have altogether missed the specifically post-Revolutionary meanings encoded in the play's treatment of Puritan "bigotry" and "the generalities of prejudice and superstition."[39]

Barker undoubtedly approached these problems with a particular sense of urgency, given that his tenure as mayor of Philadelphia in 1819–20 was plagued by rampant rioting, arson, and violent crime.[40] When *The Tragedy of Superstition* opened at Philadelphia's Chestnut Street Theater in March 1824, it unsurprisingly dramatized the problem of mob violence, specifically the vulnerability of the people to *de nouveau* political leadership. Much of *The Tragedy of Superstition* revolves around the evils of its aptly named villain, Ravensworth, a Puritan divine who preys upon the people's passion in order to promote himself politically. From the moment the curtain rises, the dual images of Ravensworth's cottage and the Fitzroy mansion (the home of Isabella, the wealthy immigrant from England, and her son

---

[37] William Dunlap, *A History of the American Theatre* (New York: Jared J. Harper, 1832), p. 375.

[38] Paul H. Musser, *James Nelson Barker* (1929; reprinted New York: AMS, 1969), pp. 2, 12–13, 103, 122.

[39] Musser, *Barker*, pp. 87–96; Arthur Hobson Quinn, *A History of the American Drama: From the Beginning to the Civil War* (New York: F. S. Crofts, 1946), pp. 136–62, 150.

[40] Musser, *Barker*, p. 81.

Charles) symbolize the class tensions that set the plot in motion. The envious and upwardly mobile Ravensworth continually projects upon the kind-hearted Isabella all of his own vice: he hates her "pride," her "haughty mansion," her "earth-born vanity."[41] Like Whittier's tale and *The Witch, The Tragedy of Superstition* interweaves its domestic and political plots. Ravensworth, we observe, is motivated in part by a pathological fear of Charles, who has chosen to court the minister's daughter, Mary. As a means, then, to eliminating both mother and son, Ravensworth stirs up a witch-hunt.

Through his actions, Ravensworth exemplifies what appear to be Barker's irrepressible anxieties about popular politics. When the villain reveals his "suspicions" about the Fitzroys to his friend, Walford, in act 4, Walford's response carries a political message with contemporary implications:

> Ah, my friend,
> If reason in a mind like yours so form'd,
> So fortified by knowledge, can bow down
> Before the popular breath, what shall protect
> From the all-with'ring blasts of superstition
> The unthinking crowd, in whom credulity
> Is ever the first born of ignorance?

Judicious and restrained throughout the play, Walford is a credible figure; thus, his fear of "the popular breath" and his lack of confidence in "[t]he unthinking crowd" carry weight, as do his objection to Ravensworth's insistence on the reality of witchcraft and his insight that previous witch-hunts in New England have shown only "frenzy's flame, / Like fire in tow, ran thro' the minds of men, / Fann'd by the breath of those in highest places."[42] The normative voice of reason, Walford is, in effect, the text's implied reader.

The real "tragedy" of "superstition" lies, finally, in Ravensworth's success in bringing Charles Fitzroy to trial. The storm

---

[41]James Nelson Barker, *The Tragedy of Superstition,* in *Representative American Plays from 1767 to the Present Day,* ed. Arthur Hobson Quinn (New York: Appleton-Century-Crofts, 1953), pp. 127, 117, 137.

[42]Barker, *The Tragedy of Superstition,* pp. 130–31.

raging outside the courthouse during this scene serves as a perfect objective correlative to the political drama taking place within. Ravensworth's oratorical power in court recalls Walford's earlier boast—"I know thy power / Over the multitude, but fear it not"—and with that memory, the sense of doom deepens. Ravensworth manipulates a variety of discourses: the jeremiad, the metaphysical sublime, and a republican admonishment against conspiracy. "Shall we forget," he rhetorically asks, "That worldly pride and irreligious lightness / Are the provoking sins, which our grave synod / Have [sic] urg'd us to root out?" Isabella alone understands that the demagogue's fiery words "excite the passions of his auditors."[43]

Yet the play's critique of zealotry is not so simple and straightforward. Its subplot, which centers on King Philip's War, complicates an easy dismissal of zealotry. Many early national readers would, of course, have been familiar with Barker's rendition of the Angel of Hadley episode, in which one of three regicides, in America to escape those who would avenge Charles I, had supposedly defended against Indian attack the town that had protected him. Eighteenth-century histories, such as Thomas Hutchinson's *History of the Colony and Province of Massachusetts-Bay* (1764) and Ezra Stiles's *History of Three of the Judges of King Charles I* (1794), had detailed the fates of Whalley, Goffe, and Dixwell, and later writers, such as Cooper, Hawthorne, John Stone, and Delia Bacon, would follow Barker's lead in appropriating the story for their literary works.[44] One recent analysis of *The Tragedy of Superstition*'s representation of the regicide (called the "Unknown") argues that Barker merely recapitulated Thomas Hutchinson's repugnance for the regicides' political radicalism.[45] A closer look at the role of the Unknown,

---

[43]Barker, *The Tragedy of Superstition*, pp. 131, 137.

[44]For its currency in Revolutionary and early national letters, see Mark L. Sargent, "Thomas Hutchinson, Ezra Stiles, and the Legend of the Regicides," *William and Mary Quarterly*, 3rd ser. 49 (1992): 431–48; G. Harrison Orians, "The Angel of Hadley in Fiction: A Study of the Sources of Hawthorne's 'The Gray Champion,'" *American Literature* 4 (1932): 257–69; and George Dekker, "Sir Walter Scott, the Angel of Hadley, and American Historical Fiction," *American Studies* 17 (1984): 211–27.

[45]See Sargent, "Hutchinson, Stiles and the Regicides," pp. 431–38.

however, and the textual inconsistencies created by his characterization, show how Barker recycled the legend to reify a Revolutionary ethos of classical *virtu*—the patriotic courage and martial valor requisite for the republic's survival.[46]

Initially portrayed as a mournful outcast, the Unknown nonetheless asks a crucial question during his first appearance on stage:

> Did these words, receiv'd
> In thy holy cause, stream with a felon's blood,
> Was it a felon's courage nerved my arm,
> A felon's zeal that burn'd within my heart?[47]

The question here is not really whether the Unknown is a felon—he undeniably is—but rather what the status is of the "zeal" he exemplifies. There is little room for verbal irony in the passage, for the "courage" he attributes to himself is validated in the middle of the play. When the community is endangered by sudden invasion (as the legend had it), the Unknown rallies the Puritan forces and, along with Charles Fitzroy in Barker's retelling, saves the commonwealth. Isabella aptly dubs the Unknown a "patriot," one whose selfless devotion to the *res publica*, as act 3 shows, makes him a foil for Ravensworth's self-promotion. In its dual plots, then, *Superstition* explores both internal and external perils to community. The fanatic "zeal" that endangers the community from within is, paradoxically, necessary to safeguard it from military invasion without. The historical anachronism of the play, its conflation of witch-hunting and King Philip's War, now begins to make more sense: its two plots revolve around its indecision over the nature of zealotry.

The tension evident in *The Tragedy of Superstition* points to a larger cultural struggle over the nature of Revolutionary republicanism in a post-Revolutionary world. Even more tortuously than *The Witch of New England*, Barker's play roams the unstable ideological borders between zealotry and patriotism. Years

---

[46]For the classical roots of this ideal, as well as its perpetuation in Italian civic humanism and the thought of James Harrington, see Pocock, *Machiavellian Moment*.

[47]Barker, *The Tragedy of Superstition*, p. 120.

before, John Adams had captured the essence of the problem when he reminded Americans that patriotism was a "passion" and that "we must still remember, that . . . the passion, although refined by the purest moral sentiments, and intended to be governed by the best principles, is a passion still." In his "Farewell Address," Washington had tried to distinguish between an "upright zeal" and a zealotry spawned from "the strongest passions of the human mind." Noah Webster cautioned in the *American Dictionary* (1828) that only an "enthusiasm chastened by reason or experience" could qualify as true patriotism.[48] In Barker's formulation of the ideal, Charles Fitzroy combines the "manly virtues" of courage and patriotism with the tempering quality "judgment," and thus is one of those "minds well-disciplin'd." In addition, the Unknown's decidedly cool-headed leadership saves the commonwealth from destruction in act 3. Yet Barker ultimately retreats from his synthesis as he kills off Charles and banishes the Unknown to somewhere "deep in the wilderness," safely away from civilized society.[49]

In context, then, *The Witch of New England*, "The Haunted House," and *The Tragedy of Superstition* each dramatizes the hobgoblins of republican political thought. In other words, Annie Brown, Alice Knight, and Ravensworth are *early national* demons—the women differing only in the misogynistic overtones their characters must bear—and thus they are no less the product of "delusion" than the specters haunting Essex County in 1692. The various pathologies they display—kidnapping, familial murder, secret desires of incest—recapitulate early national fears of conspiracy and contamination, and only republican vigilance, the texts affirm, can shield the citizenry from the dangers of a grotesque and depraved world. Admonishing contemporary audiences to avoid the excesses of zealotry, early nationals paradoxically dramatized its fundamental necessity to the survival of the republic.

---

[48]Adams, *Davila*, p. 49; Noah Webster, *An American Dictionary of the English Language* (New York: S. Converse, 1828), unpaginated; Washington, "Farewell Address," p. 114, 104.

[49]Barker, *The Tragedy of Superstition*, pp. 132, 140.

IV

The professionalization of belles letters during the second quarter of the nineteenth century, and the romantic ideology that arose coincidentally, complicated the period's representation of witch-hunting even further, and herein lies a significant point of distinction between the early national period's literary and nonliterary discourse. As the genteel amateur slowly relinquished his place to the professional, an inchoate form of romanticism, which privileged the imagination (as opposed to "fancy") in artistic creation, made itself visible in the witchcraft fictions of the 1820s and 1830s. Romantic ideology particularly resisted republican prescriptions for communal identity; its presence in these witchcraft fictions thus inscribes alternative understandings of both faculty psychology and individual selfhood. By implication, the virtue of the imagination displaced a civic ideal with an artistic one which privileged an alienated consciousness. Literary discourse thus was the site of unique and densely complex meanings for Puritan "gloom," "superstition," and "imagination."

Critics have long recognized that Puritan superstition was entangled in larger issues of literary nationalism. Soon after the appearance of *Legends of New England*, Whittier, for example, declared that even though America lacked European ruins and other triggers for romantic melancholy, it did possess "the tale of superstition and the scenes of witchcraft" which would provide adequate material for romance. Some up-and-coming American writer, he urged, should produce "an amusing and not uninstructing work" fictively illustrating indigenous superstitions, *precisely* the kind of stuff that Upham had explicitly warned against![50] In the preface to *Legends*, Whittier had claimed that "New-England is rich in traditionary lore,—a thousand associations of superstition and manly daring and romantic adventure are connected with her green hills and her pleasant rivers"—all of which the skilled artist could draw upon to fire the audience's imagination.

---

[50]*Whittier on Writers and Writing*, ed. Edwin Cady and Harry Hayden Clark (Syracuse: Syracuse University Press, 1950), pp. 93, 106, 115; Upham, *Lectures on Witchcraft*, pp. 200–30.

After making fun of McOrne's bewitched household, the narrator of "The Haunted House" alters his tone as he comments on the role of the imagination in a contemporary, utilitarian culture:

The days of faery are over. The tale of enchantment—the legend of ghostly power—of unearthly warning and supernatural visitation, have lost their hold on the minds of the great multitude. People sleep quietly where they are placed—no matter by what means they have reached the end of their journey—and there is an end to the church-yard rambles of discontented ghosts—

Where "the poetry of Time has gone by forever . . . we have only the sober prose left us."[51] Therefore, Whittier uses the past to create poetry in the present. Time and again in *Legends of New England*, he cites a credulous anecdote of Cotton Mather's only to exploit it for imaginative effect. "The Weird Gathering," for example, is introduced with a warning about the "fearful delusion" at Salem, and yet Mather's description of secret witch-meetings affords Whittier the means to enhance the tale's supernatural effects. "The Spectre Ship" and "The Spectre Warriors" gently mock the *Magnalia Christi Americana*'s superstitious vignettes while using them to excite the imaginations of contemporary readers. The central tension throughout the *Legends*, then, is that they debunk a distinctly Puritan imagination which they in turn feed upon.

This tension between romantic and republican virtues also helps explain the inconsistent characterization of Edward Bradley, the hero of *The Witch of New England*. Virtually every major character in the novel suffers from excessive passions but none moreso than Edward, who, as an incarnation of romantic melancholy, inhabits "an ideal world" of the mind. In stressing Edward's heroic qualities, the republican discourse on witchcraft is inverted to place the imagination in a new—and positive—light: "The witchcraft of courtesy . . . the pale but lovely remnant of deceased chivalry . . . were to be seen only in the day dreams conjured by the heat and vapours of a romantic mind." The political texture of the language becomes even more dense as the

[51]Whittier, "The Haunted House," pp. 63–64.

author of *The Witch* strains to reconcile romantic ideology with the canons of republicanism. Edward's best friend initiates a tenuous synthesis by dubbing him "a republican *and* a poet," while the narrator assures early national readers that Edward is no "idle and useless visionary" (italics added). Edward is, instead, "a poet in feeling . . . indulging often in the dreams of imagination" yet a practical man of "skill and enterprise."[52] Later in the novel, Edward's indecisiveness, his oscillations between melancholy and manliness, are tested during his Indian captivity. True to the conventions of frontier romance, his status as a suitable mate for the tale's heroine is ensured when he ultimately rejects the Native American temptress. As his Byronic gloom begins to lift, it marks a movement—at once sexual, psychological, and political—towards a cultural ideal of reason and moderation.

The complex norms of faculty psychology in witchcraft literature finally give us the tools to reconsider John Neal's novel of the Salem witch trials, *Rachel Dyer* (1828). Since his own time, Neal has been seen as a romantic, an iconoclast. His kinsman and fellow Quaker, Whittier, thought Neal "a singular, erratic genius."[53] In our day, David Reynolds has called Neal the father of the nineteenth-century "Subversive Style," a democratic movement battling the canons of reason, established social hierarchies, and anything smacking of cultural deference to European tastes.[54] Critics of *Rachel Dyer* generally have noted Neal's identification with the novel's Byronic hero, George Burroughs, and his "spirit of contradiction."[55]

Originally conceived as a short story for *Blackwood's Maga-*

---

[52] *The Witch of New England*, pp. 18, 33, 35.

[53] Whittier, *Letters*, 1:436.

[54] David S. Reynolds, *Beneath the American Renaissance: The Subversive Imagination in the Age of Emerson and Melville* (Cambridge: Harvard University Press, 1989), pp. 99–104.

[55] See Benjamin Lease, *That Wild Fellow John Neal and the American Literary Revolution* (Chicago: University of Chicago Press, 1972), pp. 137–45; Donald A. Sears, *John Neal* (Boston: Twayne, 1978), pp. 79—87; Michael Davitt Bell, *Hawthorne and the Historical Romance of New England* (Princeton: Princeton University Press, 1971), pp. 99–104; Harold C. Martin, "The Colloquial Tradition in the Novel: John Neal," *New England Quarterly* 32 (December 1959): 455–75; and William J. Scheick, "Power, Authority, and Revolutionary Impulse in John Neal's *Rachel Dyer*," *Studies in American Fiction* 4 (1976): 143–55.

*zine*, an English journal to which Neal was a frequent contributor during his residence abroad in the mid 1820s, "New-England Witchcraft" was revised and expanded after Neal, back in the United States, had consulted Robert Calef's *More Wonders of the Invisible World* (which had been reprinted in 1823). After the first chapter's rather long disquisition on the history of superstition, the account of Salem carries the reader to the household of Matthew Paris (fictional equivalent of Samuel Parris), where the afflicted girls precipitate the witchcraft crisis. At the ensuing trials, Burroughs opposes the proceedings and heroically defends (with little success) Sarah Good and Martha Cory. For his defiance, Burroughs is later executed, and the novel's heroine, the deformed Quaker Rachel Dyer, dies a martyr in prison.

Burroughs emerges as a champion of the people—a "reformer," they call him, who "braved the whole power of [the magistrates] that others were so afraid of." Divested of real power in court, however, Burroughs must resort to language. Neal (a former law student) initially has fun with Burroughs, but as Burroughs's legal adviser gives him a quick lesson in how to work the crowd, the scene subtly takes on serious implications. "Do—just keep the court in play; keep the judges at work. . . . You have the jury with you now—lay it on thick—you understand the play as well as I do now—." Like the novel as a whole, Burroughs's oratorical performance rambles on, flashes brilliantly, at times glorifies itself, and ultimately resorts to romantic irony when all else fails. "Talk—talk—talk," the lawyer urges him on, "no matter what you say—don't give them time to breathe—pop a speech into 'em!" Keep them "agog."[56]

*Rachel Dyer*'s George Burroughs thus assumes the character of a demagogue. Appealing to the people's "courage" and "heroic probity," Burroughs exhorts them to "oppose the race of men that are about you and above you." Like Edward Bradley, he embodies both romantic and republican qualities, artistic power and the "vigor" of manhood, but Neal's explicit claim that Burroughs's qualities are precisely what were required in 1792 is more devil-

[56]John Neal, *Rachel Dyer* (Gainesville, Fla.: Scholars' Facsimilies and Reprints, 1964), pp. 85, 97, 99.

ishly ambiguous than anyone has yet realized. Just as in *The Tragedy of Superstition*, this ambiguity involves a profound question about the very nature of patriotism. Even the obtuse Puritan magistrates recognize in Burroughs's ranting an "extraordinary gift of speech" capable of undermining their political control. Caught up in the frenzy of his own rabble-rousing, Burroughs defiantly boasts, *"You have no power to stop me."*[57]

Although Neal appears to be recasting demagoguery in positive terms as romantic dissent, an underlying cautionary tone rings through *Rachel Dyer*. Neal's nagging uncertainties about democracy are apparent in attacks upon irrationality that bear the characteristic marks of early national republican conservatism. Many times, the novel's rhetoric ("a frightful superstition . . . was raging with irresistible power") could easily be mistaken for that of the period's didactic histories. Its descriptions of events at Salem—a "fury [that] took possession of the people," a "fearful infatuation," the "superstitious dread" persecuting Sarah Good—also inscribe early national political fears.[58]

Neal's conflicted politics produces an inconsistency in Burroughs's characterization. Occasionally Burroughs is the voice of *reason* in court, as he outflanks the magistracy and reveals the absurdity, for example, of the circumstantial evidence used to implicate Sarah Good (as Calef had done). In such moments, the Puritans' "great show of zeal" is juxtaposed with Burroughs's "gravity and moderation," which "weighed prodigiously in the court." Later, at Burroughs's own trial, zealotry reaches a crescendo when the courtroom dissolves into histrionics, disorder, and violence under—in a significant phrase—the "weight of delusion."[59]

Neal's ambivalence to the virtue of reason in *Rachel Dyer* suggests the complicated ideological relations among historical writing, political culture, and romanticism in early national New England. Like Whittier's ambiguous relationship to Cotton Mather's superstitions or *The Witch of New England*'s conflicted charac-

---

[57]Neal, *Rachel Dyer*, pp. 130–31, 149, 120.

[58]Neal, *Rachel Dyer*, pp. 34, 47, 61.

[59]Neal, *Rachel Dyer*, pp. 97, 236.

terization of Edward Bradley, the ambiguities surrounding Burroughs in *Rachel Dyer* testify to the problematic emergence of romanticism amidst a cultural climate in which reason was still associated with psychological, social, and political stability. Witchcraft fictions of the 1820s waver indecisively in the face of their own projects of cultivating melancholic nostalgia and celebrating the virtue of an unbridled imagination. Their self-conscious gestures toward romantic individualism are ultimately compromised by lingering conservative beliefs that the abandonment of reason signaled chaos for the republic.

What one critic of *The Crucible* has called its "almost oppressively instructive"[60] quality might also be used to describe the historical literature of the early republic. Depictions of the episode at Salem, in particular, were shaped by a firm—one might even say desperate—belief in the tenets of reason, deference, and consensus, which derived in large part from republican political thought. If, as one scholar of the second American party system has argued, modern politics provided early nationals with the "emotional drama" of free-spirited, popular elections, then didactic history writing was obliged to dramatize how potentially destructive such democratic emotions could be.[61] Dominated by New England elites, early national historical narratives about witch-hunting offered up political texts that, in effect, competed with the greater "text" of modern American politics, in which the values of an older world became increasingly less tenable in the open competition for the popular vote.

Early national literary production was both complicitous in and distinctive from this conservative (if not actually "dominant") politics, a relationship that reveals a great deal about the slippery, nuanced nature of language during the early national period. Words like "zeal," "superstition," "imagination," and "gloom" contained densely layered and sometimes unstable meanings that arose from the difficulties of interpreting Revolutionary patriotism in a post-Revolutionary world. For literary

---

[60]Levin, *In Defense of Historical Literature*, p. 90.
[61]McCormick, *Second American Party System*, pp. 16, 27–29, 95.

texts, such linguistic complexities were further complicated by the ambiguous requirements of the romantic imagination. Taken on its own terms, then, and not as a measure of Hawthorne's later successes, early nineteenth-century witchcraft fictions demonstrate a multivalence rooted not so much in the records of the seventeenth-century commonwealth but rather in the immediate social and political anxieties of the early American republic.

Philip Gould *is Assistant Professor of English at Oakland University in Rochester, Michigan. The present essay derives from a larger study of the historical literature of Puritanism in early national America.*

# Eros, the Devil, and the Cunning Woman: Sexuality and the Supernatural in European Antecedents and in the Seventeenth-Century Salem Witchcraft Cases

By LOUIS J. KERN*

T H E belief in the power of magic is as old as civilization itself. Magic constituted a transcendent, sacred order of knowledge that com-manded principalities of the air and infernal forces of immense scope and power. The apparent ability of its adepts to control the lives and destinies of their fellows and to sustain or destroy society as a whole gave rise to a profound aura of fear and awe that surrounds the realm of magic in the popular mind. From the earliest times, therefore, a close association arose between the rituals of magic and those of religion. Indeed, as Jules Cambarieu has observed, the magical incantation may well have been "the oldest fact in the history of civilization."[1]

In pre-Christian times, a distinction between two forms of magic—white (licit) and black (illicit)—was widely recognized. Illicit magic operated through the invocation of demons to hinder or injure its vic-tims. Licit magic sought to forfend the disastrous consequences of de-monic intervention in human affairs. The early Church Fathers blurred

*Louis J. Kern is a social, intellectual, and cultural historian. His scholarly work has focused on radical cultural critiques and alternative social organization, and he has written on sexuality and gender construction in utopian communities and on the formation of sexual identity among sexual radicals in the late nineteenth century. He is the author of *An Ordered Love: Sex Roles and Sexuality in Victorian Utopias—the Shakers, the Mormons, and the Oneida Community* (1977). He is currently working on a study of Anthony Comstock and the culture of censorship, 1870–1915. He teaches history and American Studies at Hofstra University.

1. Quoted in Lynn Thorndike, *A History of Magic and Experimental Science during the First Thirteen Centuries of Our Era,* 8 vols. (New York: Columbia University Press, 1923), 1:6.

this distinction between theurgy and diabolical magic. Saint Augustine charged all practitioners of the magical arts with "criminal tampering with the unseen world," and maintained that "both classes are the slaves of deceitful rites of the demons whom they invoke under the names of the angels."[2]

In the popular mind, however, the distinction between harmful magic, grounded in devil worship, and beneficial, propitiatory spells and incantations endured. Despite severe ecclesiastical and secular penalties for trafficking in the magic arts, the common people persisted in believing in their efficacy, and continued to consult practitioners of occult rites. The force of custom, then, sustained the practice of magic as an alternative form of spiritual power and a body of powerful, arcane lore that coexisted (albeit not very peacefully) alongside Christian beliefs and ecclesiastical rites. Such an uneasy tenure on the popular mind was not acceptable to the Church, and gradually Christian apologists were able to subsume much of traditional magical practice under the rubric of the diabolical by employing the term "witchcraft," which had theretofore constituted but one branch of the magical tree, to signify the dire spiritual threat of a far from moribund occultism.

Witchcraft, derived from the Anglo-Saxon term, *wiccian* (which meant to practice sorcery), came to include *veneficium* (compounding and/or administering drugs, potions, or philters), and *incantatio* (to recite magical words, to work charms, or to bewitch). Since these two practices, at least in their more beneficent forms, were also attributes of white (good) magic, what was taken as the essence of the detested and execrable practice of witchcraft, as defined by Christian authorities, was the implied intent of the practitioner, expressed as *maleficium*—the noxious or pernicious infliction of injury or harm upon another.[3] The Church built upon and co-opted the popular traditions and images of sorcery and magic in defining the rites and practices of witches, and effectively forged links between the vulgar persistence of ancient pre-Christian beliefs, which continued to enjoy wide popularity, and the

2. Saint Augustine, *The City of God*, trans. Marcus Dods (New York: Modern Library, 1950), 312. See also Thorndike, *History of Magic*, 1:540–41.

3. See Cecil L'Estrange Ewen, *Witch Hunting and Witch Trials: The Indictments for Witchcraft from the Records of 1373 Assizes Held for the Home Circuit, A.D. 1559–1736* (London: Kegan Paul, Trench, Trubner, & Co., 1929), 4–7; and George Lyman Kittredge, *Witchcraft in Old and New England* (New York: Russell & Russell, 1929), 4–5.

explicit inversion of Christian doctrine through the self-consciously heretical worship of Satan. Such characteristic acts of witchcraft as compacts with the Devil, the suckling of familiars, sexual relations with demon lovers or Satan himself, and the witches' Sabbat also allowed the Church to annex to the practice of the ancient religion the full corpus of mortal sins.

Witchcraft was constructed as the mirror image of orthodoxy; it constituted a deviant organization of religious and social life that gave precedence to physical over spiritual experience. It became the duty of all true believers to root out and extirpate the full panoply of its execrable practices wherever they might be found. The full weight of the ecclesiastical establishment was brought to bear against *maleficium* in an extensive, European crusade against witchcraft that spanned three centuries (1450–1750) and resulted in over 100,000 formal prosecutions. The witch-hunts and persecutions, whose primary victims were women, were greatly facilitated by Innocent VIII's bull *Summis Desiderantes* (1484), which linked the prosecution of witches to the apparatus of the Inquisition, specifically directing inquisitors and other ecclesiastical and secular authorities to execute all practitioners of witchcraft and other diabolical arts.[4]

An extensive literature of witchcraft was produced that detailed the horrors and crimes perpetrated by the adepts of this ancient art and came to comprise a set of guidebooks to the examination and trial of suspected witches. While there is a substantial variety of interpretation among these works, there is a notable orthodoxy on fundamentals. A central dogma, from which there is scant deviation, and which is sustained by an objective study of the statistical record of prosecutions and executions, is that witchcraft is a predominantly female crime. So inveterate was this belief that it became the basis for juridical expectation and popular suspicion. In places where the witch-hunts provoked mass hysteria—Geneva in 1546, Labourd in 1609, Lorraine between 1580 and 1595, and Salem in 1692, for instance—it became a virtually self-fulfilling prophecy that led to the condemnation of thousands of women.

Nicholas Remy asserted that "it is not unreasonable that this scum of humanity should be drawn chiefly from the feminine sex," for

4. Brian P. Levack, *The Witch-Hunt in Early Modern Europe* (New York: Longman, 1987), 1.

"women excel in their knowledge of witchcraft."[5] In the late fifteenth century, two Dominican inquisitors, writing under the imprimatur of the papal see, penned a popular manual for the persecution and extirpation of witches. This comprehensive volume, the *Malleus Maleficarum* (1486), inextricably linked evil, the erotic, and the feminine, and brilliantly wove together official doctrine and popular prejudice. It defined "wicked women" as those consumed by "infidelity, ambition, and lusts," and argued that

> since of these three vices the last chiefly predominates, women being insatiable, etc., it follows that those among ambitious women are more deeply infected who are more hot to satisfy their filthy lusts; and such are adultresses, fornicatresses, and the Concubines of the Great.[6]

There were two important corollaries to the basic assumption that "far more women are witches than men." Both related to the irreducibly erotic nature of witchcraft beliefs and practices. The first held that, if women were the agents of diabolical forces in their character of witches, men were their object, their victims. Therefore, "men are more often bewitched than women." The second corollary sought to explain the seeming incongruity of the ideologically prescribed superior sex being victimized by the subordinate and weaker sex. "The reason for this," we are told,

> lies in the fact that God allows the devil more power over the venereal act, by which the original sin is handed down, than over other human actions. . . . And the venereal act can be more readily and easily bewitched in a man than in a woman.[7]

The ability of the Devil, operating through his unquestioning human

---

5. Nicholas Remy, *Demonolatry*, ed. Montague Summers (1595; reprint, London: John Rodker, 1930), 56; James I estimated the ratio of female to male witches at twenty to one (King James I, *Daemonologie* [1597; reprint, London: John Lane, 1924], 44).

6. Heinrich Kramer and James Sprenger, *Malleus Maleficarum*, ed. Montague Summers (1486; reprint, New York: Dover, 1971), 47. On the popularity of this manual, see Sydney Anglo, "Evident Authority and Authoritative Evidence: The *Malleus Maleficarum*," in *The Doomed Art: Essays in the Literature of Witchcraft*, ed. Sydney Anglo (London: Routledge & Kegan Paul, 1977), 14–15.

7. Kramer and Sprenger, *Malleus*, 167.

followers, to "cast spells upon the venereal act" demonstrates that diabolical power preeminently "lies in the privy parts of men."[8]

The literature on witchcraft makes clear that witches' sorcery and sexual magic were considered essentially identical. But while traditional magical intervention in the amatory affairs of the common people may be found in this literature—use of occult powers and potions to secure affection, to enhance the libido, and to curse the faithless paramour—the overwhelming intent of sexual spells was to induce male impotence. In general, it was maintained that witches afflicted men by means of their seductive wiles, through "their dances, their obscene kisses," they "contrive[d] to send demons and evil spirits into a man's body."[9]

Those evil spirits erected potent impediments to the male's genital functions. They affected both the mental and the physical aspects of sexual behavior. In the first instance, they might "so disturb a man's perception and imagination as to make the woman appear loathsome to him." Even more devastatingly, they might destroy the basis of male sexual capacity through spermatoschesis, spermatemphraxis, or the incapacity of the erectile power.[10] But the sexual power of witches that cast a cold horror of brute, visceral fear over the male imagination was the threat of the utter and complete disappearance of the sexual organs. For, "there is no doubt," the *Malleus Maleficarum* insists, "that certain witches can do marvellous things with regard to male organs."[11] Although they cannot actually remove the organs, they can make their victim effectually incapable of perceiving them. When this apparent removal of the sexual organs is

> performed by witches, it is only a matter of glamour; although it is no illusion in the opinion of the sufferer. For his imagination can really and actually believe that something is not present, since by

---

8. Kramer and Sprenger, *Malleus*, 26.

9. Henry Boguet, *An Examen of Witches* (1603; reprint, London: John Rodker, 1929), xli. References to more traditional magic may be found in Reginald Scott, *The Discoverie of Witchcraft, wherein the Lewd Dealings of Witches and Witchmongers Is Notablie Detected* (1584; reprint, London: John Rodker, 1930), 69, 71–72 (love potions); James I, *Daemonologie*, 45 (fixing of affections), and his *Newes from Scotland, Declaring the Damnable Life and Death of Doctor Fain, a Notable Sorcerer* (1591; reprint, London: John Lane, 1924), 19 (sexual revenge); and Edward Fairfax, *Daemonologia: A Discourse on Witchcraft* (1622; reprint, New York: Barnes & Noble, 1971), 97n.

10. Kramer and Sprenger, *Malleus*, 54–55.

11. Kramer and Sprenger, *Malleus*, 58.

none of his exterior senses, such as sight or touch, can he perceive that it is present. . . . so that it seems to him that he can see and feel nothing but a smooth body with its surface interrupted by no genital organ.[12]

Passages like these are indicative of the efforts of orthodoxy to palliate male fears of female sexual power and to undermine the vestigial beliefs in the old religion of magic that were all but inseparable from popular ideas and folk custom. Indeed, the assurances of the superiority of Christianity over diabolical magic are commingled with reiterations of traditional folk belief that are but indifferently glossed and ineffectively subsumed under the orthodox construction of the powers of witchcraft. A story recounted in the *Malleus*, for example, has all the qualities of a bawdy folk tale. It arises in the context of a widespread and persistent belief that some witches

collect male organs in great numbers, as many as twenty or thirty members together, and put them up in a box, where they move themselves like living members, and eat oats and corn, as has been seen by many and is a matter of common report.

Once, so the story goes,

a certain man . . . when he had lost his member . . . approached a known witch to ask her to restore it to him. She told the afflicted man to climb a certain tree, and that he might take which he liked out of a nest in which there were several members. And when he tried to take a big one, the witch said: You must not take that one; adding, because it belonged to the parish priest.[13]

Beneath the comedy of this story, the unreasoning fear of female power exercised through the dark arts is apparent. In the first instance, it is evident that witches have coldly and calculatedly assembled their organ collections through manipulation of what is considered the hypersexuality of the female. They have worked their will on the male community "through their [men's] carnal desires and the pleasures of the flesh."[14] Secondly, it indicates a fear of male sexual loss of control—the

12. Kramer and Sprenger, *Malleus*, 58–59.
13. Kramer and Sprenger, *Malleus*, 121.
14. Kramer and Sprenger, *Malleus*, 97.

penis has an independent life of its own; it is not subject to the control of the (male) will. And it is precisely the male's inability to control his penis that has made it possible for the female as witch to seduce and unman him. Fear of male sexual inferiority is also implied in the subject's attempt to appropriate the largest penis in the collection. Finally, the story underscores the superiority of the old faith over the new in two ways. First, the witch has seduced and deprived of his virile member the local surrogate of the church universal; and then, the only recourse to having been "collected" is to propitiate the evil forces in the person of the witch. Even in cases where a male victim had been deluded by a "glamour" that merely prevented his perception of organs still attached, their restoration often required the magical contrectation of the witch herself. As a young man described the process,

> the witch touched him with her hand between the thighs, saying: "Now you have what you desire." And the young man . . . plainly felt, before he had verified it by looking or touching, that his member had been restored to him by the mere touch of the witch.[15]

As self-conscious representatives of anarchic, unbounded, and ungovernable female sexuality, witches were also believed to be a threat to male potency and self-control through their ability to seduce men into satyriasis or *philocaption* ("inordinate love"), whereby "a man is so bound in the meshes of carnal lust and desire that he can be made to desist from it by no shame, words, blows or action; and when a man often puts away his beautiful wife to cleave to the most hideous of women."[16] Women, even when promised the handsomest of lovers, are frequently depicted in this literature as virtuously resisting temptation. Females were of two types—the dangerously lascivious and diabolically cunning witches, and the upright matrons and irreproachable virgins. It was free indulgence of feminine sexuality—promiscuous and nonreproductive in nature—that separated the conventional from the deviant woman. Typically, witches were initiated into their craft through an act of sexual intercourse. For example, a woman, tutored by one of the relatively rare males executed for witchcraft, "as the price of her learning . . . had been defiled by him and made pregnant."[17]

15. Kramer and Sprenger, *Malleus*, 119.
16. Kramer and Sprenger, *Malleus*, 169.
17. Remy, *Demonolatry*, 147.

But what most characterized the hypersexuality of the female, as represented by the conventional depiction of the witch in the literature of inquisition, was copulation with the Devil. So essential was diabolical intercourse to the ideal type of the witch, that one writer could unqualifiedly maintain that

> it has been revealed in the examinations of witches that they all have this connection with Satan. The Devil uses them so because he knows that women love carnal pleasures, and he means to bind them to his allegiance by such agreeable provocations. Moreover, there is nothing which makes a woman more subject to a man than that he should abuse her body.[18]

The usual pattern in these matters was for the witch to seal her/his covenant with the Devil by a sexual union, and for carnal connections to play a major role in the rites of the Sabbat. Orthodox authors, however, could only conceive diabolical sexuality as unnatural, and therefore depicted it as unpleasurable in some degree for the women involved. The bulk of witches' testimony reported in these guides to prosecuting witches sustains the sense of acute physical distaste associated with intimate contact with Satan. As one witch confessed,

> she had several times taken in her hand the member of the Demon which lay with her, and that it was as cold as ice and a good finger's length, but not so thick as that of a man. [Nevertheless], when Satan coupled with her she had as much pain as a woman in travail.[19]

In a literature written exclusively by men, exhibiting a fascination with the intimate details of female sexuality, both psychological and physical, male sexual fears and fantasies ran rampant. Male sensitiveness about penis size and a vindictive insistence on the castigation of female sexual desire characterize the assessment of the putative unrestrained eroticism of the sex life of the typical witch. "All female witches," we are told, "maintain that the so-called genital organs of their Demons are so huge and so excessively rigid that they cannot be admitted without the greatest pain."[20] Individual witches testified that

18. Boguet, *Examen*, 29.
19. Boguet, *Examen*, 31.
20. Remy, *Demonolatry*, 14.

the Devil's organ, "even when only half in erection, was as long as some kitchen utensils," that it felt "like a spindle swollen to an immense size so that it could not be contained by even the most capacious woman without great pain," and that it was "long environ la moitié d'une aulne, de mediocre grosseur, rouge, obscur, et tortu, fort rude et comme piquant."[21] One witch asserted that "although she had many years' experience of men, she was always so stretched by the huge, swollen member of her Demon that the sheets were drenched with blood."[22]

Some male authorities were reluctantly forced to conclude, given the weight of testamentary evidence, that for most witches, "it is wholly against their will that they are embraced by Demons, but . . . it is useless for them to resist."[23] Such a conclusion, that diabolical intercourse was ravishment, soothed the bruised male ego and minimized the threat of feminine sexuality. But not all authors were willing to accept the logic of the witch-hunters and remained obdurately defiant. A Scottish woman, for instance, stoutly maintained of her demonic paramour that "he is abler for us that way than any man can be, onlie he ves heavie lyk a malt-sek; a hudg nature, verie cold, as yce."[24]

Apparently Satan, in his infinite incarnations, was not alone "abler" for witches but for their more orthodox and conventional sisters as well, for the other great strain of eroticism in the witchcraft literature was that of the demon lover or incubi and succubi. On the question of the nature and issue of the intercourse of a human being and an incubus (literally, "lying above," male) or a succubus (literally, "lying beneath," female) there was heated controversy in the literature. Some maintained that such hypostatized apparitions were fallen angels or *eudemons*, while others contended that they were the incarnation of the spirit of evil or *cacodemons*.[25] The most heated controversy, however, emerged over

21. Remy, *Demonolatry*, 14; and De Lancre, cited in Remy, 14n. An idiomatic translation of the latter passage would be: "about as long as half a meter, of moderate thickness, red, dusky and twisted, extremely rough (hard) and how icy cold."

22. Remy, *Demonolatry*, 14. See also Boguet, *Examen*, 31–32.

23. Remy, *Demonolatry*, 14.

24. Quoted in Remy, *Demonolatry*, 13n.

25. The Greek terms for incubi and succubi are *ephialtes* and *hyphialtes,* respectively. For a "fallen angel" interpretation, see Kramer and Sprenger, *Malleus*, 29. For a "devilish" interpretation, see Francesco Maria Guazzo, *Compendium Maleficarum* (1608; reprint, London: John Rodker, 1929), 30. Ludovico Maria Sinistrari entertains both hypotheses simultaneously in his *Demonality* ([late 1680s]; reprint, in Montague Summers, *Eros and Evil: The Sexual Psychopathology of Witchcraft* [Baltimore: Penguin Books, 1974]), 236.

whether such demonic-human unions could produce progeny, and if so, what the effectual means of generation was. Though there were some dissenters, the consensus of opinion seems to have held that such unions could be fruitful; but some disagreement remained over precisely how it might be possible for supernatural intervention to operate through natural means.

A Spanish medical authority of the sixteenth century claimed that the whole process was a kind of eugenics in reverse that would eventually produce the Antichrist by means of natural biological evolution. "What Incubi introduce into the womb," he asserted,

> is not any ordinary human semen in normal quantity, but abundant, very thick, very warm, rich in spirits and free from serosity. This moreover is an easy thing for them, since they merely have to choose ardent, robust men, whose semen is naturally very copious and with whom the Succubus has connexion, and then women of like constitution, with whome the Incubus copulates, taking care that both shall enjoy a more than normal orgasm, for the more abundant the semen the greater the venereal excitement.[26]

Most writers were reluctant to accept the concept of demon lovers as super progenitors since both popular culture and conventional wisdom (grounded in Aristotelian ideas about the physical world) emphasized the coldness of the Devil and his associates. But the notion of the succubus/incubus pair as a supernatural force that magically united the male and female germs of two human parents, who remained mutually unconscious of the other's role in the reproductive process, proved at once more enduring and more popular. The supernatural part of the process, predicated upon the demon's ability to change sex at will, is quite straightforward: "the devil is Succubus to a man, and becomes Incubus to a woman."[27]

The crucial distinction between witches' sexual relations with the Devil and the connection of women and incubi is consciousness of the true identity of the lover. Witches are fully aware that their lover is the Devil, having engaged themselves by ritualized covenant to him. As a

---

26. Sinistrari, *Demonality*, 215.

27. Kramer and Sprenger, *Malleus*, 26. Francesco Guazzo maintains that demons can collect semen from nocturnal emissions and employ that for procreation as well (*Compendium*, 30). This is generally denied by other authors.

consequence, the demon may be visible to the witch's eyes alone, remaining totally imperceptible to any bystanders. In the case of incubi, who essentially delude their mistresses into believing them human, they are quite visible to all human eyes. This distinction was believed to provide one basis for eyewitness identification of a witch, for

> manie times witches are seene in the fields, and woods, prostituting themselves uncovered and naked up to the navill, wagging and moving their members in everie part, according to the disposition of one being about that act of concupiscence, and yet nothing seene of the beholders upon hir; saving that after such a convenient time as is required about such a peece of worke, a blacke vapor of the length and bigness of a man, hath beene seene as it were to depart from hir, and to ascend from that place.[28]

Another example of witchery in sexual congress was the visible use of unnatural means in performing the act. It was discovered, according to a French jurist, that a woman, who had been imprisoned under suspicion of witchcraft,

> had a hole beneath her navel, quite contrary to nature. . . . the witch confessed that her Devil . . . had sexual connection with her through this hole, and her husband through the natural hole.[29]

What drove women, either witches or more conformist women, to welcome diabolical sex was their very femininity. The physiology of the female body, the delicate balance of their humors, it was believed, made them acutely susceptible to lubricity. For

> they have such an unbridled force of furie and concupiscence naturallie, that by no means is it possible for them to temper or moderate the same. . . . Women are also . . . monethlie filled full of superfluous humors, and with them the melancholike bloud boileth.[30]

In the end, the dogmatic belief in the irreducibly lascivious nature of the feminine made it logically necessary to abandon the idea of

---

28. Scott, *Discoverie*, 43–44. See also Guazzo, *Compendium*, 31.
29. Boguet, *Examen*, 32–33.
30. Scott, *Discoverie*, 158. See also Guazzo, *Compendium*, 137.

widespread insemination by incubi. Experience in examinations of witches made it clear that it was only

> rarely that the Demons act as Succubi: either because it is not the custom of women, whose modesty in this matter they evilly imitate, to take the initiative in inducing men to commit fornication with them; or because the rabble of witches is chiefly composed of that sex which, owing to its feebleness of understanding, is least able to resist and withstand the wiles of the Devil. And certainly, in all the trials of witches that I have had to do with, this has been the one and only example of a Succubus.[31]

Given this uniformly low opinion of feminine morals and women's capacity for self-control in venereal matters, the rational mind is bound to question the existence of such palpable spirits as incubi and to wonder if they are self-conscious inventions "evolved for the sole purpose of hiding the shame of the mothers." But popular belief in the early modern era adhered tenaciously to their existence and, it was maintained, "even to this day nearly all men show by their speech and their thoughts that they truly and firmly believe in the procreation of men by Demons."[32] It might perhaps have been more comforting to the male ego for a husband to believe himself cuckolded by a supernatural rather than a mortal rival, but he would have been nonplussed and disquieted by his wife's response to her dalliance with her "Bawdy Incubus" had he realized, as an English author (speaking of "honest women" in general) pointed out, that "she hath more pleasure and delight (they say) with *Incubus* that waie, than with anie mortall man."[33] This was an indication of how far the popular culture of sexuality and the supernatural diverged in the minds of the two sexes in the late sixteenth century.

The magisterial *Malleus Maleficarum* argues that not simply witches but the entire female gender is deviant, and that when its natural tendencies are enhanced by diabolical power, it threatens the subversion of society and the extermination of the true faith. Deviance and perversion are read as innate female characteristics, for in the biblical account

---

31. Remy, *Demonolatry*, 90.
32. Remy, *Demonolatry*, 20.
33. Scott, *Discoverie*, 44.

the female arises from one of the precedent male's ribs, but one "which is bent as it were in the contrary direction to a man. And since through this defect she is an imperfect animal, she always deceives."[34] Witches, as the most ambitious, cunning, deceitful, and lewd of women, were accused of every variety of what orthodoxy defined as sexual perversion. Their perversion and deviance threatened the integrity of the Christian community, and their aberrant behavior challenged the righteous order of society. The literature of witchcraft is so rife with descriptions of the diabolical deviance of witches that it virtually comprises a catalogue of contemporary sexual perversions and antisocial behavior. For contemporaries, these two aspects of witchery were integral parts of a monolithic system of demonality at work in the world.

Witches were darkly linked to incest, animal aberrations, necrophilia, anal and oral intercourse, pederasty, homoeroticism, and cross-dressing. These deviations from the sexual norm were usually considered corollaries of the primary sexual activities in which witches were believed to play a central role—sex with the Devil and the incubus/succubus pairings—or part of their general malevolent campaign to seduce the innocent and to subvert an ordered society. Charges of bestiality are a case in point. A typical case of bewitchment involved a young man who fell so "farre in love with his cow" that "for his life he could not come in where she was, but he must needes take up her tayle and kisse under it."[35] Sex with the Devil was often depicted as interspecific and unnatural. The Devil frequently assumed the form of a great goat and "a tousiours un membre de mulet, ayant choisy en imitation celuy de cet animal comme le mieux pourueu."[36] One author, though, turned the argument on its head, asserting that incubi and succubi were

> more noble than man, by reason of the greater subtilty [immateriality] of their bodies, and . . . when having intercourse with

34. Kramer and Sprenger, *Malleus*, 44.

35. George Gifford, *A Dialogue Concerning Witches and Witchcraftes* (1593; reprint, London: Oxford University Press, 1931), n.p. For examples of references to incest and anal intercourse, see Boguet, *Examen*, 57, and 26, 270–74; for instances of pederasty and homoeroticism, see Fairfax, *Daemonologia*, 89 and Boguet, *Examen*, 92; and for references to necrophilia, see Sinistrari, *Demonality*, 201 and Boguet, *Examen*, 21.

36. Remy, *Demonolatry*, 14n. The passage might be translated thus: "always had the organ of a mule, having chosen to counterfeit that of that animal as the best appointed [for its office]."

humankind, male or female, fall into the same sin as man when copulating with a beast, which is inferior to him.[37]

The psychological functions of these explanations for the popular mind are immediately apparent. In the first case, an outré sexual practice, which seems virtually incomprehensible in terms of conventional human erotic motivation, becomes immediately comprehensible and can be used to reinforce conformity to orthodox norms. Much in the same way that our contemporary popular understanding of serial killers as human "monsters" reinforces our fundamental belief in the order of our society and in fundamental human decency, the diabolical explanation of animal aberrations was comforting, and encouraged identification with conventional values. Indeed, this psychological projection mechanism constituted the basis for the popular frenzy that sustained the intellectual structures we have been discussing, i.e., the literature and folklore of witchcraft. This was nowhere more evident than in the belief that humans were analogous to lower animals in their relations with demon lovers. Given the much greater frequency of incubi among the preternatural lovers that appear in this literature, the implication of the vicious logic of this argument is certainly the bestialization of the female. Women emerge as potentially a separate, intermediate species, a meretricious, bastardized link in the Great Chain of Being, above the lower animals but below man (in both the gendered and the generic sense), and below the demons of the air.

The inveterate belief that sexual aberrations, while not unique to women, were, when practiced by women, typically more antisocial and represented a more serious threat to orthodoxy and social order, reinforced the vision of female moral inferiority and the need for social control of women. Women of power, women of knowledge—cunning women—were a threat to the established male hierarchies of power, and were frequently subsumed under the broad categories of witchcraft and demonality. Instances of cross-dressing (often in an effort to gain arcane male knowledge or to usurp male power) and the ability to change one's sex, are representative of this set of beliefs. A woman who sought to test the taboo on female presence in a monastery, and who put on male attire to secure entry, provides an example to all rash,

37. Sinistrari, *Demonality*, 257.

presumptuous females. She was resoundingly repulsed by a demon, who forcibly thrust

> her head between her thighs, so that she who had tried to imprint a false kiss upon the holy threshold was forced to kiss the filthy parts of her own body; and she had to exhibit openly to all who wished to see it that sex which she had tried to conceal beneath a man's clothing. The result of this was that no woman thereafter dared to approach the monastery.[38]

Of the limited number of cases of change of sex (which often seems to have resulted naturally from the evolution of congenital hermaphroditism) that appear in this literature, all are from female to male, and it is dogmatically assumed that such changes can be effected by diabolical influences.[39] The few cases of witches "laying on" people in their beds suggest a homoerotic variation on the incubus/succubus theme. These cases exclusively involve child victims, and the intent of the practice, apart from whatever erotic overtones are present, seems to have been to gain nefarious influence over the young. The overt threat to household order and parental authority is also clear. The sole male example involved a pupil and his schoolmaster, who "was in the habit of stretching himself upon his body, placing his mouth on the boy's mouth, which he made him open, and muttering into it."[40]

More real and more dangerously antisocial than these largely symbolic (when not merely potential or imaginary) forms of predominantly female revolt were those activities associated with the cunning women who professed and practiced witchcraft as an ancient form of knowledge and belief. These were the practice of abortion (and sometimes infanticide), "tying the points," and the evil eye. Witches, it was believed, had peculiar power over the health and life of children, and an association between "those midwives and wise women who are witches" and the diabolical rituals of infanticide and abortion is presupposed. These women, it is maintained, kill children "before they have been baptized,

38. Guazzo, *Compendium*, 121. Compare the description of a nun who tried to usurp priestly powers (141). See also Fairfax, *Daemonologia*, 106.

39. Guazzo, *Compendium*, 57–59.

40. Boguet, *Examen*, 92. For other examples, see Fairfax, *Daemonologia*, 89, 152.

by thrusting a large pin into their brains," and "they do even worse; for they kill them while they are yet in their mothers' wombs."[41]

"Tying the points" need not detain us long other than to remark that it comprised, in the popular mind, the most prominent and most feared form of sexual magic. Since we have discussed this aspect of witchcraft at some length above, it should suffice here simply to cite the definition of this practice in ecclesiastical law, which essentially constructed its juridical code in these matters on the foundation of ancient popular belief. The practice undermined the basic social unit of Christian society — the family — by rendering

> men impotent and bewitched, and therefore by this impediment brought about by witchcraft they are unable to copulate, and so the contract of marriage is rendered void and matrimony in their cases has become impossible.[42]

While this is clearly a predominantly female crime of aggression against males, the Church recognized that it might be as effectively accomplished indirectly by undermining female capacity. "It is to be noted also that impotence of the member to perform the act is not the only bewitchment; but sometimes the woman is caused to be unable to conceive, or else she miscarries." The Church followed popular belief in emphasizing the threat to male potency. The popular term for marital infertility was "tying the points," a colorful idiomatic expression that referred to magically knotting the strings ("points") that attached the codpiece to the hose so that they could not be undone by natural means and thereby preventing male sexual activity.[43]

The evil eye (*mal d'ochio*) tradition represented the survival of an ancient tradition of innate malevolent occult power. Its deleterious effect on the health of those who fell victim to a stare from someone who had the power of the eye was potentially devastating. The operative

---

41. Boguet, *Examen*, 88. See also Guazzo, *Compendium*, 25, 91; Remy, *Demonolatry*, 99–100 (associated here specifically with midwives and harlots), and 102–3; and Kramer and Sprenger, *Malleus*, 60.

42. Kramer and Sprenger, *Malleus*, 4.

43. See Adolph F. Niemoeller, *American Encyclopedia of Sex* (New York: Panurge Press, 1935), 204. The French term was "nouer l'aiguillete," "knotting the lace (string)." For a detailed discussion of the specific varieties of incapacity that might be magically imposed on a couple, see Guazzo, *Compendium*, 91–96, and 99.

principle of the evil eye and its power of fascination was believed to be vapors, "conveied out as it were by beames and streames of a certeine fierie force."[44] It was typically associated with certain women. For example, "if anybody's spirit be inflamed with malice or rage, as is often the case with old women, then their disturbed spirit looks through their eyes, for their countenances are most evil and harmful." In fact, such is the highly contagious power of infection of certain categories of women that a person might contract an optical affliction simply by looking upon her, "and although the vision be perfectly clear, yet the sight of some impurity, such as, for example, a woman during her monthly periods, the eyes will as it were contract a certain impurity."[45]

Some authorities opposed the weight of accumulated superstition as it related to occult ocular power, but insisted that a witch could seduce, fascinate, or bewitch by a mere touch of her hand (or, wielding a phallic symbol, her wand). One writer, a jurist, revealed his personal paranoia at the prospect of the male's loss of control in his remark that "if a judge lets himself be touched on the bare arm and hand by the witch, he thereby becomes her advocate."[46]

Such fears were rooted in the belief that witches had literally and completely been defiled and corrupted through their association with the powers of evil, and that the very physical essence of their bodies was imbued with highly communicable, pestilential essences. This may explain the fascination in this literature with the scatological aspects of witchcraft. Since the Devil revels in "external filth and uncleanness," he imparts to his acolytes a taste for "impurity and uncleanness." The physical touch of his body and attendance at his rituals corrupt the taste and sensibilities, for when he occupies a human body he frequently selects that of a corpse, and "often dwells in those parts of the body which . . . harbour the excremental waste of the body. . . . The gifts of the Demon also are fashioned from ordure and dung, and his banquets from the flesh of beasts that have died."[47] The holy water of the witches' Sabbat was the Devil's urine, and during that ritual as well on diverse other occasions, witches were instructed "that they should kisse his

44. Scott, *Discoverie*, 282.
45. Kramer and Sprenger, *Malleus*, 17.
46. Boguet, *Examen*, 84.
47. Remy, *Demonolatry*, 38.

Buttockes, in signe of dutye to him."[48] Satan is also able, on occasion, to "speak through the shameful parts of a woman."[49]

Since the average person might never see and hear this ventriloquist's feat of the Devil, more certain and publicly verifiable methods of identifying witches were required. This was the function of the examination and trial of suspected witches. In the European tradition, the examination was conducted to locate the Devil's mark, with which he had stigmatized his followers. Diligence and care were necessary in the search because

> the mark is not always of the same description. . . . on men it is generally found on the eye-lids, or the armpit, or lips or shoulder or posterior; whereas on women it is found on the breasts or privy parts.[50]

Satan's method of branding witches was detailed by James I of England:

> the Deuill dooth lick them with his tung in some privy part of their bodie, before he dooth receiue them to be his seruants, which marke commonly is given them vnder the haire in some part of their bodye, whereby it may not easily be found out or seene, although they be searched: and generally so long as the marke is not seene to those which search them, so long the parties that hath the marke will neuer confesse any thing.[51]

As a result of the difficulty in locating such a mark, the examination of a suspected witch required an extremely minute and probing scrutiny of her/his flesh. If the suspect did not confess, it had been common practice since ancient times to see to it that "their apparell . . . be changed, and everie haire in their body must be shaven off with a sharpe

---

48. James I, *Newes,* 14. See also Guazzo, *Compendium,* 35; Boguet, *Examen,* 56, 257. On urine at the Sabbat, see Boguet, *Examen,* 61. Since the standard sources give us no etymology for the derisory challenge, "kiss my ass," it may be that it derived from this folk tradition. It was certainly in common use by the time of Shakespeare.

49. Boguet, *Examen,* 28. The episode in William S. Burroughs's novel *Naked Lunch* (where a man teaches his anus to talk, and it eventually usurps the functions of his mouth) echoes this popular superstition.

50. Guazzo, *Compendium,* 15. He cites as one of his authorities for this belief Lambert Doneau, a sixteenth-century Calvinist theologian.

51. James I, *Newes,* 12–13. See also Remy, *Demonolatry,* 8–11.

razor."[52] The purpose of this procedure was twofold: to facilitate the location of the Devil's mark, and even more importantly to forfend the concealment of spells, charms, or drugs that would render the witch immune to torture or able to maintain silence in the face of vigorous inquisition.

The location of the Devil's mark is critical to the examination, and was believed to have unique properties. As the mark of Satan's talon, some claimed, it was scarified, and was characterized by "a slight hardening of the skin," and

> the place is entirely bloodless and insensitive, so that even if a needle be deeply thrust in, no pain is felt and not a drop of blood is shed. This fact is held to be so certain a proof of capital guilt that it is often made the base of examination and torture.[53]

Certain aspects of a woman's appearance and antecedents also figured against her in the proceedings of witchcraft tribunals. "Devils attach themselves chiefly to women who have beautiful hair," one authority maintained; while "maides having yellow haire are most combred with Incubus."[54] Intense, quarrelsome women were also suspect, as were "of all other women, leane, hollow eied, old, beetlebrowed women."[55] Of even more importance than physical appearance was family descent, for "it is taken as a great presumption of guilt against the accused if his father and mother, or one of them, are witches. [Indeed], some have maintained that this is an infallible rule; and there seems much to be said for such a view."[56]

European procedure in witchcraft cases, based on ancient tradition and medieval precedent, routinely relied on torture as a means to ascertain the truth of accusations and more particularly to elicit confessions — definitive proof of guilt and sufficient basis for condemnation and execution. On the question of trial by ordeal, there was less agreement. Trial by red-hot iron and trial by boiling water were adamantly condemned by the most authoritative Continental, fifteenth-century

52. Scott, *Discoverie*, 12. See also Boguet, *Examen*, 125–27, and 216; and Remy, *Demonolatry*, 168.

53. Remy, *Demonolatry*, 9.

54. Boguet, *Examen*, 65; Scott, *Discoverie*, 45.

55. Scott, *Discoverie*, 158.

56. Boguet, *Examen*, 155. See also Kramer and Sprenger, *Malleus*, 144; and Guazzo, *Compendium*, 96–98.

witch-hunters' manual, while an English Protestant guidebook of a century later sustained both practices. This suggests some variation in procedure in witchcraft cases by region, by doctrinal belief, and over time. As we turn our attention to the witchcraft trials in Salem, Massachusetts, in 1692, and consider in what ways and to what extent they were influenced by European tradition and practice, it will be useful to keep this divergence of belief and practice in the matter of trial by ordeal clearly in mind.

English legal tradition, from the time of Elizabeth, tended to divide the occult arts into "magicke, southsaying wizards, diuination, iuggling, inchanting and charming, and witcherie." "Witcherie" was conceived of as a uniquely feminine offense, the term "witch" signifying a "hagg" who has been "eluded by a league made with the deuil."[57] The burden of a witch's offenses was attendance at the Sabbat or Black Mass, where she would "spend all night after with her sweete hart [the Devil], in playing, sporting, bankqueting, dauncing, and diuerse other deuelish lustes and lewd desports, and to shew a thousand such monsterous mockeries."[58]

New England practice blurred the distinction between one kind of supernatural activity and another, and subsumed them all under the comprehensive category of witchcraft. This made for a pragmatic simplification of the legal code, and was quite logical in light of the fact that contemporary British statutory law ("An Acte againste Conjurations Inchantmente and Witchcrafte," 1 James I, chapter 12), mandated the death penalty for all three magical categories when their exercise led to the loss of life or property or materially affected the health or welfare of others. Second convictions of intent without the fact of such threats to society also merited capital punishment.[59] New England practice also greatly diminished the erotic concerns in witchcraft prosecutions, but could not wholly eliminate them.

Traditional folk concerns rooted in sexual magic played a role in several of the Salem cases. Bridget Bishop was said to have bewitched her first husband to death, perhaps an instance of the use of magical means to achieve revenge on a lover. Her troubled domestic relations

---

57. Ewen, *Witch Hunting*, 22, 23.

58. William West, *Symbolaeographie* (1594), quoted in Ewen, *Witch Hunting*, 23–24.

59. See Ewen, *Witch Hunting*, 25, 44. The 1604 statute was not repealed by Parliament until 1736 (9 George II, chapter 5).

are attested to by the fact that her husband at the time of the Salem outbreak, Edward Bishop, had brought charges of witchcraft against her. In the trial of Susannah Martin, William Brown deposed that his wife had been bewitched by the accused and implied that their marital relations had been supernaturally impeded. He testified that, about thirty years before the trial, upon his return from a journey to England, his

> wife would not owne him but sd they were devorst and Asked him wither he did not mett with one M. Benty Abey in England by whom he was divorst And from that time to this very day have been under a strange kind of distemper frenzy vncapibil of any resional action though strong and helthy of body.[60]

Martin's interference in the domestic life of the Browns suggests the persistence of superstitious belief in "tying the points."

Another area of witchcraft that touched on popular erotic fantasy and folklore was fortune-telling and divination. Tituba, Carib Indian slave of the Reverend Samuel Parris, and catalyst for the witchcraft hysteria in Salem, had undertaken to conjure forth the images of the future husbands of her enthralled adolescent audience in the minister's kitchen. Dorcas Hoar had been dabbling in palmistry since the 1670s, and had run into difficulties when she successfully predicted the death of her husband, William Hoar. The suspicions of the village had been aroused because she had declared at the very time she predicted his demise

> yt shee should live poorely so long as her husband willm Hoar did live but ye said will should dye before her and after yt shee should live better.[61]

She had also successfully predicted the order of deaths in other village couples, which made her suspect as one who bewitched others to death and thus feared as a threat to marital unions.

Though not so dramatic and prominent as in the European tradition, there were cases of bewitchment of the genitourinary functions and organs in the Salem records. Bray Williams testified in the proceedings

60. *Records of Salem Witchcraft, Copied from the Original Documents*, 2 vols. (1864; reprint, New York: Da Capo Press, 1969), 1:207–8.
61. *Records of Salem Witchcraft*, 1:245.

against John Willard that subsequent to his refusal to support Willard, who had been charged with witchcraft, he suffered acute urinary distress. "I cannot express the misery I was in," he told the court, "for my water was suddenly stopd & I had no benefit of nature but was like a man in a Rock." About five days later, after Willard had been arrested and imprisoned, Williams experienced relief, but "in the room of a stoppage I was vexed with a flow of water so that it was hard to keep myself dry," and finally, "I was taken in the sorest distress & misery my water being turned into real blood, or of a bloody colour and the old pain returned excessively as much as before which continued for about 24 hours together."[62]

Another suspect, Wilmott Reed (like Willard, later convicted and hanged), was accused of bewitching essential bodily functions. Charity Pitman testified that Reed, subsequent to a dispute with a Mrs. Syms over missing linen, had cursed the latter for accusing Reed's servant of theft. Reed's imprecation took the form of a wish that "she might never mingere, nor cacare," and as a consequence, "Mrs. Syms was taken with the distemper of the dry Belly-ake and so continued many months" until she removed from Salem.[63]

Benjamin Abbott was tormented, he claimed, by Martha Carrier, who inflicted upon him, amongst other ills, a "sore [that] did breede in my grine."[64] The most telling example, however, was recounted in Cotton Mather's *Memorable Providences* (1689), and provides a glimpse into the paranoid context out of which the Salem episode arose. Mather reported, unequivocally and rather sensationalistically, that in the winter of 1684 one Philip Smith had been "murdered with an hideous Witchcraft." The jury of inquest that examined his corpse "found a Swelling on one Breast, which rendered it like a Womans. His Privities were wounded or burned."[65] This episode suggests an aggressive attack on male sexuality and a conscious effort to achieve emasculation and the transformation of sex not unlike episodes recorded in the European witchcraft literature.

62. *Records of Salem Witchcraft*, 2:9–10.

63. *Records of Salem Witchcraft*, 2:105.

64. *Records of Salem Witchcraft*, 2:60.

65. Cotton Mather, *Memorable Providences, Relating to Witchcraft and Possessions* (1689), reprinted in George L. Burr, *Narratives of the Witchcraft Cases, 1648–1706* (1914; reprint, New York: Barnes and Noble, 1968), 132, 134.

There seems to have been much less overtly diabolical erotic activity in Salem than had been the case in Europe. There is not a single unequivocal reference to sexual relations between a witch and the Devil at Salem. The only supposed case was reported by Edward Bishop, who said of his wife, Bridget, "that the Devill did come bodly unto her and that she was familiar with the Deuil and that she sate up all ye night long with ye Deuill."[66]

Incubus/succubus sex was also less common than in the European tradition, but was certainly not unheard of in Salem. Mercy Short, for example, was visited by demons who would "come and sitt upon her Breast, and pull open her Jaw, and keep her without fetching a Sensible Breath, sometimes for Half-an-hour, and sometimes for several whole Hours together."[67] The specifically erotic content of this case was revealed in Short's response to the incubi: "You pretend a precious deal of Love to mee indeed! . . . Fine Promises! You'l bestow an Husband upon mee, if I'll be your Servant. An Husband! What? A Divel!"[68]

Richard Coman claimed that Bridget Bishop "in her Red paragon Bodyce," did "lay upon my Brest or body and soe oppressed him yt he could not speake nor stur noe not soe much as to awake his wife althow he Endeavured soe to do itt."[69] He was oppressed by similar visitations on two succeeding nights. Susannah Martin was also accused of acting the part of a succubus. Bernard Peach testified that when he was in bed on a Sunday night he

> saw Susanna Martin come in [at the window], and jump down upon the Floor She took hold of this Deponent's Feet, and drawing his Body up into an Heap, she lay upon him near Two Hours; in all which time he could neither speak nor stirr.[70]

---

66. *Records of Salem Witchcraft*, 1:168. Cotton Mather insinuated as much about Goody Glover in a case that predated the Salem trials. She had confessed, he reported, that she "had One, who was her Prince, with whom she maintain'd, I know not what Communion." See Cotton Mather, *Memorable Providences,* 104.

67. Cotton Mather, *A Brand Pluck'd Out of the Burning* (1693), reprinted in Burr, *Narratives,* 264.

68. Mather, *A Brand Pluck'd Out of the Burning,* 269.

69. *Records of Salem Witchcraft*, 1:164. The term "paragon" referred to the cloth of the garment. In seventeenth-century sartorial terminology, it meant "camlet," an expensive, imported fabric, a satin weave of camel's hair or angora wool.

70. Cotton Mather, *The Wonders of the Invisible World* (1693), reprinted in Burr, *Narratives,* 231. See also *Records of Salem Witchcraft*, 2:212. See also Jarvis Ring's testimony that Martin "lay upon him awhile" on several occasions, *Records of Salem Witchcraft*, 1:214.

Reports of apparitions in bedchambers with less disturbing consequences and less graphic descriptions were also not uncommon at the
height of the witchcraft craze in Salem. These apparitions provide clues
to the kinds of aggressively sexual or provocative behavior that led to
accusations of witches tormenting men as succubi. William Stacy recalled that during an illness Bridget Bishop "did give him a visitt and
withall proferred a great Love for this Deponant in his affliction more
than ordinary, at which this deponant admired."[71] At the time of these
events, Stacy was twenty-two and Bishop was twenty-seven years of
age. The forward older woman, then, visited Stacy while he slept and
he awakened to find her at the foot of his bed, whereupon she "hopt
vpon the bed and aboute the Roome and then went out."[72] Samuel
Gray also testified that he had experienced a nocturnal visit from
Bishop, and corroborated Stacy's statements about awakening with
something piercingly cold "betweene his lips Pressing hard agt his
teeth."[73] Both Stacy and Gray believed Bishop was responsible for the
deaths of their daughters.

Contrary to European experience, those accused of witchcraft in
Salem do not seem to have confessed to relations with incubi, and I
have found only a single example of a male (who was ultimately hanged
as a witch) accused of an implicitly sexual offense. John Willard used
witchcraft and sorcery upon a single woman, Susannah Sheldon, to the
extent that she was "hurt tortured afflicted."[74] His conduct may have
constituted what we would today describe as sexual harassment.

The erotic element in the Salem trials seems to have been immediately linked to social disapprobation of what contemporary community standards considered deviant and socially destructive sexual
behavior. Bridget Bishop had apparently scandalized her neighbors.
John Hale said her home was all but "a house of great profainness and
iniquity," for she "did entertain certain people in her house at unsea-
sonable hours in ye nite to keep drinking and playing at shovel board
whereby discord did arise in other families and young people were in
danger of being corrupted."[75]

71. *Records of Salem Witchcraft*, 1:150.
72. *Records of Salem Witchcraft*, 1:151.
73. *Records of Salem Witchcraft*, 1:150. Gray's statement may be found on page 153.
74. *Records of Salem Witchcraft*, 1:269.
75. *Records of Salem Witchcraft*, 1:154.

One Joseph Ring deposed that he had been inveigled by an acquaintance to an abandoned house near a forest where he encountered Susannah Martin and another woman. The group "had a good fire and drink it seemed to be sidr this continued most part of the night sd. Martin then being in her naturall shape."[76] His brother, Jarvis, had suffered several visits from Martin in her succubus form. The association of the wilderness with unrestrained sexuality is clear here, as it was in the case of Abigail Hobbs, who routinely slept out in the woods alone. She told an acquaintance, it was later learned in court, that "she was not a fraid of any thing for . . . she had sold herselfe boddy & soule to ye old boy."[77] Whether we are to understand this to mean that Hobbs had had intercourse with the Devil is not clear; in any case, her deviance by contemporary standards is quite evident.

Males, too, were accused of witchcraft because of social deviance related to sexuality. George Burroughs, former pastor of Salem Village and considered by Cotton Mather to be the ringleader of a vast diabolical plot, was charged with murdering (in collusion with his soon-to-be third wife) his second wife, "because they would have one another." He was also charged with "keeping his two Successive Wives in a strange kind of Slavery."[78]

It is a striking fact that every case of demon love, and most of the cases of natural desire resulting in sexually aggressive behavior in the Salem episode, involved the victimization of the male. This stands in stark contrast to the European tradition. Quite probably this resulted from juridical expectations of higher rates of female sexual deviance. As Carol F. Karlsen has shown, there was an increasing incidence of sexual offenses committed by females recorded in Essex County as the seventeenth century wore on. Since prosecutions for sexual offenses after 1650 increasingly focused on premarital pregnancies and illegitimate births, women came under intense scrutiny; by 1680, sixty percent of prosecutions were of women. The double standard of sexual justice was reflected in the legal practice of the colony as a whole, for sixty-three percent of those punished for fornication in Massachusetts between 1620 and 1689 were women.[79]

---

76. *Records of Salem Witchcraft*, 1:215.

77. *Records of Salem Witchcraft*, 1:177.

78. *Records of Salem Witchcraft*, 2:116. See also Mather, *Wonders of the Invisible World*, 220.

79. Carol F. Karlsen, *The Devil in the Shape of a Woman: Witchcraft in Colonial New England* (New York: W. W. Norton, 1987), 198, 329.

Deviance was also inferred in New England, as it had been in the European tradition, from familial association. The taint of witchcraft was not genetically transmitted but was absorbed by contiguity and inculcated by parental example. The most moving case in the records of the Salem trials is that of Sarah Good's daughter, aged four or five years, who was believed to afflict adolescent girls through her evil eye.[80]

The goal of the examination and trial of suspected witches was to establish definitively their deviance and to secure a confession. As John Hale, minister of Beverly, remarked retrospectively, "this matter was carried on . . . chiefly by the complaints and accusations of the Afflicted, Bewitched ones, as it was supposed, and then by the Confessions of the Accused, condemning themselves, and others."[81] Cotton Mather, in a letter written to Judge John Richards at the outset of the Salem trials, maintained that the best evidence for conviction was a "credible confession" as opposed to one that "may be the result of only a delirious brain or a discontented heart."[82]

But in the heat and light of the public spectacle, Mather's injunctions about caution were swamped by a flood of popular superstition and prejudice. In no area of the proceedings was superstition, firmly rooted in the centuries-long European tradition, more evident than in the examination of witches and the search for the Devil's mark. Unlike that tradition, however, which saw the mark as outward and visible evidence of the soul contracted to Satan and the body dedicated to spreading diabolism abroad, the Salem witch-hunters tended to emphasize a minor element of the European trials and to combine the idea of the Devil's mark with the notion of the witch's teat, upon which her diabolical familiars were suckled.

Suckling familiars was a preternatural act and therefore became a central point in the physical identification of witches. In the Salem episode as well as in the European tradition, it was never an act exclusive to females. Usually the point of attachment for the familiar's mouth was secret, and no doubt this explains why only those who were sup-

---

80. Deodat Lawson, *A Brief and True Narrative of Some Remarkable Passages Relating to Sundry Persons Afflicted by Witchcraft, at Salem Village: Which Happened from the Nineteenth of March, to the Fifth of April, 1692* (1692), reprinted in Burr, *Narratives,* 159.

81. John Hale, *A Modest Enquiry into the Nature of Witchcraft* (1702), reprinted in Burr, *Narratives,* 421.

82. Quoted in Chadwick Hansen, *Witchcraft at Salem* (New York: George Braziller, 1969), 97.

posedly witnessed in the act were credibly taken to nurse through their natural mammary glands. Giles Corey, for example, was described by Susannah Sheldon as appearing with "two turcles hang to his coat and he opened his bosom and put his turcles to his brest and gave them suck."[83]

Just as in the European tradition for the Devil's mark, the location of the more covert teats was gender specific. On the male body, they were found in Salem examinations on the inside of the mouth in the flesh of the cheek, on the shoulder blade, or on the hip. One female witch was said to have had a teat on the lower right shoulder, and Tituba supposedly suckled her familiar between her fingers, but for the most part, these fleshy excrescences were found in the genital area of women.

Bridget Bishop, Rebecca Nurse, and Elizabeth Proctor, upon examination by a committee of nine women and a male surgeon, were found to have "a preternatural Escrescence of flesh between ye pudendum and Anus [the perineum] much like to tetts and not usuall in women . . . and yt they were in all ye three women neer ye same place."[84] The location of these witches' teats on women's bodies in Salem presents a direct line of descent from the European witchcraft tradition, and suggests the persistence of certain bodies of ideas, particularly those linking conceptions of sexuality, sin, and evil to inveterate bodily taboos in the popular mind.

Custom and folk superstitions pertaining to the supernatural seem to have been transmitted somewhat erratically over time and distance. While the basic elements of the drama of the individual soul in its struggle with evil were expressed in a set of symbolic conventions and formulaic rituals associated with witchcraft, the function of particular allegorical and anagogical elements in the system was not immutable. Some associations of ideas were remarkably persistent in the social construction of diabolical magic in the popular mind, while others were

83. *Records of Salem Witchcraft*, 1:168–69. For another male example, see *Records of Salem Witchcraft*, 1:279. For women suckling familiars at their breasts, see *Records of Salem Witchcraft*, 1:168, 192, and 238.

84. *Records of Salem Witchcraft*, 1:146. Later in the afternoon on the same day (2 June 1692), the committee reversed its decision, finding the teats to be dry skin, except in the case of Proctor, whose blemish was now characterized as a "proper procedeulia Ani" [hemorrhoids?], *Records of Salem Witchcraft*, 1:147. See also Nurse's petition to the court to be reexamined, *Records of Sa' Witchcraft*, 1:98–99.

more fluid as their meanings shifted to accord with the demands social ideology placed on the systems of cultural belief that sustained it.

A good example of this was the way the incubus/succubus tradition was adapted to the socially determined realities of sexual deviance at Salem. The emphasis on female sexual aggression reflected in the preponderance of malevolent succubi that appear in the trial records represents an adaptation of a traditional cultural system of folk belief to the social construction of gender as expressed in legislation and jurisprudence governing fornication. As we have seen, the fact of sexual deviance had come to be primarily a female responsibility from 1650 on, and Puritan law after 1668 required the questioning of unmarried pregnant women during childbirth to pressure them into naming the fathers of their children. Thus, deviant women became responsible for incriminating their lovers and for reestablishing the socioeconomic balance of the community, since the child would now be supported by its father rather than becoming a burden on the common resources of the village.

The inquisitorial function in cases of unwed mothers fell to the lot of midwives, who thus played an essential role in maintaining community moral standards and protecting its citizens from undue demands on their purses and charitable sensibilities.[85] This may provide some insight into another unique aspect of witchcraft tradition at Salem. There is virtually no concern about the practice of abortion and infanticide among Salem witches and no consistent attempt to link them with midwives. Witches at Salem certainly were accused of afflicting children and, in several important instances, of bringing about their deaths, but the children are typically older (many are adolescents), and there is little interference with pregnancy or childbirth evident in the record.

Essentially, midwives were on the same side as the male magistracy in its attempts to deal effectively with sexual deviance; it would not have done to use them as symbols of witchcraft as the European tradition had done. Since witchcraft trials were part of the broader effort to control social (and especially sexual) deviance, midwives were enlisted to assist in examinations of suspects, a task analogous to their inquisition of unwed mothers. Since such examinations, given expectations

85. For a discussion of the Massachusetts law of 1668 on identifying the father of an illegitimate child, see Roger Thompson, *Sex in Middlesex: Popular Mores in a Massachusetts County, 1649-1* (Amherst: University of Massachusetts Press, 1986), 22–24.

about the location of the witch's teat, required close inspection of the genital region, it is not surprising that women often requested the presence of midwives.

Rebecca Nurse, who petitioned the court for a reexamination on 28 June 1692, is a case in point. She noted that physical phenomena discovered on her body were the results of hard travail and difficult births and requested that a new team of women be appointed to examine her. Two of the four women she suggested for the team were specifically identified as midwives.[86] It is notable, too, that the role of midwives in eliciting the name of the father of an illegitimate child partook of the spirit of persecution and the use of physical pain to secure a confession, for it was their practice to refuse assistance in easement of pain during childbirth until the mother had confessed the name of the child's father. The links to the moral and juridical use of torture in witchcraft cases underscore the role of midwives in supporting the established social order in its crusade to control deviance.

As a colonial outpost of the British empire, the immediate legal tradition that would have influenced Salem was that of England. The Act of Parliament of 1604 governed witchcraft cases in England until its repeal in 1735, and is much more specific in its provisions than any colonial statute.[87] Massachusetts statutes of 1641 and 1648 simply provided, as an operative definition of the crime, that the witch "hath or consulteth with a familiar spirit."[88] The colonial laws are skeletal and clearly give little guidance to examiners and prosecutors. The traditions of the English law, much fuller in their elaboration, were selectively applied to the colonial situation. Much more important than statutory provisions for both British and colonial witchcraft proceedings were popular attitudes and beliefs about precisely what behavior constituted witchery. The letter of the law does, however, provide a clear rationale for the most sensational aspect of the Salem prosecutions—the singular importance of the witch's teat as opposed to the Devil's mark, so central a part of European folk belief. The location of the teat provided definitive physical evidence that an individual had entertained and nourished a familiar. The witch's teat was a central element in the

---

86. *Records of Salem Witchcraft*, 1:98–99.

87. See Ewen, *Witch Hunting*, 19–21.

88. David D. Hall, ed., *Witch-Hunting in Seventeenth-Century New England* (Boston: Northeas University Press, 1991), 315–16.

juridical literature that arose in England to assist judges to distinguish the natural from the supernatural. Since this was the only characteristic of a witch cited in the law for a capital offense, it became the primary physical condition for execution in the colonial tradition.

The Puritans believed themselves to be modern and scientific in their approach to the natural and supernatural worlds, and therefore the New England tradition tended to reject some of the more colorfully fanciful and credulous beliefs associated with European witchcraft literature. European authors were closer in time and more temperamentally sympathetic to the pagan tales of animal aberrations in which the animal was an incarnation of a god or a spirit. In their compendia, these authors reflected powerful currents of folk superstition and popular magical lore flowing from the lusty sensibilities of pagan eroticism. Puritan emphasis on rationality precluded their following the lead of an author like Henri Boguet, who declared: "I thoroughly believe all that has been written of Fauns, Satyrs and woodland gods, which were no more than demons"; and who could dispute a witch's confession of having copulated with a fowl, saying

> I am of opinion that she meant to say gander instead of fowl, for that is a form which Satan often takes, and therefore we have the proverb that Satan has feet like a goose.[89]

The whole controversy so central to the European literature — whether demons could reproduce through intercourse with human beings or whether they merely provided an alternative mode of human reproduction — found no place in Puritan texts on witchcraft. The Devil was more a threat to the soul than to the body in New England, which helps to explain why there are virtually no straightforward references to intercourse between witches and the Devil in the Salem records. The succubus tradition, however, proved more useful at Salem, and though equally irrational, played a prominent role in accusations of witches. But, then, victimization of males by females, as we have seen, constituted a prominent social and legal fact in Puritan society ás related to fornication statutes, and fear of female sexual aggression seemed to be validated by the rising incidence of female offenders. In this context, it becomes easier to understand why there is a preponderance of succubi

89. Boguet, *Examen*, 33, 34.

in the Salem experience, while in the European tradition, incubi were the primary offenders.

The rational position on the incubus/succubus issue was set forth by a late sixteenth-century English author, who argued that "of the evil Spirits *Incubus* and *Succubus* there can be no firme reason or proofe brought out of scriptures," and that "in truth, this *Incubus* is a bodilie disease . . . although it extend unto the trouble of the mind."[90] His cynical rationalism about what he considered the rankest superstitious ignorance is reflected in his assumption that "lecheries [are] covered with the cloke of *Incubus* and witchcraft . . . speciallie to excuse and maintaine knaveries and lecheries of idle priests and bawdie monks; and to cover the shame of their lovers and concubines."[91] Both of the traditions implied here—use of witchcraft to explain sexual deviance and anti-Catholicism—figured prominently in the Salem episode, but that did not prevent the persistence of the succubus belief in the popular mind and, as a consequence, in personal accusations.

Despite a move toward rationality, English cases, too, from the 1580s to the end of the seventeenth century, continued to emphasize certain magical elements. From about 1645, in the English legal tradition, accusations for "entertaining" Satan, in the form of beastly familiars, became increasingly common. While Salem cases revealed little interest in the notion of sex with the Devil, they enthusiastically embraced incrimination for "entertaining."

The tradition of witches cherishing and nourishing their diabolical imps was very strong in English cases, and James I had given the imprimatur of the highest secular authority to the expectation that the teats, which were the outward physical sign of their presence, would be found in the genital region. The resulting dehumanization of the suspected witch was clear in the record of one seventeenth-century English case where, after a diligent and minute search, examiners had found "in her secret parts 2 white pieces of flesh like paps and some swore they were like the teats of an ewe, & some like the paps of a cat."[92] I have found no evidence that English practice in physical examination of witches followed European precedent in shaving the entire body of the suspects, but the remarks of James I on the location and cunning

90. Scott, *Discoverie*, 50, 49.
91. Scott, *Discoverie*, 48.
92. Ewen, *Witch Hunting*, 316.

concealment of these teats or marks strongly suggest the wisdom of thorough depilation.[93] At Salem, the strip search of witches was a standard feature of examinations in cases of witchcraft, but like English practice, there is no evidence to support the continuation of the earlier European practice of systematic removal of all body hair. The tradition of associating diabolical contact with the genital region of the female body, however, remained central to Salem belief and practice.

An idiosyncrasy of the seventeenth-century English tradition arose from its emphasis on the physicality of the relationship between the witch and Satan. Since the Devil typically appeared to women in the shape of a man, he was believed to seduce them through the lusts of the body, to seal a diabolical covenant. But whereas the European tradition had pondered the question of whether such sexual contacts resulted in diabolical progeny, the English stressed the literal indwelling presence of evil in the witch. Butterflies, bees, and mice were described as apparently emerging from the private parts of various witches, and one Margaret Mixter cried out "that Satan was within her," and onlookers "saw a thinge come from under her coats in likeness and shape of a beaver brush [tail]."[94] It is clear that these physical entities that had taken up residence within women's bodies were often considered to be their familiars, but they also seem to have been, from another point of view, the monstrous spawn of diabolical intercourse. There is no evidence of this explicit belief in the Salem records despite the prominence of familiars in accusations, yet the supposition of the location of the witches' teats in the genital area suggests at least a subliminal persistence of this tradition.

The Salem emphasis on familiars and the witch's teat represented a direct line of descent from the biblical texts and Stuart practice as determined by the king. In the early Salem cases, especially the confessions of Tituba and William Barker, detailed descriptions of the inverted rites of the unholy Sabbat, and sealings of diabolical covenants by signing the Devil's book, figured prominently. As the number of cases grew and a body of victims (the afflicted) came forward, accusations and confessions came to focus on proof of the fact of apparitional affliction; spectral evidence took precedence over customary belief. The

93. James I, *Daemonologie*, 12–13.

94. Ewen, *Witch Hunting*, 297. For other references to indwelling physical presences, see pages 296, 305, and 306.

personality of the Devil and his direct role in matters of witchcraft was downplayed, and the presence of evil became more spiritual than physical. In these ways, procedural practice at Salem diverged from the Stuart example.

In Salem, the broad Protestant tradition (as opposed to a narrowly sectarian Puritan one) played an important role in the social construction of witchcraft. Cotton Mather, for instance, linked early witches with the Catholic and specifically Irish traditions as well as with French influence and the pagan savagery of the Indian population.[95] English reticence about detailed discussions of sexual aspects of witchcraft seems to have prevailed at Salem as well, but that does not mean that sexuality did not play a significant role in the Salem trials: it was simply expressed in less direct ways. There is certainly no evidence to suggest that prudery or sexual delicacy played any role at Salem. Nevertheless, when we compare the testimony in seventeenth-century fornication cases with the witchcraft trials at Salem, the deviation of the latter from contemporary standards of popular public parlance becomes clear. Fornication trials were replete with detailed, eyewitness accounts (as the law required) of sexual acts, and not infrequently earthy Anglo-Saxon terms for sexual organs and acts were uttered openly in court.[96]

Rejection of the central Continental concept of sexual intercourse between witches and the Devil and the focus on spectral evidence, which moved witchcraft activity to a primarily supernatural plane, seems to have been grounded in the rejection of Catholic superstition and ecclesiastical precedent, for the tradition of witchcraft's power over the venereal act arose directly out of the 1484 papal bull of Innocent VIII.[97] No doubt a desire to distinguish the crimes of witchcraft from

95. Mather, *Memorable Providences*, 99, 103–4.

96. See Thompson, *Sex in Middlesex*, 130–54. It should be noted that the European manuals were compendia based on hundreds or thousands of cases of witches who were executed over a decade or more (Remy's *Demonolatry* had surveyed cases of nine hundred witches executed in Lorraine between 1580 and 1595). If the Salem trials had taken place in an area with as large a population base over such an extended period of time, they might well have produced a substantially larger number of examples of more overtly erotic descriptions. We have no way of telling how representative the cases selected for detailed treatment in a book like Remy's are. If there are fifty separate cases cited in Remy, for example, and all included significant erotic elements, that would constitute less than six percent of the total number of cases. In Salem, twenty people were killed in connection with witchcraft. A comparable rate of incidence of magical erotic behavior would be 1.2, less than two cases.

97. This connection had been specifically laid out in Kramer and Sprenger's *Malleus*, 47–48.

those less threatening and more typical, frequent forms of sexual deviance, like fornication and adultery, was also involved in the de-emphasis on witchcraft as sexual magic.

Judicial practice and standards of evidence also played important roles in establishing the nature of witchcraft proceedings at Salem. In the European tradition, inquisitorial procedure came to dominate witchcraft trials by the late fifteenth century. These trials, conducted after 1550 in secular courts, allowed the initiation of proceedings by accusers (who sustained no criminal liability in bringing such charges), and permitted judges wide discretion (including use of torture) in accumulating evidence necessary for conviction. The standards of proof in such cases were based on the Roman law of treason, and mandated either the testimony of two eyewitnesses or the confession of the accused.[98]

The English tradition was the only one in Europe that did not follow inquisitorial procedures in witchcraft trials but instead relied on the jury system. The effect of this divergence of English legal practice from that of the Continent in these matters was to allow rumor, hearsay, circumstantial evidence, and the establishment of fact by a single uncorroborated witness.[99]

Salem practice in the witchcraft trials adopted a syncretic approach. As in the inquisitorial framework, accusers played a prominent role and judges conducted the proceedings so as to confirm accusations, to elicit confessions, or to build up an overwhelming body of evidence. Two witnesses to the fact of witchcraft were required, but "one single witness to one Act of witchcraft, and another single witness to another such fact, made two witnesses against the Crime and the party suspected."[100] This standard, much closer to the English single-witness criterion than to European legal tradition, made the rule for sufficient testamentary evidence in a capital felony less rigorous than for sexual violations, much less serious criminal offenses. Two eyewitnesses of the deed were required for conviction in these cases.

Though this was common Massachusetts practice in witchcraft cases, there was precedent for establishing a stricter standard of evidence in the issue of the case of Goody Glover in 1679. Governor Simon

98. See Sinistrari, *Demonality,* 264–66; and Boguet, *Examen,* 169–70.
99. Levack, *Witch-Hunt,* 68–69.
100. Hale, *Modest Enquiry,* 411.

Bradstreet and a panel of magistrates dissented from the jury verdict and reprieved Glover on the grounds that "they did not esteem one single witness to one fact, and another single witness to another fact, for two witnesses, against the person in a matter Capital."[101]

Contrary to the long tradition of European witchcraft, but in accord with contemporary English practice, torture was generally discountenanced at Salem, and trial by ordeal, especially the popular trial by water, widely employed in England, was rejected. The New England legal code expressly rejected the use of torture, but a letter of John Proctor, one of the accused, from Salem prison in July 1692, suggests that some physical duress was used to extract confessions.

Proctor claimed two of Martha Carrier's sons were induced to confess when "they tied them neck to heels till the blood was ready to come out of their noses."[102] And, of course, there was the case of Giles Corey, pressed to death because he refused to plead when charged with witchcraft. But these were exceptions to the rule in the Salem proceedings. In general, they seemed to follow Cotton Mather's advice that "far from urging the un-English method of torture," intense questioning and other methods that "hath a tendency to put the witches into confusion" should be employed to elicit confessions.[103] In fact, the role of torture in the Salem trials was reversed. The victims of physical abuse who occupied center stage were the afflicted, whose "tortures increased continually," and were endlessly described in minute detail in court testimony.[104] Indeed, the tortures of those afflicted by spectral agents became a central body of evidence for the conviction of those accused of witchcraft at Salem.

Puritan ecclesiastical and secular authorities sincerely believed that they were conducting the Salem trials on the basis of enlightened, rational, scientific principles of jurisprudence and human behavior. Certainly, in comparison to seventeenth-century English standards — especially in regard to torture — the Salem cases were conducted in a physically more humane way. But the Puritans, despite their efforts to downplay the personal, sensual presence of the Devil (perhaps they had overused his metaphorical presence in the literature produced to

---

101. Hale, *Modest Enquiry*, 412.
102. Quoted in Hansen, *Witchcraft at Salem*, 133.
103. Quoted in Hansen, *Witchcraft at Salem*, 97.
104. Cotton Mather, *Remarkable Providences*, 101.

rationalize the Indian wars of 1636–37 and 1675–76, in which the dusky complexion of savagery was equated with that of the Black Man), had been unable finally to subdue the persistent folk beliefs about the active presence of evil in everyday life that were rooted in the popular lore and superstition of both England and Europe. Despite the inveterate Protestant bias against the irrationalities and superstition of Catholicism, the bulk of the evidence brought forward in the trials by accusers sustained important traditions associating witchcraft with sexual magic, and the examination of witches to locate the Devil's mark or witch's teat, long part of the European and English traditions of witchcraft, and carrying powerful implications (though never openly stated at Salem) of sexual congress with the Devil, fed into and reinforced (though in diminished form) popular beliefs about witchcraft and the practice of sexual magic. As the definitive European witchhunters' manual, the *Malleus Maleficarum* (1486) had observed, "witchcraft is not taught in books, nor is it practiced by the learned, but by the altogether uneducated.[105] What the Puritan elite discovered was that the beliefs as well as the practice were sustained by the common people, and once the chords of superstition had been touched in the popular mind, folk traditions, vulgar rhythms, and ancient hermetic harmonies would call the tune.

105. Kramer and Sprenger, *Malleus*, 95. The centrality of this work to the tradition of witchcraft is evident in its publication history. Between 1487 and 1520, fourteen editions were published; between 1574 and 1669, sixteen editions were produced (*Malleus*, vii–viii).

# Acknowledgments

Unsworth, C. R. "Witchcraft Beliefs and Criminal Procedure in Early Modern England." In *Legal Record and Historical Reality*, edited by Thomas Watkin (London: Hambledon Press, 1989): 71–98. Reprinted with the permission of Hambledon Press.

Levack, Brian P. "Possession, Witchcraft, and the Law in Jacobean England." *Washington and Lee University Law Review* 52 (1996): 1613–1640. Reprinted with the permission of the Washington and Lee Law Review.

Sharpe, Jim. "Women, Witchcraft, and the Legal Process." In *Women, Crime, and the Courts in Early Modern England*, edited by Jenny Kermode and Gartine Walker (Chapel Hill: University of North Carolina Press, 1994): 106–124. Reprinted with the permission of UCL Press.

Swain, J. T. "The Lancashire Witch Trials of 1612 and 1634 and the Economics of Witchcraft." *Northern History* 30 (1994): 64–85. Reprinted with the permission of the University of Leeds, The School of History.

Gregory, Annabel. "Witchcraft, Politics, and 'Good Neighbourhood' in Early Seventeenth-Century Rye." *Past & Present* 133 (1991): 31–66. Reprinted with the permission of the Past and Present Society and the author.

Windt, Anne Reiber de. "Witchcraft and Conflicting Visions of the Ideal Village Community." *Journal of British Studies* 34 (1995): 427–463. Reprinted with the permission of the University of Chicago Press, publisher.

Gaskill, Malcolm. "Witchcraft in Early Modern Kent: Stereotypes and the Background to Accusations." In *Witchcraft in Early Modern Europe: Studies in Culture and Belief*, edited by Jonathan Barry, Mariann Hester, and Gareth Roberts (Cambridge: Cambridge University Press, 1996): 257–287. Reprinted with the permission of Cambridge University Press.

Sharpe, J. A. *Witchcraft in Seventeenth-Century Yorkshire: Accusations and Countermeasures.* Borthwick Papers, 81 (1992). (Peasholme Green, York:Borthwick Institute of Historical Research, University of York, 1992): 1–28. Reprinted from Borthwick Paper 81.

Willis, Deborah. "Shakespeare and the English Witch Hunts: Enclosing the Maternal Body." In *Enclosure Acts: Sexuality, Property, and Culture in Early Modern Culture*, edited by Richard Burt and John Michael Archer (Ithaca: Cornell University Press, 1994): 96–120. Copyright © 1994 by Cornell University. Used by permission of the publisher, Cornell University Press.

Bennett, Gillian. "Ghost and Witch in the Sixteenth and Seventeenth Centuries." *Folklore* 97, 1 (1986): 3–14. Reprinted by kind permission of The Folklore Society.

Purkiss, Diane. "Desire and Its Deformities: Fantasies of Witchcraft in the English Civil War." *Journal of Medieval and Early Modern Studies* 27 (1997): 103–132. Reprinted with the permission of Duke University Press.

Gaskill, Malcolm. "Witchcraft and Power in Early Modern England: The Case of Margaret Moore." In *Women, Crime, and the Courts in Early Modern England*, edited by Jenny Kermode and Gartine Walker (Chapel Hill: University of North Carolina Press, 1994): 125–145. Reprinted with the permission of UCL Press.

Sharpe, Jim. "The Devil in East Anglia: The Matthew Hopkins Trials Reconsidered." In *Witchcraft in Early Modern Europe: Studies in Culture and Belief*, edited by Jonathan Barry, Mariann Hester, and Gareth Roberts (Cambridge: Cambridge University Press, 1996): 237–254. Reprinted with the permission of Cambridge University Press.

Bostridge, Ian. "Witchcraft Repealed." In *Witchcraft in Early Modern Europe: Studies in Culture and Belief*, edited by Jonathan Barry, Mariann Hester, and Gareth Roberts (Cambridge: Cambridge University Press, 1996): 309–334. Reprinted with the permission of Cambridge University Press.

Maxwell-Stuart, Peter. G. "The Fear of the King Is Death: James VI and the Witches of East Lothian." In *Fear in Early Modern Society*, edited by William G. Naphy and Penny Roberts (Manchester: Manchester University Press, 1997): 209–223. Reprinted with the permission of Manchester University Press.

MacDonald, S. W., and A. Thom. "The Bargarran Witchcraft Trial: A Psychiatric Reassessment." *Scottish Medical Journal* 41 (1996): 152ff. Reprinted with the permission of Hermiston Publications Ltd.

Lapoint, Elwyn C. "Irish Immunity to Witch-Hunting, 1534–1711." *Éire-Ireland* 27 (1992): 76–92. Reprinted with the permission of the Irish American Cultural Institute.

Clark, Michael. "Like Images Made Black with the Lightning: Discourse and the Body in Colonial Witchcraft." *Eighteenth Century: Theory and Interpretation* 34 (1993): 199–220. Reprinted with the permission of Texas Tech University Press.

Rosenthal, Bernard. "Tituba's Story." *New England Quarterly* 71 (1988): 190–203. The New England Quarterly. v. 71 1988 for "Tituba's Story" by Bernard Rosenthal. Copyright held by The New England Quarterly. Reproduced by permission of the publisher and the author.

Craker, Wendel. "Spectral Evidence, Non-Spectral Acts of Witchcraft and Confessions at Salem in 1692." *Historical Journal* 40 (1997): 331–358.

Gould, Philip. "New England Witch-Hunting and the Politics of Reason in the Early Republic." *New England Quarterly* 68 (1995): 58–82. The New England Quarterly. v. 68 1995 for "New England Witch-Hunting and the Politics of Reason in the Early Republic" by Bernard Rosenthal. Copyright held by The New England Quarterly. Reproduced by permission of the publisher and the author.

Kern, Louis J. "Eros, the Devil, and the Cunning Woman: Sexuality and the Supernatural in European Antecedents and in the Seventeenth-Century Salem Witchcraft Cases." *Essex Institute Historical Collections* 129 (1993): 3–38. Reprinted with the permission of the Essex Institute, Salem, Massachusetts.